The Guinness Sports Yearbook 1995

Cris Freddi

C000185993

GUINNESS PUBLISHING

The Author

Cris Freddi follows the England Football Fact Book and Book of Sporting Blunders with his third Guinness publication, for which he has the right credentials, twice reaching the final of ITV's Sportsmasters and working for the BBC's A Question of Sport. His articles appear in the national dailies and a variety of magazines, from When Saturday Comes to Wisden Cricket Monthly.

A published novelist, he found time in 1994 to win BBC Wildlife magazine's national nature writing competition.

© Cris Freddi 1995

The right of Cris Freddi to be identified as the Author of this Work has been asserted in accordance with the Design, Copyright and Patents Act 1988

Published in Great Britain by Guinness Publishing Ltd, 33 London Road, Enfield, Middlesex

All rights reserved. No part of this publication may be reproduced, stored in a retrieval system or transmitted in any form or by any means, electronic, mechanical, photocopying or otherwise without prior permission in writing of the publisher

Cover illustrations by Mike Hewitt/Allsport UK Ltd: Michael Schumacher (left), Damon Hill (right). By Pascal Rondeau/Allsport UK Ltd: Schumacher leads Hill at the 1994 Japanese Grand Prix

Cover design by Ad Vantage Studios

Text design and layout by Mitchell Associates, Hertford

Printed and bound in Great Britain by The Bath Press, Bath, Avon

'Guinness' is a registered trademark of Guinness Publishing Ltd

A catalogue record for this book is available from the British Library

ISBN 0-85112-790-8

Contents

Introduction & Acknowledgements

The second edition of the Guinness Sports Yearbook introduces a few firsts. For a start, it covers a calendar year as opposed to essentially a winter season. (Actually, it goes back to October 1993, where last year's edition ended, and encroaches into January 1995, but the point's made, I hope: it's a real *year*book.)

Secondly, whereas last time the pattern was a page or two of text on each major sport followed by unbroken statistics, this year we've spread things around a little. So the bare results of, say, the NFL play-offs are followed by a paragraph of notes on who did what and why it was significant – which we hope will add some immediacy as well as interest. Also, if a performance affects an event's all-time records, we've tried to highlight this too. For example, after Devon Malcolm's onslaught against South Africa, we've added a list of all bowlers to have taken nine wickets in a Test innings for England. Again, we hope this provides a little contextual flavour.

Another new addition is, or are, the Guinness 5, the competitors we feel have achieved the most in their sports during 1993-94. All very subjective, of course, as these things always are, but our nominees come with impressive credentials and are worth their place even if they simply provoke a conversation or two.

One thing that we hope *hasn't* changed is the customary Guinness commitment to accuracy. Unfortunately, even with the best will in the world, this doesn't mean we can claim to have made no errors of fact. When you spread the net as widely as this, it seems to be inevitable for one or two to slip through. Any major ones that we discover, or that readers point out, will, space permitting, find their way into a safety net, an *Errata* page in next year's book, so they'll be only temporary, as it were.

They'll also remain all my own work and have nothing to do with those who've helped stitch the whole thing together. The English national dailies generally cover sport in great detail, but of course don't have space for everything. Neither do the specialist magazines – and some sports don't even have magazines. As a result, we've had to turn to some individual contributors from a number of sports associations.

The vast majority have been only too pleased to help, often providing far more than was asked. Here's hoping that the result does them justice. Any success it may have, and enjoyment it may provide, is dedicated to them:

First and very much foremost, Steve Lynch, deputy editor of Wisden Cricket Monthly and mighty quiz league captain, for some tremendous help (again) with all sports, especially cricket, and not least for introducing me to…

…the ubiquitous, remarkably patient and simply indispensable Christine Forrest, without whose help the tennis section would have been very incomplete

Peter Oakes, the Speedway Control Board's exemplary press officer

John Goldman for some incredibly quick fixes

John Randall of the Racing Post for mapping out the whole of horse racing

Chris Rhys, rugby union expert

Dave Bainbridge, rugby league guru

Albert 'Dillard' Sanders (horse racing & Moroccan World Cup football)

Brian Mellowship as always

Helen Jeavons of the Football Association, for introducing me to...

...her colleague Sue Barwick, who generously provided all the details of women's football

Nicky Beer of the Badminton Association of England

Tracey Howard at the English Basketball Association

Wendy Blackman of the British Canoe Union

Mike Thompson of the Caledonian Curling Club

Paul West at the British Cycling Federation

Mike Getty of the British Darts Organisation

Kim Robinson at the Amateur Fencing Association

Barry Rolfe of the British Gliding Association

Frank Melville at the National Greyhound Racing Club

Lynette Hotchkiss at the British Amateur Gymnastics Association

The British Handball Association

Jim Bowyer of the British Hang Gliding Association

Gaynor Morgan at the All England Women's Hockey Association

Steve Barlow at the Hockey Association

Sonia Goggin at the Auto-Cycle Union (Moto-Cross)

Sheila Redpath at the All England Netball Association

Mrs Gregson of the British Orienteering Federation

Kate Hodson at the Tennis & Rackets Association

The Amateur Rowing Association

Mary Holloway at the National Rifle Association

Judy Mott of the Amateur Swimming Association

Rob Sinclair & Graham Carter of the English Table Tennis Association

Rob Andrews of the British Tenpin Bowling Association

Mrs Holmes of the British Trampoline Federation

Elaine Shaw at the British Triathlon Association

Joanna Cassells at the British Volleyball Federation

Buff Crisp of the Hurlingham Polo Association

Mandy Fisher of the World Ladies Billiards & Snooker Association

James Chambers, Keith Lovejoy & Marcia Stretch of the Amateur Fencing Association

Claire at the Endurance Riding Group

Candy French-Mullen at the Horse Trials Office

Nigel Oldfield of the World Professional Billiards & Snooker Association

Mary Holloway & Mrs B Dixon at the National Rifle Association

Wally Holland and Mick at the British Amateur Weight Lifters' Association

Gordon Neil of the British Disabled Sports Association

Jane Swan of the British Paralympic Association

Stan Greenberg and Peter Matthews

Elaine Shaw of the British Triathlon Association

Bob Fisher, manager of the Great Britain cerebral palsy football team

Charlotte Ibbotson of the British Olympic Association

Syd Jones of the Croquet Association

BCM Grandstand

Robert Sloman & Sheila Fairclough (golf)

Joy Woodward of the European Swimming League

Lynda Jones of the Auto-Cycle Union

Mr D Pickles, secretary of the British Ice Hockey Association

Mike Thomson, secretary of the World Curling Federation

Bill Hartston, chess correspondent of The Independent

Antionette Ellis of the National Ice Skating Association of UK

Chris at the British Handball Association

Trevor Low of The Gymnast magazine

Helen Dorey of the Royal Yachting Association

Sarah Langford of the International Yacht Racing Association

Myrna Burger of the Squash Rackets Association

Sarah Langford & Nicola Hastwell of the International Yacht Racing Union

Roddy Brooks of Motor Cycle News

Steve Small

Judy Leden, British Open paragliding champion 1994

Rob Andrews of the British Tenpin Bowling Association

The Grand National Archery Society

Joe New of the National Ice Skating Association, for all his help with speed skating

Above all, my editors at Guinness, without whom...Simon Duncan for thinking of me – and Charles Richards, patient and indefatigable as ever.

The Guinness 5

Sportspeople of the Year

Tanni Grey

In 1992 British student Tanni Grey won the London Marathon and took four gold medals in the TW3 wheelchair class at the Paralympics, setting a world record and two Paralympic records. The following year, she was in hospital. Nothing to do with the congenital spinabifida: she'd spilled hot coffee in her lap. In Casualty, she kept in shape by lifting dumbbells.

Fully recovered by 1994, she staged a virtual repeat of 1992 by winning the same four events at the world championships (this time setting two world records) and, in one of the races of the year, regaining the London Marathon title in a sprint finish after two hours eight minutes, faster than the male runners but rather longer than her combined time for all the track golds, won at 100, 200, 400 & 800 metres. She gets into this section for sheer, sustained versatility and triceps of fire.

Brian Lara

Sometime during the season, county cricket got to Brian Charles Lara. There seemed to be a clear cut-off date, when the stamina, desire and especially the runs dried up. Lessons here for the structure of the domestic game – because in the first part of the year nothing had seemed beyond him.

In the Test series at home against England, he cleared his throat with 83, 167 & 43 in the early matches before shouting from the rooftops what Garry Sobers had been saying for some time, that this was one of the great batsmen in the making. In the fifth Test his 375, which broke Sobers' world Test record, was made without giving a chance and ended only by either tiredness or satiation.

Remarkably, this was just the start, followed by innings of 147, 106, 120* & 136: 884 runs at an average of 221– and even all *that* was just a prelude to his monumental 501 not out against Durham, making him the first batsman since Bradman (comparisons, for once, are justified) to hold the records for the highest score in Test and all first-class cricket.

After that, even the technique, eyesight and appetite for runs couldn't always compensate for the drudgery of county cricket – but this is perhaps overstating the case (Warwickshire, after all, won three of the four titles, and in the final of the other, the NatWest, Lara scored 81, his highest one-day score for the county) and anyway the top form returned towards the end: his ninth Championship century (191) helped beat Hampshire and win the title.

Almost as importantly as the sheer weight of runs, his presence did wonders for the rest of the Warwicks batting, especially Dominic Ostler & Roger Twose. It goes without saying that he'll be sorely missed in 1995 when the West Indies are here. And to think the county wouldn't have hired him if Manoj Prabakhar, the very average Indian all-rounder, had passed a fitness test!

On the penultimate day of the last Test of the year, his speedy 91 helped set up the win that preserved the West Indies' record of not losing a series since 1980. Before that, he'd been suspended and fined 50% of his match fee after staying at the crease when given out, telling the umpire to consult the third official. Shades of WG Grace. Talking of whom, the sign at the Sportsman's Arms in Northampton was changed from a portrait of the good doctor to one of Lara hooking.

A boundary, of course.

Paolo Maldini

Ah, this is what it's all about. An editor with Italian parents having to write about an Italian who was the world's No.1 footballer in 1994. It's a dirty job but someone has to do it.

No.1? With Romário & Roberto Baggio around? Well, Romário missed chances in the World Cup final, did nothing in the European Cup final, and anyway always played in front of a settled team. Baggio did his messianic best, but the World Cup final was one match too many. Maldini took it, like every other one, in his stride.

He was born to the purple. His father Cesare had been an equally smooth defender for Milan & Italy, sweeper and captain of the team which won the 1963 European Cup. Paolo, who first played for Milan as a 16-y-o, eclipsed the parental successes almost immediately: three Serie A titles, two European Cups, 47 caps, acknowledged as the best left-back in the world – all this before 1993-94.

Milan started the European Cup final as clear underdogs. Stuttering in the league, struggling to score goals, they faced a Barcelona team armed with Koeman's long-range gun and the two best strikers in the world, Romário & Stoitchkov – and had to do it without their suspended central defenders Costacurta & Baresi. A slaughter in prospect.

So it proved. Maldini moved into the middle, where his height and coolness made it look as if he'd played there all his life, Romário & Stoitchkov didn't get a kick, Milan won 4-0.

In the World Cup, more of the same. After losing their first match, Italy had their goalkeeper sent off and Baresi taken off injured against Norway. Maldini went into the centre again, played superbly despite an injury, the ten men conjured an improbable win, Italy didn't look back. When Mussi was injured in the final, Maldini simply returned to the left and carried on where he'd left off. If the Milan dynasty really does die out this season, the father figure for the next generation's already there. A young dad, too. He's still only 26.

Michael Schumacher

Forget the shunt in the last race; history will. Class tells, and this year it only stopped talking when points were taken away by suspensions and disqualifications. By any law of natural justice, the title would have been won with races to spare.

Some of the talking wasn't altogether gentlemanly, but when he described Damon Hill as 'not a No.1 driver' he was only articulating what many in the sport then believed. Whereas the impression given by Hill was of a good driver in a very good car, Schumacher already looked a great one, in a car that was only very good in the right hands. In the two races from which he was banned, Benetton didn't score a point, testimony to the precision and sensitivity that had marked him out as a future champion from the start, a Grand Prix winner (and third overall) at 23. Third again in 1993, he already looked the best in the championship; all he needed was the right machine.

This year he got it, and dominated from the start, winning six of the first seven races (his gearbox cost him the other). Even the rest of the season, which should have been processional but was one complicated mess, belonged to him. The black flag incident, the comments about Hill, the final collision – this was the stuff of all the recent great, tetchy champions: Prost (who applauded the crash in Adelaide), Senna, Mansell.

Talking of Senna, would he have won the title if he'd lived? Well, Schumacher out-drove him in the first two Grands Prix and even last season had looked set to take over. There was no shadow over the title.

Not everyone in Britain believes that, but two who matter did. Federation president Max Mosley had no doubts that 'the right man won the championship. Schumacher is the quicker driver' – and one of the other contenders was just as unequivocal: 'This year he has been the class of the field.'

Not the words of a Benetton team-mate; they were the thoughts of Damon Hill.

Emmitt Smith

The Dallas Cowboys' road to a second consecutive Superbowl began with a defeat, suffered without the help of their decisive player, who was holding out for more money. High-profile owner Jerry Jones held out too, but only till the second game. Result: a 0-2 start, and a huge pay rise for Emmitt Smith.

Crudely put, running backs come in two types: elusive runners (Tony Dorsett, Marcus Allen) and bulldozers (Franco Harris, John Riggins). Occasionally an amalgam of the two materialises, manufactured from granite and turbo, and proves fearfully hard to stop.

Smith (5'9 and virtually 15 stone) wasn't stopped all season, heading the rushing table for the third year in a row, voted MVP for the two touchdowns that won the 1994 Superbowl (to go with the one he scored in 1993). His selection for the Pro Bowl again was a complete formality. Fully fit, he might well have taken Dallas to Superbowl '95; as it was, even with an injured hamstring he scored a touchdown in the NFC Championship Game.

Honours List

Sportspeople who received awards in 1993 & 1994 included the following:

Knighthood

Bobby Charlton	England footballer

DBE

Marea Hartman	Athletics official

CBE

EW 'Jim' Swanton	Cricket writer
Trevor Bailey	England cricketer
Alex Ferguson	Scottish football manager *(awarded OBE in 1984)*
Dudley Wood	Rugby union administrator

OBE

Gavin Hastings	Scotland & Lions rugby captain
Nat Lofthouse	England footballer
Karen Smithies	England cricket captain
Garry Schofield	England rugby league player
Ian Emmerson	president British Cycling Federation
Viv Richards	West Indian cricketer

Richards apparently forgot to come and pick it up.

Sue Slocombe	England hockey player
Lisa Opie	British squash player
Jimmy Hill	Football pundit
Reg Gutteridge	Boxing commentator
Jonathan Martin	TV broadcaster

MBE

Karen Pickering	UK swimmer
John Regis	UK sprinter
Ally McCoist	Scotland footballer
Gary Mabbutt	England footballer
Peter Winterbottom	England rugby union flanker
Bill Prosser	services to rugby union in Bangor, Wales
Ian Smith	N Zealand wicketkeeper
Barry McGuigan	Irish boxer
Nicola Fairbrother	British judoka
Katherine McNeil	services to golf
Kenny Colaine	sprint double gold medallist at 1992 Paralympics.

First person with a learning disability to get MBE.

Harry Brind	cricket groundsman
Mike Turner	Leicestershire CC secretary
Stephen Hilditch	Irish rugby union referee
Grant Fox	N Zealand rugby union player
Jonathan Davies	Welsh rugby league player
Steve Backley	UK javelin thrower
Neil Thomas	UK gymnast

In December 1994, Alain Prost was awarded an honorary OBE for his 'role in the development of shared technology and enhancing Franco-British collaboration' – which must have raised the Mansell eyebrows.

Abbreviations

Where a time is shown, the minutes and seconds are separated by a colon, parts of a second by a full stop, and the word 'hours' abbreviated to an 'h': e.g. 2 hours 34 minutes 56.78 seconds: 2h34:56.78.

WR	World record
ER	European record
ComR	Commonwealth record
ChR	Championship record
JR	Junior record
eq	equalled
w	wind assisted

Countries etc

Some names are written in full: Chile, Cuba, Fiji, Haiti, India, Iran, Peru.

AFR	Africa
ALG	Algeria
AMER	Americas
ARG	Argentina
ARM	Armenia
AUS	Australia
AUT	Austria
AZER	Azerbaijan
BAH	Bahamas
BEL	Belgium
BERM	Bermuda
BRZ	Brazil
BUL	Bulgaria
BYL	Belarus
CAN	Canada
COL	Colombia
CHN	China
COL	Colombia
C RICA	Costa Rica
CRO	Croatia
CYP	Cyprus
CZE	Czech Republic
DEN	Denmark

DOM	Dominican Republic
ECU	Ecuador
EG	East Germany
Eire	Republic of Ireland
ENG	England
EST	Estonia
ETH	Ethiopia
EUR	Europe
FIN	Finland
FRA	France
GEO	Georgia
GER	Germany
GHA	Ghana
GRE	Greece
GUER	Guernsey
HK	Hong Kong
HOL	Holland
HUN	Hungary
ICE	Iceland
INDO	Indonesia
IRE	Ireland
ISR	Israel
ITA	Italy
JAM	Jamaica
JAP	Japan
JERS	Jersey
KEN	Kenya
KAZ	Kazakhstan
LAT	Latvia
LIECH	Liechtenstein
LITH	Lithuania
LUX	Luxembourg
MALAY	Malaysia
MEX	Mexico
MOLD	Moldova
MOR	Morocco
MOZ	Mozambique
NAM	Namibia
NAU	Nauru
NIG	Nigeria
N IRE	Northern Ireland
N KOR	North Korea
NOR	Norway
NZ	New Zealand

PAK	Pakistan
PAN	Panama
PAR	Paraguay
PHIL	Philippines
POL	Poland
PORT	Portugal
PR	Puerto Rico
ROM	Romania
RUS	Russia
SAF	South Africa
SCOT	Scotland
SEN	Senegal
SING	Singapore
S KOR	South Korea
SLVK	Slovakia
SLVN	Slovenia
SOM	Somalia
SPA	Spain
SRI	Sri Lanka
ST LUC	St Lucia
SWE	Sweden
SWI	Switzerland
TAIW	Taiwan (Chinese Taipei)
TAJ	Tadjikistan
TAN	Tanzania
THAI	Thailand
TKM	Turkmenistan
TRIN	Trinidad & Tobago
TUN	Tunisia
TURK	Turkey
UAE	United Arab Emirates
UGA	Uganda
UK	United Kingdom
UKR	Ukraine
URU	Uruguay
USA	United States
UZB	Uzbekistan
VEN	Venezuela
VIRG	Virgin Islands
WAL	Wales
WG	West Germany
YUG	Yugoslavia
ZAM	Zambia
ZIM	Zimbabwe

American Football

All manner of records, in a sport that devours them, were broken in 1993 and 1994. Don Shula racked up his 325th win as head coach to overtake the legendary George Halas, then led the Dolphins against Cincinnati in the first NFL game ever to feature a father and son as opposition coaches. Jerry Rice caught his 127th touchdown pass, and then some. New England Patriots quarterback Drew Bledsoe attempted 70 passes, connecting with 45 of them for 426 yards, breaking his own 421 set in the season's first game, without throwing a single interception. In contrast, Joe Montana finally suffered the first shut-out of his 16-year career, in his 154th game, as Kansas City lost 16-0 at home to the Raiders. Like waiting for a bus, the Chiefs were also shut out in their next game.

But 1993-94 belonged, for the second season running, to the Cowboys and the luckless Bills (OJ Simpson got in on the act by starring in a televised car chase and standing trial for his wife's murder, but that's another media event altogether). With Troy Aikman this time taking a back seat to Emmitt Smith (see Guinness 5), Dallas retained the championship as expected, leaving Buffalo with the unenviably unique record of four Superbowl defeats in succession (poor Scott Norwood's last-minute missed field goal in 1991 growing in significance year by year). The Bills' mediocre season-after meant there wouldn't be five in '95. A mercy all round.

NFL 1993-94

American Conference (AFC)

Eastern Division	W	L	F	A
Buffalo Bills*	12	4	329	242
Miami Dolphins	9	7	349	351
New York Jets	8	8	270	247
New England Patriots	5	11	238	286
Indianapolis Colts	4	12	189	378
Central Division				
Houston Oilers*	12	4	368	238
Pittsburgh Steelers*	9	7	308	281
Cleveland Browns	7	9	304	307
Cincinnati Bengals	3	13	187	319
Western Division				
Kansas City Chiefs*	11	5	328	291
Los Angeles Raiders*	10	6	306	326
Denver Broncos*	9	7	373	284
San Diego Chargers	8	8	322	290
Seattle Seahawks	6	10	280	314

National Conference (NFC)

Eastern Division	W	L	F	A
Dallas Cowboys*	12	4	376	229
New York Giants*	11	5	288	205
Philadelphia Eagles	8	8	293	315
Phoenix Cardinals	7	9	326	269
Washington Redskins	4	12	230	345
Central Division				
Detroit Lions*	10	6	298	292
Minnesota Vikings*	9	7	277	290
Green Bay Packers*	9	7	340	282
Chicago Bears	7	9	236	230
Tampa Bay Buccaneers	5	11	237	376
Western Division				
San Francisco 49ers*	10	6	473	297
New Orleans Saints	8	8	317	343
Atlanta Falcons	6	10	316	385
Los Angeles Rams	5	11	221	367
* qualified for play-offs				

Wild Card Play-offs

Denver	24	LA Raiders	42
Pittsburgh	24	Kansas City	27 (OT)
Minnesota	10	NY Giants	17
Green Bay	28	Detroit	24

Jeff Hostetler & John Elway each throw three touchdown passes in the first half before the Raiders' Napoleon McCallum rushes for three touchdowns in the second.

Joe Montana, three times Superbowl MVP with the 49ers, pulls it out of the hat again, throwing a touchdown pass with less than two minutes remaining, after which Nick Lowery's 32-yard overtime field goal beats the Steelers.

Rodney Hampton's two touchdown runs in the third quarter win it for the Giants after they trail 10-3.

Detroit put together 410 yards but can't compete with the Packers' big plays, the last of which, Brett Favre's 40-yard touchdown pass to Sterling Sharpe with less than a minute to go, wins the game, Green Bay's first in the play-offs since 1983.

AFC Semi-finals

Buffalo	29	LA Raiders	23
Kansas City	28	Houston	20

Jim Kelly throws for 287 yards to drag the Bills back from eleven points down to reach the Championship game for the fourth time in row and the fifth in the last six years.

Joe Montana works the oracle yet again, throwing three touchdown passes after the Chiefs trail 10-0 at half-time.

NFC Semi-finals

Dallas	27	Green Bay	17
San Francisco	44	NY Giants	3

Troy Aikman throws for 302 yards & three touchdowns for Dallas, who score ten points in eighteen seconds just before half-time.

Ricky Watters rushes for five touchdowns, two more than the previous record for a play-off game, to inflict the Giants' worst ever play-off defeat.

AFC Championship Game

Buffalo	30	Kansas City	13

Thurman Thomas may have a relatively lean time of it in Superbowls, but at least he keeps getting the Bills there: here he rushes for 186 yards and three touchdowns. Buffalo out-rush the Chiefs by 229 yards to 52, and there's no compensation in the air; Montana can't produce the fairytale ending: his touchdown pass is dropped by running back Kimble Anders, he completes only nine out of 23 passes, and sits out most of the second half with concussion.

NFC Championship Game

Dallas	38	San Francisco	21

Troy Aikman throws two touchdown passes, Emmitt Smith rushes for two more, the Cowboys repeat last year's win at the same stage against the same team, the 49ers lose the Championship game for the third time in four years.

Superbowl XXVIII

30 Jan 1994 Georgia Dome, Atlanta

DALLAS COWBOYS (6)30	BUFFALO BILLS (13)13
TD: Washington, E Smith 2	TD: T Thomas
PAT: Murray 3	PAT: Christie
FG: Murray 3	FG: Christie 2

In an uncanny repeat of last year's game, some of the Bills' wounds are self-inflicted. In 1993 a fumble by Thurman Thomas led to a Cowboys touchdown; this time he loses the ball when Buffalo lead 13-6, Washington picks it up and runs 46 yards for the equalising TD. Last year Washington picked off a Kelly pass to create a touchdown; this time he does the same thing. Then Smith takes over. He deserves the MVP award, but Washington must have won a few votes: usually a reserve, called in as one of five defensive backs to counter the Bills' no-huddle offence, he makes eleven tackles and forces another fumble from poor Thomas, whose Superbowl record (despite a record-equalling four TDs) doesn't get any better. No AFC team's won the Superbowl since the Raiders in 1984. Buffalo, already the only team to lose three in a row, make it four. After the repeat of 1992 and the 'three-peat' last time, this is christened, rather unenthusiastically, the 'four-peat'. There was no dive in '95.

One small bright spot for the Bills: Steve Christie's 54-yard field goal is the longest in any Superbowl.

Offence

DALLAS		BUFFALO
Alvin Harper	WR	Don Beebe
Mark Tuinei	LT	John Fina
Nate Newton	LG	Glenn Parker
John Gesek	C	Kent Hull
Kevin Gogan	RG	John Davis
Erik Williams	RT	Howard Ballard
Jay Novacek	TE	Pete Metzelaars
Michael Irvin	WR	André Reed
Troy Aikman	QB	Jim Kelly
Emmitt Smith	RB	Thurman Thomas
Daryl Johnston	RB-WR	Bill Brooks

Defence

Tony Tolbert	LE	Phil Hansen
Tony Casillas	LT/NT	Jeff Wright
Leon Lett	RT/RE	Bruce Smith
Charles Haley	RE/LOLB	James Patton
Ken Norton	MLB/LILB	Cornelius Bennett
Darrin Smith	RLB/RILB	Mark Maddox
Darren Woodson	DB/ROLB	Darryl Talley
Kevin Smith	LCB	Mickey Washington
Larry Brown	RCB	Nate Odomes
Thomas Everett	SS	Henry Jones
James Washington	FS	Mark Kelso

Kicker

Eddie Murray	Steve Christie

Dallas subs
Offence: Bernie Kosar, Frank Cornish, Scott Galbraith, Derrick Gainer, Dale Hellestae, Lincoln Coleman, Kevin Williams
Defence: Kenneth Grant, Elvis Patterson, Dixon Edwards, Matt Vanderbeek, Godfrey Myles, Bill Bates, Joe Fishback, Russell Maryland, Chad Hennings, Dave Thomas, Robert Jones, Jim Jeffcoat, Jimmie Jones
Kicker: John Jett

Buffalo subs
Offence: Frank Reich, Jim Ritcher, Jerry Crafts, Steve Tasker, Kenneth Davis, Mike Devlin, Keith McKeller, Carwell Gardner, Adam Lingner, Russell Copeland
Defence: Kurt Schulz, Matt Darby, Mike Lodish, Monty Brown, Thomas Smith, Keith Goganious, Oliver Barnett, Jerome Henderson, Richard Harvey, Mark Pike
Kicker: Chris Mohr

Most Valuable Player (MVP): E Smith

Superbowl: some records
Not including 1995
Appearances

7	Dallas	1971-72-76-78-79-93-94
5	Miami	1972-73-74-83-85
5	Washington	1973-83-84-88-92

Wins

4	Pittsburgh	1975-76-79-80
4	SF 49ers	1982-85-89-90
4	Dallas	1972-78-93-94

Chuck Noll was Pittsburgh head coach each time.

Games as losing coach

4	Bud Grant	1970-74-75-77	Minnesota
4	Don Shula	1969-72-83-85	Baltimore/ Miami
4	Marv Levy	1991-92-93-94	Buffalo

Shula was also a winner with Miami in 1973 & 1974. Grant never won the title; nor (so far) has Levy.

Touchdowns

4	Franco Harris	1975-79-80	Pittsburgh
4	Roger Craig	1985-90	SF 49ers
4	Jerry Rice	1989-90	SF 49ers
4	Thurman Thomas	1991-92-93-94	Buffalo
3	Four others, including Emmitt Smith (Dallas) 1993-94.		

Craig (1985) & Rice (1990) are the only two to score three in one game, Thomas the only one to score in four different games, let alone four in a row.

NFL 1994-95

American Conference (AFC)

Eastern Division	W	L	F	A
Miami Dolphins*	10	6	389	327
New England Patriots*	10	6	351	312
Indianapolis Colts	8	8	307	320
Buffalo Bills	7	9	340	356
New York Jets	6	10	264	320

* qualify for play-offs

Central Division	W	L	F	A
Pittsburgh Steelers*	12	4	316	234
Cleveland Browns*	11	5	340	204
Cincinnati Bengals	3	13	276	406
Houston Oilers	2	14	226	352

Western Division	W	L	F	A
San Diego Chargers*	11	5	381	306
Kansas City Chiefs*	9	7	319	298
Los Angeles Raiders	9	7	303	327
Denver Broncos	7	9	347	396
Seattle Seahawks	6	10	287	323

National Conference (NFC)

Eastern Division	W	L	F	A
Dallas Cowboys*	12	4	414	248
New York Giants	9	7	279	305
Arizona Cardinals	8	8	235	267
Philadelphia Eagles	7	9	308	308
Washington Redskins	3	13	320	412

Central Division	W	L	F	A
Minnesota Vikings*	10	6	356	314
Detroit Lions*	9	7	357	342
Green Bay Packers*	9	7	382	287
Chicago Bears*	9	7	271	307
Tampa Bay Buccaneers	6	10	251	351

For the first time, four teams qualify from the same division.

Western Division	W	L	F	A
San Francisco 49ers*	13	3	505	296
New Orleans Saints	7	9	348	407
Atlanta Falcons	7	9	313	389
Los Angeles Rams	4	12	286	366

Wild Card Play-offs
31 Dec 1994 - 1 Jan 1995

Miami	27	Kansas City	17
New England	13	Cleveland	20
Green Bay	16	Detroit	12
Minnesota	18	Chicago	35

Dan Marino wins the battle of the great quarterbacks against Joe Montana by completing 22 of 29 passes for 257 yards and two touchdowns to bring the Dolphins back from 17-10 down.

Angling

Fly Fishing

World Championships
13-14 Aug Lillehammer

P Coquard	FRA	13 pts
H Morgan	WAL	30
P Cochito	ITA	32

Team	
Czech Republic	285
Italy	286
England	290

English National River Championships
20 Jun East & West Dart

Brian Easterbrook	West Country
Stuart Crofts	Yorkshire
Dennis Buck	North West

Coarse Angling

World Championships
3-4 Sep Holme Pierrepont

R Nudd	ENG
R Stronck	LUX
JJ Chaumet	FRA

Team
England
France
Italy

England: Nudd, Scotthorne, Gardener, White, Milsom

Archery

Goodwill Games

Men's 70m final
Gennady Mitrofanov (RUS) bt Ho Jin-su (S KOR) 112-110
Simon Terry (UK) lost to Ho in the quarter-finals

Women's 70m final
Kim Hyo-jung (S KOR) bt Cho Youn-jeong (S KOR)103-101

British Target Championships
Aug 1994 Lichfield

Men	
Steve Hallard	2356
M Evans	2246
Richard Priestman	2229

Hallard sets an unofficial British record in regaining the title he won in 1990 & 1991.

Women	
Pauline Edwards	2293
S Wooff	2292
S Snowden	2211

Edwards regains the title she won in 1990.

British Open Field Championships
May 1994 Finsthwaite, Cumbria

Men	
Traditional	R Hardy
Traditional Longbow	J Cope
Freestyle	J Shales
Compound Unlimited	D Jones
Compound Limited	J McCrea
Compound Bowhunter	D Danks
Barebow	G Edwards

Women	
Traditional	B Beriman
Traditional Longbow	R Moore
Freestyle	L Oliver
Compound Unlimited	A Shephard
Compound Bowhunter	H Watson

Athletics

In a quiet year (biennial World Championships having diluted the importance of the Commonwealth Games and even the European Championships) there were still things to admire – world records by Leroy Burrell, Sergei Bubka (yet again), Haile Gebresilasie; Colin Jackson's unbeaten run; Sally Gunnell's complete set of golds – but they were overshadowed by the case of Diane Modahl, who was found with 42 times the normal amount of testosterone in her system. Those who confirmed her suspension agreed that 'it would be naive to believe she's the only one.'

Indeed she wasn't. Solomon Wariso was briefly banned for upping his gas, John Ngugi for refusing to take a test. Others caught in 1993 & 1994 included a number of world record holders and world, Olympic and European champions: Tatyana Dorovskikh, Tsvetanka Khristova, Inessa Kravets, Lyudmila Narozhilenko, Lilia Nurutdinova, Mike Stulce (again), Dragutin Topic, Romas Ubartas and Ben Johnson (yes, the head honcho himself, caught again and at last banned for life) plus British shot putter Paul Edwards, who once complained that other shot putters won medals ahead of him because they took drugs. Opinions vary as to whether those caught constitute just the tip.

All of which means that even for those of us who've followed athletics since our teens, it's hard not to take some of the records and results with just a pinch of white powder.

European Championships
7-14 August 1994 Helsinki

Men

100 metres

Linford Christie	UK	10.14
Geir Moen	NOR	10.20
Aleksandr Porkhomovskiy	RUS	10.31

Christie becomes the first to win the event three times in a row over the regular 8-year span (Valery Borzov of the USSR won it in 1969-71-74).

200 metres

Geir Moen	NOR	20.30
Vladislav Dologodin	UKR	20.47
Patrick Stevens	BEL	20.68

Defending champion and hot favourite John Regis withdrew injured before the Championships.

400 metres

Du'aine Ladejo	UK	45.09
Roger Black	UK	45.20
Matthias Rusterholz	SWI	45.96

After yet another comeback from injury, the defending champion leads into the straight but doesn't have the conditioning to hold off Ladejo, who completes the European indoor/outdoor double and deprives Black (already the only man to win the event twice) of a hat-trick.

800 metres

Andrea Benvenuti	ITA	1:46.12
Vebjorn Rodal	NOR	1:46.53
Tomas De Teresa	SPA	1:46.57

Italy's first gold medal in the event. For the first time since 1969, no British runner wins a medal (defending champion Tom McKean goes out in the first round).

1500 metres

Fermin Cacho	SPA	3:35.27 ChR
Isaac Viciosa	SPA	3:36.01
Branko Zorko	CRO	3:36.88

The previous Championship best was set by Steve Ovett in 1978.

5000 metres

Dieter Baumann	GER	13:36.93
Rob Denmark	UK	13:37.50
Abel Anton	SPA	13:38.04

The slowest winning time since Ian Stewart in 1969.

10 000 metres

Abel Anton	SPA	28:06.03
Vincent Rousseau	BEL	28:06.63
Stephane Franke	GER	28:07.95

The first Spaniard to win the event runs a personal best (and in world terms very slow) time.

Marathon

Martin Fiz	SPA	2h10:31
Diego Garcia	SPA	2h10:46
Alberto Juzdado	SPA	2h11:18

Again, the first Spaniard to win the event, and the first time runners from the same country win all its medals. The favourite, Richard Nerurkar (UK) runs out of fizz and finishes fourth, the first time he fails to win a Marathon.

3000m Steeplechase

Alessandro Lambruschini	ITA	8:22.40
Angelo Carosi	ITA	8:23.53
William Van Dijck	BEL	8:24.86

Lambruschini wins despite falling during the race.

110m Hurdles

Colin Jackson	UK	13.08
Florian Schwarthoff	GER	13.16
Tony Jarrett	UK	13.23

Jackson, who retains the title, set a Championship record of 13.04 in the semi-final. Jarrett finished second in 1990.

400m Hurdles

Oleg Tverdokhleb	UKR	48.06
Sven Nylander	SWE	48.22
Stéphane Diagana	FRA	48.23

Nylander also finished second in 1990 (and third in 1986).

20km Walk

Mikhail Shchennikov	RUS	1h18:45 ChR
Yevgeny Misyulya	BYL	1h19:22
Valentin Massana	SPA	1h20:33

Shchennikov, four times World Indoor and three times European Indoor champion, at last wins a major outdoor championship.

50km Walk

Valery Spitsyn	RUS	3h41:07
Thierry Toutain	FRA	3h43:52
Giovanni Pericelli	ITA	3h43.55

Toutain had won the 20 km bronze in 1990.

4x100m relay

Hermann Lomba, Daniel Sangouma, Jean-Charles Trouabal, Eric Perrot	FRA	38.57
Sergey Osovich, Dmitry Vanyaikin, Oleg Kramarenko, Vladislav Dologodin	UKR	38.98
Ezio Madonia, Domenico Nettis, Giorgio Marras, Sandro Floris	ITA	38.99

France have no trouble retaining the title (Sangouma and Trouabal winning their second gold medals in the event) when a) Britain fail to qualify because Tony Jarrett and Darren Braithwaite drop the baton, and b) Russia are disqualified for two false starts in the final.

4x400m relay

David McKenzie, Brian Whittle, Roger Black, Du'aine Ladejo	UK	2:59.13
Marco Vaccari, Fabio Grossi, Ashraf Saber, Alessandro Aimar	ITA	3:03.46
Bittner, Kai Karsten, Lutz Becker, Edgar Itt	GER	3:04.15

Britain (and Black) are the first to win the event three times in a row. Whittle was also on the winning team in 1986. Saber, the world junior champion over 400m hurdles in 1992, has an Ethiopian father.

High Jump

	Steinar Hoen	NOR	2.35 ChR
2eq	Steve Smith	UK	2.33
2eq	Artur Partyka	POL	2.33

Hoen equals his personal best, Smith's is 2.37.

Long Jump

Ivalyo Mladenov	BUL	8.09
Milan Gombala	CZE	8.04
Kostas Koukodimos	GRE	8.01

Triple Jump

Denis Kapustin	RUS	17.62
Serge Hélan	FRA	17.55
Maris Bruziks	LAT	17.20

Bruziks had finished second in 1986.

Pole Vault

Rodion Gataullin	RUS	6.00 ChR
Igor Trandenkov	RUS	5.90
Jean Galfione	FRA	5.85

In the absence of Sergei Bubka, Gataullin retains the title.

Shot Putt

Aleksandr Klimenko	UKR	20.78
Aleksandr Bagach	UKR	20.34
Roman Virastyuk	UKR	19.59

Bagach, banned for drug-taking in 1989, contributes to the first clean sweep of medals in the event since East Germany in 1969.

Discus

Vladimir Dubrovshchik	BYL	64.78
Dmitry Shevchenko	RUS	64.56
Jürgen Schult	GER	64.18

Hammer

Vasily Sidorenko	RUS	81.10
Igor Astapkovich	BYL	80.40
Heinz Weis	GER	78.48

Astapkovich was the defending champion.

Javelin

Steve Backley	UK	85.20
Seppo Räty	FIN	82.90
Jan Zelezny	CZE	82.58

Backley retains the title.

Decathlon

Alain Blondel	FRA	8453
Henrik Dagaard	SWE	8362
Lev Lobodin	UKR	8201

Hot favourite Eduard Hämäläinen (BYL) falls over the first hurdle in the first event of the second day after scoring 4512 on the first.

Wheelchair 1500 metres

Hakan Ericsson	SWE	3:27.74
David Holding	UK	3:27.74
F Waque	HOL	3:27.94

Not an official event. Ericsson and Holding share title.

Women

100 metres

Irina Privalova	RUS	11.02
Zhanna Tarnopolskaya	UKR	11.10
Melanie Päschke	GER	11.28

200 metres

Irina Privalova	RUS	22.32
Zhanna Tarnopolskaya	UKR	22.77
Galina Malchugina	RUS	22.90

The first woman since 1974 to finish second in both sprints. Malchugina also won the bronze in 1990.

400 metres

Marie-José Pérec	FRA	50.33
Svetlana Goncharenko	RUS	51.24
Phylis Smith	UK	51.30

Pérec completes the set (World, Olympic and European titles).

800 metres

Lyubov Gurina	RUS	1:58.55
Natalya Dukhnova	BYL	1:58.55
Lyudmila Rogachova	RUS	1:58.69

Ann Griffiths (UK), who finishes fifth in a PB time,

qualifies after finishing last in her heat! Gurina, now 37, wins in a photo finish.

1500 metres

Lyudmila Rogachova	RUS	4:18.93
Kelly Holmes	UK	4:19.30
Yekaterina Podkopayeva	RUS	4:19.37

The 42-year-old Podkopayeva becomes the oldest ever medallist at the event.

3000 metres

Sonia O'Sullivan	EIRE	8:31.84
Yvonne Murray	UK	8:36.48
Gabriela Szabo	ROM	8:40.08

O'Sullivan beats defending champion Murray to win the Republic's first ever European Championship gold medal. Their three previous silver medallists finished behind British runners.

10 000 metres

Fernanda Ribeiro	PORT	31:08.75
Conceição Ferreira	PORT	31:32.82
Daria Nauer	SWI	31:35.96

Ribeiro and Nauer set new national records.

Marathon

Manuela Machado	PORT	2h29:54
Maria Curatolo	ITA	2h30:33
Adriana Barbu	ROM	2h30:55

Portuguese runners have won the event every time it's been held (first in 1982).

100m Hurdles

Svetla Dimitrova	BUL	12.60
Yulia Graudyn	RUS	12.78
Yordanka Donkova	BUL	12.93

400m Hurdles

Sally Gunnell	UK	53.33
Silvia Rieger	GER	54.68
Anna Knoroz	RUS	54.68

Gunnell sets the fastest time in the world this year in becoming only the second athlete (the first since Daley Thompson) to win Olympic, World, European and Commonwealth gold medals and set a world record.

10km Walk

Sari Essayah	FIN	42:37	ChR
Annarita Sidoti	ITA	42:43	
Yelena Nikolayeva	RUS	42:43	

Sidoti was the defending champion.

4x100m relay

Melanie Päschke, Bettina Zipp, Silke-Beate Knoll, Silke Lictenhagen	GER	42.90
Natalya Anisimova, Galina Malchugina, Marina Trandenkova, Irina Privalova	RUS	42.96
Svetla Dimitrova, Anelia Nuneva, Desislava Dimitrova, Petya Pendareva	BUL	43.61

4x400m relay

Francine Landre, Viviane Dorsile, Evelyne Elien,		
Marie-José Pérec	FRA	3:22.34
Natalya Khruchelyova, Yelena Andreyeva,		
Tatyana Zakharova, Svetlana Goncharenko		
	RUS	3:24.06
Karin Janke, Uta Rohländer, Heike Meissner,		
Anja Rücker	GER	3:24.10

High Jump

Britta Bilac	SLVN	2.00
Yelena Gulyayeva	RUS	1.96
Nele Zilinskiene	LITH	1.93

Long Jump

Heike Drechsler	GER	7.14
Inessa Kravets	UKR	6.99
Fiona May	ITA	6.90

May, now married to an Italian, won four AAA and three UK National titles.

Triple Jump

Ana Biryukova	RUS	14.89
Inna Lasovskaya	RUS	14.85
Inessa Kravets	UKR	14.67

The first time the event's been held in the Championships.

Shot Putt

Viktoriya Pavlysh	UKR	19.61
Astrid Kumbernuss	GER	19.49
Svetla Mitkova	BUL	19.49

The Ukraine's first European Championship gold medal as a separate country.

Discus

Ilke Wyudda	GER	68.72
Ellina Zvereva	BYL	64.46
Mette Bergmann	NOR	64.34

Javelin

Trine Hattestad	NOR	68.00
Karen Forkel	GER	66.10
Felicia Tilea	ROM	64.34

Forkel also won the silver in 1990.

Heptathlon

Sabine Braun	GER	6419
Rita Inancsi	HUN	6404
Urszula Wlodarczyk	POL	6322

Braun retains the title.

European Marathon Cup
(Held in conjunction with Marathon)

Men

1 Spain	2 Portugal	3 France

Women

1 Italy	2 Romania	3 France

European Championships gold medals
All-time list. Relay golds in brackets.

6	Marita Koch	EG	1982-86	(3)
5	Fanny Blankers Koen	HOL	1946-50	(1)
5	Irena Szewinska	POL	1966-74	(1)
5	Marlies Göhr	EG	1978-86	(2)
5	Harald Schmid	WG	1978-86	(2)
5	Roger Black	UK	1986-94	(3)

Black's won 6 medals in all, equalling the record for a male athlete set by Pietro Mennea (ITA 1971-78) and Schmid.

World Cup
9-11 September 1994 Crystal Palace

Men

100 metres

Linford Christie	UK	10.21

Christie becomes the only man to win the event three times, let alone three in a row. The slowest winning times have all been set by British runners: 10.21 Christie 1992 & 1994, 10.20 Allan Wells 1981.

200 metres

John Regis	UK	20.45

400 metres

Antonio Pettigrew	USA	45.27
2 Du'aine Ladejo	*UK*	*45.44*

800 metres

Mark Everett	USA	1:46.02
3 Craig Winrow	*UK*	*1:47.16*

1500 metres

Nourredine Morceli	AFR	3:34.70
5 Gary Lough	*UK*	*3:44.10*

Morceli, winning the event for the first time, just misses one of the oldest Cup records in the book: Steve Ovett's 3:34.45 set in 1977.

5000 metres

Brahim Lahlafi	AFR	13:27.96
2 John Nuttall	*UK*	*13:32.47*

10 000 metres

Khalid Skah	AFR	27:38.74
3 Rob Denmark	*UK*	*28:20.65*

3000m Steeplechase

Moses Kiptanui	AFR	8:28.38
4 Colin Walker	*UK*	*8:41.14*

110m Hurdles

Tony Jarrett	UK	13.23

In the absence of the injured Colin Jackson, Jarrett at last wins a major individual event for the first time.

400m Hurdles

Samuel Matete	AFR	48.77
6 Gary Cadogan	*UK*	*50.48*

4x100m relay

Darren Braithwaite, Tony Jarrett, John Regis, Linford Christie	UK	38.46

The Cup record still stands at 38.03, set (as a world record) in 1977.

4x400m relay

Dave Mackenzie, Du'aine Ladejo, Jamie Baulch, Roger Black	UK	3:01.34

Britain had never won either relay before.

High Jump

Javier Sotomayor	AMER	2.40	ChR
3 Steve Smith	*UK*	*2.28*	

Sotomayor breaks the previous Cup best by 6cm in winning the event for (rather surprisingly) the first time.

Long Jump

Fred Salle	UK	8.10

The completely unsung Salle, Commonwealth silver medallist in 1986, wins (with his last jump) a major event for the first time since the 1984 AAA.

Triple Jump

Yoelvis Quesada	AMER	17.61	ChR
2 Julian Golley	*UK*	*17.06*	

Quesada sets a British all-comers' record in winning the event for the second successive time. Golley beats the personal best he set in winning the Commonwealth Games.

Pole Vault

Okkert Brits	AFR	5.90	ChR
8 Neil Winter	*UK*	-	

Surely some kind of record, this: for the second World Cup in a row, Winter fails to clear a height or score a point. If he'd cleared his Commonwealth Games winning height (5.40) Britain might well have won the Cup. Brits, who no-heighted at the Games, is the first African to win the event and sets a new continental and Commonwealth record.

Shot Putt

CJ Hunter	USA	19.92
8 Nigel Spratley	*UK*	*17.20*

Hunter (the C stands for Cotterell, the J's his mother's name, which he won't release) registers the four longest throws of the competition.

Discus

Vladimir Dubrovshchik	EUR	64.54
7 (last) Bob Weir	*UK*	*55.86*

Hammer

Andrei Abduvaliyev	ASIA	81.72
8 Paul Head	*UK*	*68.38*

Javelin

Steve Backley	UK	85.02

Women

British placings included for interest's sake; the IAAF delete them from the record books when the result of Modahl's drug test is confirmed.

100 metres

Irina Privalova	EUR	11.32
7 Paula Thomas	*UK*	*11.67*

200 metres

Merlene Ottey	AMER	22.23
6 Paula Thomas	*UK*	*23.22*

Ottey sets a British all-comers' record.

400 metres

Irina Privalova	EUR	50.62

Privalova (who also finishes second in the 200m) completes a unique double in her first ever individual 400m race.

800 metres

Maria Mutola	AFR	1:58.27
6 Cathy Dawson	*UK*	*2:04.13*

The muscular Mutola wins the event (easily) for the second time in a row.

1500 metres

Hassiba Boulmerka	AFR	4:01.05	ChR
3 Kelly Holmes	*UK*	*4:10.81*	

3000 metres

Robin Meagher	AMER	9:05.81
1 Yvonne Murray	*UK*	*8:56.81*

10 000 metres

Elana Meyer	AFR	30:52.51	ChR
5 Suzanne Rigg	*UK*	*33:38.14*	

Meyer sets an African, Commonwealth & British all-comers' record, the fourth-fastest time ever run.

100m Hurdles

Aliuska Lopez	AMER	12.91
3 Jacqui Agyepong	*UK*	*13.02*

Lopez wins the event for the second successive time.

400m Hurdles

Silvia Rieger	GER	56.14
1 Sally Gunnell	*UK*	*54.80*

4x100m relay

Faith Idehen, Mary Tombiri, Christy Opara
Thompson, Mary Onyali (all Nigeria)
AFR 42.92

*8 Jacqui Agyepong, Geraldine McLeod, Simmone
Jacobs, Paula Thomas UK 44.45*

4x400m relay

Karin Janke, Ute Rohländer, Heike Meissner,
Anja Rücker GER 3:27.59

*1 Phylis Smith, Linda Keough, Melanie Neef,
Sally Gunnell UK 3:27.36*

High Jump

Britta Bilac	EUR	1.91
6 Debbie Martin	*UK*	*1.85*

Long Jump

Inessa Kravets	EUR	7.00
6 Yinka Idowu	*UK*	*6.51*

Triple Jump

Ana Biryukova	EUR	14.46	ChR
4 Michelle Griffith	*UK*	*13.70*	

Shot Put

Huang Zhi-hong	ASIA	19.45
5 Judy Oakes	*UK*	*17.92*

Huang regains the title she won in 1989.

Discus

Ilke Wyludda	GER	65.30
7 Jackie McKernan	*UK*	*56.28*

Javelin

Trine Hattestad	EUR	66.48
6 Sharon Gibson	*UK*	*53.32*

Men's result

Africa 116, UK 111, Americas 95, Europe 91, Germany
85.5, USA 78, Asia 75, Oceania 62.5

*Africa's strong team (a contrast with the USA's second
strings) retain the men's title, Britain finishing second
behind them again (again the highest-placed single
country).*

Women's result

Europe 111, Americas 98, Germany 79, Africa 78,
Asia 67, Oceania 57, USA 48. *UK 73*

*Asian and African athletes condemn the food,
accommodation and travel arrangements, criticisms
largely accepted by BAF spokesman Tony Ward.
Overshadowing all this is the fact that the British
women are allowed to compete: they wouldn't have
qualified if Modahl hadn't finished first in the European
Cup 800m. By the time their results are deleted, it's too
late for the Russians, who would have taken their place.*

European Cup
25-26 June 1994
Alexander Stadium, Birmingham

Men

100 metres

Linford Christie	UK	10.21

200 metres

Linford Christie	UK	20.69

400 metres

Roger Black	UK	45.09

800 metres

Nico Motchebon	GER	1:48.12
3 Craig Winrow	*UK*	*1:48.76*

1500 metres

Andrei Bulkovskiy	UKR	3:49.33
3 Gary Lough	*UK*	*3:49.57*

5000 metres

Dieter Baumann	GER	13:48.95
4 John Mayock	*UK*	*13:50.58*

10 000 metres

Francesco Panetta	ITA	28:38.45
5 Gary Staines	*UK*	*29:57.27*

3000m Steeplechase

Alessandro Lambruschini	ITA	8:24.98
3 Justin Chaston	*UK*	*8:29.99*

110m Hurdles

Florian Schwarthoff	GER	13.35
3 Andy Tulloch	*UK*	*13.65*

400m Hurdles

Sven Nylander	SWE	49.36
6 Peter Crampton	*UK*	*50.09*

4x100m relay

Jason John, Solomon Wariso, John Regis,
Linford Christie UK 38.79

4x400m relay

Du'aine Ladejo, Adrian Patrick, Brian Whittle,
Roger Black UK 3:02.50

High Jump

Hendrik Beyer	GER	2.25
3 Dalton Grant	*UK*	*2.20*

Long Jump

Stanislav Tarasenko	RUS	8.02
6 Barrington Williams	*UK*	*7.66*

Triple Jump

Denis Kapustin	RUS	17.30
4 Jonathan Edwards	*UK*	*16.88*

Pole Vault

Jean Galfione	FRA	5.70
5 eq Mike Edwards	*UK*	*5.20*

Shot Putt

Paulo Dal Soglio	ITA	19.69
7 Paul Edwards	*UK*	*18. 10*

Discus

Dmitry Shevchenko	RUS	64.74
6 Bob Weir	*UK*	*58.92*

Hammer

Vasili Sidorenko	RUS	78.76
7 Peter Vivian	*UK*	*68.44*

Javelin

Andrei Moruyev	RUS	87.34
3 Mick Hill	*UK*	*85.28*

Women

100 metres

Zhanna Tarnopolskaya	UKR	11.26
2 Katharine Merry	*UK*	*11.34*

200 metres

Silke Knoll	GER	23.04
2 Katharine Merry	*UK*	*23.38*

400 metres

Svetlana Goncharenko	RUS	52.08
2 Melanie Neef	*UK*	*52.43*

800 metres

Patricia Djaté	FRA	2:02.95

Diane Modahl (UK) finishes first but is later found to have tested positive for drugs at an earlier meeting (Lisbon 18 Jun).

1500 metres

Lyubov Kremlyova	RUS	4:05.97
2 Kelly Holmes	*UK*	*4:06.48*

3000 metres

Lyudmila Borisova	RUS	8:52.21
3 Sonia McGeorge	*UK*	*8:55.47*

10 000 metres

K Wessel	GER	32:26.85
6 Vicki McPherson	*UK*	*34:03.07*

100m Hurdles

Jacqui Agyepong	UK	13.00

400m Hurdles

Sally Gunnell	UK	54.62

4x100m relay

	UKR	43.65
2 Sandra Douglas, Katharine Merry, Simmone Jacobs, Paula Thomas	*UK*	*43.46*

4x400m relay

Melanie Neef, Tracy Goddard, Phylis Smith, Sally Gunnell	UK	3:27.33

High Jump

Tatyana Shevchik	BYL	1.94
6 Julia Bennett	*UK*	*1.85*

Long Jump

Heike Drechsler	GER	6.99
5 Denise Lewis	*UK*	*6.42*

Triple Jump

Helga Radtke	GER	13.90
4 Michelle Griffith	*UK*	*13.75*

Shot Put

Astrid Kumbernuss	GER	19.63
4 Judy Oakes	*UK*	*17.75*

Discus

Ilke Wyludda	GER	68.36
6 Jacqui McKernan	*UK*	*55.30*

Javelin

Natalya Shikolenko	BYL	69.00
8 Karen Costello	*UK*	*49.24*

Men's result

Germany 121, UK 106, Russia 101, Ukraine 87, Italy 84, Sweden 81.5, France 80, Romania 56

Women's result

Germany 98, Russia 95, Ukraine 86, Belarus 64, France 60, Romania 60, Spain 50

Both British teams qualify for the World Cup.

AAA Championships
incorporating UK National Championships

Men

100m	Linford Christie	9.91w	ChRw
200m	Solomon Wariso	20.67	
400m	Roger Black	44.94	
800m	Craig Winrow	1:48.45	
1500m	Kevin McKay	3:40.59	
5000m	Dermot Donnelly	13:52.63	
10 000m	Rob Denmark	28:03.34	
3000 St	Justin Chaston	8:46.99	
110mH	Andy Tulloch	13.70	
400mH	Peter Crampton	49.82	
High J	Brendan Reilly	2.24	
Long J	Barrington Williams	7.77	
Triple J	Jonathan Edwards	17.39	ChR
Pole V	Andy Ashurst	5.30	
Shot	Paul Edwards	18.32	
Discus	Kevin Brown	58.60	
Hammer	Peter Vivian	70.80	
Javelin	Mick Hill	84.60	

Women

100m	Katharine Merry	11.27	
200m	Katharine Merry	22.85	
400m	Melanie Neef	52.56	
800m	Diane Modahl	2:01.35	
1500m	Kelly Holmes	4:01.41	
3000m	Sonia McGeorge	9:03.80	
10 000m	Zahara Hyde	33:23.25	
100mH	Clova Court	13.06	
400mH	Gowry Retchakan	57.08	
High J	Julia Bennett	1.89	
Long J	Yinka Idowu	6.58	
Triple J	Michelle Griffith	14.08	ChR
Pole V	Kate Staples	3.65	ChR
Shot	Judy Oakes	18.38	
Discus	Jacqui McKernan	56.94	
Hammer	Lorraine Shaw	59.58	
Javelin	Shelley Holroyd	57.08	

Griffith and Staples' marks are also Commonwealth records (Griffith the first over 14m). Staples is better known as Zodiac in ITV's Gladiators, where she teams up with former Commonwealth heptathlon champion Judy Simpson, now known as Nightshade.

AAA Indoor Championships

18-19 February 1994
National Arena, Birmingham

Men

60m	Michael Rosswess	6.56
200m	Philip Goedluck	21.16
400m	Du'aine Ladejo	46.54
800m	Tom McKean	1:48.46
1500m	Atoi Boru (KEN)	3:42.25
3000m	Matt Barnes	7:56.08
60mH	Hugh Teape	7.73
High J	Brendan Reilly	2.28
Long J	Mattias Sunneborn (SWE)	7.50
Triple J	Francis Agyepong	16.55
Pole V	Peter Widén (SWE)	5.45
Shot	Paul Edwards	18.95

Women

60m	Bev Kinch	7.35
200m	Maria Staafgard (SWE)	23.78
400m	Tracy Goddard	54.05
800m	Kirsty Wade	2:05.60
1500m	Lynn Gibson	4:17.01
3000m	Erika König (AÚT)	9:25.58
60mH	Samantha Farquharson	8.19
High J	Hanne Haugland (NOR)	1.94
Long J	Denise Lewis	6.07

Triple J	Rachel Kirby	13.21
Pole V	Kate Staples	3.46
Shot	Maggie Lynes	15.82

European Indoor Championships

11-13 March 1994 Bercy, Paris

Men

60 metres
| | Colin Jackson | UK | 6.49 | ChR |
| | *3 Michael Rosswess* | *UK* | *6.54* | |

200 metres
| | Daniel Sangouma | FRA | 20.68 |

400 metres
| | Du'aine Ladejo | UK | 46.53 |

Ladejo dislocates his shoulder in diving over the line.

800 metres
| | Andrei Loginov | RUS | 1:46.38 |

1500 metres
| | David Strang | UK | 3:44.57 |

3000 metres
| | Kim Bauermeister | GER | 7:52.34 |
| | *3 Rod Finch* | *UK* | *7:53.99* |

60m Hurdles
| | Colin Jackson | UK | 7.41 |

First ever to win 60m double at these championships.

5000m Walk
| | Mikhail Shchennikov | RUS | 18:34.32 |

High Jump
| | Dalton Grant | UK | 2.37 |

Long Jump
| | Dietmar Haaf | GER | 8.15 |

Triple Jump
| | Leonid Voloshin | RUS | 17.44 |

Pole Vault
| | Piotr Bochkaryov | RUS | 5.90 | ChR |

Shot Putt
| | Aleksandr Bagach | UKR | 20.66 |

Heptathlon
| | Christian Plaziat | FRA | 6268 |

Women

60 metres
| | Nelli Cooman | HOL | 7.17 |

Cooman wins the title for the sixth time.

200 metres
Galina Malchugina	RUS	22.41

400 metres
Svetlana Goncharenko	RUS	51.62

800 metres
Natalya Dukhnova	BYL	2:00.42

1500 metres
Yekaterina Podkopayeva	RUS	4:06.46

In retaining the title, Podkopayeva becomes the oldest athlete ever (41) to win a major international track gold.

3000 metres
Fernanda Ribeiro	POR	8:50.47

60m Hurdles
Yordanka Donkova	BUL	7.85

3000m Walk
Annarita Sidoti	ITA	11:54.32

Sidoti, the 1990 European outdoor champion, is probably the shortest athlete, (barely 5') to win a major championship.

High Jump
Stefka Kostadinova	BUL	1.98

Long Jump
Heike Drechsler	GER	7.06

Triple Jump
Inna Lasovskaya	RUS	14.88	ChR

Shot Putt
Astrid Kumbernuss	GER	19.44

Pentathlon
Larisa Turchinskaya	RUS	4801	ChR

Goodwill Games
24-29 July 1994
Petrovski Stadium, St Petersburg

Men

100 metres
Dennis Mitchell	USA	10.07

200 metres
Michael Johnson	USA	20.10
3 John Regis	*UK*	*20.31*

400 metres
Quincy Watts	USA	45.21
2 Du'aine Ladejo	*UK*	*45.21*

800 metres
Andrei Loginov	RUS	1:46.65

Mile
Nourredine Morceli	ALG	3:48.67

5000 metres
Moses Kiptanui	KEN	13:10.76
3 Jon Brown	*UK*	*13:24.79*

10 000 metres
Hammou Boutayeb	MOR	28:10.89

3000m Steeplechase
Marc Davis	USA	8:14.30

110m Hurdles
Colin Jackson	UK	13.29
2 Tony Jarrett	*UK*	*13.33*

400m Hurdles
Derrick Atkins	USA	47.86

20km Walk
Bernardo Segura	MEX	1h23:28.88

High Jump
Javier Sotomayor	CUBA	2.40

Long Jump
Mike Powell	USA	8.45

Triple Jump
Kenny Harrison	USA	17.43

Pole Vault
Igor Trandenkov	RUS	5.90

Shot Putt
CJ Hunter	USA	20.35

Discus
Dmitry Shevchenko	RUS	64.68

Hammer
Lance Deal	USA	80.20

The first US hammer thrower to win any kind of global competition since Hal Connolly at the 1956 Olympics.

Javelin
Andrei Shevchuk	RUS	82.90

Decathlon
Dan O'Brien	USA	8715

Women

100 metres
Gwen Torrence	USA	10.95

200 metres
Gwen Torrence	USA	22.09

400 metres
Jearl Miles	USA	50.60

800 metres
Maria Mutola	MOZ	1:57.63

1500 metres
Yekaterina Podkopayeva	RUS	4:04.92

3000 metres
Yelena Romanova	RUS	8:41.06

Most world records in one event
Official records in Olympic events only

17	Sergei Bubka	USSR/UKR	1984-94	pole v
14	Iolanda Balas	ROM	1956-61	high j
11	Faina Melnik	USSR	1971-76	discus
10	Matti Järvinen	FIN	1930-36	javelin
10	Parry O'Brien	USA	1953-59	shot
10	Nadyezhda Chizhova			
		USSR	1968-73	shot

10 000 metres
Tecla Lorupe   KEN   31:52.39

2000m Steeplechase
Marina Pluzhnikova   RUS   6:11.84   WR

100m Hurdles
Brigita Bukovic   SLVN   12.83

400m Hurdles
Sally Gunnell   UK   53.51

10km Walk
Olympiada Ivanova   RUS   42:30.31

High Jump
Silvia Costa   CUB   1.95

Long Jump
Heike Drechsler   GER   7.12

Triple Jump
Ana Biryukova   RUS   14.57

Pole Vault
Sun Cai-yun   CHN   4.00

Shot Putt
Sui Xin-mei   CHN   20.15

Discus
Barbara Echevarria   CUB   64.84

Javelin
Trine Hattestad   NOR   65.74

Heptathlon
Jackie Joyner Kersee   USA   6606

JJK is accused of putting beer on her javelin to get a better grip.

Grand Prix final
3 September 1994 Charlety, Paris

Men
100m	Dennis Mitchell	USA	10.12
	2 Linford Christie	UK	10.13
400m	Derek Mills	USA	45.22

1500m	Nourredine Morceli	ALG	3:40.89
5000m	Khalid Skah	MOR	13:14.63
110mH	Colin Jackson	UK	13.08
400mH	Samuel Matete	ZAM	48.02
High J	Javier Sotomayor	CUBA	2.33
Triple J	Mike Conley	USA	17.68
Pole V	Sergei Bubka	UKR	5.90
Shot	Randy Barnes	USA	20.60
Hammer	Andrei Abduvaliyev	TAJ	81.46

Women
100m	Merlene Ottey	JAM	10.78
400m	Marie-José Pérec	FRA	49.77
1500m	Angela Chalmers	CAN	4:01.61
5000m	Sonia O'Sullivan	EIRE	15:12.94
	3 Alison Wyeth	*UK*	*15:15.45*
100mH	Svetla Dimitrova	BUL	12.66
Long J	Jackie Joyner Kersee	USA	7.21
Discus	Ilke Wyludda	GER	65.84
Javelin	Natalya Shikolenko	BYL	68.26

Final standings

Men
1	Morceli	78 pts
2	Matete	72
3	Conley	72

Women
1	Joyner Kersee	72
2	Dimitrova	72
3	O'Sullivan	72

IPC (Paralympic) World Championships
22-31 July 1994 Berlin

Leading medal winners
	Gold	Silver	Bronze
Germany	26	31	27
Australia	23	20	12
UK	22	25	19
USA	20	26	26
Canada	20	17	12

41 of the 43 medal-winning countries win gold.

British gold medallists
Nigel Bourne	T20	200	22.56	WR
Nigel Bourne	T20	Long J	6.92	WR
Ken Churchill	F36	Discus	36.28	
Ken Churchill	F36	Javelin	44.56	WR

Esther Cruice	T37	400	1:10.26	
Keith Gardner	F35	Club	54.14	WR
Tanni Grey	T52	100	17.93	
Tanni Grey	T52	200	30.75	WR
Tanni Grey	T52	400	58.28	WR
Tanni Grey	T52	800	2:00.23	

Grey also won the London Marathon.

Tracy Hinton	T10	100	13.44	
Janice Lawton	F33	Javelin	14.08	WR
Stephen Payton	T37	100	11.94	
Stephen Payton	T37	200	25.09	
Stephen Payton	T37	400	54.84	WR
Clare Pearce	F34	Javelin	14.66	
Sally Reddin	F53	Shot	5.76	
Gordon Robertson	T35	400	1:03.23	
Noel Thatcher	T11	5000	15:48.64	
Noel Thatcher	T11	10 000	33:15.73	
Paul Williams I	F37	Javelin	38.46	WR
Paul Williams II	&32	400	1:25.15	

European Clubs Cup

Men

28-29 May 1994 Malaga

Larios	SPA	129
Fiamme Azzurre	ITA	116
Racing Club de Paris	FRA	97
Ujpesti Dozsa	HUN	95
Dukla Prague	CZE	90
Haringey	UK	86
Fenebahçe	TURK	61.5
CSKA Sofia	BUL	60

Haringey are once again at a disadvantage as Larios, packed with overseas stars as always, win the title for the fourth time in the last five years.

Women

28-29 May Vienna

CSKA Sofia	BUL

Sofia win the competition for the first time.

British club titles

LEAGUE DIVISION 1 Winners

Men	Thames Valley Harriers
Women	Sale Harriers

CUP FINAL 17 September 1994 Bedford

Men

Thames Valley Harriers	133
Shaftesbury Barnet	113

Birchfield Harriers	108
Belgrave Harriers	106
Blackheath	104
Woodford Green	95
Windsor, Slough & Eton	54

Thames Valley do the double by taking the Cup for the first time. Haringey are barred because Solomon Wariso failed that drugs test.

Women

Essex Ladies	100
Sale Harriers	96
Shaftesbury Barnet	80
Coventry Godiva	76
Birchfield Harriers	74.5
Edinburgh Woollen Mills	74.5
Aldershot, Farnham & District	63
Cardiff	25

Essex retain the title.

Road running

Major marathons

Eindhoven 10 October 1993

Men	Mohamed Salmi	ARG	2h12:47
Women	Liesbeth van Ast	HOL	2h40:57

Chicago 31 October 1993

Men	Luis Dos Santos	BRZ	2h13:14
Women	Ritva Lemettinen	FIN	2h33:18

World Cup San Sebastián 31 October 1993

Men	Richard Nerurkar	UK	2h10:03
Women	Wang Jun Xia	CHN	2h28:16

Nerurkar becomes the first British runner to win a championship Marathon since Ian Thompson's 1974 Commonwealth-European double.

New York 14 November 1993

Men	Andrés Espinosa	MEX	2h10:04
Women	Uta Pippig	GER	2h26:24

45-y-o Zoe Koplowitz finishes last (in 27h 45m) for the sixth year in a row. A victim of multiple sclerosis, she gets along with the help of two sticks.

New York 6 November 1994

Men	German Silva	MEX	2h11:21
Women	Tecla Lorupe	KEN	27:39

The closest men's race in the history of the event (Silva wins by two seconds) owes something to his running an extra 200 metres after taking a wrong turn near the end. Lorupe runs a Marathon for the first time. Neither of the defending champions takes part. Two runners die during the race.

Fukuoka 5 December 1993

Men	Dionicio Cerón	MEX	2h08:51
Women	No race		

London 18 April 1994

Men	Dionicio Cerón	MEX	2h08:53
	Abebe Mekkonen	ETH	2h09:17
	German Silva	MEX	2h09:18
	8 Eamonn Martin	UK	2h11:05
Women	Katrin Dörre	GER	2h32:34
	Lisa (Martin) Ondieki	AUS	2h33:17
	Janet Mayal	BRZ	2h34:21
	4 Sally Ellis	UK	2h37:06

In becoming the first runner (of either sex) to win the event three years in a row, Dörre runs the slowest winning time in the race's history.

Men wheelchair

	David Holding	UK	1h46:06
	Ivan Newman	UK	1h46:08
	Haakan Eriksson	SWE	

Holding, who outsprints Newman in the last ten metres, was also the last previous British winner (1989).

Women wheelchair

	Tanni Grey	UK	2h08:26
	Rose Hill	UK	2h08:30
	Tracey Lewis	UK	2h28:34

Grey, winner in 1992, regains the title from Hill, whose chair hits a sleeping policeman. None of the competitors appreciate the cobbles near the finish.

Rotterdam 18 April 1994

Men	Vincent Rousseau	BEL	2h07:51
Women	Miyoko Asahina	JAP	2h25:52

Boston 18 April 1994

Men	Cosmas Ndeti	KEN	2h07:51
Women	Uta Pippig	GER	2h21:45

Ndeti wins the race for the second year in a row. Both winners run the fastest times ever for the event.

Berlin 25 September 1994

Men	António Pinto	PORT	2h08:31
Women	Katrin Dörre	GER	2:25:15

Half-marathon World Championship 1993

3-4 October Brussels

Men

Vincent Rousseau	BEL	1h 01m 06
Steve Moneghetti	AUS	1h 01m 10
Carl Thackery	UK	1h 01m 13

Team: Kenya

Women

Conceição Ferreira	PORT	1h 10m 07
Mari Tanigawa	JAP	1h 10m 09
Tecla Lorupe	KEN	1h 12m 00

Team: Romania

Half-marathon World Championship 1994

24 September Oslo

Men

Khalid Skah	MOR	1h00:27
German Silva	MEX	1h00:28
Ronaldo da Costa	BRZ	1h00:54

Team: Kenya

Skah, the 1990 & 1991 world cross-country champion and 1992 Olympic 10 000 gold medallist, breaks the course record set by Hugh Jones (UK) in 1982 in becoming the first man to win global titles on three surfaces. The only actual world champion on all three was Ingrid Kristiansen (NOR). The event's been held three times, Kenya predictably winning every team title.

Women

Elana Meyer	SAF	1h08:36
Iulia Negura	ROM	1h09:15
Anuta Catuna	ROM	1h08:35

Team: Romania

Meyer becomes the first S African to win a senior world title since the end of the boycott. Romania retain the team title. The highest placed British runner in each event finishes 29th, the men's team 12th, the women 9th.

Great North Run

18 Sep 1994 Newcastle to South Shields.
Over 30 000 take part, apparently a record for any half-marathon anywhere.

Men

Benson Masya	KEN	1h00.02
Moses Tanui	KEN	1h00:02
Paul Tergat	KEN	1h00.42
4 Paul Evans	UK	1h01.30

Masya, who wins the event for the third time in four years, has now won his last eight road races. He and Tanui set the second fastest time in history (Tanui the only runner to go under an hour for the distance: 59:47 in 1993).

Women

Rosanna Munerotto	ITA	1h11:29
Andrea Wallace	UK	1h11:34
Manuela Machado	PORT	1h11:48

Evans & Wallace win the British half-marathon championships.

Men wheelchair

Dave Holding	UK	50:33
Jack McKenna	UK	50:37
Chris Madden	UK	50:38

Road walking

NATIONAL CHAMPIONSHIPS 1993 16 Oct Horsham

| Men 50km | Les Morton | 4h03:20 |
| Women 20km | Elaine Callinan | 1h45:11 |

NATIONAL CHAMPIONSHIPS 1994 4 Sep Chesterfield

| Men 50km | Les Morton | 4h32:25 |
| Women 20km | Vicky Lupton | 1h44:48 |

Cross country

World Championships

26 March 1994 Budapest

Men 12060m

William Sigei	KEN	34:29
Simon Chemoiywo	KEN	34:30
Haile Gebresilasie	ETH	34:32

Sigei retains the title. First non-African: 13 Paulo Guerra (POR). First UK: 32 John Nuttall.
Last non-African winner: 1985 Carlos Lopes (POR).

Team
Kenya 34, Morocco 83, Ethiopia 133. *8th UK 439*

Kenya win the title for the eighth consecutive year. The last European winners were England in 1980.

Junior men 8140m

Philip Mosima	KEN	24:15
Daniel Komen	KEN	24:17
Abreham Tsige	ETH	24:46

Mosima retains the title.
First European: 14 Benoit Zwierzchlewski (FRA)

Team
Kenya 18, Ethiopia 27, Morocco 78

Women 6220m

Helen Chepngeno	KEN	20:45
Catherina McKiernan	EIRE	20:52
Conceição Ferreira	POR	20:52

The first African winner of the event. McKiernan is the first woman to finish runner-up three years in a row.

Team
Portugal 55, Ethiopia 65, Kenya 75

Junior women 4300m

Selina (Sally) Barsosio	KEN	14:04
Rose Cheruiyot	KEN	14:05
Elizabeth Cheptanui	KEN	14:15
11 Nicola Slater	*UK*	*14:49*

Team
Kenya 11, Ethiopia 46, Japan 60. *5th UK 119*

For the second successive year, Kenya win seven of the eight titles.

European Championships

10 Dec 1994 Alnwick Castle, Northumberland

An inaugural event, apparently organised (in the face of African domination) to allow Europeans (but not yet the British) to actually win races.

Men

Paulo Guerra	PORT	27:43
Domingos Castro	PORT	27:59
Antonio Serrano	SPA	28:03
11 Andrew Pearson	*UK*	*28:20*

Women

Catherina McKiernan	EIRE	14:28
Julia Vaquero	SPA	14:30
Elena Fidatov	ROM	14:36
26 Andrea Wallace	*UK*	*15:10*

Men's Team		**Women's Team**	
Portugal	20	Portugal	26
Spain	27	France	28
France	50	Portugal	29
4 UK	*77*	*9 UK*	*84*

British National Championships

MEN
12 March 1994 Temple Park, South Shields (14km)

Dave Lewis	42:36
John Nuttall	42:52
John Downes	43:18

Team: Blackheath

WOMEN
13 March 1994 Witton Park, Blackburn (6 km)

Paula Radcliffe	20:51
Alison Wyeth	20:54
Laura Adam	21:04

Team: Parkside

Australian Rules Football

Australian Football League (AFL)

Play-offs
West Coast 82 (11-16), Collingwood 80 (12-8)
Melbourne 123 (18-15), Carlton 96 (14-12)
North Melbourne 114 (15-24), Hawthorn 91 (13-13) aet
Geelong 106 (15-16), Footscray 101 (15-11)

Preliminary finals
Geelong 109 (16-13), North Melbourne 103 (14-19)
West Coast 117 (16-21), Melbourne 52 (8-4)

Final, 1 October 1994
West Coast 143 (20-23)
G: Evans 3, Heady 2, Kemp 2, Sumich 2, Wilson 2, Bond 2, Ball 2, Lewis 2
Geelong 63 (8-15)
G: Brownless 4, Wills, Ablett, Couch, Riccardi

Same teams, same result as the 1992 final, when the Eagles became the first club from outside Victoria to win the AFL. Geelong, who can't repeat their feat of winning each of their last two matches with the very last kick, haven't won the title since 1963.

British League

Regular season
Champions Wandsworth. 2nd West London. 3rd Bristol.

BARFL play-offs
August-September 1994
Popefield Reserve, Acton, London

Elimination final
London Hawks 148 (21-22), North London 10 (0-10)

Qualifying final
West London 150 (23-12), Bristol 25 (3-7)
Wandsworth bye

Semi-finals
Bristol 70 (10-10), London Hawks 115 (18-7)
Wandsworth 50 (6-14), West London 76 (11-10)

Grand Final
London Hawks 98 (15-8), West London 53 (7-11)

The Hawks, regular season champions the previous year, are gifted the final by the four West London players who get themselves sent off: Darren Isaacs, Bruce Williams, Darren Zoccoli, Teague Higham.

Badminton

World Team Championships
May 1994 Djakarta

For the first time ever, Britain fail to qualify for the final stages of both competitions, the men losing 3-2 to Finland, the women 4-1 to Sweden, both in zone finals in Glasgow.

Thomas Cup (men)

Semi-finals

Malaysia	4	China	1
Indonesia	3	S Korea	1

Final

INDONESIA	3	MALAYSIA	0
Ardy Wiranata	beat	Ong Ewe Hock	15-11 15-5
Heryanto Arbi	beat	Rashid Sidek	15-6 15-11
Bambang Suprianto	beat	Soo Beng Kiang	15-10 6-15 15-8

Uber Cup (women)

Semi-finals

Indonesia	4	S Korea	1
China	3	Sweden	1

Final

INDONESIA	3	CHINA	2
Susi Susanti	beat	Ye Zhao Ying	11-4 12-10
L Tampi, Finarsih	beat	Wu Yu Hong, Chen Ying	15-13 17-16
Yuliani Sentosa	lost to	Han Jing Na	5-11 5-11
Eliza & Z Resiana	lost to	Ge Fei, Gu Jun	10-15 8-15
M Audina	beat	Zhang Ning	11-7 10-12 11-4

World Grand Prix Finals 93
Dec, Kuala Lumpur

Men's singles
Joko Suprianto (INDO) bt Heryanto Arbi (INDON) 11-15 15-2 15-1

Women's singles
Susi Susanti (INDO) bt Ye Zhao Ying (CHN) 11-3 12-9

Susanti sets a record by winning a fourth World Grand Prix Finals title.

Men's doubles
Rudi Gunawan & B Suprianto (INDO) bt R Mainaky & Ricky Subagya (INDO) 11-15 15-10 15-9

Women's doubles
Finarsih & Lili Tampi (INDO)

Mixed doubles
Thomas Lund (DEN) & Catrine Bengtsson (SWE) bt Nick Ponting & Gill Clark (UK) 15-9 15-7

In their last world circuit tournament together, Ponting & Clark lead 4-0 in the first game against the reigning world champions. After winning the mixed doubles against China in October '94, Clark retires from international badminton with 145 England caps, breaking Steve Baddeley's record of 143.

World Grand Prix Finals 94
Dec, Bangkok

Men's singles
Ardy Wiranata (INDO) bt Allan Budi Kusuma (INDO) 9-15 15-7 15-5

Women's singles
Susi Susanti (INDO) bt Ye Zhao Ying (CHN) 4-11 12-10 11-4

Same players and result as last year's final.

Men's doubles
Ricky Subagya & R Mainaky (INDO) bt R Gunawan & B Suprianto (INDO) 15-10 15-7

Revenge for last year's final.

Women's doubles
G Fei & G Jun (CHN) bt Finarsih & Lili Tampi (INDO) 13-15 15-8 15-5

Mixed doubles
Thomas Lund (DEN) & M Thomson (DEN) bt JE Antonsen (SWE) & A Crabo (SWE) 12-15 15-4 15-9

3rd-place final: Nick Ponting (ENG) & Joanne Wright (ENG) bt Michael Sogaard (DEN) & Gillian Gowers (ENG) 15-9 15-4

All-England Championships
15-19 March 1994 Birmingham

Men's singles

Darren Hall, the only home seed in either singles, pulls out with a long-standing back injury. Only one British player, Steve Butler, reaches the last 16.

Quarter-finals

Ardy Wiranata	INDO	Fung Permadi	AUS	14-18 15-4 15-4
Hermawen Susanto	INDO	Thomas Stuer-Lauridsen	DEN	15-12 14-18 15-7
Heryanto Arbi	INDO	Rashid Sidek	MALAY	15-1 15-5
Allan Budi Kusuma	INDO	Poul-Erik Hoyer Larsen	DEN	15-10 15-3

Semi-finals

Wiranata	Susanto	15-8 15-3
Arbi	Budi Kusuma	15-5 15-7

Final

Arbi	Wiranata	15-12 17-14

Arbi retains the title.

Women's singles

Quarter-finals

Susi Susanti	INDO	Ra Kyun Min	S KOR	11-5 11-2
Bang Soo Hyun	S KOR	Han Jing Na	CHN	11-8 11-6
Ye Zhao Ying	CHN	Yuni Kartika	INDO	12-11 11-7
C Martin	DEN	Liu Yu Hong	CHN	11-4 11-6

Semi-finals

Ye	Martin	11-6 11-8
Susanti	Bang	11-8 11-9

Final

Susanti	Ye	15-5 15-9

Susanti regains the title she won in 1990 & 1991.

Men's doubles

Final

Rudi Gunawan & B Suprianto bt R Mainaky & Ricky Subagya	15-12 15-12

All four players are Indonesian.

Women's doubles

Final

Chung So-Young & Gil Young-Ah bt Jang Hye-Ock & Shim Eun-Jung	7-15 15-8 15-4

All four players are South Korean.

Mixed doubles

Final

Nick Ponting & Joanne Wright bt Chris Hunt & Gill Clark	15-10 15-11

England's first title at the Championships since 1985. The same two pairs had contested the National Championship final.

European Championships
11-17 April 1994 Den Bosch, Holland

Men's singles

Quarter-finals

Poul-Erik Hoyer-Larsen	DEN	Oliver Pongratz	GER	15-4 15-9
Jens Olsson	SWE	Jyri Aalto	FIN	15-9 15-10
Tomas Johansson	SWE	Michael Sogaard	DEN	18-14 14-17 15-1
Anders Nielsen	ENG	Jeroen van Dijk	HOL	15-9 14-18 15-8

Semi-finals

Hoyer-Larsen	Olsson	15-9 15-9
Johansson	Nielsen	17-14 15-6

Final

Hoyer-Larsen	Johansson	15-9 15-5

Hoyer-Larsen wins in the absence of his team mate and No.1 seed Thomas Stuer-Lauridsen who withdraws injured before the competition.

Men's doubles

Semi-finals

Chris Hunt & Simon Archer	ENG	15-12 7-15 15-12
Christian Jakobsen & Jens Eriksen	DEN	
Andrej Antropov & Nikolai Zuev	RUS	15-11 6-15 15-7
Henrik Svarrer & Jim Laugesen	DEN	

Final

Hunt & Archer	Antropov & Zuev	18-16 15-4

The first British pair to win the event since Mike Tredgett & Martin Drew in 1984.

Women's singles

Quarter-finals

Christine Magnusson	SWE	Astrid van der Knaap	HOL	11-2 11-4
Pernille Nedergaard Jessen	DEN	Jo Muggeridge	ENG	11-7 11-6
Lim Xiao Qing	SWE	Marina Andrievskaya	RUS	11-3 11-1
Catrine Bengtsson	SWE	Camilla Martin	DEN	3-11 12-10 11-7

Semi-finals

Lim	Nedergaard Jessen	11-1 6-11 11-6
Bengtsson	Magnusson	5-11 11-0 11-4

Final

Lim	Bengtsson	11-5 12-9

Women's doubles

Semi-finals

Lim Xiao Qing & Christine Magnusson	SWE	15-11 12-15 18-14
Gillian Clark & Julie Bradbury	ENG	
Lisbet Stuer-Lauridsen & Lotte Olsen	DEN	15-2 15-8
Erica van der Heuvel (HOL) & Maria Bengtsson (SWE)		

Final

| Lim & Magnuson | Stuer-Lauridsen & Olsen | 17-14 15-12 |

Lim & Magnusson retain the title.

Mixed doubles

Semi-finals

| Michael Sogaard (DEN) & Catrine Bengtsson (SWE) | 15-6 15-6 |
| Par-Gunnar Jönsson & Maria Bengtsson (SWE) | |

| Christian Jacobsen & Lotte Olsen (DEN) | 15-5 15-2 |
| Ron Michels & Erica van der Heuvel (HOL) | |

Final

| Sogaard & Bengtsson | Jacobsen & Olsen | 15-6 15-9 |

English National Championships

11-13 Feb 1994 Norwich

Men's singles

Semi-finals

| Darren Hall | Peter Bush | w.o |
| Peter Knowles | Anders Nielsen | 15-12 15-8 |

Final

| Hall | Knowles | 15-3 15-13 |

A record seventh singles title for Hall, in his tenth consecutive final in the event.

Men's doubles

Final

| Simon Archer & Chris Hunt | Nick Ponting & Julian Robertson | 15-8 18-17 |

Women's singles

Semi-finals

| Suzanne Louis Lane | Alison Humby | 6-11 11-6 11-2 |
| Fiona Smith | Sara Hore | 11-3 12-10 |

Final

| Louis Lane | Smith | 11-4 11-1 |

Women's doubles

Final

| Gillian Gowers & Joanne Wright | Gill Clark & Julie Bradbury | 15-7 ret |

Baseball

Major League 1993

Each team plays 162 games, placings decided on number of wins (draws don't exist).

National League

East

Philadelphia	97
Montreal	94
St Louis	87
Chicago	84
Pittsburgh	75
Florida	64
New York	59

West

Atlanta	104
San Francisco	103
Houston	85
Los Angeles	81
Cincinnati	73
Colorado	67
San Diego	61

Championship Series

6 Oct	Philadelphia	4	Atlanta	3
7 Oct	Philadelphia	4	Atlanta	14

The Braves hit four home runs on the way to scoring the most runs by one team in a League Championship Series game.

9 Oct	Atlanta	9	Philadelphia	4
10 Oct	Atlanta	1	Philadelphia	2
11 Oct	Atlanta	3	Philadelphia	4

Len Dykstra's home run wins it after Atlanta come back from 0-3 to 3-3.

13 Oct	Philadelphia	6	Atlanta	3

The Phillies stop Atlanta winning the title for a third consecutive year and reach the World Series themselves for the first time since 1984.

American League

East

Toronto	95
New York	88
Baltimore	85
Detroit	85
Boston	80
Cleveland	76
Milwaukee	69

West

Chicago	94
Texas	86
Kansas City	84
Seattle	82
California	71
Minnesota	71
Oakland	68

Championship Series

5 Oct	Chicago	3	Toronto	7
6 Oct	Chicago	1	Toronto	3

Mistakes by Dan Pasqua & Joey Cora conribute to two of the Blue Jays' runs.

8 Oct	Toronto	1	Chicago	6
9 Oct	Toronto	4	Chicago	7
10 Oct	Toronto	5	Chicago	3
12 Oct	Chicago	3	Toronto	6

Two more errors give Toronto a 3-2 lead in the fourth inning. Dave Stewart has now pitched eight games in Championship Series (the first seven with the Oakland Athletics) without conceding a run.

World Series

16 Oct	Toronto	8	Philadelphia	5

The Phillies make things hard for themselves from the start. They lead 3-2 when two of their outfielders, Milt Thompson & Len Dykstra, collide under an easy catch to let Toronto equalise. John Olerud, the Blue Jays' first baseman who recovered from a brain aneurism, seals the game with a 373-foot home run.

17 Oct	Toronto	4	Philadelphia	6

Philadelphia square the Series with home runs by Jim Eisenreich and (making up for Game One) Len Dykstra, but their famously unreliable pitching almost allows Toronto to come back from 5-0 down.

19 Oct	Philadelphia	3	Toronto	10

Angela Carmello, a 23-y-o nurse, wins a Madonna lookalike contest (first prize: tickets for the great lady's show in Philadelphia on the same night as the game) wearing a Holy Mary outfit (Like A Virgin, geddit?) and

a Phillies baseball cap. The highlight of the game itself
is Paul Molitor's huge home run.

| 20 Oct | Philadelphia | 14 | Toronto | 15 |

The pivotal game, it sets several Series records: longest
game (4 hrs 14 mins), most runs, most runners left on
base (18), the first team to reach double figures and
lose. Philadelphia's relief pitcher Mitch Williams saved
43 games during the season, but here he helps the Blue
Jays recover from 15-10 down. Dykstra, continuing his
improvement, scores two home runs and comes within
inches of joining Babe Ruth & Reggie Jackson in
scoring three in a single World Series game. He scores
five in the Series in a losing cause.

| 21 Oct | Philadelphia | 2 | Toronto | 0 |

Curt Schilling wins it by pitching a 5-hit shut-out.

| 23 Oct | Toronto | 8 | Philadelphia | 6 |

After Dykstra's fourth home run of the Series helps pull
the Phillies back from 5-1 down to lead 6-5, Joe
Carter's three-run homer run wins the title for the Blue
Jays, the first team to retain it since the New York
Yankees in 1978. The only other instance of a World
Series being finished off with a home run was in 1960
(Bill Mazerowski for the Pittsburgh Pirates v the
Yankees).

Major League 1994

On Sep 14, after 34 days of a players' strike, the whole
show (leagues, play-offs, World Series) is cancelled,
for the first time since 1904. WJMP radio station in
Akron, Ohio, who promise to broadcast the song Take
Me To The Ball Game over and over until the strike's
over, call it off after 57,161 plays.

1993 Leaders

Batting

BATTING AVERAGE
.370	Andres Galarraga	Colorado	NL
.363	John Olerud	Toronto	AL
.358	Tony Gwynn	San Diego	NL

SLUGGING AVERAGE
.677	Barry Bonds	San Fran.	NL
.632	Juan Gonzalez	Texas	AL
.617	Ken Griffey	Seattle	AL

HOME RUNS
46	Barry Bonds	San Fran.	NL
46	Juan Gonzalez	Texas	AL
40	David Justice	Atlanta	NL

Winning is the drug

Dwight Gooden, the New York Mets pitcher,
World Series winner in 1986, is suspended for a
whole 60 days. After failing two tests.

Meanwhile, examples of bat-tampering abound.
Albert Belle of the Cleveland Indians is banned
for ten games, reduced to seven, for putting
cork inside his bat.

RUNS BATTED IN
129	Albert Belle	Cleveland	AL
128	Frank Thomas	Chicago	AL
123	Barry Bonds	San Fran.	NL

HITS
211	Paul Molitor	Toronto	AL
200	Carlos Baerga	Cleveland	AL
200	John Olerud	Toronto	AL

Best NL: 194 Len Dykstra (Philadelphia) 4th

Pitching

WINNING %
.818	Mark Portugal	Houston	NL
.800	Tommy Greene	Philadelphia	NL
.786	Tom Glavine	Atlanta	NL

Best AL: .750 Jimmy Key (New York) 5th eq

EARNED RUN AVERAGE
2.36	Greg Maddux	Atlanta	NL
2.48	José Rijo	Cincinnati	NL
2.56	Kevin Appier	Kansas City	AL

Maddux, who sets an all-time record with an ERA more
than 2.5 below the average, becomes the first to win the
NL Cy Young award (best all-round pitcher) for the third
year in a row. David Cone (Toronto) wins the AL award.

WINS
22	John Burkett	San Fran.	NL
22	Tom Glavine	Atlanta	NL
22	Jack McDowell	Chicago	AL

SAVES
53	Randy Myers	Chicago	NL
48	Rod Beck	San Fran.	NL
45	Bryan Harvey	Florida	NL
45	Jeff Montgomery	Kansas City	AL
45	Duane Ward	Toronto	AL

Dec 6 1993, San Juan: in the Central American
& Caribbean Games, the 100-game winning
streak of world champions Cuba is ended by a
4-3 defeat by hosts Puerto Rico - partly due to
the defection of 40 players.

Basketball

World Championships (Men)
August 1994 Toronto

For the first time ever, the championships are held in North America - and for the first ever, the American professionals are allowed to enter, which brings in the crowds (330 000, including 32 616 for the final, both records) to see the Dream Team carry on what they started in the 1992 Olympics. The Shaq & Co score 19 three-pointers against Russia and are simply unapproachable. The only contest worthy of the name is for second place, which Croatia are disappointed not to win.

Group A

China	97	Brazil	93
USA	115	Spain	100
Spain	73	Brazil	67
USA	132	China	77
China	78	Spain	76
USA	105	Brazil	82

	P	W	L	F	A	Pts
USA	3	3	0	352	259	6
China	3	2	1	252	301	5
Spain	3	1	2	249	260	4
Brazil	3	0	3	242	275	3

Group B

Croatia	85	Cuba	65
Australia	87	S Korea	85
Croatia	104	S Korea	53
Australia	93	Cuba	87
Cuba	92	S Korea	79
Croatia	83	Australia	69

	P	W	L	F	A	Pts
Croatia	3	3	0	272	187	6
Australia	3	2	1	249	255	5
Cuba	3	1	2	244	257	4
S Korea	3	0	3	217	283	3

Group C

Canada	83	Angola	52
Russia	84	Argentina	64
Canada	91	Argentina	73
Russia	94	Angola	57
Argentina	67	Angola	59
Russia	73	Canada	66

	P	W	L	F	A	Pts
Russia	3	3	0	251	187	6
Canada	3	2	1	240	198	5
Argentina	3	1	2	204	234	4
Angola	3	0	3	168	244	3

Group D

Puerto Rico	102	Egypt	74
Greece	68	Germany	58
Greece	69	Egypt	53
Germany	81	Puerto Rico	74
Puerto Rico	72	Greece	64
Germany	78	Egypt	56

	P	W	L	F	A	Pts
Greece	3	2	1	201	183	5
Puerto Rico	3	2	1	248	219	5
Germany	3	2	1	217	198	5
Egypt	3	0	3	183	249	3

Ashraf Mahmoud (EGY) is caught taking steroids.

Quarter-finals

Group W

Russia	101	Puerto Rico	85
USA	130	Australia	74
USA	134	Puerto Rico	83
Russia	103	Australia	76
Australia	94	Puerto Rico	81
USA	111	Russia	94

	P	W	L	F	A	Pts
USA	3	3	0	375	271	6
Russia	3	2	1	298	272	5
Australia	3	1	2	244	314	4
Puerto Rico	3	0	3	249	329	3

Group X

Croatia	105	China	73
Greece	74	Canada	71
Croatia	92	Canada	61
Greece	77	China	61
Croatia	81	Greece	55
Canada	90	China	58

	P	W	L	F	A	Pts
Croatia	3	3	0	278	189	6
Greece	3	2	1	206	213	5
Canada	3	1	2	222	224	4
China	3	0	3	192	272	3

Semi-finals

USA	97	Greece	58
Russia	66	Croatia	64

3rd-place final

Croatia	78	Greece	60

16 teams take part. Cuba beat Angola 75-67 to finish 15th.

Final

USA	137	Russia	91

USA squad: Derrick Coleman, Joe Doumars, Tim Hardaway, Larry Johnson, Shawn Kemp, Dan Majerle, Reggie Miller, Alonzo Mourning, Shaquille O'Neal, Mark Price, Steve Smith, Isiah Thomas, Dominique Wilkins

World Championships (Women)

Sydney June 1994

Group A

Spain	117	N Zealand	54
USA	108	S Korea	64
S Korea	97	N Zealand	58
USA	92	Spain	71
USA	97	N Zealand	47
Spain	89	S Korea	88

	P	W	F	A	Pts
USA	3	3	297	182	6
Spain	3	2	277	234	5
S Korea	3	1	249	255	4
N Zealand	3	0	159	311	3

Group B

Cuba	71	France	68
Canada	109	Kenya	34
Cuba	90	Canada	72
France	108	Kenya	44
Canada	66	France	55
Cuba	122	Kenya	51

	P	W	F	A	Pts
Cuba	3	3	283	191	6
Canada	3	2	247	179	5
France	3	2	231	181	4
Kenya	3	0	129	339	3

Group C

Slovakia	94	Poland	52
Brazil	112	Taiwan	83
Poland	102	Taiwan	64
Slovakia	99	Brazil	88
Slovakia	86	Taiwan	73
Brazil	87	Poland	77

	P	W	F	A	Pts
Slovakia	3	3	279	213	6
Brazil	3	2	287	259	5
Poland	3	1	231	245	4
Taiwan	3	0	220	300	3

Group D

Italy	65	China	60
Australia	60	Japan	58
Italy	77	Japan	65
China	87	Australia	67
Australia	73	Italy	51
China	82	Japan	65

	P	W	F	A	Pts
China	3	2	229	197	5
Australia	3	2	200	196	5
Italy	3	2	193	198	5
Japan	3	0	188	219	3

Quarter-finals

Group 1

USA	88	Australia	70
Slovakia	66	Canada	63
USA	98	Canada	65
Australia	86	Slovakia	77
USA	103	Slovakia	96
Australia	90	Canada	72

Group 2

Brazil	111	Cuba	91
Spain	76	China	60
Cuba	68	Spain	65
China	97	Brazil	90
Brazil	92	Spain	87
China	86	Cuba	84

Semi-finals

Brazil	110	USA	107
China	66	Australia	65

Shelley Gorman's huge long shot in the very last second just fails to win it for Australia, who'd led by 15 pts.

3rd-place final

USA	100	Australia	95

Final

12 June Entertainment Centre

Brazil	96	China	87

Brazil, who lead by 19 pts halfway through the second half on the way to winning the title for the first time, are indebted to their great veteran Hortencia Marcari Oliva, who retires from international basketball after scoring 19 pts in the first 20 mins and 13 out of 14 free throws.

NBA 1993-94

Eastern Conference

All teams play 82 matches, places decided by number of wins.

Atlantic Division	W
New York Knicks	57
Orlando Magic	50
New Jersey Nets	45
Miami Heat	42
Boston Celtics	32
Philadelphia 76ers	25
Washington Bullets	24

Central Division	
Atlanta Hawks	57
Chicago Bulls	55
Cleveland Cavaliers	47
Indiana Pacers	47
Charlotte Hornets	41
Detroit Pistons	20
Milwaukee Bucks	20

Western Conference

Midwest Division	
Houston Rockets	58
San Antonio Spurs	55
Utah Jazz	53
Denver Nuggets	42
Minnesota Timberwolves	20
Dallas Mavericks	13

By winning their first 15 games, Houston equal an NBA record (Washington 1948), as do Dallas by losing 20 in a row (Philadelphia 1973); their 19 successive home defeats set another record (16 Orlando 1990).

Pacific Division	
Seattle SuperSonics	63
Phoenix Suns	56
Golden State Warriors	50
Portland Trail Blazers	47
Los Angeles Lakers	33
Sacramento Kings	28
Los Angeles Clippers	27

Play-offs

May 1994

Eastern Conference

Atlanta   3   Miami   2
88-93, 104-86, 86-90, 103-89*, 102-91*
* in overtime

New York   3   New Jersey   1
91-80, 90-81, 92-93*, 102-92
Chicago   3   Cleveland   0
104-96, 105-96, 95-92*
Indiana   3   Orlando   0
89-88, 103-101, 99-86

Semi-finals
Indiana   4   Atlanta   2
96-85, 69-92, 101-81, 102-86, 76-88, 98-79
New York   4   Chicago   3
90-86, 96-91, 102-104, 83-95, 87-86, 79-93, 87-77

One man doesn't make a team? In the regular season, the Bulls ride Michael Jordan's sudden retirement (6 Oct 1993) but could have done with him here. Defeat in a close series ends their three-year reign as NBA champions.

Finals
New York   4   Indiana   3
100-89, 89-78, 68-88, 77-83, 86-93, 98-91, 94-90

Western Conference

Denver   3   Seattle   2
106-82, 97-87, 93-110, 85-94*, 94-98*
Houston   3   Portland   1
114-104, 115-104, 115-118, 92-89
Phoenix   3   Golden State   0
111-104, 117-111, 140-133
Utah   3   San Antonio   1
89-106, 96-84, 105-72, 95-90

Semi-finals
Houston   4   Phoenix   3
87-91, 117-124*, 118-102, 107-96, 107-96, 86-103, 104-94
Utah   4   Denver   3
100-91, 104-94, 111-109*, 82-83, 109-101*, 94-91, 91-81

Finals
Houston   4   Utah   1
100-88, 104-99, 86-95, 80-78, 94-83

NBA Finals

Game 1 *8 June 1994 Houston*
Houston   85   New York   78
Olajuwon 28   *Ewing 23*

Game 2 *10 June 1994 Houston*
Houston   83   New York   91
Olajuwon 25, Maxwell 20

Game 3 *12 June 1994 New York*
New York   89   Houston   93
Harper 21, Starks 20   *Olajuwon 21*

Game 4 *15 June 1994 New York*

New York	91	Houston	82
Harper 21, Starks 20		*Olajuwon 32*	

Game 5 *17 June 1994 New York*

New York	91	Houston	84
Ewing 25		*Olajuwon 27*	

Game 6 *19 June 1994 Houston*

Houston	86	New York	84
Olajuwon 30		*Starks 27*	

Game 7 *22 June 1994 Houston*

Houston	90	New York	84
Olajuwon 25		*Harper 23*	
Maxwell 21			

As well as all the points, Hakeem Olajuwon, voted player of the series, picks up ten rebounds in the decider to help the Rockets win the title for the first time. He also produces the winning play in Game 6: with the score 84-84, he steals John Starks' shot to claim the two free throws that level the series. The Knicks, who haven't won it since 1973, regret Patrick Ewing's mediocre (by his standards) series. For the first time since the 24-second rule was introduced in 1954, neither team scores 100 points in a Finals match. Derek Harper equals the Finals record by shooting 17 three-pointers in the series (out of a record 50 attempts).

NBA: some 1993-94 statistics

Points

2383	David Robinson	San Antonio
2377	Shaquille O'Neal	Orlando
2184	Hakeem Olajuwon	Houston

Assists

1031	John Stockton	Utah
789	Mookie Blaylock	Atlanta
780	Tyrone Bogues	Charlotte

European club titles (Men)

Club Championship
Final stages Tel Aviv

Semi-finals *19 April 1994*
Joventut Badalona (SPA) 79 Barcelona (SPA) 65
Olympiakos Piraeus (GRE) 77 Panathinaikos (GRE) 65
Badalona recover from a 36-31 half-time deficit.

3rd-place final *21 April 1994*
Panathinaikos 100 Barcelona 83

Final *21 April 1994*
Badalona 59 Olympiakos 57
Again Badalona win it in the second half: the teams are level (39-39) at half-time.

European Cup

Semi-finals
Aris Salonica (GRE) 83 Olimpija Ljubljana (SLVN) 79
Olimpija Ljubljana 84 Aris Salonica 78
Olimpija Ljubljana 74 Aris Salonica 61
Taugres, Vitoria Alava (SPA) 81 Cholet (FRA) 67
Cholet 103 Taugres 90
Cholet 83 Taugres 90

Final *15 March 1994 Lausanne*
Olimpija 91 Taugres 81

Hard to know exactly what this event proves. It's a plate competition, for clubs knocked out in the early rounds of the Club Championship.

Korac Cup

Semi-finals
Stefanel Trieste (ITA) 96 OR Milan (ITA) 79
Milan 103 Trieste 96
Panionios (GRE) 83 PAOK Salonika (GRE) 85
PAOK 82 Panionios 64

Final
PAOK 75 Trieste 66
Trieste 91 PAOK 100

Neither Olimpija nor PAOK defend their title the following season.

European club titles (Women)

Champions' Cup
Final stages Poznan

Semi-finals
SFT Como (ITA) 79 Olimpia Poznan (POL) 62
Dorna Valencia (SPA) 75 BTV Wuppertal (GER) 62

3rd-Place final
Poznan 72 Wuppertal 63

Final
Como 79 Valencia 68

Como do it in stages. Third in 1992, second in 1993, their revenge stops Valencia winning the title for the third time in a row.

Ronchetti Cup

Final
Cesena (ITA) 78 Parma Primixie (ITA) 65
Parma 68 Cesena 66

An Italian team wins the cup for the fifth successive season. In the second leg, Parma lead by 14 pts before Catherine Pollini celebrates her 28th birthday by putting together 12 consecutive pts, the only ones she scores in the game.

British titles (Men)

National League

	W	L	F	A	Pts
Thames Valley Tigers	31	5	3356	2777	62
Worthing Bears	30	6	3342	3031	60
Manchester Giants	29	7	3516	2903	58
Guildford Kings	24	12	3100	2845	48
London Towers	21	15	3093	3124	42
Birmingham Bullets	21	15	3044	2914	42
Leicester Riders	20	16	2974	2917	40
Derby Bucks	17	19	3139	3132	34
Doncaster Panthers	13	23	2917	3105	26
Sunderland Scorpions	13	23	3190	3394	26
Chester Jets	11	25	2927	3073	22
Hemel Hempstead	3	33	2998	3552	6
Oldham Celtics	1	35	2729	3558	2

Thames Valley win the title for the first time.

League Play-offs

Birmingham 76 Manchester 93
Manchester 90 Birmingham 88
London 60 Guildford 61
Guildford 77 London 79
Derby 83 Thames Valley 81
Thames Valley 79 Derby 91
Leicester 83 Worthing 96
Leicester 77 Worthing 104
Play-off: Guildford 66 London 53

Championship semi-finals
30 April 1994 Wembley Arena
Guildford 82 Manchester 72
Worthing 77 Derby 75
Worthing score the last three points of the match from the free-throw line before Mike Landell misses a three-pointer for Derby with two seconds left.

Championship final
1 May 1994 Wembley Arena

Worthing	71	Guildford	65
Cunningham 16		*Byrd 15*	
Irish 15		*Politi 13*	
Harried 12		*Cummings 12*	
Lewis 11		*Henlan 12*	

Guildford lose their franchise at the end of the season.

Division 1 Play-offs

Semi-finals
Coventry Crusaders 76 Sheffield Forgers 74
Cardiff Heat 67 Crystal Palace Mavericks 65

Final

Coventry	75	Cardiff	69
M Donaldson 24		*Harper 31*	
Smith 19, Salvason 17		*Longman 13*	

Coventry also finished top of the division table.

Division 2 Play-offs

Semi-finals
Swindon Sonics 82 Mid-Sussex Magic 81
Guildford Storm 63 Nottingham Cobras 55

Nottingham finished top of the division table.

Final
Guildford 69 Swindon 54

Disabled League
Winners: Milton Keynes 26 pts

Simon Munn's rebound basket in the last second of their last match gives Milton Keynes the title for the first time in five years.

National Cup

Quarter-finals
Leicester Riders 55 Guildford Kings 64
Manchester Giants 99 Birmingham Bullets 85
Sunderland Scorpions 80 Thames Valley Tigers 89
Chester Jets 79 Worthing Bears 102

Colin Irish scores 35 pts for Worthing.

Semi-finals
Manchester Giants 72 Thames Valley Tigers 93
Thames Valley Tigers 98 Manchester Giants 80
Guildford 77 Worthing 93
Worthing 71 Guildford 68

Worthing knock out the holders.

Final *5 March 1994 Sheffield*
Worthing Bears 92 Thames Valley Tigers 83

Herman Harried scores 33 pts for Worthing.

League Trophy

Final *16 Jan 1994 National Indoor Arena, Birmingham*
Thames Valley Tigers 79 Manchester Giants 73

The Tigers retain the title.

National Trophy

Quarter-finals
Bury 84 Stockton 66
Sheffield 92 Coventry 89
Plymouth 100 Brixton 84
Crystal Palace 76 Solent 62

Semi-finals
Plymouth 87 Crystal Palace 74
Sheffield 88 Bury 79

Final
Sheffield 62 Plymouth 60

British titles (Women)

Division 1

	W	L	F	A	Pts
Sheffield Hatters	21	1	1610	1128	42
Northampton 76ers	20	2	1709	1195	40
Thames Valley Ladies	14	8	1492	1204	28
Barking & Dagenham Bobcats	14	8	1477	1402	28
Ipswich	12	10	1270	1332	24
Birmingham Quality Cats	11	11	1254	12031	22
Nottingham Wildcats	11	11	1081	1206	22
Chester Cats	8	14	1203	1407	16
London Jets	8	14	1280	1384	16
Rhondda	6	16	1149	1451	12
Brixton Lady Top Cats	5	17	1098	1327	10
South Tyneside	2	20	1226	1582	4

Championship Play-offs

Semi-finals
Thames Valley 63 Northampton 62
Sheffield 81 Barking & Dagenham 63

Final
Thames Valley 60   Sheffield 56
Josey 14, Smith 11   *Castle 16, V Ellis 15*
Paris 10

TV win the final for the third time in four years to stop Sheffield achieving a second successive League-Cup-Championship treble.

Division 2

	W	L	F	A	Pts
London Heat	17	1	1237	774	34
Cardiff Flyers	15	3	1093	943	30
Leicester Ladies	13	5	1085	929	26
Spelthorne Acers	10	8	1041	993	20
Doncaster Free Press	9	9	931	937	18
Luton Accs Raiders	8	10	947	1109	16
Sunderland Ladies	7	11	883	877	14
Manchester Flames	6	12	910	1027	12
Harlesden Amazons	4	14	855	1000	8
Plymouth Racers	1	17	819	1212	2

Play-offs

Semi-finals
Leicester 54 Cardiff 47
London 69 Spelthorne 66

Final
London 83 Leicester 59

National Cup

Quarter-finals
Barking & Dagenham Bobcats 90 Brixton Lady Top Cats 57

Thames Valley Ladies 77 London Jets 55
Northampton 76ers 86 Chester Jets 62
Sheffield Hatters 71 Birmingham Quality Cats 48

Semi-finals
Sheffield 79 Barking & Dagenham 71
Northampton 79 Thames Valley 63

Final
Sheffield 81 Northampton 79

Karen Goodrich misses the free throw that would have prevented Sheffield's fifth successive win in the event.

National Trophy

Quarter-finals
Cardiff 51 Kings Lynn 41
Leicester 99 Luton 46
Sunderland 56 Manchester 53
London Heat 60 Harlesden 36

Semi-finals
Cardiff 56 Leicester 53
London Heat 55 Sunderland 31

Final
Cardiff 59 London Heat 54

Commonwealth Championships

July 1994 Sungei Petani, Malaysia (men only)

	P	W	L	F	A	Pts
Canada	5	4	1	436	259	9
England	5	4	1	354	253	9
Nigeria	5	4	1	383	289	9
Malaysia	5	2	3	362	418	7
Hong Kong	5	1	4	313	446	6
Singapore	5	0	5	262	445	5

Canada beat defending champions England 64-50.

Goodwill Games

July 1994 St Petersburg

Men

Final
Puerto Rico 94 Italy 80

Women

Final
USA 87 France 63

World Invitation Club Tournament 1994

Crystal Palace

Semi-finals

Manchester Giants (ENG) 103 Worthing Bears (ENG) 90
Broceni Riga (LAT) 92 Thames Valley Tigers (ENG) 89

Final *3 Jan 1994*
Broceni Riga 118 *Bakatskis 36, Zeidaks 18, Pehka 17*
Manchester 95 *Hillman 25, Gordon 24, Samuels 20*

World Invitation Club Tournament 1995

Jan, Crystal Palace

FINAL

Thames Valley Tigers (ENG) 99
London Towers (ENG) 85

Steve Bucknall plays in a winning team for the third time with a third different club, following University of North Carolina in 1988 and Sunderland in 1991.

Wheelchair Basketball

World Championships (Gold Cup)

Men

July 1994 Edmonton, Canada

Pool A	P	W	L	F	A
France	5	5	0	338	260
Canada	5	4	1	260	226
Holland	5	3	2	313	260
Sweden	5	2	3	278	259
Japan	5	0	5	210	320

Pool B	P	W	L	F	A
USA	5	0	0	395	247
G Britain	5	4	1	322	261
Australia	5	3	2	336	316
Spain	5	2	3	340	293
Germany	5	1	4	301	309
Brazil	5	0	5	184	452

Brazil finish last of the twelve teams after losing 63-54 to Japan.

Semi-finals

USA	80	Canada	50
GB	48	France	47

Britain's finest hour (or finest half-minute). France, the defending champions, lead by five pts with only 23 secs to go, then Joe Jayaratne scores a three-pointer, Simon Munn from a free throw, and Dan Johnson the winning two points from twelve yards in the very last second.

3rd-Place final

Canada	72	France	62

Final

USA 67
Schlappi 14, Shepherd 14, Colton 14, Johnson 13, Waller 12
GB 53
Gordon 12, Caine 12, Jayaratne 8, Johnson 6, Price 5, Munn 4, Cheaney 2, Bramley 2, Woollard 2

British squad: Dave Bramley, Calum Gordon, Gary Peel, Tony Woollard (c), Simon Munn, Dan Johnson, Colin Price, Nigel Smith, Joe Jayaratne, Steve Caine, Malcolm Tarkenter, Mark Cheaney

The USA lead only 30-26 at half-time and by just five pts until the last few minutes.

Women

6-13 Aug 1994 Guttman SC, Stoke Mandeville

Semi-finals

Canada	39	Holland	30
USA	33	Australia	29

3rd-place final

Australia	38	Holland	36

Final

Canada	45	USA	34

A repeat of the 1992 Olympic final. Britain finish sixth (out of the ten) after beating Israel 36-26 & Japan 38-37 (recovering from a 17-pt deficit) and losing 51-19 to Australia, 51-26 to Canada and 43-24 & 35-18 to Germany. British squad: Karen Aspey, Sarah Baillie, Ann Bingham, Laura Bleakley, Josie Cichockyj, Susan Conroy, Kath Davies, Linda Morton, Niki Stanton, Yvonne Walker, Ann Wild.

European Cup (Men)

Final *Milton Keynes*
Sheffield 53 Meaux 51
Sheffield, who lead by ten pts at half-time, become the first British team to win the event (which has been held since 1975) when Michel Fahrafmaneo misses two free throws which would have tied the scores in the last minute.

Billiards

World Professional Championship 1993

Oct, Bombay

Semi-finals

Geet Sethi	INDIA	Roxton Chapman	ENG	1598-1024
Mike Russell	ENG	Norman Dagley	ENG	1317-1237

Final *5 Oct 1993*

Sethi	Russell	2139-1140

Same players and result as in the previous year's final.

World Professional Championship 1994

Oct, Bombay

Semi-finals

Peter Gilchrist	ENG	Geet Sethi	INDIA	1312-916
Mike Russell	ENG	Ian Williamson	ENG	1556-806

Final

Gilchrist	Russell	1539-645

Gilchrist, beaten by fellow Teessider Russell in the 1989 final, wins the title for the first time. Russell, still only 24, takes part in the final for the fifth time in a row, losing the last three.

Grand Slam Championship

July 1994 Madras

Semi-finals

Mike Russell	ENG	Roxton Chapman	ENG	5-2
Robbie Foldvari	AUS	Geet Sethi	INDIA	5-3

Final

Russell	Foldvari	6-3

U K Professional Championship

Semi-finals

Peter Gilchrist	ENG	Bob Close	ENG	699-418
Mike Russell	ENG	Geet Sethi	INDIA	787-653

Final *7 April 1994 Plymouth Pavilions*

Russell	Gilchrist	1072-330

Russell wins the title for the fourth time.

English Amateur Championship

Semi-finals

Martin Goodwill	P Shelley	1739-561
David Causier	D Burgess	2093-771

Final *28 March 1994 Bulwell, Notts*

Goodwill	Causier	1127-1105

Goodwill beats the defending champion.

British Bar Billiards Championships

Men's final

Kevin Tunstall bt Chris Saville

The 47-y-o Saville, playing in the final for the first time, loses by a massive margin to the England captain and tournament favourite (ten years his junior), who becomes only the second player to win the title more than once (his other win was back in 1980). Sue Banting, who chooses to enter the men's event, finishes second in Saville's group after winning the first leg of her match against him.

Women's final

Jan Taylor bt Pauline Withey

Taylor beats the England captain (who comes close to scoring the required but virtually impossible 4710 points in the last three mins) to regain the title she won in 1992.

Women's doubles

Gail Woods & Sue Banting bt Jan Taylor & Jill O'Brien

Taylor & O'Brien lose in the final for the second successive year.

Bobsleigh & Luge

Bobsleigh

Two Man World Cup

Pierre Lueders & David MacEachern	CAN	136
Christoph Langen & Günter Eger	GER	124
Günther Huber & Stefano Ticci	ITA	122
6 Mark Tout & Lenny Paul	*UK*	*100*

European Championships 1993-94

19 Jan La Plagne, France

Two Man

Christoph Langen & Peer Jöchel	GER	2:00.45
Günther Huber & Stefano Ticci	ITA	2:00.51
Gustav Weder & Donat Acklin	SWI	2:00.69

Four Man

Günther Huber	ITA	1:57.92
Mark Tout	UK	1:58.11
Dirk Wiese	GER	1:58.19

The British team of Tout, George Farrell, Jason Wing & Lenny Paul leads at halfway but makes a mistake at the start of the second run.

1994-95

Dec, Altenberg, Germany

Two Man
Standings after four races

Günther Huber & A Tartaglia	ITA	114
Reto Goetschi & Donat Acklin	SWI	112
Pierre Lueders & J Pyc	CAN	106

Four Man

Wolfgang Hoppe	GER	1:51.26
Mark Tout	UK	1:51.64
B Shimer	USA	1:51.68

Tout (with Dean Ward, Courtney Rumboldt and the perennial Paul) again finishes second to one of the best: Hoppe won two Olympic golds in 1984.

Two Man British Championship

Jan 1994 La Plagne, France

Mark Tout, Lenny Paul	2:02.89
Sean Olsson, Paul Field	2:03.15
R Pope, E Sekwalor	2:04.36

Luge

World Cup

Men's Single		
Markus Prock	AUT	160
Duncan Kennedy	USA	148
Georg Häckl	GER	140

Women's Single		
Gabriele Köhlisch	GER	83
Jana Böde	GER	82
Susi Erdmann	GER	60
Andrea Tagwerker	AUT	60

Men's Double		
S Krause, J Behrendt	GER	95
T Schiegl, M Schiegl	AUT	71
S Skel, S Wöller	GER	65

European Championships

Jan 1994 Königsee, Germany

Men's Single		
Markus Prock	AUT	1:35.907

Men's Double		
Jorg Raffl, Norbert Huber	ITA	1m30.137
K Brugger, Wilfried Huber	ITA	1m30.313
Y Hankel, T Rudolph	GER	1m30.627
The Hubers are brothers.		

Women's Single		
Gerda Weissensteiner	ITA	1m30.185
Jana Bode	GER	1m30.209
Gabriele Kohlisch	GER	1m30.422

Bowls

World Indoor Championships

Men
21 Feb - 6 March 1994 Guild Hall, Preston

Quarter-finals

Andy Thomson	ENG	Willie Wood	SCOT	7-0 7-3 5-7 6-7 7-4
Mark McMahon	HK	Graham Robertson	SCOT	7-5 7-4 7-3
Steve Rees	WAL	Wynne Richards	ENG	7-2 7-5 7-6
Richard Corsie	SCOT	Ian Taylor	AUS	7-6 5-7 3-7 7-4 7-4

Semi-finals

Thomson	Rees	1-7 1-7 7-4 7-4 7-1
Corsie	McMahon	7-3 7-1 2-7 7-4

Final

Thomson	Corsie	7-2 7-0 6-7 7-6

Thomson, the best indoor player of the last decade, wins a televised event for the first time.

Doubles semi-finals

Gary Smith	ENG	Steve Rees	WAL	7-0 7-4 7-3
Andy Thomson	ENG	John Price	WAL	
Cameron Curtis	AUS	David Bryant	ENG	7-0 5-7 7-4 7-4
Ian Schuback	AUS	Tony Allcock	ENG	

Doubles final

Curtis & Schuback		Smith & Thomson	7-1 7-6 5-7 7-0

In both the singles (Corsie) and the doubles, the holders lost in the final.

Women
22-24 April 1994 Cymbernauld

Quarter-finals

Jan Woodley	SCOT	Kate Adams	SCOT	1-7 0-7 7-6 7-5 7-0
Anne Simon	GUER	Jenny Nicolle	GUER	7-0 6-7 7-6 0-7 7-2
Mary Price	ENG	Margaret Johnston	IRE	7-1 7-2 7-4
J Conlan	SCOT	Val Stead	JERS	7-2 7-6 7-3

Woodley causes a big surprise by surviving an early pounding to knock out the holder, who'd looked unbeatable in the round-robin matches.

Semi-finals

Woodley	Simon	7-3 7-6 7-5
Price	Conlan	7-3 0-7 7-2 7-5

Final

Woodley	Price	5-7 7-1 7-5 5-7 7-5

Woodley beats the 1991 champion to win the title for the first time. In 1995 she and Johnston will compete, controversially for some, in the men's event.

British Outdoor Titles

Men

BRITISH ISLES CHAMPIONSHIPS
July 1994 Ayr

Singles semi-finals

Colin Best	IRE	R Rowans	WAL	w.o
George Whitelaw	SCOT	John Wickham	ENG	21-5

Whitelaw wins the last 18 points in a row.

Singles final

Best	Whitelaw	21-20

Pairs final

P Howells & G Jones (WAL) bt Sandy Grant & Robert Grant (SCOT)   25-9

Triples final

IRE (B Moffet, J Henry, Ian McClure) bt WAL   16-15

Fours

SCOT (W Wells, S Wilson, G Lyall, N Amos) bt ENG (skip: Mike Newman)   23-21

Teams

England beat Scotland 127-103, Ireland 129-96 & Wales 125-86 to win the title for the eleventh time in the last twelve years, a sequence interrupted only by Wales in 1992. Scotland haven't won it since 1980, Ireland since 1981.

EBA NATIONAL CHAMPIONSHIPS
Sep 1994 Worthing

Singles semi-finals

Brett Morley	A Manton	21-16
Paul Wilkinson	Wynne Richards	21-18

Singles final

Morley	Wilkinson	21-14

Morley's the first Notts player to take part in the final. The favourite, world outdoor champion Tony Allcock, loses 21-18 to Graham Hatherall in the 2nd round.

Pairs semi-finals

Keith Wood & Mike Bennett	H Barker & J Thompson	26-13
Alan Theobald & David Webb	Dean Morgan & Russell Morgan	25-14

Pairs final

Wood & Bennett	Theobald & Webb	26-6

The first Northumberland pair since 1978 to win the title.

Women

BRITISH ISLES CHAMPIONSHIPS
24-27 June 1994 Llandrindod Wells

Singles semi-finals

Dorothy Prior	ENG	J Cormack	SCOT	25-13
M Rosser	WAl	M Barber	IRE	25-14

Singles final

Prior	Rosser	25-9

Pairs final

J Davies & B Morgan (WAL) bt IRE (I Minnis, F Elliott) 30-19

Triples final

ENG (Wendy Buckingham, Val Haste, Jill Polley) bt WAL (S Proctor, P John, Margaret Pomeroy) 16-13

Fours final

IRE (M Killen, M McGarrity, M Hand, M Martin) bt SCOT (P Hunter, F Allan, M Strachan, N Hunter) 23-17

Teams

England	110	Scotland	107
Wales	130	Ireland	114
England	131	Ireland	84
Scotland	147	Wales	110
England	125	Wales	119
Scotland	143	Ireland	94

England regain the title.

EWBA NATIONAL CHAMPIONSHIPS
July-Aug 1994 Victoria Park, Leamington Spa

Singles semi-finals

Ingrid Betke	Caroline Duarte	21-19
Pat Kirk	Lisa Francis	

Duarte led 19-15.

Singles final

Betke	Kirk	21-12

The 65-y-o Betke becomes the first ever German-born EWBA champion.

Triples final

Egham (Chrissie Winter, Pam Garden, Doreen Hankin) bt Penryn (Liz Swadling, Pat Jose, Judith Reynolds) 17-8

Fours final

Peterborough (Sarah Newson, Valerie Newson, Mandy Brundle, Catherine Anton) bt Carlton Conway (J Turner, A Parker, S Keeling, Brenda Atherton) 25-8

Sarah Newson (17) becomes the youngest ever winner of a EWBA championship. Valerie, her mother, also wins her first title. The trade marquee is set on fire the night before the final.

British Indoor Championships

Men

ENGLAND INDOOR CLUB CHAMPIONSHIPS

Semi-finals

Ely	72	Cambridge Park	70
Stanley	85	Teignbridge	61

Final *20 Feb 1994 Lawson Park, Bedford*

Ely	80	Stanley	79

Ely win the title for the third time in seven seasons.

BRITISH ISLES INDOOR CHAMPIONSHIPS
March 1994 Nottingham

Singles semi-finals

Jeremy Henry	IRE	Alex Marshall	SCOT	21-10
Russell Morgan	ENG	David Harding	WAL	21-3

Singles final

| Henry | Morgan | 21-18 |

Henry becomes the youngest ever winner (20) of the event.

Pairs final

Steve Rees & John Price (WAL) bt Ian Bell & Graham Robertson (SCOT) 21-12

The first pair ever to retain the title.

Triples final

SCOT (A Binnie, J Jeans, W Galloway) bt ENG (W Tomlinson, G Hufton, J Mills) 17-13

Fours final

ENG (C Yelland, N Thompson, S Tuohy, Wynne Richards) bt IRE (B Moffat, J Henry, R Weir, Ian McClure) 20-15

Teams

England	120	Wales	105
Scotland	125	Ireland	83
Scotland	125	England	113
Ireland	116	Wales	94
Scotland	132	Wales	116
England	160	Ireland	73

Scotland win the title for the fourth year in a row.

NATIONAL INDOOR CHAMPIONSHIPS
Melton Mowbray

Singles final *16 April 1994*

| M King | P Bennett | 21-12 |

Doubles final *15 April 1994*

Gary Smith & Brian Vickers bt Mike Newman & Robert Newman 23-22

Smith, the first player to win the event three times, wins his tenth national indoor title, one short of Andy Thomson's record. The Newmans are father and son.

EPA (ENGLISH PLAYERS' ASSOCIATION) SINGLES

Final 24 April 1994 Wellingborough

| Russell Morgan | Mel Biggs | 1-7 7-1 7-0 |

Women

INDOOR (EWIB) CHAMPION OF CHAMPIONS
March 1994 Darlington

Singles semi-finals

| Sharon Rickman | Margaret Knight | 21-6 |
| Sue Curtis | Jean Baker | 21-20 |

Singles final

| Rickman | Curtis | 21-2 |

Rickman, runner-up in 1991 and 1992, wins the title for the first time.

Pairs final

Joan Hills & Janet Tester bt Joan Beardsley & Jean Baker 18-17

Triples

Val Mitchell, Pam Sutton, Julie Meakin (Barwell) bt Di Gray, Denise Marshall, Jill Young (Taunton) 21-14

Fours final

| Swinton | Crystal Palace | 21-20 |

INDOOR (EWIB) NATIONAL SINGLES CHAMPIONSHIP
March 1994 Darlington

Final

Mary Price	Diana Hunt	21-18

The 1991 champion regains the title. In the semi-finals, Hunt beat Norma Shaw, who was trying to win the title for the seventh time.

BRITISH ISLES CHAMPIONSHIPS
March 1994 Blackpool

Singles final

Julie Davies	WAL	Jan Woodley	SCOT	21-18

Pairs final
Anne Erridge & Mary Price (ENG) bt Julie Forrest & Joyce Foster (SCOT) 25-15

Triples final
SCOT (Heather Mackay, Pat Clarke, Minnie Naismith) bt WAL (S Proctor, M Jones, M Pomeroy) 21-19

Fours final
SCOT (J McCreath, A Gilmour, D Jeffrey, E Smith) bt IRE (M Wilkinson, G Law, O Paisley, B Cameron) 17-14

Teams

Scotland	147	Ireland	77
England	117	Wales	106
Scotland	129	Wales	102
Ireland	128	England	122
Scotland	132	England	111
Ireland	133	Wales	112

Scotland retain the title. Ireland had never previously beaten England in the competition, which began in 1967.

EIBA NATIONAL MIXED FOURS

Final *27 March 1994 Church Gresley*
Sunderland (Judith Moran, Emma Baker, Jim Lambert, Richard McKie) beat
Cambridge Park (Pat Launders, Jean Staples, Steve Tuohi, Gary Little) 18-14

EIBA NATIONAL MIXED TEAMS

Semi-finals

South Forest	Tilbury	94-78
Rugby Thornfield	Atherley	102-70

Final *28 March 1994 Church Gresley*

South Forest	Rugby Thornfield	99-70

Winning is the drug?
Jane Gooday had to withdraw from the Scottish Championships because she was taking banned substances. She wasn't the only miscreant. 'Most of us,' she announced, 'take drugs for something. Half the club will have to be banned.' 'Retire' might be more apt. None of the team is under fifty. Gooday, who takes diuretics prescribed for her heart condition, is 73.

Boxing

Bradley Stone's death should have changed something – anything – but it didn't really. Breasts were beaten, genuine regret and sadness aired – but the show went on as it always does.

Whatever you think of all the punching, there was an awful lot of it in 1994 – or at least there were an awful lot of bodies governing it, and a lot of awful boxers involved. By the end of the year, there were at least 136 world champions, with more to come (Jon Robinson, former IBF vice-president, recently formed the WBU) and the odds are that they'll all become acceptable in the near future. After all, when the IBF staged its first title fight, in 1983, it wasn't taken seriously. When the WBO appeared, it was given much the same reception. Now it's the biggest source of British world champions and therefore passes as the real thing over here – though the Danish PBF banned it for having 'no class, no credibility' and the French followed suit.

There are still a few class fighters around (Roy Jones, Naseem Hamed, the declining Chávez), but with so many titles and mediocre title holders in that multitude, small wonder that the oldies are making comebacks or staying around: Larry Holmes (44), Roberto Duran (43), Stephen Muchoki (42), Alexis Arguello (42), Bonecrusher Smith (41), Trevor Berbick (40), Mike Weaver (NBA heavyweight champion at 42), Leon Spinks (41), Dennis Andries (heaven only knows), and the grandaddy of 'em all, George Foreman (soon to be 47).

World Title Fights
(PROFESSIONAL)

Heavyweight

WBC
2 Oct 1993 Arms Park, Cardiff
Lennox Lewis (UK, holder) bt Frank Bruno (UK) rsf 7
The end of another comeback pantomime.

WBO
30 Oct 1993 Tulsa
Michael Bentt (USA) bt Tommy Morrison (USA, holder) ko 1
Morrison, latest of the Great White Hope champions, is knocked down three times. Bentt, born in London, proclaims himself a life-long Millwall fan.

WBA & IBF
7 Nov 1993 Caesar's Palace, Las Vegas
Evander Holyfield (USA) bt Riddick Bowe (USA, holder) pts 12 (115-114, 115-113, 114-114)
The veteran Holyfield fights bravely and shrewdly to regain the title, only to find himself upstaged by one James Miller, who parachutes onto the ring apron just before the fight and is charged with 'dangerous flying.' He may have done it for a bet: for the first time ever, more than $100 million changes hands in Lost Wages. In January, Miller's arrested for flying over the LA Raiders v Buffalo Bills NFL play-off game.

WBF
18 Nov Auckland
Johnny Nelson (UK) bt Jimmy Thunder (NZ) pts 12 (119-111 115-114 115-112) (vacant title)
Nelson's the first fighter ever to become a 'world' heavyweight champion after previously holding a version (also WBF) of the cruiser title. He previously lost fights for the British (2), WBC & IBF titles.

WBO
19 March 1994 New Stadium, Millwall FC
Herbie Hide (UK) bt Michael Bentt (USA, holder) ko 7
Bentt is visibly short of peak condition. The crowd exhort Hide to 'go for the tits, hit him under the tits.' Bentt, said to have fought better in the set-to after the weigh-in (for which both boxers were fined £10 000) is released from hospital after the fight, with strict instructions to retire.

WBA & IBF

22 April 1994 Caesars Palace, Las Vegas
Michael Moorer (USA) bt Evander Holyfield (USA, holder) pts 12 (115-114 116-112 114-114)
Moorer, surprisingly the first southpaw ever to win a world heavyweight title (WBO in 1992), gets up from a second-round knockdown to beat Holyfield, a lay preacher, who'd apparently said he was told by God to remain champion till Mike Tyson gets out of prison. Mills Lane referees his 73rd world title fight.

WBC

7 May 1994 Convention Center, Atlantic City
Lennox Lewis (UK, holder) bt Phil Jackson (USA) rsf 8

IBO

4 Aug 1994 Ledyard
Danell Nicholson (USA) bt John Ruiz (USA) pts 12

WBC

25 Sep 1994 Wembley Arena
Oliver McCall (USA) bt Lennox Lewis (UK, holder) rsf 2
Lewis, the first British boxer to take part in four world heavyweight title fights, soon joins the ranks of British horizontal heavyweights (31 secs of the second round) as he meets a hungry fighter, losing for the first time in 30 pro fights. McCall's trainer Emanuel Steward, producing his 19th world champion, is just one of many who've seen no development since Lewis' Olympic gold medal: 'He's just a very predictable, big strong amateur kid.' Still, there's little doubt about the talent. Steward again: 'It's an unbelievable waste, because the boy's got everything...Lewis is the best heavy out there – he just needs a good trainer.' Oh yes, and who would that be? The unsubtle job application works: Lewis' trainer Pepe Correa is sacked and Steward leaves McCall to work with Lewis. Not before time: the three main world champions don't exactly have a ring to them – McCall, Foreman, Hide – and some of the prospective challengers make gloomy reading: Morrison, the 44-y-o Holmes and the inevitable Bruno.

IBO

29 Oct 1994 Atlantic City
Jimmy Thunder (NZ) bt Richard Mason (USA) pts 12 (116-111 115-112 114-113) (vacant title)

IBF

5 Nov 1994 MGM Grand, Las Vegas
George Foreman (USA) bt Michael Moorer (USA, holder) ko 10
The 46-y-o grandfather claims he decided to take the fight against a man virtually 20 years younger after seeing flaws while commentating on Moorer's fight v Holyfield – but can't put the knowledge to any use in the first nine rounds, before a short right hand brings about the first pro defeat for a blown-up light-heavy who owned only a piece of the world title. Foreman finds a place in a host of all-time lists.

Longest spans in world title fights

yrs days

21 287	George Foreman	1973-94	heavy
17 164	Roberto Duran	1972-89	light/spr middle
16 220	Muhammad Ali	1964-80	heavy
15 170	Emile Griffith	1961-76	welter/jnr middle

Griffith lost his last five world title fights spread over more than eight years. Larry Holmes (first heavyweight title fight 1978) will join the club when he fights Oliver McCall.

Oldest in world title fights

yrs days

47 179	Archie Moore	1961	light-heavy
46 287	George Foreman	1994	heavy
42 208	Bob Fitzsimmons	1905	light-heavy
42 229	Larry Holmes	1992	heavy
40 236	Jem Mace	1871	heavy

Moore was stripped of the remains of his title in 1962 when he was 48y 59, though it's possible that he was actually three years younger, which would make Foreman the oldest of the lot. Mace, who fought in the bare knuckle era, retired as generally accepted world best immediately after his last fight. Some sources said Foreman was 45; he was born on 22 Jan 1948. Definitely.

World Champion after a gap

yrs days

20 06	George Foreman	1974-94	heavy
7 353	Eder Jofre	1965-73	bantam/ feather
7 174	Muhammad Ali	1967-74	heavy
7 164	Bobby Chacon	1975-82	feather/jnr light

Foreman wore the same shorts in each fight. Ali's first date: the day he was stripped of the title by the WBA.

Regained world heavyweight title

Floyd Patterson	1956-59	1960-62
Muhammad Ali	1964-67	1974-78
Tim Witherspoon	1984	1986
George Foreman	1973-74	1994-

WBF
5 Nov 1994 Bangkok
Johnny Nelson (UK, holder) bt Nikolai Kulpin (KAZ) pts
12

IBO
8 Dec 1994 Michigan
Jimmy Thunder (NZ, holder) bt Tony Tubbs (USA) pts
10
*No misprint: held over ten rounds. The 35-y-o Tubbs
last fought for a world title in 1988.*

Cruiserweight

WBF
1 Oct 1993 Waregem
Franco Wanyama (UGA) bt Johnny Nelson (UK, holder)
disq 10
*The WBF is made even more risible by announcing the
weight limit as 13st 13 instead of the required 13st 8.*

WBC
16 Oct 1993 Marcel Cerdan Sports Palace, Levallois
Anaclet Wamba (FRA, holder) bt Akim Tafer (FRA) ret 8
The third all-French world title fight.

WBA
6 Nov 1993 Winter Circus, Paris
Orlin Norris (USA) bt Marcelo Figueroa (ARG) rsf 6
(vacant title)
*Injury forces Bobby Czyz (USA) to give up the title, but
Norris has long been considered a king without a crown,
which he now picks up after knocking Figueroa down
within two seconds (no misprint) of the first round.*

IBF
17 Nov 1993 Caesars, Atlantic City
Alfred Cole (USA, holder) bt Vincent Boulaware (USA)
rsf 5

WBO
20 Nov 1993 Alsterdorfer Sportshalle, Hamburg
Nestor Giovannini (ARG, holder) bt Markus Bott (GER)
pts 12
*Giovannini makes the first defence of the title he took
from Bott in June 1993. On the same bill, 37-y-o actor
Mickey Rourke (USA) stops 25-y-o Thomas McCoy
(USA) in the third.*

WBA
4 March 1994 MGM Grand, Las Vegas
Orlin Norris (USA, holder) bt Arthur Williams (USA) pts
12 (114-112 112-114 118-110)
*Williams, knocked down in the first round, loses a
controversial decision.*

WBF
April
Kenny Keene (USA) bt Bobby Crabtree (USA) rsf 4
Keene recovers from a second-round knockdown.

WBA
2 July 1994 MGM Grand, Las Vegas
Orlin Norris (USA, holder) bt Arthur Williams (USA) ko
3

WBC
14 July 1994 Monaco SC, Monte Carlo
Anaclet Wamba (FRA, holder) drew with Adolpho
Washington (USA) 12 (116-114 116-116 115-115)

IBF
23 July 1994 Bismarck, North Dakota
Alfred Cole (USA, holder) bt Nate Miller (USA) pts 12
(117-111 115-113 117-111)

IBO
4 Aug 1994 Ledyard
David Izeqwire (NIG) bt Bobby Czyz (USA) rsf 4

WBO
1 Oct 1994 Buenos Aires
Nestor Giovannini (ARG, holder) bt Larry Carlisle (USA)
ret 6

WBA
12 Nov 1994 Mexico City
Orlin Norris (USA, holder) bt James Heath (USA) ko 2

WBC
2 Dec 1994 Estadio Polideportivo, Salta, Argentina
Anaclet Wamba (FRA, holder) bt Marcelo Dominguez
(ARG) pts 12 (117-115 115-113 114-114)

WBO
17 Dec 1994 Hamburg
Dariusz Michalczewski (GER) bt Nestor Giovannini
(ARG, holder) rsf 10
*The WBO light-heavyweight champion moves up to win
at the higher weight.*

Light-heavyweight

IBO
20 Aug 1993 Melrose Park
Lenny Lapaglia (USA) bt Darayl Fromm (USA) rsf 5
(vacant title)
Fromm had lost five of his last six fights.

WBO
29 Sep 1993 Palazzo dello Sport, Pesaro
Leeonzer Barber (USA, holder) bt Andrea Magi (ITA) pts
12 (115-114, 116-113 115-113)
Magi's first defeat as a professional, in his 17th fight.

WBF
23 Oct 1993 Nashville
Ken Atkin (USA) bt Carlos Cantu (MEX, holder) ko 5

WBA
9 Nov 1993 FargoDome, Fargo, N Dakota
Virgil Hill (USA, holder) bt Saul Montana (MEX) rsf 10
*Hill's 14th successful defence, against a man
celebrating (or something) his 23rd birthday.*

IBF
11 Dec 1993 Düsseldorf
Henry Maske (GER) bt David Vedder (USA) pts 12 (118-109 120-107 120-108)
Vedder lost previous attempts at WBA & WBC light-heavy and WBC cruiser titles.

WBA
17 Dec 1993 Municipal Auditorium, Minot, N Dakota
Virgil Hill (USA, holder) bt Guy Walters (AUS) pts 12 (120-108 119-110 120-108)
Hill breaks Bob Foster's record number of world light-heavy defences (Hill's 15th).

WBO
29 Jan 1994 National Ice Rink, Cardiff
Leeonzer Barber (USA, holder) bt Nicky Piper (UK) rsf 9
Piper, typically enough, leaves a gap for the left hook that saves Barber, whose swollen right eye would probably have forced him to retire at the end of the round.

IBF
26 March 1994 Westfalenhalle, Dortmund
Henry Maske (GER, holder) bt Ernie Magdelano (USA) rsf 9

WBF
28 April 1994 Yalta
Ali Saidi (TUN) bt Sergei Klokov (RUS) rsf 7 (vacant title)

IBF
4 June 1994 Westfalenhalle, Dortmund
Henry Maske (GER, holder) bt Andrea Magi (ITA) pts 12 (117-112, 119-110, 117-114)
Maske's knocked down (10th) for the first time in 15 years.

WBC
23 July 1994 Bismarck, North Dakota
Mike McCallum (JAM) bt Jeff Harding (AUS, holder) pts 12 (116-114 116-113 117-113)
The 37-y-o McCallum, who first won a world title (at light-middleweight) in 1984, beats a champion who hasn't fought for 19 months.

WBA
23 July 1994 Bismarck, North Dakota
Virgil Hill (USA, holder) bt Frank Tate (USA) pts 12 (119-108 119-107 118-110)

WBO
10 Sep 1994 Alsterdorf, Hamburg
Dariusz Michaczewski (POL) bt Leeonzer Barber (USA, holder) pts 12
The fight's suspended when the lights go out during the tenth round.

IBC
17 Sep 1994 Aalborg
Ole Klemetsen (NOR) bt Rick Gannon (USA) rsf 1

IBC
7 Oct 1994 Copenhagen
Ole Klemetsen (NOR, holder) bt Erik Brown (USA) rsf 3

IBF
8 Oct 1994 Halle
Henry Maske (GER, holder) bt Iran Barkley (USA) rsf 9
The 34-y-o Barkley, in his ninth world title fight, a former champion at WBC middle, IBF super-middle & WBA light-heavy, is advised to retire after the sixth round.

Super-middleweight

WBO
10 Oct 1993 Old Trafford
Chris Eubank (UK, holder) & Nigel Benn (UK) draw 12 (Eubank 115-113 113-114 114-114)
Benn's WBC title not at stake
Eubank: 'Please don't criticise the decision because pugilism is a gentleman's sport and all involved should behave honourably.' Benn: 'I am pissed off good and proper. I feel I was ripped off.'

IBF
29 Oct 1993 Tulsa
James Toney (USA, holder) bt Tony Thornton (USA) pts 12 (118-110 116-112 118-110)

WBA
18 Dec 1993 Cuauhtemoc Stadium, Puebla
Michael Nunn (holder) bt Merqui Sosa (DOM) pts 12 (116-113 116-112 116-113)

IBO
28 Dec 1993 Aspen, Colorado
Vinny Pazienza (USA) bt Dan Sherry (CAN) ko 11 (vacant title)
The crowd figure says it all: 80.

WBO
5 Feb 1994 Deutschlandshalle, Berlin
Chris Eubank (UK, holder) bt Graciano Rocchigiani (GER) pts 12 (115-113 114-113 118-109)
Eubank's tenth title defence is his 38th pro fight without defeat. Rocchigiani, once the IBF super-middle champion, was previously unbeaten in 35.

WBC
26 Feb 1994 Earl's Court
Nigel Benn (UK, holder) bt Henry Wharton (UK) pts 12 (116-114 116-113 117-112)
Watched by Michael Watson at ringside, Wharton knocks Benn down before losing for the first time as a professional.

WBA
26 Feb 1994 Earl's Court
Steve Little (USA) bt Michael Nunn (USA, holder) pts 12 (115-112 113-115 116-114)
Nunn's former sparring partner, fighting for the first time in fourteen months, knocks the hot favourite down in the first 30 seconds.

IBF

5 March 1994 Olympic Auditorium, Los Angeles
James Toney (USA, holder) bt Tim Littles (USA) rsf 4
*Littles, knocked down three times, loses for the first
time as a professional.*

WBO

21 May 1994 King's Hall, Belfast
Chris Eubank (UK, holder) bt Ray Close (UK) pts 12
(118-112, 117-114, 115-114)
*Judge Clark Sammarino apparently hands in her score
as 105-104, which leads to calls for a rematch. Close
later starts legal proceedings against the WBO, who
retaliate by threatening to sue his manager.*

WBO

9 July 1994 Olympia, Kensington
Chris Eubank (UK, holder) bt Mauricio Amaral (BRZ) pts
12 (116-113, 115-113, 116-114)

IBF

29 July 1994 MGM Grand, Las Vegas
James Toney (USA, holder) bt Charles Williams (USA)
ko 12
*Williams once held the IBF light-heavyweight title,
Toney's unbeaten in 45 pro fights, the current record
after Chávez' first defeat.*

WBA

12 Aug 1994 Tucuman
Frank Liles (USA) bt Steve Little (USA, holder) pts 12
(118-114 118-113 116-114)

WBF

20 Aug 1994 Valinho, Brazil
Luciano Torres (BRZ, holder) bt Tomás Quinones
(MEX) pts 12
*Quinones had been stopped in one round by Pat Barrett
(UK) and by lightweight Billy Schwer.*

WBO

27 Aug 1994 International Arena, Cardiff
Chris Eubank (UK) bt Sam Storey (UK) rsf 7
*Eubank's now unbeaten in 42 pro fights, including 13
title defences. Storey (who fractures an ankle during the
fight) earns £40 000 against Eubank's £1 million.*

WBC

10 Sep 1994 NEC, Birmingham
Nigel Benn (UK, holder) bt Juan Carlos Gimenez (PAR)
pts 12 (117-112 118-112 119-115)
*From the second round to the seventh, the main event's
disturbed by fighting between fans of Robert
McCracken & Steve Foster (see British Title Fights).
Gimenez loses a world title challenge for the third time.*

WBF

15 Oct 1994 Belem, Brazil
Luciano Torres (BRZ, holder) bt Don Penelton (USA)
pts 12
*If the WBO fights are poor, this company's bankrupt.
Penelton came in with four wins in 23 fights.*

WBO

15 Oct 1994 Superbowl, Sun City
Chris Eubank (UK, holder) bt Desperate Dan Schommer
(USA) pts 12(116-114 116-113 117-113)
*The customary stinker, even down to the controversial
points decision. Schommer's not the only desperate
one here.*

IBF

18 Nov 1994 MGM Grand, Las Vegas
Roy Jones (USA) bt James Toney (USA) pts 12
(119-108 118-109 117-111)
*Both go in unbeaten as professionals, Jones having
given up the middleweight title to fight Toney, who's
unhappy with his manager Jackie Kellen, claiming that
she pressurised him to take the fight despite 'flu and
trouble making the weight. Jones knocks him down in
the third on the way to an easy points win that
establishes him as one of the best fighters in the world.*

WBO

10 Dec 1994 G-Mex Centre, Manchester
Chris Eubank (UK, holder) bt Henry Wharton (UK) pts
12 (118-112 116-112 114-113)
*Eubank boxes well for a change, perhaps stoked by the
comments of Wharton's manager Mickey Duff at a pre-
fight press conference: 'You are scum' etc.*

WBA

16 Dec 1994 Ruminahui Coliseum, Quito
Frank Liles (USA, holder) bt Michael Nunn (USA) pts 12

Middleweight

WBA

2 Oct 1993 Buenos Aires
John David Jackson (USA) bt Reggie Johnson (USA,
holder) pts 12
*Jackson gives up the WBO light-middle title to
challenge for this one.*

WBO

9 Feb 1994 Brentwood
Chris Pyatt (UK, holder) bt Mark Cameron (SAF) ko 1
Pyatt knocks Cameron down with his first two punches.

WBC

5 March 1994 Las Vegas
Gerald McClellan (USA) bt Gilbert Baptiste (USA) rsf 1
*The fight lasts 1 min 37 sec, during which Baptiste is
knocked down three times.*

WBC

7 May 1994 MGM, Las Vegas
Gerald McClellan (USA, holder) bt Julian Jackson (USA)
ko 1
*McClelland, who stopped Jackson to win the title in May
1993, ends proceedings in 83 seconds, his fourteenth
KO victory in a row, including ten in the first round.*

WBO
11 May 1994 Ponds Forge Centre, Sheffield
Steve Collins (UK) bt Chris Pyatt (UK, holder) rsf 5
Collins wins a world title at the third attempt.

IBF
27 May MGM Grand, Las Vegas
Roy Jones (USA, holder) bt Thomas Tate (USA) rsf 2
Jones later gives up the title to challenge Toney at the next weight up.

WBA
12 Aug 1994 Tucuman
Jorge Castro (ARG) bt Reggie Johnson (USA) pts 12
(116-14 115-116 116-114) (vacant title)
John David Jackson wins a court order to stop the WBA stripping him of the title, but the fight goes on regardless. By all accounts, it's a hometown verdict.

WBA
5 Nov 1994 Caleta Olivia, Argentina
Jorge Castro (ARG, holder) bt Alex Ramos (USA) ko 2
The challenger is knocked down in each round.

WBA
10 Dec 1994 Monterrey
Jorge Castro (ARG, holder) bt John David Jackson (USA) rsf 9
Jackson, trying to regain the title he didn't lose in the ring, gives the holder a terrible hiding only to be knocked down three times in the ninth by Castro, who's taking part in his 102nd pro fight.

IBF
17 Dec 1994 Ruminahui Coliseum, Quito
Bernard Hopkins (USA) drew with Segundo Mercado 12
(vacant title)

Light-middleweight
JUNIOR MIDDLEWEIGHT, SUPER-WELTERWEIGHT

WBO
30 Oct 1993 America West Arena, Phoenix
Verno Phillips (USA) bt Lupe Aquino (MEX) rsf 7
Aquino's a former WBC champion.

WBF
1 Nov 1993 Izegem, Belgium
Patrick Vungbo (BEL) bt Pat Barrett (UK) pts 12 (117-113 114-116 119-114) (vacant title)
Title vacated by Craig Trotter (AUS) who'd been due to fight Vungbo. Dutch officials are drafted in when the Belgian BA refuse to handle a WBF bout.

WBC
18 Dec 1993 Cuauhtemoc Stadium, Puebla
Simon Brown (JAM) bt Terry Norris (USA, holder) ko 4

WBF
25 Dec 1993 Izegem, Belgium
Godfrey Nyakana (USA) bt Patrick Vungbo (BEL) pts 12
(120-109 120-110 118-111)

WBA
22 Jan 1994 Alm Ata, Kazakhstan
Júlio César Vásquez (ARG, holder) bt Juan Medina Padilla (DOM) pts 12
Hard to know how Padilla lasts the fight - or wins any points in it: Vásquez knocks him down seven times.

WBC
29 Jan 1994 Las Vegas
Simon Brown (JAM, holder) bt Troy Walters (AUS) pts 12 (118-111 116-112 114-114)

IBF
4 March 1994 MGM Grand, Las Vegas
Gianfranco Rosi (ITA, holder) drew with Vincent Pettway (USA) 6
Rosi, in his first fight for more than a year, survives his eleventh title defence when a clash of heads cuts his eye.

WBA
4 March 1994 MGM Grand, Las Vegas
Júlio César Vásquez (ARG) bt Armand Picar (PHIL) rsf 2

WBA
8 April 1994 Buenos Aires
Júlio César Vásquez (ARG, holder) bt Ricardo Nuñez (ARG) pts 12

WBC
7 May 1994 MGM Grand, Las Vegas
Terry Norris (USA) bt Simon Brown (JAM, holder) pts 12 (116-112 117-111 119-109)

WBA
21 May 1994 King's Hall, Belfast
Júlio César Vásquez (ARG, holder) bt Ahmet Dottuev (UKR) rsf 10
Vásquez survives his eighth title defence by knocking Dotuyev down four times after being put down twice himself.

WBO
25 July 1994 Great Western Forum, Inglewood, California
Verno Phillips (USA, holder) bt Jaimes Llanes (MEX) ko 7
Llanes is knocked down four times.

WBA
21 Aug 1994 St Jean de Luz
Júlio César Vásquez (ARG, holder) bt Ronald Wright (USA) pts 12
Vásquez (knocked down in the second round) makes his ninth successful defence. Wright (knocked down four times) suffers his first defeat as a pro.

IBF
17 Sep 1994 MGM Grand, Las Vegas
Vincent Pettway (USA) bt Gianfranco Rosi (ITA, holder) ko 4
The 37-y-o Rosi won the European welter title in 1984 and the first of his world titles, the WBC light-middle, in 1987. This, his twelfth defence of a title he won in 1989, is his first defeat since 1988.

WBO
9 Nov 1994 New Orleans
Verno Phillips (USA, holder) bt Santos Cardona (PR)
pts 12 (114-113 116-112 116-110)
Phillips recovers from a second-round knockdown.

WBA
11 Nov 1994 Tucuman
Júlio César Vásquez (ARG, holder) bt Tony Marshall
(USA) pts 12 (118-110 119-112 117-111)
Vásquez' twelfth successful defence of the title.

WBC
12 Nov 1994 Plaza del Toro, Mexico City
Luis Santaña (DOM) bt Terry Norris (USA, holder)
disq 5
*The 35-y-o Santaña is knocked out by a rabbit punch
which leads to the disqualification.*

Welterweight

WBA
10 Oct 1993 Old Trafford
Crisanto España (VEN, holder) bt Donovan Boucher
(CAN) rsf 10

WBO
16 Oct 1993 King's Hall, Belfast
Eamonn Loughran (UK) bt Lorenzo Smith (USA) pts 12
(116-112, 118-110, 117-112) (vacant title)
*The champion, Gert Bo Jacobsen (DEN), was stripped
of the title for pulling out of a defence v Loughran at
only three days' notice. Smith lost a challenge for the
WBO light-welter title in Nov 1992. Loughran's the first
Irishman to hold a WBO title.*

WBO
17 Oct 1993 Brisbane
Jeff Malcolm (AUS, holder) bt Tata Regatuna (FIJI) rsf 3

IBF
23 Oct 1993 Fort Lauderdale, Florida
Félix Trinidad (PR) bt Anthony Stephens (USA) rsf 10
*Trinidad, unbeaten as a professional, recovers from a
third-round knockdown in the first world title fight ever
to feature a 'no draw' rule (a 13th round would have
been staged if necessary).*

WBO
22 Jan 1994 King's Hall, Belfast
Eamonn Loughran (UK, holder) bt Alessandro Duran
(ITA) pts 12 (117-112, 117-111, 117-112)
*The points margin seems generous; some think Duran
does enough to win.*

IBF
29 Jan 1994 MGM Grand, Las Vegas
Félix Trinidad (PR, holder) bt Hector Camacho (PR) pts
12 (118-106 117-109 116-110)
Camacho won the first of his three world titles in 1983.

IBO
13 March 1994 Erie
John Boy Bizzarro (USA, holder) bt Tom Hanks (USA)
pts 12
*Despite Mickey Rourke (see Cruiserweight), this isn't
the Tom Hanks of course, though it's that kind of title.*

WBF
19 March 1994 Fiji
Jeff Malcolm (AUS) bt Sovita Tabuarua (FIJI) pts 12
(vacant title)

WBC
9 April 1994 The Scope, Norfolk, Virginia
Pernell Whitaker (USA, holder) bt Santos Cardona (PR)
pts 12 (119-109 119-111 119-109)

IBC
29 April 1994 Newcastle, Pennsylvania
Roland Cummings (USA) bt Tom Alexander (USA)
pts 12

WBA
4 June 1994 Palais des Sports Marcel Derdan,
Levallois-Perret, Paris
Ike Quartey (GHA) bt Crisanto España (VEN) rsf 11
*The first African to win a world welter title inflicts
España's first defeat as a professional.*

WBF
18 June 1994 Brisbane
Jeff Malcolm (AUS, holder)) bt Tata Regatuna (FIJI)
ko 3
Same fighters, same result, same round as on 17 Oct.

IBF
17 Sep 1994 MGM Grand, Las Vegas
Félix Trinidad (PR, holder) v Ramón 'Yori Boy' Campas
(MEX) rsf 4
*Both went into the fight unbeaten as professionals,
Trinidad after 23 fights, Campas after 56.*

WBA
1 Oct 1994 Carpentras, France
Ike Quartey (GHA, holder) bt Alberto Cortes (ARG) ko 5

WBC
1 Oct 1994 Norfolk, Virginia
Pernell Whitaker (USA, holder) bt James 'Buddy' McGirt
(USA) pts 12 (117-113 118-112 117-110)
*Whitaker recovers from a second-round knockdown to
outpoint McGirt (who can't use his left hook any more)
for the second time in 18 months.*

IBF
10 Dec 1994 Monterrey
Félix Trinidad (PR, holder) bt Oba Carr (USA) rsf 8
*In a battle of big punchers, Trinidad recovers from a
second-round knockdown.*

WBO
13 Dec 1994 G-Mex Centre, Manchester
Eamonn Loughran (UK, holder) bt Manning Galloway (USA) tko 5
Galloway, a previous holder of the title, has to retire with a cut over each eye, caused by clashes of heads.

Light-welterweight
JUNIOR WELTERWEIGHT, SUPER LIGHTWEIGHT

WBA
24 Sep 1993 Tucuman
Juan Martín Coggi (ARG, holder) Guillermo Cruz (MEX) rsf 10

IBF
19 Nov 1993 Convention Hall, Atlantic City
Charles Murray (USA, holder) bt Courtney Hooper (USA) ret 6
Hooper's a substitute for former IBF champion Rafael Pineda (COL).

WBO
19 Nov 1993 Arezzo
Zack Padilla (USA, holdr) bt Efrem Calamati (ITA) ret 8

WBO
16 Dec 1993 Foxwoods Casino, Ledyard, Conn.
Zack Padilla (USA, holder) bt Ray Oliveira (USA) pts 12 (118-110, 116-113 117-112)

WBA
17 Dec 1993 Estádio Villa Lujan, Tucuman
Juan Martín Coggi (ARG, holder) bt Eder Gonzalez (COL) rsf 7
An early Xmas present for the champion. Two different rounds are ended many seconds early to save him from being KO'd - and when referee Isidoro Rodriguez (VEN) isn't holding Gonzalez back as he's about to finish things off, Coggi's cornermen are doing it. Rodriguez and the timekeeper are later banned for life by the WBA, Coggi's trainer for 60 days, but the result stands.

WBC
20 Dec 1993 Cuauhtemoc Stadium, Puebla
Júlio César Chávez (MEX, holder) bt Andy Holligan (UK) ret 6
Chávez, once the best professional boxer in the world, has now won 26 of his 27 world title fights, more bouts than Holligan's had in his entire career. Arthur Mercante referees his 109th world title fight.

WBC
29 Jan 1994 MGM Grand, Las Vegas
Frankie Randall (USA) bt Júlio César Chávez (MEX, holder) pts 12 (116-111 113-114 114-113)
Chávez, knocked down in the eleventh (for the first time in his professional career), has two points taken away for low blows, the difference between retaining the title and losing for the first time as a professional - after an incredible 90 unbeaten fights.

IBF
13 Feb 1994 Bally's Casino, Atlantic City
Jake Rodriguez (USA) bt Charles Murray (USA, holder) pts 12 (116-112 115-113 114-114)
Rodriguez was a 20-1 underdog.

WBA
18 March 1994 MGM Grand, Las Vegas
Juan Martín Coggi (ARG, holder) bt Eder Gonzalez (COL) rsf 3
Less controversial than the 17 Dec fight, but almost as dramatic. Coggi recovers, in desperation, from a first-round knockdown and cut eye.

WBO
18 April 1994 Rotterdam
Zack Padilla (USA, holder) bt Harold Miller (USA) ret 6
The first world title fight ever staged in Holland.

IBF
21 April 1994 Ledyard, Connecticut
Jake Rodriguez (USA, holder) bt Ray Oliveira (USA) pts 12 (116-111 115-112 119-108)
Oliveira lost a WBO title fight on 16 Dec.

WBC
7 May 1994 MGM Grand, Las Vegas
Júlio César Chávez (MEX) bt Frankie Randall (USA, holder) pts 8
A clash of heads leaves Chávez with a cut right eye and ends the fight. The referee, Mills Lane, deciding the butt was intentional, deducts a point from Randall's score, the difference between retaining and losing the title.

WBO
24 July 1994 Grand Olympic Auditorium, LA
Zack Padilla (USA, holder) bt Juan LaPorte (PR) ret 11 (TKO 10)

IBF
27 Aug 1994 Fernwood Resort, Bushkill, Pennsylvania
Jake Rodriguez (USA) bt George Scott (SWE) rsf 9
Only the second 'Swede' (he was born in Liberia) to fight for a world pro title, following Ingemar Johansson, the 1959-60 heavyweight champion.

IBO
4 Aug 1994 Ledyard
Roger Mayweather (USA) bt Johnny Bizarro (USA) pts 12
Mayweather won the WBA junior-light title in 1983.

WBC
17 Sep 1994 MGM Grand, Las Vegas
Júlio César Chávez (MEX, holder) bt Meldrick Taylor (USA) rsf 8
Taylor was ahead on points when his 1990 title fight with Chávez was very controversially stopped with only two secs remaining. He later won the WBA welter title, but here Chávez knocks him down in the eighth.

WBA
17 Sep 1994 MGM Grand, Las Vegas
Frankie Randall (USA) bt Juan Martín Coggi (ARG, holder) pts 12
Comeuppance at last for Coggi, knocked down three times by Randall, who wins his second version of the title in the same year.

WBA
10 Dec 1994 Monterrey
Frankie Randall (USA, holder) bt Rodney Moore (USA) rsf 7
Moore's knocked down in the first round.

WBC
10 Dec 1994 Monterrey
Júlio César Chávez (MEX, holder) bt Tony Lopez (USA) rsf 10
Chávez is relieved to win his 94th pro fight, against a fighter who once held the IBF super-feather & WBA lightweight titles.

Most world title fights

31	Júlio César Chávez jr light, light, lt welter	MEX	1984-94
27	Joe Louis heavy	USA	1937-50
26	Henry Armstrong feather, welter, light, middle	USA	1937-41
25	Muhammad Ali heavy	USA	1964-80
25	Larry Holmes heavy	USA	1978-92

Most without defeat:

20   Kaosai Galaxy (THAI) 1984-91 (jr bantam)

Lightweight

WBO
24 Sep 1993 PalaEur, Rome
Giovanni Parisi (ITA, holder) bt Antonio Rivera (PR) pts 12
Parisi's only pro defeat was v Rivera (ko 3) in 1990.

WBF
16 Oct 1993 Hyfia, Israel
Johar Lashin (ISR, holder) bt Hector Ramirez (MEX) rsf 7

WBA
30 Oct 1993 NEC, Johannesburg
Olzubeck Nazarov (RUS) bt Dingaan Thobela (SAF, holder) pts 12 (115-114 117-111 118-108)

WBC
27 Nov 1993 Arena Coliseo, Mexico City
Miguel Angel González (MEX, holder) bt Wilfrido Rocha (COL) rsf 10
González is now unbeaten in 31 professional fights.

IBF
19 Feb 1994 Great Western Forum, Inglewood, California
Rafael Ruelas (USA) bt Freddie Pendleton (USA, holder) pts 12 115-110 114-112 116-111)
Ruelas recovers from two first-round knockdowns.

WBA
19 March 1994 Carousel, Hammanskraal, S Africa
Olzubek Nazarov (RUS, holder) bt Dingaan Thobela (SAF) pts 12 (118-110 118-111 18-108)

WBC
29 March 1994 Palais des Sports Marcel Cerdan, Levallois-Perret, Paris
Miguel Angel González (MEX, holder) bt Jean-Baptiste Mendy (FRA) rsf 5
Mendy, the European champion, is knocked down three times.

IBF
27 May 1994 MGM Grand, Las Vegas
Rafael Ruelas (USA, holder) bt Mike Evgen (USA) rsf 3
Evgen, six inches shorter than Ruelas at 5'5, comes in as a late substitute for Carl Griffith (USA).

WBO
29 July 1994 MGM Grand, Las Vegas
Oscar De la Hoya (USA) bt Jorge Paez (MEX) ko 2 (vacant title)
De la Hoya, in his fourteenth pro fight, wins his second world title (see WBO super-feather).

WBC
6 Aug 1994 Ciudad Juarez, Mexico
Miguel Angel Gonzalez (MEX) bt Leavander Johnson (USA) rsf 8

WBO
18 Nov 1994 MGM Grand, Las Vegas
Oscar de la Hoya (USA, holder) bt Carl Griffith (USA) rsf 3
Griffith is knocked down twice.

9 Dec 1994 Los Angeles
Oscar de la Hoya (USA, holder) bt Johnny Avila (USA) rsf 9

WBA
10 Dec 1994 Portland, Oregon
Olzubek Nazarov (RUS, holder) bt Joey Gamache (USA) ko 2

WBC
13 Dec 1994 Albuquerque
Miguel Angel Gonzalez (MEX, holder) bt Calvin Grove (USA) rsf 5

Super featherweight
JUNIOR LIGHTWEIGHT

IBF
9 Oct 1993 San Juan, Puerto Rico
Juan 'John John' Molina (PR, holder) bt Bernard Taylor (USA) ko 8
Taylor, now 36, lost a world title fight to Barry McGuigan in 1985 after drawing another with Eusebio Pedroza in 1982.

WBA
11 Oct 1993 Inglewood, Calif.
Genaro Hernandez (USA, holder) bt Harold Warren (USA) pts 12 (119-109, 118-110, 118-115)
Hernandez is now unbeaten in 30 pro fights.

IBO
21 April 1994 North Las Vegas
Jeff Mayweather (USA) bt John Roby (USA, holder) pts 12
Mayweather's brother Roger was WBA champion at the same weight 1983-84 and held two other world titles 1987-89.

IBF
22 Jan 1994 Cardiff
Juan 'John John' Molina (PR, holder) bt Floyd Havard (UK) ret 6

WBA
31 Jan 1994 Forum, Inglewood, Calif.
Genaro Hernandez (USA, holder) bt Jorge Ramirez (MEX) rsf 8
Hernandez' eighth title defence.

WBO
5 March 1994 Olympic Auditorium, Los Angeles
Oscar De la Hoya (USA) bt Jimmi Bredahl (DEN, holder) rsf 10
Bredahl, brother of WBO super-fly champion Johnny, is knocked down three times.

IBF
22 April 1994 Caesars Palace, Las Vegas
Juan 'John John' Molina (PR, holder) bt Gregorio (Goyo) Vargas (MEX) pts 12 (118-110 117-112 118-110)

WBC
7 May 1994 MGM, Las Vegas
Jesse James Leija (USA) bt Azumah Nelson (GHA, holder) pts 12 (114-113 117-109 117-110)
When the two fought in September, Nelson kept his title thanks to a disputed draw. Now the curtain's probably come down: he suffers a second-round knockdown on the way to losing a title he'd held for six years. He fought his first world title fight in 1982 and first won one in 1984.

WBO
27 May MGM Grand, Las Vegas
Oscar De la Hoya (USA, holder) bt Giorgio Campanella (ITA) rsf 3

De la Hoya, knocked down after only fifteen seconds, returns the compliment four times then relinquishes the title.

IBO
7 July 1994 Las Vegas
Jeff Mayweather (USA, holder) bt Gabriel Castro rsf 8

WBF
15 Sep 1994 Village Green, Durban
Ditau Moleyfane (SAF, holder) bt Noe Hernandez (MEX) rsf 6
Moleyfane almost fails to make the weight.

WBC
17 Sep 1994 MGM Grand, Las Vegas
Gabriel Ruelas (MEX) bt Jesse James Leija (USA, holder) pts 12 (116-108 115-109 115-111)

WBO
24 Sep 1994, Ahoy Sports Palace, Rotterdam
Regilio Tuur (HOL) bt Eugene Speed (USA) pts 12 (118-110 117-109 118-108 (vacant title)
Tuur wins despite a bad cut over his left eye.

WBA
12 Nov 1994 Mexico City
Genaro Hernandez (USA, holder) bt Jimmy Garcia (COL) pts 12

IBF
26 Nov 1994 Rubén Rodríguez Coliseum, Bayamon, Puerto Rico
Juan 'John John' Molina (PR, holder) bt Wilson Rodriguez (DOM) ko 10

Featherweight

WBO
23 Oct 1993 National Ice Rink, Cardiff
Steve Robinson (UK, holder) bt Colin McMillan (UK) pts 12 (117-113 117-111 116-113)
McMillan's first fight since losing the title thirteen months earlier.

IBF
30 Nov 1993 Palais des Sports, Marseilles
Tom Johnson (USA, holder) bt Stéphane Haccoun (FRA) rsf 9

WBC
4 Dec 1993 Sparks Convention Centre, Reno, Nevada
Kevin Kelley (USA) bt Gregorio (Goyo) Vargas (MEX, holder) pts 12 (115-112 116-111 115-112)
Kelley recovers from a ninth-round knockdown.

WBA
4 Dec 1993 Kwangmyong, S Korea
Eloy Rojas (VEN) bt Park Yung-kyun (S KOR) pts 12 (113-112 111-114 115-111)
Park makes his ninth defence of the title he won in 1991.

IBF
12 Feb 1994 St Louis
Tom Johnson (USA, holder) bt Orlando Soto (PAN) pts 12

WBO
12 March 1994 National Ice Rink, Cardiff
Steve Robinson (UK, holder) bt Paul Hodkinson (UK) rsf 12
Hodkinson, WBC feather champion 1992-93, is knocked down twice in the last round.

WBA
19 March 1994 Kobe
Eloy Rojas (VEN, holder) bt Seji Asakawa (JAP) rsf 5

WBC
6 May 1994 Atlantic City
Kevin Kelley (USA, holder) bt Jesse Benavides (US) pts 12 (116-112 116-111 117-111)
For the second fight in a row, Kelley wins despite being knocked down, this time in the second.

WBO
4 June 1994 National Ice Rink, Cardiff
Steve Robinson (UK, holder) bt Freddy Cruz (DOM) pts 12 (116-112, 117-110, 118-109)

IBF
11 June 1994 Bally's, Atlantic City
Tom Johnson (USA, holder) bt Benny Amparo (DOM) ko rsf 12

WBA
11 Sep 1994 Trang, Thailand
Eloy Rojas (VEN, holder) bt Samart Payakaroon (THAI) rsf 8
Payakaroon, who won the WBC super-bantam title in 1986, hadn't fought for a world title since 1987.

WBC
24 Sep 1994 Atlantic City
Kevin Kelley (USA, holder) bt José Vidal Ramos (DOM) ko 2
Kelley still unbeaten after 40 pro fights.

WBO
1 Oct 1994 National Ice Rink, Cardiff
Steve Robinson (UK, holder) bt Duke McKenzie (UK) ko 9
A short left to the body ends a rough fight in which McKenzie fails to become the first British boxer to win world titles at four different weights.

IBF
22 Oct 1994 Ballys Park Place Atlantic City
Tom Johnson (USA, holder) bt Pancho Segura (USA) pts 12 (118-110 117-111 118-110)

WBA
3 Dec 1994 Bogotá
Eloy Rojas (VEN, holder) bt Luis Mendoza (COL) pts 12 (116-114 115-113 117-111)

Rojas makes sure with two knockdowns in the last round.

Super-bantamweight
JUNIOR FEATHERWEIGHT

WBC
25 Sep 1993 Poughkeepsie, NY
Tracy Patterson (USA, holder) bt Daniel Zaragoza (MEX) rsf 7
Zaragoza fails to regain the title.

IBF
17 Oct 1993 Lake Tahoe, Nevada
Kennedy McKinney (USA, holder) bt Jesus Salud (USA) pts 12 (119-109, 118-110, 119-109)
Salud had previously won the WBA title.

WBO
29 Oct 1993 Zaragoza
Daniel Jimenez (PR, holder) bt Félix Garcia Losada (SPA) rsf 5

WBA
18 Nov 1993 Tokyo Dome
Wilfredo Vasquez (PR, holder) bt Horoaki Yokota (JAP) pts 12
Yokota, who's been fighting since 1979, is knocked down in the fifth.

WBO
7 Jan 1994 Palma, Majorca
Daniel Jimenez (PR, holder) bt Félix Garcia Losada (SPA) pts 12

IBF
19 Feb 1994 Carousel Casino, Hammanskraal, S Africa
Kenedy McKinney (USA, holder) bt José Rincones (VEN) ko 5

WBA
2 March 1994 Metropolitan Gym, Tokyo
Wilfredo Vásquez (PR, holder) bt Yuichi Kasai (JAP) rsf 1
The tall skinny Kasai lasts only 2:05 of Vásquez' sixth title defence.

WBC
9 April 1994 Reno, Nevada
Tracy Harris Patterson (USA, holder) bt Richard Duran (USA) pts 12

IBF
16 April 1994 South Padre Island, Texas
Kennedy McKinney (USA, holder) bt Welcome Ncita (SAF) pts 12 (117-110 117-111 114-114)
Ncita's a former world champion at the weight.

WBO
25 June 1994 Utrera, Sevile
Daniel Jimenez (PR, holder) bt Cristobal Pascual (SPA) pts 12

WBA
2 July 1994 Mirage, Las Vegas
Wilfredo Vásquez (PTR, holder) bt Choi Jae-won (S KOR) rsf 2
Choi's first defeat as a pro, but he crumples under Vásquez' first few jabs.

IBF
20 Aug 1994 Carousel Casino, Hammanskraal, S Africa
Vuyani Bungu (SAF) bt Kennedy McKinney (USA, holder) pts 12 (116-112 117-111 116-112)

WBC
27 Aug 1994 Atlantic City
Hector Acero (DOM) bt Tracy Patterson (USA, holder) pts 12 (114-113 112-113 114-113)
Patterson, managed by his father, former world heavyweight champion Floyd, lives to regret taking on a voluntary title defence.

WBO
3 Sep 1994 Domplatz, Wiener Neustadt
Daniel Jimenez (PR, holder) bt Harald Geier (AUT) ko 1
The first world title fight held in Austria since 1936 begins and ends with a single punch. The official time, including the count, is given as 19 seconds, making this the shortest world title fight of all time.

WBA
13 Oct 1994 Palais des Sports Marcel Cerdan, Paris
Wilfredo Vásquez (PR, holder) bt Juan Polo-Perez (COL) pts 12
Vásquez is outboxed in at least ten of the rounds. The decision's booed for nearly fifteen mins.

IBF
19 Nov 1994 Hammanskraal, S Africa
Vuyani Bungu (SAF, holder) bt Felix Camacho (PR) pts 12 (117-111 119-110 118-111)
Camacho isn't in the same league as his older brother, Hector 'Macho', who won three world titles.

Bantamweight

WBA
23 Oct 1993 Sands Hotel, Atlantic City
Junior Jones (USA) bt Jorge Elicier Júlio (COL, holder) pts 12 (116-111, 117-109, 116-111)
Both were undefeated before the fight, Jones after 30 pro fights, Júlio after 26. Jones was the WBA, WBC & IBF's No.1 contender.

IBF
20 Nov 1993 Hammanskraal, S Africa
Orlando Canizales (USA, holder) bt Juvenal Berrio (COL) pts 12 (116-112 116-110 116-112)

WBC
23 Dec 1993 Nagoya
Yasuei Yakushiji (JAP) bt Byun Jung-il (S KOR, holder) pts 12 (116-115 113-115 115-113)

WBA
8 Jan 1994 Friar Tuck Inn, Catskill, NY
Junior Jones (USA, holder) bt Elvis Alvarez (COL) pts 12

IBF
26 Feb 1994 San José
Orlando Canizales (USA, holder) bt Gerardo Martínez (USA) rsf 4

IBF
7 June 1994 Convention Centre, South Padre Island, Texas
Orlando Canizales (USA, holder) bt Rolando Bohol (PHI) ko 5
Canizales, who hasn't lost in almost eight years, makes his fifteenth consecutive successful defence of a title he won in 1988 to equal Manuel Ortiz' world record (1943-46) for the division.

WBC
16 April 1994 Nagoya
Yasuei Yakushiji (JAP, holder) bt Josefino Suarez (MEX) rsf 10

WBA
22 April 1994 Caesar's Palace, Las Vegas
John Michael Johnson (USA) bt Junior Jones (USA, holder) rsf 11
Revenge for Johnson, beaten by Jones in 1989.

WBA
16 July 1994 Bangkok
Daorung Chuwatana (THAI) bt John Michael Johnson (USA, holder) ret 1
Chuwatana's now known as Daorung MP Petroleum.

WBO
30 July 1994 York Hall, Bethnal Green
Alfred Kotey (GHA) bt Rafael Della Valle (PR, holder) pts 12 (118-111 116-111 116-112)
Della Valle's first defeat as a professional.

WBC
1 Aug 1994 Nagoya
Yasuei Yakushiji (JAP, holder) bt Byun Jung-il (S KOR) rsf 11
The former champion, is knocked down five times.

IBF
15 Oct 1994 Laredo, Texas
Orlando Canizales (USA, holder) v Sergio Reyes (USA) pts 12 (114-113 115-112 116-111)
Canizales duly makes his record-breaking sixteenth defence of the title: Reyes is a former Olympic boxer but a light puncher.

WBF
22 Oct 1994 Bangkok
Faprakob Sithkwan-in (THAI) bt Boualem Belkif (ALG) pts 12

WBO
25 Oct 1994 Town Hall, Middlesbrough
Alfred Kotey (GHA, holder) bt Armando Castro (MEX)
pts 12 (120-108 119-111 120-108)

WBA
20 Nov 1994 Bangkok
Daorung Chuwatana (THAI, holder) bt Koh In-sik
(S KOR) rsf 5

WBC
4 Dec 1994 Municipal Gymnasium, Nagoya
Yasuei Yakushiji (JAP, holder) bt Joichiro Tatsuyoshi
(JAP) pts 12 (115-114 11-112 114-114)
Yakushiji beats the former champion.

Super flyweight
JUNIOR BANTAMWEIGHT

WBO
29 Oct 1993 Korsoer, Denmark
Johnny Bredahl (DEN, holder) bt Eduardo Nazario (PR)
disq 4

WBA
6 Nov 1993 Tokyo
Katsuya Onizuka (JAP, holder) bt Thanomsak
Sithbaobay (THAI) pts 12 (116-114 115-113 116-111)

WBC
13 Nov 1993 Seoul
José Luis Bueno (MEX) bt Moon Sung-kil (S KOR,
holder) pts 12
Bueno recovers from a third-round knockdown.

IBF
19 Nov 1993 Sonora
Júlio César Borboa (MEX, holder) bt Rolando Pascua
(PHIL) rsf 5
*Borboa recovers from a second-round knockdown to
beat the 1990 WBC light-fly champion.*

WBO
25 March 1994 Akirkeby, Denmark
Johnny Bredahl (DEN, holder) bt Eduardo Nazario (PR)
pts 12 (118-111 119-110 118-109)
The WBO strip Bredahl of the title on 13 July.

WBA
3 April 1994 Ryogoko Arena, Tokyo
Katsuya Onizuka (JAP, holder) bt Lee Seung-koo (S
KOR) pts 12 (115-114 115-112 115-114)
Onizuka recovers from a fifth-round knockdown.

IBF
25 April 1994 Great Western Forum, Inglewood,
California
Júlio César Borboa (MEX, holder) bt Jorge Luis Román
(MEX) rsf 4
*A mismatch. No-one understands why Román, a
natural light-fly, is fighting at super-fly.*

WBC
4 May Yokohama
Hiroshi Kawashima (JAP) bt José Luis Bueno (MEX,
holder) pts 12 (116-110 114-113 114-112)

IBF
21 May Carousel, Hammanskraal, S Africa
Júlio César Borboa (MEX, holder) bt Jaji Sibali (SAF)
rsf 9

WBC
7 Aug 1994 Ariake Coliseum, Tokyo
Jiroshi Kawashima (JAP, holder) bt Carlos Salazar
(ARG) pts 12 (118-110 115-113 117-113)

IBF
29 Aug 1994 Great Western Forum, Inglewood,
California
Harold Grey (COL) bt Júlio César Borboa (MEX, holder)
pts 12 (116-112 111-117 114-113)
*The differences in the judges' scoring don't reflect a
deserved win for Grey.*

WBF
17 Sep 1994 Bangkok
Samson Elite Gym (THAI) bt Colin Nelson (AUS) rsf 3
(vacant title)
*The new champion's real name is Saenmuangnoi
Lookchaopormahesak.*

WBA
18 Sep 1994 Tokyo
Lee Hyung-chul (S KOR) bt Katsuya Onizuka (JAP,
holder) rsf 9
Onizuka loses for the first time as a professional.

WBO
12 Oct 1994 The Pit, Albuquerque
Johnny Tapia (USA) bt Henry Martínez (USA) (USA) rsf
11 (vacant title)

IBF
17 Dec 1994 Cagliari
Harold Grey (COL, holder) bt Vincenzo Belcastro (ITA)
pts 12

Flyweight

IBF
3 Oct 1993 PE College, Bangkok
Pichit Sithbangprachan (THAI, holder) bt Miguel
Martínez (MEX) rsf 9
*The challenger's knocked down in the second & eighth,
the champion in the fifth.*

WBA
4 Oct Puerto La Cruz, VEN
David Griman (VEN, holder) bt Alvaro Mercado (COL)
pts 12 (117-113 115-112 117-113)

WBO
4 Dec 1993 Sun City
Baby Jake Matlala (SAF, holder) bt Luigi Camputaro
(ITA) ret 8
Matlala's only 4'10.

WBC
13 Dec 1993 Kyoto
Yuri Arbachakov (RUS, holder) bt Cha Nam-hoon
(S KOR) pts 12 (117-113 118-111 116-112)
Arbachakov has won all his 17 professional fights.

IBF
23 Jan 1994 Surat Thani
Pichit Sithbangprachan (THAI, holder) bt Arthur
Johnson (USA) pts 12 (115-113 118-110 115-113)

WBA
13 Feb 1994 Bangkok
Saen Sor Ploenchit (THAI) bt David Griman (VEN,
holder) pts 12 (115-114 117-112 120-111)

WBA
10 April 1994 Bangkok
Saen Sor Ploenchit (THAI, holder) bt Jesus Rojas (VEN)
pts 12

IBF
8 May 1994 Rajaburi Province, Thailand
Pichit Sithbangprachan (THAI, holder) bt José Luis
Zepeda (MEX) pts 12 (115-113 112-115 115-113)

WBO
11 June 1994 York Hall, Bethnal Green
Baby Jake Matlala (SAF, holder) bt Francis Ampofo (UK)
ret 10
*Ampofo, who had his licence revoked by the British
Board of Control after failing a brain scan in 1993, has
further neurological tests after the fight.*

WBA
12 June 1994 Bangkok
Saen Sor Ploenchit (THAI, holder) bt Aquiles Guzman
(VEN) pts 12

WBC
1 Aug 1994 Tokyo
Yuri Arbachakov (RUS, holder) bt Hugo Rafael Soto
(ARG) ko 8

WBA
25 Sep 1994 Kanchanaburi, Thailand
Saen Sor Ploenchit (THAI, holder) bt Kim Young-kang
(S KOR) pts 12

WBO
15 Oct 1994 Superbowl, Sun City
Baby Jake Matlala (SAF, holder) bt Domingo Lucas
(PHIL) pts 12 (118-110 119-110 118-110)

WBF
Oct 1994 Bangkok
Fahlan Sakkririn (THAI) bt Kasimir Tcholakov (BUL) pts 12

WBA
26 Dec 1994 Rayong, Thailand
Saen Sor Ploenchit (THAI, holder) bt Danny Nuñez
(DOM) rsf 11
*Nuñez, who loses consciousness after the fight, is
taken to hospital suffering from a haemorrhage and
swelling of the brain.*

Light-flyweight
JUNIOR FLYWEIGHT

WBA
21 Oct 1993 Korakuen Hall, Tokyo
Leo Gamez (VEN) bt Shiro Yahiro (JAP) ret 9
(vacant title)
*Gamez, a previous WBA strawweight champion, knocks
Yahiro down twice in the 9th.*

WBC & IBF
30 Oct 1993 America West Arena, Phoenix
Michael Carbajal (USA, holder) bt Domingo Sosa (DOM)
rsf 5

WBO
2 Feb 1994 Kelvin Hall, Glasgow
Josue Camacho (PR, holder) bt Paul Weir (UK) pts 12
(115-114 118-111 116-112)
*Camacho makes his first defence of the title he won
back in July 1992.*

WBA
6 Feb 1994 New Panama Gym, Panama City
Leo Gamez (VEN, holder) bt Juan Torres (PAN) rsf 7

WBC & IBF
19 Feb 1994 Great Wester Forum, Inglewood, California
Humberto Gonzalez (MEX) bt Michael Carbajal (USA,
holder) pts 12 (117-113 115-114 115-113)
*Carbajal becomes the first flyweight to win a £1 million
purse.*

WBA
27 June 1994 Rajadamnern Stadium, Bangkok
Leo Gamez (VEN, holder) drew with Kaj Ratchabandit
(THAI) 12 (115-14 114-115 114-114)
*Gonzalez recovers from a 7th-round knockdown to beat
a man now calling himself Hadao CP Gym.*

WBC & IBF
9 July 1994
Humberto Gonzalez (MEX, holder) bt A Diaz (MEX) rsf 3

WBF
9 July 1994 Bangkok
Sairung Oh Surwanasing (THAI) bt Azardin Anhar
(INDO) rsf 5

WBO
15 July 1994 Phoenix
Michael Carbajal (USA) bt Josue Camacho (PR, holder)
pts 12 (119-108 119-110 118-108)

WBC & IBF
10 Sep 1994 Lake Tahoe
Humberto Gonzalez (MEX, holder) bt Juan Domingo
Cordoba (ARG) rsf 8

WBA
9 Oct 1994 Thailand
Leo Gamez (VEN, holder) bt Pichitnoi Sitbangprachan
(THAI) ko 6

WBF
30 Oct 1994 Bangkok
Sairung Oh Suwanasing (THAI, holder) bt Andrés
Tavares (DOM) rsf 3

WBC & IBF
12 Nov 1994 Plaza del Toro, Mexico City
Humberto Gonzalez (MEX) bt Michael Carbajal (USA)
pts 12 (117-114 116-113 114-114)
*Carbajal, who gives up the WBO title to take the fight,
loses to Gonzalez for the second successive time.*

WBO
23 Nov 1994 Magnum Centre, Irvine
Paul Weir (UK) bt Paul Oulden (SAF) pts (119-110 117-
111 116-112) (vacant title)
*In only his ninth professional fight (his fourth for a
world title), Weir wins his second WBO championship.*

Strawweight
MINI-FLYWEIGHT

IBF
26 Sep 1993 Hua Mark, Bangkok
Ratanapol Sor Vorapin (THAI, holder) bt Domingues
Siwalette (INDON) rsf 4

WBO
25 Oct 1993 St Andrew's SC, Glasgow
Paul Weir (UK, holder) bt Lindi Memani (SAF) pts 12
(116-113, 117-112, 116-111)
Weir makes his only defence before relinquishing the title.

WBA
28 Nov 1993 Pichit, Thailand
Chana Porpaoin (THAI, holder) bt Rafael Torres (DOM)
ko 4
*Popaoin, who recovers from a first-round knockdown,
is now unbeaten in 30 pro fights.*

IBF
10 Dec 1993 Suphanburi
Ratanapol Sor Vorapin (THAI, holder) bt Félix Naranjo
(COL) rsf 2
*Naranjo, knocked down twice in the first round, lasts
only 24 seconds into the second.*

WBC
18 Dec 1993 Caesars, Lake Tahoe
Ricardo Lopez (MEX, holder) bt Manny Melchior (PHIL)
ko 11

WBO
22 Dec 1993 San Juan, P Rico
Alex Sánchez (PR) bt Orlando Malone (USA) ko 1
(vacant title)

WBO
7 Jan 1994 Palma, Majorca
Alex Sánchez (PR, holder) bt Arturo Garcia Mayen
(MEX) rsf 1
*One of the more preposterous world title fights: after 90
seconds, Garcia Mayen turns and runs back to his
corner. His background? No-one's sure if he's a Mex or
a Tex, and this is said to be his third professional fight,
though there seems to be no record of any at all.*

IBF
27 Feb 1994 Bangkok
Ratanapol Sor Vorapin (THAI, holder) bt Ronnie
Magramo (PHIL) pts 12

WBA
27 March Chonburi
Chana Porpaoin (THAI, holder) bt Carlos Murillo (PAN)
pts 12 (116-113 117-114 114-114)

WBC
7 May 1994 MGM Grand, Las Vegas
Ricardo Lopez (MEX, holder) bt Kermin Guardia (COL)
pts 12 (117-110 119-109 117-110)
*Both come into the ring unbeaten, Lopez after 35 fights,
Guardia after 21.*

IBF
14 May 1994 Bangkok
Ratanapol Sor Vorapin (THAI, holder) bt Roger
Easpañola (PHIL) ko 6

WBF
9 July 1994 Bangkok
Ronnie Magramo (PHIL) bt Wanwin Charoen (THAI)
ko 2

IBF
13 Aug 1994 Bangkok
Ratanapol Sor Vorapin (THAI, holder) bt Marcelino
Bolivar (VEN) rsf 4
*Sor Vorapin gets up from a second-round knockdown
to put Bolivar down twice in the fourth.*

WBO
13 Aug 1994 Bayamon, Puerto Rico
Alex Sánchez (PR, holder) bt Carlos Juan Rodriguez
(DOM) ko 1
Rodriguez lasts 2:12.

WBA
27 Aug 1994 Petchaboon, Thailand
Chana Porpaoin (THAI, holder) bt Kang Keun-young (S
KOR) pts 12

WBO
10 Sep 1994 Hamburg
Alex Sánchez (PR, holder) bt Oscar Andrade (MEX) ko 4

WBC
17 Sep 1994 MGM Grand, Las Vegas
Ricardo Lopez (MEX, holder) bt Yodsing Au
Saengmorokot (THAI) ko 1
Lopez makes his tenth successful defence of the title he
won in 1990, but it's little surprise that the challenger
lasts just two punches spread over 1:53.

WBF
22 Oct 1994 Bangkok
Falan Sakkririn (THAI) bt Krasimir Chokalov (BUL)
pts 12

WBA
5 Nov 1994 Hat Yai, Thailand
Chana Porpaoin (THAI, holder) bt Miguel Herrera
(DOM) pts 12 (115-111 112-114 115-113)
Porpaoin makes his seventh successful defence of the
title by winning a split decision after being knocked
down in the sixth.

IBF
12 Nov 1994 Khon Kaen, Thailand
Ratanapol Sor Vorapin (THAI, holder) bt Carlos
Rodriguez (VEN) ko 3

WBC
12 Nov 1994 Mexico City
Ricardo Lopez (MEX, holder) bt Javier Varguez (MEX)
rsf 8

WBO
18 Nov 1994 Tandil, Argentina
Alex Sánchez (PR, holder) bt Carlos Elualza

WBA
10 Dec 1994 Monterrey
Ricardo Lopez (MEX, holder) bt Yamil Caraballo (COL)
ko 1
Caraballo lasts 70 seconds.

European Title Fights

Heavyweight

1 Dec 1993 Albert Hall London
Henry Akinwande (UK, holder) bt Biagio Chianese (ITA)
rsf 4

23 July 1994 Berlin
Henry Akinwade (UK, holder) bt Mario Schiesser (GER)
rsf 7
No German's held the title since Joe Bugner beat
Jürgen Blin in 1972.

Cruiserweight

2 Feb 1994 Ferrara
Carl Thompson (UK) bt Massimiliano Duran (ITA,

holder) rsf 8
Thompson recovers after being knocked down twice to
become the first British boxer to win a European title in
Italy since Pat Barrett in 1990 (eleven failed attempts in
between). Duran's brother Alessandro fought Eamonn
Loughran for the WBO welter title on 22 Jan.

14 June 1994 Epernay
Carl Thompson (UK, holder) bt Akim Tafer (FRA) rsf 6

13 Oct 1994
Carl Thompson (UK, holder) v Ralf Rocchigiani (GER)
Thompson's stripped of the title when a hand injury
prevents him defending it in early December.

Light-heavyweight

13 Nov 1993 Palais des Sports, Castelnau-le-Nez,
Montpellier
Eddy Smulders (HOL, holder) bt Eric Nicoletta (FRA) pts
12 (117-113 118-114 115-114)
Smulders remains unbeaten after 25 pro fights...

5 March 1994 Palais des Sports, Lyon
Fabrice Tiozzo (FRA) bt Eddy Smulders (HOL, holder) rsf 7
...but not 26. Tiozzo's brother Christophe won the WBA
super-middle title in the same ring in 1990.

25 Oct 1994 Palais des Sports, Besançon
Fabrice Tiozzo (FRA, holder) bt Maurice Core (UK) rsf 4
Knockdowns in the third & fourth rounds force Core's
corner to throw in the towel. He loses for the first time
as a professional.

Super-middleweight

26 Nov 1993 Ice Palace, Marino
Vincenzo Nardiello (ITA) bt Mauro Galvano (ITA) pts 12
(118-113 117-112 117-113)
Nardiello regains the (vacant) title.

11 June 1994 Zenith, Toulon
Frédéric Seillier (FRA) bt Vincenzo Nardiello (ITA,
holder) ret 5
Seillier, who lost two previous attempts at the European
middleweight title, knocks Nardiello down three times.

8 Oct 1994 Berck-sur-mer, France
Frédéric Seillier (FRA, holder) bt Bernard Bonzon (SWI)
rsf 9
Seillier wins every round but survives a cut over each eye.

Middleweight

11 Dec 1993 Berck-sur-Mer
Agostino Cardamone (ITA, holder) bt Frédéric Seillier
(FRA) pts 12 (117-114 115-113 117-114)

20 July 1994 Piazza Onsini, Solofra, nr Naples
Agostino Cardamone (ITA, holder) bt Neville Brown
(UK) rsf 7

Brown's knocked down three times.

9 Nov 1994 Ariston Theatre Complex, San Remo
Agostino Cardamone (ITA, holder) bt Shaun Cummins
(UK) pts 12 (117-111 119-109 118-110)
The unbeaten Cardamone recovers from an eighth-round knockdown.

Light-middleweight

5 Oct 1993 Dijon
Bernard Razzano (FRA) bt Laurent Boudouani (FRA, holder) ko 9

11 Jan 1994 Palais des Sports, Dijon
Javier Castillejo (SPA) bt Bernard Razzano (FRA, holder) ret 6

19 Feb 1994 Madrid
Javier Castillejo (SPA, holder) bt Santo Colombo (ITA)
rsf 3

25 March 1994 Cordoba
Javier Castillejo (SPA, holder) bt Valentino Manca (ITA)
ret 3
Castillejo knocks Manca down twice.

20 May 1994 Las Palmas
Javier Castillejo (SPA, holder) bt Patrick Vungbo (BEL)
pts 12

23 July Boiro, Spain
Javier Castillejo (SPA, holder) bt Ludovic Proto (FRA)
ret 8
Proto's a former European welterweight champion.

Welterweight

22 Sep 1993 Wembley Arena
Gary Jacobs (UK, holder) bt Daniel Bicchieray (FRA)
rsf 5

1 Feb 1994 Stade Marcel Cerdan, Levallois-Perret, Paris
Gary Jacobs (UK, holder) bt Tek N'Kalankete (FRA) pts
12 (118-114 117-114 117-112)

13 April 1994 Kelvin Hall, Glasgow
Gary Jacobs (UK, holder) bt Alessandro Duran (ITA)
rsf 8
Only 850 pay to come and watch, which may be a factor in Jacobs' decision to give up the title in October.

18 Dec 1994 Córdoba
José Luis Navarro (SPA) bt Del Bryan (UK) rsf 10
(vacant title)

Light-welterweight

4 Dec 1993 Palais des Sports Marcel Cerdan, Levallois
Perret, Paris
Christian Merle (FRA) bt Valéry Kayumba (FRA, holder)
rsf 2

17 April 1994 Clermont-Ferrand
Válery Kayumba (FRA) bt Christian Merle (FRA, holder)
rsf 3
Kayumba, who was born in Zaire, regains the title when the British Board withhold a licence from the original challenger Tony Ekubia (who's 34 and hasn't boxed for a year) after doubts raised by a brain scan.

4 June 1994 Palais des Sports Marcel Cerdan, Levallois-Perret, Paris
Khalid Rahilou (FRA) bt Valéry Kayumba (FRA) pts 12
(118-112 115-113 117-115)

11 Nov 1994 Randers
Khalid Rahilou (FRA, holder) bt Gert Bo Jacobsen (DEN)
ret 3
A bad cut on the nose forces Jacobsen out after the end of the second round.

Lightweight

Jean-Baptiste Mendy (FRA, holder) bt Angel Mona
(FRA) ret 9

22 April 1994 Copenhagen
Racheed Lawal (DEN) bt Paul Burke (UK) ko 4 (vacant title)
No British fighter's won a European title in Denmark since Colin Jones in 1982.

4 Dec 1994 Palais Omnisports, Thiais
Jean-Baptiste Mendy (FRA) bt Racheed Lawal (DEN, holder) rsf 9
Lawal is knocked down twice in the second round.

Super-featherweight

2 Oct 1993 Cayenne
Jacobin Yoma (FRA, holder) bt Areski Bakir (FRA) rsf 8
A rarity: a European title fight in South America (French Guiana).

28 Jan 1994 Cayenne
Jacobin Yoma (FRA, holder) bt Rimvidas Bilius (LITH)
rsf 8

14 May 1994 Cayenne
Jacobin Yoma (FRA, holder) bt Neil Haddock (UK) ret 7

7 Oct 1994 Copenhagen
Jacobin Yoma (FRA, holder) bt Jimmi Bredahl (DEN)
pts 12 (119-111 118-112 119-111)

Featherweight

24 Sep 1993 Palais des Sports, Marseille
Stéphane Haccoun (FRA) bt Maurizio Stecca (ITA, holder) ret 8

22 March 1994 Charleroi, Belgium
Stefano Zoff (ITA) bt Stéphane Haccoun (FRA, holder)
ret 9

9 Sep 1994 Fontenay-sous-bois
Medhi Labdouni (FRA) bt Stefano Zoff (ITA, holder) pts 12 (117-114 116-113 116-114)

Bantamweight

2 Feb 1994 Kelvin Hall, Glasgow
Vincenzo Belcastro (ITA, holder) bt Drew Docherty (SCOT) pts 12 (116-113 118-112 117-115)
Belcastro celebrates his 33rd birthday by retaining the title despite being knocked down after only ten seconds.

11 May 1994 Sheffield
Naseem Hamed (UK) bt Vincenzo Belcastro (ITA, holder) pts 12 (119-110 120-109 120-107)
The flashily brilliant 20-y-o becomes the first opponent to knock Belcastro down in a professional fight. Towards the end, he openly mocks the veteran champion, which gets up a few broken noses.

17 Aug 1994 Hillborough Leisure Centre, Sheffield
Naseem Hamed (UK, holder) bt Antonio Picardi (ITA) rsf 3

Flyweight

22 Sep 1993 Oristano
Luigi Camputaro (ITA) bt Salvatore Fanni (ITA) pts 12 (116-114, 116-113, 115-113) (vacant title)

27 April 1994 York Hall, Bethnal Green
Luigi Camputaro (ITA, holder) bt Mickey Cantwell (UK) pts 12 (115-114 116-113 115-114)

3 Aug 1994 Whitchurch Leisure Centre, Bristol
Luigi Camputaro (ITA, holder) bt Darren Fifield (UK) pts 12 (117-111, 118-110, 118-111)
Fifield, although already the Commonwealth champion, is having only his ninth pro fight.

19 Nov 1994 National Ice Rink, Cardiff
Robbie Regan (UK) bt Luigi Camputaro (ITA, holder) pts 12 (115-114 113-116 115-113)
Regan regains the title he relinquished.

Commonwealth Title Fights

Cruiserweight

28 Jan 1994 Waregem, Belgium
Franco Wanyama (UGA) bt Tony Booth (UK) rsf 2
Wanyama gives up the WBF title (who wouldn't?) to take the fight.

Light-heavyweight

Brent Kosolofski (CAN) is stripped of the title in July.

30 Sep 1994 York Hall, Bethnal Green
Garry Delaney (ENG) bt Arigoma Chiponda (ZIM) ko 2 (vacant title)
Delaney's now unbeaten after eighteen pro fights.

Super-middleweight

26 Oct 1994 Town Hall, Leeds
Henry Wharton (ENG, holder) bt Sipho Moyo (ZIM) ko 1
A complete mismatch. The 35-y-o Moyo folds under the very first punch, thrown after about twenty seconds. Harry Warner of the Commonwealth Boxing Council agrees: 'Moyo was clearly not championship standard.'

Middleweight

27 Oct 1993 Gala Baths, West Bromwich
Richie Woodhall (ENG, holder) bt Gerry Meekison (CAN) pts 12 (119.5 - 114.5)

5 Oct 1994 Civic Hall, Wolverhampton
Richie Woodhall (ENG, holder) bt Jacques Le Blanc (CAN) pts 12 (120-114.5)
Woodhall, unbeaten as a professional but fighting for the first time in seven months after operations on each hand, beats a man who's never been stopped or knocked down in 35 pro fights but once lost five in a row.

30 Nov 1994 Civic Hall, Wolverhampton
Richie Woodhall (ENG, holder) bt Art Serwano (UGA) rsf 11
Woodhall has to work for it against a 30-y-o late replacement for Chris Pyatt.

Light-middleweight

26 Feb 1994 Earl's Court
Lloyd Honeyghan (ENG, holder) bt Kevin Adamson (ENG) rsf 6
Honeyghan is stripped of the title in July.

30 Oct 1994 Tweed Heads
Leo Young (AUS) bt Fitzgerald Bruney (CAN) pts 12 (vacant title)

Welterweight

5 Oct 1993 Grosvenor House Hotel, London
Andrew Murray (GUY) bt Tony Swift (ENG) rsf 6 (vacant title)
Swift's father Wally fought for the same title, losing to Brian Curvis (WAL) in 1960 & 1961.

Light-welterweight

25 May 1994 Colston Hall, Bristol
Ross Hale (ENG) bt Andy Holligan (ENG, holder) rsf 3
Also for Holligan's British title.

Lightweight

10 Nov 1993 Town Hall, Watford
Billy Schwer (ENG) bt Paul Burke (ENG, holder) pts 12
(118.5-116) (see British Titles)

16 Feb 1994 Ice Bowl, Stevenage
Billy Schwer (ENG, holder) bt Sean Murphy (ENG) rsf 3
Schwer retains British as well as Commonwealth title.

11 May 1994 Ice Bowl, Stevenage
Billy Schwer (ENG, holder) bt Howard Grant (CAN) rsf 9
*Grant, once a world-class amateur, loses for the first
time as a professional.*

Super-featherweight

30 July 1994 York Hall, Bethnal Green
Tony Pep (CAN, holder) bt John (JT) Williams (WAL)
rsf 1
*Williams is knocked down twice in a fight that lasts
92 seconds.*

Featherweight

24 May 1994 Crowtree Leisure Centre, Sunderland
Billy Hardy (ENG, holder) bt Alan McKay (ENG) rsf 8
Also for vacant British title.

15 Oct 1994 Superbowl, Sun City
Billy Hardy (ENG, holder) bt Stanford Ngcebeshe (SAF)
pts 12 (118-112 115-114 117-112)
*The first Commonwealth title fight held in South Africa
since 1960.*

Bantamweight

14 Jan 1994 York Hall, Bethnal Green
Johnny Armour (ENG, holder) bt Rufus Adebayo (NIG)
rsf 7

23 Sep 1994 York Hall, Bethnal Green
Johnny Armour (ENG, holder) bt Shaun Anderson
(SCOT) rsf 11
*Anderson comes in as a late replacement for Steve
Mwele (KEN) who failed a medical.*

Flyweight

13 Oct 1993 York Hall, Bethnal Green
Daren Fifield (ENG) bt Danny Porter (ENG) rsf 9
(vacant title)
Fifield's first professional title.

9 Feb 1994 York Hall, Bethnal Green
Daren Fifield (ENG, holder) bt Danny Porter (ENG) rsf 6

20 Dec 1994 York Hall, Bethnal Green
Francis Ampofo (ENG) bt Daren Fifield (ENG, holder) rsf
2 *(Ampofo also retains the British title).*
Fifield's knocked down twice in the second round.

British Title Fights

Heavyweight

19 Nov 1994 National Ice Rink, Cardiff
James Oyebola bt Clifton Mitchell ko 4
*The 6'8 giant cuts Mitchell's unbeaten record down
to size.*

Light-heavyweight

1 Dec 1993 Albert Hall, London
Maurice Core (holder) bt Simon Harris rsf 11
*Core's first defence since winning the title in Sep 1992.
He relinquishes it in 1994.*

19 Nov 1994 National Ice Rink, Cardiff
Crawford Ashley bt Nicky Piper pts 12 (vacant title)
117.5-116
*Ashley, who regains the title, knocks Piper down in
the eighth.*

Super-middleweight

11 March 1994 York Hall, Bethnal Green
Cornelius Carr bt James Cook (holder) pts 12 (118-
116.5)
*Cook needed a successful defence to win a Lonsdale
Belt outright.*

Middleweight

10 Nov 1993 York Hall, Bethnal Green
Neville Brown bt Frank Grant (holder) rsf 7
A cut over the right eye costs Grant the title.

26 Jan 1994 Aston Villa Leisure Centre, Birmingham
Neville Brown (holder) bt Andy Flute ret 8

29 Nov 1994 Leisure Centre, Cannock
Neville Brown (holder) bt Antonio Fernandez rsf 9
*Brown wins a Lonsdale Belt outright, again thanks to a
cut eye, sustained by Fernandez in the eighth when he's
taking control.*

Light-middleweight

23 Feb 1994 Watford Town Hall
Robert McCracken bt Andy Till (holder) pts 12 (118.5-116.5)
McCracken's now unbeaten in nineteen fights. Some of his fans stampede towards the ring after the fight, but don't hit their peak till the Steve Foster fight on 10 Sep.

10 Sep 1994 NEC, Birmingham
Robert McCracken (holder) bt Steve Foster pts 12 (118.5-116)
The real action goes on outside the ring. Rival supporters throw seats and barriers, hospitalise eight people, and threaten the cancellation of Nigel Benn's world title defence. Conservative Party chairman Jeremy Hanley begins a famous sequence of gaffes by calling the riot 'just exuberance'.

11 Oct 1994
Robert McCracken (holder) bt Dean Cooper rsf 4
The late replacement leaves early.

Welterweight

22 Sep 1993 York Hall, Bethnal Green
Del Bryan bt Pat Barrett pts 12 (118-116.5) (vacant title)
Bryan wins a Lonsdale Belt outright (he won two title fights before losing to Gary Jacobs)

17 Feb 1994 Goresbrook Leisure Centre, Dagenham
Del Bryan (holder) bt Derek Grainger ko 7

10 Sep 1994 NEC, Birmingham
Del Bryan (holder) bt Lindon Scarlett pts 12 (118.5-117)

Light-welterweight

25 May 1994 Colston Hall, Bristol
Ross Hale bt Andy Holligan (holder) rsf 3
Holligan, knocked down in the first round, also loses his Commonwealth title. Hale's the first Bristolian ever to win a British title.

3 Aug 1994 Whitchurch Leisure Centre, Bristol
Ross Hale (holder) bt Hughie Forde rsf 7
Forde's a former British & Commonwealth super-feather champion.

Lightweight

10 Nov 1993 Town Hall, Watford
Billy Schwer bt Paul Burke (holder) pts 12 (118.5-116) (also for Commonwealth title)
Schwer regains the title from the man who took it from him.

16 Feb 1994 Ice Bowl, Stevenage
Billy Schwer (holder) bt Sean Murphy rsf 3
Schwer, who wins a Lonsdale Belt outright (and retains his Commonwealth title) against the former British featherweight champion, relinquishes the title in Dec 1994.

Super-featherweight

23 March 1994 Star Leisure Centre, Splott, Cardiff
Floyd Havard bt Neil Haddock (holder) rsf 10
Haddock needed a successful defence to win a Lonsdale Belt outright.

13 Dec 1994 The Island, Ilford
Floyd Havard (holder) bt Davey McHale rsf 10
Havard wins it instead.

Featherweight

18 Dec 1993 Wythenshawe Forum
Duke McKenzie bt John Davison rsf 4 (vacant title)
The first boxer to win British titles at both flyweight & featherweight, McKenzie (who also held world titles at fly, bantam & super-bantam) sends the 35-y-o Davison into retirement.

24 May 1994 Crowtree Leisure Centre, Sunderland
Billy Hardy bt Alan McKay rsf 8 (vacant title)
Also for Hardy's Commonwealth title.

Super-bantamweight

26 April 1994 York Hall, Bethnal Green
Richie Wenton bt Bradley Stone rsf 10
Wenton wins the inaugural British title fight at this weight, then pulls out during his next fight, in October, unable to think of anything but Stone, who dies in hospital.

Bantamweight

23 Nov 1994 Magnum Centre, Irvine
Drew Docherty (holder) bt Adey Benton pts 12 (119-116.5)
Docherty wins a Lonsdale Belt outright by beating the man who knocked out his corner man Pat Clinton in the first round.

Flyweight

21 Sep 1994 Musselburgh
Francis Ampofo (holder) bt James Drummond rsf 3

20 Dec 1994
Francis Ampofo (holder) bt Daren Fifield rsf 2 *(Also for Fifield's Commonwealth title).*
Fifield's knocked down twice in the second round.

Amateur Boxing

World Cup
3-10 June 1994 Bangkok

Light-Fly	Nshan Munchian	ARM	Rafael Lozano Muñoz	SPA	pts 15-6
Fly	Rovshan Guseinov	AZER	Vichai Khadpo	THAI	pts 15-10
Bantam	Alexander Christov	BUL	Clausia Cristache	ROM	pts 17-8
Feather	Falk Huste	GER	Joel Casamayor	CUBA	pts 11-6
Light	Marco Rudolph	GER	Júlio González	CUBA	pts 15-11
Light-Welter	Oktay Urkal	GER	Abdullah Ben Biar	MOR	pts 14-5
Welter	Nariman Atayev	UZB	Arkom Chenglai	THAI	ko 3
Light-Middle	Francisc Vastag	ROM	Ratanabek Chagatayev	KAZ	pts 16-7
Middle	Arkady Topayev	KAZ	Bert Schenk	GER	pts 16-10
Light-Heavy	Rostislav Zaoulitschniy	UKR	Sven Ottke	GER	pts 16-14
Heavy	Félix Savón	CUBA	René Monse	GER	rsf 4
Super-Heavy	Roberto Balado	CUBA	Oleg Mascayev	UZB	w.o.

The USA, who lost 11-1 at home to Cuba in Sep 1993, send ten boxers, only one of whom survives his first fight.

Goodwill Games
July 1994 St Petersburg

Light-Fly	Manuel R Mantilla	CUBA	Choi Joon-wook	S KOR	pts 30-3
Fly	Waldemar Font	CUBA	Carlos Navarro	USA	pts 18-14
Bantam	Vladyslav Antonov	RUS	Enrique Carrion	CUBA	pts 6-2
Feather	Ramaz Paliani	RUS	Joel Casamayor	CUBA	pts 15-8
Light	Paata Gvasalia	RUS	Heiko Hinz	GER	pts 12-3
Light-Welter	Hector Vinent	CUBA	Nurhan Suleymanoglu	TURK	pts 21-6
Welter	Juan Hernandez	CUBA	Aleksandr Shkalikov	RUS	pts 16-6
Light-Middle	Sergei Karavayev	RUS	Juan Lemus	CUBA	pts 15-7
Middle	Ariel Hernandez	CUBA	Shane Swartz	USA	pts 8-0
Light-Heavy	Benjamin McDowell	USA	Dihosvani Figueroa	CUBA	pts 9-7
Heavy	Félix Savón	CUBA	Sergei Moichalov	RUS	ko 1
Super-Heavy	Aleksandr Lezin	RUS	Lance Whitaker	USA	pts 17-0

Savón proves himself, yet again, probably the best heavyweight outside the Indiana Youth Detention Centre.
Moichalov goes down from a single punch. Rodriguez Mantilla & Font are banned for two years after failing tests.

ABA Finals
4 May 1994 National Indoor Arena, Birmingham

Light-Fly	Gary Jones	Darren Fox	pts
Fly	Danny Costello	Owen Spensley	pts
Bantam	Spencer Oliver	John McLean	rsf 2
Feather	Dean Pithie	Stephen Smith	pts
Light	Andy Green	Ian Smith	pts
Light-Welter	Alan Temple	Richie Edwards	rsf 3
Welter	Kevin Short	Mark Santini	pts
Light-Middle	Wayne Alexander	Steven Bendall	rsf 1
Middle	David Starie	Eddie Stuart	pts
Light-Heavy	Kelly Oliver	Paul Rogers	pts
Heavy	Steve Burford	Israel Ajose	pts
Super-Heavy	Danny Watts	Mohammed Khamkhoer	pts

McLean was also the losing finalist in 1987 & 1989. Temple won the 1992 featherweight title. Santini was the 1992
champion. Starie won the 1993 light-middleweight title. K Oliver, who also beat Rogers in the 1992 final, wins the title
for the third successive year. Burford was the losing finalist in 1993. Costello's only 18, Khamkhoer a Russian.

Canoeing

World Cup
Final standings 1994

Wild water

C1 Men

Vladi Panato	ITA
Dominique Rouvel	FRA
Stefan Steinenhöfer	GER
16 Rob Pumphrey	*UK*

C2 Men

Danjek & Knittel	GER
Simon & Eich	GER
Kennel & Müller	GER
14 Bebin & Caunt	*UK*

K1 Men

Robert Ponarolo	ITA
Markus Gickler	GER
Philippe Graile	FRA
10 Ian Tordoff	*UK*

K1 Women

Profanta Uschi	AUT
Amore Bringard	FRA
Myriam Legallo	FRA
8 Cynthia Berry	*UK*

Slalom

C1 Men

Gareth Marriott	UK
Lukas Pollert	CZE
Danko Herceg	CRO

C2 Men

Simek & Rohan	CZE
Saidi & Delray	FRA
Haller & Haller	USA

K1 Men

Shaun Pearce	UK
Ian Raspin	UK
Scott Shipley	USA

K1 Women

Lynn Simpson	UK
Rachel Crosbee	UK
Kordula Striepecke	GER

World Marathon Championships
4 Sep 1994 Bosban Lake, Amsterdam 42.7 km

C1 Men

Arne Neilsen	DEN	3h20:38
Gabor Kolozsvari	HUN	3h28:41
Karsten Scales	DEN	3h28:56
14 James Lee	*UK*	*3h42:13*

C2 Men

Zsolt Bohacs & István Gyulai	HUN	3h06:31
Stephen Train & Andy Train	UK	3h06.33
Pedro Areal & Beinvenido Perez	SPA	3h14:58

The Trains do well to finish second: their boat's sabotaged (two holes drilled into the bow) before the race.

K1 Men

Lars Koch	DEN	2h59:46
Tom Krantz	SWE	2h59:50
Robert Herreveld	SAF	2h59:59
8 Gregory Slater	*UK*	*3h03:43*

Koch won the K2 world title in 1988 and 1990.

K2 Men

Steven Harris & Ivan Lawler	UK	2h46:50
László Ceaba & László Tóth	HUN	2h46:51
Thomas Christensen & Karsten Solgard	DEN	2h46:52

Lawler exchanges his K1 world title for this one.

K1 Women

Susanne Gunnarsson	SWE	3h16:13
Denise Cooper	AUS	3h18:9
Andria Pitz	HUN	3h19:12
5 Anna Hemmings	*UK*	*3h23:48*

Hemmings is still young enough (17) to compete as a junior.

K2 Women

Denise Cooper & Shelly Jesney	AUS	3h00:57
Hanne Selmer & Bettina Larsen	DEN	3h10:37
Andria Biró & Agnes Erdodi	HUN	3h11:47
5 Helen Gilby & Alison Thorogood	*UK*	*3h13:40*

British Open Slalom

1994 titles

Men	Overall	Shaun Pearce
	Kayak	Andrew Raspin
Women	Overall	Lynn Simpson
	Slalom	Lynn Simpson

1994 Championships

23 Oct 1994 Llangollen

Men C1	M Delaney
Men C2	M Millar & S Pitt
Men K1	Ian Raspin
Women K1	Rachel Crosbee

Devizes to Westminster

2 April 1994 125 miles

Mark Philips, Richard Lewis   15h43

Only 8 minutes outside the record of Tim Cornish, who finishes 2nd with Robin Belcher.

British Marathon Championships

28 Aug 1994 River Severn, Worcester

Men K1 15 km	G Mawer
Men K2 15 km	Steven Harris & Ivan Lawler
Women K1 10 km	Anna Hemmings
Women K2 10 km	Andrea Dallaway & Helen Gilby

Canoe Polo

World Championships

6-10 July 1994 Ponds Forge, Sheffield

The inaugural championships. Britain win the first ever World Cup match, beating Italy 2-0.
Brazil, taking part in their first ever canoe polo event, lose 20-0 to Australia, 17-0 to Belgium, and 12-0 to New Zealand.

Men

Semi-finals

Australia	5	Holland	1
Germany	2	G Britain	1

Holland lead at half-time and are level until they concede a penalty with only five minutes left. Britain

equalise in the last few minutes but concede the winner with only seconds left.

3rd-place final

G Britain	2	Holland	1

Final

Australia	6	Germany	1

The Pacific champions beat the European champions in much the same way as they won their semi, pulling away from 1-1 in the second half.

Women

Semi-finals

G Britain	2	France	1
Australia	6	Germany	4

3rd-place final

France	5	Germany	3

Final

Australia	2	G Britain	0

In the second half, a broken paddle leads to so much confusion that Britain are caught with one player too many on the water. The subsequent penalty leaves them one player short (4) for two minutes, during which Australia score the second goal.

British Championships

Crystal Palace

Men

Semi-finals

St Albans	2	Luton	1
Meridian	2	Wimps	1 aet

Final

St Albans	5	Meridian	1
Vessey 2,		Hammond	
Rackham 2, Smale,			

Alex Vessey doesn't score the first goal of the game until ten seconds from half-time.

Women

Semi-finals

St Albans	2	Wimpy Dragon	0
Mutineers	2	Woodmill	1 aet

Final

St Albans	2	Mutineers	1
Parkes,		Wright	
Marlow			

A missed penalty by the Mutineers allows Jackie Marlow to score the last-minute goal that gives St Albans the title for the third year in a row.

Chess

World Championship

PCA Men – title match
London 1993

Garry Kasparov	RUS	12.5
WDWWDDWDWDDDDDWLDDDD		
Nigel Short	UK	7.5

Short, the first British-born player to play off for the title (Isidor Gunsberg, a Hungarian emigrant, played Wilhelm Steinitz in 1890-91), loses the first game when his clock runs out, misses chances to win several of the early games, and sacks his trainer Lubos Kavalek, who admires Kasparov's play in Game 15 but 'beating a corpse hardly deserves cheers.' Kasparov, undisputed world No.1, later loses to a £90 computer program.

FIDE Men – title match
Sep-Nov 1993 Oman & Djakarta

Anatoly Karpov	RUS	12.5
WLDDDWDDDWDDDWWWDDDLD		
Jan Timman	HOL	8.5

After Timman misses several chances of closing to within a point in Game 14, Karpov regains the (vacant) title he first won on a walkover v Bobby Fischer in 1975 and lost to Kasparov ten years later. Timman: 'Kasparov is clearly No.1.' Karpov: no argument about that.

FIDE Women – title match
Oct-Nov 1993 Monaco

Xie Jun	CHN	8.5
WWDWWLWDWDW		
Nana Ioseliani	GEO	2.5

23-y-o Xie makes the first defence of her title, against a player who qualified to meet her by drawing lots in the Monte Carlo casino after her semi-final with Zsusza

Longest spans as world champion

28 yrs	Emanuel Lasker	1894-1921
19	Aleksandr Alekhine	1927-46
19	Anatoly Karpov	1975-94...
17	Vera Menchik	1927-44

Menchik (the first ever women's champion), and Alekhine both died 'in office.'

Polgar, the eldest of the famous Hungarian sisters, one of whom, Judith, is universally recognised as the best woman player in the world: at Madrid in 1994 she becomes the first woman ever to win a top class Grandmaster tournament, ahead of Kamsky, Shirov, Salov & Bareyev.

FIDE Men 1994 –

QUARTER-FINALS
July-Aug 1994 Sanghi Nagar, India

Gata Kamsky	USA	6
DDLLDWWDWW		
Viswanath Anand	INDIA	4
Boris Gelfand	BYL	4.5
DDLWDDDW		
Vladimir Kramnik	RUS	3.5
Valery Salov	RUS	4.5
LDDWDDWD		
Jan Timman	HOL	3.5

Anatoly Karpov, the reigning champion, has a bye into the semi-finals.

PCA Men 1994 –

QUARTER-FINALS

Gata Kamsky	USA	4.5
WWDDDW		
Vladimir Kramnik	RUS	2.5

Kamsky becomes the only player to reach the semi-finals of both the FIDE & PCA cycles.

Viswanathan Anand	INDIA	5
DWWDDDW		
Oleg Romanishin	RUS	2

The chain-smoking 42-y-o Romashinin discovers to his horror that he's in a non-smoking venue.

Nigel Short	UK	6.5
DLWDDDDDDDWD		
Boris Gulko	USA	5.5
Michael Adams	UK	7.5
WWLLDWLDDDDDW		
Sergei Tiviakov	RUS	6.5

The British players go through after quick-play tie-breakers, Adams winning the decider on the 67th move.

SEMI-FINALS
Sep 1994 Linares

Gata Kamsky	USA	5.5
Nigel Short	UK	1.5
Viswanathan Anand	INDIA	5.5
Michael Adams	UK	1.5

The winner of the final (not a Briton this time) qualifies to play Kasparov for the title.

World Team Championship
Nov 1993 Lucerne

USA	22.5
Ukraine	21
Russia	20.5
Armenia	19
Iceland	18.5
Latvia, China	18
Uzbekistan	16
Switzerland	13.5
Cuba	13

For the first time since 1978, a Soviet team fails to win a global title, but there are reasons: the republics now enter individually, Kasparov & Karpov don't take part, and four of the six US players are former Soviets! England surprisingly failed to qualify.

Olympiad
Dec 1994 Hotel Cosmos, Moscow

Russia I	37.5
Bosnia	35
England & Russia II	34.5
Bulgaria, Holland & USA	34
Belarus, China, Georgia, Hungary & Ukraine	33.5
Ireland	29
Scotland	29
Wales	27.5

124 teams take part. After a bad start (draws with Scotland & Indonesia), England take the lead in the twelfth round but lose it in the next, going down 3-1 to Russia I, Kasparov beating Short yet again. Earlier, England drew 2-2 with Hungary, Short being held to a draw by Judit Polgar, who yet again eschews a women's event (if she'd taken part, Hungary would probably have won). Hungary may well be the team of the future: the rest of the team includes former world junior champion Zoltán Almasi and the world's youngest ever GM, Peter Leko.

Women	
Georgia	32
Hungary	31

China & Romania	27
Ukraine	25
England & Estonia	24.5
Ireland	20.5
Scotland	20.5
Wales	19

81 teams take part. England, with the 16-y-o Harriet Hunt in the team, achieve their highest ever finish.

British Championship '93
Play-off

Michael Hennigan	DDWD	2.5
Dharshan Kumaran		1.5

The 23-y-o Hennigan wins the third game in 52 moves.

British Championship '94
1-13 Aug Norwich Sports Centre, Hellesdon

William Watson	9
James Howell	8.5
Keith Arkell	7.5
Christopher Ward	7.5
Mark Hebden	7
Andrew Ledger	7
Andrew Webster	7

In the absence of Short, Adams, Nunn, Speelman & Co, Watson (no longer a chess professional) goes through the tournament unbeaten to win the title for the first time. The 17-y-o Ledger achieves International Master status. The event takes place amid a plague of wasps; John Abd-Mariam loses fifteen minutes on his clock by taking a stung junior to the first-aid station, then suffers a wasp down the back of his T-shirt. He finishes 39th.

Conkers

World Championship
9 Oct 1994 Ashton, Northants

FINAL

Jimmy Marsh bt Bob Jenner

Marsh, who wins despite having only half a conker left, took up the noble craft only five weeks earlier. Ashton, where the greatest event in the calendar's been held for thirty years, is the logical site: hundreds of horse chestnut trees were planted there in 1900.

Cricket

In a muddled, indeterminate twelve months or so, at least at Test level, order was restored at the very end. The West Indies, for so long the dominant power, had beaten England easily enough at home but lost the first Test in India and were within a day of losing a series for the first time since 1980 - whereupon, as always, as we should have expected, their fast bowlers rose up and blew the batting away. The unbeaten run has to end sometime - surely - but few expect England to do it in '95.

Meanwhile, back in '94, Australia drew 1-1 with South Africa at home and away before losing in Pakistan, whose claims to top spot don't survive an examination of their West Indian tour in the spring of 1993. Hard to say whether England, at long last, were on the way up. Results improved in relation to the disasters in India and at home to Australia, but that wasn't saying too much - and the win in Barbados, the series win over New Zealand, and the comeback which squared the next against South Africa were offset by three successive defeats in the Caribbean (including that total of 46), another by 356 runs against South Africa, and two at the start of the series in Australia. Progress wasn't so much slow as complicated. It was that kind of year.

It wasn't even possible to identify the bad guys with certainty any more. Although Imran Khan resigned from a cricket committee after admitting that ball-tampering had gone on in his time, and Pakistani pace bowler Asadullah Butt was suspended for the same activity in a match in November 1994, the New Zealand Test player Willie Watson admitted his country had scraped the surface of the ball during a Test *against* Pakistan in 1990. Above all, of course, Mike Atherton was caught with dirt in his pocket, which must have warmed a few cockles in Rawalpindi. Time, perhaps, to admit it's always gone on, at all levels (Brad Donelan, the Somerset spinner, was fined £250 by the club for ball-tampering in a 2nd XI match in late June 1994), and let it rest. Certainly it's doubtful whether England gained anything from whatever Atherton was trying to do, and the reputations of Wasim & Waqar are built on genuine world-class talent rather than strategic use of the bottle top.

If Pakistan were as much sinned against as sinning, the same went for Phil Tufnell, who was in court in June on charges of assaulting his girlfriend, then received £500 in damages against her father and went on the Ashes trip. That kind of year, alright.

The English domestic scene was altogether less equivocal. There was only one team (Warwickshire) and arguably one individual (the remarkable Lara) in it, one helping the other to win three competitions and reach the final of the fourth, amassing the highest scores in Test and first-class cricket on his way. Cynics will say 'follow that', but neither the team nor the individual have anything to prove after that kind of year.

While Lara arrived, Gower departed, his Test career cut unnecessarily short by disciples of the great god Sweat. Enduringly world-class batsman though he is, Gooch will also be remembered for his part in the loss of the best-loved batsman of his generation. It's been that kind of career.

West Indies v England

1st Test

19-24 Feb 1994 Sabina Park, Kingston
Toss: England
Umpires: SA Bucknor (WI), ID Robinson (ZIM)

England

MA Atherton*	c Murray b K Benjamin	55	c Adams b Walsh		28
AJ Stewart	c Murray b K Benjamin	70	run out		19
GP Thorpe	b K Benjamin	16	(7) b W Benjamin		14
RA Smith	b Walsh	0	(3) c Adams b Walsh		2
GA Hick	b Adams	23	(4) c sub (RA Harper) b K Benjamin		96
MP Maynard	lbw b K Benjamin	35	(5) c Murray b W Benjamin		0
RC Russell†	lbw K Benjamin	0	(6) c Adams b W Benjamin		32
CC Lewis	c Adams b Ambrose	8	lbw b Ambrose		21
AR Caddick	c Adams b K Benjamin	3	not out		29
AP Igglesden	not out	3	c Adams b K Benjamin		0
DE Malcolm	run out	6	b Walsh		18
Extras	b2 lb5 w4 nb4	15	b1 lb3 w2 nb2		8
		234			267

Fall: 121, 133, 134, 172, 172, 172, 194, 209, 227

34, 39, 58, 63, 126, 155, 213, 226, 228

1st inns: Ambrose 22-8-46-1, Walsh 23-6-41-1, K Benjamin 24-7-66-6, W Benjamin 19.1-7-43-0, Adams 10-1-31-1

2nd inns: Ambrose 24-6-67-1, Walsh 24.5-6-67-3, W Benjamin 20-3-56-3, K Benjamin 18-2-60-2, Adams 2-0-9-0, Simmons 3-1-4-0

W Indies

DL Haynes	c Thorpe b Malcolm	4	not out		43
PV Simmons	c Russell b Caddick	8	lbw b Igglesden		12
RB Richardson*	c Maynard b Malcolm	5	(4) not out		4
BC Lara	b Hick	83	(3) b Caddick		28
KL Arthurton	c Lewis b Malcolm	126			
JC Adams	not out	95			
JR Murray†	lbw b Igglesden	34			
WKM Benjamin	b Caddick	38			
CEL Ambrose	b Caddick	0			
KCG Benjamin	b Lewis	0			
CA Walsh	lbw b Lewis	0			
Extras	lb10 w1 nb3	14	b5 lb3		8
		407	2 wkts		95

Fall: 12, 12, 23, 167, 256, 319, 389, 389, 390

38, 87

Malcolm 23-3-113-3, Caddick 29-5-94-3, Lewis 26-4-82-2, Igglesden 24-5-53-1, Hick 21-4-55-1

Malcolm 5-1-19-0, Caddick 6-1-19-1, Lewis 3-0-6-0, Igglesden 7-0-36-1, Hick 3-1-2-0, Stewart 2.2-0-5-0

Man of the Match: Adams

West Indies won by 9 wickets

England's splendid start, as so often recently, doesn't last, either with bat or ball – and Lara's just warming to the task. Atherton passes 2000 Test runs, Hick 1000. Arthurton's century is the 100th by West Indies in Tests v England. Adams' six catches equal the W Indies record for a single Test.

2nd Test

17-22 March 1994 Bourda, Georgetown
Toss: West Indies
Umpires: CR Duncan (WI), S Venkataraghavan (IND)

England

MA Atherton*	c Murray b Ambrose	144	b Ambrose		0
AJ Stewart	b Walsh	0	b K Benjamin		79
MR Ramprakash	lbw b Walsh	2	b Ambrose		5
RA Smith	c Lara b K Benjamin	84	c Richardson b Ambrose		24
GA Hick	c Richardson b Ambrose	33	b K Benjamin		5
GP Thorpe	b Ambrose	0	b Walsh		20
IDK Salisbury	lbw b W Benjamin	8	(9) b Walsh		19
RC Russell†	c Richardson b Ambrose	13	(7) c Murray b Ambrose		6
CC Lewis	c Richardson b K Benjamin	17	(8) c Adams b K Benjamin		24
ARC Fraser	not out	0	b K Benjamin		0
AP Igglesden	b K Benjamin	0	not out		1
Extras	lb14 nb7	21	b2 lb2 w1 nb2		7
		322			190

Fall: 0, 2, 173, 245, 253, 276, 281, 322, 322   0, 30, 91, 96, 129, 140, 150, 185, 186

Ambrose 30-8-54-4, Walsh 26-7-69-2, K Benjamin 23,5-5-60-3, W Benjamin 26-9-62-1, Adams 3-1-10-0, Chanderpaul 16-2-49-0

Ambrose 23-5-37-4, Walsh 25-4-71-2, W Benjamin 16-4-44-0, K Benjamin 19-6-34-4, Adams 2-2-0-0

W Indies

DL Haynes	c Russell b Salisbury	63
RB Richardson*	c Lewis b Fraser	35
BC Lara	c Atherton b Lewis	167
KLT Arthurton	c Thorpe b Salisbury	5
JC Adams	lbw b Igglesden	137
S Chanderpaul	b Salisbury	62
JR Murray†	lbw b Salisbury	0
WKM Benjamin	b Fraser	44
CEL Ambrose	c Russell b Lewis	10
KCG Benjamin	c Russell b Lewis	1
CA Walsh	not out	10
Extras	b2 lb6 w1 nb13	22
		556

Fall: 63, 177, 203, 315, 441, 441, 505, 520, 532

Lewis 28-1-110-3, Igglesden 24.3-3-94-1, Fraser 29-5-85-2, Salisbury 37-4-163-4, Hick 20-1-61-0, Ramprakash 15-1-35-0

Man of the Match: Lara

West Indies won by an innings & 44 runs

Lara scores his 1000th Test run, Ambrose takes his 200th Test wicket. Chanderpaul is the first teenager capped by the W Indies since 1973.

3rd Test

25-30 March 1994 Queen's Park Oval, Port-of-Spain
Toss: W Indies
Umpires: SA Bucknor (WI), S Venkataraghavan (IND)

W Indies

Batsman	Dismissal (1st)	1st	Dismissal (2nd)	2nd
DL Haynes	b Salisbury	38	b Lewis	19
RB Richardson*	lbw b Salisbury	63	c&b Caddick	3
BC Lara	lbw b Lewis	43	c Salisbury b Caddick	12
KL Arthurton	lbw b Lewis	1	c Stewart b Caddick	42
JC Adams	c Smith b Lewis	1	c Russell b Salisbury	43
S Chanderpaul	b Fraser	19	c Fraser b Caddick	50
JR Murray†	not out	27	c Russell b Caddick	14
WKM Benjamin	b Fraser	10	c Fraser b Lewis	35
CEL Ambrose	c Thorpe b Fraser	13	b Caddick	12
KCG Benjamin	b Fraser	9	not out	5
CA Walsh	lbw b Lewis	0	lbw b Lewis	1
Extras	b1 lb13 w1 nb12	27	b8 lb13 nb12	33
		252		269

Fall: 66, 158, 158, 163, 164, 201, 212, 241, 251

15, 37, 51, 131, 143, 167, 227, 247, 267

Fraser 24-9-49-4, Caddick 19-5-43-0, Lewis 25.2-3-61-4, Salisbury 22-4-72-2, Ramprakash 2-1-8-0, Hick 3-1-5-0

Fraser 25-6-71-0, Caddick 26-5-65-6, Lewis 27.5-6-71-3, Salisbury 9-1-41-1

England

Batsman	Dismissal (1st)	1st	Dismissal (2nd)	2nd
MA Atherton*	c Murray b W Benjamin	48	lbw b Ambrose	0
AJ Stewart	b Ambrose	6	b Ambrose	18
MR Ramprakash	c&b W Benjamin	23	run out	1
RA Smith	lbw b Ambrose	12	b Ambrose	0
GA Hick	lbw b Walsh	40	c Murray b Ambrose	6
GP Thorpe	c Lara b Ambrose	86	b Ambrose	3
RC Russell†	b Ambrose	23	(8) c sub (PV Simmons) b Ambrose	4
CC Lewis	b Ambrose	9	(9) c W Benjamin b Walsh	6
IDK Salisbury	c Lara, b Walsh	36	(7) c Lara b Walsh	0
AR Caddick	c Lara b W Benjamin	6	c Lara b Walsh	1
ARC Fraser	not out	8	not out	0
Extras	b10 lb9 w1 nb11	31	lb6 nb1	7
		328		46

Fall: 16, 82, 87, 115, 167, 249, 273, 281, 294

0, 1, 5, 21, 26, 27, 37, 40, 45

Ambrose 29-6-60-5, Walsh 27.2-3-77-2, K Benjamin 20-5-70-0, W Benjamin 24-3-66-3, Adams 4-0-18-0, Chanderpaul 5-0-13-0, Arthurton 3-0-5-0

Ambrose 10-1-24-6, Walsh 9.1-1-16-3

Man of the Match: Ambrose

West Indies won by 147 runs

Walsh suffers his 19th Test duck, a West Indies record, but his reputation as a world class No.2 to Ambrose doesn't suffer. The series is wrapped up with brutally swift efficiency.

England's lowest Test innings totals

45	1887	v Australia	Sydney
46	1994	v W Indies	Port-of-Spain
52	1948	v Australia	The Oval
53	1888	v Australia	Lord's

4th Test

8-13 April 1994 Kensington Oval, Bridgetown
Toss: W Indies
Umpires: LH Barker (WI), DB Hair (AUS)

England

MA Atherton*	c Lara b K Benjamin	85	c Lara Walsh	15
AJ Stewart	b W Benjamin	118	b Walsh	143
MR Ramprakash	c Murray b W Benjamin	20	c Chanderpaul b Walsh	3
RA Smith	c Murray b W Benjamin	10	lbw b K Benjamin	13
GA Hick	c Murray b Ambrose	34	c Lara b Walsh	59
GP Thorpe	c sub (PV Simmons) b K Benjamin	7	c Arthurton b Walsh	84
RC Russell†	c Chanderpaul b Ambrose	38	not out	17
CC Lewis	c Murray b Ambrose	0	c Walsh b Adams	10
AR Caddick	b Ambrose	8		
ARC Fraser	c Chanderpaul b Walsh	3		
PCR Tufnell	not out	0		
Extras	lb8 nb24	32	b8 lb6 nb36	50
		355	7 wkts dec	394

Fall: 171, 223, 242, 265, 290, 307, 307, 327, 351   33, 43, 79, 194, 344, 382, 394

Ambrose 24.2-5-86-4, Walsh 24-3-88-1, W Benjamin 22-4-76-, K Benjamin 20-5-74-2, Chanderpaul 10—23-0

Ambrose 22-4-75-0, Walsh 28-5-94-, W Benjamin 22-3-58-0, K Benjamin 20-1-92-1, Chanderpaul 10-3-30-0, Adams 6.5-0-31-1

W Indies

DL Haynes	c Atherton b Fraser	35	(8) c Thorpe b Tufnell	15
RB Richardson*	c Atherton b Fraser	20	(1) c Ramprakash b Caddick	33
BC Lara	c sub (N Hussain) b Lewis	26	c Tufnell b Caddick	64
KLT Arthurton	c Russell b Fraser	0	(5) b Tufnell	52
JC Adams	c Thorpe b Fraser	26	(2) c Russell b Caddick	12
S Chanderpaul	c Ramprakash b Tufnell	77	c sub (N Hussain) b Hick	5
JR Murray†	c Thorpe b Fraser	0	c Thorpe b Caddick	5
WKM Benjamin	c Hick b Fraser	8	(9) c Stewart b Tufnell	3
CEL Ambrose	c Hick b Fraser	44	(10) b Lewis	12
KCG Benjamin	not out	43	(4) c Hick b Caddick	0
CA Walsh	c Tufnell b Fraser	13	not out	18
Extras	lb1 nb11	12	b1 lb7 nb10	18
		304		237

Fall: 55, 55, 95, 126, 126, 126, 134, 205, 263   43, 43, 128, 150, 164, 179, 195, 199, 216

Fraser 28.5-7-75-8, Caddick 24-2-92-0, Lewis 17-2-60-1, Tufnell 32-12-76-1

Fraser 17-7-40-0, Caddick 17-3-63-5, Tufnell 36-12-100-3, Lewis 8.2-1-23-1, Hick 4-2-3-1

Man of the Match: Stewart

England won by 208 runs

England, in their 700th official Test, become the first team to win a Test in Barbados since 1935. West Indies had lost only once in 29 Tests there, winning the last twelve. Fraser's 8-75 are the best figures for any England bowler in a Barbados Test, Stewart becomes the first player to score a century in each innings of a Test for England v W Indies. West Indies are fined 65% of their match fee for a slow over rate, Ambrose £1000 for knocking over his one standing stump after being bowled at the very end.

5th Test

16-21 April 1994 Recreation Ground, St John's
Toss: W Indies
Umpires: SA Bucknor (WI), DB Hair (AUS)

W Indies

PV Simmons	lbw b Caddick	8	not out	22
SC Williams	c Caddick b Fraser	3	not out	21
BC Lara	c Russell b Caddick	375		
JC Adams	c sub (N Hussain) b Fraser	59		
KLT Arthurton	c Russell b Caddick	47		
S Chanderpaul	not out	75		
Extras	lb3 nb23	26		0
	5 wkts dec	593	0 wkt	43

DNB: JR Murray†, WKM Benjamin, CEL Ambrose, KCG Benjamin, CA Walsh*

Fall: 11, 12, 191, 374, 593

Fraser 43-4-121-2, Caddick 47.2-8-158-3, Tufnell 39-8-110-0, Lewis 33-1-140-0, Hick 18-3-61-0

Fraser 2-1-2-0, Caddick 2-1-11-0, Tufnell 6-4-5-0, Hick 8-2-11-0, Ramprakash 3-1-5-0, Thorpe 2-1-1-0, Stewart 1-0-8-0

England

MA Atherton*	c Murray b Ambrose	135
AJ Stewart	c Ambrose b K Benjamin	24
MR Ramprakash	lbw b K Benjamin	19
RA Smith	lbw b K Benjamin	175
GA Hick	b K Benjamin	20
GP Thorpe	c Adams b Chanderpaul	9
RC Russell†	c Murrayb Benjamin	62
CC Lewis	not out	75
AR Caddick	c W Benjamin b Adams	22
ARC Fraser	b Adams	0
PCR Tufnell	lbw b W Benjamin	0
Extras	b9 lb20 nb23	52
		593

Fall: 40, 70, 373, 393, 401, 417, 535, 585, 589

Ambrose 40-18-66-1, Walsh 40-9-123-0, W Benjamin 41.1-15-93-2, K Benjamin 37-7-110-4, Chanderpaul 24-1-94-1, Adams 22-4-74-2, Arthurton 2-1-4-0

Man of the Match: Lara. Man of the Series: Ambrose

Drawn

Atherton & Smith's partnership of 303 sets a new record for England v West Indies, who set two firsts in their 305th Test: a specialist bowler as captain, and no players from Barbados.

Highest Test score: progression

165*	Charles Bannerman	Australia	1877	v England	Melbourne
211	Billy Murdoch	Australia	1884	v England	Oval
287*	RE 'Tip' Foster	England	1903	v Australia	Sydney
325	Andy Sandham	England	1930	v W Indies	Kingston
334	Don Bradman	Australia	1930	v England	Headingley
336*	Wally Hammond	England	1933	v N Zealand	Auckland
364	Len Hutton	England	1938	v Australia	Oval
365*	Garry Sobers	W Indies	1958	v Pakistan	Kingston
375	Brian Lara	W Indies	1994	v England	St John's

Test averages

WEST INDIES batting & fielding

	M	I	NO	HS	Runs	Av	100	50	Ct
Brian Lara	5	8	-	375	798	99.75	2	2	9
Jimmy Adams	5	7	1	137	374	62.33	1	2	8
Shivnarine Chanderpaul	4	6	1	77	288	57.60	-	4	3
Keith Arthurton	5	7	-	126	273	39.00	1	1	1
Desmond Haynes	4	7	1	63	217	36.17	-	1	-
Richie Richardson	4	7	1	63	163	2.17	-	1	4
Winston Benjamin	5	6	1	44	138	23.00	-	-	3
Phil Simmons	2	4	1	22*	50	16.67	-	-	-
Junior Murray	5	6	1	34	80	16.00	-	-	13
Curtly Ambrose	5	6	-	44	91	15.17	-	-	1
Kenny Benjamin	5	6	2	43*	58	14.50	-	-	-
Courtney Walsh	5	6	2	18*	42	10.50	-	-	1

*Played in one match: Stuart Williams 3, 21**

WEST INDIES bowling

	O	M	R	W	Av	BB	5/i	10/m
Ambrose	224.2	61	519	26	19.96	6-24	2	1
K Benjamin	181.5	38	566	22	25.73	6-66	1	-
Walsh	227.2	44	646	19	34.00	5-94	1	-
W Benjamin	190.2	48	498	12	41.50	3-56	-	-
Adams	49.5	8	173	4	43.25	2-74	-	-
Chanderpaul	65	10	209	1	209.00	1-94	-	-

Also bowled: Arthurton 5-1-9-0, Simmons 3-1-4-0

ENGLAND batting & fielding

	M	I	NO	HS	Runs	Av	100	50	Ct
Mike Atherton	5	9	-	144	510	56.67	2	2	3
Alec Stewart	5	9	-	143	477	53.00	2	2	2
Robin Smith	5	9	-	175	320	35.56	1	1	1
Graeme Hick	5	9	-	96	316	35.11	-	2	3
Graham Thorpe	5	9	-	86	239	26.56	-	2	7
'Jack' Russell	5	9	1	62	195	24.38	-	1	10
Chris Lewis	5	9	1	75*	170	21.25	-	1	2
Ian Salisbury	2	4	-	36	63	15.75	-	-	1
Andrew Caddick	4	6	1	29*	69	13.80	-	-	2
Mark Ramprakash	4	7	-	23	73	10.43	-	-	2
Angus Fraser	4	6	3	8*	11	3.67	-	-	2
Alan Igglesden	2	4	2	3*	4	2.00	-	-	-
Phil Tufnell	2	2	1	0*	0	0.00	-	-	2

Played in one match: Devon Malcolm 6,18; Matthew Maynard 35, 0 (1 ct)

ENGLAND bowling

	O	M	R	W	Av	BB	5/i	10/m
Fraser	168.5	39	443	16	27.69	8-75	1	-
Caddick	170.2	30	545	18	30.28	6-65	2	-
Salisbury	68	9	276	7	39.43	4-163	-	-
Lewis	168.3	18	553	14	39.50	4-61	-	-
Malcolm	28	4	132	3	44.00	3-113	-	-
Igglesden	55.3	8	183	3	61.00	1-36	-	-
Tufnell	113	36	291	4	72.75	3-100	-	-
Hick	77	14	198	2	99.00	1-3	-	-

Also bowled: Ramprakash 20-3-48-0, Stewart 3.2-0-13-0, Thorpe 1-1-0-0

Catches as substitute: Roger Harper (1) & Simmons (2) for W Indies, Nasser Hussain (3) for England Neither side made a stumping throughout the series.

England v New Zealand

1st Test

2-6 June 1994 Trent Bridge
Toss: N Zealand
Umpires: HD Bird (ENG), SJ Bucknor (WI)

N Zealand

BA Young	c Hick b DeFreitas	15	(2) c Rhodes b Fraser	53
BR Hartland	c Hick b DeFreitas	6	(1) lbw DeFreitas	22
KR Rutherford*	lbw b DeFreitas	25	c Atherton b Such	14
MD Crowe	c Rhodes b White	16	lbw b DeFreitas	28
SP Fleming	c White b DeFreitas	54	c White b Hick	11
SA Thomson	c Hick b Fraser	14	c White b Such	6
AC Parore†	c Rhodes b Malcolm	38	c Rhodes b DeFreitas	42
GR Larsen	c Fraser b Such	8	c Stewart b DeFreitas	2
MN Hart	c Hick b Fraser	36	lbw b Fraser	22
DJ Nash	c Rhodes b Malcolm	19	c Rhodes b DeFreitas	5
HT Davis	not out	0	not out	0
Extras	lb6 nb14	20	lb1 nb20	21
		251		226

Fall: 13, 37, 66, 78, 108, 169, 188, 194, 249

59, 95, 95, 122, 141, 141, 147, 201, 224

Malcolm 17.4-5-45-2, Fraser 21-10-40-2, DeFeitas 23-4-94-4, Such 19-7-28-1, White 13-3-38-1

Malcolm 10-2-39-0, Fraser 23-8-53-2, DeFreitas 22.3-4-71-5, Such 34-12-50-2, Hick 14-6-12-1, White 3-3-0-0

England

MA Atherton*	c Parore b Larsen	101
AJ Stewart	c Larsen b Davis	8
GA Gooch	c Crowe b Thomson	210
GA Hick	b Nash	18
RA Smith	run out	78
C White	c Larsen b Hart	19
SJ Rhodes†	c Thomson b Nash	49
PAJ DeFreitas	not out	51
ARC Fraser	c Fleming b Larsen	8
Extras	lb9 w6 nb10	25
	8 wkts ec	567

DNB: PM Such, DE Malcolm

Fall: 16, 279, 314, 375, 414, 482, 528, 567

Davis 21-0-93-1, Nash 36-5-153-2, Larsen 44.4-11-116-2, Hart 35-7-123-1, Thomson 38-6-73-1

Man of the Match: Gooch

England won by an innings & 90 runs

Larsen makes his Test debut after playing in 55 one-day internationals, Steve Bucknor becomes the first overseas umpire to stand in a Test in England. Davis' second name is the broadest on the international scene: Te-Ihi-O-Te-Rangi (Salutations to Rangi, God of the Sky). His first ball in Test cricket goes for 4 wides.

2nd Test

16-20 June 1994 Lord's
Toss: N Zealand
Umpires: SA Bucknor (WI), NT Plews (ENG)

N Zealand

BA Young	lbw b Fraser	0	(2) c Hick b Such		94
BA Pocock	c Smith b Such	10	(1) lbw b DeFreitas		2
KR Rutherford*	c Stewart b DeFreitas	37	lbw b DeFreitas		0
MD Crowe	c Smith b DeFreitas	142	b DeFreitas		9
SP Fleming	lbw b Fraser	41	lbw b Taylor		39
SA Thomson	run out	69	not out		38
AC Parore†	c Rhodes b Taylor	40	not out		15
MN Hart	b Such	25			
DJ Nash	b White	56			
C Pringle	c Hick b DeFreitas	14			
MB Owens	not out	2			
Extras	b3 lb15 w1 nb21	40	lb4 nb10		14
		476	5 wkts dec		211

Fall: 0, 39, 67, 138, 318, 350, 391, 397, 434   9, 9, 29, 144, 170

Fraser 36-9-102-2, DeFreitas 35-8-102-3, Taylor 20-4-64-1, Such 30-8-84-2, White 21.1-4-84-1, Gooch 5-1-13-0, Hick 2-0-9-0

Fraser 15-0-50-0, DeFreitas 16-0-63-3, Such 25-5-55-1, White 4-1-21-0, Hick 2-2-0-0, Taylor 6-2-18-1

England

MA Atherton*	lbw b Hart	28	c Young b Nash		33
AJ Stewart	c Parore b Nash	45	c Crowe b Nash		119
GA Gooch	lbw b Nash	13	lbw b Nash		0
RA Smith	c&b Nash	6	c Parore b Nash		23
GA Hick	c Young b Pringle	58	lbw b Pringle		37
C White	run out	51	c Thomson b Nash		9
SJ Rhodes	not out	32	not out		24
PAJ DeFreitas	c Parore b Thomson	11	lbw b Owens		3
ARC Fraser	c&b Nash	0	lbw b Hart		2
JP Taylor	c Parore Nash	0	not out		0
P Such	c Parore b Nash	23			
Extras	b4 lb12 nb7	23	b2 lb1 nb1		4
		281	8 wkts		254

Fall: 65, 95, 95, 101, 193, 225, 241, 265, 271   60, 60, 136, 210, 217, 240, 244, 250

Owens 7-0-34-0, Nash 25-6-76-6, Pringle 23-5-65-1, Hart 44-21-50-1, Thomson 22-8-40-1

Nash 29-8-93-5, Owens 10-3-35-1, Hart 41-23-55-1, Pringle 16-5-41-1, Thomson 12-4-27-0

Man of the Match: Nash

Drawn

In scoring his first first-class fifty and taking ten wickets in a Test for the first time, Dion Nash becomes the first player to achieve both feats in the same Lord's Test. Martin Crowe passes 5000 runs in Tests, Ken Rutherford sets a record by being out for a duck in each of his three Tests at Lord's. Gooch's duck is his first for 60 Test innings.

3rd Test

30 June – 5 July 1994 Old Trafford
Toss: England
Umpires: SB Lambson (SAF), DR Shepherd (ENG); TV replays: AGT Whitehead (ENG)

England

MA Atherton*	lbw b Nash	111
AJ Stewart	c Pringle b Nash	24
GA Gooch	c Young b Nash	0
RA Smith	b Owens	13
GA Hick	c Nash b Owens	20
C White	c Hart b Owens	42
SJ Rhodes†	c Parore b Nash	12
PAJ DeFreitas	b Owens	69
D Gough	c sub (HT Davis) b Pringle	65
ARC Fraser	c Thomson b Hart	10
PM Such	not out	5
Extras	lb8 w1 nb2	11
		382

Fall: 37, 37, 68, 104, 203, 224, 235, 365, 372

Nash 39-9-107-4, Owens 34-12-99-4, Pringle 39-12-95-1, Hart 27.3-9-50-1, Thomson 7-1-23-0

N Zealand

BA Young	c Rhodes b DeFreitas	25	lbw b DeFreitas	8
MJ Greatbatch	c Hick b Gough	0	c DeFreitas b White	21
KR Rutherford*	c Gooch b DeFreitas	7	c Rhodes b Gough	13
SP Fleming	c Rhodes b Gough	14	c Hick b Fraser	11
MD Crowe	c Gooch b White	70	c Hick b DeFreitas	115
MN Hart	c Atherton b Gough	0	(8) not out	16
SA Thomson	c Rhodes b DeFreitas	9	(6) c Smith b Gough	21
AC Parore†	c Rhodes b White	7	(7) c Gooch b DeFreitas	71
DJ Nash	not out	8	not out	6
C Pringle	b White	0		
MB Owens	c Stewart b Gough	4		
Extras	nb7	7	b8 lb13 nb5	
		151	7 wkts	308

Fall: 2, 12, 47, 82, 93, 113, 125, 140, 140   8, 34, 48, 73, 132, 273, 287

Fraser 12-3-17-0, Gough 16.3-2-47-4, DeFreitas 17-2-61-3, Such 5-2-8-0, White 7-1-18-3

DeFreitas 30-6-60-3, Gough 31.2-5-105-2, Fraser 19-7-34-1, White 14-3-36-1, Such 10-2-39-0

Man of the Match: DeFreitas

Men of the Series: DeFreitas, Nash

Drawn

Gooch takes his 100th Test catch.

Test averages

ENGLAND batting & fielding

	M	I	NO	HS	Runs	Av	100	50	Ct
Mike Atherton	3	4	-	111	273	68.25	2	-	2
Steven Rhodes	3	4	2	49	117	58.50	-	-	12
Graham Gooch	3	4	-	210	223	55.75	1	-	3
Alec Stewart	3	4	-	119	196	49.00	1	-	3
Phillip DeFreitas	3	4	1	69	134	44.67	-	2	1
Graeme Hick	3	4	-	58	133	33.25	-	1	9
Craig White	3	4	-	51	121	30.25	-	1	3
Robin Smith	3	4	-	78	120	30.00	-	1	3
Peter Such	3	2	1	5*	9	9.00	-	-	-
Angus Fraser	3	4	-	10	30	7.50	-	-	1

*Played in one match: Darren Gough 65, Devon Malcolm DNB, Paul Taylor 0, 0**

ENGLAND bowling

	O	M	R	W	Av	BB	5/i	10/m
DeFreitas	143.3	24	451	21	21.48	5-71	1	-
Gough	47.5	7	152	6	25.33	4-47	-	-
White	62.1	15	197	6	32.83	3-18	-	-
Fraser	126	37	296	7	42.29	2-40	-	-
Such	123	36	264	6	44.00	2-50	-	-

Also bowled: Gooch 7-1-26-0, Hick 18-8-21-1, Malcolm 27.4-7-84-2, Taylor 26-6-82-2

NEW ZEALAND batting & fielding

	M	I	NO	HS	Runs	Av	100	50	Ct
Martin Crowe	3	6	-	142	380	63.33	2	1	2
Adam Parore	3	6	1	71	213	42.60	-	1	7
Brian Young	3	6	-	94	195	32.50	-	2	3
Shane Thomson	3	6	1	69	157	31.40	-	1	3
Dion Nash	3	5	2	56	94	31.33	-	1	3
Stephen Fleming	3	6	-	54	170	28.33	-	1	1
Matthew Hart	3	5	1	36	99	24.75	-	-	1
Ken Rutherford	3	6	-	37	96	16.00	-	-	-
Chris Pringle	2	2	-	14	14	7.00	-	-	1
Michael Owens	2	2	1	4	6	6.00	-	-	-

Played in one match: Heath Davis 0, 0*, Mark Greatbatch 0, 21, Blair Hartland 6, 22, Gavin Larsen 8, 2 (2 ct), Blair Pocock 10, 2*

Catch as substitute: Davis (1)

NEW ZEALAND bowling

	O	M	R	W	Av	BB	5/i	10/m
Nash	129	28	429	17	25.24	6-76	2	1
Owens	51	15	168	5	33.60	4-99	-	-
Larsen	44.4	11	116	2	58.00	2-116	-	-
Pringle	78	22	201	3	67.00	1-41	-	-
Hart	147.3	60	278	4	69.50	1-50	-	-
Thomson	79	19	163	2	81.50	1-40	-	-

Also bowled: Davis 21-0-93-1

Neither side made a stumping throughout the series

England v South Africa

1st Test
21-25 July 1994 (no play 25) Lord's
Toss: S Africa
Umpires: HD Bird (ENG), SG Randell (AUS); TV replays: MJ Kitchen (ENG)

South Africa

AC Hudson	c Gooch b Gough	6	(2) lbw b Fraser	3
G Kirsten	c DeFreitas b Hick	72	(1) st Rhodes b Hick	44
WJ Cronje	c Crawleyb Fraser	7	c Fraser b Gough	32
KC Wessels*	c Rhodes b Gough	105	c Crawley b Salisbury	28
PN Kirsten	c Rhodes b Gough	8	b Gough	42
JN Rhodes	b White	32	b Gough	32
BM McMillan	c Rhodes b Fraser	29	not out	39
DJ Richardson†	lbw b Gough	26	c Rhodes b Fraser	3
CR Matthews	b White	41	b Gough	25
PS De Villiers	c Rhodes b Fraser	8		
AA Donald	not out	5		
Extras	lb9 nb9	18	b8 lb10 nb12	30
		357	8 wkts dec	278

Fall: 18, 35, 141, 164, 239, 241, 281, 334, 348   14, 73, 101, 141, 208, 209, 220, 278

DeFreitas 18-5-67-0, Gough 28-6-76-4, Salisbury 25-2-68-0, Fraser 24.5-7-72-3, Hick 10-5-22-1, White 13-2-43-2

Fraser 23-5-62-2, Gough 19.3-5-46-4, DeFreitas 14-3-43-0, Hick 24-14-38-1, Salisbury 19-4-53-1, White 3-0-18-0

England

MA Atherton*	c Wessels b Donald	20	c McMillan b De Villiers	8
AJ Stewart	b Donald	12	c Richardson b Matthews	27
JP Crawley	c Hudson b De Villiers	9	c Hudson b McMillan	7
GA Hick	c Richardson b De Villiers	38	lbw b McMillan	11
GA Gooch	lbw b De Villiers	20	lbw b Donald	28
C White	c Richardson b Donald	10	c Wessels b Matthews	0
SJ Rhodes†	b McMillan	15	not out	14
IDK Salisbury	not out	6	(10) lbw b Donald	0
PAJ DeFreitas	c Wessels b Donald	20	(8) c G Kirsten b Matthews	1
D Gough	c&b Donald	12	(9) ret hurt	0
ARC Fraser	run out	3	lbw b McMillan	1
Extras	b2 lb5 nb8	15	b1 lb1	2
		180		99

Fall: 19, 41, 68, 107, 119, 136, 141, 161, 176   16, 29, 45, 74, 74, 82, 85, 88, 99

Donald 19.3-5-74-5, De Villiers 16-5-28-3, Matthews 16-6-46-0, McMillan 10-1-25-1

Donald 12-5-29-2, De Villiers 12-4-26-1, Matthews 14-6-25-3, McMillan 6.5-2-16-3, Cronje 1-0-1-0

Man of the Match: Wessels

South Africa won by 356 runs

South Africa's comeback is not so much that of a prodigal son as some kind of returning hero. Indeed the BBC catch some eye-opening flak for not showing live the moment when their openers set foot on the hallowed turf.
South Africa's biggest win (by a runs margin) in any Test. Wessels (24 Tests for Australia) becomes the only batsman to score a century for two different countries against England (each time in his first innings against them). The last South African to score a Test century at Lord's was Roy McLean (142) in 1955. Gooch's first innings is his 200th in all Tests. He becomes the first batsman to score 2000 Test runs on any one ground. The third day of the match is his 41st birthday. The Kirstens are half-brothers.

2nd Test

4-8 Aug 1994 Headingley
Toss: England
Umpires: DR Shepherd (ENG), RS Dunne (NZ); TV replays: JC Balderstone (ENG)

England

GA Gooch	c McMillan b De Villiers	23	c Richardson b Matthews	27
MA Atherton*	c&b McMillan	99	c sub (DJ Cullinan) b De Villiers	17
GA Hick	c McMillan b De Villiers	25	lbw b McMillan	110
GP Thorpe	c Rhodes b McMillan	72	run out	73
AJ Stewart	b McMillan	89	not out	36
JP Crawley	lbw b Matthews	38	c Cronje b McMillan	0
SJ Rhodes†	not out	65		
PAJ DeFreitas	b Donald	15		
D Gough	run out	27		
ARC Fraser	c Cronje b De Villiers	6		
Extras	b1 lb5 nb12	18	lb1 nb3	4
	9 wkts dec	477	5 wkts dec	267

DNB: PCR Tufnell

Fall: 34, 84, 226, 235, 350, 367, 394, 447, 477   39, 57, 190, 267
Donald 29-2-135-1, De Villiers 39.3-12-108-3, Matthews 39-7-97-1, McMillan 37-12-9-3, Cronje 16-3-38-0
De Villiers 25-3-98-1, McMillan 15.3-0-66-2, Matthews 24-8-53-1, G Kirsten 2-1-10-0, Cronje 12-3-39-0

South Africa

AC Hudson	c Atherton b Gough	9	(2) c&b Tufnell	12
G Kirsten	c Rhodes b DeFreitas	7	(1) c Rhodes b DeFreitas	65
DJ Richardson†	b Fraser	48		
WJ Cronje	b DeFreitas	0	(3) not out	13
KC Wessels*	c Crawley b Fraser	25	(4) b Tufnell	7
PN Kirsten	c Stewart b DeFreitas	104	(5) not out	8
JN Rhodes	c Rhodes b Gough	46		
BM McMillan	b Tufnell	78		
CR Matthews	not out	62		
PS de Villiers	st Rhodes b Tufnell	13		
AA Donald	c Crawley b DeFreitas	17		
Extras	b8 lb7 nb13	28	b2 lb2 nb7	11
		447	3 wkts	116

Fall: 13, 31, 31, 91, 105, 199, 314, 391, 410   43, 93, 104
Gough 37-3-153-2, DeFreitas 29.1-6-89-4, Fraser 31-5-92-2, Tufnell 32-13-81-2, Gooch 2-0-3-0, Hick 1-0-8-0
DeFreitas 14-3-41-1, Gough 10-5-15-0, Tufnell 23-8-31-2, Fraser 7-2-19-0, Hick 6-3-6-0

Man of the Match: P Kirsten

Drawn

The first drawn Test at Headingley since 1980. Hick scores his second Test century (his first in England). Atherton's only the fifth player to twice score 99 in Tests.

Oldest to score a maiden Test century

yrs	days				
42	294	AW 'Dave' Nourse	S Africa	1921	v Australia
39	256	Ted Bowley	England	1930	v N Zealand
39	191	Andy Sandham	England	1930	v W Indies
39	173	Harry Makepeace	England	1921	v Australia
39	163	Eric Rowan	S Africa	1948	v England
39	84	Peter Kirsten	S Africa	1994	v England

3rd Test

18-22 Aug 1994 The Oval
Toss: South Africa
Umpires: KE Palmer (ENG) & RS Dunne (NZ) T replays: AGT Whitehead (ENG)

South Africa

G Kirsten	c Rhodes b DeFreitas	2	(2) c&b Malcolm		0
PN Kirsten	b Malcolm	16	(1) c DeFreitas b Malcolm		1
WJ Cronje	lbw b Benjamin	38	b Malcolm		0
KC Wessels*	lbw b Benjamin	45	c Rhodes b Malcolm		28
DJ Cullinan	c Rhodes b DeFreitas	7	c Thorpe b Gough		94
JN Rhodes	ret hurt	8	(9) c Rhodes b Malcolm		10
BM McMillan	c Hick b DeFreitas	93	(6) c Thorpe b Malcolm		25
DJ Richardson†	c Rhodes b Benjamin	58	(7) lbw b Malcolm		3
CR Matthews	c Hick b Benjamin	0	(8) c Rhodes b Malcolm		0
PS De Villiers	c Stewart b DeFreitas	14	not out		0
AA Donald	not out	14	b Malcolm		0
Extras	b8 lb10 w1 nb18	37	lb5 nb9		14
		332			175

Fall: 2, 43, 73, 85, 136, 260, 266, 301, 332
DeFreitas 26.2-5-93-4, Malcolm 25-5-81-1, Gough 19-1-85-0, Benjamin 17-2-42-4, Hick 5-1-13-0
DeFreitas 12-3-25-0, Malcolm 16.3-2-57-9, Gough 9-1-39-1, Benjamin 11-1-38-0, Hick 2-0-11-0

England

GA Gooch	c Richardson b Donald	8	b Matthews		33
MA Atherton*	lbw b De Villiers	0	c Richardson b Donald		63
GA Hick	b Donald	39	not out		81
GP Thorpe	b Matthews	79	not out		15
AJ Stewart	b De Villiers	62			
JP Crawley	c Rhodes b Donald	5			
SJ Rhodes†	lbw b De Villiers	11			
PAJ DeFreitas	run out	37			
D Gough	not out	42			
JE Benjamin	lbw b De Villiers	0			
DE Malcolm	c sub (Shaw) b Matthews	4			
Extras	b1 w1 nb15	17	lb6 nb7		13
		304	2 wkts		205

Fall: 1, 33, 93, 145, 165, 219, 222
Donald 17-2-76-3, De Villiers 19-3-62-4, Matthews 20.5-4-82-2, McMillan 12-1-67-0, Cronje 8-3-16-0
Donald 12-1-96-1, De Villiers 12-0-66-0, Matthews 11.3-4-37-1

Man of the Match: Malcolm

Men of the Series: Malcolm & McMillan

England won by 8 wickets

Benjamin, who didn't play county cricket till he was 27, wins his first cap at 33 (the oldest debutant England pace bowler since Robin Jackman (35) in 1981) after taking 71 wickets in the season so far. J Rhodes is hospitalised by a short ball from Malcolm, which probably deprives McMillan of a maiden Test century. For showing dissent after being lbw to the first ball he receives, Atherton becomes the first England captain to be fined by a match referee (£1250 by Peter Burge of Australia). Wessels is the first batsman to score 1000 Test runs for each of two countries. Gooch rubs another one into David Gower's retirement: his 205th Test innings breaks the England record they shared. Malcolm, galvanised by a blow on the helmet from a short ball by De Villiers, maintains a ferocious pace (and at last gets the radar consistently right) to become the first bowler since Jim Laker in 1956 to take nine wickets in an innings for England in a home Test. More importantly, he's the first player to appear in six consecutive Tests against six different countries, the kind of thing cricket statisticians lap up. Great stuff.

9 Wickets in a Test Innings for England

10-53	Jim Laker	1956	v Australia
9-28	George Lohmann	1896	v S Africa
9-37	Jim Laker	1956	v Australia
9-57	Devon Malcolm	1994	v S Africa
9-103	Sydney Barnes	1913	v S Africa

The top three are the best for any country. Laker's figures were set in the same Test.

Test averages

ENGLAND batting & fielding

	M	I	NO	HS	Runs	Av	100	50	Ct	St
Graham Thorpe	2	4	1	79	239	79.66	-	3	2	
Graeme Hick	3	6	1	110	304	60.80	1	1	2	
Alec Stewart	3	5	1	89	226	56.50	-	2	2	
Steven Rhodes	3	4	2	65*	105	52.50	-	2	2	2
Darren Gough	3	4	2	42*	81	40.50	-	-	-	
Mike Atherton	3	6	0	99	207	34.50	-	2	1	
Graham Gooch	3	6	0	33	139	23.16	-	-	1	
Phil DeFreitas	3	4	0	37	73	18.25	-	-	2	
John Crawley	3	5	0	38	59	11.80	-	-	4	
Angus Fraser	2	3	0	6	10	3.33	-	-	1	

Played in one Test: Ian Salisbury 6*, 0; Craig White 10, 0; Devon Malcolm 4 (1 ct); Joey Benjamin 0; Phil Tufnell DNB (1 ct)

ENGLAND bowling

	O	M	R	W	Av	BB	5/i	10/m
Malcolm	41.3	7	138	10	13.80	9-57	1	1
Benjamin	28	3	80	4	20.00	4-42	-	-
Tufnell	55	21	112	4	28.00	2-31	-	-
White	16	2	61	2	30.50	2-43	-	-
Fraser	85.5	19	245	7	35.00	3-72	-	-
Gough	122.3	21	414	11	37.63	4-46	-	-
DeFreitas	113.3	25	358	9	39.77	4-89		
Hick	48	23	98	2	49.00	1-22	-	-
Salisbury	44	6	121	1	121.00	-	-	-

Also bowled: Gooch 3-0-9-0

SOUTH AFRICA batting & fielding

	M	I	NO	HS	Runs	Av	100	50	Ct
Brian McMillan	3	5	1	93	264	66.00	-	2	4
Kepler Wessels	3	6	0	105	238	39.66	1	-	3
Peter Kirsten	3	6	1	104	179	35.80	1	-	-
Jonty Rhodes	3	5	1	46	128	32.00	-	-	1
Craig Matthews	3	5	1	62*	128	32.00	-	1	-
Gary Kirsten	3	6	0	72	190	31.66	-	2	1
Dave Richardson	3	5	0	58	138	27.60	-	1	7
Allan Donald	3	4	2	27	46	23.00	-	-	1
Johan (Hansie) Cronje	3	6	1	38	90	18.00	-	-	2
Stephanus (Fanie) De Villiers	3	4	1	14	35	11.66	-	-	-
Andrew Hudson	2	4	0	12	30	7.50	-	-	2

Played in one match: Darryl Cullinan 7, 94
Catches as substitute: Cullinan, Tim Shaw

SOUTH AFRICA bowling

	O	M	R	W	Av	BB	5/i	10/m
McMillan	81.2	16	267	9	29.66	3-16	-	-
De Villiers	123.3	27	388	12	32.33	4-62	-	-
Donald	89.3	15	410	12	34.16	5-74	1	-
Matthews	125.3	35	340	8	42.50	3-25	-	-

Also bowled: Cronje 37-9-94-0, G Kirsten 2-1-10-0

Australia v England

1st Test

25-29 Nov 1994 Woolloongabba, Brisbane
Toss: Australia
Umpires: Steve Randall (AUS) & Cyril Mitchley (SAF); TV replays PD Parker

Australia

MJ Slater	c Gatting b Gooch	176	c Stewart b Tufnell		58
MA Taylor*	run out	59	lbw b Gough		45
DC Boon	b Gough	3	b Tufnell		28
ME Waugh	c Stewart b Gough	140	b Tufnell		15
MG Bevan	c Hick b Gough	7	c Rhodes b DeFreitas		21
SK Warne	c Rhodes b Gough	2	(8) c sub (C White) b DeFreitas		0
SR Waugh	c Hick b DeFreitas	19	(6) c sub (C White) b Tufnell		7
IA Healy†	c Hick b DeFreitas	7	not out		7
CJ McDermott	c Gough b McCague	2	c Rhodes b Gough		6
TBA May	not out	3	not out		9
G McGrath	c Gough b McCague	0			
Extras	b5 lb2 nb1	8	b2 lb9 w2 nb1		14
TOTAL		426	8 wkts dec		248

Fall: 99, 126, 308, 326, 352, 379, 407, 419, 425   109, 117, 139, 174, 183, 190, 191, 201

DeFreitas 31-8-102-2, McCague 19.2-4-96-2, Gough 32-7-107-4, Tufnell 25-3-72-0, Hick 4-0-22-0, Gooch 9-0-20-1

DeFreitas 22-10-74-2, Gough 23-3-78-2, Tufnell 38-10-79-4, Gooch 3-2-5-0, Hick 2-1-1-0

England

MA Atherton*	lbw	54	lbw b Warne		23
AJ Stewart	c Healy b McDermott	16	b Warne		33
GA Hick	c Healy b McDermott	3	c Healy b Warne		80
GP Thorpe	c&b Warne	28	b Warne		67
GA Gooch	c Healy b May	20	c Healy b Warne		56
MW Gatting	lbw b McDermott	10	c Healy b McDermott		13
MJ McCague	b McDermott	1	(10) lbw b Warne		0
SJ Rhodes†	lbw b McDermott	4	(7) c Healy b McDermott		2
PAJ DeFreitas	c Healy b Warne	7	b Warne		11
D Gough	not out	17	c M Waugh b Warne		10
PCR Tufnell	c Taylor b Warne	0	not out		2
Extras	lb1 nb6	7	b9 lb5 nb12		26
TOTAL		167			323

Fall: 22, 35, 82, 105, 131, 133, 140, 147, 151   50, 59, 219, 220, 250, 280, 309, 310, 310

McDermott 19-3-53-6, McGrath 10-2-40-0, May 17-3-34-1, Warne 21.2-7-39-3

McDermott 23-4-90-2, McGrath 19-4-61-0, Warne 50.2-22-71-8, May 35-16-59-0, M Waugh 7-1-17-0, Bevan 3-0-11-0

Man of the Match: Warne

Australia won by 184 runs

Having lost his first series as captain, in Pakistan, Mark Taylor puts his place on the line by not enforcing the follow-on, reasoning that England, batting last on a spinner's pitch, won't be able to keep out Shane Warne. So it proves - eventually. Hick & Thorpe's partnership of 160, a record for any England wicket in a Brisbane Test, keeps him at bay for a while, but he dismisses both in five balls on the last day on the way to his best Test figures and the best match figures for any bowler in a Test in Brisbane. The omens aren't too good for England - since 1982-83, the country winning the Brisbane Test has won the series, and Warne's been Australia's leading wicket taker in their last six series before this one - but at least Devon Malcolm's coming back after becoming the first England player to miss a Test through chickenpox since Bruce French in 1987, and Angus Fraser's call-up may help steady things. Malcolm's replacement McCague struggles to withstand the 'traitor' taunts (he learned his cricket in Australia), conceding 80 runs in his first fourteen overs, unable to bowl in the second innings because of an upset stomach, bowled first ball at the death, invalided back to Britain with a stress fracture of the leg. In contrast, McDermott comes back after being written off for not taking five wickets in an innings for 25 Tests. Michael Slater & Mark Waugh hit their best Test scores, Waugh scoring his 50th first-class century. Stewart passes 3000 runs in Tests, Boon 2000 v England. Healy takes his 200th Test catch and equals the Australian & Ashes record of 9 catches in a Test. Gough, who has a defiant match after becoming a father the night before the first day, christens his son Liam plus the first names of the batsmen he dismisses on the first day: David (Boon) and Michael (Bevan).

2nd Test

24-29 Dec 1994 Melbourne Cricket Ground
Toss: England
Umpires: Steve Randall (AUS) & Steve Bucknor (WI)

AUSTRALIA

MJ Slater	run out	3	lbw b Gough	19
MA Taylor*	lbw b DeFreitas	9	st Rhodes b Tufnell	44
DC Boon	c Hick b Tufnell	41	lbw b DeFreitas	131
ME Waugh	c Thorpe b DeFreitas	71	c&b Gough	29
MG Bevan	c Atherton b Gough	3	c sub b Tufnell	35
SR Waugh	not out	94	not out	26
IA Healy†	c Rhodes b Tufnell	17	c Thorpe b Tufnell	17
SK Warne	c Hick b Gough	6	c DeFreitas b Gough	0
TBA May	lbw b Gough	9		
CJ McDermott	b Gough	0	(9) not out	2
DW Fleming	c Hick b Malcolm	16		
Extras	lb 7 nb3	10	b1 lb9 nb6	17
		279	7 wkts dec	320

Fall: 10, 39, 91, 100, 171, 208, 220, 242, 242   61, 81, 157, 269, 275, 316, 317

Malcolm 28.3-4-78-1, DeFreitas 23-4-66-2, Gough 26-9-60-4, Tufnell 28-7-59-2, Hick 2-0-9-0

Malcolm 22-3-86-0, DeFreitas 26-2-70-1, Tufnell 48-8-90-3, Gough 25-6-59-3, Hick 3-2-5-0

ENGLAND

MA Atherton*	lbw b Warne	44	(2) c Healy b McDermott	25
AJ Stewart	c&b Warne	16	(7) not out	8
GA Hick	c Healy b McDermott	23	b Fleming	2
GP Thorpe	c M Waugh b Warne	51	c Healy b McDermott	9
GA Gooch	c&b McDermott	15	(1) c Healy b Fleming	2
MW Gatting	c S Waugh b Warne	9	(5) c Taylor b McDermott	25
D Gough	c Healy b McDermott	20	(9) c Healy b Warne	0
SJ Rhodes†	c M Waugh b Warne	0	(6) c M Waugh b McDermott	16
PAJ DeFreitas	st Healy b Warne	14	(8) lbw b Warne	0
DE Malcolm	not out	11	c Boon b Warne	0
PCR Tufnell	run out	0	c Healy b McDermott	0
Extras	lb7 nb2	9	lb2 nb3	5
		212		92

Fall: 40, 119, 124, 140, 148, 151, 185, 189, 207   3, 10, 23, 43, 81, 88, 91, 91, 91

McDermott 24-6-72-3, Fleming 11-5-30-0, M Waugh 3-1-11-0, Warne 27.4-8-64-6, May 18-5-28-0

McDermott 16.5-5-42-5, Fleming 9-1-24-2, Warne 13-6-16-3, May 4-1-8-0

Australia won by 295 runs

Yet again England fail to capitalise on a good start, this time excelling themselves with a descent steeper than most even by their own recent standards, losing their last six wickets in 75 balls and helping the opposition to pass some

Test milestones: Boon's 20th century, Warne's 150th Test wicket in only his 31st Test, spiced by his first first-class hat-trick. When Warne sees Malcolm coming out to face the third ball, he must think it's his birthday. Actually, it's Boon's (his 34th); his one-handed catch completes the hat-trick. For the fourth Ashes series in a row, England (dismissed for their lowest total v Australia since 1959) fall 2-0 behind. The only team to win a series after such a deficit (1936-37) had Bradman in it. Stewart breaks the same part of the same finger for the second time in a week.

3rd Test

1-5 Jan 1995 Sydney Cricket Ground
Toss: England
Umpires: SA Bucknor (WI) & DB Hair (Aus)

ENGLAND

GA Gooch	c Healy b Fleming	1	lbw b Fleming		29
MA Atherton*	b McDermott	88	c Taylor b Fleming		67
GA Hick	b McDermott	2	not out		98
GP Thorpe	lbw b McDermott	10	not out		47
JP Crawley	c M Waugh b Fleming	72			
MW Gatting	c Healy b McDermott	0			
ARC Fraser	c Healy b Fleming	27			
SJ Rhodes	run out	1			
D Gough	c Fleming b McDermott	51			
Malcolm	b Warne	29			
Tufnell	not out	4			
Extras	b8 lb7 nb9	24	lb6 w1 nb7		14
		309	2 wkts dec		255

Fall: 1,10, 20, 194, 194, 196, 197, 255, 295

54, 158

McDermott 30-7-101-5, Fleming 26.2-12-52-3, Warne 36-10-88-1, May 17-4-35-0, M Waugh 6-1-10-0, Bevan 4-1-8-0

McDermott 24-2-76-0, Fleming 20-3-66-2, M Waugh 2-1-4-0, Warne 16-2-48-0, May 10-1-55-0

AUSTRALIA

MJ Slater	b Malcolm	11	c Tufnell b Fraser		103
MA Taylor*	c&b Gough	49	b Malcolm		113
DC Boon	b Gough	3	c Hick b Gough		17
ME Waugh	c Rhodes b Malcolm	3	lbw b Fraser		25
MG Bevan	c Thorpe b Fraser	8	c Rhodes b Fraser		7
SR Waugh	b Gough	1	c Rhodes b Fraser		0
IA Healy†	c Hick b Gough	10	c Rhodes b Fraser		5
SK Warne	c Gatting b Fraser	0	not out		36
TBA May	c Hick b Gough	0	not out		10
CJ McDermott	not out	21			
DW Fleming	b Gough	0			
Extras	b6 lb1 nb3	10	b12 lb3 w1 nb12		28
		116	7 wkts		344

Fall: 12, 15, 18, 38, 39, 57, 62, 65, 116208, 239, 265, 282, 286, 289, 292

Malcolm 14-4-34-2, Gough 18.5-4-49-6, Fraser 11-1-26-2

Malcolm 21-4-75-1, Gough 28-4-72-1, Fraser 25-3-73-5, Tufnell 35-3-9-61-0, Hick 5-0-21-0, Gooch 7-1-27-0

Drawn

Australia's spin twins do little with the ball (though Warne again takes more wickets than any other spinner in the match!) but hold out to retain the Ashes after bad light prevents Atherton from using his pace bowlers in the last hour. The first Australian wicket to fall is Malcolm's 100th in Tests.

Longest England Test Careers

yrs days

30	315	Wilfred Rhodes	1899-1930
26	356	Brian Close	1949-76
25	13	Frank Woolley	1909-34
22	233	Jack Hobbs	1908-30
22	120	George Gunn	1907-30
21	336	Freddie Brown	1931-53
20	79	Colin Cowdrey	1954-75
19	221	Fred Titmus	1955-75
19	203	Denis Compton	1937-57
19	179	Graham Gooch	1975-94
19	91	Wally Hammond	1927-47
19	14	Cyril Washbrook	1937-56

The top three are the longest for any country, the only ones over 25 years.

Hat Tricks in Ashes Tests

1879	Fred Spofforth	Australia
1883	Billy Bates	England
1892	Johnny Briggs	England
1899	Jack T Hearne	England
1902	Hugh Trumble	Australia
1904	Hugh Trumble	Australia
1994	Shane Warne	Australia

Spofforth's was the first in any Test, Bates' the first for England. Trumble took his second hat-trick in his last Test.

Test 100s

34	Sunil Gavaskar	India	1971-86
29	Don Bradman	Australia	1929-48
27	Allan Border	Australia	1979-94
26	Garry Sobers	W Indies	1958-73
24	Greg Chappell	Australia	1970-84
24	Viv Richards	W Indies	1974-89
23	Javed Miandad	Pakistan	1976-92
22	Wally Hammond	England	1928-39
22	Colin Cowdrey	England	1954-69
22	Geoff Boycott	England	1964-81
21	Neil Harvey	Australia	1948-63
20	Ken Barrington	England	1960-68
20	Graham Gooch	England	1980-94
20	David Boon	Australia	1985-94

One day internationals

West Indies v England

16 Feb 1994 Kensington Oval, Bridgetown

Toss: England

Umpires: LH Barker (WI), CR Duncan (WI)

England		
MA Atherton*	c Richardson b Cummins	86
AJ Stewart†	c Lara b Benjamin	11
GP Thorpe	c Adams b Benjamin	4
RA Smith	c&b Harper	12
GA Hick	c Simmons b Cummins	47
MP Maynard	not out	22
CC Lewis	not out	6
Extras	b4 lb7 nb3	14
	5 wkts, 50 overs	202

DNB: SL Watkin, AP Igglesden, PCR Tufnell, DE Malcolm

Fall: 35, 45, 73, 166, 176

Ambrose 10-2-35-0, Walsh 10-0-42-0, Benjamin 10-2-38-2, Cummins 10-1-28-2, Harper 10-0-48-1

W Indies		
DL Haynes	c Malcolm b Igglesden	17
BC Lara	c Igglesden b Malcolm	9
RB Richardson*	c Maynard b Lewis	12
KLT Arthurton	b Lewis	6
PV Simmons	b Lewis	0
JC Adams†	c Thorpe b Igglesden	29
RA Harper	lbw b Watkin	11
AC Cummins	c Thorpe b Malcolm	24
WKM Benjamin	c Thorpe b Tufnell	0
CEL Ambrose	c Smith b Malcolm	10
CA Walsh	not out	1
Extras	b1 lb10 w11	22
	40.4 overs	141

Fall: 17, 43, 48, 48, 55, 82, 121, 122, 136

Malcolm 8.4-1-41-3, Watkin 8-1-27-1, Lewis 8-2-18-3, Igglesden 8-2-12-2, Tufnell 8-0-32-1

Man of the Match: Atherton

England won by 61 runs

West Indies v England

26 Feb 1994 Sabina Park, Kingston

Toss: W Indies

Umpires: LH Barker (WI), SA Bucknor (WI)

England		
MA Atherton*	c Arthurton b Harper	46
AJ Stewart†	run out	66

RA Smith	c Harper b K Benjamin	56
GA Hick	c Cummins b Arthurton	31
MP Maynard	b Cummins	22
N Hussain	c Richardson b Cummins	10
CC Lewis	b K Benjamin	0
SL Watkin	b K Benjamin	0
AP Igglesden	not out	2
PCR Tufnell	not out	2
Extras	lb9 w7 nb2	18
	8 wkts, 50 overs	253

DNB: ARC Fraser

Fall: 112, 128, 209, 214, 247, 248, 248, 249
Walsh 5-1-26-0, K Benjamin 10-01-44-3, Cummins 8-1-42-2, W Benjamin 8-0-33-0, Harper 8-0-45-1, Simmons 7-0-32-0, Arthurton 4-0-22-1

W Indies

DL Haynes	c&b Hick	53
BC Lara	lbw b Watkin	8
PV Simmons	b Fraser	39
KLT Arthurton	st Stewart b Hick	12
RB Richardson*	c Fraser b Watkin	32
JC Adams†	not out	52
RA Harper	lbw b Watkin	0
AC Cummins	c Smith b Watkin	16
WKM Benjamin	not out	9
Extras	b3 lb7 w6 nb3	19
	7 wkts, 45.5 overs	240

DNB: KCG Benjamin, CA Walsh

Fall: 13, 111, 128, 130, 186, 186, 223
Igglesden 7-1-29-0, Watkin 9.5-1-49-4, Fraser 9-0-50-1, Lewis 9-0-48-0, Tufnell 4-0-22-0, Hick 7-0-32-2

Man of the Match: Adams

W Indies won on faster scoring rate

West Indies v England

2 March 1994 Arnos Vale, St Vincent
Toss: England
Umpires: LH Barker (WI), GT Johnson (WI)

W Indies

DL Haynes	c Lewis Tufnell	83
PV Simmons	c Hussain b Tufnell	63
BC Lara	Stewart b Fraser	60
KLT Arthurton	c Smith b Watkin	28
RB Richardson*	not out	52
JC Adams†	c Smith b Watkin	6
RA Harper	run out	15
AC Cummins	not out	0
Extras	lb4 w2	6
	6 wkts, 50 overs	313

DNB: WKM Benjamin, CEL Ambrose, KCG Benjamin

Fall: 145, 156, 230, 242, 256, 300

Igglesden 10-1-65-0, Watkin 9-0-61-2, Lewis 9-0-67-0, Fraser 10-0-46-1, Hick 3-0-18-0, Tufnell 9-0-52-2

England

CC Lewis	lbw b Cummins	2
AJ Stewart†	c Adams b K Benjamin	13
RA Smith	b Ambrose	18
GA Hick	c Cummins b Harper	32
MP Maynard	c Simmons b Cummins	6
N Hussain	c&b Harper	16
MA Atherton*	not out	19
SL Watkin	c Lara b Arthurton	4
AP Igglesden	c Ambrose b Lara	18
ARC Fraser	st Adams b Lara	1
PCR Tufnell	not out	0
Extras	b1 lb12 w6	19
	9 wkts, 50 overs	148

Fall: 7, 24, 41, 64, 99, 105, 119, 144, 148
K Benjamin 6-0-21-1, Cummins 8-1-22-2, W Benjamin 5-1-15-0, Ambrose 6-2-13-1, Simmons 7-1-18-0, Harper 10-0-29-2, Arthurton 6-1-12-1, Lara 2-0-5-2

Man of the Match: Haynes

W Indies won by 165 runs

The highest total conceded and heaviest defeat suffered by England in their 222 one-dayers.

West Indies v England

5 March 1994 Queen's Park Oval, Port-of-Spain
Toss: England
Umpires: SA Bucknor (WI), CE Cumberbatch (WI)

W Indies

DL Haynes	b Lewis	115
PV Simmons	c Hick b Lewis	16
BC Lara	lbw Fraser	19
KLT Arthurton	c Stewart b Fraser	0
RB Richardson*	c Ramprakash b Caddick	13
JC Adams†	c Caddick b Fraser	40
RA Harper	b Lwis	23
AC Cummins	not out	13
WKM Benjamin	not out	0
Extras	b4 lb4 w13 nb5	26
	7 wkts, 45.4 overs	265

DNB: CEL Ambrose, KCG Benjamin

Fall: 45, 75, 75, 98, 222, 38, 265
Igglesden 3-0-16-0, Caddick 10-0-60-1, Fraser 10-0-31-3, Lewis 9.4-1-59-3, Salisbury 9-0-58-0, Hick 4-0-33-0

England

MA Atherton*	b K Benjamin	41
AJ Stewart†	b K Benjamin	2
RA Smith	b Harper	45
GA Hick	c&b Harper	10

93

MP Maynard	b Harper	8
MR Ramprakash	b Ambrose	31
CC Lewis	c Lara b Harper	4
AR Caddick	not out	21
IDK Salisbury	b Cummins	5
AP Igglesden	run out	0
ARC Fraser	not out	4
Extras	b1 lb9 w11 nb2	23
	9 wkts, 36 overs	194

Fall: 23, 86, 110, 121, 130, 145, 177, 184, 184
K Benjamin 8-0-37-2, Cummins 6-0-34-1, Ambrose 8-0-35-1, W Benjamin 7-0-38-0, Harper 7-0-40-4

Man of the Match: Haynes

W Indies won on faster scoring rate

West Indies v England

6 March 1994 Queen's Park Oval, Port-of-Spain
Toss: W Indies
Umpires: SA Bucknor (WI), CE Cumberbatch (WI)

W Indies
PV Simmons	b Salisbury	84
JC Adams†	c Atherton b Salisbury	23
BC Lara	c Stewart b Caddick	16
KLT Arthurton	b Ramprakash b Lewis	17
RB Richardson*	c Stewart b Salisbury	15
RIC Holder	run out	26
RA Harper	c&b Lewis	37
AC Cummins	c Smith b Lewis	11
WKM Benjamin	c Ramprakash b Lewis	8
KCG Benjamin	not out	0
Extras	b1 lb10 w1 nb1	13
	9 wkts, 50 overs	250

DNB: CA Walsh

Fall: 89, 126, 13, 164, 164, 230, 232, 248, 250
Fraser 10-2-41-0, Watkin 10-0-56-0, Lewis 10-0-35-4, Caddick 10-2-66-1, Salisbury 10-0-41-3

England
MA Atherton*	b K Benjamin	51
AJ Stewart†	b Cummins	53
RA Smith	lbw b Cummins	4
GA Hick	not out	47
MP Maynard	c Adams b K Benjamin	1
MR Ramprakash	c Adams b Walsh	10
CC Lewis	not out	16
Extras	b2 lb9 w4 nb4	19
	5 wkts, 36.4 overs	201

DNB: R Caddick, IDK Salisbury, SL Watkin, ARC Fraser

Fall: 62, 83, 151, 156, 174
W Benjamin 8-1-33-0, Walsh 10-0-58-1, Cummins 7.4-0-36-2, K Benjamin 9-0-55-2, Harper 2-0-8-0

Man of the Match: Stewart

England won on faster scoring rate

England v New Zealand

19 May 1994 Edgbaston
Toss: N Zealand
Umpires: R Palmer (ENG), NT Plews (ENG); TV replays:
BJ Meyer (ENG)

England
MA Atherton*	run out	81
AJ Stewart	c Nash b Pringle	24
RA Smith	c Parore b Thomson	15
GA Gooch	b Thomson	23
GA Hick	b Pringle	18
DA Reeve	c Fleming b Pringle	16
SJ Rhodes†	c Thomson b Pringle	12
CC Lewis	b Pringle	19
SD Udal	not out	3
Extras	b1 lb5 w7	13
	9 wkts, 55 overs	224

DNB: D Gough, ARC Fraser

Fall: 33, 84, 140, 161, 180, 199, 199, 224

Morrison 6-0-31-0, Pringle 11-1-45-5, Nash 6-1-20-1, Larsen 10-1-43-0, Hart 11-0-45-0, Thomson 11-0-34-2

N Zealand
BA Young	b Gough	65
MD Crowe	c Stewart b Gough	0
AC Parore†	b Udal	42
KR Rutherford*	lbw b Udal	0
SP Fleming	c&b Hick	17
SA Thomson	c Lewis b Hick	7
GR Larsen	c&b Lewis	0
DJ Nash	b Lewis	0
MN Hart	c Stewart b Lewis	13
C Pringle	c Hick b Fraser	3
DK Morrison	not out	17
Extras	lb4 w1	5
	52.5 overs	182

Fall: 2, 78, 81, 110, 134, 136, 136, 149, 152

Fraser 10-0-37-1, Gough 11-1-36-2, Udal 11-0-39-2, Reeve 4-0-15-0, Lewis 9.5-2-20-3, Hick 7-0-31-2

Man of the Match: Atherton

England won by 42 runs

England v New Zealand

21 May 1994 Lord's

For only the second time, a one-day international in England is washed out, allowing Rutherford, a Man Utd fan, to watch the FA Cup final.

England v South Africa

25 Aug 1994 Edgbaston

Toss: South Africa

Umpires: JC Balderstone, HD Bird (ENG); TV replays: P Willey (ENG)

South Africa

KC Wessels*	b DeFreitas	4
G Kirsten	c DeFreitas b Lewis	30
PN Kirsten	c Rhodes b DeFreitas	8
JN Rhodes	c Thorpe b Cork	35
DJ Cullinan	b DeFreitas	45
WJ Cronje	b Lewis	36
DJ Richardson†	not out	20
RP Snell	c Gough b Lewis	2
TG Shaw	not out	17
Extras	lb6 w10 nb2	18
	7 wkts, 55 overs	215

DNB: CR Matthews, FS De Villiers

Fall: 5, 30, 58, 103, 174, 176, 182

DeFreitas 9-1-38-3, Gough 11-2-40-0, Lewis 8-0-32-3, Udal 11-0-34-0, Cork 11-0-46-1, Hick 5-1-19-0

England

MA Atherton*	run out	49
AJ Stewart	c De Villiers b Shaw	32
GA Hick	c Shaw b Snell	81
GP Thorpe	run out	26
NH Fairbrother	not out	19
SJ Rhodes†	not out	0
Extras	b9 w1 nb1	12
	4 wkts	219

DNB: CC Lewis, DG Cork, PAJ DeFreitas, D Gough, SD Udal

De Villiers 11-2-27-0, Matthews 11-1-42-0, Shaw 11-0-34-1, Cronje 9-0-50-0, Snell 11-0-49-1, G Kirsten 1-0-8-0

Man of the Match: Hick

England won by 6 wkts

England v South Africa

27 Aug 1994 Old Trafford

Toss: England

Umpires: MJ Kitchen, KE Palmer (ENG); TV replays: B Duddleston (ENG)

South Africa

G Kirsten	c Lewis b Cork	30
KC Wessels*	lbw b DeFreitas	21
WJ Cronje	run out	0
JN Rhodes	lbw b Cork	0
DJ Cullinan	run out	54
BM McMillan	st Rhodes b Udal	0
DJ Richardson†	c Lewis b Gough	14
TG Shaw	b Gough	6
CR Matthews	b Cork	26
PS De Villiers	not out	14
AA Donald	not out	2
Extras	lb6 w4 nb4	14
	9 wkts, 55 overs	181

Fall: 43, 47, 47, 64, 68, 113, 121, 163, 163

DeFreitas 11-4-12-1, Gough 10-1-39-2, Lewis 9-0-4-0, Udal 11-2-17-1, Cork 11-1-49-3, Hick 3-0-14-0

England

MA Atherton*	c Wessels b Matthews	19
AJ Stewart	c Cullinan b Donald	11
GA Hick	lbw b Donald	0
GP Thorpe	c Cullinan b Shaw	55
NH Fairbrother	run out	3
SJ Rhodes†	run out	56
CC Lewis	not out	17
PAJ DeFreitas	not out	7
Extras	w4 nb10	14
	6 wkts	182

DNB: DG Cork, D Gough, SD Udal

Fall: 27, 28, 42, 60, 130, 171

Donald 10.2-1-47-2, De Villiers 8-1-29-0, McMillan 10-1-53-0, Matthews 9-2-20-1, Shaw 11-0-33-1

Man of the Match: S Rhodes

Men of the Series: DeFreitas, Cullinan

England won by 4 wickets

Australia v England

World Series Cup

6 Dec 1994 Sydney Cricket Ground

Toss: Australia

Umpires: D Hair (AUS) & P Parker (AUS)

Australia

MA Taylor*	c& b Hick	57
MJ Slater	c Hick b Udal	50
ME Waugh	b Udal	4
DC Boon	not out	64
MG Bevan	c Gooch b Gough	46
SG (Stuart) Law	not out	0
Extras	lb2 w1	3
	4 wkts	224

DNB: IA Healy†, SK Warne, CJ McDermott, TBA May, GD McGrath

Fall: 96, 106, 125, 218

Benjamin 6-0-25-0, DeFreitas 9-1-43-0, Gough 10-0-51-1, White 5-0-22-0, Udal 10-1-37-2, Hick 10-0-44-1

England

MA Atherton*	lbw b Law	60
AJ Stewart	c Law b May	48
GA Hick	c Boon b May	6
GP Thorpe	c Bevan b McDermott	21
GA Gooch	c McDermott b Warne	21
C White	b McDermott	0
SJ Rhodes†	c Warne b Law	8
PAJ DeFreitas	run out	6
D Gough	not out	8
SD Udal	b McGrath	4
JE Benjamin	b McDermott	0
Extras	lb7 w6 nb1	14
		196

Fall: 100, 112, 133, 147, 149, 164, 180, 187, 195

McDermott 9.3-0-34-3, McGrath 9-4-22-1, Warne 10-0-46-1, Law 10-0-52-2, May 10-1-35-2

Australia won by 28 runs

Australia 'A' v England

World Series Cup

13 Dec 1994 Melbourne Cricket Ground

Toss: England
Umpires: S Randall (AUS) & A McQuillan (AUS)

England

GA Gooch	c Emery b Hughes	6
AJ Stewart*	c Emery b Reiffel	5
GA Hick	c Emery b Moody	32
GP Thorpe	run out	29
MW Gatting	st Emery b Robertson	23
C White	run out	43
SJ Rhodes†	run out	21
PAJ DeFreitas	c Hayden b Hughes	11
SD Udal	run out	9
PCR Tufnell	not out	0
Extras	lb7 w2	9
	9 wkts, 50 overs	188

DNB: ARC Fraser

Fall: 9, 23, 55, 95, 97, 137, 170, 187, 188

Hughes 10-3-22-2, Reiffel 10-0-45-1, Moody 10-0-33-1, Angel 9-1-45-0, Robertson 10-0-31-1, Martyn 1-0-5-0

Australia 'A'

DS Lehmann	c Rhodes b Fraser	3
ML Hayden	c Rhodes b Fraser	12
DR Martyn*	c Gooch b Tufnell	40
JL Langer	run out	55
RT Ponting	b White	31
TM Moody	b White	2
P Emery†	c Rhodses b DeFreitas	2
GR Robertson	run out	2
PR Reiffel	c Rhodes b DeFreitas	1

MG Hughes	b White	2
J Angel	not out	3
Extras	lb2 w1 nb1	4
		157

Fall: 7, 20, 79, 138, 142, 145, 151, 152, 153

DeFreitas 10-2-24-2, Fraser 9-1-31-2, White 8.5-1-35.3, Udal 8-0-33-0, Tufnell 10-0-32-1

England won by 31 runs

Zimbabwe v England

World Series Cup

15 Dec 1994 Sydney Cricket Ground

Toss: Zimbabwe
Umpires: D Hair (AUS) & S Doull (NZ)

Zimbabwe

A Flower *†	c Stewart b Fraser	12
GW Flower	not out	84
ADR Campbell	b Gough	23
GJ Whittall	c Stewart b Gough	0
DL Houghton	c Stewart b Gough	57
MH Dekker	c DeFreitas b Fraser	5
GC Martin	b DeFreitas	7
PA Strang	run out	0
HH Streak	run out	1
SG Peall	c Stewart b Gough	0
DH Brain	b Gough	7
Extras	lb7 w1 nb1	9
	49.3 overs	205

Fall: 24, 61, 61, 171, 179, 192, 192, 198, 198

DeFreitas 10-2-27-1, Fraser 10-0-45-2, Gough 9.3-0-44-5, Tufnell 10-0-42-0, Udal 8-0-32-0, Hick 2-0-8-0

England

GA Gooch	c&b Strang	38
MA Atherton*	c A Flower b Whittall	14
GA Hick	run out	64
GP Thorpe	lbw b Strang	0
JP Crawley	lbw b Dekker	18
AJ Stewart†	b Streak	29
PAJ DeFreitas	run out	5
D Gough	b Streak	2
SD Udal	run out	10
ARC Fraser	b Dekker	2
PCR Tufnell	not out	0
Extras	lb5 w5	10
		192

Fall: 49, 60, 60, 105, 169, 178, 179, 181, 192

Brain 8-1-27-0, Streak 8.1-1-36-2, Whittall 4-1-21-1, Strang 10-2-30-2, Peall 10-2-29-0, Dekker 9-0-44-2

Zimbabwe won by 13 runs

TV replays show that Grant Flower's run out on 26.

County cricket

County Championship 1994

		P	W	D	L	Bt	Bwl	Pts	1993
1	Warwicks	17	11	5	1	41	55	272	16th
2	Leics	17	8	2	7	42	60	230	9
3	Notts	17	8	4	5	39	51	218	7
4	Middx	17	7	7	3	43	57	212	1
5	Northants	17	8	5	4	28	53	209	4
6	Essex	17	7	5	5	32	63	207	11
7	Surrey	17	7	3	7	32	57	201	6
8	Sussex	17	7	5	5	28	60	200	10
9	Kent	17	6	4	7	44	58	198	8
10	Lancs	17	8	3	6	32	59	194	13
11	Somerset	17	7	3	7	32	47	191	5
12	Gloucs	17	5	4	8	28	56	172	17
13	Yorks	17	4	7	6	38	57	159	12
14	Hants	17	4	6	7	32	55	159	13
15	Worcs	17	4	7	6	42	52	158	2
16	Durham	17	4	3	10	32	57	153	18
17	Derbys	17	4	4	9	25	54	143	15
18	Glamorgan	17	2	7	8	29	50	111	3

Gloucs & Hants include eight points batting last in matches where the scores finished level. Lancs 25 points deducted for a substandard pitch.

Warwickshire win the championship for the first time since 1972. When they beat Hampshire to seal the title, regular captain Dermot Reeve stands aside for Tim Munton to collect the trophy: with Reeve out injured, he captained Warwicks to eight of their eleven wins up to then.

Phil Simmons' 261 breaks the record for a debut innings in the County Championship, for professional cricket in England (the latter set in 1826) and for Leicester, breaking Samuel Coe's 252 set in 1914.

Against Derbyshire in early July, 19-y-o Middlesex seamer Richard Johnson becomes the first bowler since Ian Thompson in 1964 to take all ten wickets in a County Championship innings. His figures: 18.5-6-45-10.

Also against against Derbyshire, also in July, two Leicestershire bowlers do the hat-trick: Vince Wells and (on his county championship debut) Alamgir Sheriyar.

In July yet again, Jamie Hall scores 85 for Sussex v Surrey, including the slowest ever first-class half-century: 5hrs 4mins, breaking by 14 minutes the record set by England Test cricketer Dick Barlow of Lancs, v Kent in 1889.

Derbyshire are on the receiving end again when Keith Piper of Warwickshire dismisses eleven of their batsmen to equal the County Championship record for a wicketkeeper.

Derbys strike back through Dominic Cork's hat-trick v Kent.

Bob Woolmer, Warwickshire's all-conquering coach, leaves to become national coach of the South African Test team.

Nat West Trophy 1994

60 overs

1st Round

21 June Finchampstead
KENT 384-6 (Hooper 136*, Ward 120; Oxley 5-87)
BERKSHIRE 241-5 (Wood 88, Shaw 57)
Kent won by 143 runs
MoM: Carl Hooper

21-22 June Northampton
IRELAND 182-6 (Smyth 61)
NORTHAMPTONSHIRE 183-3 (Warren 100*)
Northants won by 7 wkts
MoM: Russell Warren

21 June March
CAMBRIDGESHIRE 107
HAMPSHIRE 110-1 (R Smith 59*)
Hants won by 9 wkts
MoM: Cardigan Connor

Connor, in his eleventh season with Hants, becomes a NatWest man of the match for the first time. March is a Cambridgeshire town, of course, not the month.

21-22 June The Oval
STAFFORDSHIRE 165-8 (Myles 71)
SURREY 166-1 (Thorpe 84*, Bicknell 56)
Surrey won by 9 wkts
MoM: Joey Benjamin (Surrey)

21-22 June Hove
ESSEX 272-5 (Gooch 86, Stephenson 55)
SUSSEX 256 (Lenham 82, Smith 64)
Essex won by 16 runs
MoM: Ronnie Irani (Essex)

21-22 June Exmouth
DEVON 242-5 (Roebuck 83)
YORKSHIRE 246-6 (White 65*)
Yorks won by 4 wkts
MoM: Peter Roebuck

21-22 June Aston Rowant
SOMERSET 349-4 (Trescothick 116, Harden 105*, Lathwell 64)
OXFORDSHIRE 130 (Van Troost 5-22)
Somerset won by 219 runs
MoM: Marcus Trescothick

21-22 June Edgbaston
WARWICKSHIRE 361-8 (Twose 110, Ostler 81)
BEDFORDSHIRE 164
Warwicks won by 197 runs
MoM: Roger Twose

21-22 June Northrop Hall
WELSH MINOR COUNTIES 104
MIDDLESEX 108-1 (Haynes 64)
MoM: Keith Brown (Middlesex)

21-22 June Lakenham
WORCESTERSHIRE 309-8 (Haynes 98, Curtis 78)
NORFOLK 172 (Plumb 57)
Worcs won by 137 runs
MoM: Gavin Haynes

22 June Bowdon
CHESHIRE 107-9 [47 overs] (Gray 51*)
DURHAM 108-5
Durham won by 5 wkts
MoM: Simon Brown (Durham)

22 June Netherfield
CUMBERLAND 188
LEICESTERSHIRE 192-3 (Whitaker 73*, Smith 63*)
Leics won by 7 wkts
MoM: Ben Smith

22 June Swansea
GLAMORGAN 344-5 (James 123, Dale 110, Maynard 75)
LINCOLNSHIRE 184-9
Glamorgan won by 160 runs
MoM: Stephen James

22 June Bristol
GLOUCESTERSHIRE 228-8 (Dawson 60)
DERBYSHIRE 229-7 (Barnett 113*, Adams 52)
Derbyshire won by 3 wkts
MoM: Kim Barnett

22 June Old Trafford
SCOTLAND 178-9 (Reifer 72)
LANCASHIRE 179-5 (Atherton 50)
Lancs won by 5 wkts
MoM: George Reifer

Reifer was born in Barbados.

22 June Jesmond
NOTTINGHAMSHIRE 344-6 (Johnson 146, Lewis 89, Robinson 62)
NORTHUMBERLAND 116 (Evans 6-10)
Notts won by 228 runs
MoM: Paul Johnson

2nd Round

6 July Southampton
HAMPSHIRE 187 (Nicholas 62)
KENT 188-6 (Ward 42)
Kent won by 4 wkts
MoM: Mark Nicholas

6 July Uxbridge
MIDDLESEX 259-6 (Roseberry 67)
NORTHAMPTONSHIRE 262-3 (Bailey 52, Lamb 129*)
Northants won by 7 wkts
MoM: Allan Lamb

6 July The Oval
SURREY 343-6 (Thorpe 145*, Ward 87)
LANCASHIRE 218 (Wasim Akram 50, Austin 57)
Surrey won by 125 runs
MoM: Graham Thorpe

6-7 July Darlington
DURHAM 278 (Morris 67, Bainbridge 88; Cork 5-43)
DERBYSHIRE 280-6 (O'Gorman 89, Azharuddin 74*)
Derbyshire won by 4 wkts
MoM: Tim O'Gorman

6 July Cardiff
GLAMORGAN 316-8 (Maynard 78, Cottey 57, Croft 50; Kasprowicz 5-60)
ESSEX 240 (Shahid 85*)
Glamorgan won by 76 runs
MoM: Ottis Gibson (Glam)

6 July Leicester
WARWICKSHIRE 296-6 (Twose 40, P Smith 50, Penney 65*)
LEICESTERSHIRE 168 (Boon 55)
Warwicks won by 128 runs
MoM: Trevor Penney

6 July Worcester
WORCESTERSHIRE 263-6 (Hick 97)
NOTTINGHAMSHIRE 174
Worcs won by 89 runs
MoM: Graeme Hick

6 July Headingley
YORKSHIRE 215 (Byas 71)
SOMERSET 216-7 (Harden 64)
Somerset won by 3 wkts
MoM: Andrew Hayhurst (Somerset)

Quarter-finals
26 July Taunton
SOMERSET 124
WARWICKSHIRE 125-2
Warwicks won by 8 wkts
MoM: Neil Smith (Warwicks)

26 July Derby
DERBYSHIRE 128 (Cork 62)
KENT 129-5
Kent won by 5 wkts
MoM: Mark Ealham (Kent)

26 July Worcester
NORTHAMPTONSHIRE 128
WORCESTERSHIRE 129-8
Worcs won by 2 wkts
MoM: Steven Rhodes (Worcs)

27 July (postponed from 26) Swansea
GLAMORGAN 161 (Murphy 6-26)
SURREY 165-5 (Thorpe 56)
Surrey won by 5 wkts
MoM: Tony Murphy

Murphy leaves the county three weeks later, after being left out of the semi-final. Alec Stewart sets a new record for the competition by taking seven catches behind the stumps.

Semi-finals
9 Aug The Oval
WORCESTERSHIRE 357-2 (Curtis 136*, Moody 180*)
SURREY 350 (Bicknell 89, Brown 52, Hollioake 60)
Worcs won by 7 runs
MoM: Tom Moody

Curtis & Moody's unbroken partnership of 309 sets a new world record for any wicket in first-class one-day cricket. Moody hits the highest individual score against a first-class county in the Gillette/NatWest, then takes two wickets and catches Joey Benjamin on the boundary (needing all of his 6'6) after the latter hits two sixes in the last over.

9 Aug Edgbaston
WARWICKSHIRE 265-8 (Moles 105*)
KENT 257 (Ward 80, Taylor 64)
Warwicks won by 8 runs
MoM: Andy Moles

Final
3-4 Sep Lord's
Toss: Worcs
Umpires: NT Plews & DR Shepherd
(TV replays: AA Jones)

Warwickshire

Andy Moles	c Rhodes b Newport	8
Dominic Ostler	c Lampitt b Newport	4
Brian Lara	c Hick b Haynes	81
Paul Smith	c Haynes b Moody	13
Roger Twose	c Leatherdale b Newport	22
Trevor Penney	lbw b Radford	18
Dermot Reeve*	c Rhodes b Newport	13
Neil Smith	c Illingworth b Lampitt	20
Keith Piper†	not out	16
Gladstone Small	run out	5
Tim Munton	not out	0
Extras	b1 lb8 w10 nb4	23
	9 wkts	223

Fall: 8, 17, 50, 90, 150, 171, 188, 215, 222

Moody 12-4-17-1, Newport 12-2-38-4, Radford 12-1-45-1, Lampitt 11-1-45-1, Illingworth 6-0-35-0, Haynes 7-0-34-1

Worcestershire

Tim Curtis*	b Reeve	11
Damien D'Oliveira	c Lara b Munton	12
Graeme Hick	not out	93
Tom Moody	not out	88
Extras	lb6 w11 nb6	23
	2 wkts	227

DNB: Gavin Haynes, David Leatherdale, Steven Rhodes†, Stuart Lampitt, Phil Newport, Richard Illingworth, Neal Radford

Fall: 29, 29

Small 12-2-40-0, Munton 12-3-23-1, Reeve 6-1-30-1,

P Smith 7-1-54-0, Twose 5-0-36-0, N Smith 7-0-34-0, Penney 0.1-0-4-0

Man of the Match: Moody

Worcestershire won by 8 wickets

A later start seems to be needed, to avoid the early moisture which helps the side batting first lose the trophy for the ninth successive year. Worcs beat the holders to win the competition for the first time and leave Warwicks to finish the season with a mere three titles. The unbroken partnership of 198 between Hick & Moody is the second-highest in any final.

B&H Cup 1994
55 overs

1st Round
26 April The Parks, Oxford
COMBINED UNIVERSITIES 191-3 (Montgomerie 52)
LANCASHIRE 193-3 (Crawley 73)
Lancs won by 7 wkts
Gold Award: John Crawley

26 April Leicester
IRELAND 160 (Warke 53)
LEICESTERSHIRE 164-1 (Simmons 64, Briers 70*)
Leics won by 9 wkts
GA: Phil Simmons

26 April Lord's
NORTHAMPTONSHIRE 232-7 (Loye 68*)
MIDDLESEX 236-4 (Ramprakash 119*)
Middx won by 6 wkts
GA: Mark Ramprakash

26 April Trent Bridge
MINOR COUNTIES 191-4 (Cockbain 54*)
NOTTINGHAMSHIRE 195-7
Notts won by 3 wkts
GA: Ian Cockbain

26 April The Oval
SURREY 288-3 (Stewart 167*, Ward 50)
SOMERSET 253 (Lathwell 120)
Surrey won by 35 runs
GA: Alex Stewart

26 April Hove
SCOTLAND 157-7 (Love 53)
SUSSEX 161-2 (D Smith 65*, A Wells 51*)
Sussex won by 8 wkts
GA: David Smith

2nd Round
10 May Derby
LANCASHIRE 280-5 (Atherton 100, Crawley 73)
DERBYSHIRE 282-6 (Rollins 70, Cork 63*)
Derby won by 4 wkts
GA: Dominic Cork
Cork's 63 comes off just 34 balls.

10 May Stockton
DURHAM 190-8
WORCESTERSHIRE 191-2 (Hick 104*, Moody 65*)
Worcs won by 8 wkts
GA: Phil Newport (Worcs)

10 May Chelmsford
LEICESTERSHIRE 241-9 (Simmons 57, Whitaker 53)
ESSEX 246-2 (Gooch 130*, Hussain 59)
Essex won by 8 wkts
GA: Graham Gooch
Gooch's 21st Gold Award, a record.

10 May Southampton
YORKSHIRE 178-6
HAMPSHIRE 182-2 (Middleton 63*, R Smith 58)
Hants won by 8 wkts
GA: Tony Middleton

10 May Canterbury
GLOUCESTERSHIRE 189-9 (Wright 55)
KENT 193-6
Kent won by 4 wkts
GA: Matthew Fleming (Kent)

10 May Lord's
MIDDLESEX 150
WARWICKSHIRE 151-7
Warwicks won by 3 wkts
GA: Tim Munton (Warwicks)

10 May Trent Bridge
SUSSEX 239-9 (A Wells 51)
NOTTINGHAMSHIRE 241-3 (Adams 86, Robinson 91*)
Notts won by 7 wkts
GA: Tim Robinson

10 May The Oval
GLAMORGAN 236-6 (Morris 55)
SURREY 240-7 (Dicknell 90, Thorpe 51)
Surrey won by 3 wkts
GA: Darren Bicknell

Quarter-finals
24 May Derby
DERBYSHIRE 98 (Lampitt 6-26)
WORCESTERSHIRE 100-1
Worcs won by 9 wkts
GA: Stuart Lampitt
Derbyshire's lowest ever total in the competition.

24-25 May Southampton
ESSEX 124-3 (19 overs)
HAMPSHIRE 127-1 (17.2 overs) (R Smith 73*)
Hampshire won by 9 wkts
GA: Robin Smith

24 May Trent Bridge
NOTTINGHAMSHIRE 275-8 (Pollard 104)
SURREY 278-4 (Bicknell 109, Ward 73)
Surrey won by 6 wkts
GA: David Ward
Ward wins the Gold Award despite the twelve fours in

Darren Bicknell's first B&H century.

24 May Edgbaston
WARWICKSHIRE 5
KENT 4

After Warwicks decide not to use the 'Brumbrella' for fear of causing fungal grass disease, they beat the visitors 5-4 in a bowling competition, all five of their bowlers hitting a set of unguarded stumps while Nigel Llong misses.

Semi-finals
7 June The Oval
SURREY 267-7 (Thorpe 87, Ward 61)
WARWICKSHIRE 270-6 (Lara 70)
Warwicks won by 4 wkts
GA: Dermot Reeve (Warwicks)

7-8 June Worcester
HAMPSHIRE 244-6 (R Smith 108)
WORCESTERSHIRE 245-7 (Moody 56, Haynes 65)
Worcs won by 3 wkts
GA: Gavin Haynes

Final
9 July Lord's
Toss: Warwickshire
Umpires: HD Bird, KE Palmer (TV: B Leadbeater)

Worcestershire

Tim Curtis*	c Piper b Small	13
Adam Seymour	b Munton	3
Graeme Hick	lbw b P Smith	27
Tom Moody	run out	47
Gavin Haynes	c Piper b N Smith	22
David Leatherdale	c Ostler b P Smith	4
Steven Rhodes†	lbw b Twose	0
Stuart Lampitt	c Penney b P Smith	1
Richard Illingworth	lbw b Reeve	18
Neal Radford	not out	23
Phil Newport	not out	1
Extras	lb2 w5 nb4	11
	9 wkts, 55 overs	170

Fall: 10, 28, 55, 100, 124, 124, 125, 126, 168
Small 11-4-26-1, Munton 11-3-29-1, P Smith 11-1-34-3, Reeve 9-1-38-1, N Smith 5-0-16-1, Twose 8-1-25-1

Warwickshire

Dominic Ostler	run out	55
Roger Twose	run out	37
Brian Lara	c Hick b Newport	8
Paul Smith	not out	42
Asif Din	c Rhodes b Moody	15
Dermot Reeve*	not out	9
Extras	lb1 w5	6
	4 wkts, 44.2 overs	172

DNB: Trevor Penney, Keith Piper†, Neil Smith, Gladstone Small, Tim Munton

Fall: 91, 98, 103, 147

Moody 11-2-31-1, Newport 8-0-29-1, Lampitt 9.2-1-38-0, Illingworth 6-0-22-0, Radford 8-0-39-0, Hick 2-0-12-0

Gold Award: P Smith

Warwickshire won by 6 wickets

Sunday League 1994

	P	W	L	T	NR	Pts	1993
Warwicks	17	13	3	0	1	54	10th
Worcs	17	12	4	0	1	50	16
Kent	17	12	5	0	0	48	2
Lancs	17	11	5	0	1	46	6
Yorks	17	10	6	0	1	42	9
Surrey	17	9	5	0	3	42	3
Glamorgan	17	9	6	1	1	40	1
Derbys	17	8	7	0	2	36	11
Durham	17	6	7	1	3	32	7
Leics	17	7	9	0	1	30	14
Notts	17	6	8	0	3	30	17
Hants	17	7	10	0	0	28	15
Northants	17	6	9	1	1	28	5
Middx	17	6	10	0	1	26	8
Sussex	17	5	11	0	1	22	4
Somerset	17	5	12	0	0	20	18
Essex	17	4	11	1	1	20	12
Gloucs	17	4	12	0	1	18	13

Minor Counties

MCC Trophy (Cup Final)
24 Aug 1994 Lord's 55 overs
DEVON 281-5 (Nick Gaywood 106)
LINCOLNSHIRE 263 (Mark Fell 73, David Gillett 53)

Devon won by 18 runs.

Devon, the 1992 winners, appearing in the final for the third time in four years, beat the 1990 finalists.

Championship final
11-12 Sep 1994 Lord's
CAMBRIDGESHIRE 153-6 dec (N Gadsby 62) & 165-4 ded (N Gadsby 60*)
DEVON 150-4

Abandoned as a draw (rain on 2nd day); Devon win 3-2 on first-innings bonus points.

The decision to add a second day to the final allows Devon captain Peter Roebuck to set defensive fields in the second innings and essentially play out time, despite Cambs captain Gadsby's efforts.

English Area Championship

Final

3 Aug 1994 Fenner's, Cambridge University
YORKSHIRE 233 (Maybury 68, Ellder 50)
EAST MIDLANDS 123

Yorkshire win the title for the third consecutive time.

English National Knockout Trophy

Final

4 Sep 1994 Christchurch, Oxford
SHEPPERTON 118-6 (20 overs)
SHERWOOD & NEWARK 118-2 (20 overs, Ella Donnison 59)

S&N win the title for the first time by virtue of losing fewer wickets.

Women's Cricket

World Cup final

1 Aug 1993 Lord's
Toss: N Zealand
Umpires: J West & V Williams

England

JA Brittin	c Gunn b McLauchlan	48
WA Watson	b McLauchlan	5
CA Hodges	st Illingworth b Campbell	45
HC Plimmer	run out	11
JM Chamberlain	b Harris	38
BA Daniels	not out	21
K Smithies*	not out	10
Extras	b8 lb7 w2	17
	5 wkts, 60 overs	195

DNB: J Smit†, CE Taylor, GA Smith, SJ Kitson

Fall: 11, 96, 114, 118, 175

Turner 8-1-32-1, McLauchlan 10-2-25-2, Campbell 12-2-45-1, Gunn 12-5-33-0, Drumm 6-1-14-0

New Zealand

PD Kinsella	st Smit, b Taylor	15
DA Hockley	run out	24
K Bond	c Kitson b Chamberlain	12
MAM Lewis	lbw b Taylor	28
SL Illingworth*†	c&b Smithies	4
EC Drumm	c Chamberlain b Smith	0
KV Gunn	b Smith	19
S McLauchlan	c Brittin b Kitson	0
JA Turner	c Taylor b Smith	2
JE Harris	not out	5
CA Campbell	c Brittin b Kitson	6
Extras	lb8 w5	13
	55.1 overs	128

Fall: 25, 51, 60, 70, 71, 110, 112, 114, 120

Taylor 12-3-27-2, Hodges 5-2-11-0, Chamberlain 9-2-28-1, Smithies 12-4-14-1, Smith 12-1-29-3, Kitson 5.1-1-11-2

England won by 67 runs

Player of the Match: Jo Chamberlain

Wendy Watson is dropped twice, Carole Hodges & Chamberlain once each as England win the Cup for the first time (in the first final without Australia) since the very first, in 1973.

Other Test Matches

Sri Lanka v India

1st Test
17-22 July 1993 Asgiriya, Kandy
Sri Lanka 24-3

Drawn

Only 50 mins play possible, all on second day

2nd Test
27 July-1 Aug 1993 Sinhalese SC, Colombo
India 366 (Kambli 125, Sidhu 82) & 359-4 dec (Sidhu 104, Tendulkar 104*, Prabhakar 95)
Sri Lanka 254 (Ranatunga 88; Kumble 5-87) & 236 (A de Silva 93)

India won by 235 runs

3rd Test
4-9 Aug 1993 P Saravanamuttu, Colombo
Sri Lanka 351 (A de Silva 148, Gurusinha 56, Tillekeratne 51) & 352-6 (Mahanama 151, Tillekeratne 86)
India 446 (Kambli 120, Tendulkar 71, Prabhakar 55, Azharuddin 50)

Drawn

Sri Lanka v South Africa

1st Test
25-30 Aug 1993 T Fernando, Moratuwa
Sri Lanka 331 (Tillekeratne 92, Mahanama 53; Donald

5-69) & 300-6 dec (Ranatunga 131, A de Silva 68)
S Africa 267 (Hudson 90; Muralidharan 5-104) & 251-7
(Rhodes 101*)

Drawn

2nd Test
6-10 Sep 1993 Sinhalese SC, Colombo
Sri Lanka 168 (Schultz 5-48) & 119
S Africa 495 (Cronje 122, Wessels 92, Hudson 58,
Cullinan 52, Symcox 50; Muralidharan 5-101)

S Africa won by an innings & 208 runs

3rd Test
14-19 Sep 1993 (No play 19)
P Saravanamuttu, Colombo
S Africa 316 (Cullinan 102, Richardson 62) & 159-4
(Cronje 73)
Sri Lanka 296 (A de Silva 82, Jayasuriya 65, Ranatunga
50; Schultz 6-63)

Drawn

Australia v New Zealand

1st Test
12-16 Nov 1993 WACA, Perth
Australia 398 (Healy 113, Taylor 64, Reiffel 51) & 323-1
dec (Taylor 142*, Slater 99, Boon 67*)
N Zealand 419-9 dec (Jones 143, Cairns 78) & 166-4

Drawn

Martin Crowe scores 31 to save the match for N Zealand,
but aggravates a well documented knee injury and misses
the rest of the series, Ken Rutherford taking over as
captain. Craig McDermott takes his 200th Test wicket.

2nd Test
26-29 Nov 1993 Bellerive Oval, Hobart
Australia 544 (Slater 168, M Waugh 111, Boon 106,
Border 60)
N Zealand 161 (May 5-65) & 161 (Rutherford 55;
Warne 6-31)

Australia won by an innings & 222 runs

N Zealand's heaviest defeat in any Test match (apart
from their women's innings & 337 defeat by England
in 1935).

3rd Test
3-7 Dec 1993 Woolloongabba, Brisbane
N Zealand 233 (Jones 56) & 278 (Rutherford 86,
Young 53)
Australia 607-6 dec (S Waugh 147, Border 105, Boon
89, Warne 74, M Waugh 68, Taylor 53)

Australia won by an innings & 96 runs

Allan Border adds to two of his world records by
holding his 150th catch in his 150th Test. Steve Waugh
passes 3000 runs in Tests and 10 000 in first-class

cricket. For only the second time in Test history, five
bowlers concede 100 runs apiece in the same innings:
Danny Morrison, Chris Cairns, Simon Doull, Richard de
Groen, Dipak Patel.

Sri Lanka v West Indies

Only Test
8-13 Dec 1993 (no play 8, 12, 13)
T Fernando, Moratuwa
Sri Lanka 190 (A e Silva 53) & 43-2
W Indies 204 (Hooper 62, Richardson 51)

Drawn

W Indies' 300th Test, Sri Lanka's 50th.

Australia v South Africa

1st Test
26-30 Dec 1993 (no play 27) MCG, Melbourne
Australia 342-7 dec (Taylor 170, M Waugh 84)
S Africa 258-3 (Cronje 71, Hudson 64, Wessels 63*)

Drawn

Mark Taylor, in his 50th Test, passes 4000 runs and
becomes only the second batsman to score a century
against seven different countries. Kepler Wessels, S
Africa's captain, but capped by Australia 1982-85, is the
first player since 1882 to play for and against Australia.
Allan Border's 151st Test is his first v S Africa

2nd Test
2-6 Jan 1994 SCG, Sydney
S Africa 169 (G Kirsten 67; Warne 7-56) & 239 (Rhodes
76; Warne 5-72)
Australia 292 (Slater 92, Martyn 59) & 111 (de Villiers
6-43)

S Africa won by 5 runs

Australia, struggling at 75-8, are dismissed for the
deadly Nelson (111, the three stumps).

3rd Test
28 Jan - 1 Feb 1994 Oval, Adelaide
Australia 469-7 dec (S Waugh 164, Border 84, Taylor
62, Slater 53, Boon 50) & 124-1 dec
S Africa 273 (Hudson 90, P Kirsten 79) & 129

Australia won by 191 runs

Shane Warne takes his 100th wicket in only his 23rd
Test, Ian Healy makes his 200th Test dismissal. Steve
Waugh, who takes 4-26 to go with his century, is voted
Player of the Series despite appearing in just this one
match. Allan Border plays in his last home Test.

India v Sri Lanka

1st Test
18-22 Jan 1994 Babu, Lucknow
India 511 (Tendulkar 142, Sidhu 124, Manjrekar 61; Muralidharan 5-162)
Sri Lanka 218 (Mahanama 73) & 174 (Kumble 7-59)

India won by an innings & 119 runs

India's 50th win, in their 286th Test, at the latest (72nd) Test venue. Sidhu hits an Indian record eight sixes, six off Muralidharan, whose bowling action is regarded as suspect by some. Tendulkar, still only 20, scores his seventh Test century. Hashan Tillekeratne passes 1000 runs in Tests for Sri Lanka.

2nd Test
26-30 Jan 1994 Chinnaswamy, Bangalore
India 541-6 dec (Azharuddin 108, Sidhu 99, Tendulkar 96, Kambli 82, Kapil Dev 53)
Sri Lanka 231 (Kalpage 63) & 215 (Tillekeratne 80)

India won by an innings & 95 runs

Don Anurasiri, caught by Mohammed Azharuddin at first slip, provides Kapil Dev with his 431st Test wicket, equalling Richard Hadlee's world record. India make sure he achieves it: Kumble bowls wide of the stumps to be certain of not taking a wicket, Sanjay Manjrekar's scolded by his team mates for attempting a run-out!

3rd Test
8-12 Feb 1994 Gujarat, Ahmedabad
Sri Lanka 119 (Raju 5-38) & 222 (Mahanama 63; Raju 6-87)
India 358 (Azharuddin 152, Kambli 57)

India won by an innings & 17 runs

Kapil Dev's only wicket of the match (Tillekeratne c Manjrekar) breaks Hadlee's record.

New Zealand v Pakistan

1st Test
10-12 Feb 1994 Eden Park, Auckland
N Zealand 242 (Jones 66) & 110 (Wasim Akram 6-43)
Pakistan 215 (Doull 5-66) & 141-5 (Aamir Sohail 78)

Pakistan won by 5 wickets

Wasim Akram, in his 51st Test, takes his 200th wicket; Waqar Younis, in only his 26th, takes his 150th.

2nd Test
17-20 Feb 1994 Basin Reserve, Wellington
N Zealand 175 & 361 (Blain 78, Jones 76, Rutherford 63; Wasim Akram 7-119)
Pakistan 548 (Saeed Anwar 169, Salim Malik 140, Inzamam-ul-Haq 135*)

Test Wickets: progression of the world record

1	Allen Hill
England 1877	
10	Tom Kendall
Australia 1877	
50	Fred Spofforth
Australia 1883	
100	Johnny Briggs
England 1895	
101	Charlie Turner
Australia 1895	
103	Johnny Briggs
England 1895	
112	George Lohmann
England 1896	
118	Johnny Briggs
England 1899	
141	Hugh Trumble
Australia 1904	
189	Sydney Barnes
England 1914	
216	Clarrie Grimmett
Australia 1936	

Pakistan won by an innings & 12 runs

Imran Khan suggests, apparently in all seriousness, that the 42-y-o Hadlee should make a Test comeback.

3rd Test
24-28 Feb 1994 Lancaster Park, Christchurch
Pakistan 344 (Basit Ali 103, Saeed Anwar 69, Aamir Sohail 60) & 179 (Bsit Ali 67)
N Zealand 200 (Jones 81; Waqar Younis 6-78) & 324-5 (Young 120, Thomson 120*)

N Zealand won by 5 wickets

New Zealand v India

Only Test
19-23 March 1994 Trust Bank Park, Hamilton
N Zealand 187 (Rutherford 63) & 368-7 dec (Fleming 92, Young 85, Rutherford 59)
India 246 (Azharuddin 63) & 177-3 (Sidhu 98)

Drawn

Stephen Fleming comes close to a century in his first Test innings. Ken Rutherford & Sachin Tendulkar pass 2000 runs in Tests. Kapil Dev takes his world record number of Test wickets to a final 434.

South Africa v Australia

1st Test
4-8 March 1994
S Africa 251 (Rhodes 69) & 450-9 dec (Cronje 122,
Hudson 60, P Kirsten 53, Wessels 50)
Australia 248 & 256 (Boon 83)

S Africa won by 197 runs

Shane Warne & Merv Hughes are fined (by the
Australian board as well as the match referee) for
verbal abuse.

2nd Test
17-21 March 1994 Newlands, Cape Town
S Africa 361 (Hudson 102, McMillan 74, P Kirsten 70)
& 164 (S Waugh 5-28)
Australia 435 (Boon 96, S Waugh 86, Taylor 70, Healy
61; Matthews 5-80) & 92-1

Australia won by 9 wickets

Australia's seventh win in eight visits to Newlands.
Healy passes 2000 runs in Tests.

3rd Test
25-29 March 1994 Kingsmead, Durban
Australia 269 (S Waugh 64) & 297-4 (M Waugh 113,
Slater 95)
S Africa 422 (McMillan 84, Rhodes 78, Hudson 65,
Richardson 59)

Drawn

Andrew Hudson becomes the first batsman to score
1000 runs for S Africa since their return to Test cricket.
Steve Waugh finishes top of the Australian batting and
bowling averages. Allan Border ends his Test career with
11174 runs in 156 matches, both world records.
Typically enough, he's not out (for 42) in his last innings.

Sri Lanka v Pakistan

1st Test
9-14 Aug 1994 (no play 14) P Saravanamuttu, Colombo
Pakistan 390 (Saeed Anwar 94, Inzamam-ul-Haq 81;
Dharmasena 6-99) & 318-4 dec (Saeed Anwar 136,
Aamir Sohail 65, Salim Malik 50*)
Sri Lanka 226 (A de Silva 127) & 181 (Wasim Akram 5-43)

Pakistan won by 301 runs.

2nd Test
19-23 Aug 1994

Cancelled...

...because of the 'tense atmosphere' in the wake of the
general election. Replaced by two one-day
internationals.

Tests

156	Allan Border	Australia	1978-94
131	Kapildev Nikhanj	India	1978-94
125	Sunil Gavaskar	India	1971-87
124	Javed Miandad	Pakistan	1976-94
121	Viv Richards	W Indies	1974-91
117	David Gower	England	1978-92
116	Dilip Vengsarkar	India	1976-92
116	Desmond Haynes	W Indies	1978-94
115	Graham Gooch	England	1975-94
114	Colin Cowdrey	England	1954-75
110	Clive Lloyd	W Indies	1966-85
108	Geoff Boycott	England	1964-82
108	Gordon Greenidge	W Indies	1974-91
102	Ian Botham	England	1977-92

Test Runs

11174	Allan Border	Australia	1978-94
10122	Sunil Gavaskar	India	1971-87
8832	Javed Miandad	Pakistan	1976-93
8780	Graham Gooch	England	1975-94
8540	Viv Richards	W Indies	1974-91
8231	David Gower	England	1978-92
8114	Geoff Boycott	England	1964-82
8032	Garry Sobers	W Indies	1954-74

Test Catches

156	Allan Border	Australia	1978-94
122	Greg Chappell	Australia	1970-84
122	Viv Richards	W Indies	1974-91
120	Colin Cowdrey	England	1954-75
120	Ian Botham	England	1977-92
110	Wally Hammond	England	1928-47
110	Bobby Simpson	Australia	1957-78
109	Garry Sobers	W Indies	1955-74
108	Sunil Gavaskar	India	1971-87
105	Ian Chappell	Australia	1964-80
102	Graham Gooch	England	1975-94

Border averaged exactly one catch per match

3rd Test
26-30 Aug 1994 (no play 29, 30) Asgiriya, Kandy
Sri Lanka 71 (Waqar Younis 6-34) & 234 (Tillekeratne
83*, Kalpage 62; Waqar Younis 5-85)
Pakistan 357-9 dec (Inzamam-ul-Haq 100*, Aamir
Sohail 74, Basit Ali 53)

Pakistan won by an innings & 52 runs

It can't get much worse for Sri Lanka (who record their
lowest ever Test total) but it nearly does: they're 46-9.
Although a record seventh-wicket stand drags them up

from 78-6 in their second innings, they nevertheless lose within four days for the fifth Test in a row. Tillekeratne again comes close to a maiden Test century. A dropped catch by 19-y-o debutant Kabir Khan prevents Waqar from improving on his best Test figures of 7-76. For only the second time, a pair of Pakistanis bowls unchanged throughout a completed Test innings, following Fazal Mahmoud & Khan Mohammed who dismissed Australia for 80 in 1956.

Pakistan v Australia

1st Test
28 Sep - 2 Oct 1994 National Stadium, Karachi
Australia 337 (Bevan 82, S Waugh 73, Healy 57) & 232 (Boon 114*, M Waugh 61)
Pakistan 256 (Saeed Anwar 85) & 315-9 (Saeed Anwar 77, Inzamam-ul-Haq 58*; Warne 5-89)

Pakistan won by 1 wkt

Off the last delivery of the match, bowled by Shane Warne, Ian Healy misses a chance to stump Inzamam with Pakistan still two runs behind. The ball goes for four byes and Inzamam & Mushtaq Ahmed's improbable last-wicket partnership of 57 wins the match to preserve Pakistan's record in Karachi, where they've played Test matches since 1955 without losing any. Mark Taylor becomes the only batsman to make a pair in his first Test as captain. Michael Bevan, Yorkshire's overseas player for 1995, makes 82 and a first-ball duck on his Test debut.

One-Wicket Test Wins			
1902	England	bt Australia	The Oval
1906	S Africa	bt England	Jo'burg
1908	England	bt Australia	Melbourne
1923	England	bt S Africa	Cape Town
1951-52	Australia	bt W Indies	Melbourne
1980	N Zealand	bt W Indies	Dunedin
1994	Pakistan	bt Australia	Karachi

The 57-run partnership by Inzamam & Mushtaq is the highest to win such a match.

2nd Test
5-9 Oct 1994 Rawalpindi Stadium
Australia 521-9 dec (Slater 110, S Waugh 98, Bevan 70, Taylor 69, M Waugh 68, Healy 58) & 14-1
Pakistan 260 (Aamir Sohail 80) & 537 (Salim Malik 237, Saeed Anwar 75, Aamir Sohail 72, Aamir Malik 65)

Drawn

In the first Test staged at the new ground, Salim Malik redeems himself (he makes the mistake of fielding first, Taylor & Michael Slater put on 176 for the first wicket, a record for Australia v Pakistan) by scoring his first

Test double century, the highest innings for Pakistan v Australia (in the highest total amassed by Pakistan at home against the same country) before being dismissed by Damien Fleming, who thereby completes a hat-trick. After his pair in Karachi, Taylor drops Salim on 20, his seventh (and most costly) dropped catch in three matches. Pakistan haven't lost a Test series at home for ten years. They somehow escape punishment despite bowling twelve overs fewer than required in the day. A 20-run penalty for each missing over would probably solve the problem once and for all.

Hat-trick on Test debut			
Maurice Allom	England	1930	v N Zealand
Peter Petherick	N Zealand	1976	v W Indies
Damien Fleming	Australia	1994	v Pakistan

Allom took four wickets in five balls.

3rd Test
1-5 Nov 1994 Gaddafi Stadium, Lahore
Pakistan 373 (Moin Khan 115*, Salim Malik 75, Inzamam-ul-Haq 66) & 422 (Salim Malik 143, Aamir Sohail 105)
Australia 455 (Bevan 91, Slater 74, M Waugh 71, Langer 69)

Drawn

Wicketkeeper Ian Healy, who flies home after breaking a thumb, is replaced by Test debutant Phil Emery, who has to go off on the third day - with a badly bruised thumb! For the first time since Nov 1989, Pakistan are without both Wasim Akram & Waqar Younis. The other wicketkeeper, the recalled Moin Khan, is cautioned for wrongly appealing against the light on the first day then completes his first Test century on the second. Bevan comes within nine runs of his first. On the last day, with Pakistan 137-5 overnight, Salim Malik & Aamir Sohail's record partnership of 196 saves the match.

Zimbabwe v Sri Lanka

1st Test
11-16 Oct 1994 Sports Club, Harare
Sri Lanka 383 (Gurusinha 128, S Ranatunga 118, A Ranatunga 62)
Zimbabwe 319-8 (Extras 65, Houghton 58)

Drawn

Rain puts a merciful end to the match (the first ever between the countries) at lunch on the last day. Sri Lanka's innings, against an attack that strikes little terror in Test hearts (rugby international Malcolm Jarvis is 38, David Brain breaks down after five overs), takes up the entire first two days; they amass only 157, about one run for every spectator (yes, honestly) on the first. Sanjeewa Ranatunga, brother of captain Arjuna, scores

Slowest Test Centuries
hrs:mins

9:37	Mudassar Nazar	Pakistan v England	1977
9:05	Jackie McGlew	S Africa v Australia	1958
8:50	Asanka Gurusinha	Sri Lanka v Zimbabwe	1994
8:36	Jeff Crowe	N Zealand v Sri Lanka	1987
8:20	Sanjay Manjrekar	India v Zimbabwe	1992
8:08	Peter Richardson	England v S Africa	1956

Slowest in England:

7:38	Keith Fletcher	v Pakistan	1974

his maiden Test fifty (in only his second Test) on his way to his first century. Zimbabwe benefit from 44 no-balls.

2nd Test
20-24 Oct 1994 Queen's Club, Bulawayo
Zimbabwe 462-9 dec (Houghton 266, A Flower 50)
Sri Lanka 218 (Gurusinha 63, Dharmasena 54) & 193-4 (S Ranatunga 100*)

Drawn

In their ninth Test, put back two days because of bad weather, Zimbabwe enforce a follow-on for the 1st time but fail to win a match in which Sri Lanka were 30-2 at the end of the fourth day, mainly because Ranatunga bats 7 hrs 2 mins for a century he reaches off the last ball of the match. Houghton shatters his own national record for runs in a Test innings (previously 121, in Zimbabwe's first ever Test, v India in 1992).

3rd Test
26-31 Oct 1994 Sports Club, Harare
Sri Lanka 402 (Tillekeratne 116, Gurusinha 54) & 89-3

Highest Test Score for each country

W Indies	375	Brian Lara	1994	v E
England	364	Len Hutton	1938	v A
Pakistan	337	Hanif Mohammad	1958	v WI
Australia	334	Don Bradman	1930	v E
N Zealand	299	Martin Crowe	1991	v SL
S Africa	274	Graeme Pollock	1970	v A
Sri Lanka	267	Aravinda da Silva	1991	v NZ
Zimbabwe	266	Dave Houghton	1994	v SL
India	236*	Sunil Gavaskar	1983	v WI

Zimbabwe 375 (Houghton 142, Campbell 99, Whittal 61*)

Drawn

Rain and bad light put a blessedly early end to the last day of another dismal affair. Tillekeratne's maiden Test century is the only bright spot in another Sri Lankan crawl: again their first innings uses up virtually two whole days. Campbell spends nearly five hours in an unavailing bid for his first Test century. Each of the ten days of Test cricket at Harare is watched by fewer than 1000 spectators. Arjuna Ranatunga hits a six off the last ball of the Test, but it hasn't been that kind of series.

India v West Indies

1st Test
18-22 Nov 1994 Wankhede, Bombay
India 272 (Mongia 80, Manjrekar 51; Walsh 6-79) & 333 (Tendulkar 85, Manjrekar 66, Srinath 60)
W Indies 243 (Raju 5-60) & 266 (Murray 85, Adams 81)

India won by 96 runs

India win a home Test for the tenth successive time and for only the seventh in all (out of 63) against W Indies. Mohammed Azharuddin's ten wins as captain break the Indian record.

2nd Test
1-5 Dec 1994 Vidarbha CA Ground, Nagpur
India 546-9 dec (Tendulkar 179, Sidhu 107, Azharuddin 97, Kumble 52*; Hooper 5-116) & 208-7 dec (Sidhu 76, Tendulkar 54)
W Indies 428 (Adams 125*, Hooper 81, Murray 54, Simmons 50, Lara 50; Raju 5-127) & 132-5 (Hooper 67)

Drawn

Two long stoppages almost lead to the first day being abandoned: Courtney Walsh leads the team off after spectators pelt his fielders: Phil Simmons with an unripe guava, Shivnarine Chanderpaul more seriously with a brick. Tendulkar makes his highest Test score so far. Even the leg-spinning tailender makes an unbeaten fifty. India drop catches after reducing W Indies to 22-3 on the last day.

3rd Test
10-14 Dec 1994 Chandigarth
W Indies 443 (Adams 174, Cummins 50) & 301-3 dec (Lara 91, Adams 78*)
India 387 (Prabhakar 120) & 114 (K Benjamin 5-65)

W Indies won by 243 runs

On the last day of their last Test of the year, West Indies avoid losing a series for the first time since 1980 (the longest sequence ever: 29 series - and they'll always believe they were robbed in 1980!) and the first to India since 1978-79. Jimmy Adams, who makes his highest Test score so far and passes 1000 runs in only his twelfth Test, is adjudged Man of the Series for his 520 runs. In the first innings, Sachin Tendulkar scores 40 without having to run: 2 sixes, 7 fours. In the second, Manoj Prabhakar is hospitalised by an important rising ball from Walsh which breaks his nose.

S Africa v N Zealand

1st Test
25-29 Nov 1994 Wanderers, Johannesburg
N Zealand 411 (Thomson 84, Crowe 83, Rutherford 68) & 194 (Matthews 5-42)
S Africa 279 (Richardson 93, Cullinan 58) & 189 (Cronje 62; Hart 5-77)

N Zealand won by 137 runs

The first Test between the two countries since the drawn series of 1961-62 (2-2, NZ's only two wins v S Africa in 17 Tests prior to this one); N Zealand are trying to win a series v S Africa for the first time. Against an attack without Allan Donald, only a dubious lbw decision prevents Crowe from becoming the first player to score a century against each of the other eight Test-playing countries; he's bowled for a duck in the second innings. Matthew Hart takes five wickets in a Test innings for the first time, but Simon Doull is made man of the match for his six wickets and 45 runs without being dismissed.

Slowest Test 50s
hrs:mins
5:57	Trevor Bailey	England	1958	v Australia
5:50	Chris Tavaré	England	1982	v Pakistan
5:33	Bryan Young	N Zealand	1994	v S Africa

2nd Test
26-30 Dec 1994 Kingsmead, Durban
New Zealand 185 (Thomson 82; De Villiers 5-64) & 192 (Young 51)
South Africa 226 (Doull 5-73) & 153-2 (G Kirsten 66*)

South Africa won by 8 wkts

New Zealand don't recover from 114-8 in the first innings. During his second innings of only 10 runs, Martin Crowe breaks John Wright's New Zealand record total of 5334.

3rd Test
2-6 Jan 1995 Newlands, Cape Town
New Zealand 288 (Fleming 79, Rutherford 56) & 239 (Fleming 53, De Villiers 5-61)
South Africa 440 (Cronje 112, Richardson 109, G Kirsten 64) & 89-3

South Africa won by 7 wkts

Matthew Hart's dropped catch off Simon Doull proves costly: captain Hansie Cronje, then on 59, plays a major part in making S Africa only the second country (the first since WG Grace's England in 1888) to win a three-Test series from 1-0 down.

Croquet

World Championship
10-17 Aug 1994 Carden Park, Cheshire

Quarter-finals

Robert Fulford	ENG	bt	Reg Bamford	SAF
Aaron Westerby	NZ	bt	Michael Taylor	AUS
Steve Cornish	ENG	bt	Mark Kobelt	AUS
Chris Clarke	ENG	bt	Colin Irwin	ENG

Semi-finals

Fulford	bt	Westerby
Clarke	bt	Cornish

Final

Fulford	bt	Clarke

Fulford recovers from losing the first game to avenge his British Open defeat against his doubles partner, retain the title, and win it for the third time out of the five it's been held.

British Open
July 1994 Hurlingham Club, London

Quarter-finals

Reg Bamford	SAF	bt	J Dawson	ENG
Chris Clarke	ENG	bt	David Maugham	ENG
Steve Mulliner	ENG	bt	Michael Taylor	AUS
Robert Fulford	ENG	bt	Paul Day	ENG

Day was English table tennis champion in 1978.

Semi-finals

Bamford	bt	Mulliner
Clarke	bt	Fulford

Final

Bamford	bt	Clarke

Bamford retains the title.

ENGLISH CHAMPIONSHIPS *June 1994 Cheltenham*

Men:	Michael Taylor	AUS
Women:	Debbie Cornelius	ENG

PRESIDENT'S CUP *Sep 1994 Parkstone*

David Maugham   ENG
Maugham retains the trophy.

INTER-COUNTIES *May 1994 Southwick & Compton*
Cheshire

Curling

World Championships
April 1994, Obersdorf, Germany

Men's final

Canada (Rick Folk)	Sweden (Jan-Olov Nassen)	5-1

After a gap of 14 yrs, Folk skips a world title winning team for the second time.

Women's final

Canada	Scotland	5-2
(Sandra Peterson)	(Christine Gannon)	

Canada (and Peterson) retain the title.

European Championships
Dec 1993 Leukerbad, Switzerland

Men's final

Norway	Denmark	7-6
(Eigil Ramsfjell)	(Tommy Stjerne)	

Ramsfjell, world champion skip in 1984 & 1988, wins the European title for the first time.

Women's final

Sweden	Switzerland	8-4
(Elizabet Johansson)	(Diana Kaufmann)	

Johansson wins the title for the second time. In 1992 she was the world as well as the European champion.

Scottish Championships
Feb 1994, Glasgow

Men's final

Colin Hamilton	Peter Wilson	7-3

After a gap of 13 yrs, Hamilton wins the title for the second time.

Women's final

Christine Gannon	Rhona Martin	7-4

Gannon wins the title for the fifth time.

Cycling

Tour de France 1994

Men

Prologue - 2 July - 7 km/4.5m - Lille-Euralille time trial
Chris Boardman   UK   GAN   7:49   YJ: Boardman
Boardman rides the fastest Prologue in the history of the Tour to beat defending champion and time-trial expert Miguel Induráin (SPA) and become only the second British rider to lead the Tour (after Tommy Simpson in 1962).

Stage 1 - 3 July - 229 km/143m - Lille-Euralille to Armentières
Djamolidin Abdoujaparov   UZB   Polti   5h46:16   YJ: Boardman
Boardman, who finishes 29th, becomes the first British rider to wear the Yellow Jersey (YJ) for more than a day.

Stage 2 - 4 July - 201km/126m - Roubaix to Boulogne
Jean-Paul van Poppel   HOL   Festina   5h05:40   YJ: Boardman
If Van Poppel hadn't beaten the famous sprinter Olaf Ludwig (GER) by the width of a tyre, Boardman would have lost the overall lead.

Stage 3 - 5 July - 66.5km/41.5m - Calais to Channel Tunnel team time trial
GB MG team   1h20:31   YJ: Johan Museeuw (BEL)
Boardman, riding like a Trojan but with little support ('If we'd had eight of him,' says team mate Greg Lemond, 'we'd have gained ten minutes on everyone else') drops back to 20th overall and won't lead the Tour into England.

Stage 4 - 6 July - 204km/127m - Dover to Brighton
Francisco Cabello   SPA   Kelme   5h12:53   YJ: Flavio Vanzella (ITA)
Estimates vary, but it's possible that a million specators line the route. Sean Yates, the 'other British rider' (an unfair title for a veteran of eleven Tours), is allowed to lead the race into Ashdown Forest, where his parents live.

Stage 5 - 7 July - 187km/117m - Portsmouth out-and-home
Nicola Minali   ITA   Gewiss Ballan   4h10:49   YJ: Vanzella
Ludwig loses another sprint finish by inches. Ominously, Induráin moves to within 14 sec of the lead.

Stage 6 - 8 July - 265km/165m - Cherbourg to Rennes
Gianluca Bertolami   ITA   Mapei Clas   6h58:47   YJ: Yates
Bertolami wins the Tour's longest stage to move up to second place overall, just one second behind Yates, who becomes the third British rider to wear the Yellow Jersey. Lemond, winner of the Tour in 1986-89-90, retires from the race through exhaustion (or metal fatigue: 35 lead pellets were left in his body by a hunting accident in 1987)

Stage 7 - 9 July - 259km/162m - Rennes to Futuroscope
Jan Svorada   SLVK   Lampre   5h56:50   YJ: Museeuw
Yates drops to second, six seconds behind, after Rolf Sorensen (DEN) holds him back by the jersey, which Yates never wears again.

Stage 8 - 10 July - 216km/135m - Poitiers to Trélissac
Bo Hamburger   DEN   TVM   5h09:27   YJ: Museeuw
Hamburger's first ever stage win.

Stage 9 - 11 July - 63km/39m - Périgueux to Bergerac time trial
Miguel Induráin   SPA   Banesto   1h15:58   YJ: Induráin
Induráin, leading by 2m 28s, already looks unbeatable.

Stage 10 - 12 July - 170km/106m - Bergerac to Cahors

Jacky Durand	FRA	Castorama	3h 38:11	YJ: Induráin

Stage 11 - 13 July - 263km/164m - Cahors to Lourdes

Luc Leblanc	FRA	Festina	6h58:04	YJ: Induráin

Boardman drops out of the Tour after 62 km, but his time may come...

Stage 12 - 15 July - 205km/128m - Lourdes to Luz Ardiden

Richard Virenque	FRA	Festina	6h08:32	YJ: Induráin

Induráin increases his overall lead over Tony Rominger (SWI) to 7m 56s. Claudio Chiappucci (ITA), runner-up in 1990 & 1992, abandons the race.

Stage 13 - 16 July - 233km/146 - Bagnères de Bigorre to Albi

Bjarne Riis	DEN	Gewiss Ballan	5h14:48	

Rominger, lying second overall but suffering from viral gastroenteritis, pulls out of a race he's in no shape to win. The rest of the week is purely processional.

Stage 14 - 17 July - 192km/120m - Castres to Montpellier

Rolf Sorensen	DEN	GB MG	5h11:04	YJ: Induráin

More big names accept the inevitable and withdraw: Durand, Pavel Tonkov (RUS, fourth in the Giro d'Italia), Gianni Bugno (ITA), world champion Lance Armstrong (USA).

Stage 15 - 18 July - 231km/144m - Montpellier to Carpentras

Eros Poli	ITA	Mercatone Uno	6h31:59	YJ:Induráin

A wreath's laid at the spot where Tommy Simpson died of heat exhaustion and drugs in 1967. Poli, an Olympic gold medallist 10 years earlier, is an untypical long-distance cyclist: he stands 6'6 and weighs 16st.

Stage 16 - 19 July - 224.5km/140m - Valreas to L'Alpe d'Huez

Roberto Conti	ITA	Lampre	6h06:45	YJ: Induráin

Stage 17 - 20 July - 147km/92m - Bourg d'Oisans to Val Thorens

Nelson Rodriguez	COL	ZG Mobili	5h13:52	YJ: Induráin

Stage 18 - 21 July - 174km/109m - Moutiers to Cluses

Piotr Ugrumov	LAT	Gewiss Ballan	4h52:19	YJ: Induráin

Stage 19 - 22 July - 47.5km/29m - Cluses to Morzine time trial

Piotr Ugrumov	LAT	Gewiss Ballan	1h22:59	YJ: Induráin

Stage 20 - 23 July - 225km/141m - Morzine to Lac Saint-Point

Djamolidin Abdujaparov	UZB	Polti	5h50:37	YJ: Induráin

Stage 21 - 24 July - 188km/117.5m - EuroDisney to Paris

Eddy Seigneur	FRA	GAN	4h43:34	YJ: Induráin

Overall

Miguel Induráin	SPA	Banesto	103h38:38
Piotr Ugrumov	LAT	Gewiss Ballan	5:39 behind
Marco Pantani	ITA	Carrera	7:19
71 Sean Yates	*UK*	*Motorola*	*2h04:55*

Induráin, who turns 30 during the race, wins the event for the fourth time in a row. Ugrumov is the first rider from any of the old Soviet republics to finish in the top three. Pantani finishes third in his first Tour de France.

Points

Djamolidin Abdujaparov	UZB	Polti	322
Silvio Martinello	ITA	Mercatone Uno	273
Jan Svorada	SLVK	Lampre	230

The Tashkent Terror wins the title for the third time in four years.

King of the Mountains

Richard Virenque	FRA	Festina	392
Marco Pantani	ITA	Carrera	243
Piotr Ugrumov	LAT	Gewiss Ballan	219

Teams

Festina	AND	311h28:53
Gewiss Ballan	ITA	312h11:50
Mapei-Clas	SPA	312h12:31

Tour de France: most wins

5	Jacques Anquetil	FRA	1957-61-62-63-64
5	Eddy Merckx	BEL	1969-70-71-72-74
5	Bernard Hinault	FRA	1978-79-81-82-85
4	Miguel Induráin	SPA	1991-92-93-94

Anquetil, Merckx & Induráin share the record of 4 consecutive wins.

Women: Tour Cycliste Féminin

Prologue	24 July		Ile de Groix time trial	Clara Hughes	CAN	7:32
Stage 1	25 July	124km/77.5m	Lanester-Lorient	Michela Fanini	ITA	3h10:51
Stage 2	26 July	127km/79m	Grand-Champ - Pontchâteau	Yvonne Brunnen	HOL	3h26:24
Stage 3	27 July	147km/92m	Pontchâteau-Commequiers	Anne Samplonius	CAN	3h53:40

Samplonius holds off Fanini by half a metre.

Stage 4	28 July	134km/84m	Castiloon-la-Bataile - Agen	Michela Fanini	ITA	3h31:44
Stage 5	29 July	145km/90.5m	Moissac-Tarbes	Cécile Odin	FRA	4:02:15
Stage 6a	30 July	59km/37m	Barèges-Bagnères de Bigorre	Michela Fanini	ITA	1h31:56
Stage 6b	31 July	28km/12m	Campan-Le Tourmalet	Iolanta Polikiaviciute	LITH	1:15:22
Stage 7			Saint-Gaudens - Cugnaux	abandoned		
Stage 8a	1 Aug	60km/37.5m	Toulouse-Salles du Salat	Guo Xing-hong	CHN	1h28:42
Stage 8b	2 Aug		Salles du Salat - Aix les Thermes	Liuda Triabaite	LITH	
Stage 9	3 Aug	29.6km/18.5m	St Paul Trois Château time trial	Valentina Polhanova	RUS	42:41

Polhanova takes the Yellow Jersey which she keeps to the end.

Stage 10	4 Aug	127km/79m	Pierrelatte-Davezieux	Svetlana Samohvalova	RUS	3h19:20
Stage 11	5 Aug	62.5km/39m	Eybens-Vaujany	Rasa Polikiaviciute	LITH	1h41:03

The other Polikiaviciute twin finishes second to install herself as favourite, but abandons the race after crashing on the final stage.

Stage 12		105km/65.5m	Vaujany-l'Alpe d'Huez	Rasa Polikiaviciute	LITH	3h36:50

Overall

Valentina Polhanova	RUS	34h52:37
Rasa Polikiaviciute	LITH	2:52
Cécile Odin	FRA	4:17

Previous winner Jeannie Longo (FRA) and defending champion Leontine Van Moorsel don't take part. One British rider does: Cherie Pridham.

Giro d'Italia (Tour of Italy) 1994

Stage

1a	22 May	Bologna prologue	Endrio Leoni	ITA
1b	22 May	Bologna time trial	Armand de las Cuevas	FRA

Armand takes the overall lead after the first day. Miguel Induráin lies second.

2	23 May	Bologna to Osimo	Moreno Argentin	ITA
3	24 May	Osimo to Loreto Aprutino	Gianni Bugno	ITA
4	25 May	Montesilvano to Campitello Matese	Yevgeny Berzin	RUS

Berzin takes the overall lead.

5	26 May	Campitello Matese to Melfi	Endrio Leoni	ITA
6	27 May	Potenza to Caserta	Marco Saligari	ITA

| 7 | 28 May | Caserta-Fiuggi | L Cubino | SPA |
| 8 | 29 May | Fiuggi time trial | Yevgeny Berzin | RUS |

Induráin suffers the worst time trial defeat of his career, finishing 2m34 behind Berzin, who retains the Pink Jersey.

9	30 May	Castiglione della Pescaia-Pontedera	Jan Svorada	SLVK
10	31 May	Marostica circuit	Djamoldine Abdujaparov	UZBEK
11	1 June	Marostica to Bibione	Jan Svorada	SLVK
12	2 June	Bibione-Kranj (Slovenia)	Andrea Ferrigato	ITA
13	3 June	Kranj to Lienz (Austria)	Michele Bartoli	ITA
14	4 June	Lienz to Merano	Marco Pantani	ITA
15	5 June	Merano to Aprica	Marco Pantani	ITA
16	6 June	Sondrio to Stradella	Max Sciandri	ITA
17	7 June	Sta. Maria della Versa to Lavagna	Jan Svorada	SLVK
18	8 June	Passo del Bocco time trial	Yevgeny Berzin	RUS
19	9 June	Lavagna to Bra	Massimo Ghirotto	ITA
20	10 June	Cuneo to les Deux Alpes (FRA)	V Poulnikov	UKR
21	11 June	Les Deux Alpes to Sestriere	Pascal Richard	FRA
22	12 June	Turin to Milan	Stefano Zanini	ITA

Overall

Yevgeny Berzin	RUS	100h41:21
Michele Pantani	ITA	2:51
Miguel Induráin	SPA	3:23

King of the Mountains

| Pascal Richard | SWI |

In depriving Induráin of a third successive win in the Giro, Berzin, in only his second season as a professional, becomes the first Eastern European rider to win one of the major national tours.

Women

July 1994

Overall

Michela Fanini	ITA	18h30:58
Kathy Watt	AUS	40 sec
L Zberg	SWI	1:00

Fanini, just 21, dies in a car crash in October.

Vuelta a España (Tour of Spain) 1994

Stage

| 1 | 25 April | Valladolid 9 k time trial | Tony Rominger | SWI |
| 2 | 26 April | Valladolid to Salamanca | Laurent Jalabert | FRA |

Adriano Baffi (ITA), who finishes first, is disqualified for causing a crash.

3	27 April	Salamanca to Caceres	Laurent Jalabert	FRA
4	28 April	Almendralejo to Córdoba	Endrio Leoni	ITA
5	29 April	Córdoba to Granada	Laurent Jalabert	FRA
6	30 April	Grenada to Sierra Nevada	Tony Rominger	SWI
7	1 May	Baza to Alicante	Simone Biasci	ITA
8	2 May	Benidorm time trial	Tony Rominger	SWI
9	3 May	Benidorm to Valencia	Jean-Paul Van Poppel	HOL
10	4 May	Igualada to Ordino Arcalis	Angel Camargo	COL
11	5 May	Ordino Arcalis to Cerler	Tony Rominger	SWI
12	6 May	Benasque to Zaragoza	Laurent Jalabert	FRA
13	7 May	Zaragoza to Pamplona	Laurent Jalabert	FRA
14	8 May	Pamplona to Alto Cruz	Tony Rominger	SWI

15	9 May	Santo Domingo to Santander	Alessio Di Basco	ITA
16	10 May	Santander to Covadonga	Laurent Jalabert	FRA
17	11 May	Onis to Alto del Naranco	Bart Voskamp	HOL
18	12 May	Avila back and home	Giuseppe Calcaterra	ITA
19	13 May	Avila to Segovia	Marino Alonso	SPA
20	14 May	Segovia time trial	Tony Rominger	SWI
21	15 May	Palazuelos to Madrid	Laurent Jalabert	FRA

Final standings

Tony Rominger	SWI	92h07:48
Mikel Zarrabeitia	SPA	7:28
Pedro Delgado	SPA	9:27

Rominger, who leads from start to finish, becomes the first rider to win the race three years in a row.

King of the Mountains
Luc Leblanc (FRA)

Tour of Britain 1994

Stage

| 1 | 8 Aug | Glasgow back and home | Maurizio Fondriest | ITA |
| 2 | 9 Aug | Carlisle to Blackpool | Wiebren Veenstra | HOL |

The riders stop the race, complaining of inadequate security, after a bad crash involving the whole field.

| 3a | 10 Aug | Bolton time trial | Maurizio Fondriest | ITA |
| 3b | 10 Aug | Liverpool city centre | André Tchmil | UKR |

Tchmil withdraws from the race the following day.

| 4 | 11 Aug | Chester to Leicester | Olaf Ludwig | GER |
| 5 | 12 Aug | Nottingham to Manchester | Jan Svorada | SLVK |

Overall

Maurizio Fondriest	ITA	20h54:53
Vyacheslav (Slava) Ekimov	RUS	21s
Olaf Ludwig	GER	27s
6 Sean Yates	*UK*	*55s*

Fondriest overcomes a bad back to lead from start to finish.

Points

Olaf Ludwig	GER	47
Jan Svorada	SLVK	47
Gary Coltman	UK	33

Sprints

Ben Luckwell	UK	24
Mark Walsham	UK	11
Slava Ekimov	RUS	10

Mountains

Scott Sunderland	AUS	68
Maurizio Fondriest	ITA	31
Malcolm Elliott	UK	30

Teams

Lampre	57h24:35
TVM	17s
GB MG Maglifico	17s

World Championships

15-28 Aug 1994 Sicily (track: Palermo)
Previously divided into professional & amateur, now mainly Open.

Men

Sprint

Marty Nothstein	USA	2
Darryn Hill	AUS	0
Michael Hübner	GER	

The first American to win the title since Fred Kramer in 1912, initially disqualified in the semi-final against Hübner (1990 & 1992 champion who beat him in the same round last year), Nothstein's reinstated on appeal.

Tandem sprint

Fabrice Colas & Frédéric Magne	FRA
Jens Glücklich & Emanuel Raasch	GER
Roberto Chiappa & Federico Paris	ITA

Colas & Magne win the event (the last tandem to be held at the championships) for the fourth time, the first since their 1987-88-89 hat-trick.

Keirin

Marty Nothstein	USA
Michael Hübner	GER
Federico Paris	ITA

Hübner, boxed in at the final bend, finishes only a wheel length behind.

4000m pursuit

Chris Boardman	UK	4:27.742
Francis Moreau	FRA	4:39.301
Jens Lehmann	GER	4:30.004
		(in semi)

Olympic champion Boardman wins a world title for the first time by beating the 1991 professional champion in the final, but is perhaps lucky that defending champion Graeme Obree isn't allowed to compete.

4000m team pursuit

Andreas Bach, Guido Fulst, Danilo Hondo, Jens Lehmann	GER	4:15.668
Carl Sundquist, Mariano Friedrik, Matt Hamon, Dirk Copeland	USA	4:17.372
Brett Aitken, Stuart O'Grady, Tim O'Shannessey, Rod McGee	AUS	4:18.417
		(in semi)

In the semi-final, the USA beat the defending champions and favourites Australia by two hundredths of a second in controversial circumstances.

1000m time trial

Florian Rousseau	FRA	1:03.163
Erin Hartwell	USA	1:03.795
Shane Kelly	AUS	1:03.846

Rousseau retains the title. Kelly finished second the previous year.

100km team time trial

Gianluca Colombo, Dario Andriotto, Gianfranco Contri, Christian Salvato	ITA	1h57:54.1
Jean-François Anti, Dominique Bozzi, Pascal Derame, Christophe Moreau	FRA	2h:00:42.5
	GER	2h00:55.7

Italy, who won last year and the first world title at this event (1962), now win the last (it's to be replaced by mountain biking in future championships).

Points

Bruno Risi	SWI	35
Jan-Bo Petersen	DEN	18
Franz Stocher	AUT	14

Amateur champion in 1991, professional champion in 1992, Risi wins the first Open title when defending champion Etienne De Wilde (BEL) withdraws after injuring his arm in a training fall.

Motor paced

motorcyclist's name in brackets

Carsten Podlesch (Dieter Durst)	GER	85 pts
Roland Königshofer (Carl Igl)	AUT	57
Alessandreo Tresin (Mauro Valentini)	ITA	42

Professional road race 250 km Agrigento

Luc Leblanc	FRA	6h33:54
Claudio Chiappucci	ITA	9s
Richard Virenque	FRA	9s

The first Frenchman to win the event since Bernard Hinault in 1980. Gianni Bugno (ITA), winner in 1991 & 1992, withdraws before the race after failing a drug test. Only 56 of the 172 starters complete the course. The one British rider to finish, Robert Millar, is 51st.

Amateur road race 185 km Capo d'Orlando

Alex Pedersen	DEN	4h24:38
Milan Dvorscik	SLVK	0s
Christophe Mengin	FRA	0s

The first reinstated amateur ever to win a world championship title. A heart problem forced Pedersen to abandon professional racing in 1991.

Road time trial (42 km) Catania

Chris Boardman	UK	49:34
Andrea Chiurato	ITA	50:22
Jan Ullrich	GER	51:25

The inaugural event brings mixed results for the leading Brits: while Boardman becomes the first British rider ever to win two titles at the same world championships, Obree's still out of luck: after dropping his threat of legal action, fitting tri-bars to his bike, and testing a variety of saddle positions, he struggles in the 42° heat and finishes 30th. Ullrich won the amateur road race the previous year.

Women

Sprint

Galina Eniukhina	RUS	2
Felicia Ballanger	FRA	1
Oksana Grishina	RUS	

Eniukhina was caught taking steroids at the last world championships; she was banned for the standard three months.

3800m pursuit

Marion Clignet	FRA	3:43.399
Svetlana Samokhvalova	RUS	3:50.898

Defending champion Rebecca Twigg (USA) withdrew with toothache.

Road time trial (30 km) Catania

Karen Kurreck	USA	38:22.8
Anne Samplonius	CAN	39:07.7
Jeannie (Longo) Ciprelli	FRA	39:44.1

Kurreck came to cycling from triathlon & gymnastics (cf Yvonne McGregor at the Commonwealth Games)

50km team time trial

Russia	1h04:55

Olga Sokolova, Aleksandra Ilaliaseva, Svetlana Bubenkova, Valentina Polhanova

Lithuania	1h05:39

Rasa Polikiavichiute, Jolanda Polikiaviciute, Diana Zilite, Luda Triabaite

USA	1h05:53

Dede Demet, Eve Stephenson, Jeane Golay, Alison Dunlap

Russia retain the title. The Polikiaviciutes are twins.

Points (24 km)

Ingrid Haringa	HOL	24
Svetlana Samohvalova	RUS	18
Lyudmila Gorojanskaya	BYL	16

Haringa wins the title for the fourth successive year, Gorojanskaya the first world championship medal for Belarus.

Amateur road race 84 km Capo d'Orlando

Monica Valvik	NOR	2h08:03
Patsy Maegerman	BEL	0s
Jeanne Golay	USA	0s

The first Norwegian to win a world title since 1973.

World Cup 1994

Milan-San Remo 19 March:	Giorgio Furlan ITA
Tour of Flanders 3 April:	Gianni Bugno ITA
Paris-Roubaix 10 April:	André Tchmil MOLD

The first Moldovan to win the the most prestigious as well as the hardest ('Hell of the North') European one-day race, now in its 102nd year.

Liège-Bastogne-Liège 17 April:	Yevgeny Berzin RUS

The first Russian to win the event, which was first staged in 1892.

Amstel Gold Race 23 April:	Johan Museeuw BEL
San Sebastian 6 August:	Armand de las Cuevas FRA
Leeds International Classic 14 August:	
	Gianluca Bertolami ITA
Championship of Zürich 21 Aug:	Gianluca Bertolami ITA
Paris-Tours 2 Oct:	Eric Zabel GER

Zabel, who wins a Classic for the first time, finishes inches ahead of Gianluca Bortolami (ITA) who takes the overall World Cup lead from Museeuw.

Tour of Lombardy 8 Oct:	Vladislav Bobrik RUS

The first Russian ever to win a World Cup event. Museeuw forfeits any chance of the overall title by not starting the race.

Final standings

156	Gianluca Bortolami	ITA
125	Johan Museeuw	BEL
115	André Tchmil	MOLD

Teams

89	GB-MG	ITA
53	Motorola	USA
51	Gewiss	ITA

Winning is the drug

If athletics has grubs in its apple, cycling at times seems a complete can of pharmaceutical worms. But this is set to change, according to the Union Cycliste Internationale, who in 1994 announced tougher drug penalties. Currently, for a first offence, a rider can expect a suspended ban (3 months for amateurs). This now shoots up to a six months to a year suspension, plus a maximum fine of £2000 and the loss of 50 ranking points.

During the Tour d'Oise, Miguel Induráin, no less, was caught using a Ventoline inhaler, which contains salbutamol, banned in France but not by the ICU. When big Mig was acquitted, justice seemed to have been done. Persecution of a man taking medication for asthma, it was said, a hammer to crack the biggest nut. But with other luminaries caught taking the same substance, it seemed that suddenly the world's best had all contracted respiratory problems. Then retire, lads, before it kills you...

Gianni Bugno, caught taking an excess of caffeine in August 1994, was pulled out of the World Championships at the last minute and banned by the Italian federation for two years, commuted by the ICU to three months. World pursuit champion Marion Clignet (FRA) was also temporarily banned for caffeine abuse.

Caffeine abuse? You can't be serious. Jeez, half the business community overdoses on the stuff. Surely it can't be ranked alongside all the anabolic horrors?

Well, as in athletics, one has to assume these things are ingested for a reason, an advantage, however slight or imagined. Jacques Anquetil, five times winner of the Tour de France, once said that 'Everyone in cycling dopes himself. Those who claim they don't are liars.' Against this background, even those who want to believe the sport's clean are having to backpedal.

Other major races 1994

Paris-Nice 6-13 March	Tony Rominger SWI
Criterium International 26-27 March	Giorgio Furlan ITA
Ghent-Wevelgem 6 April	Wilfried Peeters BEL
Flèche Wallonne 20 April	Moreno Argentin ITA
Tour of Romandy 3-8 May	Pascal Richard SWI
Dauphiné Libéré 30 May - 6 June	Laurent Dufaux FRA
Midi Libre 14-18 June	Jan Svorada SLVK
Tour of Switzerland 14-23 June	Pascal Richard SWI
Tour of Luxembourg 9-12 June	F Maessen HOL
Tour of Holland 15-19 Aug	Jesper Skibby DEN
Tour of Catalonia 9-14 Sep	Claudio Chiappucci ITA

The first Italian to win the event since Francesco Moser in 1978.

Paris-Brussels 15 Sep	Rolf Sorensen DEN
Tour de l'Avenir 6-16 Sep	Angel Casero SPA
Nations GP 24 Sep	Tony Rominger SWI
Tour of Piedmont 6 Oct	N Miceli ITA

UK National Track Championships

July 1994 Leicester

Men

Sprint
Stewart Brydon
Gary Hibbert
Craig Percival

Brydon retains the title.

Tandem sprint
P Boyd & Garry Hibbert
L Rowe & M Phillips
S Paulding & M Librizzi

1000m Time trial
Robert Hayles
Glen Sword
R Prince

4000m Pursuit
Graeme Obree
Bryan Steel
Stuart Dangerfield

The same three medallists as last year. Obree's 4:34.656 in the final breaks his own championship record.

4000m Team pursuit
North Wirral Velo
Team Haverhill
City of Edinburgh

Simon Lillistone, Stuart Dangerfield, Matthew Illingworth & Paul Jennings retain the title

20km Scratch
Anthony Stirrat
Gary Coltman
Russell Williams

Stirrat's 24:00.05 breaks the championship record by 21 secs.

40km
Simon Lillistone
Tony Doyle
Anthony Stirrat

Keirin
Paul McHugh
P Jacques
M Libbrizzi

McHugh was disqualified in the semi-final of the Sprint.

Omnium series
A Wallis	12 pts
Gary Coltman	17
Russell Williams	20

Women

Sprint
Wendy Everson
Sally Boyden
G Danson

Everson sets a championship record of 12.136 in beating defending champion Boyden by 0.60 secs.

1000m Time trial
Maxine Johnson
R Jones
Sally Dawes

25 km Points race
Sally Hodge	53 pts
Sally Dawes	38
Maria Lawrence	13

Mountain bikes

World Championships

Vail, Colorado

Men's cross-country 17 Sep 1994
Henrik Djernis	DEN	2h33:57.90
Tinker Juarez	USA	2h34:35.49
Bart Brentjens	HOL	2h37:32.39
23 Nick Craig	*UK*	*2h43:53.44*

In the closest ever men's world championship, Juarez stays with Djernis on the climbs but can't match the smooth descents of the Dane, who wins the title for the third successive year.

Women's cross-country 17 Sep 1994

Alison Sydor	CAN	2h12:07.08
Susan DeMattei	USA	2h15:26.55
Sara Ballantyne	USA	2h12:52.19
10 Caroline Alexander	*UK*	*2h19:42.74*

Sydor, silver medallist in 1992 (and at the 1994 Commonwealth Games), leads virtually from the start to win the title for the first time. Reigning world & European champion Paola Pezzo (ITA) crashes out. Juliana (Jules) Furtado (USA) has never managed to repeat her win at the first world championships (1991) despite starting as favourite every time.

Men's downhill 18 Sep 1994 5 km

François Gachet	FRA	6:22.52
Tommy Johansson	SWE	6:27.00
Corrado Herin	ITA	6:27.65
12 Steven Peat	*UK*	*6:35.72*

Women's downhill 18 Sep 1994 5 km

Missy Giove	USA	6:58.03
Sophie Kempf	FRA	7:03.03
Giovanna Bonazzi	ITA	7:04.47

Bonazzi was the defending champion.

Junior Men Cross-Country	Miguel Martinez	FRA
Junior Women Cross-Country	Karin Römer	GER
Junior Men Downhill	Nicolas Vouilloz	FRA
Junior Women Downhill	Anne-Caroline Chausson	FRA
Veteran Men Downhill	Walter Brändli	SWI
Veteran Women Downhill	Lisa Muhich	USA
Men Dual Slalom	Brian Lopes	USA
Women Dual Slalom	Anne-Caroline Chausson	FRA

The remarkable Römer finishes four minutes ahead of European champion Mona Fee (FRA) to win the title for the third time (the first was as a 14-y-o in 1991). She also finished second in 1992. Vouilloz also wins his event for the third time (in a time just 0.01 slower than the senior winner Gachet). Chausson's time is almost two seconds faster than Giove's.

World Cup

Men's cross-country

Bart Brentjens	HOL	343
Ned Overend	USA	307
Tinker Juarez	USA	305
5 Tim Gould	*UK*	*291*

Women's cross-country

Jules Furtado	USA	239
Caroline Alexander	UK	166
Alison Sydor	CAN	163

Men's downhill

François Gachet	FRA	240
Jürgen Beneke	GER	192
Nicolas Vouilloz	FRA	181
No British riders in the top 20.		

Women's downhill

Kim Sonier	USA	119
Anne-Caroline Chausson	FRA	117
Missy Giove	USA	113
10 Karen Van Merbeeck	*UK*	*49*

European Championships

Aug 1994 Métabief, France

Men's cross-country 50.5 km

Albert Iten	SWI	2h57:51
Gary Foord	UK	2h58:02
Benny Heylen	BEL	2h58:14

Pierre Lollo (FRA) dies after crashing in practice.

Women's cross-country 30 km

Paola Pezzo	ITA	2h02:45
Sophie Eglin	FRA	2h04:47
Maria Paola Turcutto	ITA	2h04:47
7 Siân Roberts	*UK*	*2h08:14*

Junior Men	Miguel Martinez	FRA
Junior Women	Mona Fee	FRA
Veteran Men	Mario Noris	ITA
Veteran Women	Danny Bonnoront	FRA

Fee takes advantage of Karin Römer's absence.

Men's downhill

Nicolas Vouilloz	FRA	4:07.8
Tommy Johansson	SWE	4:13.0
Corrado Herin	ITA	4:13.9
14 Rob Warner	*UK*	*4:21.7*

Like the winner of the women's race, the 18-y-o Vouilloz was eligible for the Junior event.

Women's downhill

Anne-Caroline Chausson	FRA	4:31.1
Giovanna Bonazzi	ITA	4:40.0
Brigitta Kasper	SWI	4:46.0
10 Karen Van Merbeeck	*UK*	*5:00.5*

The 1993 world downhill champion's beaten into second place by a 16-y-o.

Junior Men	Florent Poussin	FRA
Junior Women	*Cancelled as a medal event (too few entries)*	
Veteran Men	Lorenzo Orlando	ITA

British Hill Climb Championship

1993
Individual: Stuart Dangerfield (Leo RC)
Team: Leo RC

1994
Individual: J Wright (North East RT)
Team: North East RT

Wright breaks the course record to push defending champion Dangerfield into second place.

One hour record 1993-94

km

51 596	Graeme Obree	UK	18 Jul 1993
52 270	Chris Boardman	UK	23 Jul 1993
52 713	Graeme Obree	UK	27 Apr 1994
53 040	Miguel Induráin	SPA	2 Sep 1994
53 832	Tony Rominger	SWI	22 Oct 1994
55 291	Tony Rominger	SWI	5 Nov 1994

The previous record, set by Francesco Moser (ITA), lasted since 1984. The last five are all set at sea level on the same Bordeaux track.

Obree's tuck position is later banned, though the record stays in the books. He gets the attempt in before the ICU meet to discuss things.

Induráin breaks the record at his first ever attempt, on a bike made of a lightweight material with a carbon disc rear wheel, in front of a limited crowd (so that the spectators won't use up 'his' oxygen!)

24 riders, spread over 101 years, have now set the record. Induráin & Eddy Merckx (1972) are the only two to win the Tour de France in the same year.

Cyclo cross

World Championships (Men)

30 Jan 1994 Koksibje, Belgium

Senior 15 miles

Paul Herijgers	BEL	1h00:38
Richard Groenendaal	HOL	1h00:44
E Verveccken	BEL	1h01:15
33 Roger Hammond	*UK*	*1h05:54*

Herijgers is also the inaugural World Cup champion.

Junior 9 miles

Gretienus Gommers	HOL	39:48
Kamil Ausbuher	CZE	40:12
B Berden	BEL	40:48
22 R Thackray	*UK*	*43:03*

Gommers, who first competed in the event in 1991, wins it at his third attempt, ahead of defending champion Ausbuher.

British Championships

9 Jan 1994 Southampton

Men

Roger Hammond	1h11:43
Nick Craig	1h11:57
Steve Douce	1h12:35

Women

Caroline Alexander	44:59
Sally Hibberd	48:30
Isla Rowntree	49:04

Darts

BDO World Professional Championship 1993-94

1-8 Jan 1994 Lakeside CC, Frimley Green
Seeding numbers in brackets.

1st round

John Part	CAN	Ronnie Baxter (2)	ENG	3-0
Paul Lim	USA	Jim Damore	USA	3-0
Steve McCollum	ENG	Shayne Burgess (7)	ENG	3-0
Colin Monk	ENG	Jan Hoffmann	DEN	3-0
Troels Rusel	DEN	Alan Brown	SCOT	3-1
Ian Sarfas	ENG	Dave Askew (6)	ENG	3-0
Roland Scholten (3)	HOL	Sean Palfrey	WAL	3-0
Ronnie Sharp	SCOT	Trevor Nurse	SCOT	3-2
Martin Adams	ENG	Per Skau (5)	DEN	3-0
Bob Taylor	SCOT	Tony Payne	USA	3-0
Leo Laurens	BEL	Eric Burden	WAL	3-0
Magnus Caris	SWE	Wayne Weening (4)	AUS	3-2
Kevin Kenny	ENG	Kevin Painter	ENG	3-2
Nick Gedney	ENG	Steve Beaton (1)	ENG	3-2
Martin Phillips	WAL	Richard Herbert	WAL	3-2
Bobby George	ENG	Russell Stewart (8)	AUS	3-0

2nd round

Part	Lim	3-0
McCollum	Monk	3-1
Rusel	Sarfas	3-1
Sharp	Scholten	3-1
Adams	Taylor	3-1
Caris	Laurens	3-0
Kenny	Gedney	3-2
George	Phillips	3-1

Quarter-finals

Part	McCollum	4-0
Sharp	Rusel	4-1
Caris	Adams	4-2
George	Kenny	4-2

Semi-finals

Part	Sharp	5-1
George	Caris	5-4

Final

Part	George	6-0

Part, 20 years younger than the 47-y-o George, who reached the final in 1980, enters the championship for the first time and becomes the first player from outside Britain to reach the final – but wins a devalued title: the best players take part in their own world championship.

BDO World Professional Championship 1994-95

Lakeside CC, Frimley Green
Seeding numbers in brackets.

1st round

Richie Burnett (2)	WAL	Peter Wright	ENG	3-1
Russell Stewart	AUS	Alan Brown	SCOT	3-2
Sean Palfrey (7)	WAL	Andy Jenkins	ENG	3-1
Paul Hogan	ENG	Per Skau	DEN	3-1
Paul Williams	ENG	Bob Taylor	SCOT	3-0
John Part (3)	SCOT	Paul Knighton	ENG	3-2
Ronnie Sharp	SCOT	Bobby George	ENG	3-0
Andy Fordham (6)	ENG	Nicky Turner	ENG	3-2
Ian Brand	ENG	Wayne Atkins	AUS	3-0
Mike Gregory (5)	ENG	Yves Chamberland	CAN	3-2
Kevin Painter	ENG	Magnus Caris	SWE	3-2
Martin Adams (4)	ENG	Bruno Raes	BEL	3-1
Peter Hunt	NZ	Stefan Eeckelaert	BEL	3-0
Colin Monk (8)	ENG	Roland Scholten	HOL	3-1
Dave Askew	ENG	Steve Beaton (1)	ENG	3-2
Raymond Berneveld	HOL	Les Wallace	SCOT	3-2

Beaton, No.1 seed for the second year in a row, again goes out in the first round, again after leading 2-0.

2nd round

Burnett	Stewart	3-2
Hogan	Palfrey	3-0
Williams	Part	3-2
Fordham	Sharp	3-2
Gregory	Brand	3-2
Adams	Painter	3-0
Monk	Hunt	3-2
Berneveld	Askew	3-0

Beaton's conqueror lasts only 34 minutes against a Dutch postman who'd already booked his ferry home.

Quarter-finals

Burnett	Hogan	4-2
Fordham	Williams	4-2
Adams	Gregory	4-3
Berneveld	Monk	4-2

Burnett wins the last six legs, giving Hogan only one shot at a double. At 3-3, Gregory misses several chances of forcing a tie-break

Semi-finals

Burnett	Fordham	5-2
Berneveld	Adams	5-4

Adams misses the double 18 which would have given him a 4-1 lead. Burnett beats his room-mate to become only the second Welshman to reach the final, the first since Leighton Rees in 1979. The bearded players lose both semis.

Final

Burnett	Berneveld	6-3

Burnett, entering the championship for the first time, becomes the first Welshman to win it since Rees won the very first in 1978. Berneveld pulls back to 3-3 from 1-3 but must regret missing the double 16 which would have put him 2-0 ahead.

WDC World Professional Championship 1993-94

29 Dec 1993 – 2 Jan 1994 Purfleet

Quarter-finals

Dennis Priestley	T Kirby	4-2
Peter Evison	Rod Harrington	4-1
Phil Taylor	Bob Anderson	4-2
Steve Brown (USA)	Alan Warriner	4-3

Semi-finals

Priestley	Evison	5-3
Taylor	Brown	5-0

3rd-place final

Brown	Evison	5-1

Final

Priestley	Taylor	6-1

Both are former official world champions, Priestley (1991) beating the player who preceded and succeeded him.

WDC World Professional Championship 1994-95

Circus Tavern, Purfleet, Essex

Quarter-finals

Rod Harrington	Jamie Harvey	4-1
Peter Evison	Kevin Spiolek	4-1
Phil Taylor	Bob Anderson	4-1
John Lowe	Dennis Smith	4-0

Harrington wins on his 37th birthday. Defending champion and No.1 seed Dennis Priestley fails to reach the quarter-finals after losing his first group match 3-0 (all nine games) to Lowe, now 50 and unseeded.

Semi-finals

Taylor	Lowe	5-4
Harrington	Evison	5-1

Evison: 'I've never seen Rod hit so many doubles.' Harrington: 'I've never seen Peter miss so many doubles.'

3rd-PLACE FINAL

Lowe	Evison	4-2

FINAL

Taylor	Harrington	6-2

In a final of no great quality, Taylor recovers from 1-2 down to win a third world title comfortably despite hitting only 19 out of 58 doubles.

World Matchplay

Aug 1994 Blackpool

Quarter-finals

Dennis Priestley	Jamie Harvey	11-4
Rod Harrington	J Watkins (USA)	11-7
Larry Butler (USA)	Jocky Wilson	11-4
Shayne Burgess	Bob Anderson	11-8

Semi-finals

Priestley	Harrington	11-4
Butler	Burgess	11-7

3rd-place final

Harrington	Burgess	11-9

Final

Butler	Priestley	16-12

Priestley, the WDC world champion, was 15-8 on to win.

British Open 1993

Dec London

Men's final

Martin Adams	Stefan Nagy (SWE)	2-0

Pairs final

R Chettur & M Landers	S Palfrey & M Savvery	3-2

Women's final

Sandra Greatbatch	Sue Talbot	3-0

Pairs final

Jane Phillips & L Searle		
H Ernst (GER) & F Hoesnlaar (HOL)		3-2

British Open 1994

Dec Park Inn Hotel, London

Men's final

AHedman	Andy Fordham	2-1

Women's final

Frances Hoenselaar	Pauline Dyer	3-2

Equestrianism

World Games

27 July - 7 Aug 1994 Zuiderpark,
The Hague & De Vlasekkers
World Championships in all major disciplines

Showjumping

INDIVIDUAL

Franke Sloothaak	GER
Michel Robert	FRA
Sören von Ronne	GER

All four finalists ride each other's horses (for the first time, all 4 are mares); Sloothaak & Robert both jump four clear rounds, but the Frenchman incurs half a time fault on Sloothaak's horse Weihaiwei. Von Ronne picks up his only fault when riding his own horse Taggi.

TEAM

Germany	16.88 faults
France	31.63
Switzerland	45.69
6 UK	*63.66*

The winning team: Franke Sloothaak (San Patrignano Weihaiwei), Sören von Ronne (Taggi), Dirk Hafemeister (Priamos) and Olympic champion Ludger Berbaum (Almox Ratina). Kelly Brown's the first woman to be chosen for a British showjumping team at a major event since Liz Edgar at the 1981 Euopeans, but it doesn't help: for the first time since the championships began, in 1978, Britain fail to finish in the top three. Brazil, with father and son Nelson & Rodrigo Pessoa in the team, finish fourth. The course, designed by Jon Doney of Britain, features windmills at the water jump, Gouda cheeses at the eighth fence, and other assorted icons of 'typical Dutch everyday life'.

Dressage

INDIVIDUAL

Anky van Grunsven	HOL	Olympic Bonfire	pts:1819
Isabell Werth	GER	Gigolo	1810
Nicole Uphoff-Becker	GER	Rembrandt	1742
10 Emile Faurie	*UK*	*Virtu*	*1635*

TEAM

Germany	5269

Holland	5196
USA	4787
7 UK	*4578*

Germany win the event for the seventh time out of the eight it's been held.

SPECIAL INDIVIDUAL

Isabell Werth	GER	Gigolo	1605
Nicole Uphoff-Becker	GER	Rembrandt	1592
Sven Rothenberger	GER	Dondolo	1495
Emile Faurie	UK	Virtu	1469

INDIVIDUAL FREESTYLE

Anky van Grunsven	HOL	Olympic Bonfire	83.08
Klaus Balkenhol	GER	Goldstern	82.4
Karin Rehbein	GER	Donnerhall	77.07
11 J Bredin	*UK*	*Cupido*	*67.72*

Three day event

INDIVIDUAL

Vaughn Jefferis	NZ	Bounce	pens:55.6
Dorothy Trapp	USA	Molokai	56.8
Karen Dixon	UK	Get Smart	60.8

Mary Thomson (UK, on King William) leads after the first day but finishes fourth. Prue Cribb (AUS, in her first major Three-Day Event competition) leads after the second day but has a disaster in the showjumping ring. Defending champion Blyth Tait (NZ) has to retire when his horse Delta III is injured during the cross-country section.The USA, close second after the cross-country, are eliminated when two of their horses are withdrawn by vets. Britain, in contrast, take the cross-country easily, incurring time faults but producing clear rounds and clean bills of health.

TEAM

UK	198.8
France	213.2
Germany	279.6

The all-woman British team (Dixon, Thomson, Charlotte Bathe, Tina Gifford) lead from Day One.

Carriage driving

INDIVIDUAL

Michael Freund	GER
George Bowman	UK

Ijsbrand Chardon	HOL

If Freund had made a single mistake on the final day, the 59-y-o Bowman (16 times British national champion) would have won the title.

TEAM
Germany
Belgium
France

Endurance (100 miles)

INDIVIDUAL

Valerie Kanavy	USA	Pierax
Dennis Pesce	FRA	Melfenik
Stéphane Fleury	FRA	Roc H

TEAM
France
Spain
Australia

Vaulting

MEN

T Fiskbaek	DEN
C Lensing	GER
T Focking	GER

WOMEN

T Benedetto	GER
Lemon	USA
M Lorentz	GER

TEAM
Switzerland
Germany
Sweden

After the success of the first Games (Stockholm 1990), the future of the combined event may be in some doubt after riders criticise the courses (being used for the first time), conditions for horses, and travel arrangements. The next Games are scheduled for Ireland in 1998.

Showjumping

World Cup Final
14-17 April 1994 Hertogenbosch, Holland

FIRST LEG

Jos Lansink	HOL	Bollvorm's Libero
Nick Skelton	UK	Everest Limited Edition
Lesley McNaught-Mandli	SWI	Panok Goldrausch

Lansink had won a record five qualifying rounds. McNaught-Mandli was born in Britain.

SECOND LEG

Jos Lansink	HOL	Bollvorm's Libero
Franke Sloothaak	GER	San Patrignano Weihaiwej
Eddie Macken	IRE	Schalkhaar

THIRD LEG

1eq Jos Lansink	HOL	Bollvorm's Libero
1eq Dirk Hafemeister	GER	Priamos

FINAL PLACINGS

Jos Lansink	Bollvorm's Libero	0 flts
Franke Sloothaak	San Patrignano Dorina	9.5
Michael Whitaker (UK)	Everest Midnight Madness	14

Lansink becomes only the second rider (after Ian Millar (CAN) on Big Ben in 1989) to win all three legs of the final.

Horse of the Year Show 1993
Oct, Wembley Arena

Whitbread International Cup	Everest My Mesieur	Michael Whitaker
Middlewood Horseboxes 21	Miniature Quickstep	Andrew Davies
Senior Newcomers	Pennwood Fleetway	Geoff Glazzard
Junior Newcomers	Ultra Gold	S Scott
National Grade A SectionC	It's The Business	Geoff Glazzard
National Grade A Section C	Impressionist	D Inglis
Working Hunter	Lightwater What Fun	D Bartram
BSPS Pony Championship	Cringle Laughter	L Hillyard
Leading Jumper	Everest Grannusch	John Whitaker
Touch of Class Accumulator	Everest Vantage	Geoff Luckett
Olympic Star Spotters	Endeavour	Alison Bradley

Foxhunter	Fleurance	John Popely
Junior Foxhunter	Ultra Gold	S Scott
Toggi Grand Prix	Everest Grannusch	John Whitaker
Everest Championship	Everest Showtime	Nick Skelton
Knockout	Fire One	Geoff Luckett
Dressage Grand Prix	Quarryman	Laura Fry
The 1st dressage event ever held at the Show.		
Dressage Freestyle to Music 1	Ushin	J Haazan
Dressage Freestyle to Music 2	Quarryman	Laura Fry
Champion of Champions	College Jester	R Creber
Hunter of the Year	College Jester	R Creber
Ladies' Hunter	College Jester	R Creber
Pony Club Games	Eglington club	
Speed Horse of the Year	Monterrey II	James Fisher
Speed Stakes	Everest Monsanta	Michael Whitaker
Danco International	Everest Hopscotch	John Whitaker
Abstract Junior Challenge	Everest My Mesieur	Michael Whitaker
Grade B Championship	Grischunda	T Priest
Jump & Drive	Fire One	Geoff Luckett
British Ladies' Championship	Endeavour	Alison Bradley
Daily Maul Christy Beaufort Junior	Ballymoss	L Henderson
Daily Mail Christy Beaufort Grade C	Moneymore	C Edwards
Puissance	Benjumin	Warren Clarke

Horse of the Year Show 1994

Oct, Wembley Arena

Nissan Grand Prix	Everest Grannusch	John Whitaker
Ride & Drive	Toggi Interview	Tim Stockdale
Power & Speed Classic	Lusius	Elmer Gundel (GER)
Riding Horse	Madam Victoria	C Mackness
Pony Club Games	Eglington club	
Dressage Grand Prix	Bo	Sven Rothenberger (HOL)
Dressage Freestyle to Music	Olympic Cocktail	Anky van Grunsven (HOL)
Also a World Cup qualifier.		
Dressage Intermediaire	My Lord	N Capellmann-Biffar (GER)
Leading Jumper	Everest Midnight Madness	Michael Whitaker
Puissance	Gold	Robert Smith
Grade B Championship	Everest Magic Carpet	Michael Whitaker
Speed Stakes	Tip Toe	James Fisher
Woodhouse International Stakes	Rossport Aquila	Mark McCourt
Under 21	High Flyer II	Joanna Dennis
Everest Championships	Everest Grannusch	John Whitaker
Olympic Star Spotters	Abbervail Dream	Di Lampard
International Trophy	FAN Skyview	Eddie Macken
National Grade A	Wessex Zakatak	P Sutton
National Grade B	Everest Magic Carpet	Michael Whitaker
Foxhunter	Valentino R	Peter Murphy
Christy National	Sagase	Paul Barker
Christy Junior Championship	Maltstreet Mystic	Paul Barker
Show Hunter	King's Warrior	F Rapson
Small Hunter	Small Print	J Hutchinson
British Women's Indoor	Bond Gringo	Emma-Jane Brown
Cob Champion	Superted	H Griffiths
Hack Champion	Nobility	J Friswell
Snowflake International Cup	Flo Jo	Mario Hughes

Olympia 1993

MAIN EVENTS

Brandy Butter Stakes	Everest Limited Edition	Nick Skelton
Christmas Candle Stakes	Everest Mon Santa	Michael Whitaker
Mini/Major Relay	Everest Lifestyle	Michael Whitaker
1eq	Half A Penny	Robert Whitaker
Christmas Turkey Stakes	Everest Dollar Girl	Nick Skelton
Young Showjumper award	Closewood Again	Sarah Winterbottom
Christmas Cracker	Adelfos AC Folien/Singapur	Markus Fuchs (SWI)
Christmas Pudding Accumulator	Everest Lifestyle	Michael Whitaker
Christmas Cake Challenge	San Patrignano Corrado	Franke Sloothaak (GER)
Holly Bareback Puissance	Everest If Ever	Geoff Luckett
	1 eq Bockmann's Town	Lesley McNaught
	1 eq Everest Lifestyle	Michael Whitaker
World Cup Preliminary	Everest Two Step	Michael Whitaker
Mistletoe Top Score	Everest Major Wager	Nick Skelton
Father Christmas Stakes	Michael Whitaker	Everest Lifestyle
Christmas Hamper	Toggi Santa's Echo	Tim Stockdale
Christmas Knockout	Athlet	Willi Melliger (SWI)
Christmas Stocking Stakes	Everest Major Wager	Nick Skelton
Snowman Stakes (own line)	Everest Challenge	Geoff Luckett
Mince Pie Puissance	Everest Limited Edition	Nick Skelton
	1 eq San Patrignano Mister	Franke Sloothaak (GER)
Christmas Carol Stakes	Everest Limited Edition	Nick Skelton
Christmas Eve Six Bar	San Patrignano Mister	Franke Sloothaak (GER)
Grand Prix	Impulse	Peter Charles
Fancy Dress Relay	Everest Major Wager	Nick Skelton
	1 eq Everest Bikker	John Whitaker

I think we get the message about the festive season – and which double-glazing salesmen have been calling.

Olympia 1994

15-19 Dec

MAIN EVENTS

Christmas Turkey Stakes	Endeavour	Alison Bradley
Holly Stakes	Everest Elton	Michael Whitaker
Christmas Stocking Stakes	Wunderknabe	Rob Ehrens (HOL)
Father Christmas Stakes	Sprehe It's Me	Ludger Beerbaum (GER)
Christmas Candle Stakes	Tip Toe & Rose Princess	James Fisher
Christmas Hamper Stakes	Everest Welham	John Whitaker
Young Showjumper award	Count Bellair	Paul Barker
Christmas Pudding Accumulator	Alex H	Markus Beerbaum (GER)
Christmas Cracker Stakes	Rose Princess	James Fisher
World Cup qualifier	Sonora La Silla	Jan Tops (HOL)
Mistletoe Top Score	Goodwill Boy	Markus Beerbaum (GER)
Snowman Stakes (own line)	Showtime	Nick Skelton
Christmas Cake Stakes	Everest Dollar Girl	Nick Skelton
Christmas Knockout	Everest Randi	John Whitaker
Christmas Carol Stakes	Everest My Mesieur	Michael Whitaker
Mince Pie Puissance	Gold	Robert Smith
Christmas Eve Speed Stakes	Interpane Shandor	Markus Fuchs (SWI)
Brandy Butter Six Bar	Adelfos AC Folien	Markus Fuchs (SWI)
Grand Prix	Sprege Gaylord	Ludger Beerbaum (GER)

Bradley, making her debut in senior competition, lost an eye when a horse kicked her two years ago.

Hickstead 1994

SPEED DERBY 28 Aug

John Ledingham	EIRE	Castlepollard
Robert Splaine	EIRE	Bluegrass
Hervé Godignon	FRA	Si Jolie II

Ledingham & Castlepollard retain the title. The 1990-91-92 winners, David Bowen & Delsey, finish 5th (in Delsey's last Speed Derby), the only British combination in the top 8.

DERBY 29 Aug

John Ledingham	EIRE	Kilbaha
Katie Monahan-Prudent	USA	Partly Cloudy
Ralf Schneider	GER	Almox Come On

Ledingham completes the Speed Derby/Derby double by winning a jump-off to regain the title he won in 1984.

Aachen Grand Prix

19 June 1994

Rodrigo Pessoa	BRZ	Loro Piana Special Envoy
Thomas Fuchs	SWI	Major AC Folien
Nelson Pessoa	BRZ	Loro Piana Chouman
6 John Whitaker	*UK*	*Everest Gammon*

Nelson, Rodrigo's father, now 58, won the event in 1964 & 1972.

Three day eventing

World Rankings

A kind of World Cup; points awarded for a series of competitions.

Blyth Tait	NZ	360
Karen Dixon	UK	354
Mark Todd	NZ	330
6 Mary Thomson	UK	307

Tait regains the title he won in 1992.

Badminton

5-8 May 1994

Mark Todd	NZ	Horton Point	41.4
Blyth Tait	NZ	Delta III	53.8
Vaughn Jefferis	NZ	Bounce	57.0

Todd, who also places fifth on Just An Ace, also won in 1980 and finished second in 1984 & 1985. He rides Horton Point (a 16-y-o castrated stallion taking part in his sixth and last Badminton) only because Lynne Bevan (WAL) broke her collarbone.

British Championships

12-14 Aug 1994 Gatcombe Park

OPEN

Karen Dixon	UK	Too Smart	48 pens
William Fox-Pitt	UK	Chaka	51
Mark Todd	NZ	Bertie Blunt	53

INTERMEDIATE

Mark Todd	NZ	Chessman	46
Andrew Nicholson	UK	Walk On Top	47
Leslie Law	UK	Welton Envoy	47

Burghley

1-4 Sep 1994

William Fox-Pitt	UK	Chaka	49.8
Mary Thomsen	UK	King Kong	51.4
Karen Dixon	UK	Too Smart	52.4

Thomsen also finishes fourth on Star Appeal.

Bramham

10-12 Sep 1994

Blyth Tait	NZ	Aspyring	50
Ian Stark	UK	Kilcoran	52
Andrew Nicholson	UK	Walk On Cloud	56

Blenheim

16-18 Sep 1994

Bruce Davidson	USA	Squelch	52.95
Rodney Powell	UK	Comic Relief	57.00
Sharon Ridgeway	AUS	Kilkenny Castle	59.80

Davidson wins an event in Britain for the first time since his first world title in 1974.

Dressage

World Cup Final

31 March - 4 April 1994 Gothenburg

Monica Theodorescu	GER	Gaimedes Tecrent
Nicole Uphoff-Becker	GER	Herrmann's Grand Gilbert
Kyra Kyrklund	FIN	Edinburgh

British Championships

24-25 Sep 1994 Addington, Bucks

Emile Faure	Virtu
Jane Bredin	Cupido
F Eilberg	Arun Tor

Faure retains the title.

Carriage Driving

British Championships

9-11 Sep 1994 Windsor Great Park

Horse Teams	George Bowman
Pony Teams	G Frith
Horse Pairs	B Capstick
Pony Pairs	I Barlow
Horse Tandems	J French
Pony Tandems	A Graystone
Single Horse	K Trout
Single Pony	A Douglas

Bowman wins a record 17th national title.

Endurance

British Championships

23 July 1994 Cirencester Park

Jackie Taylor	Sally
Jo Trego	Oliver's Taboo
Jane James	Master Fiddler

Taylor beats Trego in a sprint finish after 100 miles. In hot and humid conditions, only four of the fourteen entrants finish. Questions may need to be asked.

JUNIORS

Saskie Lovell	Pensilva Sparkle
Emma Froehlich	Earl Grey
Christie Passant	Solaglass Hero

Froehlich was the defending champion.

Winning Junior Team: South Down (West)

World Disabled Championships

23-24 July 1994 Hartpury College, Gloucester

INDIVIDUAL

M Gray	USA	89.3 faults
C Bernd-Kaesgen	GER	89.8
D Ahern	ENG	97.0

TEAM

Germany	194.2
England	199.6
USA	217.9

GOLD MEDALS

borrowed horses

Grade 1	Diane Tubbs	UK	Louis
Grade 2	D Rice	CAN	Wellington Ebenezer
Grade 3 1eq)	Liz Stone	UK	Otter
Grade 3 (1eq)	S Townsend	USA	Dexter
Grade 4	Jo Jackson	UK	Fosseway Farmer

own horses

Grade 1	Allison Hasley	UK	Monty
Grade 2	Anne Dunham	UK	RDA Oberon
Grade 3	B Seifried	GER	Alouette
Grade 4	I de Groot	HOL	Titon

At the last World Championships, in 1991, Britain failed to win a medal. Tubbs, who has multiple sclerosis, won a gold at the first championships, in 1987.

Fencing

World Championships
July 1994 Athens

Foil

Men

1	Rolando Tucker	CUBA
2	Alessandro Puccini	ITA
3eq	Thorsten Weidner	GER
3eq	Oscar Perez Garcia	CUBA

Men's team

1	Italy
2	Germany

Women

1	Reka Szabo Lazar	ROM
2	Valentina Vezzali	ITA
3eq	Francesca Bortolozzi	ITA
3eq	Laurence Modaine	FRA

Bortolozzi was the defending champion.

Women's team

1	Romania
2	Italy

Epée

Men

1	Pavel Kolobkov	RUS
2	Olivier Jaquet	SWI
3eq	Arnd Schmitt	GER
3eq	Jean-Michel Henry	FRA

Kolobkov retains the title. Schmitt was runner-up last year. Angelo Mazzoni (ITA), yet again the winner of the World Cup, yet again fails to win the World Championship: second in 1990, he finishes fifth this time.

Men's team

1	France
2	Germany
3	S Korea

Women

1	Laura Chiesa	ITA
2	Katja Nass	GER
3eq	Mina Lehtola-Kaariainen	FIN

3eq	Corinna Panzeri	ITA

Chiesa finished second the previous year.

Women's team

1	Spain
2	Hungary
3	Romania

Sabre
(men only)

Individual

1	Felix Becker	GER
2	Stanislav Posdniakov	RUS
3eq	Grigory Kiriyenko	RUS
3eq	Bence Szabo	HUN

Surprisingly, the first German ever to win the event. Kiriyenko was the defending champion.

Men's team

1	Russia
2	Hungary

Commonwealth Championships
21-26 June 1994 Whistler, BC, Canada

Foil

Men

1	Tsan Wong	HK
2	David Waller	CAN
3eq	Paul Walsh	ENG
3eq	Donnie McKenzie	SCOT

Walsh is only 17.

Women

1	Marie-France Hervieu	CAN
2	Sarah Mawby	ENG
3eq	Shelley Wetterberg	CAN
3eq	Lucy Harris	ENG

Men's team

1	Canada
2	England
3	Hong Kong

Women's team

1	England
2	Scotland
3	Canada

Epée

Men

1	Laurie Shong	CAN
2	Simon Austin	WAL

3eq	Simon Weymouth	AUS
3eq	Simon Aspinall	ENG

Women

1	Charlotte Read	ENG
2	Ho Ka-lai	HK
3eq	Heather Landymore	CAN
3eq	Carol Greenaway	ENG

Men's team

1	Canada
2	England
3	Australia

Women's team

1	England
2	Canada
3	Hong Kong

Overall team

1	Canada
2	England
3	Scotland

Sabre

Men

1	Leszek Nowosielski	CAN
2	Paul Hoenigman	SCOT
3eq	Nick Fletcher	ENG
3eq	John Tanner	ENG

Men's team

1	Scotland
2	Wales
3	Canada

British Foil Championships

6 May 1994 West London Institute, Isleworth

Men

1	Laurent Harper
2	Mark Heath
3eq	Khaled Beydoun
3eq	Tony Bartlet

Women

1	Linda Strachan
2	Fiona McIntosh
3eq	Sarah Mawby
3eq	Sarah Kellett

British Epée Championship

Jan 1994 Hendon

Men

1	John Llewellyn
2	Steven Paul

3eq	Quentin Berriman
3eq	John Chalmers

Women

1	Carol Greenway
2	Sheila Pearce
3eq	Helen Nicholas
3eq	Kate Young

British Open Epée Championship

May 1994 Met Police College, Hendon

Men

1	Tony Perity
2	Chris Howser
3eq	Keith Lovejoy
3eq	Mark Kingston

British Sabre Championships

March 1994 King Edward's School, Bath

Men

1	Nick Fletcher
2	James Williams
3eq	Richard Cohen
3eq	Ian Williams

Cohen, now 46, takes part in the finals for the 25th consecutive year, a record.

Women

1	Sue Benney
2	Lynne Bornewmisza

Martini International (foil)

5-6 March 1994

1	Marius Strzalka	GER
2	Olivier Jaquet	SWI
3eq	Stefano Pantano	ITA
3eq	Kaido Kaaberma	EST

Strzalka improves on last year's second place. No British competitor finishes in the top ten.

Corble Cup (sabre)

29 May 1994 Met. Police College, Hendon

1	Kirk Zavieh
2	Ian Williams
3eq	Gary Fletcher
3eq	Peter Ujvario (AUS)

A small overseas entry and the absence of British No.1 James Williams helps make Zavieh the first home winner of the event since 1984.

Figure Skating

World Championships
22-27 March 1994 Makahari, Chiba, Japan

Men
Elvis Stojko	CAN	1.5
Philippe Candeloro	FRA	3.0
Vyacheslav Zagorodniuk	UKR	4.5
10 Steven Cousins	*UK*	*14.5*

Women
Yuka Sato	JAP	1.5
Surya Bonaly	FRA	3.0
Tanja Szewczenko	GER	5.0
18 Charlene von Saher	*UK*	*26.0*

Bonaly finishes runner-up for the second year in a row. Von Saher was twelfth the previous year.

Pairs
Yevgenia Shiskova, Vadim Naumov	RUS	1.5
Isabelle Brasseur, Lloyd Eisler	CAN	3.0
Marina Yeltsova & Andrei Bushkov	RUS	4.5
25 Dana Meldrick, Jason Briggs	*UK*	*12.5*

In their last competition before retirement, the defending champions do well to take silver: Brasseur competes despite a cracked rib.

Dance
Oksana Gritschuk, Yevgeny Platov	RUS	2.0
Sophie Moniotte, Pascal Lavanchy	FRA	4.0
Susanna Rahkamo, Petri Kokko	FIN	6.0
16 Marika Humphreys, Justin Lanning	*UK*	*32.0*

European Championships
16-23 Jan 1994 Copenhagen

Men
Viktor Petrenko	UKR	1.5
Vyacheslav Zagorodniuk	UKR	3.5
Alexei Urmanov	RUS	6.0
11 Steven Cousins	*UK*	*16.5*

Women
Surya Bonaly	FRA	1.5
Oksana Bayul	UKR	3.0
Olga Markova	RUS	4.5
23 Stephanie Main	*UK*	*33.0*

Pairs
Yekaterina Gordeeva & Sergei Grinkov	RUS	1.5
Yevgenia Shishkova & Vadim Naumov	RUS	4.0
Natalya Mishkutienok & Artur Dmitriyev	RUS	4.5
17 Dana Mednick, Jason Briggs	*UK*	*24.5*

Dance
Jayne Torvill, Christopher Dean	UK	3.6
Oksana Gritschuk, Yevgeny Platov	RUS	3.8
Maria Usova, Aleksandr Zhulin	RUS	4.6

After T&D finish behind Usova & Zhulin, Gritschuk & Platov win the free dance to jumble the final standings and let a quirk of the rules give the British favourites the gold. Suddenly the Olympic path doesn't look quite so smooth.

British Championships 1993
Singles & Pairs 8-9 Dec Basingstoke, Dance 7-8 Jan 1994 Sheffield Arena

Men
Steven Cousins	1.5
John Martin	3.0
David Ings	4.5

Women
Stephanie Main	2.5
Natalia Gorbenko-Risk	3.0
Emma Warmington	5.0

17-y-o Main, who finished 24th and last in the World Juniors, takes advantage of the absence of defending champion Charlene Von Saher, who gives up British eligibility before the 1994 championships.

Pairs

Diana Mednick & Jason Briggs	2.0
Jacqui Soames & John Jenkins	2.5
Lesley Rogers & Michael Aldred	4.5

Dance

Jayne Torvill & Christopher Dean	2.0
Marika Humphreys & Justin Lanning	4.0
Michelle Fitzgerald & Vincent Kyle	7.0

As it turns out, an illusory start. T&D take a clean sweep of 6.0s for their free dance, Courtney Jones, president of the National Ice Skating Association, calls it the greatest day in British skating.

British Championships 1994

28 Nov - 3 Dec 1994 Humberside Ice Arena

Men

Steven Cousins	2.0
Clive Shorten	2.5
Stuart Bell	4.5

Despite a heavy fall in the free programme, Cousins overtakes Shorten, who leads after the compulsories, to win the title for the sixth successive year.

Women

Jenna Arrowsmith	2.0
Zoe Jones	3.5
Stephanie Main	3.5

Two 14-y-o girls, taking part in the championships for the first time, relegate the holder (herself only 18) to third after she wins all seven judges' votes on the first day but has a highest technical mark of only 4.8 in the free programme.

Pairs

Lesley Rogers & Michael Aldred	2.0
Jacqui Soames & John Jenkins	2.5
N Thomas & D Thomas	5.5

This sport in life
Katarina Witt revealed that the Stasi, the East German secret police, used to bug even her sex life: 'Sexual Intercourse from 20.00 to 20.07.' Staying power only on the rink, it seems.

Dance

Michelle Fitzgerald & Vincent Kyle	2.2
Clair Wileman & Andrew Place	3.8
Lynn Burton & Duncan Lenard	6.0

World Junior Championships 1993

Dec, Colorado Springs

Men

Michael Weiss	USA	1.5
Naoki Shigematsu	JAP	6.0
Jere Michael	USA	6.5

Women

Michelle Kwan	USA	1.5
Krisztine Czako	HUN	3.0
Irina Slutskaya	RUS	4.5

Pairs

Maria Petrova & Anton Sikharulidze	RUS	1.5
Caroline Haddad & Jean-Sebastien Fecteau	CAN	3.5
Galina Maniachenko & Yevgeny Gigursky	UKR	4.0

Dance

Sylwia Nowak & Sebastien Kolasinski	POL	2.4
Yekaterina Svirina & Sergei Sahnovskiy	RUS	3.6
Agnes Jacquemard & Alexis Gayet	FRA	7.2

Goodwill Games

Aug 1994 St Petersburg

Men	Alexei Urmanov	RUS
Women	Surya Bonaly	FRA
Pairs	Natalya Mishkutenok & Artur Dmitriyev	RUS
Dance	Irina Romanova & Igor Yaroshenko	UKR

Football

Money, which has been doing the talking for several years now, positively shouted from the rooftops in 1994. Rangers, it almost goes without saying, were the big noise in Scotland again. Manchester United retained the League title (in some style, let it be said), did the Double, and in time would smash the British transfer record newly set by Blackburn, who finished second. Romantics everywhere hoped for Tottenham, Everton & Man City to go down, but weren't surprised when those on relative shoestrings (Swindon, Oldham, Sheffield United) did instead.

With four to go down in 1994-95, the need to stay in the Premier Division, which has gathered most of the riches to itself, led to a string of managerial sackings: Ardiles, Walker, Atkinson. The Sun endeared itself further to Merseysiders by accusing Bruce Grobbelaar of taking bribes to fix matches, and the Premier League staged an investigation into John Jensen's transfer to Arsenal from Brondby.

Meanwhile the *real* money men of Barcelona & Milan again dominated the European Cup, with quality football but largely thanks to their foreign imports: Stoitchkov, Koeman, Romário, Desailly, Savicevic.

Money and muscle, the pillars of the British game, let it down badly as far as international competition's concerned. Arsenal's flesh-and-bone defence did tremendously well in the Cup-Winners' Cup, but Man Utd flopped against Barcelona & Gothenburg, Blackburn against some other Swedish part-timers, Rangers against the Greeks. Oh, and for the first time since the War, none of the four Home countries made it to the finals of a tournament being held in the land of the dollar.

World Cup

USA 94: 17 June - 17 July

FIFA seemed to have got it right. You may want to read that again, but it seems true enough. Whether it was the three points for a win, the refereeing clampdown (including the outlawing of the tackle from behind), the ban on passing back to the 'keeper, the invalid carts, or any permutation thereof, the result was one of the best tournaments of all time.

There were no more talented players than in any other World Cup, but those that were there were given a stage and an audience (the largest in the history of the event) and revelled in the part. The ones who had nothing to prove proved it anyway: Hagi, Stoitchkov, Romário, Roberto Baggio, Brolin, Dahlin, Bergkamp, Klinsmann. Defenders, too: Babb, Belodedici, Maldini, Philippe Albert, the incredible Baresi, the bionic McGrath.

There were sparkling goals, there were impressive and expressive haircuts, and there was always someone in the news. Big Jack fined £10 000 for unscheduled touchline appearances. Leonardo, perhaps the left-back of the tournament, missing the final after nearly killing Tab Ramos with his elbow. Maradona sent home and banned for 18 months after imbibing a peppy cocktail. More terribly, Andres Escobar murdered in his drug-infested home town.

There was, in an event with hardly a dull moment, a dull final. It was a tournament with some great players but not a great team. The nearest thing, or at least the one with the most world-class players, was eliminated to almost universal glee, but at least their string of all-time greats – Matthäus, Klinsmann, Kohler, Brehme, Buchwald, Berthold, the remarkable Völler – could take comfort in having won the thing already. Their successors as champions kept a tight ship: four very good defenders and four good all-rounders in midfield, entrusting the goalscoring to two small skilful strikers, one of whom had been a match-winning genius for several years. It worked (Romário took all his goals with a kind of economical brilliance, and Brazil never really looked like losing to anyone), but it was somehow out of keeping with the tone of the tournament.

Watching Italy in 1994 was like following England in 1990: overcoming poor early form and several important injuries, under a manager who didn't seem sure what his best team was, riding some luck, winning a sequence of heart-stoppers by a single goal apiece, losing on penalties to a slightly better team. They also provided the best moment of the tournament *[a subjective thing, but one of the perks of editorship. Here goes.]*

Picture it. You've been voted European Footballer of the Year and FIFA World Player of the Year; your team, one of the supposed big names, looks to you for all its inspiration, and so far you haven't provided it: marked out of two matches, taken off in another so your goalkeeper can be substituted. Now, after another anonymous performance, a goal down with less than two minutes left, one of your team mates rolls the ball across to you in front of goal.

Hard to believe that anyone else, even the best, would do anything but hit it as hard as possible. Instead you aim carefully for the absolute bottom corner of the goal, between goalkeeper and defender. If you miss, they'll say you didn't even have the bottle to really go for your shot, and your career will always have a big minus alongside it. In all the pressure, Roberto Baggio backed his talent to the end, scored, and resuscitated his and Italy's tournament. Courage and class. His penalty miss in the final was forgiven as soon as it happened.

It was a tournament that deserved players like that, and got the refereeing they wanted. Yes yes, Kurt Röthlisberger should have awarded Belgium a penalty, and Jamal Al Sharif ruined a match that started as promisingly as any (Bulgaria-Mexico), but too many critics couldn't make one (a record 227 bookings) and one (an exciting, forwards' tournament) make two.

Relative failures? We had a few to mention. Scifo, Raí, Matthäus out of position, Koeman forever a liability in defence, Asprilla & Valderrama in mitigating circumstances. Among the teams, not so many. Greece apart, everyone dipped their bread a bit. Even some of the disappointments, and others who were eliminated early, won a match: Mexico, Switzerland, the USA, Norway, Colombia.

The biggest disappointments? Two. Nigeria, a goal down with twenty minutes to go, faced with a ten-man Italy, keeping five and six men permanently in defence. Above all, the Irish, who have played nine matches in the World Cup finals, winning one, scoring four goals. It's all wearing a bit thin.

So too, one day, may the idea that this was a great World Cup. 'FIFA seemed to have got it right', but once again the successful teams had to play one match too many – and the heat and humidity were appalling. To force teams to play at noon, for the benefit of European TV, was callous to the point of cruelty.

Don't take this word for it. If you believe Mexico were happy to play the Irish in the mid-day heat of Orlando, listen to their manager Miguel Mejia Baron: 'I would tell those gentlemen from FIFA to take their suits off and play soccer...If FIFA were to think about the player, if it were to think more about football and less about business, there would be night games.' Footballers rarely show how much conditions take out of them (except perhaps poor Steve Staunton) so we can persuade ourselves that they're not suffering all that much, but some lungs must have been burning out there. It was attractive, it was unforgettable, but it wasn't right.

Group A

18 June Pontiac Silverdome, Detroit
attendance 73 425, referee Francisco Lamolina (ARG)

| U.S.A. (1)1 | Wynalda 44 |
| SWITZERLAND (1)1 | Bregy 3 |

USA: Tony Meola, Cle Kooiman, Alexi Lalas, Marcelo Balboa, Paul Caligiuri, Tab Ramos, Tom Dooley, John Harkes, Mike Sorber, Ernie Stewart [Cobi Jones 80], Eric Wynalda [Roy Wegerle 57]

Switzerland: Marco Pascolo, Marc Höttiger, Dominique Herr, Alain Geiger, Yvan Quentin, Christophe Ohrel, Ciriaco Sforza [Thomas Wyss 76], Georges Bregy, Thomas Bickel [Nestor Subiat 71], Alain Sutter, Stéphane Chapuisat

18 June Rose Bowl, Pasadena
91 865, Alberto Tejada (PERU)

| ROMANIA (2)3 | Raducioiu 16, 89, Hagi 34 |
| COLOMBIA (1)1 | Valencia 43 |

Romania: Bogdan Stelea, Dan Petrescu, Miodrag Belodedici, Gheorghe Popescu, Daniel Prodan, Gheorghe Mihali, Ionut Lupescu, Dorinel Munteanu, Gheorghe Hagi, Ilie Dumitrescu [Tibor Selymes 67], Florin Raducioiu [Corneliu Papura 89]

Colombia: Oscar Cordoba, Andres Escobar, Luis Herrera, Wilson Perez, Luis Perea, Leonel Alvarez, Carlos Valderrama, Gabriel Gomez, Fredy Rincón, Adolfo Valencia, Faustino Asprilla

22 June Pontiac Silverdome, Detroit
61 428 Neji Jouini (TUN)

SWITZERLAND (1)4	Sutter 16, Chapuisat 53,
	Knup 66, Bregy 72
ROMANIA (1)1	Hagi 36

Switzerland: Pascolo, Höttiger, Herr, Geiger, Quentin, Ohrel [Patrick Sylvestre 82], Sforza, Bregy, Sutter [Bickel 70], Adrian Knup, Chapuisat

Romania: Stelea, Mihali, Popescu, Prodan, Hagi, Petrescu, Lupescu [Basarab Panduru 84], Belodedici, Munteanu, Dumitrescu [Ioan Vladoiu 69], Raducioiu

SENT OFF: Vladoiu [and sent home, after a World Cup career lasting 3 mins]

Some sources credit Knup with Switzerland's fourth, but slow-motion replays show that the last touch came from a Romanian defender. The Swiss credit it to Bregy.

22 June Rose Bowl, Pasadena
93 194, Fabio Baldas (ITS)

| U.S.A. (1)2 | Escobar og 33, Stewart 50 |
| COLOMBIA (0)1 | Valencia 89 |

USA: Meola, Kooiman, Balboa, Lalas, Caligiuri, Ramos, Dooley, Harkes, Sorber, Stewart [Jones 63], Wynalda [Wegerle 61]

Colombia: Cordoba, Herrera, Perea, Escobar, Perez, Valderrama, Rincón, Hernán Gaviria, Alvarez, Anthony De Avila [Valencia ht], Asprilla [Ivan Valenciano ht]

26 June Palo Alto
83 769 Peter Mikkelsen (DEN)

| COLOMBIA (1)2 | Gaviria 44, Lozano 89 |
| SWITZERLAND 0 | |

Colombia: Cordoba, Herrera, Escobar, Alex Mendoza, Perez, Valderrrama, Gaviria [Harold Lozano 78], Rincón, Alvarez, Valencia [De Avila 63], Asprilla

Switzerland: Pascolo, Höttiger, Herr, Geiger, Quentin, Ohrel, Sforza, Bregy, Sutter [Marco Grassi 81], Chapuisat, Knup [Subiat 81]

26 June Rose Bowl, Pasadena
93 869 Mario van der Ende (HOL)

| ROMANIA (1)1 | Petrescu 16 |
| U.S.A. 0 | |

Romania: Florian Prunea, Prodan, Belodedici [Mihali 87], Lupescu, Petrescu, Munteanu, Popescu, Hagi, Selymes, Dumitrescu, Raducioiu [Constantin Gilca 84]

USA: Meola, Fernando Clavijo, Balboa, Lalas, Caligiuri, Ramos [Jones 63], Dooley, Sorber [Wegerle 74], Harkes, Stewart, Wynalda

	P	W	D	L	F	A	Pts
Romania	3	2	0	1	5	5	6
Switzerland	3	1	1	1	6	4	4
USA	3	1	1	1	3	3	4
Colombia	3	1	0	2	4	6	3

Romania, Switzerland & USA qualify for the 2nd Round.

Group B

19 June Rose Bowl, Pasadena
83 959 Alberto Tejada (PERU)

SWEDEN (1)2	Ljung 7, Dahlin 74
CAMEROON (1)2	Embe 29, Omam Biyick 46

Sweden: Thomas Ravelli, Roland Nilsson, Patrik Andersson, Joachim Bjorklund, Roger Ljung, Klas Ingesson [Kennet Andersson 75], Jonas Thern, Stefan Schwarz, Jesper Blomqvist [Henrik Larsson 59], Martin Dahlin, Tomas Brolin

Cameroon: Joseph-Antoine Bell, Stephen Tataw, Raymond Kalla, Rigobert Song, Hans Agbo, Thomas Libiih, Émile Mbouh, Louis-Paul Mfede [Kessack Maboang 86], Marc Vivien Foe, François Omam Biyick, David Embe [Mouyeme 79]

20 June Palo Alto
81 061 Lee Kim Chong (MALAY)

BRAZIL (1)2	Romário 26, Raí pen 53
RUSSIA 0	

Brazil: Claudio Taffarel, 'Jorginho' (Jorge Amorim de Oliveira), Ricardo Rocha [Aldair (Nascimento Santos) 74], Marcio Santos, Leonardo (Nascimento de Araújo), Raí (Souza de Oliveira), Mauro Silva, 'Dunga' (Carlos Bledorn Verri) ['Mazinho' (Iomar do Nascimento) 85], 'Zinho' (Crizam de Oliveira), 'Bebeto' (José Roberto Gama de Oliveira), Romário (de Souza Faria)

Russia: Dmitry Kharin, Vladislav Ternavski, Yuri Nikiforov, Sergei Gorlukovich, Valery Karpin, Andrei Piatnitski, Dmitry Radchenko [Aleksandr Borodyuk 77], Dmitry Kuznetsov, Ilya Tsimbalar, Dmitry Khlestov, Sergei Yuran [Oleg Salenko 55]

Raí's brother Sócrates captained Brazil in the World Cup finals (1982 & 1986).

24 June Palo Alto
83 401 Arturo Brizio Carter (MEX)

BRAZIL (1)3	Romário 38, Marcio Santos 64, Bebeto 72
CAMEROON 0	

Brazil: Taffarel, Jorginho, Aldair, Marcio Santos, Leonardo, Raí ['Muller' (Luis Correa da Costa) 80], Dunga, Mauro Silva, Zinho [Paulo Sergio (Silvestre Nascimento) 74], Bebeto, Romário

Cameroon: Bell, Tataw, Song, Kalla, Agbo, Libiih, Mfede [Maboang 70], Mbouh, Foe, Omam Biyick, Embe [Roger Miller [Milla] 63]

SENT OFF: Song 63 (the youngest in any World Cup finals match)

24 June Pontiac Silverdome, Detroit
71 528 Joël Quiniou (FRA)

SWEDEN (1)3	Brolin pen 38, Dahlin 59, 81
RUSSIA (1)1	Salenko pen 3

Sweden: Ravelli, R Nilsson, P Andersson, Bjorklund [Magnus Erlingmark 88], Ljung, Ingesson, Schwarz, Brolin, Thern, Dahlin, K Andersson [Larsson 84]

Russia: Kharin, Gorlukovich, Nikiforov, Khlestov, Kuznetsov, Dmitry Popov [Karpin 40], Borodyuk [Dmitry Galiamin 51], Aleksandr Mostovoi, Viktor Onopko, Salenko, Radchenko

SENT OFF: Gorlukovich 49

28 June Palo Alto
74 914 Jamal Al Sharif [SYRIA]

RUSSIA [3]6	Salenko 16, 41, 44, 73, 75, Radchenko 82
CAMEROON [0]1	Milla 47

Russia: Stanislav Cherchesov, Omari Tetradze,

Goals in a single World Cup finals match

						pens
5	Oleg Salenko	Russia	1994	v Cameroon		1
4	Ernest Wilimowski	Poland	1938	v Brazil		0
4	Gustav Wetterström	Sweden	1938	v Cuba		0
4	Juan Schiaffino	Uruguay	1950	v Bolivia		0
4	Ademir (Menezes)	Brazil	1950	v Sweden		0
4	Sándor Kocsis	Hungary	1954	v W Germany		0
4	Just Fontaine	France	1958	v W Germany		0
4	Eusébio (da Silva)	Portugal	1966	v N Korea		2
4	Emilio Butragueño	Spain	1986	v Denmark		1

Virtually every source outside Brazil credits Leônidas (da Silva) with four goals in that 1938 Brazil-Poland game, but recent research by the leading Brazilian statisticians indicates that he scored three.

Nikiforov, Ternavski, Karpin, Tsimbalar, Igor Ledyakhov [Vladimir Beschastnikh 77], Khlestov, Onopko, Salenko, Igor Korneyev [Radchenko 64]

Cameroon: Jacques Songo'o, Tataw, Kalla, Victor Ndip, Agbo, Libiih, André Kana Biyick, Mfede [Milla ht], Foe, Embe [Alphonse Tchami 47], Omam Biyick

Salenko becomes the first player to score five goals in any World Cup finals match. Milla (42) is the oldest player (and goalscorer) to take part in the World Cup.

28 June Pontiac Silverdome, Detroit
77 217, Sándor Puhl [HUN]

| SWEDEN (1)1 | K Andersson 21 |
| BRAZIL (0)1 | Romário 47 |

Sweden: Ravelli, R Nilsson, P Andersson, Pontus Kamark, Ljung, Larsson [Blomqvist 62], Thern, Schwarz [Hakan Mild 75], Ingesson, Brolin, K Andersson

Brazil: Taffarel, Jorginho, Aldair, Marcio Santos, Leonardo, Raí [Paulo Sergio 86], Dunga, Mauro Silva [Mazinho ht], Zinho, Bebeto, Romário

	P	W	D	L	F	A	Pts
Brazil	3	2	1	0	6	1	7
Sweden	3	1	2	0	6	4	5
Russia	3	1	0	2	7	6	3
Cameroon	3	0	1	2	3	11	1

Brazil & Sweden qualify for the 2nd Round.

Group C

17 June Soldier Field, Chicago
63 117, Arturo Brizio Carter (MEX)

| GERMANY (0)1 | Klinsmann 61 |
| BOLIVIA 0 | |

Germany: Bodo Illgner, Jürgen Kohler, Lothar Matthäus, Thomas Berthold, Thomas Hässler [Thomas Strunz 82], Stefan Effenberg, Matthias Sammer, Andreas Möller, Andreas Brehme, Jürgen Klinsmann, Karlheinz Riedle [Mario Basler 59]

Bolivia: Carlos Trucco, Marco Sandy, Miguel Rimba, Gustavo Quinteros, Luis Cristaldo, Carlos Borja, José Melgar, Vladimir Soría, Júlio Baldivieso [Jaime Moreno 65], Erwin Sánchez, William Ramallo [Marco Etcheverry 78]

SENT OFF: Etcheverry 82 (Bolivia's great hope, only recently returned from a long injury lay-off, plays only four minutes in the finals.)

17 June Cotton Bowl, Dallas
56 247, Peter Mikkelsen (DEN)

SPAIN (0)2	Salinas 51, Goikoetxea 56
SOUTH KOREA (0)2	Hong Myung-bo 85,
	Seo Jung-won 89

Consecutive internationals

86	Andoni Zubizarreta	Spain	1985-94
70	Billy Wright	England	1951-59
60	Franz Beckenbauer	W Germany	1970-77
57	Ferenc Sipos	Hungary	1957-63
55	Gerhard Hanappi	Austria	1948-56
50	József Bózsik	Hungary	1948-54
50	Louis Carré	Belgium	1949-56

Spain: Santiago Canizares, Albert Ferrer, Rafael Alkorta, Abelardo (Fernandez), Julen Guerrero [José Luis Caminero ht], Jon Andoni Goikoetxea, Miguel Angel Nadal, Fernando Hierro, Sergi (Barjuan), Júlio Salinas [Felipe (Minambres) 62], Luis Enrique (Martínez)

S Korea: Choi In-young, Kim Pan-keun, Park Jung-bae, Lee Young-jin, Shin Hong-gi, Noh Jung-yoon [Ha Seok-ju 72], Kim Joo-sung [Seo Jung-won 58], Ko Jeong-woon, Choi Young-il, Hwang Sun-hong, Hong Myung-bo

SENT OFF: Nadal 25.

Goalkeeper and regular captain Andoni Zubizarreta misses the game as a result of his sending-off in the last qualifying match, v Denmark. To give Canizares a game before the finals, Zubizarreta was left out of the match immediately before them, putting an end to his world record run of consecutive internationals.

21 June Soldier Field, Chicago
63 113, Ernesto Filippi Cavani (URU)

| GERMANY (0)1 | Klinsmann 48 |
| SPAIN (1)1 | Goikoetxea 14 |

Germany: Illgner, Kohler, Matthäus, Berthold, Hässler, Strunz, Sammer, Möller [Rüdi Völler 61], Effenberg, Brehme, Klinsmann

Spain: Andoni Zubizarreta, Alkorta, Hierro, Abelardo, Goikoetxea [José María Bakero 63], Ferrer, Guardiola [Francisco Camarasa 76], Luis Enrique, Sergi, Salinas

23 June Foxboro, Boston
53 456, Leslie Mottram (SCOT)

| BOLIVIA 0 | |
| SOUTH KOREA 0 | |

Bolivia: Trucco, Sandy, Rimba, Quinteros, Cristaldo, Borja, Melgar, Soría, Baldivieso, Sánchez, Ramallo [Alvaro Peña 62]

S Korea: Choi IY, Kim PK, Park, Shin, Hong, Lee, Kim JS, Seo [Ha 65], Ko, Noh [Choi 71], Hwang

SENT OFF: Cristaldo 83

The first goalless draw of the tournament.

27 June Cotton Bowl, Dallas
63 998, Joël Quiniou (FRA)

| GERMANY (3)3 | Klinsmann 11, 35, Riedle 18 |
| SOUTH KOREA (0)2 | Hwang Sun-hong 52, Hong Myung-bo 63 |

Germany: Illgner, Kohler, Matthäus [Möller 63], Berthold, Effenberg [Thomas Helmer 74], Sammer, Guido Buchwald, Brehme, Hässler, Klinsmann, Riedle

S Korea: Choi IY [Lee Won-jae ht], Choi Young-il, Hong, Park, Shin, Kim PK, Lee [Chung Jong-son 39], Ko, Kim JS, Cho Jin-ho, Hwang

27 June Soldier Field, Chicago
63 089, Rodrigo Badilla (C RICA)

| SPAIN (1)3 | Guardiola pen 19, Caminero 66, 71 |
| BOLIVIA (0)1 | Sánchez |

Spain: Zubizarreta, Ferrer, Salvador Voro, Abelardo, Goikoetxea, Caminero, Guardiola [Bakero 67], Felipe [Hierro ht], Sergi, Salinas, Guerrero

Bolivia: Trucco, Sandy, Rimba, A Peña, Ramos [Moreno ht], Borja, Soruco, Melgar, Soría [Castillo 61], Ramallo, Sánchez

In their sixth World Cup finals match, spread over 64 years, Bolivia score their first goal, a deflected one at that.

	P	W	D	L	F	A	Pts
Germany	3	2	1	0	5	3	7
Spain	3	1	2	0	6	4	5
S Korea	3	0	2	1	4	5	2
Bolivia	3	0	1	2	1	4	1

Germany & Spain qualify for the 2nd Round.

Group D

21 June Cotton Bowl, Dallas
44 932, Rodrigo Badilla (C RICA)

| NIGERIA (2)3 | Yekini 21, Amokachi 43, Amunike 55 |
| BULGARIA 0 | |

Nigeria: Peter Rufai, Chidi Nwanu, Augustin Eguavoen, Uche Okechukwu, Ben Iroha, Finidi George [Emeka Ezuego 76], Samson Siasia [Mutiu Adepoju 68], Sunday Oliseh, Emmanuel Amunike, Rashidi Yekini, Daniel Amokachi

Bulgaria: Borislav Mikhailov, Emil Kremenliev, Petar Khubchev, Trifon Ivanov, Tzanko Tzvetanov, Zlatko Yankov, Daniel Borimirov [Ivailo Yordanov 72], Yordan Letchkov [Nasko Sirakov 58], Krasimir Balakov, Emil Kostadinov, Christo Stoitchkov

Yekini, apparently described as 'a humble and religious stud', scores Nigeria's first ever goal in the World Cup finals.

21 June Foxboro, Boston
53 486, Arturo Angeles (USA)

| ARGENTINA (2)4 | Batistuta 2, 44, 89 pen, Maradona 60 |
| GREECE 0 | |

Argentina: Luis Islas, Néstor Sensini, Fernando Caceres, Oscar Ruggeri, José Chamot, Diego Simeone, Diego Maradona [Arnaldo Ortega 82], Fernando Redondo, Abel Balbo [Alejandro Mancuso 79], Gabriel Batistuta, Claudio Caniggia

Greece: Antonis Minou, Stratos Apostolakis, Thanasios Kolitsidakis, Stelios Manolas, Iannis Kalitzakis, Dimitris Saravakos, Nikos Noblias, Panayotis Tsaluhidis, Nikos Tsiantakis [Spiros Maragos ht], Savas Kofidis, Nikos Machlas [Tasos Mitropoulos ht]

The following season, Batistuta, who scores within two minutes of his World Cup finals debut, breaks Ezio Pascutti's 1962 record by scoring in eleven consecutive Italian Serie A matches.

25 June Foxboro, Boston
54 453, Bo Karlsson (SWE)

| ARGENTINA (2)2 | Caniggia 22, 29 |
| NIGERIA (1)1 | Siasia 8 |

Argentina: Islas, Sensini [Hernán Diaz 87], Ruggeri, Caceres, Chamot, Simeone, Redondo, Balbo [Mancuso 71], Maradona, Batistuta, Caniggia

Nigeria: Rufai, Nwanu, Eguavoen, Okechukwu, Mike Emenalo, George, Siasia, Oliseh, Amunike, Yekini, Amokachi

26 June Soldier Field, Chicago
63 160, Ali Mohamed Bujsaim (UAE)

| BULGARIA (1)4 | Stoitchkov 5 pen, 55 pen, Letchkov 66, Borimirov 89 |
| GREECE 0 | |

Bulgaria: Mikhailov, Kremenliev, Ivanov, Khubchev, Tzvetanov [Ilian Kiriakov 76], Balakov, Letchkov, Yankov, Kostadinov [Borimirov 81], Sirakov, Stoitchkov

Greece: Ilias Atmatzidis, Apostolakis, Kalitzakis, Vaios Karaiannis, Kiriakos Karataidis, Noblias, Maragos, Minas Hantzidis [Mitropoulos 47], Kofidis, Machlas, Alexandros Alexoudis [Vasilis Dimitriadis 57]

In their 18th World Cup finals match, spread over 32 years, Bulgaria at last achieve their first win, passing their famous unwanted mantle on to S Korea, who haven't won any of their 11 games in the finals. Greek manager Alketas Panagoulias has his own succint version of the debâcle: 'Beaten by that flat-footed poof Ivanov or whatever his name is.' His genuine success in taking Greece to the finals already seems to be forgotten.

30 June Cotton Bowl, Dallas
63 998, Neji Jouini (TUN)

BULGARIA (0)2   Stoitchkov 61, Sirakov 89
ARGENTINA 0

Bulgaria: Mikhailov, Kremenliev, Khubchev, Ivanov, Tzvetanov, Balakov, Letchkov [Borimirov 73], Sirakov, Yankov, Kostadinov [Kiriakov 73], Stoitchkov

Argentina: Islas, Diaz, Ruggeri, Caceres, Chamot, Simeone, Redondo, Balbo, Leonardo Rodriguez [Ramón Medina Bello 66], Batistuta, Caniggia [Arnaldo Ortega 26]

30 June Foxboro, Boston
53 001, Leslie Mottram (SCOT)

NIGERIA (1)2   George 44, Amokachi 90
GREECE 0

Nigeria: Rufai, Stephen Keshi, Okechukwu, Nwanu, Emenalo, George [Adepoju 83], Siasia, Oliseh, Amunike, Amokachi, Yekini [Augustine Okocha 68]

Greece: Christos Karkamanis, Kalitzakis, Karaiannis, Alexis Alexiou, Tsaluhidis, Noblias, Mitropoulos [Tsiantakis 79], Hantzidis, Kofidis, Alexis Alexandris, Machlas [Dimitriadis 79]

	P	W	D	L	F	A	Pts
Nigeria	3	2	0	1	6	2	6
Bulgaria	3	2	0	1	6	3	6
Argentina	3	2	0	1	6	3	6
Greece	3	0	0	3	0	10	0

Nigeria, Bulgaria & Argentina qualify for the 2nd Round.

Group E

18 June Giants Stadium, New Jersey
74 826, Mario van der Ende (HOL)

REP. IRELAND (1)1   Houghton 12
ITALY 0

Ireland: Pat Bonner, Dennis Irwin, Phil Babb, Paul McGrath, Terry Phelan, Ray Houghton [Jason McAteer 67], Roy Keane, John Sheridan, Andy Townsend, Steve Staunton, Tommy Coyne [John Aldridge 89]

Italy: Gianluca Pagliuca, Mauro Tassotti, Paolo Maldini, Dino Baggio, Alessandro Costacurta, Franco Baresi, Roberto Donadoni, Demetrio Albertini, Giuseppe (Beppe) Signori [Nicola Berti 83], Roberto Baggio, Alberigo Evani [Daniele Massaro ht]

19 June Robert F Kennedy Stadium, Washington DC
52 359, Sándor Puhl (HUN)

NORWAY (0)1   Rekdal 85
MEXICO 0

Norway: Erik Thorstvedt, Alf-Inge Haland, Rune Bratseth, Stig-Inge Bjornebye, Erik Mykland [Kjetil Rekdal 77], Oyvind Leonhardsen, Henning Berg, Jan Ivar Jakobsen [Gunnar Halle ht], Lars Bohinen, Jostein Flo, Jan-Åge Fjortoft

Mexico: Jorge Campos, Cláudio Suarez, Raúl Gutierrez [Marcelino Bernal 70], Ignacio Ambriz, Ramón Ramirez, Luis Garcia, Joaquin Del Olmo, Juan Ramirez, Luis Valdes [Benjamin Galindo ht], Hugo Sánchez, 'Zaguinho' (Luis Alves Zague)

23 June Giants Stadium, New Jersey
74 624, Heinz Hellmut Krug (GER)

ITALY (0)1   D Baggio 69
NORWAY 0

Italy: Pagliuca, Antonio Benarrivo, Maldini, D Baggio, Costacurta, Baresi [Luigi Apolloni 48], Berti, Albertini, Signori, R Baggio [Luca Marchegiani 22], Pier Luigi Casiraghi [Daniele Massaro 68]

Norway: Thorstvedt, Haland, Berg, Bratseth, Bjornebye, Sigurd Rushfeldt [Jakobsen ht], Bohinen, Mykland [Rekdal 80], Leonhardsen, Flo, Fjortoft

SENT OFF: Pagliuca (the first goalkeeper in any World Cup finals match; R Baggio's taken off to make way for reserve keeper Marchegiani)

24 June Citrus Bowl, Orlando
61 219, Kurt Röthlisberger (SWI)

MEXICO (1)2   L Garcia 44, 66
REP. IRELAND (0)1   Aldridge 84

Mexico: Campos, Rodriguez [Gutierrez 79], Suarez, J Ramirez, Del Olmo, Bernal, L Garcia, Ambriz, Alberto Garcia Aspe, Carlos Hermosillo [Luis Miguel Salvador 79], Zaguinho

Ireland: Bonner, Irwin, McGrath, Babb, Phelan, Houghton, Townsend, Keane, Sheridan, Staunton[McAteer 65], Coyne [Aldridge 66]

A delay in getting Aldridge onto the field leads to some heated words ('You f***ing cheat' being more or less the coolest) which cost manager Jack Charlton £10 000, mainly for getting under FIFA's skin with his comments about bringing water to players on the pitch.

28 June Giants Stadium, New Jersey
76 322, José Torres Cadena (COL)

NORWAY 0
REP. IRELAND 0

Norway: Thorstvedt, Halle [Jakobsen 33], Erland Johnsen, Bratseth, Bjornebye, Flo, Berg, Leonhardsen [Bohinen 67], Mykland, Rekdal, Goran Sorloth

Ireland: Bonner, Gary Kelly, Babb, McGrath, Staunton, McAteer, Houghton, Keane, Townsend [Ronnie Whelan 74], Sheridan, Aldridge [David Kelly 64]

28 June RFK Stadium, Washington DC
53 186, Francisco Lamolina (ARG)

ITALY (0)1   Massaro 48
MEXICO (0)1   Bernal 58

Italy: Marchegiani, Benarrivo, Maldini, Costacurta, Apolloni, Berti, Albertini, D Baggio [Donadoni 64], Signori, R Baggio, Casiraghi [Massaro ht]

Mexico: Campos, Rodriguez, Suarez, J Ramirez, Del Olmo, Bernal, Ambriz, L Garcia [Juan Carlos Chavez 80], Hermosillo, Garcia Aspe, Zaguinho

Massaro, who won his first cap in 1982, scores his first senior international goal.

	P	W	D	L	F	A	Pts
Mexico	3	1	1	1	3	3	4
Rep. Ireland	3	1	1	1	2	2	4
Italy	3	1	1	1	2	2	4
Norway	3	1	1	1	1	1	4

Mexico, Ireland & Italy qualify for the 2nd Round.

Group F

19 June Citrus Bowl, Orlando
60 790, José Torres Cadena (COL)

BELGIUM (1)1   Degryse 11
MOROCCO 0

Belgium: Michel Preud'homme, Georges Grün, Michel De Wolf, Rudi Smidts, Lorenzo Staelens, Franky Van der Elst, Marc Degryse, Vincenzo (Enzo) Scifo, Danny Boffin [Vital Borkelmans 84], Josip Weber, Luc Nilis [Marc Emmers 53]

Morocco: Khalil Azmi [Zakaria Alaoui 88], Abdellah (Nacer), Ismail Triki, Larbi Hababi, Abdelkrim Hadrioui, Nourredine Naybet, Mustafa El Haddaoui [Ahmed Bahja 68], Rachid Azzouzi, Rachid Daoudi, Mustafa Hadji, Mohamed Chaouch [Aziz Samadi 81]

20 June RFK Stadium, Washington DC
52 535, Manuel Diaz Vega (SPA)

HOLLAND (0)2   Jonk 50, Taument 86
SAUDI ARABIA (1)1   Amin 19

Holland: Ed De Goey, Ulrich van Gobbel, Ronald Koeman, Frank De Boer, Wim Jonk, Frank Rijkaard, Jan Wouters, Marc Overmars [Gaston Taument 57], Dennis Bergkamp, Brian Roy [Peter van Vossen 80], Ronald De Boer

Saudi: Mohamed Al Deaye, Abdullah Al Dosari, Mohammed Al Khlawi, Mohammed Al Jawad, Ahmed Madani, Faud Amin, Fahad Al Bishi, Khalid Al Muwalid, Talal Al Jebreen, Majed Abdullah Mohammed [Hamzah Falatah 44], Saeed Owairan [Saleh (Al Daoud) 68]

25 June Citrus Bowl, Orlando
62 387, Renato Marsiglia (BRZ)

BELGIUM (0)1   Albert 65
HOLLAND 0

Belgium: Preud'homme, Emmers [Dirk Medved 77], Grün, De Wolf, Philippe Albert, Borkelmans [Smidts 60], Scifo, Van der Elst, Staelens, Degryse, Weber

Holland: De Goey, Stan Valckx, Koeman, F De Boer, Rijkaard, Jonk, Wouters, Taument [Overmars 63], Bergkamp, Roy, R De Boer [Rob Witschge ht]

25 June Giants Stadium, New Jersey
72 404, Philip Don (ENG)

SAUDI ARABIA (2)2   Al Jaber pen 8, Amin 44
MOROCCO (1)1   Chaouch 27

Saudi: Al Deaye, Al Khlawi, Al Jawad, Awad Al Anazi [Abdullah Zebermawi 29], Madani, Amin, Al Bishi, Al Muwalid, Al Jebreen, Owairan, Sami Al Jaber [Fahd Al Ghesheyan 79]

Morocco: Azmi, Abdellah [Abdelsalam Laghrissi 56], Tahar El Khalej, Triki, Naybet, Azzouzi, Hadrioui, Daoudi, Hababi [Hadji 72], Chaouch, Bahja

29 June Citrus Bowl, Orlando
60 578 Alberto Tejada (PERU)

HOLLAND (1)2   Bergkamp 42, Roy 79
MOROCCO (0) 1   Nader 46

Holland: De Goey, Valckx, Koeman, F De Boer, Aron Winter, Jonk, Wouters, Witschge, Overmars [Taument 57], Bergkamp, Van Vossen [Roy 68]

Morocco: Alaoui, Samadi, Rachid Negrouz, Triki, Hadrioui, Abdelmajid Bouyboub [Hadji ht], El Khalej, Azzouzi [Daoudi 62], Hababi, Hassan Nader, Bahja

29 June RFK Stadium, Washington DC
52 959, Heinz Hellmut Krug (GER)

SAUDI ARABIA (1)1   Owairan 5
BELGIUM 0

Saudi: Al Deaye, Al Khlawi, Zebermawi, Al Jawad, Madani, Al Bishi, Jebreen, Saleh, Majed Abdullah [Al Muwalid ht], Owairan [Al Dosari 61], Falatah

Belgium: Preud'homme, Medved, Albert, De Wolf, Smidts, Staelens, Van der Elst, Boffin, Scifo, Degryse [Nilis 23], Marc Wilmots [Weber 53]

	P	W	D	L	F	A	Pts
Holland	3	2	0	1	4	3	6
Saudi Arabia	3	2	0	1	4	3	6
Belgium	3	2	0	1	2	1	6
Morocco	3	0	0	3	2	5	0

Holland, Saudi & Belgium qualify for the 2nd Round.

2nd round

2 July Soldier Field, Chicago
60 246, Kurt Röthlisberger (SWI)

GERMANY (3)3   Völler 6, 40, Klinsmann 11
BELGIUM (1)2   Grün 8, Albert 89

Germany: Illgner, Helmer, Matthäus [Brehme ht], Kohler, Berthold, Buchwald, Hässler, Sammer, Martin Wagner, Völler, Klinsmann [Stefan Kuntz 85]

Belgium: Preud'homme, Grün, Albert, De Wolf, Smidts [Boffin 65], Staelens, Van der Elst, Emmers, Scifo, Nilis [Alex Czerniatynski 77], Weber

Germany haven't lost to Belgium since 1954 and are the better side here - but they get a little help: Röthlisberger's sent home by FIFA for being honest enough to admit that he should have awarded a penalty for a foul by Helmer on Weber.

2 July RFK Stadium, Washington DC
53 121, Mario Van der Ende (HOL)

SPAIN (1)3   Hierro 15, Luis Enrique 74, Beguiristain 87
SWITZERLAND 0

Spain: Zubizarreta, Alkorta, Nadal, Camarasa, Ferrer, Abelardo, Hierro [Jorge Otero 75], Bakero, Sergi, Goikoetxea [Beguiristain 60], Luis Enrique

Switzerland: Pascolo, Höttiger, Herr, Geiger, Quentin [Jürg Studer 57], Ohrel [Subiat 72], Sforza, Bregy, Bickel, Knup, Chapuisat

In 18 matches Switzerland have never beaten Spain.

3 July Cotton Bowl, Dallas
60 277, Renato Marsiglia (BRZ)

SWEDEN (1)3   Dahlin 5, K Andersson 50, 87
SAUDI ARABIA (0)1   Al Gheshayan 85

Sweden: Ravelli, R Nilsson, P Andersson, Bjorklund [Kamark 54], Ljung, Brolin, Thern [Mild 69], Schwarz, Ingesson, Dahlin, K Andersson

Saudi: Al Deaye, Zebermawi, Madani, Al Jawad [Al Gheshayan 54], Al Khlawi, Al Jaber, Amin, Saleh, Owairan, Al Bishi [Al Muwalid 62], Falatah

3 July Rose Bowl, Pasadena
90 469, Pierluigi Pairetto (ITA)

ROMANIA (2)3   Dumitrescu 11, 18, Hagi 56
ARGENTINA (1)2   Batistuta pen 16, Balbo 75

Romania: Prunea, Prodan, Belodedici, Lupescu, Petrescu, Selymes, Popescu, Munteanu, Mihali, Hagi [Constantin Gilca 86], Dumitrescu [Papura 85]

Argentina: Islas, Sensini [Medina Bello 63], Caceres, Ruggeri, Chamot, José Basualdo, Simeone, Redondo, Ortega, Batistuta, Balbo

4 July Citrus Bowl, Orlando
61 355, Peter Mikkelsen (DEN)

HOLLAND (2)2   Bergkamp 11, Jonk 41
REP. IRELAND 0

Holland: De Goey, Winter, Valckx, Koeman, F De Boer, Rijkaard, Jonk, Witschge [Arthur Numan 78], Overmars, Bergkamp, Van Vossen [Roy 69]

Ireland: Bonner, G Kelly, McGrath, Babb, Phelan, Houghton, Keane, Sheridan, Townsend, Staunton [McAteer 62], Coyne [Tony Cascarino 73]

4 July Palo Alto
84 147, Joël Quiniou (FRA)

BRAZIL (0)1   Bebeto 74
U.S.A. 0

Brazil: Taffarel, Jorginho, Aldair, Marcio Santos, Leonardo, Mazinho, Mauro Silva, Dunga, Zinho ['Cafú' (Marcos Evangelista) 68], Bebeto, Romário

USA: Meola, Clavijo, Balboa, Lalas, Caligiuri, Ramos [Wynalda ht], Dooley, Hugo Perez [Wegerle 65], Sorber, Jones, Stewart

SENT OFF: Leonardo 44, Clavijo 87 (the oldest, at 37, to be sent off in any World Cup finals match)

5 July Foxboro, Boston
54 367, Arturo Brizio Carter (MEX)

ITALY (0)(1)2   R Baggio 88, 102 pen
NIGERIA (1)(1)1   Amunike 27

Italy: Marchegiani, Roberto Mussi, Benarrivo, Berti [D Baggio ht], Costacurta, Maldini, Donadoni, Albertini, Signori [Gianfranco Zola 64], R Baggio, Massaro

Nigeria: Rufai, Eguavon, Okechukwu, Nwanu, Emenalo, George, Oliseh, Okocha, Amunike [Adepoju 34], Yekini, Amokachi [Thompson Oliha 56]

SENT OFF: Zola 76 (on his 28th birthday!)

5 July Giants Stadium, New Jersey
71 030, Jamal Al Sharif (SYR)

BULGARIA (1)1   Stoitchkov 8
MEXICO (1)1   Garcia Aspe pen 17

Bulgaria: Mikhailov, Kremenliev, Borimirov, Khubchev, Kiriakov, Letchkov, Yordanov, Balakov, Stoitchkov, Sirakov [Bontcho Guentchev 103], Kostadinov [Petar Mikhtarski 118]
Mexico: Campos, Rodriguez, Suarez, J Ramirez, R Ramirez, Bernal, Garcia Aspe, Ambriz, L Garcia, Galindo, Zaguinho

SENT OFF: Kremenliev 50, L Garcia 58
Penalty shoot-out: Garcia Aspe missed, Balakov saved, Bernal saved, Guentchev 1-0, L Garcia saved, Borimirov 2-0, Suarez 1-2, Letchkov 3-1 (note Luis Garcia took one despite having been sent off).

Quarter-finals

9 July Foxboro, Boston
54 605, Sándor Puhl (HUN)

ITALY (1)2	D Baggio 26, R Baggio 88
SPAIN (0)1	Caminero 59

Italy: Pagliuca, Tassotti, Benarrivo, D Baggio, Costacurta, Maldini, Albertini [Signori ht], Antonio Conte [Berti 65], Donadoni, R Baggio, Massaro

Spain: Zubizarreta, Alkorta, Nadal, Abelardo, Ferrer, Caminero, Jorge Otero, Bakero [Hierro 64], Sergi [Salinas 64], Goikoetxea, Luis Enrique

Tassotti, who isn't booked in the match, is banned for eight internationals after elbowing Luis Enrique in the face.

9 July Cotton Bowl, Dallas
63 998, Rodrigo Badilla (C RICA)

BRAZIL (0)3	Romário 52, Bebeto 62, Branco 81
HOLLAND (0)2	Bergkamp 64, Winter 76

Brazil: Taffarel, Jorginho, 'Branco' (Cláudio Vaz Leal) [Cafú 89], Mazinho [Raí 80], Aldair, Marcio Santos, Mauro Silva, Dunga, Zinho, Bebeto, Romário

Holland: De Goey, Winter, Koeman Valckx, Wouters, Rijkaard [R De Boer 64], Jonk, Witschge, Overmars, Bergkamp, Van Vossen [Roy 53]

10 July Giants Stadium, New Jersey
72 416, José Torres (COL)

BULGARIA (0)2	Stoitchkov 75, Letchkov 78
GERMANY (0)1	Matthäus pen 48

Bulgaria: Mikhailov, Ivanov, Khubchev, Tzvetanov, Kiriakov, Letchkov, Yankov, Sirakov, Balakov, Kostadinov [Guentchev 90], Stoitchkov [Yordanov 84]

Germany: Illgner, Helmer, Matthäus, Kohler, Berthold, Hässler [Brehme 82], Buchwald, Möller, Wagner [Strunz 57], Klinsmann

All of the Germans' enormous international experience doesn't help in the end. They average more than 57 previous caps between them (probably a world record), but some surely win their last here...

10 July San Francisco
81 715, Philip Don (ENG)

SWEDEN (0)(1)2	Brolin 78, K Andersson 115
ROMANIA (0)(1)2	Raducioiu 88, 100

Sweden: Ravelli, R Nilsson, P Andersson, Bjorklund [Kamark 83], Ljung, Brolin, Schwarz, Mild, Ingesson, K Andersson, Dahlin [Larsson 106]

Romania: Prunea, Prodan, Belodedici, Selymes, Lupescu, Petrescu, Munteanu [Pandaru 83], Hagi, Popescu, Dumitrescu, Raducioiu

SENT OFF: Schwarz 102

Penalty shoot-out: Mild shot over, Raducioiu 1-0, K Andersson 1-1, Hagi 2-1, Brolin 2-2, Lupescu 3-2, Ingesson 3-3, Petrescu saved, Nilsson 4-3, Dumitrescu 4-4. Sudden death: Larsson 5-4, Belodedici saved.

Semi-finals

13 July Giants Stadium, New Jersey
77 094, Joël Quiniou (FRA)

ITALY (2)2	R Baggio 20, 25
BULGARIA (1)1	Stoitchkov pen 42

Italy: Pagliuca, Mussi, Benarrivo, Berti, Costacurta, Maldini, Donadoni, Albertini, D Baggio [Conte 55], R Baggio [Signori 70], Casiraghi

Bulgaria: Mikhailov, Kiriakov, Khubchev, Ivanov, Tzvetanov, Letchkov, Yankov, Sirakov, Balakov, Kostadinov [Yordanov 71], Stoitchkov [Guentchev 78]

13 July Rose Bowl, Pasadena
84 569, José Torres (COL)

BRAZIL (0)1	Romário 80
SWEDEN 0	

Brazil: Taffarel, Jorginho, Branco, Mazinho [Raí ht], Aldair, Marcio Santos, Dunga, Mauro Silva, Zinho, Bebeto, Romário

Sweden: Ravelli, R Nilsson, P Andersson, Bjorklund, Ljung, Brolin, Thern, Mild, Ingesson, Dahlin [Stefan Rehn 68], K Andersson

3rd-place final

16 July Rose Bowl, Pasadena
83 716, Ali Mohamed Bujsaim (UAE)

SWEDEN (4)4	Brolin 8, Mild 30, Larsson 37, K Andersson 39
BULGARIA 0	

Sweden: Ravelli, R Nilsson, P Andersson, Bjorklund, Kamark, Brolin, Mild, Schwarz, Ingesson, Larsson [Anders Limpar 78], K Andersson

Bulgaria: Mikhailov [Plamen Nikolov ht], Kiriakov, Ivanov [Kremenliev 41], Khubchev, Tzvetanov, Letchkov, Yankov, Sirakov, Balakov, Stoitchkov, Kostadinov [Yordanov ht]

Final

17 July Rose Bowl, Pasadena
94 194, Sándor Puhl (HUN)

BRAZIL   0
ITALY   0

Brazil: Taffarel, Jorginho [Cafú 20], Branco, Mazinho ['Viola' (Paulo Sergio Rosa) 106], Aldair, Marcio Santos, Mauro Silva, Dunga, Zinho, Bebeto, Romário

Italy: Pagliuca, Mussi [Apolloni 34], Benarrivo, Berti, Maldini, Baresi, Donadoni, Albetini, D Baggio [Evani 94], R Baggio, Massaro

Penalty shoot-out: Baresi shot over, Marcio Santos saved, Albertini 1-0, Romário 1-1, Evani 2-1, Branco 2-2, Massaro saved, Dunga 3-2, R Baggio shot over.

The first goalless World Cup final and the first decided on penalties.

World Cup: some records
Finals tournaments only.

MATCHES
21 Uwe Seeler	W Germany	1958-70
21 Wladyslaw Zmuda	Poland	1974-86
21 Diego Maradona	Argentina	1982-94
21 Lothar Matthäus	WG/Germany	1982-94
20 Grzegorz Lato	Poland	1974-82

CAPTAIN IN MOST TOURNAMENTS
3 Billy Wright	England	1950-54-58
3 Diego Maradona	Argentina	1986-90-94

Maradona 16 matches, Wright 10.

YOUNGEST PLAYERS
yrs days
17 41	Norman Whiteside
N Ireland 1982	
17 235	Pelé Brazil
1958	
17 353	Rigobert Song
Cameroon1994	

OLDEST PLAYERS
42 34	Roger Miller
(Milla)Cameroon	1994
41 00	Pat Jennings N
Ireland1986	
40 292	Peter Shilton
England 1990	
40 133	Dino Zoff Italy
1982	
39 260	Angelito Labruna
Argentina 1958	
39 259	Joseph-Antoine
BellCameroon	1994
39 145	Stanley Matthews

Cerebral Palsy World Cup
6-13 Aug 1994 Dublin

GROUP 1
Portugal	2	G Britain	0
Spain	8	Brazil	2
Portugal	2	Argentina	0
G Britain	2	Brazil	0
Spain	3	Argentina	1
Spain	1	G Britain	0
Portugal	3	Brazil	0
Argentina	0	G Britain	0
Portugal	2	Spain	1
Argentina	1	Brazil	0

	P	W	D	L	F	A	Pts
Portugal	4	4	0	0	9	1	8
Spain	4	3	0	1	13	5	6
G Britain	4	1	1	2	2	3	3
Argentina	4	1	1	2	2	5	3
Brazil	4	0	0	4	2	14	0

GROUP 2
Belgium	2	France	0
Holland	5	Ireland	0
Belgium	1	Holland	0
Ireland	8	France	0
Holland	7	France	0
Ireland	2	Belgium	1

	P	W	D	L	F	A	Pts
Holland	3	2	0	1	12	1	4
Ireland	3	2	0	1	10	6	4
Belgium	3	2	0	1	3	2	4
France	3	0	0	3	0	17	0

SEMI-FINALS
Holland	3	Spain	0
Ireland	3	Portugal	0

3rd-PLACE FINAL
Spain	2	Portugal	1

FINAL
Holland	2	Ireland	0

England 1993-94

8 Sep 1993 Wembley
World Cup qualifier
70 220, Frans Van den Wijngaert (BEL)

ENGLAND (1)3   Ferdinand 5, Gascoigne 49,
                      Pearce 53

POLAND 0

England: David Seaman, Rob Jones, Stuart Pearce (c),
David Platt, Tony Adams, Gary Pallister, Paul Ince, Paul
Gascoigne, Les Ferdinand, Ian Wright, Lee Sharpe

Poland: Jaroslaw Bako, Andrzej Lesiak, Piotr
Czachowski, Marek Kozminski, Dariusz Adamczuk
[Jacek Bak 77], Jerzy Brzeczek, Robert Warzycha, Piotr
Swiercewski, Roman Kosecki (c), Jan Furtok [Jacek
Ziober ht], Marek Lesniak

*Gascoigne thumps the clinching goal but the old Adam
can't help rising: an unnecessary booking rules him out
of the next game. The last shreds of midfield creativity
(and realistic hopes of qualifying) go with him.*

13 Oct 1993 Feyenoord, Rotterdam
World Cup qualifier
48 000, Karl-Josef Assenmacher (GER)

HOLLAND (0)2   R Koeman 61, Bergkamp 68
ENGLAND 0

Holland: Ed De Goey, Ronald Koeman (c), Frank De
Boer, John De Wolf, Jan Wouters, Frank Rijkaard, Marc
Overmars [Aron Winter 74], Dennis Bergkamp, Ronald
De Boer [Ulrich van Gobbel 91], Erwin Koeman, Bryan
Roy

England: Seaman, Paul Parker, Tony Dorigo, Carlton
Palmer [Andy Sinton ht], Adams, Pallister, Platt (c),
Ince, Alan Shearer, Paul Merson [Ian Wright 68], Lee
Sharpe

*England have no luck – Pearce & Ferdinand are injured,
Gazza suspended, Dorigo & Merson hit a post – and
wuz arguably robbed – R Koeman should have been
sent off for fouling Platt (Assenmacher's left out of the
finals for showing only the yellow card) but stays on to
score from a twice-taken free-kick after Ince is booked
for charging the first shot – but Holland are clearly, if
only just, the better side: Rijkaard has a goal wrongly
disallowed and forces Seaman to a tremendous save.
The following season, Graham Taylor buys De Wolf for
de Wolves.*

17 Nov 1993 Renato Dall'Ara, Bologna
World Cup qualifier
2378, Muhammed Nazri (MALAY)

SAN MARINO (1)1   Gualtieri 1
ENGLAND (3)7   Ince 22, 72, Wright 33, 46,
                      78, 88, Ferdinand 38

This sport in life
*Some extreme racists, those who don't count
goals scored by black players, presumably have
to look back on a 1-0 win for San Marino...*

S Marino: Pierluigi Benedettini, Pier Angelo Manzaroli,
Mauro Valentini [Luca Gobbi 47], Claudio Canti, William
Guerra, Mirco Gennari, Loris Zanotti, Pier Domenico
Della Valle, Massimo Bonini (c), Davide Gualtieri, Nicola
Bacciocchi [Paolo Mazza 61]

England: Seaman, Lee Dixon, Pearce (c), Ince, Des
Walker, Pallister, Platt, Stuart Ripley, Ferdinand, I
Wright, Sinton

*England need to win by seven goals while Holland lose
in Poland, but neither half of the equation ever looks
very likely, especially after Pearce's back pass leads to
the fastest goal ever scored in any England match
(no later than 8.82 secs), in front of the smallest crowd
to watch a senior England game since 1883. Ripley
wins his only cap so far. Wright's the first black player
to score four goals in an England match.*

9 March 1994 Wembley
Friendly
71 970, Jacobus (Jaap) Uilenberg (HOL)

ENGLAND (1)1   Platt 16
DENMARK 0

England: Seaman, Parker, Graeme Le Saux, Ince [David
Batty 66], Adams, Pallister, Platt (c), Gascoigne [Matt
Le Tissier 66], Peter Beardsley, Darren Anderton

Denmark: Peter Schmeichel, Lars Olsen (c), Carsten
Dethlefsen, John Jensen, Marc Rieper Jensen, Jakob
Kjeldbjerg, Henrik Larsen, Kim Vilfort [Jes Hogh 70],
Bent Christensen [Soren Frederiksen 70], Michael
Laudrup, Brian Laudrup

*The new dawn creeps up slowly but pleasantly enough.
Venables' first match in charge ushers in some good
things, most of them playing to feet: Beardsley, recalled
for his 50th cap; the new caps Anderton, who has a
shot kicked off the line, and Le Saux; Shearer, alone up
front, making the goal. Promises, promises. Le Saux &
Le Tissier are the first Channel Islanders to win senior
England caps.*

17 May 1994 Wembley
Friendly
23 659, Jim McCluskey (SCOT)

ENGLAND (3)5   Anderton 23, Beardsley 37,
                      Platt 44 pen, 54, Shearer 65

GREECE 0

England: Tim Flowers, Jones [Pearce 82], Le Saux,
Kevin Richardson, Steve Bould, Adams, Platt (c),
Merson, Shearer, Beardsley [I Wright 70],
Anderton [Le Tissier 62]

Greece: Christos Karkamanis, Stratos Apostolakis, Vaios Karayiannis, Thanasis Kolitsidakis [Kiriakos Karataidis ht], Panayiotis Tsalouhidis (c), Minas Hantzidis [Tasos Mitropoulos ht], Nikos Noblias, Nikos Machlas [Dimitris Saravakos ht], Savas Kofidis [Christos Kostis 70], Nikos Tsiantakis

Hm, some early blossoming (though there's something worryingly Tayloresque about the choice of two 30-y-o debutants, Richardson & Bould), but no-one's unduly carried away: Greece only reached the finals because Yugoslavia were kept out, and it shows. Saravakos' 73rd cap equals the national record.

22 May 1994 Wembley
Friendly
64 327, Kim Nielsen (DEN)

ENGLAND 0
NORWAY 0

England: Seaman, Jones, Le Saux, Ince [Le Tissier 76], Bould, Adams, Platt (c), Beardsley, Shearer, Dennis Wise, Anderton [I Wright 76]

Norway: Erik Thorstvedt [Ola By Rise 86], Henning Berg, Erland Johnsen, Rune Bratseth (c), Roger Nilsen [Alf Inge Haland ht], Jostein Flo, Orjan Berg [Kare Ingebrigtsen 67], Lars Bohinen, Jan Age Fjortoft [Goran Sorloth ht], Kjetil Rekdal, Jahn Ivar Jakobsen

Norway pour some cold water on the parade, and probably think they've achieved something, but if this is how they intend to play in the finals...Eight of the team (seven of the starting line-up) play in the English league. The last time England played fewer matches in a season was in 1934-35.

England 1994-95

7 Sep 1994 Wembley
Friendly
38 629, Antonio Jesus Lopez Nieto (SPA)

ENGLAND (2)2   Shearer 33, 39
U.S.A. 0

England: Seaman, Jones, Le Saux, Platt (c), Adams, Pallister, Barry Venison, Shearer [I Wright 81], Teddy Sheringham [Ferdinand 81], John Barnes, Anderton

USA: Brad Friedel [Jürgen Sommer 81], Paul Caligiuri, Jeff Agoos [Mike Lapper 71], Tom Dooley (c), Alexi Lalas, Marcelo Balboa, Hugo Perez [Eric Wynalda h/t], Mike Sorber, Ernie Stewart [Frank Klopas 81], Cobi Jones, Claudio Reyna [Joe-Max Moore 81]

Attempts by Friedel (Newcastle) & Jones (Coventry) to join Premier League clubs are being frustrated by the Home Office. The English FA rather crassly offer a $25,000 win bonus to the Americans.

12 Oct 1994 Wembley
Friendly
48 754, Joël Quiniou (FRA)

ENGLAND (1)1   Lee 45
ROMANIA (1)1   Dumitrescu 36

England: Seaman, Jones [Pearce 59], Le Saux, Ince, Adams (c), Pallister, Robert Lee [Wise 71], Le Tissier, Barnes, I Wright [Sheringham 71], Shearer

Romania: Bogdan Stelea [Florian Prunea 87], Dan Petrescu, Daniel Prodan, Miodrag Belodedici, Ionut Lupescu, Gheorghe (Gica) Popescu, Ilie Dumitrescu, Florin Raducioiu [Daniel Timofte 77], Marius Lacatus [Florin Cîrstea 80], Gheorghe Hagi (c)[Tibor Selymes h/t], Dorinel Munteanu

Lee scores on debut. A player from the Premier League scores the first goal conceded by Venables' England. Romania have drawn all four of their matches in England (all at Wembley), a record.

16 Nov 1994 Wembley
Friendly
37 196, Leif Sundell (SWE)

ENGLAND (1)1   Platt 41
NIGERIA 0

England: Flowers, Jones, Le Saux, Platt (c), Steve Howey, Neil Ruddock, Wise, Beardsley [Le Tissier 78], Shearer [Sheringham 78], Lee [Steve McManaman 26], Barnes

Nigeria: Peter Rufai (c), Uche Okechukwu, Uche Okafor, Benedict (Ben) Iroha, Augustin Eguavon, Mutiu Adepoju [Nwanko Kanu 85], Augustine Okocha, Emanuel Amunike [Victor Ikpeba 61], Rashidi Yekini [Efan Ekoku 61], Daniel Amokachi, Finidi George

A little respite for Venables after a second Panorama programme (he issued a writ against the first) investigates his financial dealings (this, he says, while the BBC were offering him a four-year contract). Howey, Ruddock & McManaman win their first caps, Platt his 50th.

Most times only England scorer in a match

17	Gary Lineker	1986-91
11	David Platt	1990-94
6	Jimmy Greaves	1959-65

England goals

49	Bobby Charlton	1958-70	3 pen
48	Gary Lineker	1985-92	4 pen
44	Jimmy Greaves	1959-67	
24	David Platt	1990-94	2 pen

Scotland 1993-94

8 Sep 1993 Pittodrie
World Cup qualifier
24 000, Joël Quiniou (FRA)

SCOTLAND (0)1   Collins 50
SWITZERLAND (0)1   Bregy pen 69

Scotland: Bryan Gunn, Stewart McKimmie, Brian Irvine, Craig Levein, John Robertson, Pat Nevin, Dave Bowman [Phil O'Donnell 75], Gary McAllister, John Collins, Scott Booth [Eoin Jess 75], Gordon Durie

Switzerland: Marco Pascolo, Yvan Quentin, Dominique Herr, Alain Geiger, Régis Rothenbühler [Marco Grassi 55], Christophe Ohrel, Georges Bregy, Ciraco Sforza, Alain Sutter, Adrian Knup, Stéphane Chapuisat

13 Oct Olimpico, Rome
World Cup qualifier
61 178, Ion Craciunescu (ROM)

ITALY (2)3   Donadoni 3, Casiraghi 16, Eranio 80
SCOTLAND (1)1   Gallacher 18

Italy: Gianluca Pagliuca, Roberto Mussi [Marco Lanna 68], Antonio Benarrivo, Dino Baggio, Alessandro Costacurta, Franco Baresi (c), Stefano Eranio, Roberto Donadoni, Pierluigi Casiraghi, Roberto Baggio, Giovanni Stroppa [Gianfranco Zola 90]

Scotland: Gunn, McKimmie, Tommy Boyd, Alan McLaren, Brian Irvine, Bowman [Paul McStay 70], Durie, Stuart McCall, Jess [Ian Durrant ht], McAllister, Kevin Gallacher

17 Nov 1993 National Stadium, Ta'Qali, Valletta
World Cup qualifier
7000, Vasilakis (GRE)

MALTA 0
SCOTLAND (1)2   McKinlay 15, Hendry 74

Malta: David Cluett, Silvio Vella, Richard Buhagiar [Nicky Saliba ht], Joe Galea, Joe Brincat, John Buttigieg, Carmel Busuttil, Michael Spiteri, Hubert Suda [Charlie Scerri 74], Christian Laferla, Martin Gregory

Scotland: Jim Leighton, McLaren, Rob McKinnon, Durrant [Boyd 74], Colin Hendry, Irvine, Ferguson, Billy McKinlay [Booth ht], Nevin, McAllister, Gallacher

23 March 1994 Hampden Park, Glasgow
Friendly
35 000, Ib Nielsen (DEN)

SCOTLAND 0
HOLLAND (1)1   Roy 22

Scotland: Andy Goram, McKimmie, Robertson [Collins 65], McLaren, Hendry, Levein [Jess 66], McCall, McStay [McKinlay ht], Durie, McAllister, Nevin [Boyd ht]

Holland: Ed De Goey, Ulrich Van Gobbel, Frank De Boer, Danny Blind, Rob Witschge, Wim Jonk, Gaston Taument [Marc Overmars 78], Frank Rijkaard, Johnny Bosman [Aron Winter ht], Dennis Bergkamp [Hans Gillhaus ht], Bryan Roy

20 April 1994 Prater, Vienna
Friendly
35 000, Albrecht (GER)

AUSTRIA (1)1   Hütter 13
SCOTLAND (1)2   McGinlay 35, McKinlay 60

Austria: Franz Wohlfahrt [Michael Konsel ht], Peter Schöttel, Walter Kogler, Walter Hochmaier, Christian Prosenik, Peter Stöger [Dietmar Kuhbauer ht], Michael Baur, Andreas Herzog, Adolf Hütter, Harald Cerny, Toni Polster [Thomas Weissenberger 62]

Scotland: Leighton, McKimmie, Hendry, McLaren, Irvine, McKinlay, McAllister, Collins [McCall 85], Boyd [Ferguson ht], John McGinlay [Duncan Shearer 76], Jess [Nevin 84]

27 May Nieuw Galgewaard, Utrecht
Friendly
15 000, Ansuategui (SPA)

HOLLAND (1)3   Roy 17, Van Vossen 61, Irvine og 72
SCOTLAND (0)1   Shearer 81

Holland: De Goey, Stan Valckx, F De Boer, Ronald De Boer [Numan ht], Jonk, Rob Witschge, Jan Wouters, Winter, Overmars, Ruud Gullit [Peter Van Vossen ht], Roy [Taument 71]

Scotland: Leighton [Gunn ht], Steve Clarke, McKimmie, McCall, Hendry, Irvine, Durie [Jess ht], McKinlay [Nevin 81], McGinlay [Shearer 75], McAllister, Collins [Ferguson 61]

Scotland 1994-95

7 Sep Olympic, Helsinki
European Ch qualifier
12 845, R Wijcik (POL)

FINLAND 0
SCOTLAND (1)2   Shearer 29, Collins 66

Finland: Petri Jakonen, Janne Mäkelä, Aki Hyryláinen, Markku Kanerva, Antti Heinola [Erik Holmgren 29], Kim Suominen, Jari Litmanen, Janne Lindberg, Rami Rantanen [Petri Järvinen 41], Ari Hjelm (c), Mika-Matti (Mixu) Paatelainen

Scotland: Goram, McKimmie, Hendry, Levein [McCall 78], Boyd, McStay, McAllister (c), McLaren, Collins, Andy Walker [Jess 65], Shearer

The 32-y-o Shearer starts an international for the first time.

12 Oct 1994 Hampden Park, Glasgow
European Ch qualifier
20 885, T Hauge (NOR)

SCOTLAND (3)5	McGinlay 4, Booth 34, Collins 40, 72, McKinlay 61
FAEROE ISLANDS (0)1	Muller 75

Scotland: Goram, McLaren, Hendry [McKinlay 58], Levein, McKimmie, Nevin, McStay (c), Collins, Boyd, McGinlay, Booth [Walker 69]

Faeroes: Jens Martin Knudsen, Julian Hansen, Tummas Eli Hansen, Jon Johannesen, Ossur Hansen, Jan Dam [Joensen 53], Magni Jarnskor (c), Morkore, Henning Jarnskor, Jan Muller, Todi Jonsson

Easy as expected for the Scots, though they're indebted to Goram's save when Jonsson breaks clear with the score 1-0. Faeroes' manager Allan Simonsen, the great Danish international, bans Knudsen from wearing his celebrated bobble hat, whereupon he concedes ten goals in two games.

16 Nov 1994 Hampden Park, Glasgow
European Ch qualifier
31 254, Bo Karlsson (SWE)

SCOTLAND (1)1	Booth 19
RUSSIA (1)1	Radchenko 25

Scotland: Goram, McKimmie, Levein, McLaren, Boyd, McKinlay [Nevin 83], McAllister (c), McCall, Collins, McGinlay [John Spencer 64], Booth

Russia: Stanislav Cherchesov, Yuri Nikiforov, Sergei Gorlukovich, Viktor Onopko (c), Vasily Kulkov, Andrei Kanchelskis, Valery Karpin, Andrei Piatnitski [Omari Tetradze 71], Igor Shalimov, Vladislav Radimov, Dmitry Radchenko

18 Dec 1994 Olympic, Athens,
European Ch qualifier
20 000 John Blankenstein (HOL)

GREECE (1)1	Apostolakis pen 18
SCOTLAND 0	

Greece: Ilias Amatzidis, Theodoros Zagorakis, Yannis Kalitzakis, Mihalis Vlahos, Stratos Apostolakis (c), Mihalis Kasapis, Nikos Noblias (Aristidis Karasavidis 88), Panayotis Tsalouhidis, Yorgos Tursinidis, Alexandros Alexandris (Spiros Maragos 72), Nikos Machlas

Scotland: Goram (Leighton 78), McKimmie, Boyd, McCall, Hendry, McLaren, McKinlay (Spencer ht), McAllister (c), Collins, Ferguson, McGinlay

A harsh penalty, awarded for a foul by Hendry on Alexandris, gives the World Cup whipping boys maximum points from four games and leaves Scotland struggling to qualify.

Wales 1993-94

8 Sep 1993 National Stadium, Cardiff
World Cup qualifier
37 558, Ansuategui (SPA)

WALES (2)2	Giggs 21, Rush 35
CZECHOSLOVAKIA (1)2	Kuka 16, Dubovsky 67

Wales: Neville Southall, David Phillips, Mark Bowen, Mark Aizlewood, Eric Young, Kit Symons, Barry Horne (c), Dean Saunders, Ian Rush, Mark Hughes, Ryan Giggs

Czechoslovakia: Petr Kouba, Radoslav Látal, Jan Suchopárek, Ivan Hasek, Miroslav Kadlec, Václav Nemecek, Pavel Hapal, Jirí Novotny, Pavel Kuka, Peter Dubovsky, Lubomír Moravcík

13 Oct 1993 National Stadium, Cardiff
World Cup qualifier
30 825, Philip Don (ENG)

WALES (0)2	Saunders 70, Rush 86
CYPRUS 0	

WAles: Southall, Phillips, Symons [Jeremy Goss 70], Aizlewood, Young, Horne, Gary Speed, Saunders, Rush, M Hughes, Giggs

Cyprus: Andros Petrides, Costas Costa, Charalambos Pittas [Panayiotis Xiourouppas 78], Costas Constantinou, Evagoras Christofi, Yiannis Yiangoudakis (c) [George Panayi 78], Dimitris Ioannou, Neophytos Larkou, Andros Sotiriou, Nikos Papavasiliou, Marios Charalambous

Costa (50m) & Constantinou (80m) both sent off. Yiangoudakis wins his 68th (and to date last) cap, adding to his national record.

17 Nov 1993 National Stadium, Cardiff
World Cup qualifier
40 000, Kurt Röthlisberger (SWI)

WALES (0)1	Saunders 61
ROMANIA (1)2	Hagi 32, Raducioiu 83

Wales: Southall, Phillips, Paul Bodin [Malcolm Allen 71], Andy Melville, Young, Symons [Goss 53], Horne, Saunders, Rush, Speed, Giggs

Romania: Florian Prunea, Dan Petrescu, Daniel Prodan, Miodrag Belodedici, Ionut Lupescu, Gheorghe Popescu, Tibor Selymes [Dorinel Munteanu 74], Ioan Ovidiu Sabau, Florin Raducioiu, Gheorghe Hagi, Ilie Dumitrescu [Gheorghe Mihali 89]

Bodin, whose three goals for Wales have all been penalties, misses one in an international for the first time, hitting the bar with the scores level (63m).

9 March 1994 National Stadium, Cardiff
Friendly
10 000, John Ferry (N IRE)

WALES (0)1   Coleman 89
NORWAY (1)3   Flo 6, Mykland 49, Jacobsen 51

Wales: Southall, Phillips, Young, Melville, Chris
Coleman, Perry, Horne (c), Blake [Mark Pembridge 59],
Speed [Saunders 59], Rush, M Hughes [Ceri Hughes ht]

Norway: Frode Grodas, Karl Petter Loken, Tore
Pedersen, Henning Berg, Stig Bjornebye, Jostein Flo,
Erik Mykland, Lars Bohinen, Jan Age Fjortoft [Geir
Frigard 79], Kjetil Rekdal [Stale Solbakken 68], Jan Ivar
Jakobsen

John Toshack must have seen enough: he resigns as
national coach after just this one match.

20 April 1994 Racecourse, Wrexham
Friendly
4694, Shorte (EIRE)

WALES 0
SWEDEN (0)2   Larsson 83, Brolin 90

Wales: Southall, Bowen [Clayton Blackmore 60], Alan
Neilson, Melville, Bodin, Horne (c), Phillips, Goss (C
Hughes 81], Speed, Rush, Iwan Roberts [Blake 81]

Sweden: Thomas Ravelli, Roland Nilsson [Mikael
Nilsson 72], Patrik Andersson, Joachim Bjorklund,
Roger Ljung, Stefan Schwarz, Anders Limpar [Jesper
Blomqvist 70], Klas Ingesson, Kennet Andersson
[Niklas Kindvall 81], Henrik Larsson, Tomas Brolin

'No, no regrets.' (JB Toshack)

23 May 1994 Tallinn
Friendly
3500

ESTONIA (0)1   Reim pen
WALES (0)2   Rush, Phillips

Estonia: Mart Poom, Toomas Kallaste, Marek Lemsalu,
Igor Prins, Urmas Kaljend, Dzintar Klavan Indro
Olumets [Mati Pari 78], Tarmo Linnumae, Marko
Kristal, Martin Reim, Meelis Lindmaa

Wales: Southall, Melvile, Melville [Bodin 72], Neilson,
Coleman, Phillips, Horne, Ryan Jones, Hughes, Rush,
Jason Bowen

Wales 1994-95

7 Sep 1994 National Stadium, Cardiff
European Ch qualifier
6500, G Beschin (ITA)

WALES (1)2   Coleman 9, Giggs 67
ALBANIA 0

Wales: Southall, Adrian Williams, Melville, Coleman,
Bodin, Phillips, Goss [Pembridge 75], Speed, Giggs,
Rush, Blake [I Roberts 80]

Albania: Foto Strakosha, Ilir Shulku, A Xhumba, Rudi
Vata, Salvador Kacaj, A Kola [Indrit Fortuzi 53], A Bellai,
Ledio Pano, Besnik Kola, Sulejman Demollari, Ylli
Shehu [Eduard Dosti 82]

12 Oct 1994 Stadionul Republican, Kishinev
European Ch qualifier
15 000, I Vad (HUN)

MOLDOVA (2)3   Belous 9, Seku 29,
                     Pogorelov 79
WALES (1)2   Speed 6, Blake 70

Moldova: Vasili Koshelev, Serghei Secu, Sergei Belous,
Valery Pogorelov, Rabeja, Sergei Stroenko, Igor Oprea,
Kurican, Nani, Alexandru Spiridon (c), Miterev [Vladimir
Kosse h/t]

Wales: Southall, Symons, Bowen, A Williams, Coleman,
Phillips, Horne (c), Pembridge, I Roberts, Speed, Blake
[Melville 87]

Not as embarrassing as it looks. Wales are without
Rush, Giggs, Hughes, Saunders & Goss, and Moldova
have some classy players. Their first goal (Belous' 30-
yard volley) and their last (Pogorelov's persistent run
and fine shot) are both featured on BBC's Goal Of The
Month. Speed (in his 27th international) & Blake score
their first international goals, Blake has another
disallowed at 1-2 after shooting over when clear
through in the first half.

16 Nov 1994 Boris Paichadze, Tbilisi
European Ch qualifier
45 000, A Sars (FRA)

GEORGIA (2)5   Ketsbaia 31, 49, Kinkladze 41,
                     Gogrichiani 59, Arveladze 67
WALES 0

Georgia: Devadze, Revichvilki, Khakhaber (Khaki)
Tskadadze, Cheliya, Chikhradze, Gogichaichvili,
Nehsadze [Inalichili 42], Gogrichiani, Temur Ketsbaia
[Kavelachvili 75], Kinkladze, Arveladze

Wales: Southall, Neilson [Symons h/t], Bowen, Melville,
Coleman, Phillips, Horne, Saunders, Rush, Hughes,
Speed

Yet again, the use of so many attacking players doesn't
work: Wales suffer their worst defeat for 41 years.

14 Dec 1994 National Stadium Cardiff
European Ch qualifier

WALES 0
BULGARIA (2)3   Ivanov 3, Kostadinov 15,
                     Stoitchkov 51

Wales: Southall, Phillips, Melville, Aizlewood, Coleman,
Bowen, Speed, Hughes, Vinny Jones, Saunders, Rush (c).

Bulgaria: Borislav Mikhailov, Emil Kremenliev, Zlatko Yankov, Trifon Ivanov, Ivailo Yordanov, Tzanko Tzvetanov, Yordan Letchkov, Emil Kostadinov [Ilian Kiriakov 73], Krasimir Balakov, Liuboslav Penev [Nasko Sirakov], Christo Stoitchkov

The Welsh manager on Vincent Peter Jones: 'Some of his tackles are rash and dreadful' (they've won him 42 yellow and two red cards in the last four years). Despite this - no, because of it, of course - he adds an estimated 10 000 (worth £100 000) to the crowd, but ultimately he's just Jones the Red Herring, outclassed like all the rest by the World Cup thoroughbreds.

N Ireland 1993-94

8 Sep 1993 Windsor Park, Belfast
World Cup qualifier
6400, Correia (SPA)

N IRELAND (1)2   Quinn 35, Gray 80
LATVIA 0

N Ireland: Tommy Wright, Gary Fleming, Nigel Worthington, Gerry Taggart, Mal Donaghy, Jim Magilton, Kevin Wilson, Jimmy Quinn, Michael Hughes, Iain Dowie, Philip Gray

Latvia: Oleg Karavayev, Igor Troiitsky, Oleg Alexelenko, Valery Ivanov, Einars Gnedoy, Yuri Popkov, Alexei Sharando, Yuri Shevliakov, Vladimir Babichev, Ainars Linards, Aleksandr Yeliseyev

13 Oct 1993 Parken, Copenhagen
World Cup qualifier
40 200, Vadim Zhuk (BYL)

DENMARK (0)1   B Laudrup 81
N IRELAND 0

Denmark: Peter Schmeichel, Kim Vilfort, Marc Rieper Jensen, Lars Olsen (c), Jakob Kjeldberg, Brian Steen Nielsen, John Jensen, Frank Pingel [Henrik Larsen 87], Flemming Povlsen, Brian Laudrup, Michael Laudrup

N Ireland: Wright, Fleming, Alan McDonald, Taggart, Worthington, Wilson [Kingsley Black 85], Donaghy, Magilton, M Hughes, Dowie [Quinn 61], Gray

17 Nov 1993 Windsor Park, Belfast
World Cup qualifier
10 200, Ahmet Çakar (TURK)

N IRELAND (0)1   Quinn 73
REP IRELAND (0)1   McLoughlin 78

N Ireland: Wright, Fleming, Worthington, Taggart, Alan McDonald, Donaghy, Wilson [Kingsley Black 82], Magilton, Quinn, Gray [Dowie 72], Hughes

Ireland: Pat Bonner, Dennis Irwin, Terry Phelan, Paul McGrath, Roy Keane, Andy Townsend, Ray Houghton

[Alan McLoughlin 70], Niall Quinn, Aldridge [Tony Cascarino 81], Eddie McGoldrick

23 March 1994 Windsor Park, Belfast
Friendly
5 500, Keith Burge (WAL)

N IRELAND (1)2   Morrow 42, Gray 49
ROMANIA 0

N Ireland: Wright, Fleming, Taggart, Donaghy, C Wilson, Magilton, Steve Morrow, Lomas, M Hughes [Black ht], Quinn [Dowie 76], Gray

Romania: Florian Prunea [Bogdan Stelea 73], Miodrag Belodedici, Daniel Prodan, Gheorghe Popescu [Constantin Gilca 76], Dan Petrescu [Moldovan 70], Ioan Ovidiu Sabau [Mihali 70], Ionut Lupescu, Gheorghe Hagi, Dorinel Munteanu, Florin Raducioiu, Ilie Dumitrescu

SENT OFF: Hagi.

20 April 1994 Windsor Park, Belfast
European Ch qualifier
4 500, Lingue (HOL)

N IRELAND (3)4   Quinn 5, 33, Lomas 23,
                        Dowie 48
LIECHTENSTEIN (0)1   Hasler 84

N Ireland: Wright, Fleming, Taggart, Donaghy, Worthington, K Wilson, Magilton, Lomas [Michael O'Neill 81], M Hughes, Quinn, Dowie [P Gray 78]

Liechtenstein: Martin Oehry, Heini Stocker [Daniel Hasler 68], Christoph Frick, Wolfgang Ospelt, Roland Moser, Jürg Ritter, Alexander Quaderer, Harry Zech, Mario Frick, Daniel Telser, Christian Matt [Thomas Hanselmann 64]

4 June 1994 Foxboro, Boston
Friendly
4000

COLOMBIA (2)2   Perez 30, Valencia 44
N IRELAND 0

Colombia: Oscar Cordoba, Andres Escobar, Luis Herrera, Gabriel Gomez, Carlos Valderrama (c), Adolfo Valencia [Antony De Avila 61], Leonel Alvarez, Luis Perea, Fredy Rincón, Wilson Perez, Faustino Asprilla [Victor Aristizábal 62]

N Ireland: Wright, Fleming, Worthington, Taggart, Donaghy, Magilton [Robbie Dennison 76], Wilson [Lomas 59], Morrow, Quinn [O'Boyle 59], Dowie [Paterson ht], Hughes

11 June 1994 Miami
Friendly 8498

MEXICO (2)3   L Garcia 18 pen, 30,
                     Hermosillo 77
N IRELAND 0

Mexico: Jorge Campos, Ignacio Ambriz (c), Raúl Gutierrez, Juan Ramirez, Ramón Ramirez, Cláudio Suarez, Gabriel Bernal, Joaquin Del Olmo, 'Zaguinho' (Luis Zague Alves), Luis Garcia [Benjamin Galindo 47], Hugo Sánchez [Carlos Hermosillo 69]

N Ireland: Alan Fettis [Wright ht], Fleming [Morrow 74], Worthington, Taggart, Donaghy, Magilton [Patterson ht], Hughes, K Wilson [N Lennon ht], Quinn [Dowie ht], O'Boyle, Lomas

N Ireland 1994-95

7 Sep 1994 Windsor Park
European Ch qualifier
6000, R Pedersen (NOR)

| N IRELAND (0)1 | Quinn pen 58 |
| PORTUGAL (1)2 | Costa 8, Domingos 81 |

N Ireland: Fettis, Fleming, McDonald [Taggart 82], Morrow, Worthington, Keith Gillespie [O'Boyle 82], Magilton, Lomas, Hughes, Gray, Quinn

Portugal: Vitor Baía, João Pinto I, Paulo Madeira, Hélder, Paulinho Santos, Tavares, Paulo Sousa, Vítor Paneira [Folha 63], Luis Figo, Rui Costa, Sa Pinto [Domingos 68]

12 Oct 1994 Prater, Vienna
European Ch qualifier
20 000, Antonio Jesus Lopez Nieto (SPA)

| AUSTRIA (1)1 | Polster pen 24 |
| N IRELAND (2)2 | Gillespie 3, Gray 36 |

Austria: Franz Wohlfarth, Wolfgang Feiersinger, Werner-Klausriegler, Johann Kogler, Peter Schöttel, Christian Prosenik [Heimo Pfeifenberger 67], Anton Ogris [Ralph Hasenhüttl h/t], Peter Artner, Anton (Toni) Ploster (c), Peter Stöger, Adolf Hütter

N Ireland: Kee, Fleming, Worthington, Taggart, McDonald, Lomas, Gillespie [O'Neill 56], Magilton, Dowie [Quinn 74], Gray, Hughes

In his second international, N Ireland's best young prospect for a generation announces himself to a wider audience with a full-blooded early volleyed goal.

16 Nov 1994 Windsor Park, Belfast
European Ch qualifier
10 336, Serge Muhmenthaler (SWI)

| N IRELAND 0 | |
| REP IRELAND (3)4 | Aldridge 6, Keane 11, Sheridan 38, Townsend 54 |

N Ireland: Kee, Fleming, Taggart, Morrow (c), O'Neill [Patterson h/t], Worthington, Gillespie [Wilson 62], Magilton, Hughes, Dowie, Gray

Rep Ireland: Alan Kelly, Gary Kelly, Paul McGrath, Phil

Babb, Dennis Irwin, John Sheridan, Roy Keane [Jason McAteer h/t], Andy Townsend (c), Steve Staunton, John Aldridge [Tommy Coyne 80], Niall Quinn

N Ireland, weakened by the loss of Quinn and especially Wright & McDonald, lose to the Republic in Belfast for the first time. Kee, a hero in Vienna, is at fault with three of the goals, Keane (in his 27th match) scoring his first at this level.

Rep Ireland 1993-94

8 Sep 1993 Lansdowne Road, Dublin
World Cup qualifier
30 000, Petersen (DEN)

| REP IRELAND (2)2 | Aldridge 4, Kernaghan 25 |
| LITHUANIA 0 | |

Ireland: Pat Bonner, Dennis Irwin, Kevin Moran, Alan Kernaghan, Terry Phelan, Ray Houghton, Roy Keane, Andy Townsend [Ronnie Whelan 67], Steve Staunton, John Aldridge, Niall Quinn [Tony Cascarino 74]

Lithuania: Gintaras Stauce, Tomas Ziukas, Virginijus Baltusnikas, Girius Kalvaitis, Andreius Tereskinas, Vytautas Apanavicius, Stasys Baranauskas, Aurelijus Skarbalius [Dalius Staleliunas 84], Irmantas Stumbrys, Igoris Kirilovas [Darius Maciulevicius 68], Vaidotas Slekys

13 Oct 1993 Lansdowne Road, Dublin
World Cup qualifier
33 000, Fabio Baldas (ITA)

| REP IRELAND (0)1 | Sheridan 72 |
| SPAIN (3)3 | Caminero 11, Salinas 14, 26 |

Ireland: Bonner, Irwin, Phelan, Moran [John Sheridan 22], Kernaghan, Keane, Paul McGrath, Houghton, Quinn, Whelan, Staunton [Cascarino ht]

Spain: Andoni Zubizarreta (c), Albert Ferrer, Salvador Voro, Miguel Angel Nadal, Fernando Giner, Fernando Hierro, Jon Andoni Goikoetxea, Francisco Camarasa, Júlio Salinas [Josep Guardiola ht], José Luis Caminero [José María Bakero 31], Luis Enrique (Martínez)

17 Nov 1993

N IRELAND 1
REP IRELAND 1

see N Ireland section

23 March 1994 Lansdowne Road, Dublin
Friendly
34 550, Fallström (SWE)

REP IRELAND 0
RUSSIA 0

Ireland: Bonner [Alan Kelly ht], Gary Kelly, McGoldrick,

Phil Babb, Brian Carey, Ronnie Whelan, Jason McAteer, Liam O'Brien, Cascarino, David Kelly [Tommy Coyne ht], McLoughlin

Russia: Dmitry Kharin, Dmitry Kuznetsov, Sergei Gorlukovich, Rashid Rakhimov, Yuri Kovtun, Omari Tetradze, Igor Korneyev [Andrei Chernishev 60], Dmitry Popov, Oleg Salenko, Aleksandr Borodyuk, Dmitry Radchenko [Aleksei Kosolapov 88]

20 April 1994 Gemeentelijk Sportpark,Tilburg
Friendly
14 000, Strampe (GER)

HOLLAND 0
REP IRELAND (0)1   Coyne 55

Holland: Ed De Goey, Stan Valckx, Ronald Koeman [John De Wolf ht], Frank De Boer, Frank Rijkaard, Wim Jonk [Aron Winter ht], Edgar Davids, Marc Overmars, Dennis Bergkamp [Gaston Taument ht], Ronald De Boer

Ireland: Bonner, G Kelly, Moran, Babb, Phelan [McLoughlin 84], McGoldrick [McAteer 71], Sheridan, Whelan, Townsend, Staunton, Coyne [Owen Coyle 86]

24 May 1994 Dublin
Friendly
32 500

REP IRELAND (0)1   Sheridan
BOLIVIA 0

Ireland: Bonner, Irwin [G Kelly], Moran [Kernaghan], Babb, Phelan, Houghton [McAteer], Keane, Townsend, Sheridan, Staunton, Coyne [Cascarino]

Bolivia: Carlos Trucco, Miguel Rimba, Gustavo Quinteros, Marco Sandy, Sporuco [J Peña], Júlio Baldivieso, José Melgar, Luis Cristaldo, Piñedo [Borja], Alvaro Peña [Castillo], Ramos [Jaime Moreno]

29 May 1994 Hanover
Friendly
50 000, G Aranba (SPA)

GERMANY 0
REP IRELAND (1)2   Cascarino 31, G Kelly 68

Germany: Bodo Illgner, Thomas Strunz, Jürgen Kohler [Stefan Effenberg ht], Lothar Matthäus (c), Guido Buchwald [Thomas Berthold 36], Andreas Möller [Thomas Hässler ht], Martin Wagner, Matthias Sammer, Mario Basler, Jürgen Klinsmann, Karlheinz Riedle [Rüdi Völler 68}

Ireland: A Kelly, Irwin [G Kelly ht], Phelan, McGrath, Babb, Keane, Townsend, McAteer, Sheridan [Whelan ht], Staunton, Cascarino [Houghton 86]

5 June 1994 Lansdowne Road, Dublin
Friendly
43 465, Leif Sundell (SWE)

REP IRELAND (1)1   Townsend 43

CZECH REP (1)3   Kuka pen 25, 53,
                        Suchoparek 84

Ireland: Bonner, G Kelly, McGrath [Babb 77], Kernaghan, Phelan, McGoldrick [Keane 53], Sheridan, Townsend, Staunton, Cascarino [Coyne 64], Aldridge [McAteer 53]

Czech Rep: Petr Kouba, Lubos Kubík, Martin Kotulek, Tomás Repka, Jan Suchopárek, Karel Poborsky, Jirí Nemec [Pavel Nedved 88], Martin Frydek [Petr Samec 89], Jirí Novotny, Daniel Smejkal, Pavel Kuka

Rep Ireland 1994-95

7 Sep 1994 Daugava, Riga
European Ch qualifier
3226, A Frisk (SWE)

LATVIA 0
REP IRELAND (2)3   Aldridge 16, 75 pen,
                        Sheridan 29

Latvia: Oleg Karavajevs, Igor Troitskiy, Vitaly Astafjevs, Mihail Zemlinskis, Yury Sevlakovs, Valentin Lobanjovs, Alexey Sarando, Mikuckis [Alexandr Yelisejevs 63], Vladimir Babicevs, Milevskis [Igor Stepanovs h/t], Rolands Bulders

Ireland: A Kelly, G Kelly, Irwin, McGrath, Babb, McAteer [McGoldrick 81], Townsend, Aldridge, Quinn [Cascarino 71], Sheridan, Staunton

Aldridge has now scored six in three games v Latvia.

12 Oct 1994 Lansdowne Road, Dublin
European Ch qualifier
32 980, Bergmann (ICE)

REP IRELAND (3)4   Coyne 2, 4, Quinn 30, 82
LIECHTENSTEIN

Ireland: Bonner, G Kelly, Kernaghan, Babb, Irwin [McLoughlin h/t], McGoldrick, McAteer, Sheridan, Staunton, Coyne, Quinn

Liechtenstein: Martin Heeb, Patrik Hefti, Daniel Telser, Jürg Ritter, Roland Moser, Wolfgang Ospelt, Thomas Hanselmann, Harry Zech, Modestus [Peter Klaunzer 77], Mario Frick, Heidegger [Christian Matt 71]

Surprisingly (perhaps not), the first international under floodlights at Lansdowne Road. Coyne hits the woodwork twice, including a post after only twelve minutes.

16 Nov 1994

N IRELAND 0
REP IRELAND 4

see N Ireland section

English leagues 1993-94

Premiership

	P	Home					Away					Pts
		W	D	L	F	A	W	D	L	F	A	
Man Utd	42	14	6	1	39	13	13	5	3	41	25	92
Blackburn	42	14	5	2	31	11	11	4	6	32	25	84
Newcastle	42	14	4	3	51	14	9	4	8	31	27	77
Arsenal	42	10	8	3	25	15	8	9	4	28	13	71
Leeds	42	13	6	2	37	18	5	10	6	28	21	70
Wimbledon	42	12	5	4	35	21	6	6	9	21	32	65
Sheff Weds	42	10	7	4	48	24	6	9	6	28	30	64
Liverpool	42	12	4	5	33	23	5	5	11	26	32	60
QPR	42	8	7	6	32	29	8	5	8	30	32	60
Aston Villa	42	8	5	8	23	18	7	7	7	23	32	57
Coventry	42	9	7	5	23	17	5	7	9	20	28	56
Norwich	42	4	9	8	26	28	8	8	5	39	32	53
West Ham	42	6	7	8	26	31	7	6	8	21	27	52
Chelsea	42	11	5	5	31	20	2	7	12	18	33	51
Tottenham	42	4	8	9	29	33	7	4	10	25	26	45
Man City	42	6	10	5	24	22	3	8	10	14	27	45
Everton	42	8	4	9	26	30	4	4	13	16	33	44
Southampton	42	9	2	10	30	31	3	5	13	19	35	43
Ipswich	42	5	8	8	21	32	4	8	9	14	26	43
Sheff Utd	42	6	10	5	24	23	2	8	11	18	37	42
Oldham	42	5	8	8	24	33	4	5	12	18	35	40
Swindon	42	4	7	10	25	45	1	8	12	22	55	30

Man Utd retain the championship, Sheff Utd, Oldham & Swindon are relegated, Swindon after only one season (their first ever) in the highest division.

Leading scorers

	Premiership		pens
34	Andy Cole	Newcastle	0
31	Alan Shearer	Blackburn	3
25	Matthew Le Tissier	Southampton	6
25	Chris Sutton	Norwich	1

Cole's total of 41 (one in the FA Cup, six in the League Cup) sets a new club record.

Division 1

25	John McGinlay	Bolton	3
22	Chris Armstrong	C Palace	0
21	John Aldridge	Tranmere	3

Division 2

35	Jimmy Quinn	Reading	6
32	Gary Bennett	Wrexham	8
28	Kevin Francis	Stockport	2

Quinn finishes as overall league top scorer.

Division 3

26	Tony Ellis	Preston	3
20	Mark Carter	Bury	3
19	Steve Norris	Chesterfield	3

Play-offs

DIVISION 1 SEMI-FINALS 15 & 18 May 1994l

Derby	2	Millwall	0
Cowans, Johnson			
Millwall	1	Derby	3
Berry		Gabbiadini, Johnson, Van den Hauwe og	
Tranmere	0	Leicester	0
Leicester	2	Tranmere	1
Ormondroyd, Speedie		Nevin	

DIVISION 1 FINAL 30 May 1994 Wembley

Leicester	2	Derby	1
Walsh 2		Johnson	

DIVISION 2 SEMI-FINALS 15 & 18 May 1994

Burnley	0	Plymouth	0
Plymouth	1	Burnley	3
Marshall		Francis 2, Joyce	
York	0	Stockport	0
Stockport	1	York	0
Beaumont			

DIVISION 2 FINAL 29 May 1994 Wembley

Burnley	2	Stockport	1
Eyres, Parkinson		Beaumont	

Division 1

	P	W	D	L	F	A	W	D	L	F	A	Pts
Crystal Palace	46	16	4	3	39	18	11	5	7	34	28	90
Nottm Forest	46	12	9	2	38	22	11	5	7	36	27	83
Millwall	46	14	8	1	36	17	5	9	9	22	32	74
Leicester	46	11	9	3	45	30	8	7	8	27	29	73
Tranmere	46	15	3	5	48	23	6	6	11	21	30	72
Derby	46	15	3	5	44	25	5	8	10	29	43	71
Notts Co	46	16	3	4	43	26	4	5	14	22	43	68
Wolves	46	10	10	3	34	19	7	7	9	26	28	68
Middlesbrough	46	12	6	5	40	19	6	7	10	26	35	67
Stoke	46	14	4	5	35	19	4	9	10	22	40	67
Charlton	46	14	3	6	39	22	5	5	13	22	36	65
Sunderland	46	14	3	6	35	22	5	6	12	19	35	65
Bristol City	46	11	7	5	27	18	5	9	9	20	32	64
Bolton	46	10	8	5	40	31	5	6	12	23	33	59
Southend	46	10	5	8	34	28	7	3	13	29	39	59
Grimsby	46	7	14	2	26	16	6	6	11	26	31	59
Portsmouth	46	10	6	7	29	22	5	7	11	23	36	58
Barnsley	46	9	3	11	25	26	7	4	12	30	41	55
Watford	46	10	5	8	39	35	5	4	14	27	45	54
Luton	46	12	4	7	38	25	2	7	14	18	35	53
West Brom	46	9	7	7	38	31	4	5	14	22	38	51
Birmingham	46	9	7	7	28	29	4	5	14	24	40	51
Oxford	46	10	5	8	33	33	3	5	15	21	42	49
Peterborough	46	6	9	8	31	30	2	4	17	17	46	37

Palace & Forest are promoted, Millwall, Leicester, Tranmere & Derby go into the play-offs, Birmingham, Oxford & Peterborough are relegated.

Division 2

	P	W	D	L	F	A	W	D	L	F	A	Pts
Reading	46	15	6	2	40	16	11	5	7	41	28	89
Port Vale	46	16	6	1	46	18	10	4	9	33	28	88
Plymouth	46	16	4	3	46	26	9	6	8	42	30	85
Stockport	46	15	3	5	50	22	9	10	4	24	22	85
York	46	12	7	4	33	13	9	5	9	31	27	75
Burnley	46	17	4	2	55	18	4	6	13	24	40	73
Bradford City	46	13	5	5	34	20	6	8	9	27	33	70
Bristol Rovers	46	10	8	5	33	26	10	2	11	27	33	70
Hull	46	9	9	5	33	20	9	5	9	29	34	68
Cambridge	46	11	5	7	38	29	8	4	11	41	44	66
Huddersfield	46	9	8	6	27	26	8	6	9	31	35	65
Wrexham	46	13	4	6	45	33	4	7	12	21	44	62
Swansea	46	12	7	4	37	20	4	5	14	19	38	60
Brighton	46	10	7	6	38	29	5	7	11	22	38	59
Rotherham	46	11	4	8	42	30	4	9	10	21	30	58
Brentford	46	7	10	6	30	28	6	9	8	27	27	58
Bournemouth	46	8	7	8	26	27	6	8	9	25	32	57
Leyton Orient	46	11	9	3	38	26	3	5	15	19	45	56
Cardiff	46	10	7	6	39	33	3	8	12	27	46	54
Blackpool	46	12	2	9	41	37	4	3	16	22	38	53
Fulham	46	7	6	10	20	23	7	4	12	30	40	52
Exeter	46	8	7	8	38	37	3	5	15	14	46	45
Hartlepool	46	8	3	12	28	40	1	6	16	13	47	36
Barnet	46	4	6	13	22	32	1	7	15	19	54	28

Reading & Port Vale are promoted, Plymouth, Stockport, York & Burnley go into the play-offs, Fulham, Exeter, Hartlepool & Barnet are relegated.

Division 3

	P	W	D	L	F	A	W	D	L	F	A	Pts
Shrewsbury	42	10	8	3	28	17	12	5	4	35	22	79
Chester	42	13	5	3	35	18	8	6	7	34	28	74
Crewe	42	12	4	5	45	30	9	6	6	35	31	73
Wycombe	42	11	6	4	34	21	8	7	6	33	32	70
Preston	42	13	5	3	46	23	5	8	8	33	37	67
Torquay	42	8	10	3	30	24	9	6	6	34	32	67
Carlisle	42	10	4	7	35	23	8	6	7	22	19	64
Chesterfield	42	8	8	5	32	22	8	6	7	23	26	62
Rochdale	42	10	5	6	38	22	6	7	8	25	29	60
Walsall	42	7	5	9	28	26	10	4	7	20	27	60
Scunthorpe	42	9	7	5	40	26	6	7	8	24	30	59
Mansfield	42	9	3	9	28	30	6	7	8	25	32	55
Bury	42	9	6	6	33	22	5	5	11	22	34	53
Scarborough	42	8	4	9	29	28	7	4	10	26	33	53
Doncaster	42	8	6	7	24	26	6	4	11	20	31	52
Gillingham	42	8	8	5	27	23	4	7	10	17	28	51
Colchester	42	8	4	9	31	33	5	6	10	25	38	49
Lincoln	42	7	4	10	26	29	5	7	9	26	34	47
Wigan	42	6	7	8	33	33	5	5	11	18	37	45
Hereford	42	6	4	11	34	33	6	2	13	26	46	42
Darlington	42	7	5	9	24	28	3	6	12	18	36	41
Northampton	42	6	7	8	25	23	3	4	14	19	43	38

*Shrewsbury, Chester & Crewe are promoted, Wycombe, Preston, Torquay & Carlisle go into the play-offs.
Northampton avoid relegation because Kidderminster Harriers' ground is judged unfit for League football.*

Play-offs

DIVISION 3 SEMI-FINALS 15 & 18 May 1994

Carlisle	0	Wycombe	2
		Thompson, Garner	
Wycombe	2	Carlisle	1
Carroll, Garner		*Davey pen*	
Torquay	2	Preston	0
Darby, Moore			
Preston	4	Torquay	1
Ellis, Moyes, Hicks,		*Nevin*	
Raynor			

DIVISION 3 FINAL 28 May 1994 Wembley

Wycombe	4	Preston	2
Thompson, Garner,		*Bryson, Raynor*	
Carroll 2			

Autoglass Trophy 1993-94

Final 24 April 1994 Wembley

Swansea	(1)1	Huddersfield	(0)1
McFarlane 15		*Logan 60*	

aet Swansea 3-1 pens

Swansea: Roger Freestone, Steve Jenkins, Mark Clode (Steve Torpey 83), Mike Basham, Mark Harris, Colin Pascoe, Jason Bowen, Kwame Ampadu, Andy McFarlane, John Cornforth (c), John Hodge (John Ford 68)

Huddersfield: Steve Francis, Chris Billy, Tom Cowan, Phil Starbuck, Pat Scully, Graham Mitchell, Richard Logan, Phil Robinson, Andy Booth, Darren Bullock (Iain Dunn h/t), Simon Baldry

In the shoot-out, Huddersfield twice hit the woodwork then Freestone saves Cowan's penalty to make Swansea only the second Welsh league club to win a trophy at Wembley.

Non-league winners 1993-94

GM Vauxhall Conference	Kidderminster H
FA Challenge Trophy	Woking
FA Challenge Vase	Diss Town
Drinkwise Cup	Macclesfield
Northern Premier	Marine
Northern Premier (Division 1)	Guiseley
Northern Premier Cup	Hyde Utd
Northern Premier President's Cup	Guiseley
Northern Premier Division 1 Cup	Ashton Utd
Beazer Homes Premier	Farnborough Town
Beazer Homes Midland	Rushden & Diamonds
Beazer Homes Southern	Gravesend & Nthfleet
Diadora Premier	Stevenage Borough
Diadora Division 1	Bishop's Stortford
Diadora Division 2	Newbury Town
Diadora Division 3	Bracknell Town
Diadora Cup	Chertsey Town
Carlsberg Trophy	Chertsey Town

FA Cup 1993-94

1st Round

Accrington S (0)2 Connor 65, Wood 89	Scunthorpe (1)3 Toman 31, Goodacre 82, 89	Kidderminster (0)3 Brindley 66, Forsyth pen 68, Davies 89	Kettering 0
Barnet (0)2 Haag 56, Close 72	Carshalton (1)1 Annon 15	Knowsley (1)1 Joyce og 29	Carlisle (3)4 Arnold 8, 66, Davey 28, Reeves 33
Bournemouth (3)4 McGorry 13, Pennock 42 Masters 44, Wood 75	Brighton (1)2 Kennedy 1, 66	Leek (0)2 D Sutton (2)	Wigan (1)2 Skipper, Morton
Bradford City 0	Chester 0	Wigan (1)3 McKearney pen 17, Diskin og 50, Duffy 82	Leek 0
Chester (1)1 Lightfoot 12	Bradford 0	Leyton Orient (1)2 Lakin 42, Hackett 77	Gravesend (1)1 Portway 40
Bristol Rovers (1)1 Archer 25	Wycombe (1)2 Langford 34, Carroll 78	Macclesfield (2)2 Sorvel 39, Macdonald 44	Hartlepool 0
Burnley 0	York 0	Mansfield (0)1 Wilkinson 55	Preston (0)2 Ellis 63 pen, 89
York (1)2 Canham44, McCarthy 89	Burnley (2)3 Heath 5, Joyce 29, Eyres 89	Marlow 0	Plymouth (0)2 Dalton 64, 89
Cambridge City 0	Hereford (0)1 Pike 85	Met Police 0	Crawley (0)2 Whitington 52, Van Sittart 61
Cambridge Utd 0	Reading 0	Molesey 0	Bath (4)4 Mings 13, Boyle 14, Adcock 34, 44
Reading (1)1 Gooding 32	Cambridge Utd (1)2 Nyamah 20, Heathcote 74	Northampton (0)1 Aldridge 89	Bromsgrove (1)2 Shilvock 35, Carter 85
Chesterfield 0	Rochdale (0)1 Stuart pen 73	Port Vale (2)2 Kerr 12, Foyle 27	Blackpool 0
Colchester (1)3 McGavin 40, S Brown 52 English 86	Sutton (2)4 Quail 18, Smart 31 Newman 84, Morah 88	Rotherham (0)1 Wilder pen 58	Stockport (0)2 Todd 84, Pearce 89
Crewe (2)4 Edwards 22,Rowbotham 35 Gardiner 63, S Smith pen 74	Darlington (2)2 Ellison 18, Painter 20	Rugby 0	Brentford (1)3 Allon 38 pen, 79, Gayle 54
Enfield 0	Cardiff 0	Runcorn 0	Hull 1 (abandoned) Atkinson 29
Cardiff (0)1 Blake 89	Enfield 0	Runcorn 0	Hull (0)2 Brown , Hargreaves
Farnborough (1)1 Jones 42	Exeter (0)3 Worthington 76, Jepson 81, Ross 83	Scarborough (0)1 Young 64	Bury 0
Gretna (2)2 Townsley 11, Dobie 25	Bolton (1)3 McGinlay pen 14, Coyle 79, 84	Shrewsbury (0)1 Gallen 84	Doncaster (0)1 Williamson 54
Halifax (2)2 Peake 6, Saunders 36	West Brom (0)1 Hunt 80	Doncaster (0)(1)1 Williamson 89	Shrewsbury (0)(1)2 Spink 63, Walton 101
		Slough (0)1 M Scott 65	Torquay (2)2 Sale 10, Moore 40
		Stalybridge (1)1 Aspinall 27	Marine (1)1 Rowlands 20

Marine (2)(3)4
Camden 29, 32
Murray 83, Doherty pen 103
Stalybridge 4-2 pens

Swansea (0)1
Torpey 89

Nuneaton (0)(1)2
Simpson 82, 98

Telford (1)1
Bignot 17

Huddersfield (0)1
Jackson 50

Witton 0

Woking (1)2
S Wye 8, Dennis 53

Weston Super Mare 0

Wrexham (1)1
Watkin

Walsall (0)2
Lightbourne 70, McDonald 76

Yeading 0

Gillingham (3)3
Smith 11, Micklewhite 28
Baker 38

Yeovil (0)1
Wallace 89

2nd Round

Bath (1)2
Brooks, Batty

Bournemouth (0)1
Watson 51

Nuneaton 0

Brentford (0)1
Gayle 74

Burnley (2)4
Ryan og 25, Eyres 42, 72, 88

Carlisle (2)3
Edmondson 23, Gallimore 38
Arnold 50

Chester (2)2
Preece 8, Leonard 26

Crawley (0)1
Ford 86

Stalybridge (2)(3)4
Hill 6, Shaughnessy 30
Aspinall 62, Kirkham 113

Nuneaton (0)1
Shearer 79

Swansea (1)(1)1
Torpey 9

Huddersfield (1)1
Rowe 5

Telford 0

Lincoln (0)2
West 72, Lormor 89

Weston Sup Mare (2)2
Elson 20, Bowering 30

Woking (0)1
Clement 57

Walsall (1)1
Lightbourne

Wrexham 0

Gillingham 0

Yeading (0)1
James 85

Fulham 0

Hereford (0)1
Hall

Nuneaton (0)1
Green 79

Bournemouth (1)1
Cotterill 11

Cardiff (1)3
Westley og 40,
Stant 64, Bird 68

Rochdale (0)1
Whitehall pen 78

Stalybridge (0)1
Kirkham 68

Hull 0

Barnet (0)2
Rowe 53, Hoddle 71

Crewe (2)2
Lennon 25, Whalley 30

Kidderminster (0)1
Forsyth pen 81

Leyton Orient (1)1
Cooper 37

Exeter (0)(1)2
Exeter 5-4 pens
Storer 54, Harris 98

Lincoln (1)1
D Johnson 33

Plymouth (1)2
Nugent 28, 59

Port Vale (0)1
Tankard 89

Shrewsbury 0

Stockport (1)5
Frain 39, Francis 51, 73
Beaumont 80, Wallace 87

Torquay 0

Walsall (1)1
Wright 38

Scunthorpe 0

Wigan (0)1
Gavin 74

Wycombe (0)1
Hemmings 56

Yeovil 0

3rd Round

Birmingham (1)1
Harding 9

Blackburn (1)3
Shearer 21, Gallacher 71
Sherwood 85

Portsmouth (0)1
McLoughlin 73

Bolton (0)1
Patterson 47

Everton (1)(2)2
Barlow 28, 46

Macclesfield (0)1
Askey 48

Woking 0

Exeter (1)1
Bailey 28

Leyton Orient (0)(1)2

Carter 51, Hackett 95

Bolton (1)3
Thompson 24, Brown
69, Coyle 72

Gillingham 0

Huddersfield 0

Preston (1)1
Raynor 3

Halifax (0)1
Barr pen 85

Sutton (0)1
Jones 77

Scunthorpe (1)1
Carmichael 25

Walsall 0
aet Scunthorpe 7-6 pens

Scarborough 0

Cambridge Utd 0

Bromsgrove (2)2
Webb 4, Radburn 7

Kidderminster (1)2
Cartwright 28, Purdie 64

Portsmouth (0)3
McLoughlin 49, 82, 89

Blackburn (1)3
Shearer 44, May 68,
Wilcox 78

Everton (1)1
Rideout 44

Bolton (0)(2)3
McGinlay 51, Stubbs
82, Coyle 100

Bristol City (1)1
Allison 39

Liverpool (1)1
Rush 12

Liverpool 0

Bristol City (0)1
Tinnion 66

Bromsgrove (1)1
Crisp 31

Barnsley (0)2
Rammell 88,
Archdeacon 89

Cardiff (0)2
Stant 67, Thompson 85

Middlesbrough (1)2
Wilkinson 24, Moore 82

Middlesbrough (0)(1)1
Kavanagh 89

Cardiff (1)(1)2
Stant 10, Blake 116

Charlton (1)3
Pardew 18, Leaburn 49,
Grant 59

Burnley 0

Chelsea 0
Barnet, who came out of the hat first, chose to play at
Stamford Bridge

Barnet 0

Chelsea (2)4
Burley 29, Peacock 44,
Stein 48, Shipperley 76

Barnet 0

Exeter 0

Aston Villa (0)1
Saunders pen 60

Grimsby (0)1
Croft 88

Wigan 0

Leeds (1)3
Deane 17, Forrester 58, 83

Crewe (1)1
Naylor 31

Luton (0)1
Telfer 50

Southend 0

Man City (0)4
Ingebrigtsen 51, 52,
Kernaghan 57

Leicester (0)1
Oldfield 87

Millwall 0

Arsenal (0)1
Adams 89

Newcastle (1)2
Cole 21, Beardsley 76

Coventry 0

Notts County (2)3
Draper 2, Agana 10, Devlin 78

Sutton (0)2
Barrowcliffe 61,
Smart 69

Oldham (0)2
Beckford 60, Holden 71

Derby (1)1
Johnson 44

Oxford (1)2
Elliott 41, Byrne 71

Tranmere 0

Peterborough (0)1
Brissett 60

Tottenham (1)1
Dozzell 86

Tottenham (1)(1)1
Barmby 12
Spurs 5-4 pens

Peterborough (1)(1)1
Charlery 24

Plymouth (0)1
Nugent 84

Chester 0

Preston (0)2
Moyes 50, Conroy 86

Bournemouth (0)1
Aspinall pen 89

Sheffield Utd 0

Man Utd (0)1
Hughes

Sheffield Weds (1)1
Bright 9

Nottm Forest (0)1
Cooper 88

Nottm Forest 0

Sheffield Weds (0)2
Pearce 46,
Bart-Williams 54

Southampton (1)1
Dowie 44

Port Vale (1)1
Porter 14

Port Vale (1)1
Slaven 18

Southampton 0

Stockport (1)2
Francis 39, Preece 74

QPR (1)1
Barker 19

Stoke 0

Bath 0

Bath (0)1
Chenoweth 89

Stoke (2)4
Regis 5, 57,
Cranson 38,
Orlygsson 83

Sunderland (1)1
Ferguson 31

Carlisle (0)1
Edmondson 80

Carlisle 0

Sunderland (0)(1)1
Howey 101

Swindon (1)1
Mutch 44

Ipswich (1)1
Marshall 28

Ipswich (1)(1)2
Stockwell 44, Marshall 107

Swindon (0)(1)1
Fjortoft 75

West Ham (0)2
M Allen 65, Marsh 85

Watford (1)1
Porter pen 27

Wimbledon (2)3
Holdsworth 11, 44, 71

Scunthorpe 0

Wolves (0)1
D Kelly 74

Crystal Palace 0

Wycombe 0

Norwich (1)2
Sutton 37, 87

4th Round

Bolton (1)2
McAteer 31, Coyle 86

Arsenal (0)2
Wright 51, Adams 66

Arsenal (1)(1)
Smith 36

Bolton (1)(1)3
McGinlay 20, McAteer 99,
Walker 115

Cardiff (0)1
Blake 63

Man City 0

Charlton 0

Blackburn 0

Blackburn 0

Charlton (1)1
Pitcher 15

Chelsea	(1)1	Sheffield Weds	(0)1
Peacock 14		*Hyde 63*	
Sheffield Weds	(1)(1)	Chelsea	(1)(1)3
Bright 37		*Spencer 7, Peacock 96, Burley 115*	
Grimsby	(0)1	Aston Villa	(1)2
Groves 58		*Houghton 13, Yorke 78*	
Ipswich	(0)3	Tottenham	0
Marshall 53, Johnson 64, Thompson 85			
Kidderminster	(0)1	Preston	0
Humphreys 47			
Newcastle	(0)1	Luton	(1)1
Beardsley pen 65		*Thorpe 35*	
Luton	(1)2	Newcastle	0
Hartson 16, Oakes 77			
Norwich	0	Man Utd	(1)2
		Keane 18, Cantona 73	
Notts County	(1)1	West Ham	(1)1
Lund 38		*Jones 41*	
West Ham	(0)(0)1	Notts County	0
Chapman 118			
Oldham	0	Stoke	0
Stoke	0	Oldham	(1)1
		Beckford 31	
Oxford	(2)2	Leeds	(1)2
Dyer 15, Elliott 36		*Speed 43, Wetherall 64*	
Leeds	(0)(2)2	Oxford	(0)(2)3
Strachan 88, White 89		*Byrne 57, Allen 62, Magilton 111*	
Plymouth	(0)2	Barnsley	(1)2
Marshall 50, Dalton 59		*Payton 41, Taggart 71*	
Barnsley	(0)1	Plymouth	0
O'Connell 65			
Port Vale	0	Wolves	(1)2
		Blades 25, Keen 89	
Stockport	0	Bristol City	(1)4
		Shail 4, Allison 47, 59, 66	
Wimbledon	(1)2	Sunderland	(1)1
Scales 3, Fashanu 59		*Smith 44*	

5th Round

Bolton	(0)1	Aston Villa	0
Stubbs 82			
Bristol City	(1)1	Charlton	(0)1
Tinnion 12		*Robson 59*	
Charlton	(1)2	Bristol City	0
Pitcher pen 36, Grant 89			
Cardiff	(0)1	Luton	(1)2
Stant 65		*Oakes 39, Preece 70*	
Kidderminster	0	West Ham	(0)1
		Chapman 69	
Oldham	(0)1	Barnsley	0
Ritchie 61			
Oxford	(1)1	Chelsea	(2)2
Beauchamp 5		*Spencer 22, Burley 30*	
Wimbledon	0	Man Utd	(1)3
		Cantona 42, Ince 63, Irwin 71	
Wolves	(0)1	Ipswich	(1)1
D Kelly 81		*Wark 28*	
Ipswich	(0)1	Wolves	(2)2
Palmer 46		*Mills 8, Thompson 38*	

6th Round

Bolton	0	Oldham	(0)1
		Beckford 84	
Chelsea	(0)1	Wolves	0
Peacock 58			
Man Utd	(0)3	Charlton	(0)1
Hughes 46, Kanchelskis 71, 75		*Leaburn 77*	
West Ham	0	Luton	0
Luton	(1)3	West Ham	(1)2
Oakes 35, 47, 73		*M Allen 29, Bishop 57*	

Semi-finals

Both at Wembley

Chelsea	(1)2	Luton	0
Peacock 13, 47			
Man Utd	(0)(0)1	Oldham	(0)(0)1
Hughes 119		*Pointon 106*	

Replay at Maine Road

Man Utd	(2)4	Oldham	(1)1
Irwin 9, Kanchelskis 15 Robson 62, Giggs 68		*Pointon 39*	

Final

14 May 1994 Wembley 79 634

Man Utd	(0)4	Chelsea	0
Cantona 60 pen, 65 pen Hughes 68, McClair 89			

Man Utd: Peter Schmeichel, Paul Parker, Dennis Irwin (Lee Sharpe 84), Roy Keane, Steve Bruce (c), Gary

The Double: English League & FA Cup

1988-89	Preston
1896-97	Aston Villa
1960-61	Tottenham
1970-71	Arsenal
1985-86	Liverpool
1993-94	Man Utd

FA Cup wins

8	Tottenham, Man Utd
7	Aston Villa
6	Arsenal, Blackburn Rovers, Newcastle

Goals in FA Cup & League Cup Finals in same season

| 1983 | Norman Whiteside | Man Utd |
| 1994 | Mark Hughes | Man Utd |

Pallister, Andrei Kanchelskis (Brian McClair 84), Paul Ince, Mark Hughes, Eric Cantona, Ryan Giggs

Chelsea: Dmitry Kharin, Steve Clarke, Frank Sinclair, Jakob Kjeldberg, Erland Johnsen, Craig Burley (Glenn Hoddle 65), John Spencer, Eddie Newton, Mark Stein (Tony Cascarino 78), Gavin Peacock, Dennis Wise (c)

Referee: David Elleray

The game turns on Peacock's bad luck (scorer of both goals when Chelsea twice beat United 1-0 in the League, he now hits the bar in the first half) and Newton's rush of blood, unnecessarily bringing down Irwin in the box. Chelsea haven't won the Cup since 1970.

League Cup 1993-94

1st round

| Birmingham | (2)3 | Plymouth | 0 |
| Parris, Frain, Peschisolido | | | |

| Plymouth | (0)2 | Birmingham | 0 |
| Barlow, Marshall | | | |

| Bolton | 0 | Bury | (2)2 |
| | | Powell, Blissett | |

Bury	(0)	Bolton	(1)(2)2
		Bolton 3-0 pens	
		Coyle, McGinalay	

| Bournemouth | (2)3 | Cardiff | (1)1 |
| Fletcher, Masters, Beardsmore | | Bird | |

| Cardiff | (1)1 | Bournemouth | (1)1 |
| Morris og | | Parkinson | |

| Brentford | (0)2 | Watford | (1)2 |
| Peters, Westley | | Furlong, Dyer | |

| Watford | (1)3 | Brentford | (1)1 |
| Holdsworth, Solomon, Dyer | | Westley | |

| Bristol Rovers | (1)1 | West Brom | (2)4 |
| Sterling | | Burgess, Hunt, Donovan 2 | |

| West Brom | 0 | Bristol Rovers | 0 |

| Cambridge | (1)1 | Luton | 0 |
| Claridge | | | |

| Luton | 0 | Cambridge | (0)1 |
| | | Claridge | |

| Chesterfield | (1)3 | Carlisle | (1)1 |
| Turnbull pen, Norris, Morris | | Davey | |

| Carlisle | (1)1 | Chesterfield | (1)1 |
| Thomas | | Jules | |

| Crewe | 0 | Wrexham | (0)1 |
| | | Paskin | |

| Wrexham | (2)3 | Crewe | (1)3 |
| Connolly, Bennett pen Wilson og | | Lyons, Rowbotham, Ward | |

| Darlington | (1)1 | Bradford | (2)5 |
| Juryeff | | McCarthy 3, Reid, Jewell | |

| Bradford | (3)6 | Darlington | 0 |
| Jewell 2, McCarthy 2, Steele, Showler | | | |

| Doncaster | 0 | Blackpool | (0)1 |
| | | Watson | |

| Blackpool | (1)3 | Doncaster | (3)3 |
| Watson, Quinn, Bamber | | Hulme, Harper, Wilcox | |

| Fulham | (0)2 | Colchester | (1)1 |
| Betts og, Farrell | | Kinsells | |

| Colchester | (1)1 | Fulham (0)2 |
| McDonough | | Brazil, Farrell |

| Gillingham | (0)1 | Brighton | 0 |
| Reinelt | | | |

| Brighton | (1)2 | Gillingham | 0 |
| Kennedy, Nogan | | | |

| Hereford | 0 | Torquay | (2)2 |
| | | Trollope, Foster | |

Torquay	0	Hereford	(0)(2)2
		Hereford 4-3 pens	
		May, Hall pen	

| Huddersfield | 0 | Scarborough | 0 |

Scarborough	0	Huddersfield	(1)3
		Dunn 2, Roberts	
Leyton Orient	0	Wycombe	(1)2
		Thompson, Langford	
Wycombe	(1)1	Leyton Orient	0
Scott			
Notts County	(2)2	Hull	0
Lund, Cox			
Hull	(3)3	Notts County	(0)1 aet
Abbott, Atkinson, Windass		*Draper*	
		Notts County away goals	
Port Vale	(0)2	Lincoln	(0)2
Taylor, Slaven		*Lormor 2*	
Lincoln	0	Port Vale	0
aet Lincoln away goals			
Preston	(1)1	Burnley	(1)2
Ellis		*Eyres pen, Davis*	
Burnley	(1)4	Preston	(0)1
Russell, Eyres,		*Cartwright*	
Francis, Deary			
Reading	(0)3	Northampton	0
Quinn, Lovell, Parkinson			
Northampton	0	Reading	(1)2
		Gray, Dillon	
Rochdale	(0)2	York	0
Stuart, Flounders pen			
York	0	Rochdale	0
Shrewsbury	(1)1	Scunthorpe	0
Evans			
Scunthorpe	(0)1	Shrewsbury	(1)1
Martin		*Griffiths*	
Southend	0	Barnet	(0)2
		Lynch, Walker	
Barnet	(0)1	Southand	(0)1
Haag		*Angell*	
Stockport	(1)1	Hartlepool	(1)1
Ryan		*West*	
Hartlepool	(0)2	Stockport	(1)1
Tait, Honour		*Francis*	
Stoke	(1)2	Mansfield	(2)2
Gleghorn, Carruthers		*Noteman, McLoughlin*	
Mansfield	(1)1	Stoke	(1)3
Stant		*Stein 2, Regis*	
Sunderland	(0)3	Chester	(1)1
Goodman 2, Power		*Rimmer*	
Chester	0	Sunderland	0

Swansea	0	Bristol City	(0)1
		Robinson	
Bristol City	0	Swansea	(1)2
		Bowen 2	
Walsall	0	Exeter	0
Exeter	(1)2	Walsall	(1)1
Jepson 2 (1 pen)		*McDonald*	
Wigan	0	Rotherham	(0)1
		Hazel	
Rotherham	(3)4	Wigan	(1)2
Banks, Gavin og, Varadi,		*Gavin, Morton*	
Law			

2nd round

Barnet	(0)1	QPR	(2)2
Lynch		*Ferdinand, Barker*	
QPR	(2)4	Barnet	0
Allen 2, 67, 76, Impey 28			
Barnsley	(0)1	Peterborough	(0)1
Archdeacon pen		*Brissett*	
Peterborough	(1)(1)3	Barnsley	(0)(1)1
Philliskirk 21, McGlashan		*Bryson 75*	
93, Oliver 119			
Birmingham	0	Aston Villa	(0)1
		Richardson	
Aston Villa	(0)1	Birmingham	0
Saunders 82			
Blackburn	(1)1	Bournemouth	0
Shearer			
Bournemouth	0	Blackburn	0
Blackpool	(2)3	Sheffield Utd	0
Bamber 2, Watson			
Sheffield Utd	(0)2	Blackpool	0
Davison 57, Ward 84			
Bolton	(0)1	Sheffield Weds	(0)1
Kelly pen		*Bart-Williams*	
Sheffield Weds	(0)1	Bolton	0
Bright 80			
Bradford	(1)2	Norwich	(0)1
McCarthy 2		*Fox*	
Norwich	(0)3	Bradford	0
Ekoku 65, Fox 67,			
Sutton 70			
Burnley	0	Tottenham	0
Tottenham	(1)3	Burnley	(1)1
Sheringham 4, 89,		*Eyres 8*	
Howells 73			

Coventry (2)3
Morgan 2, Quinn

Wycombe 0

Wycombe (1)(3)4
Ryan 31, Scott 63,
Evans 87, Cousins 92

Coventry (0)(0)2 aet
Morgan 111, Babb 117

Crystal Palace (1)3
Gordon, Southgate, Whyte

Charlton (0)1
Leaburn

Charlton 0

Crystal Palace (0)1
Armstrong 78

Exeter (1)1
Storer

Derby (1)3
Kitson, Simpson,
Gabbiadini

Derby (1)2
Gabbiadini, 14 Johnson 63

Exeter 0

Fulham (0)1
Farrell

Liverpool (2)3
Rush, Clough, Fowler

Liverpool (2)5
Fowler 13, 20, 47, 55, 70

Fulham 0

Grimsby (1)3
Dobbin, Mendonca 2

Hartlepool 0

Hartlepool 0

Grimsby (1)2
Groves 24, Dobbin 89

Hereford 0

Wimbledon (1)1
Clarke

Wimbledon (3)4
Ardley 6, Jones 32,
Holdsworth 43, Earle 89

Hereford (0)1
Hall 69

Huddersfield 0

Arsenal (2)5
Wright 3, Campbell,
Merson

Arsenal (0)1
Smith 63

Huddersfield (1)1
Dunn 44

Ipswich (1)2
Milton, Whitton

Cambridge (0)1
Claridge pen

Cambridge 0

Ipswich (0)2
Marshall 49, Kiwomya 85

Lincoln (1)3
D Johnson, Matthews,
Brown

Everton (1)4
Rideout 3, Cottee

Everton (1)4
Rideout 2, Snodin 65
Cottee 75 78

Lincoln (0)2
D Johnson 48,
Baraclough pen 72

Man City (1)1
White

Reading (1)1
Lovell

Reading (0)1
J Quinn 48

Man City (1)2
Lomas 42, N Quinn 81

Middlesbrough (4)5
Hignett 4, Hendrie

Brighton 0

Brighton (0)1
Nogan 76

Middlesbrough (2)3
Wilkinson 26, Hignett 36,
Hendrie 65

Newcastle (1)4
Cole 3, Bracewell

Notts County (1)1
Srnicek og

Notts County (0)1
McSwegan 51

Newcastle (3)7
Allen 21, pen 26,
Beardsley 44
Cole 59, 61, 83, Lee 85

Rochdale (1)1
Carey og

Leicester (1)6
Whitlow, Walsh,
Thompson, Oldfield
Speedie, Ormondroyd

Leicester (1)2
Ormondroyd 44,
Joachim 76

Rochdale (1)1
Lancaster 6

Rotherham 0

Portsmouth 0

Portsmouth (3)5
Richardson og 15,
McLoughlin 18, Durnin 35,
Walsh 60, Burns 86

Rotherham 0

The own goal also credited to Stimson.

Southampton (1)1
Moore

Shrewsbury 0

Shrewsbury (1)2
Summerfield 36, Brown 71

Southampton 0

Stoke (1)2
Stein 2

Man Utd (0)1
Dublin

Man Utd (0)2
Sharpe 46, McClair 88

Stoke 0

Sunderland (1)2
Goodman, P Gray

Leeds (1)1
Speed

Leeds (0)1
Whelan 56

Sunderland (2)2
Goodman 17, P Gray 33

Swansea (2)2
Torpey, Pascoe

Oldham (1)1
Sharp

Oldham (2)2
Halle 4, Bernard 7

Swansea 0

Swindon (1)2
Summerbee, Mutch

Wolves 0

Wolves (0)2
Mountfield 81, Burke 88

Swindon (0)1
Summerbee 59

Tranmere (1)5
Aldridge 2, Nevin 3

Oxford (0)1
Beauchamp

Oxford (0)1
Wanless 69

Tranmere (1)1
Irons 44

Watford 0

Millwall 0

Millwall	(2)(3)4	Watford	(2)(3)3

Huxford 39, Murray 44, Moralee 79, Verveer 119 / *Porter 1, Nogan 20, Hessenthaler 64*

West Brom	(1)1	Chelsea	(0)1

Donovan / *Shipperley*

Chelsea	(1)2	West Brom	(1)1

Wise 8, 89 / *Taylor 44*

West Ham	(3)5	Chesterfield	(0)1

Morley 2 (1 pen), Chapman 2, Burrows / *Norris*

Chesterfield	0	West Ham	(0)2

M Allen 65, Boere 83

Wrexham	(0)3	Nottm Forest	(2)3

Bennett 2 (1 pen), Puskin / *Collymore 3*

Nottm Forest	(1)3	Wrexham	(0)1

Black 16, Crosby 55, Collymore 57 / *Pejic 56*

3rd round

Arsenal	(0)1	Norwich	(1)1

Wright / *Crook*

Norwich	0	Arsenal	(2)3

Wright 14, 65, Merson 34

Blackburn	0	Shrewsbury	0

Shrewsbury	(1)(3)3	Blackburn	(1)(3)4

Summerfield 20, 25, MacKenzie pen 52 / *Newell 7, 58 pen, May 85, Pearce 102*

Blackpool	(1)2	Peterborough	(1)2

Watson 2 / *Hackett, Adcock*

Peterborough	(2)2	Blackpool	(1)1

Rush 3, Bradshaw 30 / *Howarth og 14*

Derby	0	Tottenham	(0)1

Barmby 71

Everton	(0)2	Crystal Palace	(0)2

Beagrie, Watson / *Thorn, Southgate*

Crystal Palace	(1)1	Everton	(0)4

Southgate 20 / *Watson 31, 54, Ward pen 82, Young og 84*

Liverpool	(2)3	Ipswich	(1)2

Rush 1, 16, 64 / *Marshall 22, Mason pen 77*

Man City	(0)1	Chelsea	0

White

Man Utd	(2)5	Leicester	(0)1

Bruce 7, 86, McClair 14, Sharpe 53, Hughes 62 / *Hill 64*

Middlesbrough	(0)1	Sheffield Weds	(0)1

Hendrie 52 / *Palmer 88*

Sheffield Weds	(1)(1)2	Middlesbrough	(1)(1)1

Watson 16, Palmer 115 / *Mustoe 22*

Nottm Forest	(1)2	West Ham	(0)1

Black 28, Collymore 55 / *Morley 84*

Oldham	(1)2	Coventry	0

Beckford, Sharp

Portsmouth	(0)2	Swindon	0

Durnin, Walsh

QPR	(2)3	Millwall	0

Sinclair 31, Barker 42, Ferdinand 54

Sunderland	(0)1	Aston Villa	(2)4

P Gray / *Atkinson 2, Richardson, Houghton*

Tranmere	(2)4	Grimsby	(0)1

Aldridge 2, Vickers, Irons pen / *Okorie*

Wimbledon	(1)2	Newcastle	(1)1

Burton 23, Holdsworth 68 / *Sellars 28*

4th round

Arsenal	0	Aston Villa	(1)1

Atkinson 4

Everton	0	Man Utd	(1)2

Hughes 13, Giggs 46

Liverpool	(1)1	Wimbledon	(0)1

Molby pen 15 / *Earle 84*

Nottm Forest	0	Man City	0

Man City	(1)1	Nottm Forest	(2)2

Vonk 16 / *Webb 74, Cooper 87*

Peterborough	0	Portsmouth	0

Portsmouth	(0)(0)1	Peterborough	0

Kristensen 119

QPR	(1)1	Sheffield Weds	(1)2

Meaker 41 / *Jemson 32, Jones 86*

Tottenham	(0)1	Blackburn	0

Campbell 65

Tranmere	(0)3	Oldham	0

Brannan 52, 60, Aldridge 89

Wimbledon	(1)(2)2	Liverpool	(1)(2)2

Holdsworth 18, Earle 70, Wimbledon 4-3 pens / *Ruddock 38, Segers og 89*

5th round

Man Utd	(1)2	Portsmouth	(1)2

Giggs 29, Cantona 60 / *Walsh 32, 71*

| Portsmouth | 0 | Man Utd | (1)1 |
| | | *McClair 27* | |

| Nottm Forest | (0)1 | Tranmere | (0)1 |
| *Gemmill 74* | | *Malkin 51* | |

| Tranmere | (1)2 | Nottm Forest | 0 |
| *Nevin 26, Thomas 89* | | | |

| Tottenham | (0)1 | Aston Villa | (0)2 |
| *Caskey 64* | | *Houghton 57, Barrett 69* | |

Villa set a new record by reaching the semi-finals for the 9th time.

| Wimbledon | (0)1 | Sheffield Weds | (0)2 |
| *Holdsworth 77* | | *Watson 46, Bright 82* | |

Semi-finals

| Man Utd | (1)1 | Sheffield Weds | 0 |
| *Giggs 19* | | | |

| Sheffield Weds | (1)1 | Man Utd | (3)4 |
| *Hirst 33* | | *McClair 4, Kanchelskis 10, Hughes 38, 82* | |

| Tranmere | (2)3 | Aston Villa | (0)1 |
| *Nolan 5, Hughes 23, Aldridge 78* | | *Atkinson 89* | |

| Aston Villa | (2)(3)3 | Tranmere | (1)(1)1 |
| *Saunders 19, Teale 23 Atkinson 88* | | *Aldridge pen 29* Villa 5-4 pens | |

Final

27 March 1994 Wembley 77 231

| Aston Villa | (1)3 | Man Utd | (0)1 |
| *Atkinson 25, Saunders 75, 89 pen* | | *Hughes 83* | |

Villa: Mark Bosnich, Earl Barrett, Steve Staunton (Neil Cox 78), Shaun Teale, Paul McGrath, Kevin Richardson, Tony Daley, Andy Townsend, Dean Saunders, Dalian Atkinson, Graham Fenton

Man Utd: Les Sealey, Paul Parker, Dennis Irwin, Roy Keane, Steve Bruce (Brian McClair 84), Gary Pallister, Andrei Kanchelskis, Eric Cantona, Paul Ince, Mark Hughes, Ryan Giggs (Lee Sharpe 61)

Villa's fourth League Cup win equals the record set by Liverpool & Nottm Forest. All three have reached a record six finals each.

Footballers of the Year 1993-94

| PFA | Eric Cantona | Man Utd |
| PFA Young Player | Andy Cole | Newcastle |

Ryan Giggs, who was voted third best, had won the award for the past two seasons.

| Football Writers' | Alan Shearer | Blackburn |

Transfer records *at 15 Jan 1995*

Between British clubs

£ million		from	to	
7.00	Andy Cole	Newcastle	Man Utd	1995
5.00	Chris Sutton	Norwich	Blackburn	1994
4.00	Duncan Ferguson	Dundee Utd	Rangers	1993
4.00	Duncan Ferguson	Rangers	Everton	1994
3.75	Roy Keane	Nottm Forest	Man Utd	1993
3.60	Phil Babb	Coventry	Liverpool	1994
3.30	Alan Shearer	Southampton	Blackburn	1992
3.00	Daniel Amokachi	Bruges	Everton	1994
3.00	John Scales	Wimbledon	Liverpool	1994

Involving British players

7.00	Andy Cole	Newcastle	Man Utd	1995
6.50	David Platt	Bari	Juventus	1992
5.50	David Platt	Aston Villa	Bari	1991
5.50	Paul Gascoigne	Tottenham	Lazio	1992
5.20	David Platt	Juventus	Sampdoria	1993
5.00	Trevor Steven	Rangers	Marseille	1991
5.00	Chris Sutton	Norwich	Blackburn	1994
4.50	Chris Waddle	Tottenham	Marseille	1989

World records

13.00	Gianluigi Lentini	Torino	Milan	1992
12.00	Gianluca Vialli	Sampdoria	Juventus	1992
10.00	Jean-Pierre Papin	Marseille	Milan	1992
8.00	Igor Shalimov	Foggia	Inter	1992

The long hot-headed summer. All four took place in June of the same year.

Scottish leagues 1993-94

Premier League

	P	Home					Away					Pts
		W	D	L	F	A	W	D	L	F	A	
Rangers	44	12	6	4	43	22	10	8	4	31	19	58
Aberdeen	44	11	9	2	33	12	6	12	4	25	24	55
Motherwell	44	11	7	4	31	20	9	7	6	27	23	54
Celtic	44	8	11	3	25	17	7	9	6	26	21	50
Hibs	44	11	7	4	29	15	5	8	9	24	33	47
Dundee Utd	44	5	11	6	26	25	6	9	7	21	23	42
Hearts	44	6	9	7	22	24	5	11	6	15	19	42
Kilmarnock	44	6	10	6	18	19	6	6	10	18	26	40
Partick	44	9	8	5	23	17	3	8	11	23	40	40
St Johnstone	44	7	7	8	24	26	3	13	6	11	21	40
Raith	44	3	12	7	25	35	3	7	12	21	45	31
Dundee	44	6	7	9	26	26	2	6	14	16	31	29

Rangers win the title for the sixth successive season, the longest sequence since Celtic's nine consecutive championships 1966-74. Aberdeen finish as runners-up for the fifth time in the last six seasons. St Johnstone, Raith & Dundee are relegated.

Division 1

Falkirk	44	16	4	2	47	16	10	10	2	34	16	66
Dunfermline	44	18	2	2	61	18	11	5	6	32	17	65
Airdrie	44	9	9	4	28	18	11	5	6	30	20	54
Hamilton	44	13	5	4	43	20	6	7	9	23	34	50
Clydebank	44	11	5	6	30	28	7	9	6	26	20	50
St Mirren	44	10	3	9	30	25	11	5	6	31	30	50
Ayr Utd	44	6	8	8	20	28	8	6	8	22	24	42
Dumbarton	44	5	8	9	25	29	6	6	10	23	30	36
Stirling Albion	44	7	6	9	23	30	6	3	13	18	38	35
Clyde	44	6	7	9	18	20	4	5	13	17	38	32
Morton	44	3	11	8	22	29	3	6	13	22	46	29
Brechin	44	4	3	15	13	34	2	4	16	17	47	19

Falkirk are promoted, Dumbarton, Stirling, Clyde, Morton & Brechin relegated.

Division 2

Stranraer	39	15	2	3	38	18	8	8	3	25	17	56
Berwick	39	9	7	4	40	23	9	5	5	35	23	48
Stenhousemuir	39	9	7	4	35	15	9	3	8	27	29	47
Meadowbank	39	9	8	2	36	24	8	5	7	26	24	47
Queen of the South	39	9	3	7	36	20	8	6	6	33	28	43
East Fife	39	9	5	5	33	23	6	6	8	25	29	41
Alloa	39	6	8	6	16	17	6	9	4	25	22	41
Forfar	39	6	6	8	27	32	8	5	6	31	26	39
East Stirling	39	7	3	9	29	31	6	8	6	25	26	37
Montrose	39	6	5	8	24	25	8	3	9	32	36	36
Queen's Park	39	10	4	6	34	32	2	6	11	18	44	34
Arbroath	39	6	8	5	24	28	6	1	13	18	39	33
Albion	39	3	5	12	18	33	4	5	10	19	33	24
Cowdenbeath	39	1	4	15	19	39	5	4	10	21	33	20

Stranraer are promoted, Alloa-to-Cowdenbeath relegated to the new Division 3.

Premier Division leading scorers

			pens
22	Mark Hateley	Rangers	2
17	Duncan Shearer	Aberdeen	0
16	Craig Brewster	Dundee Utd	0
16	Keith Wright	Hibs	0

Scottish Cup 1993-94

3rd round

Airdrie	(0)1	Dunfermline	(0)1
Kirkwood pen 53		Tod 89	
Dunfermline	(0)1	Airdrie	(2)3
Tod 80		Kirkwood 6 pen, 84 pen, Ferguson 11	
Alloa	(2)2	Ross County	0
McAnenay 17, McAvoy 25			
Arbroath	(0)2	Dundee Utd	(2)3
Sorbie 56, McKinnon 78		Crabbe 10, Brewster 42, McKinlay pen 59	
Clydebank	(1)1	Dundee	(0)1
Henry 30		Tosh 83	
Dundee	(2)2	Clydebank (0)1 at Stirling	
Britton 19, Shaw 39		Sweeney 86	
East Stirling	(0)1	Aberdeen	(0)3
Geraghty 80		Craig og 57, Shearer 66, 72	
Hibs	(0)2	Clyde	(1)1
O'Neill 68, McAllister 88		McCheyne 30	
Kilmarnock	(1)2	Ayr Utd	(1)1
McSkimming 10, Black pen 50		Bryce 35	
Morton	(0)2	Cowdenbeath	(2)2
McEwan 88, Lilley 89		Henderson 6, 20	
Cowdenbeath	(0)1	Morton	(1)2
Callaghan 82		Anderson 10, McEwan 50	
Motherwell	(0)1	Celtic	0
Coyne 82			
Partick	0	Hearts	(1)1
		M Johnston 44	
Raith	(2)2	Brechin	0
Dair 24, McStay 31			
Rangers	(3)4	Dumbarton	(0)1
Durie 3, Hateley pen 20, Steven 39, Robertson 67		Mooney pen	
St Johnstone	(0)2	Hamilton	0
Dodds 55, McMartin 85			

St Mirren	(1)2	Montrose	0
Elliot 21, Bone 57			
Stirling Albion	(0)1	Berwick	0
Pew 84			
Stranraer	(1)2	Falkirk	(0)1
Sloan 6, Ferguson 68		Hughes 62	

4th round

Aberdeen	(0)1	Raith	0
Miller 81			
Airdrie	(0)1	Stranraer	0
Kirkwood pen 64			
Dundee	(1)3	St Mirren	(1)1
Britton 38 pen, 89, Shaw 57		Laverty 16	
Dundee Utd	(1)2	Motherwell	(1)2
Brewster 41, 56		Kirk 31, Philliben 89	
Hibs	(1)1	Hearts	(1)2
Wright 42		Robertson 2, Foster 86	
Motherwell	0	Dundee Utd	(0)1
		Welsh 67	
Morton	0	Kilmarnock	(1)1
		Williamson 17	
Rangers	(2)6	Alloa	0
I Ferguson 32, McPherson 44, McCoist 48, 71, 83 pen, Newbigging og 73			
St Johnstone	(1)3	Stirling Albion	(2)3
Dodds 2, Ferguson		Roberts 2, Armstrong	
Stirling Albion	0	St Johnstone	(2)2
		Scott 22, Ferguson 42	

Quarter-finals

Airdrie	0	Dundee Utd	0
Dundee Utd	(2)2	Airdrie	0
McLaren, McKinlay			
Kilmarnock	(1)1	Dundee	0
Brown 40			
Rangers	(0)2	Hearts	0
Brown 49, Hateley 74			
St Johnstone	(0)1	Aberdeen	(1)1
Dodds 60		Booth 30	
Aberdeen	(2)2	St Johnstone	0
Shearer, Richardson			

Semi-finals

All, including replays, at Hampden Park

Dundee Utd	(0)1	Aberdeen	(1)1
Welsh 88		Shearer 7	

| Dundee Utd | (0)1 | Aberdeen | 0 |
| McInally 70 | | | |

| Rangers | 0 | Kilmarnock | 0 |

| Rangers | (0)2 | Kilmarnock | (1)1 |
| Hateley 47, 52 | | Black 17 | |

Final

21 May 1994 Hampden Park 37 450

| Dundee Utd | (0)1 | Rangers | 0 |
| Brewster 47 | | | |

Dundee Utd: Guido Van De Kamp, Alec Cleland, Maurice Malpas, Jim McInally, Gordan Petric, Brian Welsh, David Bowman, David Hannah, Andy McLaren (Nixon 83), Brewster, Christian Dailly

Rangers: Ally Maxwell, Gary Stevens (Alexei Mikhailichenko 24), David Robertson, Richard Gough (c), Dave McPherson, Stuart McCall, Neil Murray, Ian Ferguson, Ally McCoist (Duncan Ferguson 73), Mark Hateley, Gordon Durie

Referee: Douglas Hope

In their seventh appearance in the final, United at last win the Cup for the first time and stop Rangers a) winning it for the third consecutive year, and b) winning a second successive Treble.

Scottish League Cup 1993-94

Quarter-finals

| Celtic | (0)1 | Airdrie | 0 |
| McAvennie | | | |

Dundee Utd	(1)3	Falkirk	(3)3
Clark 2, McLaren		Cadette 3	
aet Utd 4-2 pens			

Partick	(1)2	Hibs	(0)2
Grant, Craig		McAllister 2	
aet Hibs 3-2 pens			

| Rangers | (1)2 | Aberdeen | (0)1 aet |
| Hateley pen, I Ferguson | | Miller | |

Semi-finals

| Hibs | (1)1 | Dundee Utd | 0 |
| D Jackson | | | |

| Rangers | (0)1 | Celtic | 0 |
| Hateley | | | |

The holders win at home.

Final

24 Oct 1993 Celtic Park 47 632

| Rangers | (0)2 | Hibs | (0)1 |
| Durrant, McCoist | | McPherson og | |

Rangers: Ally Maxwell, Gary Stevens, David Robertson, Richard Gough (c), Dave McPherson, Stuart McCall, Trevor Steven, Ian Ferguson, Ian Durrant, Mark Hateley, Pieter Huistra (Ally McCoist)

Hibs: Jim Leighton, Graeme Miller, Graham Mitchell, David Farrell, Steven Tweed, Gordon Hunter, McAllister, Brian Hamilton, Keith Wright, Darren Jackson (Gareth Evans), O'Neill

Referee: Jim McCluskey

Rangers retain the Cup when McCoist, out of action for virtually a whole year with a broken leg, scores almost immediately after coming on.

Scottish League Cup 1994-95

1st round

Arbroath	(0)1	Alloa	(1)1
Riley 55		Morrison 28	
aet Arbroath 5-4 on pens			

| Berwick | 0 | Montrose | 0 |
| aet Montrose 3-2 on pens | | | |

| East Fife | (0)1 | Forfar | 0 |
| Allan 80 | | | |

| East Stirling | 0 | Caledonian Thistle | (2)2 |
| | | Robertson 34, Hercher 44 | |

| Queen of South | (0)2 | Albion Rovers | 0 |
| McLaren 81, Bryce 88 | | | |

Ross County	(1)3	Queen's Park	(0)2
Grant 39, 89,		Orr 76, Maxwell 86	
McPherson 50			

Stenhousemuir	0	Meadowbank	(1)4
		Bailey 7, McLeod pen 58,	
		Hutchinson 76, Little 87	

Stranraer	(1)2	Cowdenbeath	(0)2
Cody 28, Ferguson 66		Black 50, Soutar 73	
aet Stranraer 4-2 on pens			

2nd round

Aberdeen *Shearer 71*	(0)1	Stranraer	0
Arbroath *McKinnon 20*	(1)1	Rangers *Hateley 1, 55, D Ferguson 19, 74, 84, McCall 42*	(3)6
Ayr	0	Celtic *Grant 2*	(1)1
Dumbarton	0	Hearts *Millar 20, Robertson 36, Johnston 53, 68*	(2)4
Dundee *Shaw 28, Tosh 70, 82*	(1)3	Caledonian Thistle	0
Dunfermline *McCathie 27, Bieman 44 Petrie 63, Ward 73*	(2)4	Meadowbank *Sorbie 55*	(0)1
Falkirk *aet Falkirk 5-4 on pens Cadette 84*	(0)1	Montrose *Kennedy 70*	(0)1
Greenock *aet Airdrie 5-3 on pens Lilley 23*	(1)1	Airdrie *Smith 11*	(1)1
Hamilton *McEntegart 3, Bapptie 63, McLean 82, Campbell 87, Sherry 89*	(1)5	Clyde	0
Kilmarnock *Henry 22, McCluskey 37 Maskrey 46, 55*	(2)4	East Fife *Hope 56*	(0)1
Motherwell *Coyne pen 44, Kirk 74, Burns 79*	(1)3	Clydebank *Grady 87*	(0)1
Partick *Taylor 14, Jamieson 36, Charnley 44, 72 pen, 90*	(3)5	Brechin	0
Queen of South	0	Hibernian *Evans 42, Tweed 44, O'Neill 67*	(2)3
Ross County	0	Raith *Cameron 55, Graham 65, 83, 88, Dalziel 74*	(0)5
St Mirren *aet*	0	Dundee Utd *Ristic 97*	(0)1
Stirling	0	St Johnstone *O'Boyle 13, Scott 89*	(1)2

3rd Round

Hibs *O'Neill 28, 89*	(1)2	Dunfermline	0
Partick	0	Aberdeen *Shearer 29, 33 62 pen, Kane 60, Dodds 69*	(2)5
Dundee *Farningham 19*	(1)1	Celtic *Collins 8, Walker 78*	(1)2
Hamilton *aet Utd 5-3 pens Cleland og 75, Duffield 118*	(0)2	Dunde Utd *Hannah 41, 97*	(1)2
Hearts *Locke 9, Colquhoun 31*	(2)2	St Johnsone *O'Neil 46, Millar 68, O'Boyle 79, Irons 87*	(0)4
Motherwell *McCart 77*	(0)1	Airdrie *Boyle 33, 118*	(1)2 aet
Raith *Cameron 35, 41, 77*	(2)3	Kilmarnock *Montgomerie 33, Williamson 80*	(1)2
Rangers *Laudrup 64*	(0)1	Falkirk *Cadette 28, 76*	(1)2

Rangers had won the Cup for the last two seasons.

Quarter-finals

St Johnstone *O'Neill 50*	(0)1	Raith *Dennis 19, Graham 31, Lennon 83*	(2)3
Celtic *Collins 86*	(0)1	Dundee Utd	0
Falkirk *McDonald 23*	(1)1	Aberdeen *Booth 6, 20, 63, Rice og 83*	(2)4
Hibs *Evans 75*	(0)1	Airdrie *Smith 18, Lawrence 31*	(2)2

Semi-finals

Airdrie *Cooper 74 Raith 5-4 pens*	(0)(1)1	Raith *Graham 39 (Thomson sent off 69)*	(1)(1)1

*Goalkeeper Scott Thomson's sending-off does Raith no
harm: 17-y-o substitute Brian Porter is chaired off after
saving Airdrie's last kick in the shoot-out to send Rovers
to a major final for only the second time in their 111-year
history (they lost the 1948-49 League Cup final).*

Celtic *O'Neil 99*	(0)(0)1	Aberdeen	0

Final

27 Nov 1993 Ibrox 47 000

Raith *Crawford 18, Dalziel 86 Raith 6-5 pens*	(1)(2)2	Celtic *Walker 31, Nicholas 84*	(1)(2)2

Raith: Scott Thomson, Davie Sinclair, Dennis, David Narey, McAnespie, Colin Cameron, Jason Dair, Stephen Crawford, Broddle (Rowbotham 93), Gordon Dalziel (Ian Redford 112), Graham

Celtic: Gordon Marshall, John O'Neill, Tony Mowbray, Mark McNally, Mike Galloway, Paul McStay (c), Charlie Nicholas (Paul Byrne 98), John Collins, Tom Boyd, Donnelly (Willie Falconer 93), Andy Walker

A broken foot keeps regular captain Danny Lennon out of the game (the third time he's missed a League Cup final) which his club win to become the first team from outside the top division to take a trophy since East Fife in the 1947-48 League Cup. Even hard man Sinclair ('tattoos on his teeth') can't hold back the tears. Celtic haven't won any competition since 1988-89. In the shoot-out, the first eleven kicks go in, then Thomson makes up for his semi-final sending-off by saving from McStay, one of two survivors (Nicholas the other) from the last time Celtic won the League Cup (1982-83). Dalziel & Redford won League Cup winners' medals with Rangers, the 38-y-o Narey with Dundee Utd.

League of Wales 1993-94

	P	W	D	L	F	A	Pts
Bangor City	38	26	5	7	82	26	83
Inter Cardiff	38	26	3	9	97	44	81
Ton Pentre	38	21	8	9	62	37	71
Flint Town Utd	38	20	6	12	70	47	66
Holywell Town	38	18	10	10	74	57	64
Newtown	38	18	9	11	52	48	63
Connah's Quay Nomads	38	16	11	11	59	47	59
Cwmbran Town	38	16	9	13	51	46	57
Ebbw Vale	38	16	9	13	68	66	57
Aberystwyth Town	38	15	10	13	57	56	55
Porthmadog	38	14	7	17	90	71	49
Llanelli	38	14	4	20	76	100	46
Conwy Utd	38	13	6	19	55	70	45
Mold Alexandra	38	12	7	19	59	75	43
Haverfordwest County	38	10	10	34	40	81	40
Afan Lido	38	8	15	15	52	66	39
Caersws	38	9	12	17	39	56	39
Llansantffraid	38	9	7	22	46	77	34
Maesteg Park Athletic	38	8	9	21	43	71	33
Briton Ferry Athletic	38	8	9	21	53	84	33

Welsh League

Division 1 champions: Barry Town
Division 2 champions: Taffs Wells
Division 3 champions: Penrhiwceiber
Bottom of the League: Trelewis (on goal difference from Panteg)

Welsh Cup 1993-94

5th round

Bangor City	1	Inter Cardiff	1
Inter Cardiff	0	Bangor City	1
Barry Town	1	Flint Town Utd	0
Ebbw Vale	1	Cardiff City	1
Cardiff City	3	Ebbw Vale	0
Swansea City	1	Hereford Utd	0

Semi-finals (2 legs)

Bangor City	1	Barry Town	1
Barry Town	1	Bangor City	0
Swansea City	2	Cardiff	1
Cardiff City	4	Swansea City	1

Final 15 May National Stadium, Cardiff

Barry Town	(1)2	Cardiff City	(0)1
D'Auria 40, Hough 60		*Stant 51*	

Barry: Morris, Hough, Griffiths, Boyle, Williams, Curtis (Smith 80), Wimbleton, Beattie, D'Auria, Lilygreen, Bertschin (Sanderson 71)

Cardiff: Steve Williams, Wayne Fereday, Jason Perry, Mark Aizlewood, Damon Searle, Paul Millar, Nick Richardson (Darren Adams 60), Kevin Brock, Cohen Griffith, Phil Stant, Garry Thompson (Anthony Bird 75)

Referee: John Lloyd

Irish League 1993-94

	P	W	D	L	F	A	Pts
Linfield	30	21	7	2	63	22	70
Portadown	30	20	8	2	76	21	68
Glenavon	30	21	5	4	69	29	68
Crusaders	30	17	7	6	53	30	56
Bangor	30	14	3	13	45	49	45
Ards	30	13	2	15	59	55	41
Distillery	30	11	8	11	41	40	41
Cliftonville	30	11	10	9	40	32	40
Glentoran	30	10	7	13	46	43	37
Coleraine	30	10	7	13	41	50	37
Balymena Utd	30	9	6	15	36	58	33
Ballyclare Comrades	30	9	6	15	36	58	33
Carrick Rangers	30	6	7	17	42	81	25
Newry Town	30	5	9	16	26	52	24
Omagh Town	30	6	5	19	32	58	23
Larne	30	5	7	18	30	62	22

Linfield retain the title. Cliftonville have three points deducted for fielding an unregistered player.

Irish Cup 1993-94

6th round

Ballymena	0	Cliftonville	3
Coleraine	2	Glenavon	3
Distillery	1	Abbey Villa	0
Glentoran	4	Dundela	3
Linfield	2	Carrick Rangers	0
Loughgall Utd	1	Bangor	2
Portadown	4	Donegal Celtic	0
Newry Town	0	Omagh Town	0
Omagh Town	1	Newry Town 0 abandoned	
Omagh Town	2	Newry Town	2

aet Omagh 6-5 pens

Quarter-finals

Linfield	0	Cliftonville	0
Cliftonville	1	Linfield	0 aet
Omagh Town	1	Portadown	2
Distillery	2	Glenavon	4
Glentoran	0	Bangor	2

Semi-finals

Bangor	2	Portadown	0
Linfield	3	Glenavon	0

Final

7 May 1994 The Oval, Belfast 10 000

Linfield	2	Bangor	0

Haylock, Fenlon

Linfield: Wesley Lamont, Alan Dornan, John Easton, Peebles, Jeff Spiers (Lee Doherty), Stephen Beatty, Robert Campbell, Dessie Gorman, Garry Haylock, Pat Fenlon, Noel Bailie

Bangor: Tim Dalton, Tony Canning, Mark Glendinning, Eddie Spiers, Stephen Brown, John O'Connor, Raymond Hill, Conor McCaffrey, David McCallan, Jonathan Magee (Michael Surgeon), Ricky McEvoy

Linfield beat the holders to win the Cup for the first time since 1982.

Ulster Cup

Crusaders	1	Bangor	0
Hunter			

Gold Cup

Distillery	3	Bangor	2
Calvin, Cleland, Armstrong		*Glendinning, Spiers*	aet

Budweiser Cup

Linfield	3	Ards	0
Doherty, Haylock, Campbell			

Ulster Cup 1994-95

Bangor	2	Linfield	1

League of Ireland 1993-94

Qualifying table

	P	W	D	L	F	A	Pts
Shamrock R	22	15	3	4	43	16	48
Cork City	22	12	5	5	43	24	41
Shelbourne	22	10	6	6	33	27	36
Galway Utd	22	9	7	6	30	26	34
Bohemians	22	8	7	7	23	17	31
Derry City	22	8	7	7	21	21	31
Monaghan Utd	22	9	3	10	27	27	30
Dundalk	22	7	8	7	25	20	29
St Patrick's A	22	6	9	7	24	24	27
Cobh Ramb.	22	5	4	13	20	34	19
Limerick City	22	3	8	11	15	40	17
Drogheda Utd	22	4	5	13	16	44	17

Final table

	P	W	D	L	F	A	Pts
Shamrock R	32	21	3	8	62	30	66
Cork City	32	17	8	7	60	36	59
Galway Utd	32	14	8	10	47	42	50
Derry City	32	12	10	10	37	35	46
Shelbourne	32	11	10	11	42	42	43
Bohemians	32	11	8	12	34	35	41

Shamrock win the title for the 15th time, adding to their own record.

Promotion/relegation

	P	W	D	L	F	A	Pts
Monaghan Utd	32	13	8	11	41	38	47
Dundalk	32	10	13	9	37	27	43
St Patrick's A	32	9	12	11	32	38	39
Cobh Ramb.	32	8	8	16	31	41	32
Limerick City	32	6	11	15	23	50	29
Drogheda Utd	32	7	7	18	26	58	28

Limerick & Drogheda are relegated.

Cup final

Sligo Rovers	1	Derry City	0

European Cup 1993-94

Preliminary round

B68 (FAER)	0-5, 0-6	Croatia Zagreb (CRO)
Cwmbran Town (WAL)	3-2, 1-2	Cork City (EIRE)
Ekranas (LITH)	0-1, 0-1	Floriana (MALTA)
HJK (FIN)	1-1, 1-0	Norma Tallinn (EST)
Omonia (CYP)	2-1, 0-2	Aarau (SWI)
Avenir Beggen (LUX)	0-2, 0-1	Rosenborg
Skonto Riga (LAT)	0-1, 1-0	Olim. Ljubljana (SLVN)

Riga 12-11 pens

Dynamo Tbilisi (GEO) 2-1, 1-1 Linfield (N IRE)

Tbilisi are thrown out of the competition for trying to bribe Turkish referee Erman Toroglu.

Zimbrul (MOLD)	1-1, 0-2	Beitar Jerusalem (ISR)
Partizani Tirana (ALB)	0-0, 0-3	Akranes (ICE)

1st round

Aarau	0	Milan (ITA)	(0)1
		Papin 54	

Milan	0	Aarau	0

AIK (SWE)	(1)1	Sparta Prague (CZE)	0
Lidman 36			

Sparta Prague	(1)2	AIK	0
Siegl 15, 80			

Akranes	(0)1	Feyenord (HOL)	0
Thordarson 75			

Feyenoord	(1)3	Akranes	0
Refos 25, Obiku 65, Blinker 83			

Galatasaray (TURK)	(1)2	Cork City	0
Turkiylmaz 31, Arif 51			

Cork City	0	Galatasaray	(0)1
		Turkiylmaz 76	

HJK	0	Anderlecht (BEL)	(0)3
		Bosman 49, Versavel 74, Boffin 80	

Anderlecht	(3)3	HJK	0
Nilis 16, 21, 42			

Dinamo Kiev (UKR)	(2)3	Barcelona (SPA)	(1)1
Shkapenko 6, Leonerko 45 pen, 56		*Koeman pen 28*	

Barcelona	(2)4	Dinamo Kiev	(1)1
Laudrup 8, Bakero 16, 47 Koeman 67		*Rebrov 28*	

Kispest Honvéd(HUN)	(1)2	Man Utd (ENG)	(3)3
Szabados 40, Stefanov 70		*Keane 9, 43, Cantona 44*	

Man Utd	(0)2	Kispest Honvéd	(0)1
Bruce 55, 64		*Salloi 78*	

Lech Poznan (POL)	(2)3	Beitar Jerusalem	0
Moskai 6, Podbrozny pen 32, Trzeciak 60			

Beitar Jerusalem	(1)2	Lech Poznan	(3)4
Ohana 11, Schwartz 72		*Wilkashik 4, Scheczik 23, Brojana 31, Tapinski 70*	

Linfield	(2)3	FC Copenhagen (DEN)	0
Haylock 38, McConnell 42, Johnston 60			

FC Copenhagen	(2)4	Linfield	0 aet
Moller 2, Michael Johansen 26, Hojer 90, Mikkelsen 96			

Copenhagen level the tie deep into some very generous injury time.

Monaco (FRA)	(0)1	AEK (GRE)	0
Vlahos og 81			

AEK	(1)1	Monaco	(1)1
Siskovic 12		*Djorkaeff 5*	

Porto (PORT)	(1)2	Floriana	0
Kostadinov 8, Semedo 78			

Floriana	0	Porto	0

Rangers (SCOT)	(1)3	Levski Sofia (BUL)	(0)2
McPherson 44, Hateley 56, 79		*Borimirov 77, Todorov 83*	

Levski Sofia	(1)2	Rangers	(1)1
Sirakov 36, Todorov 90		*Durrant 44*	

Rosenborg	(3)3	FK Austria (AUT)	(0)1
Tangen pen 29, Leonhardsen 35, Loeken 42		*Zsak pen 33*	

FK Austria	(1)4	Rosenborg	(1)1
Nabekovas 12, Schmid 50 Zsak 74, Kögler 81		*Dahlum 32*	

Skonto Riga	0	Spartak Mscw (RUS)	(4)5
		Pogodin 2, 39, Rodionov 7, 41 Bestchastnykh 67	

Spartak Moscow	(3)4	Skonto Riga	0
Tsymbalar 4, 40, Pisarev 15, Onopko 87			

Steaua (ROM)	(1)1	Croatia Zagreb	(1)2
Pandaru 35		*Cvitanovic 19, Jelicic 62*	

Croatia Zagreb	(1)2	Steaua	(1)3
Vlaovic 7, Adziz 71		*Pandaru 14, Vladoiu 49, 61*	

Werder Bremen (GER)	(2)5	Dinamo Minsk (BYL)	(0)2
Hobsch 26, 32, 60, Rufer 55, 89		*Gerasimov 52, Velichko 77*	

Dinamo Minsk	(1)1	Werder Bremen	(0)1
Byelkevich 41		*Rufer pen 80*	

European Cup Finals: biggest wins

7-3	Real Madrid	1960	v Eintr Frankfurt
4-0	Bayern Munich	1974	v Atletico Madrid
4-0	Milan	1989	v Steaua
4-0	Milan	1994	v Barcelona

2nd round

Barcelona	(1)3	FK Austria	0
Koeman 37 pen, 68, Quique 89			

FK Austria	(1)1	Barcelona	(1)2
Ogris 39		*Stoitchkov 6, 78*	

FC Copenhagen	0	Milan	(3)6
		Papin 1, 71, Simone 5,14, Laudrup 43, Orlando 60	

Milan	(1)1	FC Copenhagen	0
Papin 44			

Lech Poznan	(1)1	Spartak Moscow	(3)5
Podbrozny 44		*Pisraev 8, 62, Karpin 10, Onopko 30, 53*	

Spartak Moscow	(1)2	Lech Poznan	(1)1
Karpin 6, Khlestov 81		*Dembilski 28*	

Levski Sofia	(0)2	Werder Bremen	(0)2
Yankov 75, Ginchev 89		*Bode 50, Rufer 52*	

Werder Bremen	(0)1	Levski Sofia	0
Basler 75			

Man Utd	(2)3	Galatasaray	(2)3
Robson 3, Hakan og 13, Cantona 81		*Arif 16, Turkiylmaz 31, 63*	

Galatasaray	0	Man Utd	0

United's descent into Hell. Cantona, assaulted by police after the match, is banned for the next four European matches, and a hundred United fans are imprisoned for a month.

Monaco	(0)4	Steaua	(1)1
Ikpeba 50, 75, Klinsmann 52, 64		*Dumitrescu pen 22*	

Steaua	(0)1	Monaco	0
Dumitrescu 84			

Porto	(0)1	Feyenoord	0
Domingos 89			

Feyenoord	0	Porto	0

Sparta Prague	0	Anderlecht	(0)1
		Nilis 74	

Anderlecht	(1)4	Sparta Prague	(1)2
Bosman 2, Nilis 47, 71, Versavel 89		*Dvirnik 18, Vonasek 60*	

Champions' League

Group A

Monaco	(2)4	Spartak Moscow	(0)1
Klinsmann 17, Ikpeba 41, Djorkaeff pen 62, Thuram 89		*Pisarev*	

Galatasaray	0	Barcelona	0

Barcelona	(2)2	Monaco	0
Beguiristain 16, 27			

Spartak Moscow	0	Galatasaray	0

Monaco	(2)3	Galatasaray	0
Scifo 36, Djorkaeff 41, Klinsmann 52			

Spartak Moscow	(0)2	Barcelona	(1)2
Rodionov 77, Karpin 88		*Stoitchkov 10, Romário 66*	

Barcelona	(1)5	Spartak Moscow	(1)1
Stoitchkov 34, Amor 75, Koeman 78, 80, Romário pen 86		*Karpin 3*	

Galatasaray	0	Monaco	(0)2
		Scifo 54, Gnako 89	

Barcelona	(1)3	Galatasaray	0
Amor 22, Koeman pen 71, Eusebio 77			

Spartak Moscow	0	Monaco	0

Galatasaray	(0)1	Spartak Moscow	(0)2
Cihat 86		*Onopko 55, Karpin 83*	

Monaco	0	Barcelona	(1)1
		Stoitchkov 13	

	P	W	D	L	F	A	Pts
Barcelona	6	4	2	0	13	3	10
Monaco	6	3	1	2	9	4	7
Spartak	6	1	3	2	6	12	5
Galatasaray	6	0	2	4	1	10	2

Group B

Werder Bremen	(0)5	Anderlecht	(3)3
Rufer 66, 89, Bratseth 72, Hobsch 81, Bode 83		*Albert 16, Boffin 18, 33*	

Milan	(2)3	Porto	0
Raducioiu 16, Panucci 39, Massaro 63			

Milan	(0)2	Werder Bremen	(0)1
Maldini 48, Savicevic 68		*Basler 54*	

Anderlecht	(0)1	Porto	0
Nilis 88			

Werder Bremen	(0)1	Milan	(0)1
Rufer pen 52		*Savicevic 74*	

Porto   (1)2   Anderlecht   0
Drulovic 10, Secretario 89

Milan   0   Anderlecht   0

Werder Bremen   0   Porto   (2)5
Rui Felipe 11, Kostadinov 35, Secretario 70, Domingos 74, Timofte pen 89

Anderlecht   (1)1   Werder Bremen   (1)2
Bosman 44   *Bode 33, 65*

Porto   0   Milan   0

	P	W	D	L	F	A	Pts
Milan	6	2	4	0	6	2	8
Porto	6	3	1	2	10	6	7
Werder	6	2	1	3	11	15	5
Andrlecht	6	1	2	3	5	9	4

Semi-finals

Barcelona   (2)3   Porto   0
Stoitchkov 10, 35 Koeman 72

Milan   (1)3   Monaco   0
Desailly 14, Albertini 48, Massaro 66

Final

18 May 1994 Olympic, Athens
70 000, referee Philip Don (ENG)

MILAN   (2)4   BARCELONA   0
Massaro 22, 44, Savicevic 47, Desailly

MILAN: Sebastiano Rossi, Mauro Tassotti (c), Christian Panucci, Marcel Desailly, Filippo Galli, Paolo Maldini [Stefano Nava 83], Demetrio Albertini, Dejan Savicevic, Daniele Massaro, Zvonimir Boban, Roberto Donadoni

BARCELONA: Andoni Zubizarreta, Albert Ferrer, Josep Guardiola, Guillermo Amor, Miguel Angel Nadal, Ronald Koeman, José María Bakero (c), Sergi (Barjuan) [Quique (Estebaranz) 72], Romário (de Souza Faria), Christo Stoitchkov, Aitor Beguiristain [Eusebio (Sacristán) 51]

Stoitchkov's prediction that he'll score the goal in Barcelona's 1-0 win rebounds in spectacular fashion. Savicevic is brilliant, his goal preposterously so, Desailly massive in midfield, Maldini (in the absence of Costacurta and the great Baresi) as dominant in central defence as he is on the left. Stoitchkov & Romário are blotted out, Massaro, who missed important early chances in last year's final, redeems himself by scoring twice and hitting a post. The last hat-trick in a European Cup final was scored by Pierino Prati, also of Milan, in 1969.

On the winning side in European Cup finals with different clubs
Miodrag Belodedici   1986 Steaua, 1991 Red Star
Ronald Koeman   1988 PSV, 1992 Barcelona
Dejan Savicevic   1991 Red Star, 1994 Milan
Marcel Desailly   1993 Marseille, 1994 Milan

Six others played in European Cup finals with more than one club, winning & losing.

European Cup-Winners' Cup 1993-94

Preliminary round

Balzers (LIECH)   3-1, 0-0   Albpetrol (ALB)
RAF Jelgava (LAT)   0-1   Havn. Boltfelag (FAER)
HB won the second leg on a walk-over.
Stade Dudelange (LUX)0-1, 1-6   Maccabi Haifa (ISR)
Lugano (SWI)   5-0, 1-2   Neman Grodno (BYL)
Valur Rekjavik (ICE)   3-1, 1-0   MyPa (FIN)
Sliema Wdrs (MALTA) 1-3, 0-3   Degerfors (SWE)
Bangor (N IRE)   1-1, 1-2   Apoel (CYP)
Nikol Tallinn (EST)   0-4, 1-4   Lillestrom (NOR)
Kosice (SLVK)   2-0, 1-0   Zalgiris Vilnius (LITH)
Karpaty Lvov (UKR)   1-0, 1-3   Shelbourne (EIRE)
Publikum Celje (SLVN) 0-1, 0-1   Odense (DEN)

1st round

Apoel   0   Paris SG (FRA)   (0)1
    Sassus 78

Paris Saint-Germain (2)2   Apoel   0
Le Guen 1, Gravelaine 32

Bayer Leverkusen (GER)(1)2   Boby Brno (CZE)   0
Hapal 32, Thom 66

Boby Brno   0   Bayer Leverkusen   (1)3
    Kirsten 16, Fischer 57, Wörns 75

Degerfors   (0)1   Parma (ITA)   (0)2
Berger 72   *Asprilla 87, 88*

Parma   (1)2   Degerfors   0
Balleri 2, Brolin 67

Valur   0   Aberdeen (SCOT)   (2)3
    Shearer 9, Jess 28, 56

Aberdeen   (0)4   Valur   0
Miller 51, Jess 60, 69, Irvine 65

Benfica (PORT)	(0)1	Katowice (POL)	0
Aguas 88			
Katowice	(0)1	Benfica	(0)1
Kucz 46		Vitor Paneira 70	
CSKA Sofia (BUL)	(3)8	Balzers	0
Shishkov 12, 21, 57, 69			
Andenov 41, 52,			
Nankov 67 pen, 80			
Balzers	(0)1	CSKA Sofia	(1)3
Kuster 63		Andenov 31, Tanev 54,	
		Ciric 89	
Hajduk Split (CRO)	(1)1	Ajax (HOL)	0
Mornar 44			
Ajax	(2)6	Hajduk	0
R de Boer 11, Davids 36, 76,			
Litmanen 57, F de Boer 61,			
Pettersson 71			
Innsbruck (AUT)	(0)3	Ferencvaros (HUN)	0
Danek 48, Westerhaler 58,			
Carracedo 65			
Ferencvaros	(0)1	Innsbruck	(1)2
Detari 50		Westerhaler 19, 89	
Kosice	(0)2	Besiktas (TURK)	(1)1
Danko 70 pen, 79		Sergen 2	
Besiktas	(1)2	Kosice	0
Metin 44, 72			
Lillestrom	0	Torino (ITA)	(1)2
		Silenzi 26, Jarni 58	
Torino	(1)1	Lillestrom	(0)2
Silenzi 44		Sinigaglia og 48,	
		Mjielde 58	
Torpedo Mscw (RUS)	(0)1	Maccabi Haifa	0
Borisov 88			
Maccabi Haifa	(1)3	Torpedo Moscow	(1)1
Mizrahi 6, Petz 71,		Kalaychev 12	
Holzman 85			
Odense	(1)1	Arsenal (ENG)	(1)2
Keown og 18		Wright 35, Merson 68	
Arsenal	(0)1	Odense	(0)1
Campbell 52		Nielsen 86	
Panathinaikos (GRE)	(2)3	Shelbourne	0
Donis 13, Saravakos 37,			
Warzycha 48			
Shelbourne	(0)1	Panathinaikos	(1)2
Mooney 86		Georgiadis 26,	
		Saravakos 57	
Real Madrid (SPA)	(1)3	Lugano	0
Dubovsky 44, Michel pen			
66, Fernandez og 70			

Lugano	(0)1	Real Madrid	(1)3
Subiat 62		Hierro 40,	
		Zamorano 78, 87	
Standard Liège (BEL)	(1)5	Cardiff City (WAL)	(1)2
Bisconti 13, Wilmots 63,		Bird 39, 62	
84, André Cruz pen 71,			
Asselman 76			
Cardiff City	(0)1	Standard	(2)3
James 59		Wilmots 14, Lashaf 36,	
		Bisconti 50	
Univ. Craiova (ROM)	(0)4	HB	0
Craioveanu 47, Gane 58,			
71, Calin 82			
HB	0	Universitatea Craiova	(2)3
		Gane 27, 33, Vase 76	

The attendance is surely the lowest in the history of European competition: 74!

2nd round

Ajax	(0)2	Besiktas	(1)1
Rijkaard 60, R de Boer 81		Mehmet 41	
Besiktas	0	Ajax	(1)4
		Litmanen 19, 71, 74,	
		Pettersson 77	
Arsenal	(1)3	Standard Liège	0
Wright 39, 63, Merson 50			
Standard	0	Arsenal	(4)7
		Smith 2, Selley 20, Adams	
		36, Campbell 41, 80,	
		Merson 72, McGoldrick 82	
Benfica	(2)3	CSKA Sofia	(0)1
Babunski og 26,		Andenov 60	
Rui Costa 37, Schwarz 89			
CSKA Sofia	(0)1	Benfica	(1)3
Andenov 56		Rui Costa 37,	
		João Pinto 73, Yuran 89	
Innsbruck	(0)1	Real Madrid	(1)1
Streiter pen 69		Alfonso 50	
Real Madrid	(1)3	Innsbruck	0
Michel 6, Butragueño 46,			
Alfonso 65			
Maccabi Haifa	0	Parma	(0)1
		Brolin 89	
Parma	0	Maccabi Haifa	(0)1 aet
		Mizrahi 51	
Parma 3-1 pens			
Panathinaikos	(1)1	Bayer Leverkusen	(1)4
Warzycha 44		Paulo Sergio 42, Thom 52,	
		Kirsten 59, Hapal 72	

Bayer Leverkusen	(0)1	Panathinaikos	(1)2
Kirsten 83		*Saravakos pen 6,*	
		Georgiadis 66	
Paris SG	(2)4	Universitatea Craiova	0
Guérin 12, Ginola pen 17,			
Bita og, Valdo 71			
Universitatea	0	Paris SG	(1)2
		Guérin 29, 48	
Torino	(1)3	Aberdeen	(2)2
Sergio 44, Fortunato 51,		*Paatelainen 9, Jess 24*	
Aguilera 88			
Aberdeen	(1)1	Torino	(1)2
Richardson 12		*Carbone 39, Silenzi 53*	

Quarter-finals

Benfica	(0)1	Bayer Leverkusen	(0)1
Isaias 89		*Happe 64*	
Bayer Leverkusen	(1)4	Benfica	(0)4
Kirsten 24, 80		*Xavier 59, João Pinto 60*	
Schuster 58, Hapal 80		*Kulkov 78, 86*	
Torino	0	Arsenal	0
Arsenal	(0)1	Torino	0
Adams 66			
Ajax	0	Parma	0
Parma	(1)2	Ajax	0
Minotti 15, Brolin 48			
Real Madrid	0	Paris SG	(1)1
		Weah 32	
Paris SG	(0)1	Real Madrid	(1)1
Ricardo 51		*Butragueño 20*	

Semi-finals

Paris SG	(0)1	Arsenal	(1)1
Ginola 50		*Wright 35*	
Arsenal	(1)1	Paris SG	0
Campbell 6			
Benfica	(1)2	Parma	(1)1
Isaias 7, Rui Costa 60		*Zola 13*	
Parma	(0)1	Benfica	0
Sensini 77			

Final

4 May 1994 Parken, Copenhagen
33 765, referee Václav Krondl (CZE)

ARSENAL	(1)1	PARMA	0
Smith 20			

Arsenal: David Seaman, Lee Dixon, Nigel Winterburn, Paul Davis, Steve Bould, Tony Adams (c), Steve Morrow, Ian Selley, Alan Smith, Kevin Campbell, Paul Merson [Eddie McGoldrick 86]

Parma: Alberto Benarrivo, Alberto Di Chiara, Lorenzo Minotti (c), Roberto Sensini, Gabriele Pin [Alessandro Melli 70], Massimo Crippa, Tomas Brolin, Faustino Asprilla, Gianfranco Zola, Luigi Apolloni

Arsenal, after a post thwarts Brolin at 0-0, stop Parma becoming the first club ever to retain the Cup.

UEFA Cup 1993-94

1st round

Aalborg (DEN)	(0)1	Dep. La Coruña (SPA)	0
Thorst 66			
Deportivo La Coruña	(1)5	Aalborg	0
Bebeto 18, 51, 71,			
Barragan 66, 86			
Antwerp (BEL)	(0)2	Maritimo (PORT)	0
Severeyns 57, Bursac 89			
Maritimo	(0)2	Antwerp	(2)2
Heitor Junior 66, Vado 77		*Severeyns 37, Segers 42*	
Casino Salzburg (AUT)	(1)2	Dunjaska Streda (SLVK)	0
Amerhauser 40,			
Pfeifenberger 85			
Dunjaska Streda	0	Salzburg	(1)2
		Stadler 19,	
		Pfeifenberger 58	
Bohemians (EIRE)	0	Bordeaux (FRA)	(1)1
		Dugarry 16	
Bordeaux	(2)5	Bohemians	0
Zidane 22, Vercruysse 25, 72,			
Paille 60, Fofana 67			
Crusaders (N IRE)	0	Servette (SWI)	0
Servette, Geneva	(0)4	Crusaders	0
Anderson 57, Sinval 58, 60,			
Giallanza 63			
Dnepr (UKR)	(0)1	Admira Wacker (AUT)	0
Maksimov 77			
Admira Wacker	(1)2	Dnepr	(1)3
Bacher 44, Ljung 89		*Bezhanar 43, Pokhlebayev*	
		50, Mikailenko 68	
Hearts (SCOT)	(0)2	Atletico Madrid (SPA)	(0)1
Robertson 70,		*Kosecki 77*	
Colquhoun 75			

Atletico Madrid (1)3   Hearts 0
Gonzalez 34, Manolo 72,
L Garcia 76

Karlsruhe (GER) (2)2   PSV, Eindhoven (HOL)(1)1
Schmitt 20, Kiriakov 29   *Popescu pen 35*

PSV 0   Karlsruhe 0

Kuusysi (FIN) (3)4   Waregem (BEL) 0
Annunen 17, Lius 19, 75,
Lehtinen 25

Waregem (0)1   Kuusysi (0)2
De Kneef 54   *Annunen 84, Lius 88*

Dinamo Moscow (RUS) 0   Ein. Frankfurt (GER) (3)6
  Gaudino 9, Weber 25,
  Furtok 44, Bein 48,
  Okocha 81, Yeboah 89

Eintracht Frankfurt (0)1   Dinamo Moscow (1)2
Furtok 65   *Simutenkov 22,*
  Dobvrovolski 54

Union Lux. (LUX) 0   Boavista (PORT) (1)1
  Casaca 40

Boavista (3)4   Union Luxembourg 0
Oliveira 18, 26,
M Brandão pen 30,
Ricky (Owubokiri) 88

Vac (HUN) (1)2   Apollon (CYP) 0
Szedlacsek 43, Nyilas 78

Apollon (1)4   Vac 0 aet
Scepovic 40, 65,
Spolarec pen 111,
Kricmarevic 118

Young Boys (SWI) 0   Celtic (SCOT) 0

Celtic (0)1   Young Boys 0
Baumann og 116

B Dortmund (GER) 0   S Vladikavkaz (RUS) 0

Spartak Vladikavkaz 0   Borussia Dortmund (0)1
  Chapuisat 62

Botev (BUL) (1)2   Olympiakos (GRE) (1)3
Balakov 15, Khvoinev 88   *Amanasidis 12, Tsiantakis*
  59, Batista 87

Olympiakos, Piraeus (1)5   Botev, Plovdiv (0)1
Christensen 38, 78,   *Dimitrov pen 67*
Tsiantakis 73, Mitsibonas
pen 77, Batista 85

Brondby (DEN) (1)2   Dundee Utd (SCOT) 0
Vilfort 20, Kristiansen 46

Dundee Utd (0)3   Brondby (0)1 aet
McKinlay 67, Crabbe 79,   *Kristensen 91*
Clark 119

Gloria Bistrita (ROM) 0   Maribor Branik (SLVN) 0

Maribor Branik (1)2   Gloria Bistrita 0
Stanic 5, 80

Internazionale (ITA) (1)3   Rapid Bucharest(ROM)(0)1
Bergkamp 11 pen, 74, 78   *Andrasi 52*

Rapid Bucharest 0   Inter (0)2
  Jonk 63, Battistini 75

Juventus (ITA) (0)3   Lok. Moscow (RUS) 0
R Baggio 49, 87, Ravanelli 70

Lokomotive Moscow 0   Juventus (0)1
  Marocchi 54

Kocaelispor (TURK) 0   Sporting, Lisbon (PORT) 0

Sporting (1)2   Kocaelispor 0
Cadete 6, Pacheco 57

Lazio (ITA) (1)2   Lok. Plovdiv (BUL) 0
Casiraghi 22, Cravero 55

Lokomotiv Plovdiv 0   Lazio (1)2
  Luzardi 22, Cravero 66

Norrköping (SWE) 0   Mechelen (BEL) (1)1
  Czerniatynski 44

Mechelen (0)1   Norrköping (1)1 aet
Eszenyi 113   *Biohm 33*

Norwich (ENG) (0)3   Vitesse (HOL) 0
Ekoku 51, Goss 68, Polston 71

Vitesse, Arnhem 0   Norwich 0

Osters (SWE) (1)1   Kongsvinger (NOR) (1)3
Persson 36   *Engerback 33, Francis 57,*
  Frigard 59

Kongsvinger (2)4   Osters, Vaxjö (1)1
Frigard 36, 82, 89,   *Landberg pen 41*
Engerback 44

Slavia Prague (CZE) (0)1   OFI (GRE) (0)1
Berger 52   *Georgamis 64*

OFI, Crete (1)1   Slavia Prague 0
Machlas 42

Slovan Bratislava (SLVK)0   Aston Villa (ENG) 0

Aston Villa (2)2   Slovan (0)1
Atkinson 15, Townsend 22   *Tittel 86*

Tenerife (SPA) (1)2   Auxerre (FRA) (2)2
Pinilla pen 19, Minambres 70   *Vahirua 16, Saib 21*

Auxerre 0   Tenerife (0)1
  Felipe 68

Trabzonspor (TURK) (3)3   Valletta (MALTA) (1)1
Ogun 28, 39, Hami 29   *Zarb 25*

Valletta (1)1   Trabzonspor (2)3
Zarb 8   *Hami 11, Ogun 43, Unal 66*

Twente (HOL) (0)3
Boerebach 64, Polley 70,
Vurens 75

Bayern Munich (GER) (2)4
Nerlinger 11, Ziege 27, 89,
Scholl 65

Bayern (2)3
Matthäus pen 18, Karnebeek og 44, Ziege 62

Twente 0

Din. Bucharest (ROM)(2)3
Moldovan 5, 30,
Pana pen 87

Cagliari (ITA) (2)2
Prunea og 13,
Dely Valdes 38

Cagliari (1)2
Matteoli 6, Oliveira 63

Dinamo Bucharest 0

KR (ICE) (0)1
Ingimundarsson 89

MTK Budapest (HUN) (1)2
Hamori 34, Zsivotsky 68

MTK 0

KR 0

Nantes (FRA) (1)1
Oudec 12

Valencia (SPA) (1)1
Mijatovic 15

Valencia (0)3
Penev pen 72, Galvez 104
Gomez 112

Nantes (0)1 aet
Pedros 50

2nd round

Maribor Branik 0

Borussia Dortmund 0

Borussia Dortmund (0)2
Chaouisat 48, 52

Maribor Branik (1)1
Bozgo 21

Celtic (1)1
Creaney 9

Sporting 0

Sporting (1)2
Cadete 18, 60

Celtic 0

Inter (1)1
Bergkamp 6

Apollon 0

Apollon (2)3
Spolijiarec 11, Cepovic 32
Iosephides 85

Inter (3)3
Shalimov 6, Bergkamp 8
Fontolan 38

Kongsvinger (0)1
Frigaard 89

Juventus (0)1
Kohler 61

Juventus (1)2
Moller 27, Ravanelli 68

Kongsvinger 0

Lazio (0)1
Winter 74

Boavista 0

Boavista (1)2
Owubokiri 20,52

Lazio 0

Mechelen (1)5
Eszenyi 44, 80, 83,
De Boeck 59, Leen 72

MTK 0

MTK `(0)1
Kovacs 59

Mechelen (1)1
Pereira 10

Trabzonspor (1)1
Orhan 27

Cagliari (0)1
Dely Valdes 89

Cagliari 0

Trabzonspor 0

Valencia (1)3
Mijatovic 35, Penev 47, 74

Karlsruhe (0)1
Schmitt 79

Karlsruhe (3)7
Schmitt 29, 34, 59, 63,
Schutterle 37, Schmarov
46, Bilic 89

Valencia 0

Atletico Madrid (0)1
L Garcia 58

OFI 0

OFI (0)2
Machlas 51, Tsifoutis 64

Atletico Madrid 0

Salzburg (0)1
Jurcevic 67

Antwerp 0

Antwerp 0

Salzburg (0)1
Feiersinger 84

Bayern Munich (1)1
Nerlinger 41

Norwich (2)2
Goss 13, Bowen 30

Norwich (0)1
Goss 50

Bayern (1)1
Valencia 4

Bordeaux (1)2
Paille 35, Vercruysse 56

Servette (0)1
Anderson 55

Servette 0

Bordeaux (0)1
Schepul og 66

Eintracht Frankfurt (0)2
Furtok 65, Okocha 77

Dnepr 0

Dnepr (1)1
Chukhliba 43

Eintracht Frankfurt 0

Kuusysi (1)1
Lius 13

Brondby (1)4
Okechukwu 1, Vilfort 59,
Strudal 64, 84

Brondby (1)3
Kristensen 39, Madsen 68
Hogh pen 85

Kuusysi (1)1
Annunen 6

La Coruña (0)1
Riesco 87

Aston Villa (0)1
Saunders 80

Mark Bosnich saved Bebeto's penalty.

Aston Villa 0

La Coruña (1)1
Manjarin 36

Tenerife (1)2
J Llorente 38, Del Solar 49

Olympiakos (1)1
Christensen 10

Olympiakos (2)4
Christensen 13, 34, 84
Ioannides 58

Tenerife (1)3
Minambres 23,
Chano pen 49
Amantides og 68

3rd round

Bordeaux (0)1
Zidane 77

Karlsruhe 0

Karlsruhe (1)3 Bordeaux 0
Schmitt 16, 75, Kiriakov 65

Eintracht Frankfurt (0)1 La Coruña 0
Dickhaut 89

La Coruña 0 Eintracht Frankfurt (1)1
Gaudino 15

OFI (0)1 Boavista (3)4
Velic 89 *Artur 4, 22, 54,*
Owubokiri 42

Boavista (1)2 OFI 0
Nelson 24, Nogueira 77

Brondby (1)1 Borussia Dortmund (0)1
Kristensen 19 *Chapuisat 61*

Borussia Dortmund (1)1 Brondby 0
Zorc 29

Juventus (1)3 Tenerife 0
Möller 3, R Baggio pen 69,
Ravanelli 75

Tenerife (1)2 Juventus (0)1
Aguilera 37, Del Solar 86 *Möller 85*

Quarter-finals

Boavista (1)1 Karlsruhe (0)1
Owubokiri 38 *Wittwer 77*

Karlsruhe (1)1 Boavista 0
Santos og 35

Borussia Dortmund (0)1 Inter (2)3
Schulz 83 *Jonk 33, 36, Shalimov 89*

Inter (0)1 Borussia Dortmund (1)2
Manicone 81 *Zorc 38, Zelic 46*

Cagliari (0)1 Juventus 0
Dely Valdes 59

Juventus (1)1 Cagliari (1)2
D Baggio 23 *Firicano 34, Oliveira 61*

Salzburg (1)1 Eintracht Frankfurt 0
Hütter 30

Eintracht Frankfurt (1)1 Salzburg 0
Gaudino 21

aet Salzburg 5-4 pens

Semi-finals

Salzburg 0 Karlsruhe 0

Karlsruhe (0)1 Salzburg (1)1
Krieg 54 *Stadler 12*

Cagliari (1)3 Inter (1)2
Oliveira 11, Criniti 81, *Fontolan 6, Sosa 61*
Pancaro 86

Inter (1)3 Cagliari 0
Bergkamp pen 38, Berti
54, Jonk 63

For the sixth successive year, an Italian team reaches the final.

Final

1st LEG
26 April 1994 Ernst Happel, Vienna
47 500, referee K Milton Nielsen

CASINO SALZBURG (0)0 INTERNAZIONALE (1)1
Berti 35

Salzburg: Otto Konrad, Leo Lainer, Heribert Weber, Thomas Winklhofer [Michael Steiner 61], Christian Fürstaller, Franz Aigner, Martin Amerhauser [Damir Muzek h/t], Peter Artner, 'Marquinho', Heimo Pfeifenberger, Hermann Stadler

Inter: Walter Zenga, Antonio Paganin, Angelo Orlando, Wim Jonk, Giuseppe Bergomi (c), Sergio Battistini, Alessanro Bianchi, Antonio Manicone, Nicola Berti, Dennis Bergkamp [Francesco Dell'Anno 89], Rubén Sosa [Riccardo Ferri 74]

Bianchi sent off (48m) for a second bookable offence.

2nd LEG
11 May 1994 Giuseppe Meazza, Milan

80 326, referee Jim McCluskey (SCOT)

INTERNAZIONALE (0)1 CASINO SALZBURG 0
Jonk 62

Inter: Zenga, A Paganin, Orlando, Jonk, Bergomi (c), Battistini, Davide Fontolan [Ferri 67], Manicone, Berti, Bergkamp [Massimo Paganin 89], Sosa

Salzburg: Konrad, Lainer, Weber, Winklhofer [Amerhauser 67], Fürstaller, Aigner, Nikola Jurcevic, Artner [Steiner 75], Marquinho, Wolfgang Feiersinger, Adolf Hütter

Jonk scored for Ajax in the 1992 final, Berti for Inter in the 1991 final.

Sent off in a European club final

1983	José Luis (Lopes)	Benfica v Anderlecht	UEFA
1987	Danny Blind	Ajax v Mechelen	CWC
1991	Nando (Muñoz)	Barcelona v Man Utd	CWC
1994	Alessandro Bianchi	Inter v Salzburg	UEFA

Only Blanchi was on the winning side.

European footballer of the year 1993

Roberto Baggio	Juventus & ITA	142
Dennis Bergkamp	Ajax/Inter & HOL	83
Eric Cantona	Man Utd & FRA	34
9 eq Ryan Giggs	*Man Utd & WAL*	*9*
21 eq David Platt	*Juve/Samp & ENG*	*2*

European footballer of the year 1994

Christo Stoitchkov	Barcelona & BUL	210
Roberto Baggio	Juventus & ITA	136
Paolo Maldini	Milan & ITA	109
13eq Eric Cantona	*Man Utd & FRA*	*4*

No British players in the top sixteen. Barcelona, who cried outrage when Stoitchkov finished second to Marco van Basten in 1992, can have little complaint this time: he wins the award despite his anonymity in the European Cup final.

European Cup 1994-95

Preliminary round

AEK Athens (GRE)	(1)2	Rangers (SCOT)	0
Saravakos 44, 78			

Rangers	0	AEK	(1)1
		Savevski 43	

Rangers lose an estimated £5 million from matches they won't be playing v Milan & Ajax, and – even if they win the Scottish title for the seventh successive time – may find themselves in the UEFA Cup next season, thanks to this defeat and Aberdeen's the previous night.

Avenir Beggen (LUX)	(0)1	Galatasaray (TURK)	(2)5
Zaritski 50		*Turkiylmaz 30, Safet 35, Hakan 69, Arif 76, 89*	

Galatasaray	(0)4	Avenir Beggen	0
Hakan 54, 70, 84, Safet 64			

Turkiylmaz, a Swiss international of Turkish descent, is known by his first name, Kubilay, in Turkey.

Legia Warsaw (POL)	0	Hajduk Split (CRO)	(1)1
		Rapaic 22	

Hajduk	(0)4	Legia	0
Asanovic 50, Vulic 64, Rapaic 80, ERceg 89			

Maccabi Haifa (ISR)	(0)1	Casino Salzburg (AUT)	(0)2
Revivo pen 48		*Hütter 82, Mladenovic pen 89*	

Salzburg	(0)3	Maccabi Haifa	(0)1
Mladenovic 47, 53, Jurcevic 78		*Hazan 89*	

Paris St Germain (FRA)	(1)3	Vác-Samsung (HUN)	0
Ricardo 29, Weah 47, Roche 82			

Vác	(1)1	Paris St Germain	(1)2
Fule 31		*Mboma 20, 68*	

Silkeborg (DEN)	0	Dinamo Kiev (UKR)	0

Dynamo Kiev	(2)3	Silkeborg	(0)1
Skapenko 21, Kovalets 28, Kosovski 89		*Fernandes 74*	

Sparta Prague (CZE)	(0)1	IFK Gothenburg (SWE)	0
Budka 89			

Gothenburg	(1)2	Sparta	0
Blomquist 22, Rehn 64			

Steaua (ROM)	(3)4	Servette (SWI)	(0)1
Ilie 1, Sen pen 17, Pirvu 26, Lacatus 50		*Neuville 72*	

Servette	(1)1	Steaua, Bucharest	(0)1
Schepull 15		*Pirvu 61*	

Champions League

Group A

Man Utd (ENG)	(1)4	Gothenburg	(1)2
Giggs 33, 65, Kanchelskis 48, Sharpe 71		*Pettersson 27, Rehn 50*	

Barcelona (SPA)	(1)2	Galatasaray	(1)1
Koeman 30, Amor 50		*Turkiylmaz 14*	

Jordi Cruyff, son of manager Johan, plays his first European cup match.

Galatasaray	0	Man Utd	0

Gothenburg	(0)2	Barcelona	(1)1
Erlingmark 73, Blomqvist 88		*Stoitchkov 10*	

Man Utd	(1)2	Barcelona	(1)2
Hughes 19, Sharpe 80		*Romário 34, Bakero 49*	

United are still unbeaten after 53 home games in European competition, Barcelona haven't won a European match in Britain since beating Wolves 5-2 in 1960.

Gothenburg	(0)1	Galatasaray	0
Erlingmark 75			

For the second Champions League match in a row, substitute Wahlstedt makes a vital goal.

Barcelona	(2)4	Man Utd	0
Stoitchkov 9, 52, Romário 45, Ferrer 88			

Stoitchkov's goals (including his 100th for Barcelona) take deflections off Pallister & Parker, but Barcelona (even without Hagi) deserve it all: Stoitchkov & Romário are brilliant, United don't have a clear chance all night. Alex Ferguson replaces Peter Schmeichel with Gary Walsh in goal in order to be able to use Ryan Giggs, but Giggs is substituted in the second half.

Galatasaray	0	Gothenburg	(0)1
		Mikael Nilsson 86	

Gothenburg	(1)	Man Utd	(0)
Blomqvist 10, Erlingmark		*Hughes 63*	
64, Kamark pen 72		*(Ince sent off 83)*	

United can point to the absence of Schmeichel, Keane, Giggs, Parker & Sharpe – but Ferguson has no excuses: 'We were just not good enough.'

Galatasaray	(0)2	Barcelona	(1)1
Hakan pen 72, Arif 88		*Romário 15*	

At the eleventh attempt, Galatasaray win a Champions League match for the first time, thanks to goalkeeper Carlos Busquets, who carries the ball over his line for the winner.

Man Utd	(2)4	Galatasaray	0
Davies 2, Beckham 37,			
Keane, Bülent og 88			

United's young Turks beat Galatasaray at the fourth time of asking, but are knocked out by the result in Spain.

Barcelona	(0)1	Gothenburg	(0)1
Bakero 81		*Rehn 90*	

GOTHENBURG	6	4	1	1	10	7	9
BARCELONA	6	2	2	2	11	8	6
Man Utd	6	2	2	2	11	11	6
Galatasaray	6	1	1	4	3	9	3

Group B

Paris SG	(1)2	Bayern Munich (GER)	0
Weah 41, Bravo 82			

Dinamo Kiev	(0)3	Spartak Mscw (RUS)	(2)2
Leonenko 48, 75		*Pisaryev 12, Tikhonov 39*	
Rebrov 86			

Pisaryev claims a goal that comes off defender Sergei Shmatovalenko's head. 100 000 watch the match, Kiev report that a million applied for tickets.

Bayern Munich	(1)1	Dinamo Kiev	0
Scholl 9			

Spartak Moscow	(1)1	Paris SG	(0)2
Rakhimov 39		*Le Guen 53, Valdo 61*	

Dinamo Kiev	(1)1	Paris SG	(1)2
Leonenko pen 33		*Guerin 26, Weah 90*	

Spartak Moscow	(0)1	Bayern Munich	(0)1
Pisaryev 77		*Babbel 90*	

Bayern Munich	(2)2	Spartak Moscow	(2)2
Nerlinger 29, Kuffour 36		*Tikhonov 4, Alenichev 32*	

Paris SG	(0)1	Dinamo Kiev	0
Weah 68			

Spartak Moscow	(0)1	Dinamo Kiev	0
Mukhamadiyev 52			

Bayern Munich	0	Paris SG	(0)1
		Weah 81	

Almost immediately after coming on as sub, Weah beats four men to maintain Paris SG's 100% record in the group and send them to the quarter-finals.

Dynamo Kiev	(1)1	Bayern Munich	(0)4
Shevtschenko 38		*Nerlinger 46, Papin 57,*	
		81, Scholl 87	

Paris SG	(2)4	Spartak Moscow	(0)1
Weah 28, 52, Ginola 42,			
Raí 59			

The remarkable Weah, a star in France for several years, does it again on the wider stage, beating two men to put Saint Germain ahead.

PARIS SG	6	6	0	0	12	3	12
BAYERN MUNICH	6	2	2	2	8	7	6
Spartak	6	1	2	3	8	12	4
Dynamo Kiev	6	1	0	5	5	11	2

Group C

Anderlecht (BEL)	0	Steaua	0

Hajduk	0	Benfica (PORT)	0
Stimac sent off			

Benfica	(2)3	Anderlecht	(0)1
Caniggia 27, 41,		*Madeira og 87*	
Tavares 73			

Steaua	0	Hajduk	(0)1
		Asanovic 88	

Benfica	(1)2	Steaua	(0)1
Caniggia pen 44, Pinto 60		*Militaru 89*	

Hajduk	(1)2	Anderlecht	(0)1
Pralija 34, Butorovic 88		*Weber 89*	

Steaua	(1)1	Benfica	(0)1
Pandaru 27		*Hélder 64*	

Anderlecht	0	Hajduk	0

Benfica	(0)2	Hajduk Split	(0)1
Isaias 33, João Pinto 76		*Andrijasevic 72*	

Steaua	(0)1	Anderlecht	(0)1
Dobos 52		*Bosman 42*	

Anderlecht	(0)1	Benfica	(0)1
Rutjes 48		*Edilson 83*	

Hajduk	(0)1	Steaua	(3)4
Andrijasevic 49		*Ilie 11, 33, Lacatus 23,*	
		Gilca 89	

BENFICA	6	3	3	0	9	5	9
HAJDUK	6	2	2	2	5	7	6
Steaua	6	1	3	2	7	6	5
Anderlecht	6	0	4	2	4	7	4

Group D

Ajax (HOL)   (0)2   Milan (ITA)   0
R de Boer 51, Litmanen 77

Milan's first ever defeat in the Champions League.

Salzburg   0   AEK   0

Milan   (1)3   Salzburg   0
Stroppa 39, Simone 57, 64

Although the result stands, a bottle thrown by the crowd costs Milan two pts and use of the stadium for the next two home games (which they play in Trieste), the 16th disciplinary action taken against the club by UEFA.

AEK   (1)1   Ajax   (1)2
Savevski 30   *Litmanen 33, Kluivert 63*

AEK   0   Milan   0

Ajax   0   Salzburg   0

Milan   (0)2   AEK   (1)1
Panucci 68, 74   *Savevski 16*
    (Manolas sent off)

Ajax   (0)1   Salzburg   (0)1
Litmanen 85   *Kocijan 62*

AEK   (1)1   Salzburg   (2)3
Vlachos 29   *Pfeifenberger 6, 8,*
    Hassenhüttl 76

Milan   0   Ajax   (1)2
    Litmanen 2, Baresi og 65

Ajax   (1)2   AEK   0
Oulida 7, 78

Salzburg   0   Milan   (1)1
    Massaro 26

AJAX	6	4	2	0	9	2	10
MILAN	6	3	1	2	6	5	5
Salzburg	6	1	3	2	4	6	5
AEK	6	0	2	4	3	9	2

Quarter-finals 1 & 15 March 1995
Bayern Munich   v   Gothenburg
Hajduk Split   v   Ajax
Milan   v   Benfica
Barcelona   v   Paris Saint-Germain

Cup-Winners' Cup 1994-95

Preliminary round

Bangor (N IRE)   0-1, 0-4   Tatran Presov (BUL)
Barry Town (WAL)   0-1, 0-6   Zhalgiris Vilnius (LITH)
Batey sent off 81
Bodo Glimt (NOR)   6-0, 0-0   Olimpija Riga (LAT)
Fandok Bobruisk (BYL)   4-1, 0-3   FK Tirana (ALB)
Ferencváros (HUN)   6-1, 6-1   F91 Dudelange (LUX)
Floriana (MALTA)   2-2, 0-1   Sligo Rovers (EIRE)
Pierre Brincat (Floriana) 60, Johnny Brennan 88 sent off
Keflavik (ICE)   1-2, 1-4   Maccabi Tel Aviv (ISR)
Norma Tallinn (EST)   1-4, 0-10   Maribor Branik (SLVN)
Pirin (BUL)   3-0, 1-0   Schaan (LIECH)
Sandoyar B71 (FAER)   0-5, 0-2   HJK (FIN)
Tiligul Tiraspol (MOLD)   0-1, 1-3   Omonia Nicosia (CYP)
Viktoria Zizkov (CZE)   1-0, 3-3   IFK Norrköping (SWE)

1st round

Besiktas (TURK)   (2)2   HJK   0
Oktay 27, Ertugul 35

HJK   (0)1   Besiktas   (0)1
Rantanen 67   *Oktay 88*

Bodo Glimt   (2)3   Sampdoria (ITA)   (0)2
Staurvik 1, Johnsen 32, 58   *Bertarelli 47, Platt 68*

Sampdoria   (2)2   Bodo Glimt   0
Platt 14, Lombardo 36

Brondby (DEN)   (1)3   Tirana   0
Brian Jensen pen 19,
Bo Hansen 56, Bjur 66

Tirana   0   Brondby   (1)1
    Strudal 31

Chelsea (ENG)   (2)4   Viktoria Zizkov (CZE)   (2)2
Furlong 2, Sinclair 4   *Najoros 35, 41*
Rocastle 52, Wise 69

Chelsea's first European cup match since 1971.

Viktoria Zizkov   0   Chelsea   0
36-y-o Graham Rix, who missed the decisive penalty kick in the 1980 Cup-Winners' Cup final, plays his first competitive match for eighteen months, but Chelsea's hero is Dmitry Kharin, who saves Petr Vrabec's 31st-minute penalty.

Croatia Zagreb (CRO)(2)3   Auxerre (FRA)   (1)1
Jelicic 2, Soldo 40,   *Diomede 21*
Pamic 65

Auxerre   (1)3   Croatia Zagreb   0
Diomede 41, Mahe 75, Lamouhi 89

CSKA Moscow (RUS)(0)2   Ferencváros (HUN)   (0)1
Mamchur 50, Segeyev 73   Christiansen 58

Ferencváros   (2)2   CSKA Moscow   (1)1
Ferencváros 7-6 pens
Lipscei 23, Neagoe 44   Radimov 15

Dundee Utd (SCOT)   (1)3   Tatran Presov   (2)2
Petric 16, Nixon 66,   Skalka, Zvara pen 41
Hannah 69

Tatran Presov   (2)3   Dundee Utd   (1)1
Zvara 10, 71, Kocis 18   Nixon 2

Gloria Bistrita (ROM) (0)2   Real Zaragoza (SPA)   (1)1
Raduta 49, Lungu 51   Esnaider 44

Real Zaragoza   (2)4   Gloria Bistrita   0
Pardeza 11, Aguado 42,
Poyet 49, 55

Grasshoppers (SWI) (1)3   Chernomorets (UKR)   0
Bickel 41, Koller 52,
Subiat 85

Chernomorets, Odessa(1)1   Grasshoppers   0
Khuseinov 9

Werder Bremen (GER)   0   Maccabi Tel Aviv   0

Werder Bremen   (0)2   Maccabi Tel Aviv   0
Bode 55, Basler 80

All publications show both matches played in Bremen...

Maribor Branik   (0)1   Austria Vienna (AUT) (1)1
Bozgo 46   Prosenik 23

Austria Vienna   (1)3   Maribor Branik   0
Flögel 21, Kubica 53, 56

Omonia Nicosia   (0)1   Arsenal (ENG)   (1)3
Malekos 72   Merson 37, 80, Wright 50

Arsenal   (2)3   Omonia Nicosia   0
Wright 9, 70, Schwarz 31

Pirin (BUL)   0   Panathinaikos (GRE) (0)2
  Noblias 70, Alexoudis 83

Panathinaikos   (3)6   Pirin   (1)1
Alexoudis 7, 17   Oroachev 44
Warzycha 30, 87, 90,
Borelli 66

Porto (PORT)   (0)2   LKS, Lodz (POL)   0
Domingos 72, Barros 77

LKS   0   Porto   (1)1
  Drulovic 44

Sligo Rovers   (1)1   Club Brugge (BEL)   (1)2
Kenny 44   Vermant 10, Verheyen 63

Brugge (FC Bruges) (2)3   Sligo Rovers   (1)1
Staelens 4, 44 pen,   Rooney 7
Eykelkamp 58

Zhalgiris Vilnius   (0)1   Feyenoord (HOL)   (1)1
Tereskinas 87   Larsson 9

Feyenoord   (0)2   Zhalgiris   (0)1
Larsson 55, Heus pen 65   Vencevicius 88

2nd round

Besiktas   (2)2   Auxerre   (0)2
Mehmet 39, Ertugrul 43   Moussa Saib 53,
  Martins 58

Auxerre   (1)2   Besiktas   0
Lamouchi 44, 49

Brondby   (0)1   Arsenal   (2)2
Strudal 53   Wright 16, Smith 18

Wright's now scored 104 in 132 games for Arsenal.

Arsenal   (1)2   Brondby   (1)2
Wright pen 25, Selley 46   Bo Hansen 2, Eggen 69

Brondby are dismayed that a late, apparently very good penalty appeal is turned down. Wright scores in an eleventh consecutive match; ten broke the club record set by the great David Jack in 1932.

Brugge   (1)1   Panathinaikos   0
Staelens pen 4

Panathinaikos   0   Brugge   0

Chelsea   0   Austria Vienna   0

David Rocastle hits a post (72m) soon after Manfred Schmidt's sending-off.

Austria Vienna   (0)1   Chelsea   (1)1
Narbekovas 73   Spencer 40

Spencer runs 80 yards to score.

Feyenoord   (0)1   Werder Bremen   0
Larsson 63

Werder Bremen   (1)3   Feyenoord   (2)4
Beschastnykh 12, 60,   Larsson 21, 34, 66 pen,
Basler 90   Heus pen 56

Porto   (3)6   Ferencváros   0
Costa 15, Barros 17,
Drulovic 40, 60, Oliveira 85,
Pires Alves 87

Ferencváros   (1)2   Porto   0
Zavadszky 27, Neagoe 59

Sampdoria   (1)3   Grasshoppers   0
Melli 44, Mihajlovic 76,
Maspero 83

Grasshoppers   (1)3   Sampdoria   (2)2
Willems 12, Bickel 51,   Melli 17, Lombardo 40
Koller 55

Tatran Presov	0	Real Zaragoza	(2)4
		Poyet 26, Varga 44,	
		Esnaider 49, 88	
Real Zaragoza	(1)2	Tatran Presov	(1)1
Esnaider 5, Celada 56		*Kocis 38*	

Quarter-finals 2 & 16 March 1995

Feyenoord	v	Real Zaragoza
Sampdoria	v	Porto
Arsenal	v	Auxerre
Club Brugge	v	Chelsea

Chelsea drawn at home, match moved by UEFA to avoid two games in London on the same day.

UEFA Cup 1994-95

Preliminary round

Aarau (SWI)	(0)1	Mura (SLVN)	0
Kucharski 71			
Mura	0	Aarau	(1)1
		Skrzypczak 17	
Anorthosis (CYP)	(2)2	Shumen (BUL)	0
Charalambous 19,			
Nicolic 40			
Shumen	(1)1	Anorthosis	(0)2
Iskrenov pen 43		*Ashiotis 60, Gogic 82*	
Aris Salonika (GRE)	(1)3	Hapoel Beersheba (ISR)	(1)1
Sapountzis 8, 64 pen,		*Guseyev 14*	
Ivan 89			
Hapoel Beersheba	(1)1	Aris Salonika	(1)2
Madar 44		*Bougiuklis 30,*	
		Milojevic 55	
Bangor City (WAL)	(1)1	Akranes (ICE)	(1)2
Mottram 23		*Reynisson 42, Jonsson 47*	
Akranes	(2)2	Bangor	0
Ingolfsson 8,			
Thordarsson 21			
FC Copenhagen (DEN)	0	FC Jazz (FIN)	(1)1
		Ruhanen 33	
FC Jazz	0	FC Copenhagen	(0)4
		Johansen 54, M Nielsen 81	
		Frandsen 83, A Nielsen 87	
CSKA Sofia (BUL)	(2)3	Ararat Erevan (ARM)	0
Tanev 20, Koilov 44,			
Shishkov 75			

Ararat Erevan	0	CSKA Sofia	0
Dinamo Minsk (BYL)	(0)3	Hibernians (MALTA)	(1)1
Kashantsev 69, Kachura		*Lorenz 6*	
78, Yaskovich 85			
Hibernians	(1)(3)4	Dinamo Minsk	(1)(1)3 aet
Ostrovsky og 35, Xerri 71,		*Yuravin pen 44,*	
Spiteri 89		*Plaskevich 94,*	
Miller 109		*Spiteri og 105*	

Spiteri goes from last-minute hero to villain, but the real villain's Valentin Belkevich of Dinamo: caught taking the steroid nandrolone, he's banned for a year by UEFA.

Dinamo Tbilisi (GEO)	(1)2	Univ, Craiova (ROM)	0
Kinkladze 27, S Arveladze 59			
Universitatea, Craiova	(0)1	Dinamo Tbilisi	(1)2
Pigulea 59		*Kavelashvili 3,*	
		KImbladze 86	
Fenerbahçe (TURK)	(2)5	Touran (AZER)	0
Bulent 16, Aykut 43, 66,			
Nielsen 81, Aygun 88			
Touran	0	Fenerbahçe	(0)2
		Nail pen 83, Ulgun 87	
Gornik Zabrze (POL)	(2)7	Shamrock Rovers (EIRE)	0
Szemonski 30, 83,			
Bauszynski 35 pen, 61,			
Kosea 52, Orzeszek 78,			
Kubik 80			
Shamrock Rovers	0	Gornik Zabrze	(0)1
		Baluszynski 49	
Grevenmacher (LUX)	(0)1	Rosenborg (NOR)	(1)2
A Silva 83		*Leonhardsen 4,*	
		Loken pen 89	
Rosenborg	(2)6	Grevenmacher	0
Strand 37, 87, Bergersen			
44, Jakobsen 62, Brattbakk			
77, 84			
Inter Bratislava (SLVK)	0	MyPa (FIN)	(2)3
		Kolkka 11, 30,	
		Rajamaki 49	
MyPa	0	Inter Bratislava	(1)1
		Repec 3	
Inter Cardiff (WAL)	0	GKS Katowice (POL)	(0)2
		Sermak 84 pen, 89	
GKS Katowice	(3)6	Inter Cardiff	0
Walcsak 25, 83,			
Maziejewski 33, 44 pen			
Jojko pen 75, Walny 89			
Kispest Honvéd (HUN)	(1)4	Zim. Chisinau (MOLD)	(0)1
Illes 27, 68, Pisont 60,		*Timbur 58*	
Hamar 76			

Zimbrul Chisinau	0	Kispest Honved	(0)1
		Orosz 83	

Lillestrom (NOR)	(2)4	Shakh. Donetsk (UKR)	(0)1
Hedman 2, R Johnsen 42		*Petrov 58*	
Gulbrandsen 49,			
JO Pedersen 68			

Shakhtyor Donetsk	(0)2	Lillestrom	0
Orbu 49, Petrov 58			

Motherwell (SCOT)	(2)3	Havnar Boltfelag (FAER)	0
Coyne 20, McGrillen 34,			
Kirk 83			

HB	(0)1	Motherwell	(2)4
Hansen 59		*Kirk 13, 69, Davies 20,*	
		Burns 88	

Odense (DEN)	(1)3	Flora Tallinn (EST)	0
Torup 13, Schjonberg 58,			
Madsen 89			

Flora Tallinn	0	Odense	(1)3
		Hemmingsen 19, 49,	
		Tchami 68	

Olymp. Ljubljana (SLVN)	(2)3	Levski Sofia (BUL)	(0)2
Dosti 35, 37, 73		*Sirakov 57, 72*	

Levski Sofia	(1)1	Olympija Ljubljana	(1)2
Stoilov 2		*Novak 24, Paulin 89*	

Portadown (N IRE)	0	Slov Bratislava(SLVK)	(0)2
		Timpko 58, Rosnak 75	

Slovan Bratislava	(2)3	Portadown	0
Faktor 15, Tittel 35, Rusnak			

Skonto Riga (LAT)	0	Aberdeen (SCOT)	0

Aberdeen	(0)1	Skonto Riga	(0)1
Kane 90		*Semenyov 55*	

Alexei Semenyov arrives in Scotland without his boots. Aberdeen must regret giving him a pair.

Slavia Prague (CZE)	(1)2	Cork City (EIRE)	0
Smicer 37, Suchoparek 68			

Cork City	0	Slavia Prague	(1)4
		Hogen 33, 50, Vaura 49,	
		Berger 90	

Valletta (MALTA)	(1)2	Rapid Buch. (ROM)	(2)6
Agius 16, Zerasa 68		*Cheback 5, Vladoiu 14,*	
		47, Tira 74, Chirita 77,	
		Voinea 79	

Rapid Bucharest	(1)1	Valletta	(1)1
Tira 32		*Agius 22*	

Vardar (MACEDON)	(1)1	Békéscsabai (HUN)	(1)1
Milosevski 38		*Mracko 44*	

Békéscsabai	(0)1	Vardar, Skopje	0
Csato 61			

1st round

Aarau (SWI)	0	Maritimo (PORT)	0

Maritimo	(0)1	Aarau	0
Alves 60			

Admira Wacker (AUT)	(2)5	Gornik Zabrze (POL)	(2)2
Gager pen 7, pen 60,		*Szemonski 26, Oreszek 44*	
Schiener 18, Klausz 66,			
Waldoch og 89			

Gornik	(1)1	Admira Wacker	(1)1
Baluszynski 30		*Litovchenko 44*	

AIK (SWE)	0	Slavia Prague (CZE)	0

Slavia	(1)2	AIK, Solna	(1)2
Suchopsrek 26, Bejbl 57		*Lidman 35, Sundgren 81*	

Akranes	0	Kaiserslautern	(2)4
		Hamann 32, Anders 43,	
		Kuntz 51, Kuka 58	

Kaiserslautern (GER)	4	Akranes (ICE)	1
Kuka 56, 88, Wagner 60,		*Gislasson 89*	
Haber 81			

Anorthosis (CYP)	(1)2	Athletic Bilbao (SPA)	0
Gogic 6, Tamboris 51			

Athletic Bilbao	(2)3	Anorthosis	0
Guerrero 17,			
A Panagiotou og 24,			
Andrinua 89			

Antwerp (BEL)	0	Newcastle Utd (ENG)	(3)5
		Lee 1, 9, 51, Sellars 40,	
		Watson 78	

Robert Lee marks Newcastle's first European cup match since 1977 by putting a hat-trick of headers, including one after 53 seconds, past 44-y-o goalkeeper Ratko Svilar.

Newcastle	(4)5	Antwerp	(0)2
Lee 11, Cole 26, 39, 88		*Kierkens 75, Severeyns 77*	
Beardsley pen 36			

Antwerp are (or were) no pushovers. In 1993 they reached the Cup-Winners' Cup final.

Apollon (CYP)	(1)1	Sion (SWI)	(0)3
Krcmarevic 36		*Bonvin 70, Marin 83, 85*	

Sion	(0)2	Apollon	(0)3
Marin 89, Orlando 101		*Krcmarevic 49, Spoljarich*	
		66, Csepovic 77	

The Yugoslav foreign legion comes within a minute of producing the biggest comeback by a Cypriot club in any European competition.

B Leverkusen (GER)	(4)5	PSV, Eindhoven (HOL)	(2)4
Kirsten 5, 16, 41, Dooley 14		*Ronaldo 11, 45, 61, Nilis 88*	
Schuster 73			

Ulf Kirsten's first-half hat-trick is almost overshadowed by PSV's 17-y-o Brazilian.

PSV	0	Bayer Leverkusen	0
Blackburn Rovers (ENG)	0	Trelleborgs (SWE) Sondell 71	(0)1

Blackburn lose their first ever European cup match.

Trelleborgs Karlsson 50, 85	(0)2	Blackburn Sutton 18, Shearer 84	(1)2

Trelleborgs go through despite being reduced to ten men for the last 36 mins after Jonas Brorsson's sending off.

Boavista (PORT) Oliveira 2, Gomes 53	(1)2	MyPa Laaksonen 42	(1)1
MyPa Gronholm 75	1	Boavista Artur pen 89	1

A contested last-minute refereeing decision deprives the underdogs of the bone.

Bordeaux (FRA) Dugarry 4, Johnsen og 37 Richard Witschge 84	(2)3	Lillestrom (NOR) Huard og 5	(1)1
Lillestrom	0	Bordeaux Zidane 2, Fournier 15	2
B Dortmund (GER) Möller 57	(0)1	Motherwell (SCOT) Paul McGrillen sent off 88	0
Motherwell	0	Borussia Dortmund Reidle 54, 64	(0)2
Cannes (FRA) Durix pen 49, Kozniku 56, 80, Horlaville 67	(0)4	Fenerbahçe (TURK)	0
Fenerbahçe Bulent 60	(0)1	Cannes Tayfur og 21, Horlaville 24, 63, Micoud 53, Veira 79	(2)5
CSKA Sofia (BUL) Mihtarski 44, 82, Radukanov 70	(1)3	Juventus (ITA) Porrini 39, Del Piero 76	(1)2

After the second leg, in which Fabrizio Ravanelli's goals make it irrelevant, the result's overturned by UEFA because Petar Mitarski wasn't registered by CSKA before the 31 Aug deadline.

Juventus Ravanelli 9, 65, 69, 81, 83	(1)5	CSKA Sofia Mihtarski 89	(0)1
Dinamo Minsk (BYL)	0	Lazio (ITA)	0
Lazio Ostrovski og 44, Favalli 51 Boksic 74, Fuser 84	(1)4	Dinamo Minsk Kachuro 9	(1)1

Dinamo Tbilisi (GEO) Arveladze 40	(1)1	FC Tirol (AUT)	0
Tirol Cerny 4, Stöger 32, Danek 35, 56, Janeschitz 89	(3)5	Tbilisi S Arveladze 36	(1)1
GKS Katowice (POL) Maciejewski pen 20	(1)1	Aris Salonika (GRE)	0
Aris Salonika Sapountzis 47	(0)1	GKS Katowice GKS 4-3 pens	0
Inter (ITA) Bergkamp pen 75	(0)1	Aston Villa (ENG)	0

For the third time in a row, Inter win 1-0 against an English club (twice v Norwich the previous season), each time with a goal by Bergkamp (he also converted a penalty at Carrow Road), who also scored in two matches v England in 1993.

Aston Villa Houghton 41	(0)(1)1	Inter Villa 4-3 pens	0

Villa ride their luck (Nicola Berti hits the bar early on, Rubén Sosa at the end of the penalty shoot-out) to knock out the holders, who beat them on the way to winning the 1990-91 competition.

Linfield (N IRE) Anderson 86	(0)1	Odense (DEN) Schjonberg 46	(0)1
Odense Nedergaard 5, 85, Schjonberg 25, 42 pen, Thorup 40	(4)5	Linfield	0
Napoli (ITA) Carbone 30 pen, 49	(1)2	Skonto Riga (LAT)	0
Skonto	0	Napoli Buso 31	1
Olimpija Siljak 3	(1)1	Eintr Frankfurt (GER) Legiat 84	(0)1
Eintracht Frankfurt Dickhaut 9, Yeboah 84	(1)2	Olimpija, Ljubljana	0
O Piraeus (GRE) Ivic 57	(0)1	Marseille (FRA) Ferrer 31, Marquet 79 (Durand sent off 51)	(1)2
Marseille Cascarino 53, 89, Ferreri 88	(0)3	Olympiakos Piraeus	0
Rapid Bucharest (ROM) Chirita 18, Vladoiu 70	(1)2	Kortrijk (BEL)	0
Kortrijk (Charleroi) Balog 89, Misse 90	(0)2	Rapid Bucharest Tira 47	(0)1
Real Madrid (SPA) Martín Vásquez 11	(1)1	Sporting (PORT)	0

183

Sporting, Lisbon   (2)2   Real Madrid   (1)1
Sa Pinto 2, Oceano 30   *Laudrup 15*

Rosenborg (NOR)   (0)1   La Coruña (SPA)   0
Loeken 52

La Coruña   (0)(1)4   Rosenborg   (0)(0)1 aet
Bebeto 81, 98, 114   *Brattbakk 92*
Donato da Silva pen 107

Rotor Volgograd (RUS)(1)3   Nantes (FRA)   (1)2
Gerashchenko 42,   *Quedec 28, N'doram 83*
Nechayev 65,
Veretennikov 76

Nantes   (1)3   Rotor   0
Ouedec 29, 61, Loko 75

Seraing (BEL)   (0)3   Din. Moscow (RUS) (2)4
Wamberto 67,   *Smirnov 18, Cherychev*
Schaessens 75   *25, 61, Simuntekov pen 44*
Edmilson 90

Dinamo Moscow   0   Seraing   (0)1
     Schaessens 87

Slovan (SLVK)   (0)1   FC Copenhagen (DEN) 0
Tomaschek 76

Copenhagen   (1)1   Slovan   (1)1
Hojer 44 pen   *Negro 24*

Tekstilchik (RUS)   (1)6   Bekescsabai (HUN) (1)1
Gusakov 38, Polstyanov   *Tarbash 15*
55, 90, Volguin 58,
Filipov 80, 90

Bekescsabai   (0)1   Tekstilchik Kamychin 0
Csato 77

Trabzonspor (TURK) (2)2   D Bucharest (ROM) (1)1
Orhan 7, Soner 19   *Marian 28*

Dinamo Bucharest (1)3   Trabzonspor   (1)3
Ceausila 6, Niculescu 51,   *Kuciuk 21, Buiuk 23,*
Lica 82   *Mehmet 78*

Twente (HOL)   (1)1   Kisp. Honvéd (HUN) (1)4
Mols 38   *Kovács 20, 51, 74,*
     Hamar 86

Kispest Honvéd   (0)1   Twente, Enschede (1)3
Illes 58   *Vurens 34, Ellerman 67,*
     Boerebach 87

Vitesse Arnhem (HOL)(0)1   Parma (ITA)   0
Gillhaus 51   *Fernando Couto sent off 80*

Parma   (1)2   Vitesse   0
Zola 23, 74

2nd round

Admira Wacker   (1)1   Cannes   (0)1
Gager pen 36   *Bedrossian 67*

Cannes   (0)2   Admira Wacker   (3)4
Kozniku 49, Charvet 87   *Mayrleb 8, Klausz 17, 56,*
     Schiener 24

AIK   0   Parma   (0)1
     Crippa 72

Parma   (2)2   AIK   0
Minotti 5, 16

Boavista   (1)1   Napoli   (0)1
Sánchez 26   *Carbone 58*

Napoli   (2)2   Boavista   (0)1
Agostini 18, 35   *Luciano 77*

Dinamo Moscow   (0)2   Real Madrid   (1)2
Simutenkov 65,   *Sandro 22, Zamorano 73*
Cheryshev 69

Real Madrid   (0)4   Dinamo Moscow   0
Zamorano 48, Redondo
77, Dani 89, 90

GKS Katowice   (0)1   Bordeaux   0
Strojek 85

Bordeaux   (1)1   GKS Katowice   (0)1
Histilloles 18   *Walczak pen 70*

Kaiserslautern   (0)1   Odense   (0)1
Sforza 74   *Hemmingsen 72*

Odense   0   Kaiserslautern   0

Kispest Honvéd   0   Bayer Leverkusen (1)2
     Munch 16, Sergio 80

Bayer Leverkusen (2)5   Kispest Honvéd   0
Kirsten 29, 65, 69, Hapal
31, Mario Tolkmitt 60

Maritimo   0   Juventus   (0)1
     Ravanelli 78

Maritimo hit the bar at 0-0.

Juventus   (1)2   Maritimo   (0)1
Ravanelli 34, 53   *Paulo Alves 80*

Nantes   (1)2   Tekstilchik   0
Ouedec 32 pen, 62

Tekstilchik Kamychin (0)1   Nantes   (0)2
Polstianov 67   *Ouedec 48, 64*

Newcastle   (2)3   Athletic Bilbao   (0)2
Fox 10, Beardsley pen 35,   *Ziganda 71, Suances 79*
Cole 56

Andy Cole has now scored 66 goals in 72 matches for
Newcastle, never going three in a row without scoring.

Athletic Bilbao   (0)1   Newcastle   0
Ziganda 67

Cole's absence makes all the difference. Bilbao can
even afford to miss a penalty, from José Gaitano, five
minutes from full time.

Rapid Bucharest (0)2   Eintracht Frankfurt (0)1
Vladoiu 67, Voinea 77   Furtok 64

Eintracht Frankfurt (3)5   Rapid Bucharest 0
Bommer 10, Yeboah 14,
17, Furtok 65, 67

Sion (2)2   Marseille 0
Wicky 24, Kunz 43

Vitally, as it turns out, Tony Cascarino has a goal
disallowed for Marseille.

Marseille (0)3   Sion (1)1
Libbra 46, 64, Ferreri 73   Kunz 5

Slovan Bratislava (0)2   Borussia Dortmund (1)1
Rusnak 51, Tittel 60   Möller 17

Borussia Dortmund (1)3   Slovan Bratislava 0
Möller 15, Riedle 46, 68

Tirol (1)2   La Coruña 0
Sane 30, Stöger 56

La Coruña (3)4   Tirol 0
Claudio 35, 38, Donato
pen 39, Manjarin 71

Trabzonspor (0)1   Aston Villa 0
Orhan 78

Guy Whittingham hits the bar after less than ten
minutes, Hami Mandirali in the first minute of the
second half.

Aston Villa (0)2   Trabzonspor (0)1
Atkinson 77, Ehiogu 90   Orhan 89

Villa (and Ron Atkinson, soon sacked as manager) pay
the price for missing too many chances. Literally. UEFA
fine them £9000 for a pitch invasion. Dalian Atkinson's
goal comes from a second rebound after Staunton's
penalty is saved. Ogun is sent off for handling the ball
to give away the kick.

Trelleborgs 0   Lazio 0

Lazio (0)1   Trelleborgs 0
Boksic 90 (after five minutes of injury time)

3rd Round

Admira Wacker (0)1   Juventus (3)3
Binder 56   Conte 9, R Baggio 16, 42

Juventus (1)2   Admira Wacker (0)1
Ferrara 17, Vialli 86   Wimmer 73

Athletic Bilbao (0)1   Parma 0
Ziganda 48

Parma (2)4   Athletic Bilbao (0)2
Zola 21, D Baggio 39, 47,   Vales 56, Guerrero 72
Couto 64

Eintracht Frankfurt (0)1   Napoli 0
Yeboah 56

Napoli 0   Eintracht Frankfurt (0)1
Falkenmaier 57

GKS Katowice (0)1   Bayer Leverkusen (3)4
Nikodem 54   Kirsten 30, 44, Lehnhoff
41, 65

Bayer Leverkusen (4)4   GKS Katowice 0
Schuster 11, Thom 13,
Scholz 15, Hapal 28

La Coruña (1)1   Borussia Dortmund 0
Bebeto 23

Bor. Dortmund (0)(1)3   La Coruña (0)(0)1
Zorc 50, Riedle 116,   Alfredo 102
Rikken 119

Nantes (2)4   Sion 0
Loko 15, Ferri 33,
N'Doram 51, Makelele 78

Sion (0)2   Nantes (2)2
Herr 75, Marin 81   Loko 29, N'Doram 31

Odense (1)2   Real Madrid (0)3
Schjoenberg 44, Hjorth 79   Zamorano 67, Amavisca
69, Laudrup 89

Real Madrid 0   Odense (0)2
Pedersen 72, Bisgaard 90

Morten Bisgaard wins it with ten seconds left.

Trabzonspor (0)1   Lazio (0)2
Unal Karaman 67   Rambaudi 59, Negro 61

Lazio (1)2   Trabzonspor (0)1
Cravero 25, Di Vaio 75   Soner 72

Quarter-finals 28 Feb & 14 March 1995
Eintracht Frankfurt   v   Juventus
Lazio   v   Borussia Dortmund
B Leverkusen   v   Nantes
Parma   v   Odense

World Club Cup 1992-93

12 Dec 1993 National Stadium, Tokyo
62 000, referee Joël Quiniou (FRA)

SÃO PAULO (1)3   MILAN (0)2
Palhinha 19, Cerezo 59,   Massaro 48
Muller 86   Papin 81

São Paulo: Zetti' (Armelino Donizetti), 'Cafú' (Marcos
Evangelista), Válber (de Oliveira), Ronaldo (Rodrigues),

André (Moreira), Toninho Cerezo, 'Doriva' (Dorival Guidoni), Leonardo (de Araújo), 'Dinho' (Edi Wilson), 'Palhinha' (Jorge Ferreira) ['Juninho' (Osvaldo Júnior) 64], 'Muller' (Luis Correa)

Milan: Sebastiano Rossi, Christian Panucci, Paolo Maldini, Marcel Desailly, Alessandro Costacurta, Franco Baresi (c), Roberto Donadoni, Demetrio Albertini [Mauro Tassotti 79], Jean-Pierre Papin, Florin Raducioiu [Alessandro Orlando 79], Daniele Massaro

Cerezo is the oldest outfielder ever to play in the match.

World Club Cup 1993-94

1 Dec 1994 National Stadium, Tokyo
55 860, José Torres (COL)

VELEZ SARSFIELD (0)2   MILAN   0
Trotta pen 50, Asad 57

Velez Sarsfield: José Chilavert, Roberto Trotta (c), Raúl Cardozo, Héctor Almandoz, Marcelo Gómez, Victor Sotomayor, Christian Bassedas, José Basualdo, Omar Asad, Roberto Pompei, José Flóres

Milan: Sebastiano Rossi, Mauro Tassotti, Paolo Maldini, Demetrio Albertini, Alessandro Costacurta, Franco Baresi (c), Roberto Donadoni, Marcel Desailly, Zvonimir Boban, Dejan Savicevic [Marco Simone 60], Daniele Massaro [Christian Panucci 86]

Milan, fielding virtually the same team which won the European Cup final so grandly, play like drains to become the first club to lose in successive World Club matches since Estudiantes 1969-70. In a match of eight bookings, Costacurta completes his miserable year in big matches (he missed both the European Cup & World Cup finals) by giving away both goals and being sent off five minutes from time.

World Club Cup: most appearances

4	Miguel Angel Santoro	Independiente
	1964-65-72-73	
4	Ricardo Pavoni	Independiente
	1965-72-73-74	
4	Mauro Tassotti	Milan
	1989-90-93-94	
4	Paolo Maldini	Milan
	1989-90-93-94	
4	Alessandro Costacurta	Milan
	1989-90-93-94	
4	Franco Baresi	Milan
	1989-90-93-94	
4	Roberto Donadoni	Milan
	1989-90-93-94	

Libertadores Cup 1992-93

(South American club championship)

Final 1st leg: 19 May 1993 Morumbi, São Paulo
99 000, referee José Torres (COL)

SÃO PAULO   (2)5   UNIV. CATOLICA   (0)1
Palhinha 31, Vitor 41   *Almada pen 85*
Gilmar 55, Raí 61,
Muller 66

São Paulo: 'Zetti' (Armelino Donizetti), Claudemir Vitor ['Catê' (Marcos A Leme)], Válber (de Oliveira), Gilmar (dos Santos), Ronaldo Luis (Gonçalves) [André] 'Pintado' (Luís Carlos de Oliveira), 'Dinho' (Edi Santos), Raí (Souza de Oliveira)(c), 'Cafú' (Marcos Evangelista), 'Palhinha' (José Ferreira), 'Muller' (Luís da Costa)

Universidad Catolica: Oscar Wirth, Contreras, Daniel Lopez [Rodrigo Barrera], Vasquez, Romero, Tupper, Lunari, Nelson Parraguez, Mario Leppe, Almada, Perez [Reinoso]

Final 2nd leg: 26 May 1993 Nacional, Santiago
50 000, Juan Escobar (PAR)

UNIV. CATOLICA   (2)2   SÃO PAULO   0
Lunari 10, Almada 15

Univ. Catolica: unchanged. Cardozo sub'd Contreras, Reinoso sub'd Tupper

São Paulo: Marcos Adriano (de Barros) in place of Ronaldo Luis. Toninho Cerezo sub'd Vitor c.65

Libertadores Cup 1993-94

Final 1st leg: 24 Aug 1994
42 000, José Torres (COL)

VELEZ SARSFIELD (ARG) 1   São Paulo (BRZ)   0
Asad 36

Velez: José Luis Chilavert, Zandona, Roberto Trotta (c), Victor Sotomayor, Raúl Cardozo, José Basualdo, Marcelo Gomez, Christian Bassedas, Roberto Pompei, Omar Asad [Husain], José Flores [Fernandez]

São Paulo: 'Zetti', Claudemir Vitor, Válber, 'Junior Baiano', André, 'Cafú', Gilmar, Axel, 'Palhinha' ('Juninho'), 'Muller', Euler

2nd leg: 31 Aug 1994

SÃO PAULO   (1)1   VELEZ SARSFIELD   0
Muller pen 35
Velez Sarsfield 5-3 pens

São Paulo: unchanged. Juninho came on as sub.

Velez: Héctor Almandoz in place of Sotomayor, Pellegrino in place of Pompei, who sub'd Basualdo. Husain sub'd Flores. Cardozo sent off.

Both teams won their semi-finals on penalties, but Velez are the real shoot-out masters: the final's the third round they've won that way. Chilavert who takes penalties for Paraguay, saved four and scored with three in those shoot-outs. Velez, in the final for the first time, stop São Paulo winning the title for the third year in a row and become the first Argentinian club to win it since River Plate in 1986.

African Nations' Cup

26 March – 10 April 1994 Tunisia

GROUP A

Mali	(2)2	Tunisia	0
Coulibaly 25, M Sidibe 35			
Zaire	(0)1	Mali	0
Basaula 48			
Tunisia	(1)1	Zaire	(0)1
F Rouissi pen 43		Nsumbu 55	

GROUP B

Nigeria	(1)3	Gabon	0
Yekini 18, 88, Adepoju 72			
Egypt	(2)4	Gabon	0
A Mansou 1, El Gamal 22, Samad 55, 69			
Egypt	0	Nigeria	0

GROUP C

Ivory Coast	(2)4	Sierra Leone	0
Tiehi 19, 63, 70, Guel 35			
Sierra Leone	0	Zambia	0
Zambia	(0)1	Ivory Coast	0
K Malitoli 79			

GROUP D

Ghana	(0)1	Guinea	0
Akunnor 87			
Senegal	(0)2	Guinea	(1)1
Gueye pen 46, Tendeng 50		A Camara 44	
Ghana	(0)1	Senegal	0
Opoku 88			

Quarter-finals

Nigeria	(0)2	Zaire	0
Yekini 51, 71			
Ivory Coast	(1)2	Ghana	(0)1
Tiehi 30, A Traoré 81		Akunnor 77	
Mali	(0)1	Egypt	0
S Traoré 64			

Zambia	(1)1	Senegal	0
Sakala 38			

Semi-finals

Nigeria	(2)(2)2	Ivory Coast	(2)(2)2
Iroha 26, Yekini 40		Bassole 19, 31	
Nigeria 4-2 pens			
Zambia	(2)4	Mali	0
Litana 8, Saileti 30,			
K Bwalya 47, K Malitoli			

The biters bit: defending champions Ivory Coast had won the title in a penalty shoot-out. Nigeria also reached the final in 1984 & 1988 by winning semi-finals on penalties; Peter Rufai made saves in all three shoot-outs.

3rd-place final

Ivory Coast	(1)3	Mali	(0)1
Kone 2, Quattara 67,		Diallo 46	
Sie 70			

Final

10 April 1994 El Menzah, Tunis
30 000, Lim Kee Chong (Mauritius)

NIGERIA	(1)2	ZAMBIA	(1)1
Amunike 5, 47		Litana 3	

Nigeria: Peter Rufai, Benedict Iroha, Uche Okechukwu, Augustine Eguavoen, Uchenna Okafor, Sunday Oliseh, Rashidi Yekini, Emmanuel Amunike, Austin Okacha [Nduka Ugbade 73], Daniel Amokachi, Finidi George [Samson Siasia 41]

Zambia: James Phiri, Harrison Chongo, Elija Litana, Kapambwe Mulenga [Linos Makwaza 61], Mordon Malitoli, Aggrey Chiyangi, Evans Sakala, Kalusha Bwalya, Kenneth Malitoli, Zeddy Saileti, Joel Bwalya [Johnson Bwalya 70]

Not quite the great emotional ending. Scottish coach Ian Porterfield (of 1973 FA Cup Final fame) almost brings the title to a country whose entire World Cup squad had been wiped out in an air crash. Zambia are the first losing team to score in a final since 1984, Amunike the first to score twice in a final since that same year.

African footballer of the year

1992-93
Rashidi Yekini   Vitória Setúbal (PORT) & NIG

1993-94
Emmanuel Amunike   Zamalek (Egypt) & NIG
Now with Sporting, Lisbon.

Women's Football

English Premier Division

	P	W	D	L	F	A	W	D	L	F	A	Pts
		Home					**Away**					
Doncaster Belles	18	8	1	0	60	6	8	0	1	50	10	49
Arsenal	18	6	2	1	36	11	8	1	0	49	4	45
Knowsley Utd	18	7	0	2	39	16	6	2	1	24	14	41
Wembley	18	4	1	4	17	20	5	1	3	18	14	29
Millwall Lionesses	18	5	0	4	24	29	4	1	4	18	17	28
Leasowe Pacific	18	3	2	4	17	16	4	0	5	25	32	23
Stanton Rangers	18	4	1	4	14	20	2	4	3	18	18	23
Red Star Southampton	18	1	2	6	12	36	1	1	7	13	34	6
Ipswich Town	18	1	2	6	11	38	0	1	8	3	48	6
Wimbledon	18	1	0	8	5	37	1	0	8	11	44	3

Ipswich Town & Wimbledon relegated.

Division 1 North

	P	W	D	L	F	A	W	D	L	F	A	Pts
Wolverhampton Wanderers	18	9	0	0	43	7	3	4	2	18	21	40
Sheffield Wednesday	18	6	1	2	24	10	7	0	2	22	10	40
Abbeydale	18	5	1	3	23	12	4	1	4	15	19	29
Bronte	18	5	2	2	22	11	3	2	4	24	15	28
Cowgate Kestrels	18	4	1	4	19	18	5	0	4	19	23	28
Villa Aztecs	18	4	2	3	26	18	4	1	4	11	16	27
St Helens	18	4	0	5	20	23	3	1	5	16	34	22
Langford	18	4	1	4	14	15	1	1	7	11	26	17
Nottingham Argyle	18	3	1	5	13	22	2	0	7	12	27	16
Kidderminster Harriers	18	2	2	5	14	22	1	1	7	10	27	12

Wolves promoted, Kidderminster stay up after beating Manchester Belle Vue in a play-off final.

Division 1 South

	P	W	D	L	F	A	W	D	L	F	A	Pts
Bromley Borough	18	7	1	1	27	7	7	2	0	41	9	45
Town & County	18	6	1	2	5	1	3	1	3	18	11	35
Epsom & Ewell	18	5	2	2	19	13	5	0	4	18	13	32
Bristol	17	4	0	4	25	18	6	1	2	25	16	31
Brighton & H	18	3	3	3	12	10	6	1	2	24	13	31
Maidstone T	18	4	3	2	17	13	4	2	3	20	15	29
Hemel Hempstead	18	4	1	4	24	18	0	5	4	9	26	18
Horsham	17	2	2	5	15	22	2	2	4	9	11	16
Oxford U	18	1	2	6	6	18	2	2	5	11	19	13
Hassocks	18	0	1	8	6	39	0	0	9	1	51	1

Bromley promoted. Bristol v Horsham declared void. Hassocks relegated, replaced by Brentford.

FA Cup 1993-94

6th round

Preston Rangers	2	Stanton Rangers	3 aet
Arsenal	0	Knowsley United	1
Doncaster Belles	5	Brighton & Hove Albion	1
Epsom & Ewell	2	Leasowe Pacific	3 aet

Semi-finals

at Ilkeston Town FC

Knowsley United	1	Stanton Rangers	0

at Southport FC

Doncaster Belles	6	Leasowe Pacific	0

Final

24 April 1994 Glanford Park, Scunthorpe
1 674, referee I Hemley
DONCASTER BELLES 1   KNOWSLEY UTD   0
Walker 37

DONCASTER: Davidson, Lowe, Woodhead, Ryde, Jackson, Broadhurst, Goodman, Coultard (Lisseman 35, Chipchase 88), Murray, Walker, Borman

KNOWSLEY: Thomas, Hayward, McQuigan, Taylor, Koughlin, Gallimore, Gore, Davis, Baker (Holland 82), Harper, Burke

In front of a disappointingly small crowd, in a competition that deserved better, the Belles win the Cup for the sixth time. Karen Walker is announced over the PA as 'man of the match.'

League Cup 1993-94

3rd Round

Arsenal	9	Red Star Southampton	1
Leasowe Pacific	2	Wimbledon	2

Leasowe on pens

Bromley Borough	1	Knowsley Utd	5
Millwall Lionesses	1	Doncaster Belles	6

Semi-finals

Arsenal	4	Leasowe Pacific	1
Knowsley Utd	0	Doncaster Beles	4

Final

13 Nov 1994 Abbey Stadium, Cambridge
Arsenal   (2)4   Doncaster Belles   0
Britton, Spacey, Jackson og 76, Churchman 78

If the final had been held at the end of 1993-94, Arsenal would have been underdogs - but by now they're

unbeaten in the League from the start of the new season, and Doncaster striker Tina Brannan fails to turn up for the match, all of which prevents the Belles from winning the treble.

FA Cup 1994-95

1st round

Selected results: Huddersfield Town bt Newcastle 12-0, Peterborough Diamonds bt Highfield Rangers 11-0 away, Charlton bt Milton Keynes Utd 11-1, Frome bt Sturminster Newton 10-1

2nd round

Selected results: Leyton Orient bt Slough Town 25-0, Town & County bt Chailey Mavericks 22-0 (no misprints), Huddersfield Town bt Barnsley 16-0, Manchester Belle Vue bt South Shields 11-0 away, Brighton & Hove Albion bt Reading 14-0,

England Internationals

(European qualifying Group 7 matches)

25 Sep 1993 Bezigadrom, Ljubljana
1000, Morimov (BUL)

SLOVENIA	0
ENGLAND	(5)10

Taylor 19, Spacey 21, 35, 73, 87, Borman 30, Walker 36, 47, 82, Davis 88

England: Lesley Shipp, Karen Burke, Michelle Curley, Clare Taylor, Debbie Bampton, Samantha Britton [Frances Carroll 73], Marieanne Spacey, Gillian Couthard (c), Janice (Jan) Murray, Karen Walker, Gail Borman [Kerry Davis 73]

The first competitive international ever played in Slovenia, by either sex. England equal their highest score (1986 v N Ireland), Coulthard wins her 70th cap.

6 Nov 1993 Koksijde
500, Tore Hollung (NOR)

BELGIUM	0
ENGLAND	(1)3

Walker 28, 86, Taylor 82

England: Shipp, Kirsty Pealling [Louise Waller 87], Curley, Taylor, Bampton, Hope Powell [Burke 70], Spacey, Coulthard (c), Murray, Walker, Borman

A Belgian defender's sent off two minutes before England's 2nd goal.

19 Dec 1993 Municipal, Osuna
3500

SPAIN   0   ENGLAND   0

England: Shipp, Waller, Davis, Britton, Taylor, Coulthard (c), Spacey [Powell 81], Bampton, Walker, Borman, Murray [Joanne Broadhurst 81]

20 Feb 1994 Valley Parade, Bradford

ENGLAND   0   SPAIN   0

England: Shipp, Pealling, Waller, Powell [Broadhurst 74], Taylor, Coulthard (c), Spacey, Bampton, Davis [Walker 79}, Borman, Murray

Both teams hit the woodwork in the first half, England have two goals disallowed in the second.

13 March 1994 City Ground, Nottingham

ENGLAND   (3)6
Spacey 13, 21, Walker 18, 60, Davis 56, Coulthard 87
BELGIUM   0

England: Shipp, Pealling, Waller [Samantha Hayward 75], Britton, Taylor, Coulthard (c), Spacey, Bampton, Walker, Borman, Davis [Burke 75]

17 April 1994 Griffin Park, Brentford

ENGLAND   (2)10
Taylor 4, 57, Walker 15, 60, Britton 69, 80, Coulthard 65, Powell 71, Borman 73, Spacey 86
SLOVENIA   0

England: Shipp [Tracey Davidson 58], Pealling, Waller, Britton, Taylor, Coulthard (c), Spacey, Bampton [Powell 70], Walker, Borman, Davis

England equal the record set in the away fixture against the same country. The only surprise is that the prolific Davis doesn't score (and isn't substituted).

Group 7

Other results:

Belgium	7	Slovenia	0
Belgium	0	Spain	0
Spain	17	Slovenia	0
Spain	4	Belgium	0
Slovenia	0	Belgium	8
Slovenia	0	Spain	8

Final table

	P	W	D	L	F	A	Pts
England	6	4	2	0	29	0	10
Spain	6	3	3	0	29	0	9
Belgium	6	2	1	3	15	13	5
Slovenia	6	0	0	6	0	60	0

England qualify for the quarter-finals. The Slovenian first-timers surely set records for goals conceded in one match and in a series.

Quarter-final

8 Oct 1994 National Stadium, Rekjavik

ICELAND   (1)1
Olafsdottir 30
ENGLAND   (1)2
Coulthard 7, Davis 60

Iceland: S Palsdottir, G Saemunsdottir, G Jonsdottir, V Sigurgeirsdottir, A Skuladottir, AB Gunlaugsdottir, A Helgadottir, RL Stefansdottir, Margrat Olafsdottir, S Ottarsdottir, O Faerseth

England: Shipp, Pealling, Sian Williams, Donna Smith, Taylor, Coulthard (c), Spacey (Burke 83), Bampton, Walker, Davis, Murray

Coulthard's 25-yard volley helps England win a match played in sub-zero temperatures.

30 Oct 1994 Goldstone Ground, Brighton

ENGLAND   (1)2
Coulthard 13, Spacey 65
ICELAND   (1)1
Gunnlaugsdottir 34

England: unchanged from first leg (Coulthard captain as usual). Waller sub'd Williams 74, Burke sub'd Davis 77

Iceland: unchanged except for G Kristjansdottir in place of Ottarsdottir. H Hannesdottir sub'd Skuladottir 35, K Arnsporsdottir sub'd Faerseth 80

By reaching the European semi-finals, England also qualify for the World Cup for the first time, thanks again to Coulthard, who opens the scoring with a 30-yard free kick. Gunnlaugsdottir scores in her last international before retirement.

Semi-final

11 Dec 1994 Vicarage Road, Watford

ENGLAND   (1)1
Farley 7
GERMANY   (1) 4
Möhr 32, 84, Vröcker 75, Wiegmann pen 89

England: Higgs, Pealling (Spacey 76), Karen Farley, Britton, Taylor, Coulthard (c), Burke (Easton 76), Bampton, Walker, Davis, Murray

Germany: Göller, Bernhard, Austermühl, Minnert, Fitschen, Meinert, Martina Voss, Bettina Wiegmann, Heidi Möhr, Silvia Neid (c), Patricia Bröcker

Germany, traditionally a far stronger power in the women's game, set up what should be a comfortable second leg in February - but the goal that puts them ahead is a virtual own goal by Burke. England's run to the semis deserves a better crowd than 937 with tickets costing only £2.

Gaelic Football

All-Ireland Final 1994

18 Sep 1994 Croke Park, Dublin

DOWN   (11)15   DUBLIN   (7)13

Down: Neil Collins, M Magill, Brian Burns, Paul Higgins, Eamonn Burns, Barry Breen, DJ Kane (c), Gregory McCartan, Conor Deegan (Gerard Colgan), Ross Carr, Greg Blaney, James McCartan, Mickey Linden, Aidan Farrell, Gary Mason.

Dublin: John O'Leary (c), Paddy Moran, Dermot Deasy, Paul Curran, Paul Clarke, Keith Barr, Mick Deegan, Brian Stynes, Jack Sheedy, Pat Gilroy (Paul Whelan), Vinnie Murphy, Niall Guiden Johnny Barr), Charlie Redmond, Mick Galvin, Dessie Farrell. Other sub used: Sean Cadell

Dublin lead only once, 2-1 through their leading scorer Redmond, who was also on the losing side in the finals of 1985 & 1992, missed a penalty in the latter, and misses another here, hitting it straight at Collins with the score 15-12. Dublin haven't won the title since 1983. Down, who've never lost in the final, win their fifth All-Ireland title by beating Dublin in a championship match for the first time. Eleven players from each team played in previous finals, Down winning in 1991, Dublin losing the following year. Neither the Burns, the McCartans nor the Deegans are related. J McCartan, who scores the only goal after 18 mins, was man of match in the 1991 final. HIs father Jim was in the first two Down teams to win the title (1960 & 1961).

Gliding

European Championships

July-Aug 1994 Rieti, Italy

Open

B Gantenbrink	GER	8623
JW Andersen	DEN	8540
M Heller	GER	8492
15 R May	*UK*	*7568*

15 metre

S Ghiorzio	ITA	8552
W Meuser	GER	8424
R Termaat	HOL	8173
24 J Edyvean	*UK*	*6248*

Standard

P Fischer	GER	9358
R Schramme	GER	9358
E Ziegler	GER	9358
21 D Campbell	*UK*	*7618*

A remarkable statistic with so many points involved: the three Germans share the title.

British National Championships

Standard
6-14 Aug Bicester

Andy Davis	4936
Steve Jones	4888
Mike Young	4836

Open
23 July - 2 Aug 1994 Enstone Eagles GC*

Alister Kay	4490
Steve Jones	4477
Russell Cheetham	4397

* Flights over Rutland Water, Watford Gap, Oundle, Long Mynd, Hay on Wye, etc - although in fact there were hardly any flights at all (cancelled on the 26th, 27th & 31st) due to the weather.

15 metre
9-17 July 1994 Dunstable

Justin Wills	5719
Martin Wells	5547
Tim Scott	5385

Junior
18-26 Aug 1994 Lasham

Guy Westgate	3923
Derren Francis	3914
Richie Toon	3855

Westgate is lucky to win, which he does by only nine points: a broken wrist keeps out defending champion Karina Hodgson, then David Allison suffers a mid-air collision while in the lead. A prize is awarded daily to the Dick of The Day.

British Aerobatic Championships

10-11 Sep 1994

Buckminster GC, Saltby airfield

Unlimited	Lionel Sole
Intermediate	Mike Woollard
Sports	Chris Pollard

Golf

At one stage in the international season, a case could be made for claiming that it had all been decided by a single stroke, but if so which one? Parnevik's misjudgment at the last or Price's 50-footer at the 17th? Probably the latter, which won him the British Open at last and presumably did his confidence no harm for the USPGA. Back-to-back Majors, with both Norman & Faldo going through a fallow period, should have made him player of the year.

Instead 1994 will probably come to be regarded less as Price's peak than Ernie Els' first step on the road up. Winning the US Open & World Matchplay, both in head-to-head finales, showed nerve and maturity (the strokeplay already had the critics drooling); the runaway win at the World Championship (with Price ten strokes adrift) put the seal on it. Between them, they also won five times on the US Tour.

Talking of Americans, it was a year when we didn't have to. For the first time ever, none of them won a men's Major. Still, reports of their dearth may be rather exaggerated: although Laura Davies finished top of the rankings over there as well as over here, their women easily regained the Solheim Cup – and even the men had their moments: in the team World Championships, amateur as well as professional, in the President's Cup, beating Price among others. Even at this range, this year's Ryder Cup looks a humdinger, especially if someone can get inside John Daly's head.

The Majors

US Masters
7-10 April 1994 Augusta National

279	José Maria Olazabal	SPA	74 67 69 69
281	Tom Lehmann		70 70 69 72
282	Larry Mize*		68 71 72 71
283	Tom Kite		69 72 71 71
285	Jay Haas		72 72 72 69
285	Loren Roberts		75 68 72 70
285	Jim McGovern		72 70 71 72
286	Corey Pavin		72 72 73 70
286	Ernie Els	SAF	74 67 74 71
287	John Huston		72 72 74 69
287	Ray Floyd*		70 74 71 72
287	Ian Baker Finch	AUS	71 71 71 74
288	Tom Watson*		70 71 73 74
289	Dan Forsman		74 66 76 73
291	Mark O'Meara		75 70 76 70
291	Brad Faxon		71 73 73 74
291	Chip Beck		71 71 75 74
292	Severiano Ballesteros*	SPA	70 76 75 71
292	Hale Irwin		73 68 79 72
292	Bill Glasson		72 73 75 72
292	Ben Crenshaw*		74 73 73 72
292	Lanny Wadkins		73 74 73 72
292	David Edwards		72 73 73 74
292	Greg Norman	AUS	70 70 75 77
293	Bernhard Langer*	GER	74 74 72 73
293	Jeff Sluman		74 75 71 73
294	Scott Simpson		74 74 73 73
294	Curtis Strange		74 70 75 75
294	Vijay Singh	FIJI	70 75 74 75
295	Lee Janzen		75 71 76 73
295	Craig Parry	AUS	75 74 73 73
296	Nick Faldo*	UK	76 73 73 74
297	Sam Torrance	UK	76 73 74 74
297	Russ Cochran		71 74 74 78
298	Nick Price	ZIM	74 73 74 77
298	David Frost	SAF	74 71 75 78
298	Frank 'Fuzzy' Zoeller*		74 72 74 78
299	Sandy Lyle*	UK	75 73 78 73
299	Fred Funk		79 70 75 75
299	Fulton Allem	SAF	69 77 76 77
300	Costantino Rocca	ITA	79 70 78 73

300	Mike Standly		77 69 79 75
300	Andrew Magee		74 74 76 76
300	Hajime Meshiai	JAP	71 71 80 78
300	Wayne Grady	AUS	74 73 73 80
301	Ian Woosnam*	UK	76 73 77 75
301	John Cook		77 72 77 75
304	John Daly		76 73 77 78
304	Howard Twitty		73 76 74 81
305	Jeff Maggert		75 73 82 75
305	John Harris		72 76 80 77

Olazabal, the first man to win the event while using a metal wood, wins his first Major (Europeans have won six of the last seven Masters). At the other end of the scale, Harris is the leading amateur.

Among those who miss the cut (at 149): 150 Colin Montgomerie UK 77 73, Johnny Miller 77 73, Craig Stadler 76 74, Mark Calcavecchia 75 75, Gary Player* SAF 71 79, 152 Jack Nicklaus* 78 74, 154 Charles Coody* 80 74, Billy Casper* 77 77, 155 Arnold Palmer* 78 77, 156 Payne Stewart 78 78, Tommy Aaron* 76 80. Highest of the High: 163 Gary Brewer 84 79.

* previous Masters champion.

US Open
16-19 June 1994 Oakmont, Pennsylvania

Play-off

74	Ernie Els	SAF	
74	Loren Roberts		
78	Colin Montgomerie	UK	

The youngest player to win a Major (24) since Ballesteros (22) took the 1979 British Open, and only the second South African to take the title (after Gary Player in 1965) wins at the second extra hole of the first three-way play-off for the title since 1962, which comes about when Roberts, 38 years old and winner of just one pro tournament, misses a short putt on the 72nd hole. A frustrating near-miss for the 1988 & 1989 champion Strange, but at least he's consistent.

279	Ernie Els	SAF	69 71 66 73
279	Loren Roberts		76 69 64 70
279	Colin Montgomerie	UK	71 65 73 70
280	Curtis Strange*		70 70 70 70
282	John Cook		73 65 73 71
283	Clark Dennis		71 71 70 71
283	Greg Norman	AUS	71 71 69 72
283	Tom Watson*		68 73 68 74
284	Duffy Waldorf		74 68 73 69
284	Jeff Maggert		71 68 75 70
284	Jeff Sluman		72 69 72 71
284	Frank Nobilo	NZ	69 71 68 76
285	Jim McGovern		73 69 74 69

285	Scott Hoch		72 72 70 71
285	David Edwards		73 65 75 72
286	Fred Couples		72 71 69 74
286	Steve Lowery		71 71 68 76
287	Scott Verplank		70 72 75 70
287	Seve Ballesteros	SPA	72 72 70 73
287	Hale Irwin*		69 68 71 78
288	Sam Torrance	UK	72 71 76 69
288	Steve Pate		74 66 71 77
289	Bernhard Langer	GER	72 72 73 72
289	Kirk Triplett		70 71 71 77
290	Mike Springer		74 72 73 71
290	Craig Parry	AUS	78 68 71 73
290	Chip Beck		73 73 70 74
292	Davis Love III		74 72 74 72
292	Jim Furyk		74 69 74 75
292	Lennie Clements		73 71 73 75
292	Jack Nicklaus*		69 70 77 76
292	Masashi 'Jumbo' Ozaki	JAP	70 73 69 80
293	Mark Carnevale		75 72 76 70
293	Tom Lehman		77 68 73 75
293	Fulton Allem	SAF	73 70 74 76
293	Tom Kite*		73 71 72 77
293	Ben Crenshaw		71 74 70 78
293	Brad Faxon		73 69 71 80
294	Bradley Hughes	AUS	71 72 77 74
294	Peter Baker	UK	73 73 73 75
294	Gordon Brand jnr	UK	73 71 73 77
294	Brondt Jobe		72 74 68 80
295	Francis Quinn		75 72 73 75
296	Paul Goydos		74 72 79 71
296	Fred Funk		74 71 74 77
296	Don Walsworth		71 75 73 77
297	Tim Dunlavey		76 70 78 73
297	Olin Browne		74 73 77 73
297	Barry Lane	UK	77 70 76 74
297	Mike Emery		74 73 75 75
297	Danny Berganio		73 72 76 76
297	Jim Gallagher		74 68 77 78
297	Wayne Levi		76 70 73 78
297	Phil Mickelson		75 70 73 79
298	Tommy Armour III		73 73 79 73
298	Hugh Royer		72 71 77 78
298	Scott Simpson*		73 74 73 78
299	Steve Richardson	UK	74 73 76 76
299	Frank 'Fuzzy' Zoeller*		76 70 76 77
301	Dave Rummells		71 74 82 74
301	Doug Martin		76 70 74 81
302	Ed Humenik		74 72 81 75
302	Mike Smith		74 73 78 77
302	Emlyn Aubrey		72 69 81 80

Rocco Mediate (70 76 79) withdraws after the third round.

Among those who miss the cut (at 147): 149 Larry Mize 77 72, Wayne Grady AUS 75 74, B Alexander (leading amateur) 75 74, 150 José María Olazabal SPA 76 74, Corey Pavin 77 73, 152 Ian Woosnam UK 77 75,

Craig Stadler 78 74, 157 Ian Baker-Finch AUS 83 74,
158 Arnold Palmer* 77 81. Highest of the High: 161
Joey Ferrari 82 79

* previous Open champion.

Chris Patton, who recently weighed in at 25 stone,
withdraws with heat exhaustion after only eight holes of
the first round. Arnold Palmer plays his last US Open.

British Open
14-17 July 1994 Turnberry

268	Nick Price	ZIM	69 66 67 66
269	Jesper Parnevik	SWE	68 66 68 67
271	Frank 'Fuzzy' Zoeller	USA	71 66 64 70
273	Anders Forsbrand	SWE	72 71 66 64
273	Mark James		72 67 66 68
273	David Feherty		68 69 66 70
274	Brad Faxon	USA	69 65 67 73
275	Nick Faldo*		75 66 70 64
275	Tom Kite	USA	71 69 66 69
275	Colin Montgomerie		72 69 65 69
276	Russell Claydon		72 71 68 65
276	Mark McNulty	ZIM	71 70 68 67
276	Frank Nobilo	NZ	69 67 72 68
276	Jonathan Lomas		66 70 72 68
276	Mark Calcavecchia*	USA	71 70 67 68
276	Greg Norman*	AUS	71 67 69 69
276	Larry Mize	USA	73 69 64 70
276	Tom Watson*	USA	68 65 69 74
276	Ronan Rafferty		71 66 65 74
277	Mark Brooks	USA	74 64 71 68
277	Vijay Singh	FIJI	70 68 69 70
277	Peter Senior	AUS	68 71 67 71
278	Bob Estes	USA	72 68 72 66
278	Terry Price	AUS	74 65 71 68
278	Paul Lawrie		71 69 70 68
278	Jeff Maggert	USA	69 74 67 68
278	Tom Lehman	USA	70 69 70 69
278	Ernie Els	SAF	69 69 69 71
278	Mike Springer	USA	72 67 68 71
278	Loren Roberts	USA	68 69 69 72
278	Peter Jacobsen	USA	69 70 67 72
278	Craig Stadler	USA	71 69 66 72
278	Andrew Coltart		71 69 66 72
279	Mark Davis		75 68 69 67
279	Lee Janzen	USA	74 69 69 67
279	Gary Evans		69 69 73 68
280	David Gilford		72 68 72 68
280	Domingo Hospital	SPA	72 69 71 68
280	José María Olazabal	SPA	72 71 69 68
280	Severiano Ballesteros	SPA	70 70 71 69
280	Brian Marchbank		71 70 70 69
280	Darren Clarke		73 68 69 70
280	Jean Van de Velde	FRA	68 70 71 71
280	Davis Love III	USA	71 67 68 74

280	Masashi 'Jumbo' Ozaki	JAP	69 71 66 74
281	Jim Gallagher jnr	USA	73 68 69 71
281	David Edwards	USA	68 68 73 72
281	Greg Kraft	USA	69 74 66 72
281	Howard Twitty	USA	71 72 66 72
282	David Frost	SAF	70 71 71 70
282	Mats Lanner	SWE	69 74 69 70
282	Katsuyoshi Tomori	JAP	69 69 73 71
282	Tsukasa Watanabe	JAP	72 71 68 71
283	Peter Baker		71 72 70 70
283	John Cook	USA	73 67 70 73
283	Tommy Nakajima	JAP	73 68 69 73
283	Brian Watts	USA	68 70 71 74
283	Ross McFarlane		68 74 67 74
284	Gordon Brand jnr		72 71 73 68
284	Hajime Meshiai	JAP	72 71 71 70
284	Bernhard Langer	GER	72 70 70 72
284	Christy O'Connor jnr		71 69 71 73
284	Per-Ulrik Johansson	SWE	73 69 69 73
284	Robert Allenby	AUS	72 69 68 75
284	Wayne Grady	AUS	68 74 67 75
285	Carl Mason		69 71 73 72
285	Rubén Alvarez	ARG	70 72 71 72

BRITISH OPEN: some records
Lowest totals
267	Greg Norman	1993
268	Tom Watson	1977
268	Nick Price	1994
269	Jack Nicklaus	1977
269	Jesper Parnevik	1994

Most rounds under 70
31	Jack Nicklaus
29	Nick Faldo
26	Tom Watson
21	Lee Trevino
19	Seve Ballesteros

All four rounds under 70
Greg Norman	1993
Ernie Els	1993
Nick Price	1994
Jesper Parnevik	1994

Places in the two tables only rub the salt into
Parnevik's wounds: scores like that counting for
nothing alongside the 72nd hole (where he
dropped a shot after misreading the score and
going for a birdie) which may stay with him for
the rest of his career.

285	Lennie Clements	USA	72 71 72 70
285	Mark Roe		74 68 73 70
285	Steve Elkington	AUS	71 72 73 69
286	Warren Bennett		72 67 74 73
286	Wayne Riley	AUS	77 66 70 73
287	Sandy Lyle		71 72 72 72
288	Colin Gillies		71 70 72 75
288	Craig Ronald		71 72 72 73
289	Craig Parry	AUS	72 68 73 76
289	Ben Crenshaw	USA	70 73 73 73
289	Joakim Häggman	SWE	71 72 69 77
291	Nic Henning	SAF	70 73 70 78
292	John Daly	USA	68 72 72 80

Leading amateur: Warren Bennett, the only one to make the cut.

Watson, trying to become only the second player to win the title six times, and one of the oldest to win it at all, leads after the second round and is only one shot off the lead after the third, but stages one of his recently familiar minor collapses on the last, during which Forsbrand's long putt stops on the very lip of the 18th hole, depriving him of a 63 that would have equalled the Open record.

Among those who miss the cut (at 143): 145 Jack Nicklaus* 72 73, Gary Player* SAF (his 40th consecutive appearance in the event) 72 73, 146 Scott Simpson 73 73, 147 Lee Trevino* 75 72, 147 Sam Torrance UK 74 73, 148 Payne Stewart 74 74, 150 Ian Baker-Finch* AUS 73 77, 151 Chip Beck 76 75, Corey Pavin 75 76, 152 Ian Woosnam UK 79 73, 153 Bob Charles* NZ 74 79. Highest of the High: 160 Lee Fickling 80 80

* previous Open champion.

Lane shoots a hole-in-one, the sixth of his professional career, on the fourth hole of the first round.

USPGA
11-14 Aug 1994 Southern Hills, Tulsa, Oklahoma

269	Nick Price*	ZIM	67 65 70 67
275	Corey Pavin		70 67 69 69
276	Phil Mickelson		68 71 69 69
277	Nick Faldo	UK	73 67 71 66
277	Greg Norman	AUS	71 69 67 70
277	John Cook		71 67 69 70
278	José María Olazabal	SPA	72 66 70 70
278	Steve Elkington	AUS	73 70 66 69
279	Ian Woosnam	UK	68 72 73 66
279	Tom Kite		72 68 69 70
279	Loren Roberts		69 72 67 71
279	Tom Watson		69 72 67 71
280	Jay Haas		70 67 68 75
281	Kirk Triplett		71 69 71 70

281	Larry Mize		72 72 67 70
281	Mark McNulty	ZIM	72 68 70 71
281	Glen Day		70 69 70 72
282	Frank 'Fuzzy' Zoeller		69 71 72 70
282	Craig Stadler		70 70 74 68
282	Mark McCumber		73 70 71 68
282	Bill Glasson		71 73 68 70
282	Curtis Strange		73 71 68 70
282	Craig Parry	AUS	70 69 70 73
283	Barry Lane	UK	70 73 68 72
283	Bernhard Langer	GER	73 71 67 72
283	David Frost	SAF	70 71 69 73
283	Ernie Els	SAF	68 71 69 75
283	Jeff Sluman*		70 72 66 75
284	Sam Torrance	UK	69 75 69 71
284	Brad Faxon		72 73 73 66
284	Wayne Grady*	AUS	75 68 71 70
284	Bob Boyd		72 71 70 71
284	Lennie Clements		74 70 69 71
284	Richard Zokol	CAN	77 67 67 73
285	Colin Montgomerie	UK	67 76 70 72
285	Chip Beck		72 70 72 71
285	Blaine McCallister		74 64 75 72
286	Fred Couples		68 74 75 69
286	Billy Mayfair		73 72 71 70
286	Gil Morgan		71 68 73 74
286	Tom Lehman		73 71 68 74
286	Hale Irwin		75 69 68 74
287	Neal Lancaster		73 72 72 70
287	David Edwards		72 70 74 71
287	David Gilford	UK	69 73 73 72
288	Billy Andrade		71 71 78 68
288	Fulton Allem	SAF	74 67 74 73
288	Bob Estes		72 71 72 73
288	Andrew Magee		70 74 71 73
288	Frank Nobilo	NZ	72 67 74 75
288	Greg Kraft		74 69 70 75
288	Masashi 'Jumbo' Ozaki	JAP	71 69 72 76
288	DA (Donald Albert) Weibring		69 73 70 76
289	Dudley Hart		72 71 75 71
289	Fred Funk		76 69 72 72
289	Hal Sutton*		76 69 72 72
289	Tom Dolby		73 68 75 73
289	Kenny Perry		78 67 70 74
289	Mike Springer		77 66 69 77
290	Ray Floyd*		69 76 73 72
290	Tommy Nakajima	JAP	73 71 74 72
290	Ron McDougal		76 69 72 73
290	Lanny Wadkins*		69 73 73 75
290	Bruce Fleisher		75 68 72 75
291	Lee Janzen		73 71 73 74
291	Jay Don Blake		72 71 74 74
291	Payne Stewart*		72 73 72 74
291	John Inman		70 72 73 76
291	Todd Smith		74 69 71 77
292	Donnie Hammond		74 69 76 73
292	Peter Senior	AUS	74 71 70 77
297	Sandy Lyle	UK	75 70 76 76

297	Dicky Pride		75 69 73 80
298	Hajime Meshiai	JAP	74 71 74 79
298	Brian Henninger		77 65 78 78

* former USPGA winner.

Among those who miss the cut (at 145): 146 John Daly* 73, 73, John Mahaffey 72 74, Davis Love III 73 73, Larry Nelson* 75 71, Mark Calcavecchia 74 72, 147 Scott Hoch 74 73, Mark James UK 71 76, 148 Scott Simpson 75 73, Ian Baker-Finch AUS 74 74, 149 Paul Azinger (the defending champion, recovered from cancer) 75 74, 150 Jack Nicklaus*, 152 Jesper Parnevik SWE 79 73, 154 Seve Ballesteros SPA 78 76. Highest of the High: 175 George Bowman 87 88.

After sharing the first-round lead with Montgomerie, Price is out on his own, becoming the first player since Faldo in 1990 to win two Majors in the same season, the first since Tom Watson in 1982 to win two in a row, and the first since Walter Hagen in 1924 to win the British Open & USPGA in the same year (the PGA was matchplay at the time). For the first time ever, none of the Majors is won by an American.

British Open (Amputee)

July 1994
Geoff Nicholas   AUS

US Open (Amputee)

Aug 1994 Pinehurst, N Carolina
Geoff Nicholas   AUS   215

Nicholas, who finishes one shot ahead of Bick Long (USA), holds his own among the more able-bodied: the only one-armed professional, he shoots 67 to lead the qualifiers for the Singapore Open.

World Championship 1993

16-19 Dec Tryall, Montego Bay, Jamaica

266	Larry Mize	USA	67 66 68 65
276	Fred Couples	USA	71 69 72 64
277	Bernhard Langer	GER	71 68 69 69
278	Colin Montgomerie	UK	67 69 68 74
279	Curtis Strange	USA	73 68 72 66
281	Nick Faldo	UK	70 72 69 70
281	Brad Faxon	USA	69 69 71 72
282	Vijay Singh	FIJI	72 70 71 69
282	Steve Elikington	AUS	68 65 77 72
282	Ernie Els	SAF	66 73 70 73
284	Sam Torrance	UK	73 74 67 70
285	Gordon Brand jr	UK	70 76 72 67
287	Steve Richardson	UK	73 71 73 70
292	Ian Woosnam	UK	73 73 74 72
307	Peter Baker	UK	74 78 79 76

Mize, who comes in as late replacement for Greg Norman, doesn't drop a shot in the last round on the way to setting a record total for the event. Baker collects $28 000 for finishing last.

World Championship 1994

15-18 Dec Tryall, Montego Bay, Jamaica

268	Ernie Els	SAF	64 64 71 69
274	Nick Faldo	UK	67 67 73 67
274	Mark McCumber	USA	67 70 70 67
275	Paul Azinger	USA	71 74 62 68
275	Brad Faxon	USA	72 70 69 64
275	Ian Woosnam	UK	70 68 69 68
276	David Gilford	UK	71 64 73 68
276	Bernhard Langer	GER	70 70 68 68
276	Jeff Maggert	USA	68 72 70 66
277	Robert Allenby	AUS	69 71 69 68
277	Colin Montgomerie	UK	67 74 67 69
294	Carl Mason	UK	70 74 76 74

Els climaxes his big year by leading from the start: three strokes after the first round, six after the second, seven after the third, in which Azinger's new course record confirms his recovery from cancer.

World Matchplay 1993

21-24 Oct West Course, Wentworth

ROUND 1

Steve Elkington	AUS	John Daly	USA	5&4
Nick Faldo	ENG	bye		
David Frost	SAF	Seve Ballesteros	SPA	7&6
Ian Woosnam	WAL	bye		
Corey Pavin	USA	Peter Baker	ENG	4&3
Nick Price	SAF	bye		
Colin Montgomerie	SCOT	Yoshinori Mizumaki	JAP	37th
Bernhard Langer	GER	bye		

QUARTER-FINALS

Faldo	Elkington	4&3
Frost	Woosnam	2&1
Montgomerie	Langer	6&4
Pavin	Price	2&1

SEMI-FINALS

| Faldo | Frost | 2&1 |
| Pavin | Montgomerie | 37th |

FINAL

| Pavin | Faldo | 1 hole |

Pavin holds his nerve to win both semi and final by one hole and take the title for the first time.

World Matchplay 1994

13-16 Oct West Course, Wentworth

ROUND 1

Vijay Singh	FIJI	Jesper Parnevik	SWE	4&3
Corey Pavin	USA	bye		
Colin Montgomerie	UK	Yoshinori Mizumaki	JAP	2&1
Nick Faldo	UK	bye		
Seve Ballesteros	SPA	David Frost	SAF	8&7
Ernie Els	SAF	bye		
Brad Faxon	USA	Ian Woosnam	UK	1 hole
José María Olazabal	SPA	bye		

Seve Ballesteros, annoyed at being invited only as a replacement when John Daly withdraws, takes part in the event for the 19th consecutive year. He & Montgomerie play the same opponents for the second successive year, Ballesteros taking emphatic revenge by shooting 63 in the morning and finishing 13 under par for the 29 holes, an event record.

QUARTER-FINALS

Singh	Pavin	37th
Montgomerie	Faldo	1 hole
Els	Ballesteros	2&1
Olazabal	Faxon	6&4

SEMI-FINALS

Montgomerie	Singh	1 hole
Els	Olazabal	2&1

The first South African to reach the final since Gary Player twenty years earlier.

FINAL

Els	Montgomerie	4&2

Both shoot 70 in the morning round, then Montgomerie's tiredness sets in (he's played 36 holes more than Els and this is his tenth week without a break from golf). The day before his 25th birthday, Els wins an event for the first time since the US Open (when he beat Montgomerie in a play-off) to become the first South African to win the title since Player (for a record fifth time) in 1973, and the first from any country to win it at the first attempt since Greg Norman in 1980.

European Tour 1993

GERMAN MASTERS

30 Sep - 3 Oct Stuttgart   Steve Richardson UK   271
Richardson's first tournament win for over two years.

BELGIAN OPEN

7-10 Oct Knokke-le-Stoute Darren Clarke   UK   270

MADRID OPEN

28-31 Oct Puerta de Hierro Des Smyth   EIRE 272
Smyth's first tournament win since the 1988 Jersey Open. Bad light forces the event to continue into a fourth day.

VOLVO MASTERS

4-7 Nov Valderrama   Colin Montgomerie UK   274
Montgomerie finishes as the European season's leading money winner.

European Tour 1994

MADEIRA OPEN

13-16 Jan Madeira   Mats Lanner   SWE 206
Reduced to three rounds after the third is rained off. Two other Swedes finish second equal. First round leader in the Tour: Jay Townsend (USA) 67.

MOROCCAN OPEN

20-23 Jan Agadir   Anders Forsbrand SWE 276
David Gilford, winner for the past two years, is fined by the PGA for withdrawing late. Howard Clark, who finished second eqUal in Madeira and hasn't won a Tour event since 1988, finishes second again here after holding a five-stroke lead at halfway.

DUBAI DESERT CLASSIC

27-30 Jan Emirates Club   Ernie Els   SAF   268
Els' first Tour win owes much to a round of 61, the lowest on the circuit all year (equalled by Carl Mason at the Scottish Open, but Els shoots eleven under against Mason's nine under).

JOHNNIE WALKER CLASSIC

3-6 Feb 1994
Phuket, Thailand   Greg Norman   AUS 277
Norman ends Nick Faldo's 81-week reign at the top of the world rankings.

TENERIFE OPEN

10-13 Feb Golf del Sur   David Gilford   UK   278
48-y-o Brian Barnes finishes equal fifth after leading with six holes to play.

EXTREMADURA OPEN

17-20 Feb
Guadiana, Badajoz   Paul Eales   UK   281
Eales' first Tour win. Nic Henning (SAF) sets a course record 66 in the third round.

ANDALUCIAN OPEN (TURESPAÑA MASTERS)

24-27 Feb
Montecastillo, Jerez   Carl Mason   UK   278
At the age of 40, after finishing second six times, in his 445th Tour event, Mason at last wins one for the first time.

MEDITERRANEAN OPEN

3-6 March
Villamartin, Torrevieja   José María Olazabal
SPA 276
Olazabal forces a play-off after being four shots behind runner-up Paul McGinley (EIRE) with four to play. 50-y-o Antonio Garrido (SPA) shoots 66 to lead the first round, then 75 in the second.

BALEARIC OPEN
10-13 March
Son Vida, Majorca   Barry Lane   UK   269
Lane shoots an event record 64 in the first round.

PORTUGUESE OPEN
17-20 March
Linho, Sintra   Phillip Price   UK   278
Price emulates Lane by leading from start to finish after shooting a course record 64 in the first round.

KRONENBOURG OPEN
24-27 March Gardagolf, Verona   cancelled

LYON OPEN
1-4 April
Villette D'Anthon   Stephen Ames   TRIN 282
Despite not shooting a birdie on the last round, Ames becomes the fifth first-time winner on the season's Tour so far. For the second successive tournament, Phillip Price starts with a course record: 67.

ROME MASTERS   cancelled
14-17 April Rome

CATALONIAN OPEN
21-24 April
Pals, Girona   José Coceres   ARG 275
Coceres wins a Tour event for the first time. Advance publicity centres heavily on Ballesteros & Olazabal. Neither played.

CANNES OPEN
28 April - 1 May
Mougins, Cannes   Ian Woosnam   UK   271
Woosnam, eight strokes off the lead during the second round, finishes five clear of the field.

B&H INTERNATIONAL OPEN
5-8 May
St Mellion, Plymouth   Seve Ballesteros   SPA 281
Ballesteros' first Tour win for two years.

SPANISH OPEN
12-15 May
Club de Campo   Colin Montgomerie UK 277
Twelve players walk out during the storm-affected second round, most claiming medical problems, Ronan Rafferty not claiming, just going.

ITALIAN OPEN
19-22 May
Marco Simone, Rome   Eduardo Romero   ARG 272
Romero beats the holder, Greg Turner (NZ), by one stroke for his first Tour win in three years.

VOLVO PGA
27-30 May Wentworth   José Maria Olazabal
SPA 271

DUNHILL OPEN
2-5 June
Knokke-le-Zoute, Belgium Nick Faldo   UK   279

Faldo, without a win on the Tour for nearly a year, survives a play-off with Joakim Häggman (SWE), who bogeys the 72nd and the first extra hole.

HONDA OPEN
9-12 June
Gut Kaden, Hamburg   Robert Allenby   AUS 276
Allenby beats Miguel Angel Jimenez (SPA) at the third hole of a play-off.

JERSEY OPEN
16-19 June La Moye   Paul Curry   UK   266
Curry, a professional for fifteen years, wins a tournament for the first time by shooting a second-round 62 (equalling the course record) and 63 in the last.

FRENCH OPEN
23-26 June Paris   Mark Roe   UK   274
43-y-o Mike Miller shoots 66 to share the lead in the first round. Jeremy Robinson (UK) celebrates (rather too hard?) his hole-in-one at the 16th during the third round with 86 in the last to finish on 299.

IRISH OPEN
30 June - 3 July
Mt Juliet, Co.Kilkenny   Bernhard Langer GER 275
Langer wins the title for the third time, one stroke ahead of John Daly (USA) who shoots 65 in the last round to equal the event record which Sam Torrance (UK) had equalled in the first.

SCOTTISH OPEN
6-9 July Gleneagles   Carl Mason   UK   265
After 19 years without a tournament win, Mason does it for the second time in the season (see Andalucian Open) thanks mainly to a third-round 61, one short of the course record.

BRITISH OPEN
14-17 July Turnberry   see separate entry

DUTCH OPEN
21-24 July
Hilversum   Miguel Angel Jimenez
SPA 270

SCANDINAVIAN MASTERS
28-31 July
Drottningholm, Stockholm Vijay Singh   FIJI 268

BMW INTERNATIONAL OPEN
4-7 Aug
St Eurach, Munich   Mark McNulty   ZIM 274
Seve Ballesteros finishes second, one shot behind, after twice being warned for slow play.

AUSTRIAN OPEN
11-14 Aug
Waldviertel, Litschau   Mark Davis   UK   270
Davis shoots a course record 64 in the last round to finish two shots ahead of Philip Walton (UK), who set the previous record of 65 in the second round to take the lead.

ENGLISH OPEN
18-21 Aug
Forest of Arden   Colin Montgomerie UK 274
Montgomerie's sixth tournament win but his first in Britain.

GERMAN OPEN
25-28 Aug
Hubbelrath, Düsseldorf   Colin Montgomerie UK 269
Bernhard Langer, trying to win the event for a record sixth time, finishes second, one shot behind Montgomerie, who becomes the first player since Ballesteros in 1991 to win consecutive events on the Tour (he beat Montgomerie in a play-off to win the first). His last six tournament wins have all been by a single stroke.

EUROPEAN MASTERS
1-4 Sep
Crans-sur-Sierre (SWI)   Eduardo Romero ARG 266
The 40-y-o Argentinian leads from the end of the third round. John Daly continues his rollercoaster career by dropping out with injuries from his fight with Roth snr (see US Tour).

EUROPEAN OPEN
8-11 Sep
E Sussex National, Uckfield David Gilford   UK 275
Gilford finishes five shots clear of the field.

BRITISH MASTERS
16-18 Sep Woburn   Ian Woosnam   UK 271
Woosnam repeats his Cannes Open charge. Seven shots off the lead after the second round, he shoots a course record 63, then 67, on the last day (the first is washed out by rain) to win by four strokes.

LANCÔME TROPHY
22-25 Sep
St Nom la Bretèche   Vijay Singh   FIJI 263
Singh wins by a stroke from Miguel Angel Jimenez and two from Ballesteros (trying to win the event for the sixth time). All three are level with two holes to play, then Singh birdies the 17th which Ballesteros bogeys.

GERMAN MASTERS
30 Sep - 3 Oct
Motzener See, Berlin   Seve Ballesteros SPA 270
Ballesteros birdies the second extra hole of a play-off v Olazabal & Els after the latter shoots a course record 63 in the first round, leads by seven strokes after the second, then bogeys the 72nd.

DUNHILL CUP & WORLD MATCHPLAY
see separate sections

MADRID OPEN
20-23 Oct
Puerta de Hierro   cancelled, replaced by Czech Open

CZECH OPEN
20-23 Oct
Marianske Lazne   Per-Ulrik Johansson
                                              SWE 237
The first PGA event ever held in the Czech Republic is dogged by cold weather. The first three rounds are each reduced to 15 holes and all the players start the last at the same time from different tees. Gordon Brand jnr, joint leader after the first round, wears two vests (one thermal), two sweaters (one polo neck), a waterproof jacket, thermal longjohns, two pairs of trousers (one waterproof), a woollen hat, and a Rupert Bear scarf. The event will still be held here in 1995 & 1996, but in August.

Montgomerie, who at last takes a rest from tournament play, wins the European order of merit for the second successive year (the first to do so since Sandy Lyle in 1980) when Ballesteros finishes only equal tenth, seven shots behind Johansson.

VOLVO MASTERS
27-30 Oct
Valderrama, Sotogrande   Bernhard Langer GER 276
The European season ends in comic controversy. Ballesteros, level with Langer going into the last, knocks his ball into a hole he claims was made by an animal, but is refused a free drop by referee John Paramor, who insists he 'could not find any evidence of droppings'. Except in that decision, thinks Seve. Langer, nevertheless, deserves his win: after Sam Torrance, Peter Mitchell & Miguel Angel Jimenez equal the course record of 65 in the first round, he tames the toughest venue on the Tour with a remarkable 62 in the second, during which Jimenez shoots an albatross two at the 17th.

US Tour

Regular tournaments only (no pro-ams, sharks or skins)

BUICK SOUTHERN OPEN
30 Sep - 3 Oct 1993
Pine Mountain, Georgia   John Inman   278

WALT DISNEY OLDSMOBILE CLASSIC
6-9 Oct 1993
Buena Vista, Florida   Jeff Maggert   265

TEXAS OPEN
14-17 Oct 1993
San Antonio   Jay Haas   263

LAS VEGAS INVITATIONAL
20-23 Oct 1993
Desert Inn, Las Vegas   Davis Love III   331
Played over five rounds.

TOUR CHAMPIONSHIP
27-30 Oct 1993
San Francisco   Jim Gallagher   277

KAPALUA INTERNATIONAL
3-6 Nov 1993
Maui, Hawaii   Fred Couples   274

MERCEDES CHAMPIONSHIP
6-9 Jan 1994
Carlsbad, California   Phil Mickelson   276

HAWAIIAN OPEN
14-17 Jan 1994
Honolulu   Brett Ogle (AUS)   269
Davis Love III finishes a stroke behind despite shooting 60 in the second round.

TUCSON OPEN
20-23 Jan 1994
Tucson, Arizona   Andrew Magee   270

PHOENIX OPEN
27-30 Jan 1994
Phoenix, Arizona   Bill Glasson   268

LOS ANGELES OPEN
10-13 Feb 1994
Riviera CC, LA   Corey Pavin   271
42-y-o Tom Purtzer, the 1977 winner, finishes seventh after scoring 64 to lead the first round.

BOB HOPE CHRYSLER CLASSIC
16-20 Feb 1994
Palm Springs   Scott Hoch   334
Famously played over five rounds.

BUICK INVITATIONAL
24-27 Feb 1994
Torrey Pines, San Diego   Craig Stadler   268
At the age of 40, Stadler wins a tournament in his home town for the first time.

DORAL RYDER OPEN
3-6 March 1994
Miami   John Huston   274

HONDA CLASSIC
10-13 March 1994
Fort Lauderdale   Nick Price (SAF)   276

NESTLÉ INVITATIONAL
17-20 March 1994
Bay Hill, Orlando   Loren Roberts   275
The 38-y-o Roberts, in his thirteenth season on the Tour, wins a tournament for the first time.

ATP CHAMPIONSHIP
24-27 March 1994
Sawgrass, Ponte Vedra   Greg Norman (AUS)   264
Norman (63 67 67 67) shoots only one bogey throughout.

NEW ORLEANS CLASSIC
31 March - 3 April 1994
English Turn   Ben Crenshaw   273
José-María Olázabal (SPA) shoots a course record 63 in the first round.

HERITAGE CLASSIC
14-17 April 1994
Hilton Head Island,
S Carolina   Hale Irwin   266
David Frost (SAF) shoots a course record 61 in the 2nd round.

GREATER GREENSBORO OPEN
22-25 April 1994
North Carolina   Mike Springer   275

HOUSTON OPEN
29 April - 2 May 1994
Houston   Mike Heinen   272
Heinen missed the cut in six of the ten tournaments he entered prior to this in 1994.

BELL SOUTH CLASSIC
6-9 May 1994
Marietta   John Daly   274

BYRON NELSON CLASSIC
14-15 May 1994
Irving, Texas   Neil Lancaster   132
Played over two rounds after the first two are rained off.

MEMORIAL TOURNAMENT
19-22 May 1994
Muirfield Village,
Dublin, Ohio   Tom Lehman   268

SOUTHWESTERN BELL COLONIAL
26-29 May 1994
Fort Worth   Nick Price (ZIM)   266
Start delayed by rain.

KEMPER OPEN
3-6 June 1994
Avenel, Potomac, Md.   Mark Brooks   271
Brooks, ahead after the first two days, recaptures the lead from Lanny Wadkins' brother Bobby (42) who takes a two-shot advantage into the final round but is still without a Tour win after 19 years as a professional.

BUICK CLASSIC
10-13 June 1994
Harrison, NY   Lee Janzen   268
Janzen's first tournament win since last year's US Open.

GREATER HARTFORD OPEN
23-26 June 1994
Hartford, Connecticut   David Frost (SAF)   268
John Daly finishes joint second, only to be disqualified because his playing partner Clark Dennis credits him with a three instead of a four at the fifth.

WESTERN OPEN
2-5 July 1994
Lemont, Illinois   Nick Price (ZIM)   277

ANHEUSER-BUSCH CLASSIC
8-11 July 1994
Williamsburg, Virginia   Mark McCumber   267

McCumber (67 69 65 66) wins a tournament for the first time in five years.

DEPOSIT GUARANTY
14-17 July 1994
Annandale,
Madison, Minnesota   Brian Henninger   135

NEW ENGLAND CLASSIC
21-24 July 1994
Sutton, Mass.   Kenny Perry   268
David Feherty of Ireland, having a tough time on the US Tour, finishes second, one stroke behind. John Daly, who finished last in the British Open a week earlier, pulls out of the tournament after shooting 75 in the first round. Ed Fiori, who hasn't won a tournament for twelve years, shows why by slipping back after shooting 66 66 to lead after two rounds.

St JUDE CLASSIC
28-31 July 1994
Memphis   Dicky Pride   267
Pride, in his first year on the Tour, wins his first PGA tournament by sinking a twenty-foot putt on the last hole to force a three-way play-off, then a fifteen-footer at the first extra hole.

BUICK OPEN
5-8 Aug 1994
Flint, Michigan   Fred Couples   270
Paul Azinger plays in a Tour event for the first time since being diagnosed as having cancer.

THE SPRINT INTERNATIONAL
18-21 Aug 1994
Castle Rock, Colorado   Steve Lowery   35 pts
In the only Tour event of its kind (five pts for an eagle, two for a birdie), Lowery beats Rick Fehr at the first extra hole to win a USPGA tournament for the first time. He'd been back to the qualifying school five years in a row.

WORLD SERIES of GOLF
25-28 Aug 1994
Firestone CC, Akron, Ohio José M Olazabal (SPA) 269
Olazabal shoots every round in under 70: 66, 67, 69, 67. John Daly's enormous driving sometimes gets him out of trouble, but not this time. He's involved in a fist fight with 60-y-o Bob Roth, father of another player, who alleges Daly hit close to his boy (drove into the group playing up ahead) on the 14th & 15th holes. Daly doesn't play another tournament all year.

GREATER MILWAUKEE OPEN
2-5 Sep 1994
Deer Park, Milwaukee   Mike Springer   268
Springer, who enters at the last minute, shoots 69 67 65 67 to become the first American to win two Tour events this year.

CANADIAN OPEN
9-12 Sep 1994
Glen Abbey, Oakville   Nick Price (ZIM)   275

BC OPEN
15-18 Sep 1994
Endicott, NY   Mike Sullivan   266

HARDEE'S CLASSIC
22-24 Sep 1994
Coal Valley, Illinois   Mark McCumber   265

BUICK SOUTHERN OPEN
29 Sep - 1 Oct 1994
Pine Mountain, Georgia   Steve Elkington (AUS)   200
Rain washes out the last day. Elkington's 200 is a record for the tournament.

WALT DISNEY CLASSIC
6-9 Oct 1994
Magnolia,
Lake Buena Vista, Fla.   Rick Fehr   269
Fehr wins a Tour event for the first time in eight years...

TEXAS OPEN
13-16 Oct
San Antonio   Bob Estes   265
...which seems to inspire Estes, who shoots 62 to lead from the first round, beating Gil Morgan (USA) to win a PGA tournament for the first time in seven years.

LAS VEGAS INVITATIONAL
19-23 Oct   Bruce Lietzke   332
Played over five rounds, on three separate courses, each with a different par.

TOUR CHAMPIONSHIP
27-30 Oct
Olympic Club,
San Francisco   Mark McCumber   274
McCumber, who shares the lead after the first round then seems to have fallen away, sinks a thirty-footer to beat Fuzzy Zoeller at the first extra hole after both shoot 68 in the last round.

SARAZEN WORLD OPEN
2-5 Nov 1994
Braselton, Georgia   Ernie Els (SAF)   273
Els' last round 65 equals the course record in this inaugural event.

KAPALUA INTERNATIONAL
3-6 Nov
Hawaii   Fred Couples   279
A hole-in-one on the last round helps Couples retain the title.

GRAND SLAM of GOLF
8-9 Nov 1994
Poipu Bay, Hawaii   Greg Norman (AUS)   136
Played over 36 holes. Norman retains the title.

World Cup 1993

11-14 Nov Lake Nona, Florida

556	USA	Fred Couples & Davis Love III
561	Zimbabwe	Nick Price & Mark McNulty
565	Scotland	Colin Montgomerie & Sam Torrance
566	Australia	Robert Allenby & Rodger Davis
567	Spain	José Rivero & Miguel Angel Jimenez
568	N Zealand	Frank Nobilo & Greg Turner
568	S Africa	Ernie Els & Ratief Goosen
571	Germany	Bernhard Langer & S Struver
573	Ireland	Ronan Rafferty & Paul McGinlay
573	Italy	Costantino Rocca & Silvio Grappassoni
574	England	David Gilford & Mark James
582	Wales	Ian Woosnam & Mark Mouland

World Cup 1994

10-13 Nov Dorado Beach, Puerto Rico

536	USA	Fred Couples & Davis Love III
550	Zimbabwe	Mark McNulty & Tony Johnstone
551	Sweden	Joakim Häggman & Jesper Parnevik
553	N Zealand	Frank Nobilo & Greg Turner
557	Scotland	Gordon Brand jnr & Andrew Coltart
558	Germany	Bernhard Langer & S Struver
559	Australia	Steve Elkington & Mike Clayton
559	Italy	Costantino Rocca & Silvio Grappassoni
559	Malaysia	Marimuthu Ramayah & P Gunasegaran
560	Argentina	Eduardo Romero & M Guzman
568	Ireland	Darren Clarke & Paul McGinlay
568	England	Mark Roe & Barry Lane
579	Wales	Ian Woosnam & P Price

For the second successive year, Couples & Love lead from the start, this time setting a record by winning the event for the third consecutive year. Their 40-under-par total is also a record (previously 544) and their margin of victory equals the record set by two immortals, Ben Hogan & Sam Snead, in 1956.

Dunhill Cup 1993

15-17 Oct 1993 Old Course, St Andrews

GROUP 1

Spain	2	Argentina	1
Ireland	3	Zimbabwe	0
Spain	2	Ireland	1
Zimbabwe	2	Argentina	1
Ireland	3	Argentina	0
Zimbabwe	2	Spain	1

GROUP 2

S Africa	2	Taiwan	1
England	3	Mexico	0
Mexico	2	S Africa	1
England	2	Taiwan	1
S Africa	2	England	1
Taiwan	2	Mexico	1

Chen Liang-hsi comes from three shots down to beat Nick Faldo 72-73

GROUP 3

Paraguay	2	Scotland	1
USA	3	Wales	0
USA	2	Paraguay	1
Scotland	3	Wales	0
Paraguay	2	Wales	1
USA	3	Scotland	0

Scotland & Wales are beaten by a country with only two golf courses and 500 golfers, including 400 with handicaps of eighteen or more and only eighteen professionals.

GROUP 4

Canada	2	Australia	1
Sweden	3	Japan	0
Japan	2	Australia	1
Sweden	2	Canada	1
Canada	2	Japan	1
Sweden	2	Australia	1

SEMI-FINALS

England	3	Ireland	0
USA	2	Sweden	1

FINAL

USA	2	England	1
Fred Couples	68	Nick Faldo	69
John Daly	70	Peter Baker	73
Payne Stewart	74	Mark James	70

Stewart collects £100 000, his share of the winners' prize money, despite losing both his last two matches.

Dunhill Cup 1994

6-9 Oct 1994 Old Course, St Andrews

Gale-force winds on the first day send even the successful scores sky-high: Howard Clark 80, Anders Forsbrand & Ernie Els 81, and Chen Tze-chung (TAI) 83, the highest winning round in the competition's history.

GROUP 1

USA	2	Japan	1
N Zealand	2	Ireland	1
Japan	2	N Zealand	1
Ireland	2	USA	1
USA	3	N Zealand	0
Ireland	2	Japan	1

GROUP 2

England	3	Spain	0

Australia	2	France	1
Australia	2	Spain	1
England	3	France	0
France	2	Spain	1
England	3	Australia	0

GROUP 3

S Africa	2	Taiwan	1
Scotland	2	Paraguay	1

Scotland take revenge for last year's disaster, but only when Andrew Coltart beats Raúl Fretes at the first extra hole.

Scotland	3	Taiwan	0
S Africa	2	Paraguay	1
Taiwan	2	Paraguay	1
S Africa	2	Scotland	1

Although the event's always held in Scotland, the hosts have never won it.

GROUP 4

Sweden	2	Canada	1
Zimbabwe	2	Germany	1

Canada	2	Zimbabwe	1
Germany	2	Sweden	1
Canada	2	Germany	1
Zimbabwe	2	Sweden	1

Rick Gibson's 85 v Sweden won't matter in the end...

SEMI-FINALS

Canada	2	S Africa	1
USA	3	England	0

FINAL

Canada	2	USA	1
Dave Barr	70	Tom Kite	71
Rick Gibson	74	Curtis Strange	67
Ray Stewart	71	Fred Couples	72

The 40-1 outsiders cause the biggest upset in the event's history (neither Gibson nor Stewart has played the Old Course before). The USA lose in the final for the first time since the very first year (1985). Although Stewart's 40 and Barr 42, age doesn't come into it: Kite, favoured to win his match, is older than either of them.

President's Cup

17-18 Sep 1994 Gainesville, Virginia

USA	20	Rest of World	12

Fourballs

Jim Gallagher jr & John Huston	L	Fulton Allem SAF & Mark McNulty ZIM	4&3
Jay Haas & Scott Hoch	L	Tsukasa Watanabe JAP & Vijay Singh FIJI	3&1
Loren Roberts & Tom Lehman	L	Craig Parry AUS & Brad Hughes AUS	4&3
Davis Love III & Fred Couples	W	Frank Nobilio NZ & Robert Allenby AUS	2 up
Phil Mickelson & Corey Pavin	D	Nick Price ZIM & Steve Elkington AUS	

Foursomes

Haas & Hale Irwin	L	David Frost SAF & Peter Senior AUS	6&5
Love & Gallagher	W	Nobilio & Allenby	7&5
Jeff Maggert & Huston	W	Elkington & Singh	3&2
Roberts & Pavin	W	Parry & Allem	1 up
Mickelson & Lehman	W	Hughes & McNulty	3&2

Singles

Haas	W	McNulty	4&3
Gallagher	W	Watanabe	4&3
Irwin	W	Allenby	1 up
Huston	L	Senior	3&2
Maggert	W	Hughes	2&1
Couples	W	Price	1 up
Hoch	D	Frost	
Roberts	D	Nobilio	
Love	W	Elkington	1 up
Pavin	L	Parry	1 up

Amateur Golf

Eisenhower Trophy

World amateur team championship
6-9 Oct 1994 Le Golf National, La Boulie,
Versailles

838	USA
849	UK
855	Sweden
858	Australia
860	N Zealand
866	Spain
872	Belgium
878	Austria
878	Holland
880	Canada

The USA, runners-up the last five times the event's been held, win it for the first time since 1984 thanks to a great British disaster: two shots ahead after the second round, and again after eight holes of the last round, Stephen Gallacher, Lee James, Gordon Sherry & Warren Bennett all hit balls into the water during the final four holes. The Latvian team stay in the car park of the Novotel, the hotel overlooking the 18th green; their driver Dzintars Vieglins, the father of two of the players, Elias & Joackim, is drafted into the team when another member breaks a wrist, goes out in 47 and finishes with (surely a record) 115.

INDIVIDUAL TITLE

277	Allen Doyle	USA
281	Warren Bennett	UK
282	Lee James	UK

The 46-y-o Allen is 28 years older than his more fancied team-mate Tiger Woods.

British Amateur Championship

QUARTER-FINALS

Lee James	Craig Watson	5&4
Allan Turnbull	Martin Erlandsson (SWE)	19th
Gordon Sherry	Robbie Shiels	2&1
Kalle Brink (SWE)	Carl Duke	19th

SEMI-FINALS

James	Turnbull	2&1
Sherry	Brink	4&3

James prevents the first all-Scottish final since 1921. Brink is only 18.

FINAL 4 June 1994 Nairn

James	Sherry	2&1

The first final between an Englishman and a Scotsman since Peter McEvoy beat Paul McKellar in 1978. James is 20, Sherry (6'7 and 17st) wears size 13 shoes.

English Amateur

July 1994 Moortown

SEMI-FINALS

Alan Johnson	Chris Poxon	3&2
Mark Foster	Graham Homewood	2&1

FINAL

Foster	Johnson	8&7

The 18-y-o Foster beats a player making only his second appearance in the event.

Scottish Amateur

July 1994 Renfrew

SEMI-FINALS

Hugh McKibbin	Gordon Sherry	3&2
Alan Reid	Barclay Howard	3&2

FINAL

McKibbin	Reid	39th

Reid comes close (he leads by four strokes at one stage), but in seven matches still hasn't beaten McKibbin.

Welsh Amateur

July 1994 Porthcawl

SEMI-FINALS

Craig Evans	Rhodri Price	1 hole
Mark Smith	Bradley Dredge	2&1

FINAL

Evans	Smith	5&4

Irish Amateur

6-10 Aug 1994 Portmarnock

SEMI-FINALS

David Higgins	Jody Fanagan	3&1
Padraig Harrington	John Morris	3&2

FINAL

Higgins	Harrington	20th

US Amateur

Final 28 Aug 1994 TPC Sawgrass

Tiger Woods	Trip Kuehne	2 holes

Woods, very much the favourite, comes back from six holes down after thirteen to win six of the last ten (including the last three) in the second round and become the first black winner of the event, the youngest ever (18) and the first to win both the US Amateur & US Junior.

Boys' World Championship

20-21 Aug 1994 Deeside

275	Shaun Webster	ENG	72 67 72 64
276	David Gleeson	AUS	71 69 66 70
277	Christian Aronsen	NOR	66 64 76 71

Women's Golf

USLPGA

12-15 May 1994 Wilmington, Delaware

279	Laura Davies	UK	70 72 69 68
282	Alice Ritzman		68 73 71 70
285	Amy Alcott		71 75 70 69
283	Pat Bradley		73 73 70 67
283	Elaine Crosby		76 71 69 67
283	Hiromi Kobayashi	JAP	72 73 71 67
283	Lotta Neumann	SWE	74 73 67 69
285	Beth Daniel		72 74 68 71
285	Patty Sheehan		72 68 72 73
285	Sherri Steinhauer		75 70 72 68
286	Dottie Mochrie		68 78 70 70
286	Meg Mallon		71 71 69 75
287	Val Skinner		74 69 72 72
288	Dana Dormann		71 76 71 70
288	Chris Johnson		70 74 73 71
288	Julie Inkster		69 76 74 79
289	Donna Andrews		73 76 69 71
289	Nanci Bowen		73 75 73 68
289	Tammie Green		71 76 74 68
289	Betsy King		74 73 71 71
289	Mardi Lunn	AUS	70 75 70 74
289	Missie McGeorge		75 71 70 73
289	Kris Monaghan		72 72 72 73
289	Barb Mucha		73 74 75 67
289	Robin Walton		70 70 75 74
290	JoAnne Carner		73 75 74 68
290	Michelle McGann		70 76 75 69
291	Tina Barrett		73 77 68 73
291	Missi Berteotti		75 70 75 71
291	Brandie Burton		76 70 73 72
291	Gail Graham		73 71 76 71
291	Jenny Lidback		73 73 74 71
291	Ayako Okamoto	JAP	74 72 73 72
291	Jenniffer Wyatt		72 74 73 72
292	Dale Eggeling		76 74 71 71
292	Page Dunlap		71 74 75 72
292	Amaya Arruti	SPA	75 73 71 73
292	Helen Alfredsson	SWE	73 74 71 74
293	Judy Dickinson		74 71 79 69
293	Kathy Guadagnino		72 79 69 73
293	Lisa Kiggens		75 71 76 71
293	Cindy Shreyer		76 75 71 71
293	Muffin Spencer-Devlin		76 72 74 71
293	Lori West		75 73 70 75
294	Hollis Stacey		73 76 72 73
295	Barb Bunkowsky		72 76 75 72
295	Lauri Merten		74 77 71 73
295	Mary Beth Zimmermann		74 77 71 73
296	Noelle Daghe		69 79 78 70
296	Nina Froust		76 75 70 75
296	Marianne Morris		75 76 76 69
296	Nancy Scranton		78 72 74 72
296	Kris Tschetter		75 72 74 75
297	Cindy Figg-Courier		75 75 74 73
297	Alison Finney		75 76 75 71
297	Lisa Walters		74 77 74 72
298	Pamela Allen		75 72 79 72
298	Jody Anschutz		76 73 72 77
298	Pearl Sinn		75 76 75 72
298	Michelle Estill		78 73 71 76
298	Marta Figueras-Dotti		76 75 70 77
298	Karen Noble		75 75 76 72
299	Amy Benz		75 74 75 75
299	Cindy Rarick		72 74 73 80
299	Jan Stephenson		75 76 74 74
300	Mitzi Edge		73 74 74 79
300	Cathy Johnston-Forbes		74 75 77 74
300	Caroline Keggi		74 75 72 79
300	J Larsen		71 77 80 72
300	Alice Miller		73 77 73 77
300	Nancy Ramsbottom		77 74 75 74
300	Kim Saiki		75 75 74 76
301	Vicky Goetze		73 78 73 77
301	Shelley Hamlin		71 80 79 71
301	Nancy Harvey		77 72 79 73
301	Maggie Will		72 77 75 77
303	Dawn Coe-Jones	CAN	76 75 76 76
304	Kathryn Marshall	UK	74 77 80 73
305	Lori Rinker-Graham		75 75 81 74
305	Sue Biago		76 71 78 80

US Open

21-23 July 1994 Indianwood, Lake Orion, Michigan

277	Patty Sheehan		66 71 69 71
278	Tammie Green		66 72 69 71
281	Lotta Neumann	SWE	69 72 71 69
283	Tania Abitol	SPA	72 68 73 70
284	Amy Alcott		71 67 77 69
284	Betsy King		69 71 72 72
284	Meg Mallon		70 72 73 69
285	Helen Alfredsson	SWE	63 69 76 77
285	Donna Andrews		67 72 70 76
286	Laura Davies	UK	68 68 75 75
286	Judy Dickinson		66 73 73 74
286	Michelle Estill		69 68 75 74
286	Lisa Grimes		72 73 69 72
286	Lauri Merten		74 68 75 69
286	Dottie Mochrie		72 72 71 71
287	Beth Daniel		69 74 71 73
287	Julie Inkster		75 72 69 71
287	Michelle McGann		71 70 77 69
287	Joan Pitcock		74 72 67 74
289	Pat Bradley		72 69 70 78
288	Stephanie Maynor		73 70 76 69
289	Deb Richard		68 74 72 75
288	Sherri Steinhauer		68 72 74 74
289	Kris Tschetter		71 73 72 73
288	Lisa Walters		72 73 72 71
289	Pam Wright	UK	74 65 71 79
290	Vicky Goetze		71 73 73 73
290	Karen Lunn	AUS	72 72 77 69
291	D Eggeling		67 73 79 72
291	JoAnne Carner		69 74 75 73
291	Amy Read		68 72 76 75
291	Carol Thomson		66 75 76 74
292	Dawn Coe-Jones	CAN	73 73 71 75
292	Jane Geddes		73 72 73 74
292	Nancy Lopez		73 71 73 75
292	Missie McGeorge		69 73 75 75
292	Kris Monaghan		75 69 72 76
292	Holly Vaughn		74 70 76 72
292	Colleen Walker		73 73 75 71
292	Kim Williams		72 74 72 74
293	Missi Berteotti		71 73 77 72
293	Brandie Burton		70 73 74 76
293	Elaine Crosby		74 72 73 74
293	Vicki Fergon		72 72 77 72
293	Mayumi Hirase	JAP	74 72 73 74
293	Sally Little		67 76 74 76
294	Nanci Bowen		73 74 72 75
294	Ayako Okamoto	JAP	71 72 72 79
295	Sherri Turner		72 74 75 74
295	Dana Dormann		73 73 73 76
295	Emilee Klein		71 73 69 82
296	Jan Stephenson		70 77 74 75
296	Hiromi Kobayashi	JAP	71 76 73 76
296	Nancy Ramsbottom		71 74 72 79
297	Caroline Pierce		74 73 76 74
297	Sarah Ingram		74 71 77 75
297	Tara Fleming		70 75 77 75
297	Alice Ritzman		73 74 74 76
297	Mitzi Edge		72 72 76 77
298	Tosurma Kimura		73 72 75 78
298	Lisa Kiggens		71 74 73 80
300	Page Dunlap		73 71 78 78
300	Pearl Sinn		74 73 75 78
303	Judy Sams		74 73 76 80
304	Sarah McGuire		76 71 77 80

Leading amateur: C Thomson

Among those who miss the cut (at 148): Alison Nicholas (UK) 76 73, Helen Dobson (UK) 74 77, Mardi Lunn (AUS) 77 74

Sheehan holes a brave little putt at the last to hold on to her third-round lead and regain the title she won in 1992 - but this is the Open lost by Alfredsson. Her first-round 63 sets a new record by a woman in any of the Majors and equals the best by any man. Leading by three strokes after the first round and six after the second, she drops fourteen strokes in eighteen holes. 45-y-o amateur Carole Semple Thompson lies joint second after the first round. Wright shoots a event record 30 for the second nine holes of the second round.

British Open

11-14 Aug 1994 Woburn

280	Lotta Neumann	SWE	71 67 70 72
283	Dottie Mochrie	USA	73 66 74 70
283	Annika Sorenstam	SWE	69 75 69 70
284	Laura Davies*		74 66 73 71
284	Corinne Dibnah*	AUS	75 70 67 72
285	Cindy Figg-Currier	USA	69 74 68 74
286	Helen Alfredsson*	SWE	71 76 71 68
287	Tracy Hanson	USA	74 73 66 74
288	Caroline Pierce	USA	70 75 71 72
288	Val Skinner	USA	77 71 66 74
288	Suzanne Srudwick		71 71 71 75
289	Hiromi Kobayashi	JAP	73 73 69 74
290	Sarah Gautrey	AUS	69 74 72 75
291	Marnie McGuire	NZ	71 73 78 69
291	Penny Grice-Whittaker*		77 72 72 70
291	Tania Abitbol	SPA	76 68 75 72
292	Estefania Knuth	SPA	78 69 72 73
292	Jane Geddes*	USA	74 72 72 74
292	Li Wen-lin	CHN	73 70 73 76
292	Sofia Gronberg-Whitmore	SWE	71 69 74 78
293	Pam Wright		68 75 78 72
293	Karen Pearce	AUS	70 74 75 74
293	Kris Tschetter	USA	68 76 75 74

294	Kay Cockerill	USA	71 77 73 73
294	Amy Alcott	USA	74 74 75 71
294	Betsy King*	USA	73 74 69 78
294	Alice Ritzman	USA	69 76 75 74
295	Susan Moon	USA	72 78 74 71
295	Alison Nicholas*		72 73 70 80
295	Dale Reid		76 72 75 72
295	Mardi Lunn	AUS	73 75 75 72
295	Kathryn Marshall		76 72 75 72
295	Lora Fairclough		75 72 72 76
295	Sue Redman	USA	74 71 76 74
296	Trish Johnson		75 75 72 74
296	Evelyn Orley	SWI	73 76 74 73
296	Kristi Albers	USA	75 67 74 73
297	Leigh Ann Mills	USA	72 76 73 76
297	Heidi Person	USA	75 74 72 76
297	Caroline Hall		71 77 77 72
297	Laura Navarro	SPA	74 76 76 71
297	Lori West	USA	77 73 74 73
298	Tina Barrett	USA	78 71 73 76
299	Marta Figueras-Dotti	SPA	74 73 76 76
299	Karina Orum	DEN	73 75 76 75
299	Wendy Doolan	AUS	75 76 73 75
299	Martina Fischer	GER	71 78 76 74
299	Julie Forbes		73 75 75 76
300	Marie-Laure De Lorenzi	FRA	74 76 73 77
300	Carin Hjalmarsson	SWE	75 74 75 76
300	Isabella Maconi	ITA	72 74 75 79
301	Xonia Wunsch-Ruiz	SPA	78 73 76 74
301	Laree Suggs	USA	76 74 76 75
301	Karen Noble	USA	75 73 72 81
302	Federica Dassu	ITA	78 70 78 76
302	Marjan de Boer	HOL	76 75 75 76
302	Gillian Stewart		74 77 74 77
302	Florence Descampe	BEL	76 75 78 73
302	Catrin Nilsmark	SWE	74 76 75 77
302	Sally Prosser		74 72 76 80
302	Muffin Spencer-Devlin	USA	73 74 79 76
302	Shani Waugh	AUS	76 74 75 77
302	Helen Wadsworth		73 78 78 73
302	Sandrine Mendiburu	FRA	72 77 81 72
302	Sara Robinson		73 76 74 79
303	Nancy Scranton	USA	80 70 73 80
304	Diane Barnard		75 74 77 78
304	Lisa Hackney		76 75 77 76
304	Elaine Crosby	USA	76 73 77 78
306	Mette Hageman	USA	73 77 76 80
307	Beverley New		76 74 82 75
307	Malin Burström	SWE	72 76 80 79
307	Nicola Moult		77 73 77 80
307	Mary Lawrence Wengler	USA	76 74 77 80
309	Jennifer Lawrence		74 77 77 81
309	Sophie Gustafsson	SWE	76 75 83 75

Leading Amateur: Fischer (the only one to make the cut).

Among those who miss the cut (at 151):
152 Emma Duggleby (British Amateur champion),
153 Karen Lunn AUS* (defending champion) 71 82,

162 Malin Landehag SWE (despite a hole-in-one at
the 5th).

Highest of the High: 168 A Johns 88 80.

*previous British Open winners.

Du Maurier

25-28 Aug 1994 Ottawa H&CC

279	Martha Nause		65 71 72 71
280	Michelle McGann		66 71 71 72
281	Lotta Neumann	SWE	70 67 71 73
283	Betsy King		67 69 74 73
283	Jane Geddes		74 67 70 72
283	Meg Mallon		70 72 68 73
284	Judy Dickinson		72 68 70 74
284	Kelly Robbins		66 70 73 75
284	M Morris		69 72 70 73
284	Dawn Coe Jones	CAN	72 70 71 71
285	Vicki Fergon		72 68 75 70
285	Sherri Steinhauer		68 72 73 72
285	Patty Sheehan		71 71 68 75
286	Amy Alcott		73 70 72 71
286	Dottie Mochrie		67 74 72 73
287	Jane Crafter	AUS	71 74 75 67
287	Page Dunlap		72 69 75 71
287	Alice Ritzman		76 70 68 73
287	Rosie Jones		73 70 70 74
287	Jenny Lidback		70 72 71 74
287	Alicia Dibos	PERU	71 71 70 75
288	Sally Little		74 72 73 69
288	Missi Berteotti		70 72 73 73
288	Brandie Burton		71 74 69 74
288	Barb Bunkowsky		74 69 71 74
288	Kim Williams		67 74 73 74
288	Karen Lunn	AUS	70 73 70 75
288	Annika Sorenstam	SWE	72 67 73 76
288	Nancy Lopez		67 70 75 76
288	Leigh Ann Mills		66 72 70 80
289	Tina Barrett		71 75 72 71
289	Lisa Walters		73 72 73 71
289	Alice Miller		72 71 74 72
289	Michelle Redman		72 72 72 73
289	Helen Alfredsson	SWE	71 73 71 74
289	Robin Walton		73 67 72 77
289	Jenniffer Wyatt		69 72 69 79
290	Judy Sams		71 72 76 71
290	Gail Graham		72 72 74 72
290	Lori West		75 71 71 73
290	Michelle Estill		71 72 74 73
290	Laura Davies	UK	75 69 72 74
291	Mitzi Edge		75 71 75 70
291	Lori Garbacz		74 72 74 71
291	Stephanie Maynor		72 72 76 71
291	Missie McGeorge		74 71 70 76
292	Deb Richard		68 76 78 70

292	Chris Johnson		70 74 76 72
292	Carolyn Hill		72 71 76 73
292	Caroline Pierce		70 72 74 76
292	Dale Eggeling		71 70 74 77
293	Maggie Will		75 71 75 72
293	Barb Mucha		72 74 75 72
293	Pat Bradley		73 72 76 72
293	Amy Benz		72 72 73 76
293	Marta Figueras-Dotti	SPA	73 69 75 76
294	Lisa Kiggens		73 73 77 71
294	Joan Pitcock		73 72 74 75
294	Florence Descampe	BEL	71 74 73 76
294	Colleen Walker		73 70 75 76
294	Sherri Turner		72 71 74 77
295	Hiromi Kobayashi	JAP	72 72 76 75
295	Mardi Lunn	AUS	71 73 73 78
296	Vicky Goetze		76 70 76 74
296	Katie Peterson-Parker		74 72 74 76
296	Lauri Merten		70 76 74 76
296	Jan Stephenson		74 71 75 76
296	Heather Drew		71 74 75 76
296	Nancy Scranton		75 70 72 79
297	Kristi Albers		74 71 78 74
297	Pam Wright	UK	73 70 78 76
298	Cathy Johnston-Forbes		70 74 76 78
298	Tania Abitbol	SPA	73 71 73 81
299	Penny Hammel		73 72 79 75
300	Debbie Massey		66 78 77 79

The bespectacled 39-y-o Nause, who leads after the first round, wins a Major for the first time. Mills shares the lead after the third round, Massey's in joint second place after the first. Doctors erect Smoking Kills Women signs around the course: Dr Andrew Pipe (!) contends that Du Maurier are sponsoring the event to circumvent a ban on tobacco advertising.

World Championship 1993
Oct Naples, Florida

283	Dottie Mochrie	USA
285	Donna Andrews	USA
285	Michelle McGann	USA
285	Sherri Steinhauer	USA
285	Meg Mallon	USA
286	Nancy Lopez	USA
286	Lauri Merten	USA
290	Betsy King	USA
291	Brandie Burton	USA
292	Trish Johnson	UK
292	Helen Alfredsson	SWE

World Championship 1994
13-16 Oct Naples, Florida

274	Beth Daniel	USA	68 70 71 65

279	Elaine Crosby	USA	70 66 69 72
279	Laura Davies	UK	68 73 67 71
280	Lotta Neumann	SWE	71 67 72 70
280	Dottie Mochrie	USA	67 69 73 71
282	Helen Alfredsson	SWE	71 72 68 71
283	Donna Andrews	USA	69 71 73 70
283	Sherri Steinhauer	USA	67 71 75 70
283	Martha Nause	USA	73 67 72 71

After the third round, Crosby leads Davies by three shots and Daniel by four.

European Tour

FRENCH OPEN
22-24 Oct 1993

Marie-Laure de Lorenzi	FRA	220

FORD CLASSIC
21-24 April 1994 Woburn

Catrin Nilsmark	SWE	284

Nilsmark, in her sixth year on the Tour, wins an event for the first time. Joanne Morley, in her first tournament as a professional, finishes joint second after shooting a hole-in-one on the 13th, of all places, in the second round.

COSTA AZUL OPEN
20-22 May 1994 Montado & Aroeira, Lisbon

Sandrine Mendiburu	FRA	140

Arranged for three rounds (on two separate courses), the event's decided over two after rain washes out the second day.

EVIAN MASTERS
9-12 June 1994 Evian-les-Bains

Helen Alfredsson	SWE	287

OVB OPEN
16-19 June 1994 Zell-am-See, Austria

Florence Descampe	BEL	277

Descampe wins a tournament for the first time in two years by beating Tracy Hanson (USA) at the second hole of a play-off.

EUROPEAN MASTERS
23-26 June 1994 Bercuit, Belgium

Helen Wadsworth	UK	278

Wadsworth sets a new course record total to win a Tour title for the first time. Hanson finishes second for the second successive tournament.

HENNESSEY CUP
31 June-3 July 1994 Refrath, Cologne

Lotta Neumann	SWE	277

Neumann retains the Cup by shooting a last-round

course-record 65 to beat Alison Nicholas (UK) by a single stroke.

IRISH HOLIDAYS OPEN
28-31 July 1994 St Margaret's
    Laura Davies   UK   282

A 30th tournament win for Davies, who finishes eight strokes clear.

SCOTTISH OPEN
4-7 Aug 1994 Dalmahoy
    Laura Davies   UK   278

Tina Yarwood's hole-in-one at the 15th on the last round earns her more than twice as much as she won in the whole of last year.

SWEDISH OPEN
18-21 Aug 1994 Haninge, Stockholm
    Lotta Neumann   SWE   274

ENGLISH OPEN
1-4 Sep The Tytherington, Cheshire
    Patricia Meunier   FRA   288

Meunier, in her first year as a pro, wins a Tour event for the first time.

DUTCH OPEN
9-11 Sep Rijk van Nijmegen, Groesbeck
    Liz Weima   HOL   214

The first Dutchwoman to win a Tour event.

ITALIAN OPEN
22-25 Sep Lignano, Venice
    Corinne Dibnah   AUS   277

Dibnah beats Dale Reid (UK) at the second hole of a play-off after both shoot 66 in the last round.

SPANISH OPEN
29 Sep - 2 Oct La Manga
    Marie-Laure de Lorenzi   FRA   282

De Lorenzi beats Sofia Gronberg-Whatmore (SWE) at the second hole of a play-off.

FRENCH OPEN
13-15 Oct La Motte, St Endreol
    Julie Forbes   UK   213

Defending champion Marie-Laure de Lorenzi leads (69) the first round after treatment for back trouble, but Forbes comes through to beat Dale Reid & Suzanne Strudwick at the second extra hole and win a tournament for the first time. Davies finishes as leading money winner in Europe and the USA.

US Tour (LPGA)

PALM BEACH CLASSIC
4-6 Feb 1994 Palm Beach
    Dawn Coe-Jones (CAN)   201

HAWAIIAN OPEN
18-20 Feb Honolulu
    Marta Figueras-Dotti (SPA)   209

TOURNAMENT OF CHAMPIONS
2-5 March 1994 Grand Cypress, Orlando
    Dottie Mochrie   287

PING-WELCH'S CHAMPIONSHIP
10-13 March 1994 Randolph Park, Tucson
    Donna Andrews   276

STANDARD REGISTER PING
17-20 March 1994 Moon Valley, Phoenix
    Laura Davies (UK)   277

Davies' 7th LPGA tour win and 27th worldwide.

DINAH SHORE
March 1994 Rancho Mirage, Palm Springs
    Donna Andrews   276

Andrews, whose husband John Reeves is her caddy, overtakes Laura Davies who leads going into the last hole.

ATLANTA CHAMPIONSHIP
15-17 April 1994 Stockbridge, Georgia
    Val Skinner   206

SPRINT CHAMPIONSHIP
29 April 1994 Daytona Beach
    Sherri Steinhauer   274

SARA LEE CLASSIC
7-9 May 1994 Nashville
    Laura Davies (UK)   203

Davies beats last year's winner Meg Mallon by one stroke.

LADY KEYSTONE OPEN
20-22 May Hershey, Pennsylvania
    Elaine Crosby   211

Davies, looking for a third successive Tour win, finishes second, one shot behind.

CORNING CLASSIC
26-29 May 1994 Corning, NY
    Beth Daniel   278

Start delayed by rain.

OLDSMOBILE CLASSIC
2-5 June 1994 East Lansing, Michigan
    Beth Daniel   268

Daniel, whose total (67, 63, 70, 68) equals the LPGA Tour record set in 1985, wins a Tour event for the 29th time, one short of a place in the Hall of Fame.

MINNESOTA CLASSIC
10-12 June 1994
    Lotta Neumann (SWE)

ROCHESTER INTERNATIONAL
16-19 June 1994 Rochester, NY
    Tammie Green   276

SHOPRITE CLASSIC
24-26 June 1994 Create Bay, NJ
Donna Andrews   207

YOUNGSTOWN-WARREN CLASSIC
2-3 July 1994
Tammie Green   206

*The last two rounds are played on the same day. Kim
Williams (USA) survives being shot in the neck during
the tournament.*

JAMIE FARR CLASSIC
8-10 July 1994 Toledo, Ohio
Kelly Robbins   204

*Williams finishes equal tenth despite a bullet lodged in
her ribcage (see above). Jamie Farr's the actor who
played Klinger (from Toledo) in M*A*S*H.*

BIG APPLE CLASSIC
14-17 July 1994 New Rochelle, NY
Beth Daniel   276

*Daniel beats Laura Davies (who misses from four feet)
at the first extra hole.*

PING-WELCH CHAMPIONSHIP
28-31 July 1994 Canton, Mass.
Helen Alfredsson (SWE)   274

McCALL'S CLASSIC
4-7 Aug 1994
Carolyn Hill   275

DAYTON CLASSIC
12-14 Aug 1994 CC of the North, Ohio
Maggie Will   210

*Will beats Jill Briles-Hinton & Alicia Dibos, both looking
for their first tournament win, at the second extra hole
of a sudden-death play-off.*

FARM RAIL CLASSIC
2-45 Sep 1994 Springfield
Barb Mucha   203

*Laura Davies finishes five shots behind Mucha after
losing a four-stroke lead during the last round.*

PING-CELLULAR ONE CHAMPIONSHIP
9-11 Sep 1994 Portland, Oegon
Missie McGeorge   207

SAFECO CLASSIC
15-18 Sep 1994 Kent, Washington
Deb Richard   276

HEARTLAND CLASSIC
29 Sep - 2 Oct 1994 St Louis
Lotta Neumann (SWE)   278

Solheim Cup

21-23 Oct 1994 The Greenbrier, White Sulphur Springs, West Virginia

Foursomes (Day 1)

Dottie Mochrie & Brandie Burton	W	Lotta Neumann & Helen Alfredsson		3&2
Beth Daniel & Meg Mallon	L	Annika Sorenstam & Catrin Nilsmark		1 hole
Tammie Green & Kelly Robbins	L	Dale Reid & Lora Fairclough		2&1
Donna Andrews & Betsy King	L	Laura Davies & Alison Nicholas		2&1
Patty Sheehan & Sherri Steinhauer	W	Pam Wright & Trish Johnson		2 holes
Foursomes (Day 2)				
Tammie Green & Kelly Robbins	L	Dale Reid & Lorna Fairclough		4&3
Donna Andrews & Betsy King	W	Trish Johnson & Pam Wright		3&2
Patty Sheehan & Sherri Steinhauer	L	Lotta Neumann & Helen Alfredsson		1 hole
Dottie Mochrie & Brandie Burton	W	Laura Davies & Alison Nicholas		2&1
Beth Daniel & Meg Mallon	W	Annika Soenstam & Catrina Nilsmark		6&5
Singles (Day 3)				
Betsy King	L	Helen Alfredsson		2&1
Dottie Mochrie	W	Catrin Nilsmark		6&5
Beth Daniel	W	Trish Johnson		2 holes
Kelly Robbins	W	Lora Fairclough		4&2
Meg Mallon	W	Pam Wright		1 hole
Patty Sheehan	L	Alison Nicholas		3&2
Brandie Burton	W	Laura Davies		2 holes
Tammie Green	W	Annika Sorenstam		3&2
Sherri Steinhauer	W	Dale Reid		2 holes
Donna Andrews	W	Lotta Neumann		3&2
USA	**13**	**Europe**		**7**

The USA easily regain the title they won in 1990 (the inaugural event) and lost in 1992.

Amateurs

Curtis Cup

29-30 July 1994 Chattanooga

Both teams spring surprises by leaving out world class players: Vicky Thomas, the Welsh champion, and Stephanie Neill, one of the best amateurs in the world.

Day 1

Singles

Jill McGill	D	Julie Hall	
Emilee Klein	W	Janice Moodie	3&2
Wendy Ward	L	Lisa Walton	1 hole
Carole Semple Thompson	W	Myra McKinlay	2&1
Ellen Port	W	Mhairi McKay	2&1
Stephanie Sparks	L	Catriona Matthew	1 hole

Hall leads going into the last hole(both women shoot 80). McKay's three up after eleven.

Foursomes

Semple Thompson & Klein	W	McKay & Kirsty Speak	7&5
Port & Wendy Kaupp	L	Hall & Walton	6&5
McGill & Sarah Ingram	D	Matthew & Moodie	
USA	*5*	*UK*	*4*

Day 2

Foursomes

McGill & Ingram	L	Hall & Walton	2&1
Semple Thompson & Klein	W	McKinlay & Eileen Rose	4&2

Singles

McGill	W	Hall	4&3
Port	W	McKay	7&5
Klein	L	Matthew	2&1
Kaupp	L	McKinlay	3&2
Ward	W	Walton	4&3
Semple Thompson	L	Moodie	2 holes
USA	***9***	***UK***	***9***

The UK, who keep the Cup, have won or retained it three times out of the last four. In the deciding match, Moodie (in her first Curtis Cup) beats the 45-y-o Semple Thompson (in her eighth).

World Amateur Team Championship
Sep-Oct 1994 Golf National, Versailles, Paris

USA	569
S Korea	573
Sweden	574
Spain	575
Australia	577
S Africa	581
France	582
Germany	589
UK	589
N Zealand	589

The Americans (Wendy Ward, Sara Ingram, Carole Semple Thompson) beat a Korean B team (the top players are preparing for the Asian Games) to win the title for the twelfth time out of sixteen. Ward follows her opening round of 69 with a course record 68 in the second, breaking it with 67 on the day.

British Amateur Championship
Newport, Gwent

QUARTER-FINALS 10 June 1994

Catriona Matthew	Julie Hall	2&1
Cecilia Mourgue D'Algue (FRA)	Kate Egford	2&1
Amanda-Jane Adamson (SAF)	Maitena Alsuguren FRA)	2 holes
Emma Duggleby	Karen Stupples	19th

SEMI-FINALS 11 June 1994

Duggleby	Adamson	2&1
Mourgue D'Algue	Matthew	20th

Matthew, narrowly beaten, misses the chance to become first woman to retain the title since Mickey Walker in 1972.

FINAL 11 June 1994

Duggleby	Mourgue D'Algue	3&1

Duggleby (22), subsequently left out of the Curtis Cup team, wins the title for the first time by beating a woman old enough to be most of the other competitors' mother. Mourgue D'Algue, who would have been the oldest ever winner (47), reaches the final for the first time after appearing in four semis, the last before this in 1983.

US Amateur
Homestead's Cascades, Hot Springs, Virginia

SEMI-FINALS

Wendy Ward	Baxter	7&5
Jill McGill	Emilee Klein	1 hole

FINAL 14 Aug 1994

Ward	McGill	2&1

Ward wins the last two holes to beat the defending champion.

Greyhound Racing

Puppy Derby
30 Oct 1993 Sunderland — Farloe Bid

St Leger
12 Nov 1993 Wembley — Galleydown Boy

Guineas
13 Nov 1993 Hackney — Stylefield Law

Oaks
18 Dec 1993 Wimbledon — Pearls Girl

Laurels
1993 — Slipway Jaydee

Golden Jacket
26 Feb 1994 Crayford — Wexford Minx

The Arc
5 March 1994 Walthamstow — Westmead Chick

Pall Mall
19 March 1994 Oxford — Lassa Java

Grand National
30 March 1994 Hall Green

Randy Savage	8-1	29.50
Heavenly Dream	5-2	29.66
Gis A Smile	11-10f	29.98

Blue Riband
4 April 1994 Wembley — Ardilaun Bridge

BBC Trophy
6 April 1994 Sunderland — Jubilee Rebecca

Olympic Final
14 April 1994 Brighton — Westmead Chick

Scottish Derby
21 May 1994 Shawfield — Droopys Sandy

Regency Final
21 May 1994 Brighton — Decoy Cougar

Derby
25 June 1994 Wimbledon

Moral Standards	9-4f	28.59
Ayr Flyer	3-1	28.68
Moaning Lad	7-2	28.72

Tony Meek, in charge of the previous year's winner Ringa Hustle, becomes only the second trainer to win the race in consecutive years, following Leslie Reynolds in 1952.

Scurry Gold Cup
9 July 1994 Catford — Rabatino

Circuit Final
9 July 1994 Walthamstow — Connells Cross

Champion Stakes
22 July 1994 Romford — Heres Seanie

Stanton Memorial Trophy
23 July 1994 Wimbledon — Greenane Squire

Sussex Cup
4 Aug 1994 Brighton — Unique Bay

Peterborough Derby
6 Aug 1994 Peterborough — Highway Leader

Edinburgh Cup
3 Sep 1994 Powderhall — Highway Leader

Gold Collar
17 Sep 1994 Catford — Pearls Girl

Cesarewitch
24 Sep 1994 Belle Vue — Sandollar Louie

Thanet Gold Cup
24 Sep 1994 — Bunmahon Lad

All-England Cup
26 Sep 1994 Brough Park — Toms Lodge

Midland Flat Championship
26 Sep 1994 — Just Right Kyle

Eclipse
26 Sep 1994 Nottingham — Homora Major

Grand Prix Final
8 Oct 1994 Walthamstow — Redwood Gir

Reading Masters
1994 Reading — Druids Elprado

> ### *Also ran*
> *Pat C Rendezvous' sequence of 36 consecutive wins (ended by a third place in Palm Beach) breaks the world record of 32 set by Ballyregan Bob in 1986.*

Gymnastics

World Championships
April 1994 Sports & Entertainment Centre, Brisbane

Men

OVERALL
Ivan Ivankov	BYL	57.012
Alexei Voropayev	RUS	56.924
Vitaly Scherbo	BYL	56.350
16 Neil Thomas	*UK*	*55.200*

FLOOR
Vitaly Scherbo	BYL	9.750
Ioannis Melissanidis	GRE	9.687
Neil Thomas	UK	9.687

Thomas, who finished second the previous year, this time shares the same placing with the European junior champion.

RINGS
Yuri Chechi	ITA	9.787
Paul O'Neill	USA	9.725
Dan Burinca	ROM	9.700
Valery Belenki	independent	9.700

Chechi retains the title. Burinca shares third place with Belenki, who was part of the USSR team when he won the 1991 pommel horse world title, later competes at the European Championships for Germany.

POMMEL HORSE
Marius Urzica	ROM	9.712
Eric Poujade	FRA	9.700
Li Dong-hua	SWI	9.662
Vitaly Marinich	UKR	9.662

VAULT
Vitaly Scherbo	BYL	9.674
Li Xiao-shuang	CHN	9.618
Yeo Hong-chul	S KOR	9.600

PARALLEL BARS
Huang Li-ping	CHN	9.775
Rustam Charipov	UKR	9.612
Alexei Nemov	RUS	9.575

HORIZONTAL BAR
Vitaly Scherbo	BYL	9.687
Zoltan Supola	HUN	9.537
Ivan Ivankov	BYL	9.500

Women

OVERALL
Shannon Miller	USA	39.274
Lavinia Milosevici	ROM	39.236
Dina Kochetkova	RUS	39.125
38 Karin Szymko	*UK*	*36.142*

Miller, who retains the title, has already (at 17) won more World & Olympic medals than any other US gymnast.

ASYMMETRICAL BARS
Luo Li	CHN	9.912
Svetlana Chorkina	RUS	9.875
Dina Kochetkova	RUS	9.850

No-one can match the Chinese girl's squat dislo, inverts released to Jager with double straight to dismount.

VAULT
Gina Gogean	ROM	9.812
Svetlana Chorkina	RUS	9.800
Lavinia Milosevici	ROM	9.787

BEAM
Shannon Miller	USA	9.875
Lilia Podkopayeva	UKR	9.737
Oksana Fabrichnova	RUS	9.712

FLOOR
Dina Kochetkova	RUS	9.850
Lavinia Milosevici	ROM	9.837
Gina Gogean	ROM	9.762

World Team Championships
19-20 Nov 1994 Dortmund

Men
China	283.333
Russia	282.158
Ukraine	281.086

Women
Romania	195.847
USA	194.645
Russia	194.546

The USA are without Miller, who's suffering from exhaustion.

European Championships

Men *June 1994 Prague*

TEAM
Belarus	170.286
Russia	169.848
Germany	168.911

OVERALL
Ivan Ivankov	BYL	57.549
Igor Korobchinsky	UKR	56.799
Yevgeny Chabayev	RUS	56.749

FLOOR
Ivan Ivanov	BUL	9.687
Ivan Ivankov	BYL	9.612
Dmitry Vasilenko	RUS	9.612

Ivankov & Vasilenko share second place.

POMMEL HORSE
Marius Urzica	ROM	9.787
Eric Poujade	FRA	9.762
Vitaly Marinich	UKR	9.700

RINGS
Yuri Chechi	ITA	9.787
Andreas Wecker	GER	9.725
Rustam Charipov	UKR	9.675

Chechi retains the title.

VAULT
Vitaly Scherbo	BYL	9.662
Cristian Leric	ROM	9.518
Magnus Rosengren	SWE	9.512

Scherbo retains the title.

PARALLEL BARS
Rustam Charipov	UKR	9.725
Alexei Nemov	RUS	9.725
Yevgeny Chabayev	RUS	9.600

Charipov & Nemov share first place.

HORIZONTAL BAR
Alijaz Pegan	SLVN	9.762
Vitaly Scherbo	BYL	9.662
Yevgeny Chabayev	RUS	9.600

Women *May 1994 Globe Arena, Stockholm*

TEAM
Romania	117.785
Russia	115.422
Ukraine	115.221

OVERALL
Gina Gogean	ROM	39.411
Svetalna Chorkhina	RUS	39.224
Dina Kochetkova	RUS	39.224

Chorkhina finishes second, Kochetkova third.

Milosevici, who leads the qualifiers, falls from the bars and finishes sixth overall.

VAULT
Lavinia Milosevici	ROM	9.800
Yelena Piskun	BYL	9.793
Lilia Podkopayeva	UKR	9.787

ASYMMETRIC BARS
Svetlana Chorkina	RUS	9.887
Oksana Fabrichnova	RUS	9.837
Mercedes Pacheco	SPA	9.800

BEAM
Gina Gogean	ROM	9.900
Lilia Podkopayeva	UKR	9.862
Lavinia Milosevici	ROM	9.850

FLOOR
Lilia Podkopayeva	UKR	9.937
Lavinia Milosevici	ROM	9.887
Dina Kochetkova	RUS	9.850
7 Annika Reeder	*UK*	*9.675*

British Championships 1993
1-3 Oct

Men
Liverpool

OVERALL		
Marvin Campbell		104.10
Paul Bowler		104.10
David Cox		101.90
FLOOR	Paul Bowler	8.90
HORSE	Marvin Campbell	8.85
	1eq Lee Ricketts	8.85
	1eq Robert Barber	8.85
RINGS	Paul Bowler	9.20
VAULT	Paul Bowler	9.20
BARS	Paul Bowler	9.00
HIGH BAR	Paul Bowler	9.20
	1 eq Craig Heap	9.20
UNDER 18	D Brindle	97.70
UNDER 16	T Hickey	107.05

Women
Crawley

OVERALL		
Jacky Brady		36.562
Zita Lusack		36.437
Karin Szymko		36.337
FLOOR	Jacky Brady	9.537
VAULT	Jacky Brady	9.399
BARS	Jacky Brady	9.187
BEAM	Jacky Brady	8.800

British Championships 1994

23-25 Sep Guildford

Men

Birmingham

OVERALL

Lee McDermott		98.50
Craig Heap		96.45
K Atherton		95.25

FLOOR	Craig Heap	9.25
HORSE	Lee McDermott	9.15
RINGS	Lee McDermott	9.60
VAULT	A Minshall	8.925
BARS	Lee McDermott	9.20
	1 eq Craig Heap	9.20
HIGH BAR	Lee McDermott	9.30
UNDER 18	J Smethurst	96.90
UNDER 16	K Jackson	107.85

Women

Specrum Centre, Guildford

OVERALL

Zita Lusack	73.637
Annika Reeder	72.462
Karin Szymko	71.687

Lusack improves on her second place of last year, Szymko stays third.

FLOOR	Annika Reeder	9.612
BARS	Zita Lusack	9.312
BEAM	Anna-liese Acklam	9.150
VAULT	Sonia Lawrence	9.343
	1 eq Anna-liese Acklam	9.343

Rhythmic Gymnastics

World Championships 1993

Nov, Alicante

TEAM

Bulgaria	94.750
Ukraine	94.400
Russia	94.200

OVERALL

Maria Petrova	BUL	29.00
Yekaterina Serebrianskaya	RUS	29.80
Carolina Pascual	SPA	28.65

Rope	Yekaterina Serebrianskaya	RUS
Hoop	Maria Petrova	BUL
Ball	Maria Petrova	BUL
Ribbons	Maria Petrova	BUL
Clubs	Carmen Acedo	SPA

World Championships 1994

Oct, Paris

TEAM

Russia	38.925
Spain	38.700
Bulgaria	38.675

OVERALL

Maria Petrova	BUL	38.900
Larissa Lukianenko	BYL	38.850
Amina Zaripova	RUS	38.850

Petrova retains the title, Lukianenko & Zaripova share second place. Yekaterina Serebrianskaya wins the ribbon and clubs, shares first place in the ball with Elena Vitrichenko (UKR) and with Lukianenko & Petrova in the hoop. The rope's not held as a separate event.

European Championships 1994

May, Salonica

TEAM

Ukraine	95.900
Belarus	95.000
Bulgaria	94.350

OVERALL

Maria Petrova	BUL	39.075
Elena Vitrichenko	UKR	39.050
Amina Zaripova	RUS	39.025
34 Debbie Southwick	*UK*	

Rope	Elena Vitrichenko	UKR
Hoop	Elena Vitrichenko	UKR
Ball	Amina Zaripova	RUS
Clubs	Amina Zaripova	RUS
Ribbon	Elena Vitrichenko	UKR

British Championships 1994

26 March, Bletchley

OVERALL

Debbie Southwick	36.00
Aicha McKenzie	35.25
Joanne Walker	34.30

Southwick, who retains the title, also wins all four individual apparati: rope, hoop, ball, ribbon.

Special Needs Championships

Aylestone Leisure Centre, Leicester

COMPETITION B LEVEL 1
Men: Ben Walton   Women: Gail Geddes
Junior Men: Ben McKenna
Junior Women: Michelle Bannerman
COMPETITION B LEVEL 2 (British Championships)
Men: Ronnie Broomhall
Women: Vicky Dominguez-Perez

Handball

Women's World Championship 1993

Norway

Group 1	P	W	D	L	F	A	Pts
Denmark	5	4	0	1	143	122	8
Norway	5	4	0	1	104	91	8
Russia	5	2	1	2	113	109	5
Hungary	5	1	2	2	120	135	4
Poland	5	1	1	3	117	136	3
S Korea	5	1	0	4	136	140	2

Russia, winners of the last three world titles (1982-86-90), draw with Hungary then lose to the lowly Koreans and by a single point to Poland.

Group 2	P	W	D	L	F	A	Pts
Germany	5	4	0	1	109	82	8
Romania	5	3	0	2	111	93	6
Sweden	5	3	0	2	95	80	6
Austria	5	3	0	2	83	78	6
UKR	5	2	0	3	99	99	4
USA	5	0	0	5	69	134	0

3rd-Place final

Norway	20	Romania	19

Final

Germany	22	Denmark	21 aet

Germany win the title for the first time since the good old DDR days of 1978 (many of the current team were trained in East Germany) thanks to a calamitous change in the Danish tactics. Despite the exhortations of coach Ulrik Wilbek, the favourites try to defend a 17-14 lead ('we are only strong when we attack'), are held 17-17, and lose in extra-time. They've never won the title.

Germany: Sabine Adamik, Heike Axmann, Eike Bram, Andrea Bölk, Carola Ciszewski, Cordula David, Michaela Erler, Sybille Gruner, Karen Heinrich, Franziska Heinz, Gabriele Palme, Heike Murrweiss, Michaela Schanze, Bianca Urbanke, Birgit Wagner, Renate Zienkiewicz; coach Lothar Doering

Leading scorers

58	Hong Jeong-ho	S KOR
50	Natalya Morskowa	RUS
44	Zuzana Prekopova	UKR

Hong's only 18.

Junior World Championships 1993

Men

Egypt

3rd-place final

Iceland	21	Russia	20

As in the women's senior event, the Russian favourites finish outside the medals.

Final

Egypt	22	Denmark	19

The first world handball title won by an African country.

Women

Bulgaria

3rd-place final

S Korea	28	Denmark	27

Final

Russia	24	Bulgaria	17

Goodwill Games

Men

July 1994 St Petersburg

3rd-place final

Spain	29	S Korea	25

Final

France	22	Russia	20

Hang Gliding

World Championship (women)
July 1994 Chelan, USA

Annelise Muller	SWI	6151
Kari Castle	USA	6032
Katia Schmitt	FRA	5756
5 Kathleen Rigg	*UK*	*5262*

Schmitt takes part in the championships for the first time.

TEAMS
Switzerland	17 704
France	17 491
USA	16 217
5 UK	*15 572*

Switzerland retain the title, again ahead of France

European Championships
Aug 1994 Laragne, France

TEAM	
Austria	12399
Italy	12368
France	12085
4 UK	*11420*

British Open
May 1994 Hawes, North Yorkshire

C Ashman	901
R Richardson	887
J Needham	834

British League PG Open
16-22 July Piedrahita, Spain

Paragliding

Pat Holmes
Richard Carter
John Sylvester

Sarah Fenwick (2), Pat Holmes & Judy Leden set women's world records.

Hockey

World Cup

Men
23 Nov - 4 Dec 1994 Sydney

GROUP A

England	0	Spain	0

Jon Potter, the captain, wins his 100th England cap.

Australia	2	Belarus	0
Pakistan	3	Argentina	0
England	1	Belarus	0

Potter celebrates his record 229th international (including G Britain matches), thanks to Nick Thompson's goal six minutes from time against a country with only five clubs.

Australia	2	Argentina	1
Pakistan	3	Spain	1
Argentina	1	England	1

A 44th minute equaliser by Nick Thompson does little to assuage coach David Whitaker: 'Our finishing – words fail me.'

Spain	4	Belarus	1
Pakistan	2	Australia	1
England	2	Pakistan	0

Thompson does the trick again, scoring twice (28, 49), the first just four minutes after coming on as substitute.

Australia	2	Spain	1
Argentina	4	Belarus	1
Australia	2	England	0

On the same day that Australia's cricketers win the first Test against England, their hockey team stops England reaching the semi-finals by scoring two goals in a minute – Stephen Davies 22, Paul Lewis 23 – immediately after England defender Phil McGuire is sent off for five minutes for a trivial offence.

Argentina	2	Spain	1
Pakistan	2	Belarus	0
Germany	1	S Korea	1

	P	W	D	L	F	A	Pts
Pakistan	5	4	0	1	10	4	8
Australia	5	4	0	1	9	4	8
England	5	2	2	1	4	3	6
Argentina	5	2	1	2	8	8	5
Spain	5	1	1	3	7	8	3
Belarus	5	0	0	5	2	13	0

GROUP B

Germany	1	S Africa	1
Holland	8	Belgium	1
India	2	S Korea	0
Germany	6	Belgium	0
S Africa	0	S Korea	0
Holland	4	India	2
S Korea	7	Belgium	2
S Africa	2	India	2
Germany	0	Holland	0
S Africa	1	Belgium	1
Germany	2	India	1
Holland	4	S Korea	2
India	4	Belgium	2
Holland	5	S Africa	1

	P	W	D	L	F	A	Pts
Holland	5	4	1	0	21	8	9
Germany	5	2	3	0	10	3	7
India	5	2	1	2	11	10	5
S Korea	5	1	2	2	10	9	4
S Africa	5	0	4	1	5	9	4
Belarus	5	0	1	4	6	26	1

Two goals by Bobby Crutchley and a penalty stroke by Russell Garcia give England a 3-1 win over S Korea (for whom Kim Jong-yi scores) to guarantee a place in the next World Cup (1998). The subsequent, rather irrelevant 1-0 loss to India (goal by Kumar) leaves them sixth overall.

Semi-finals

Holland	3	Australia	1
Pakistan	1	Germany	1

Pakistan 5-3 pens

Pakistan's win on penalty strokes is a repeat of the Champions Trophy final.

3rd-place final

Australia	5	Germany	2

Final
4 Dec Homebush Stadium

Pakistan	1	Holland	1

Pakistan 4-3 pens

Kamran Ahsraf 21	Bovelander 17

Already the only country to win the title three times, Pakistan win it again by taking revenge on the team who beat them in the last final (1990). Holland's coach then, Hans Jorritsma, now in charge of Pakistan, completes a unique double. The formidable Floris Jan Bovelander, who scored twice in that match, puts Holland ahead here but in the end Mansoor Ahmed saves Jeroen Delmee's penalty stroke in the shoot-out. Pakistan win their last two matches that way and are no more than firsts among equals. The only team to beat them in the tournament, if only it had got its shooting consistently right, might have been a little more than that...

Women

13-24 July Dublin

POOL A

Russia	2	Australia	1
Argentina	3	Ireland	0
Spain	3	S Korea	3
S Korea	4	Russia	0
Australia	3	Argentina	1
Ireland	1	Spain	1
Argentina	1	Russia	0
S Korea	2	Ireland	0
Australia	1	Spain	1
Argentina	1	S Korea	0
Spain	3	Russia	1
Australia	4	Ireland	0
Ireland	0	Russia	0
Argentina	1	Spain	0
Australia	4	S Korea	1

	P	W	D	L	F	A	Pts
Argentina	5	4	0	1	6	3	8
Australia	5	3	1	1	13	5	7
S Korea	5	2	1	2	10	8	5
Spain	5	1	3	1	8	7	5
Russia	5	1	1	3	3	9	3
Ireland	5	0	2	3	1	9	2

POOL B

Germany	2	Canada	0
Holland	1	China	0
USA	1	England	0
China	0	England	0
USA	1	Germany	1
Holland	3	Canada	0
Germany	3	England	0
China	2	Canada	0
USA	2	Holland	1
Canada	1	USA	0
China	2	Germany	1
Holland	1	England	0
England	3	Canada	0
USA	1	China	0
Germany	2	Holland	1

	P	W	D	L	F	A	Pts
Germany	5	3	1	1	9	4	7
USA	5	3	1	1	5	3	7
Holland	5	3	0	2	7	4	6
China	5	2	1	2	4	3	5
England	5	1	1	3	3	5	3
Canada	5	1	0	4	1	10	2

Semi-finals

| Argentina | 2 | USA | 0 |
| Australia | 2 | Germany | 0 |

3rd-place final

| USA | 2 | Germany | 1 |

Final

| Australia | 2 | Argentina | 0 |

Andrews (pen) 53
Pereira 54

Two goals in a minute (including Jackie Pereira's only goal of the tournament) beat the surprise finalists and give Australia the title for the first time. England beat Ireland 2-0 on penalties to finish 10th and win a place in the next Olympic qualifying tournament. Holland, champions since 1981 (the last three World Cup tournaments), finish sixth.

Champions Trophy

17-25 March 1994 Lahore

Pakistan	4	G Britain	1
Germany	2	Australia	1
Holland	4	Spain	4
Australia	3	Holland	2
Pakistan	3	Spain	1
Germany	1	G Britain	0
Australia	5	G Britain	4
Germany	3	Spain	2
Pakistan	2	Holland	1
Pakistan	2	Australia	0
G Britain	1	Spain	1
Germany	1	Holland	1
Holland	5	G Britain	2
Pakistan	1	Germany	1
Australia	2	Spain	0

	P	W	D	L	F	A	Pts
Pakistan	5	4	1	0	12	4	9
Germany	5	3	2	0	8	5	8
Australia	5	3	0	2	11	10	6
Holland	5	1	2	2	13	12	4
Spain	5	0	2	3	8	13	2
G Britain	5	0	1	4	8	16	1

5th-place final

Spain	4	G Britain	2

3rd-place final

Holland	2	Australia	2

Holland 8-7 on pens

Final

Pakistan	2	Germany	2

Pakistan 7-6 on pens

Shafqat, Shahbaz   *Tewes, Kunz*

Pakistan beat the holders to win the title for the first time since 1980. Their expertise and nerve in shoot-outs later serves them well in the World Cup.

Shah Trophy

Final

28 Aug 1994 Kuala Lumpur

England	(2)2	Pakistan	(1)2

Crutchley 3   *Kamran Ashraf 19, 29*
Thompson 37

England win 5-3 on pens (goals by Nick Thompson, Russell Garcia, Simon Nicklin, Phillip McGuire & Rob Crutchley, Irfan hitting a post with Pakistan's third). England's 6'6 goalkeeper Simon Mason is named Player of the Final.

European Cup (Men)

3rd-place final

Durkheim (GER)	2	Hounslow (UK)	1

Böckler, Mayerhoffer   *Knapp*

Final

23 May 1994 Bloemendaal

Uhlenhorst (GER)	2	Bloemendaal (HOL)	0

Bellenbaum, Becker

Uhlenhorst win the title for the seventh successive time.

European Cup-winners' Cup (Men)

3rd-place final

4 April 1994 Terrassa

Teddington (ENG)	5	Harvesthuder (GER)	3

Final

4 April 1994 Terrassa

Atletico Terrassa (SPA)	3	HGC (HOL)	3

Terrassa 5-4 pens

HGC had won the Cup for the last two seasons.

European Cup (Women)

3rd-place final

Ipswich (ENG)	1	Glasgow Western (SCOT)	0

Lister

Final

23 May 1994 Bloemendaal, Holland

HGC (HOL)	0	Russelheim (GER)	0

HGC 4-3 pens

European Cup-winners' Cup (Women)

3rd-place final

4 April 1994 Cardiff

Leicester (ENG)	2	Stade Français (FRA)	0

Final

4 April 1994 Cardiff

Bayer Leverkusen (GER)	0	SKIF Moscow (RUS)	0

Leverkusen 3-1 pens

English National League (Men)

Division 1

	P	W	D	L	F	A	Pts
Havant	17	14	2	1	39	13	44
Hounslow	17	12	3	2	48	14	39
Old Loughtonians	17	10	6	1	48	19	36
Southgate	17	10	4	3	45	15	34
Teddington	17	10	3	4	36	23	33
Cannock	17	7	7	3	31	21	28
Stourport	17	8	4	5	26	16	28
East Grinstead	17	8	4	5	32	23	28
Reading	17	8	2	7	30	27	26
Trojans	17	6	2	9	25	32	20
Indian Gymkhana	17	4	6	7	18	29	18
Welton	17	5	2	10	18	35	17
Bournville	17	5	1	11	23	34	16
Firebrands	17	3	7	7	15	30	16

Canterbury	17	3	5	9	20	39	14
Slough	17	4	2	11	17	37	14
St Albans	17	4	1	12	15	42	13
Bromley	17	1	1	15	8	45	4

Havant win the title for the third time in four years. St Albans & Bromley are relegated, replaced by Guildford (Div 2 champions) & Surbiton.

Hockey Association Cup (Men)

Quarter-finals
13 Feb 1994

Teddington	2	Beeston	1
Hounslow	2	Southgate	2

Hounslow 6-5 on pens

Reading	7	Harrogate	0
Old Loughtonians	3	Havant	0

Semi-finals
13 March 1994 Birmingham University

Teddington	2	Hounslow	2

Teddington 4-2 on pens

Old Loughtonians	3	Reading	2

Hounslow, holders for the last three seasons, lose in the HA Cup for the first time in 23 matches – to the club they'd beaten in the two previous finals. Reading go out in the semi-final for the second successive year.

Final
15 May 1994 Birmingham

Teddington	1	Old Loughtonians	0

Andy Billson 3

TEDDINGTON: Meredith, McGuire, Nicklin, Wallis, Colclough, Camburn, Hauck, Moore, Gibbins, Laslett, Billson. Sub: R Benzies

O LOUGHTONIANS: Seaton, Halls, Crymble, Morrison, Allen, Hector, Barker, Gladman, Thompson, Krishman, Philpot. Subs: Loftus, Donnelly.

Teddington, who lost the two previous finals, win a major HA trophy for the first time.

English Premier Division (Women)

	P	W	D	L	F	A	Pts
Leicester	14	9	3	2	23	11	30
Ipswich	14	8	4	2	24	8	28
Sutton Coldfield	14	8	3	3	19	14	27
Slough	14	7	4	3	19	8	25
Hightown	14	8	1	5	20	12	25
Clifton	14	2	3	9	10	24	9
Chelmsford	14	2	1	11	9	31	7
Ealing	14	1	3	10	10	26	4

Ealing, who forfeit a goal and two points for including an unregistered player in their squad v Clifton, are relegated. Leicester, who win the title for the first time, go into the European Club Championship.

National (AEWHA) Cup (Women)

Final
14 May 1994 Milton Keynes

Slough	1	Hightown	1

Slough on pens
Chandler 33   Marsden 50

SLOUGH: Knight, Pottow, Chandler, Burd, Hall, Wright, Brown (c), Robertson, White, Hobley, Bennett. Sub used: Thornalley

HIGHTOWN: Reid, Marsden (c), Crook, Cook, Mills, Lee, Carr, Souyave, Morton, Aspin, Cullen. Subs used: Jones, Newcombe

Slough complete the Cup double (indoor and out) v Hightown, beating them in the final of each competition on penalties.

Horse Racing

Flat Races

English Classics

1000 GUINEAS
29 April 1994 Newmarket 1m

horse	jockey	odds	trainer
Las Meninas	John Reid	12-1	Tommy Stack
Balanchine	Lanfranco Dettori	20-1	
Coup de Genie	Cash Asmussen	6-1	

A finish so tight that the judges examine the photograph for seventeen minutes before declaring a winner. Reid last won the race in 1982.

2000 GUINEAS
31 April 1994 Newmarket 1m

Mister Baileys	Jason Weaver	16-1	Mark Johnston
Grand Lodge	Lanfranco Dettori	16-1	
Colonel Collins	John Reid	13-2	

Weaver rides his first winner in a Group 1 race, let alone a Classic, the first Northern-trained success in this event since Rockavon in 1961.

DERBY
2 June 1994 Epsom 1m 4f

Erhaab	Willie Carson	7-2f	John Dunlop
King's Theatre	Michael Kinane	14-1	
Colonel Collins	John Reid	10-1	

Carson (51), in his 26th Derby, wins the race for the fourth time. Lester Piggott (58), in his 36th, 40 years after the first of his record nine wins, finishes fifth on Khamaseen. Willie Ryan breaks three ribs after being thrown from Foyer following a collision with King's Theatre.

OAKS
4 June 1994 Epsom 1m 4f

Balanchine	Lanfranco Dettori	6-1	Hilal Ibrahim
Wind In Her Hair	Richard Hills	7-1	
Hawaiiss	Walter Swinburn	9-1	

The first horse trained in the Middle East to win an English Classic. Frankie Dettori, having lost each Guineas by a short head, wins a Classic for the first time.

ST LEGER
10 Sep 1994 Doncaster 1m 6f

Moonax	Pat Eddery	40-1	Barry Hills
Broadway Flyer	Michael Hills	6-1	
Double Trigger	Jason Weaver	9-1	

While the rest of the field tires itself trying to follow Broadway Flyer's pace, Eddery plays a waiting game to win by just over a length and help Hills deprive his son of a Classic win.

<table>
<tr><td colspan="3">Oldest Derby-winning Jockeys</td><td>31</td><td>John Jackson</td><td>1791-1822</td></tr>
<tr><td colspan="3">yrs-days</td><td>31</td><td>Jem Robinson</td><td>1817-48</td></tr>
<tr><td>60-</td><td>John Forth</td><td>1829 Frederick</td><td>28</td><td>Joe Mercer</td><td>1953-81</td></tr>
<tr><td>56/57-</td><td>Frank Buckle</td><td>1823 Emilius</td><td>26</td><td>Charlie Elliott</td><td>1923-49</td></tr>
</table>

Oldest Derby-winning Jockeys

yrs-days

60-	John Forth	1829	Frederick	
56/57-	Frank Buckle	1823	Emilius	
52-25	'Scobie' Breasley	1966	Charlottown	
51-254	Charlie Smirke	1958	Hard Ridden	
51-198	Willie Carson	1994	Erhaab	

31	John Jackson	1791-1822
31	Jem Robinson	1817-48
28	Joe Mercer	1953-81
26	Charlie Elliott	1923-49

Piggott also finished second in the 1952 Derby, Osborne third in the St Leger in 1855 & 1892.

Longest Spans riding English Classic winners

yrs

38	Lester Piggott	1954-92
35	Frank Buckle	1792-1827
32	John Osborne	1856-88

Others since 1945

24	Charlie Smirke	1934-58
23	Tommy Weston	1923-46
23	Gordon Richards	1930-53
22	Rae Johnstone	1934-56
22	Willie Carson	1972-94
20	Pat Eddery	1974-94

Group One races 1993

MIDDLE PARK STAKES
30 Sep Newmarket 6f

First Trump	Michael Hills	6-1	Geoff Wragg

DUBAI CHAMPION STAKES
16 Oct Newmarket 1m 2f

Hatoof	Walter Swinburn	5-2f	Criquette Head

Group One races 1994

CORONATION CUP
3 June Epsom 1m 4f

Apple Tree	Thierry Jarnet	12-1	André Fabre

Fabre also trains the horse (Intrepidity) who finishes last.

ST JAMES'S PALACE STAKES
14 June Ascot 1m

Grand Lodge	Michael Kinane	6-1	Willie Jarvis

Kinane wins three Group races on the card before being banned for two days after hitting Grand Lodge with 'unreasonable force.'

CORONATION STAKES
15 June Ascot 1m

Kissing Cousin	Michael Kinane	13-2	Henry Cecil

ASCOT GOLD CUP
16 June Ascot 2m 4f

Arcadian Heights	Michael Hills	20-1	Geoff Wragg

Always a nippy beast, the winner. He twice tried to bite the jockey of a horse thinking of passing him in a race, and chewed off the end of an assistant trainer's finger. The only castrated horse ever to finish first in the Gold Cup, it's his first win since 1991. Shame to see him knuckling down.

ECLIPSE STAKES
2 July Sandown 1m 2f

Ezzoud	Walter Swinburn jnr	5-1	Michael Stoute

JULY CUP
7 July Newmarket 6f

Owington	Paul Eddery	3-1	Geoff Wragg

Eddery gets the ride after the suspension of regular jockey Michael Hills. Frankie Dettori's ridden Lochsong to all her major successes, but partners Catrail to third place in this. Suspicions that the extra furlong might be too much for the Queen of Speed appear to have been well-founded: Lochsong, with Willie Carson aboard, finishes second to last, but comes back to win the King George Stakes (over 5f) later in the month.

K GEORGE VI & Q ELIZABETH DIAMOND STAKES
23 July Ascot 1m 4f
King's Theatre	Michael Kinane	12-1	Henry Cecil

Ezzoud throws Walter Swinburn and gallops alongside the rest of the field. King's Theatre finished second in both the English & Irish Derbies. Japanese rider Yutaka Take finishes second on White Muzzle.

SUSSEX STAKES
27 July Goodwood 1m
Distant View	Pat Eddery	4-1	Henry Cecil

The opposition get the winner's name as Eddery (who wins the race for the fifth time) brings the 2-y-o home in a course record time.

JUDDMONTE INTERNATIONAL
16 Aug York 1m 2f
Ezzoud	Walter Swinburn jnr	4-1	Michael Stoute

Ezzoud, this time allowing Swinburn to stay in the saddle, wins the race for the second successive year.

YORKSHIRE OAKS
17 Aug York 1m 3f
Only Royale	Lanfranco Dettori	15-2	Luca Cumani

Only Royale wins the race for the second year in a row.

KEENELAND NUNTHORPE
18 Aug York 5f
Piccolo	John Reid	14-1	Mick Channon

Bad day for one owner. One of his horses, Blue Siren, is disqualified after finishing first, the other, the favourite Lochsong, finishes last after becoming tense and irritable during the pre-race parade. Ex-footballer Channon isn't complaining.

SPRINT CUP
3 Sep Haydock 6f
Lavinia Fontana	Jason Weaver	11-2	John Dunlop

Rain puts paid to the chances of the favourite Owington, who finishes third.

FILLIES' MILE
24 Sep Ascot 1m
Aqaarid	Willie Carson	11-2	John Dunlop

Q ELIZABETH II STAKES
24 Sep Ascot 1m 4f
Maroof	Richard Hills	66-1	R Armstrong

The pace setter for stablemate Mehtlaaf goes straight into the lead and holds it to win by just over a length.

CHEVELEY PARK STAKES
27 Sep Newmarket 6f
Gay Gallanta	Pat Eddery	14-1	Michael Stoute

MIDDLE PARK STAKES
29 Sep Newmarket 6f
Fard	Willie Carson	33-1	David Morley

Morley wins the first Group One race he enters.

DEWHURST STAKES
14 Oct Newmarket 7f
Pennekamp	Thierry Jarnet	5-2jf	André Fabre

CHAMPION STAKES
15 Oct Newmarket 1m 2f
Dernier Empereur	Sylvain Guillot	8-1	André Fabre

With a late run, Dernier Empereur turns the tables on last year's winner Grand Lodge, who beat him into third place.

RACING POST TROPHY (ex Futurity Stakes)
22 Oct Doncaster 1m

Celtic Swing	Kevin Darley	evens f	Herries

The unbeaten Swing wins by twelve lengths.

Group Two races 1993

SUN CHARIOT STAKES
2 Oct Newmarket 1m 2f

Talented	Willie Carson	4-1	John Dunlop

CHALLENGE STAKES
14 Oct Newmarket 7f 64y

Catrail	Michael Roberts	4-5f	Michael Stoute

Group Two races 1994

GARDNER MERCHANT MILE
22 April Sandown 1m 14y

Penny Drops	David Harrison	8-1	Huntingdon

JOCKEY CLUB STAKES
29 April Newmarket 1m 4f

Silver Wisp	Michael Hills	20-1	David Nicholson

DANTE STAKES
11 May York 1m 2f

Erhaab	Willie Carson	11-2	John Dunlop

Erhaab beats 2000 Guineas winner Mister Baileys to establish himself as 7-2 favourite for the Derby.

YORKSHIRE CUP
12 May York 1m 5f

Key To My Heart	John Reid	16-1	Dudley Moffatt

A first Group Two win for Moffatt, whose stable consists of only twenty horses, most of them jumpers.

JUDDMONTE LOCKINGE STAKES
13 May Newbury 1m

Emperor Jones	Lanfranco Dettori	11-2	John Gosden

Emperor Jones sets a new course record for the straight mile.

TEMPLE STAKES
30 May Sandown 5f

Lochsong	Lanfranco Dettori	4-9f	Ian Balding

Dettori describes the Queen of Speed as Linford without the lunchbox. Same could be said about some of the geldings.

QUEEN ANNE STAKES
14 June Ascot 1m

Barathea	Michael Kinane	3-1	Luca Cumani

P OF WALES'S STAKES
14 June Ascot 1m 4f

Muhtarram	Willie Carson	6-4f	John Gosden

K EDWARD VII STAKES
14 June Ascot 1m 4f

Foyer	Michael Kinane	7-2	Michael Stoute

RIBBLESDALE STAKES
16 June Ascot 1m 4f

Bolas	Pat Eddery	3-1f	Barry Hills

A spectator, 20-y-o James Florey, ducks under the rails into the path of Michael Kinane's horse Papago. Some racing correspondents can't resist describing his condition in hospital as stable.

HARDWICKE STAKES
17 June Ascot 1m 4f

Bobzao	John Reid	11-1	Terry Mills

KING'S STAND STAKES
17 June Ascot 5f

Lochsong	Lanfranco Dettori	30-100f	Ian Balding

The flying filly has it won from the start. Some of the most spectacular acceleration ever seen on a British racecourse leads to a win by five lengths.

P of WALES'S STAKES
5 July Newmarket 1m 4f

Wagon Master	Richard Hills	7-1	Alec Stewart

FALMOUTH STAKES
6 July Newmarket 1m

Lemon Souffle	Lester Piggott	6-5f	Richard Hannon

The winner completes her recovery from a string of operations.

RICHMOND STAKES
28 July Goodwood 6f

Sri Pekan	Richard Quinn	9-4	Paul Cole

VODAFONE NASSAU STAKES
30 July Goodwood 1m 2f

Hawajiss	Walter Swinburn jnr	4-1jf	Michael Stoute

GEOFFREY FREER STAKES
13 Aug Newbury 1m 5f

Red Route	Willie Ryan	11-10f	Henry Cecil

The favourite wins by six lengths.

GREAT VOLTIGEUR STAKES
16 Aug York 1m 4f

Sacrament	Walter Swinburn jnr	6-1	Michael Stoute

GIMCRACK STAKES
17 Aug York 1m 2f

Chilly Billy	Kieran Fallon	12-1	Jack Ramsden

LOWTHER STAKES
18 Aug York 6f

Harayir	Willie Carson	2-1jf	Dick Hern

CELEBRATION MILE
27 Aug Goodwood 1m

Mehtaaf	Willie Carson	5-2	John Dunlop

LAURENT-PERRIER STAKES
9 Sep Doncaster 7f

Sri Pekan	Michael Kinane	100-30	Paul Cole

Kinane deputises for the suspended Richard Quinn.

FLYING CHILDERS
10 Sep Doncaster 5f

Raah Algharb	Walter Swinburn jnr	7-1	Michael Stoute

MILL REEF STAKES
17 Sep Newbury 6f

Princely Hush	Michael Fenton	9-2	Michael Bell

ROYAL LODGE STAKES
24 Sep Ascot 1m

Eltish	Pat Eddery	7-4f	Henry Cecil

SUN CHARIOT STAKES
1 Oct Newmarket 1m 2f
La Confederation   Kevin Darley   5-1   David Loder

CHALLENGE STAKES
13 Oct Newmarket 7f
Zieten   Lanfranco Dettori   13-2   John Gosden

The 13-8 favourite Soviet Line finishes second after Pat Eddery laments that he 'just couldn't get out.' Zieten won the 1992 Middle Park Stakes (Group One) on the same course.

Major Handicaps

CAMBRIDGESHIRE
2 Oct 1993 Newmarket 1m 1f
Penny Drops   David Harrison   7-1f   Huntingdon

CESAREWITCH
16 Oct 1993 Newmarket 2m 2f
Aahsaylad   John Williams   12-1   John White

LINCOLN HANDICAP
26 March 1994 Doncaster 1m
Our Rita   Darryll Holland   16-1   Jon Scargill

CHESTER CUP
4 May 1994 Chester 2m 2f
Doyce   Gary Bardwell   14-1   R Williams

ROYAL HUNT CUP
15 June 1994 Ascot 1m
Face North   Alan Munro   25-1   Reg Akehurst

STEWARDS' CUP
30 July 1994 Goodwood 6f
For The Present   Jimmy Fortune   16-1   David Barron

EBOR HANDICAP
17 Aug 1994 York 1m 5f 94y
Hasten To Add   George Duffield   13-2f   Mark Prescott

AYR GOLD CUP
17 Sep Ayr 6f
Daring Destiny   Jason Tate   18-1   K Burke

FESTIVAL HANDICAP
24 Sep Ascot 7f
Wizard King   George Duffield   13-2f   Mark Prescott

ASCOT HANDICAP
24 Sep Ascot 1m 4f
Whitechapel   Michael Hills   6-1   Huntingdon

CAMBRIDGESHIRE
1 Oct 1994 Newmarket 1m
Halling   Lanfranco Dettori   8-1f   John Gosdan

CESAREWITCH
15 Oct 1994 Newmarket 2m 2f
Captain's Guest   Tony Clark   25-1   Guy Harwood

Irish Classics

2000 GUINEAS
15 May 1994 The Curragh 1m

| Turtle Island | John Reid | 5-4f | Peter Chapple-Hyam |

The turtle beats the tortoises by fifteen lengths.

1000 GUINEAS
21 May 1994 The Curragh 1m

| Mehthaaf | Wille Carson | 5-2 | John Dunlop |

Carson's 100th win in Group One races.

DERBY
26 June 1994 The Curragh 1m 4f

| Balanchine | Lanfranco Dettori | 5-1 | Hilal Ibrahim |

Only the third filly to win the race this century.

OAKS
9 July 1994 The Curragh 1m 4f

| Bolas | Pat Eddery | 5-2f | Barry Hills |

The ninth English-trained winner in the last ten years.

Vintage Crop, ridden by Michael Kinane & trained by Dermot Weld, wins the St Leger at the Curragh on 17 Sep 1994, and is widely announced as the first horse to win any European Classic twice (being castrated, and therefore no use at stud, may have something to do with it) but in fact the race apparently lost its Classic status eleven years ago when it was thrown open to older horses...

French Classics

| *horse* | *jockey* | *trainer* |

POULE D'ESSAI des POULAINS (2000 Guineas)
8 May 1994 Longchamp 1m

| Green Tune | Olivier Doleuze | Criquette Head |

POULE D'ESSAI des POULICHES (1000 Guineas)
15 May 1994 Longchamp 1m

| East Of The Moon | Cash Asmussen | François Boutin |

PRIX du JOCKEY CLUB (Derby)
5 June 1994 Chantilly 1m 4f

| Celtic Arms | Gérald Mossé | Jacques Bouchard |

PRIX de DIANE (Oaks)
12 June 1994 Longchamp 1m 4f

| East Of The Moon | Cash Asmussen | |

PRIX ROYAL-OAK (St Leger)
23 Oct 1994 Longchamp 1m 6f

| Moonax | Pat Eddery | Barry Hills |

A short-neck victory makes Moonax the first horse to win both the English and the French Legers.

Other French Races

PRIX DE L'ARC DE TRIOMPHE 1993
3 Oct Longchamp 1m 4f

Urban Sea	Eric Saint-Martin	Jean Lesbordes
White Muzzle	John Reid	
Opera House	Michael Roberts	

The favourite, Hernando, finishes eleventh. Saint-Martin's father Yves won the race in 1970-74-82-84.

GRAND PRIX de PARIS
26 June 1994 Longchamp 1m 2f
Millkom   J Dubosc

GRAND PRIX de SAINT-CLOUD
3 July 1994 Saint-Cloud
Apple Tree   Thierry Jarnet   André Fabre

PRIX MORNY
21 Aug 1994 Deauville 6f
Hoh Magic   Michael Hills   Michael Bell

GRAND PRIX de DEAUVILLE
28 Aug 1994 Deauville
White Muzzle   John Reid   Peter Chapple-Hyam

PRIX DU MOULIN
4 Sep 1994 Longchamp
Ski Paradise   Yutaka Take   André Fabre
Ski Paradise beats heavy favourite East Of The Moon into second place to give Take his biggest win outside France.

PRIX VERMEILLE
11 Sep 1994 Longchamp 1m 4f
Sierra Madre   Gérald Mossé   Pascal Bary

PRIX DE L'ABBAYE
2 Oct 1994 Longchamp 5f
Lochsong   Lanfranco Dettori   Ian Balding
The Queen of Speed, cosseted throughout her journey, wins the race for the second successive year, this time by five lengths, one short of 1993's winning margin.

PRIX DE L'ARC DE TRIOMPHE
2 Oct 1994 Longchamp 1m 4f
Carnegie   Thierry Jarnet   André Fabre
Hernando   Cash Asmussen
Apple Tree   John Reid
The three French horses produce a blanket finish. Carnegie's dam Detroit becomes the first Arc winner (1980) to give birth to a colt who also wins the race, which Jarnet wins for the second time and Fabre for the third. The latter enters five horses, including the winner, third and fifth. Much ado as Yutaka Take again replaces Reid on White Muzzle, who finishes only sixth, to the thinly disguised fury of trainer Peter Chapple-Hyam. A kick from Ezzoud costs Millkom his unbeaten record in his eleventh race.

US Races

BREEDERS' CUP RACES 1993 6 Nov, Santa Anita

Sprint 6f
Cardmania   Eddie Delahoussaye

Juvenile Fillies 1m 110y
Phone Chatter   Laffit Pincay jr

Distaff 1m 1f
Hollywood Wildcat   Eddie Delahoussaye

Mile
Lure   Mike Smith
Lure wins the race for the second time.

Juvenile 1m 110y
Brocco   Gary Stevens

Turf 1m 4f
Kotashaan   Kent Desmormeaux

Classic 1m 2f
Arcangues   Jerry Bailey

Yet again British hopes bite the dust. Only two British horses have won Breeders' Cup races so far: Pebbles (Turf 1985) and Sheikh Albadou (Sprint 1991), which is no great surprise, given that only the self-explanatory Turf is run on anything resembling a European track - and even in that, horses respected on this side of the Pond (Opera House, Hatoof) are found wanting this time. Only André Fabre's 135-1 French outsider in the Classic (the longest priced winner in Breeders' Cup history) prevents an American clean sweep. Where does that leave the Brits? Standing, it seems. None in the first three, and Oaks winner Sayyedati only twelfth in the Sprint. 'The dirt is very deep,' says Walter Swinburn. Quite so.

KENTUCKY DERBY
7 May 1994
Go For Gin   Chris McCarron   Nick Zito

ARLINGTON MILLION
27 Aug 1994 Santa Anita
Paradise Creek   Pat Day

BREEDERS' CUP RACES 1994 5 Nov, Santa Anita

Sprint 6f
Cherokee Run   Mike Smith   F Alexander
The great British hope, dubbed the Lochsong Monster by the American press after a record practice run of three furlongs in 33 secs, finishes last.

Juvenile Fillies 1m 110y
Flanders   Pat Day   Wayne Lukas

Distaff 1m 1f
One Dreamer   Gary Stevens   T Procter

Mile
Barathea   Lanfranco Dettori   Luca Cumani
The only British horse to win this year, trained and ridden by Italians.

Juvenile 1m 110y
Timber Country   Pat Day   Wayne Lukas

Turf 1m 4f
Tikkanen   Mike Smith   J Pease
White Muzzle finishes eighth.

Classic 1m 2f
Concern   Jerry Bailey   R Small

Other Races Abroad

MELBOURNE CUP 1993
2 Nov Flemington 2m
Vintage Crop   Michael Kinane   Dermot Weld
In the 133rd running of the race, the first ever European-trained entries: Drum Taps (ninth) - and the winner, the first horse from outside Australasia to win the event (despite not having had a run for 45 days), ridden by a jockey who hadn't seen the course till less than 24 hours before the race. He becomes only the second jockey (after Pat Glennon 1959-65) to win the British Derby/Arc de Triomphe/Melbourne Cup treble. Earlier in the year, Vintage Crop finished sixth in the Champion Hurdle .

MELBOURNE CUP 1994
1 Nov Flemington 2m
Jeune   Wayne Harris   David Hayes
Another British-bred winner (he's now trained in Australia), who only takes part after being refused entry into the Japan Cup. Vintage Crop, the favourite trying to become only the fourth horse to win the event twice, finishes seventh, handicapped by carrying top weight and stitches in a leg wound caused by a freak accident during his first workout since arriving in Australia.

DERBY ITALIANO
29 May 1994 Rome 1m 4f
Time Star   Richard Quinn   Paul Cole
Jockey & trainer win the race for the second time, the first since 1987.

DEUTSCHES DERBY
3 July 1994 Hamburg
Laroche   Steve Eccles   Heinz Jentzsch

PREMIO del JOCKEY CLUB
16 Oct 1994 Milan
Lando   Michael Roberts

Final standings 1994

Jockeys

Winners		Rides
233	Lanfranco Dettori	1317
200	Jason Weaver	1086
154	Kevin Darley	947
154	Pat Eddery	802
115	Richard Quinn	923
98	John Reid	698
88	Willie Carson	650
88	Michael Hills	645
83	Paul Eddery	733
82	J Carroll	641

For the first time, the championship's decided by the number of winners in a calendar year rather than a Flat season, which makes Dettori's feat of riding 100 winners earlier than it's ever been done (11 June) something of a statistical accident. Again, although he becomes only the sixth jockey to ride 200 winners in a British flat season, the other five (Richards, Eddery, Roberts, Loates & Archer) rode only from March to the beginning of November. Still, his total beats the 229 set by his father Gianfranco, the highest in Europe since the War. Weaver becomes the seventh 200 man, the first time two jockeys have each ridden that number in the same English season.

Trainers

£		Winners
1 916 479	Michael Stoute	109
1 667 263	John Dunlop	82
1 534 330	Henry Cecil	76
1 268 542	John Gosden	93
1 143 235	Richard Hannon	112
1 026 873	Mark Johnston	117
808 688	Paul Cole	69
779 538	Luca Cumani	47
735 315	Jack Berry	129
619 120	Ian Balding	51

Berry trains 100 winners in a season for the fifth successive time.

Edinburgh 4 Nov 1993: Richard Hannon equals the record for a British Flat season by training his 180th winner of the season, equalling Henry Cecil's 1987 record. Hannon, who'd never taken a runner to Edinburgh, had three winners there, all maiens: Make The Break, Stash The Cash, Western Fleet. It took him nearly 1200 runners to reach that 180.

National Hunt Races

MACKESON GOLD CUP
13 Nov 1993 Cheltenham 2m 4f 110y handicap
Bradbury Star   Declan Murphy   13-2   Josh Gifford

HENNESSEY GOLD CUP
27 Nov 1993 Newbury 2m 2f 110y handicap
Cogent   Dan Fortt   10-1   Andy Turnell
Andrew Lloyd Webber bought the favourite, Black Humour, as a present for his wife. It finishes third.

TRIPLEPRINT GOLD CUP
11 Dec 1993 Cheltenham 2m 5f handicap chase
Fragrant Dawn   Declan Murphy   14-1   Martin Pipe

BETTERWARE CUP
18 Dec 1993 Ascot 3m 110y handicap chase
Young Hustler   Carl Llewellyn   11-8f   Nigel Twiston-Davies

KING GEORGE VI CHASE
27 Dec 1993 Kempton Park 3m
Barton Bank   Adrian Maguire   9-2   David Nicholson
*Post-race controversy centres on how many times Maguire (riding his 100th winner of the season) and Declan
Murphy hit their horses (about seventeen times between them). Both jockeys are banned for two days.*

WELSH NATIONAL
28 Dec 1993 Chepstow 3m 5f 110y handicap chase
Riverside Boy   Richard Dunwoody   6-4f   Martin Pipe
Pipe trains the winner of the race for the fifth time in the last six years.

CHRISTMAS HURDLE
28 Dec 1993 Kempton Park 3m
Muse   Mark Richards   3-1   David Elsworth

AGFA DIAMOND
5 Feb 1994 Sandown 3m 110y handicap chase
Second Schedual   Richard Dunwoody   6-1   David Nicholson

TOTE GOLD TROPHY
12 Feb 1994 Newbury 2m 110y handicap hurdle
Large Action   Jamie Osborne   9-2   Oliver Sherwood

RACING POST CHASE
26 Feb 1994 Kempton Park 3m handicap chase
Antonin   John Burke   7-1   Sue Bramall

GREENALLS GOLD CUP
26 Feb 1994 Kempton Park (moved from Haydock) 3m 4f 110y
Master Oats   Norman Williamson   11-4jf   Kim Bailey

SUNDERLANDS IMPERIAL CUP
12 March 1994 Sandown 2m 110y handicap hurdle
Precious Boy   Lorcan Wyer   33-1   Michael Meagher

SUPREME NOVICES HURDLE
15 March 1994 Cheltenham 2m 110y
Artic Kinsman   Carl Llewellyn   50-1   Nigel Twiston-Davies

ARKLE CHALLENGE TROPHY
15 March 1994 Cheltenham 2m
Nakir   Jamie Osborne   9-1   Simon Christian

CHAMPION HURDLE
15 March 1994 Cheltenham 2m 110y
Flakey Dove   Mark Dwyer   9-1   Richard Price
Oh So Risky   Paul Holley   9-4f
Large Action   Jamie Osborne   8-1
*Dwyer replaces regular jockey Norman Williamson, banned after a race at Doncaster, on only the second mare ever to
win the race (after Dawn Run in 1984).*

SUN ALLIANCE NOVICE HURDLE
16 March 1994 Cheltenham 2m 5f
Danoli   Charlie Swan   7-4f   Tom Foley

QUEEN MOTHER CHAMPION CHASE
16 March 1994 Cheltenham 2m
Viking Flagship   Adrian Maguire   4-1   David Nicholson

SUN ALLIANCE CHASE
16 March 1994 Cheltenham 3m 1f
| Monsieur Le Cure | Peter Niven | 15-2 | John Edwards |

TRIUMPH HURDLE
17 March 1994 Cheltenham 2m 1f
| Mysilv | Adrian Maguire | 2-1f | David Nicholson |

STAYERS HURDLE
17 March 1994 Cheltenham 3m 110y
| Balasani | Mark Perrett | 9-2jf | Martin Pipe |

Avro Anson (Mark Dwyer) disqualified (for interfering while wandering) after finishing first.

CHELTENHAM GOLD CUP
17 March 1994 Cheltenham 3m 2f 110y
The Fellow	Adam Kondrat	7-1	François Doumen
Jodami	Mark Dwyer	6-4f	
Young Hustler	Carl Llewellyn	20-1	

The first French-trained (and Polish-ridden) winner of the event. A poor jump at the last costs Jodami a second successive win in the race and Dwyer the Champion Hurdle/Gold Cup double.

MARTELL CUP CHASE
7 April 1994 Aintree 3m 1f
| Docklands Express | Richard Dunwoody | 5-2 | Kim Bailey |

GLENLIVET ANNIVERSARY HURDLE
7 April 1994 Aintree 2m 110y
| Tropical Lake | Kevin O'Brien | 10-1 | M Hourigan |

MELLING CHASE
8 April 1994 Aintree 2m 4f
| Katabatic | Simon McNeill | 14-1 | Josh Gifford |

AINTREE CHASE
9 April 1994 Aintree 2m handicap
| Uncle Ernie | Mark Dwyer | 3-1 | Jimmy FitzGerald |

FitzGerald's 1000th winner as a trainer.

AINTREE HURDLE
9 April 1994 Aintree 2m 4f
| Danoli | Charlie Swan | 9-2 | Tom Foley |

GRAND NATIONAL
9 April 1994 Aintree
Miinnehoma	Richard Dunwoody	16-1	Martin Pipe
Just So	Simon Burrough	20-1	
Moorcroft Boy	Adrian Maguire	5-1f	

After a 1993 race organised by clowns, a winner owned by a comedian (Freddie Starr). More seriously, only six of the 36 horses finish.

WHITBREAD GOLD CUP
23 April 1994 Sandown 3m 5f 110y handicap chase
| Ushers Island | Charlie Swan | 25-1 | Howard Johnson |

Swan wins the oldest sponsored race three years after losing it on a controversial stewards' decision. The horse awarded that 1991 running, Docklands Express, finishes third this time.

MACKESON GOLD CUP
12 Nov 1994 Cheltenham 2m 4f 110y handicap
| Bradbury Star | Philip Hide | 5-1 | Josh Gifford |

It takes a photo finish to confirm only the second horse to win the race two years in a row. Declan Murphy, who rode the winner last year, is still sidelined by the injury that required brain surgery.

HENNESSEY GOLD CUP
26 Nov 1994 Newbury 2m 2f 110y handicap
| One Man | Tony Dobbin | 4-1 | Gordon Richards |

The youngest horse in the race, a grey touted as the next Desert Orchid, wins easily. The 1993 winner Cogent, ridden by amateur Chris Bonner, finishes fourth, eleven lengths behind.

TRIPLEPRINT GOLD CUP
10 Dec 1994 Cheltenham 2m 5f handicap chase

Dublin Flyer	Brendan Powell	100-30	Tim Forster

The winner, overtaken by Nuaffe near the finish, recovers to take the race by a short head. Nuaffe's rider Sean O'Donovan is suspended for seven days for improper use of the whip, trainer Pat Fahy fined a mere £220 for not telling O'Donovan that the horse is thin-skinned.

KING GEORGE VI CHASE
26 Dec 1994 Kempton Park 3m

Algan	Philippe Chevalier	16-1	François Doumen

Chevalier wins on his very first ride in England (his first on Algan in any race) and Doumen trains the winner of the race for the fourth time in eight years - all thanks to last year's winner and 10-3 favourite Barton Bank, who unseats Adrian Maguire at the last when leading by fifteen lengths.

WELSH NATIONAL
31 Dec 1994 Newbury c.3m 6f handicap chase

Master Oats	Norman Williamson	5-2jf	Kim Bailey

Run over 'three miles and about six furlongs' after being moved from a waterlogged Chepstow where it was due to take place on 27 Dec. Master Oats wins the 99th running of the race by 20 lengths.

Final Standings 1993-94

Jockeys

Winners		Rides
198	Richard Dunwoody	891
194	Adrian Maguire	915
105	Jamie Osborne	497
104	Norman Williamson	582
89	Peter Niven	409
68	Mick Fitzgerald	556
65	Graham McCourt	397
58	Declan Murphy	371
58	David Bridgwater	398
48	Lorcan Wyer	265

Dunwoody retains the title by reaching a century for the fifth consecutive season. Maguire's total, the highest ever in second place, would have won the championship in every other year except one. His runaway start to the season (40 winners ahead of Dunwoody before Christmas) is interrupted by a series of fines and suspensions (he goes more than 40 races without a win to let Dunwoody pass him in mid-May) but these things tend to even themselves out: Dunwoody is suspended for fourteen days (including the Cheltenham Festival in March) after a clash with Maguire. Along the way, Dunwoody becomes the fourth jump jockey (after Mellor, Francome & Scudamore) to ride 1000 winners in Britain. His first: Game Trust at Cheltenham in 1983. The 1000th: Flakey Dove at the same place on 29 Jan 1994.

		Winners
Conditional:	Tony Dobbin	45
Amateur:	Johnny Greenall	21
Women:	Diane Clay	17

Trainers

Prize £		Winners
754 069	David Nicholson	81
719 607	Martin Pipe	127
603 018	Nigel Twiston-Davies	72
480 164	Kim Bailey	87
416 072	Josh Gifford	51
414 383	Mary Rieveley	103
307 055	Nicky Henderson	48
274 513	Phillip Hobbs	64
252 694	Gordon Richards	48
246 958	Oliver Sherwood	41

Pipe had won the title in each of the last five seasons.

Also ran
At Newmarket on 10 Oct 1993, riding 48 horses (only two more than once each), Peter Scudamore covers 200 miles (50 times round a four-mile circuit) in 8h 37m 51, a time 4m 9s faster than Squire Osbaldeston's record.

Winning is the drug
The Jockey Club announces that random drug tests for jockeys are to begin in Oct 1994. The penalty for a first offence: suspension for up to a month. The list of banned substances is less than a page long. Michael Turner, the Jockey Club Chief Medical Officer explains that 'we're not looking for performance-enhancing drugs.'

Hurling

All-Ireland Final 1994

Croke Park, Dublin, referee Willie Barrett

OFFALY	(8)25	LIMERICK	(14)19
G: Joe Dooley, Johnny Dooley		G: Quigley 2	
G: O'Connor		P: Carey 2, Houlihan	
G: Billy Dooley 5, Joe Dooley 2		P: Kirby 6, Quigley 2	
G: J Pilkington, Johnny Dooley 4		P: 2 others	
P: D Pilkington, 1 other			

Offaly: Jim Troy, Shane McGuckin (Joe Erritty), Kevin Kinahan, Martin Hanamy (c), Brian Whelehan, Hubert Rigney, Kevin Martin, Johnny Pilkington, Daithi Regan, Johnny Dooley, John Troy, Joe Dooley, Billy Dooley, Brendan Kelly, Declan Pilkington. Subs used: Joe Erritty (for McGuckin), Pat O Connor

Limerick: Joe Quaid, Steve McDonagh, Mike Nash, Joe O'Connor, Dave Clarke, Ger Hegarty, Declan Nash, Cieron Carey, Mike Houlihan, Frankie Carroll, Gary Kirby (c), Mike Galligan, TJ Ryan, Pat Heffernan, Damian Quigley

The two teams meet in a final for the first time. Limerick, who haven't won one since 1973, lead 19-14 with only five minutes left, thanks mainly to Quigley, who scores eight points in the first half, including a brilliant reverse flick for his second goal. Two goals in a minute regain the lead for Offaly, then Billy Dooley scores three points in a row to wrap things up. Offaly have won the championship three times, all since 1981. The Dooleys are all brothers. Carroll's brothers Mossie & Brian played in the 1980 final.

Ice hockey

World Championships

Men

25 April – 8 May 1994
Bolzano, Val di Fassa, Milan
(the first time Italy host the championships since 1934)

Group A	P	W	T	L	F	A	Pts
Canada	5	5	0	0	24	7	10
Russia	5	4	0	1	30	7	8
Italy	5	3	0	2	17	15	6
Austria	5	1	1	3	15	15	3
Germany	5	1	1	3	9	14	3
G Britain	5	0	0	5	7	44	0

Britain, competing at the highest level for the first time since 1962, face Russia (for the first time ever) in their opening match and aren't disgraced by a 12-3 defeat. 3-0 down, they score their first goal (through Terry Kurtenbach) after 9 mins. Britain are the only team to concede 10 goals in a game during the qualifying stages. Their full results: Russia 3-12, Germany 0-4, Italy 2-10, Canada 2-8, Austria 0-10 (Austria qualify for the quarter-finals for the first time since 1953), and – in a play-off – Norway 2-5, which condemns them to an immediate return to Pool B, three goals in less than two minutes keeping Norway up. GB coach Alex Dampier: 'We should never have been promoted to Pool A...We're a Pool B nation.' No arguments here.

Group B	P	W	T	L	F	A	Pts
Finland	5	4	1	0	29	11	9
Sweden	5	3	1	1	22	11	7
USA	5	3	0	2	21	19	6
Czech Rep	5	1	2	2	15	17	4
France	5	1	0	4	8	25	2
Norway	5	0	2	3	9	21	2

The USA's 7-2 defeat v Finland is changed to 7-0 when one of the Americans fails a drugs test.

Quarter-finals

Canada	3	Czech	2
Sweden	7	Italy	2
USA	3	Russia	1
Finland	10	Austria	0

Semi-finals

Canada	6	Sweden	0

Finland	8	USA	0

3rd-Place final

Sweden	7	USA	2

Final

Canada	2	Finland	1

Canada win the title for the first time since 1961. Finland have never won it.

Women

11-17 April 1994 Lake Placid, NY

Group A	P	W	T	L	F	A	Pts
Canada	3	3	0	0	27	3	6
China	3	1	1	1	13	12	3
Sweden	3	1	1	1	10	13	3
Norway	3	0	0	3	2	24	0

Group B	P	W	T	L	F	A	Pts
USA	3	3	0	0	24	1	6
Finland	3	2	0	1	31	3	4
Switzerland	3	1	0	2	2	20	2
Germany	3	0	0	3	2	35	0

Finland win 13-0 v Switzerland and 17-1 v Germany, who lose 16-0 to the USA.

Semi-finals

Canada	4	Finland	1
USA	14	China	3

3rd-Place final

Finland	8	China	1

Final

Canada	6	USA	3

NHL (Stanley Cup) 1993-94

Eastern Conference

Northeast Division	W	D	L	F	A	Pts
Pittsburgh Penguins	44	13	27	299	285	101
Boston Bruins	42	13	29	289	252	97
Montreal Canadiens	41	14	29	283	248	96
Buffalo Sabres	43	9	32	282	218	95
Quebec Nordiques	34	8	42	277	292	76
Hartford Whalers	27	9	48	227	288	63
Ottawa Senators	14	9	61	201	397	37

Atlantic Division						
New York Rangers	52	8	24	299	231	112
New Jersey Devils	47	12	25	306	220	106
Washington Capitals	39	10	35	277	263	88
New York Islanders	36	12	36	282	264	84
Florida Panthers	33	17	34	233	233	83
Philadelphia Flyers	35	10	39	294	314	80
Tampa Bay Lightning	30	11	43	71	224	71

Western Conference

Central Division						
Detroit Red Wings	46	8	30	356	275	100
Toronto Maple Leafs	43	12	29	280	243	98
Dallas Stars	42	13	29	286	265	97
St Louis Blues	40	11	33	270	283	91
Chicago Blackhawks	39	9	36	254	240	87
Winnipeg Jets	24	9	51	245	344	57

Pacific Division						
Calgary Flames	42	13	29	302	256	97
Vancouver Canucks	41	3	40	279	276	85
San José Sharks	33	16	35	252	265	82
Mighty Ducks of Anaheim	33	5	46	229	251	71
Los Angeles Kings	27	12	45	294	322	66
Edmonton Oilers	25	14	45	261	305	64

Yes, seven teams in each Eastern division, six in the Western, although Anaheim's name's worth two of any other. All teams play 84 games.

1993-94: regular season statistics

Games

86	Bob Kudelski	Ottawa & Florida
85	Glenn Anderson	Toronto & NY Rangers
85	Mark Lamb	Ottawa & Philadelphia
85	Joe Reekie	Tampa Bay & Washington

Points (Goals & Assists)			Gls	Assists
130	Wayne Gretzky	LA	38	92
120	Sergei Fedorov	Detroit	56	64
112	Adam Oates	Boston	32	80

Goals

60	Pavel Bure	Vancouver
57	Brett Hull	St Louis
56	Sergei Fedorov	Detroit

Assists

92	Wayne Gretzky	LA
84	Doug Gilmour	Toronto
80	Adam Oates	Boston

By the end of the 1993-94 season, the legendary Gretzky holds more than 60 NHL all-time records, including those for most points (2458), goals (802, in 15 seasons, overtaking Gordie Howe's 801 set in 26) and assists (1655).

Quarter finals

* overtime

Eastern Conference

NY Rangers	NY Islanders	4-0

6-0, 6-0, 5-1, 5-2

Washington	Pittsburgh	4-2

5-3, 1-2, 2-0, 4-1, 2-3, 6-3

New Jersey	Buffalo	4-3

0-2, 2-1, 2-1, 3-5, 5-3, 0-1*, 2-1

Boston	Montreal	4-3

3-2, 2-3, 6-3, 2-5, 1-2*, 3-2, 5-3

Western Conference

San José	Detroit	4-3

5-4, 0-4, 2-3, 4-3, 6-4, 1-7, 3-2

Vancouver	Calgary	4-3

5-0, 5-7, 2-4, 2-3, 2-1*, 3-2*, 4-3*

Toronto	Chicago	4-2

5-1, 1-0*, 4-5, 3-4*, 1-0, 1-0

Dallas	St Louis	4-0

5-3, 4-2, 5-4*, 2-1

Vancouver, 3-1 down, win each of the last three games in overtime, Pavel Bure scoring the very last goal in the second extra period.

Semi finals

Eastern Conference

NY Rangers	Washington	4-1

6-3, 5-2, 3-0, 2-4, 4-3

New Jersey	Boston	4-2

1-2, 5-6*, 4-2, 5-4*, 2-0, 5-3

Western Conference

Toronto	San José	4-3

2-3, 5-1, 2-5, 8-3, 2-5, 3-2*, 4-2

Vancouver	Dallas	4-1

6-4, 3-0, 3-4, 2-1*, 4-2

Finals

Eastern Conference

NY Rangers	New Jersey	4-3

3-4*, 4-0, 3-2*, 1-3, 1-4, 4-2, 2-1*

Each time, the Rangers' overtime goal is scored in the second period by Stephane Matteau.

Western Conference

Vancouver	Toronto	4-1

2-3*, 4-3, 4-0, 2-0, 4-3*

Stanley Cup Play-offs

Game 1 *31 May 1994 Madison Square Garden*

NY Rangers	2	Vancouver	3*
Larmer, Kovalev		Hedican, Gelinas, Adams	

The Canucks hold out till overtime thanks to goalminder Kirk McLean, who saves 52 shots.

Game 2 *2 June 1994 Madison Square Garden*

NY Rangers	3	Vancouver	1
Lidster, Anderson		Momesso	
Leetch			

Game 3 *4 June 1994 Vancouver*

Vancouver	1	NY Rangers	5
Bure		Leetch 2, Anderson,	
		Larmer, Kovalev	

Bure puts Vancouver ahead before being sent off.

Game 4 *7 June 1994 Vancouver*

Vancouver	2	NY Rangers	4
Linden, Ronning		Leetch, Zubov, Kovalev,	
		Larmer	

Again the Rangers come back to win, this time from 2-0 down after the first period. At 2-1, Bure (it's not his series) misses a penalty.

Game 5 *9 June 1994 Madison Square Garden*

NY Rangers	3	Vancouver	6
Lidster, Larmer		Brown, Courtnall, Bure 3	
Messier		Babych	

Yet again the Canucks let a lead slip (upping the ante to 3-0), but this time come back themselves after conceding three goals in five minutes.

Game 6 *11 June 1994 Vancouver*

Vancouver	4	NY Rangers	1
Brown 2, Courtnall 2		Kovalev	

Once again goalminder MacLean keeps Vancouver in it, saving 28 shots to force the final to a seventh game for the first time since 1987.

GAME 7 *14 June 1994 Madison Square Garden*

NY Rangers	3	Vancouver	2
Leetch, Graves		Linden 2	
Messier			

The Rangers take a 2-0 first-period lead and hang on to end a sequence as famous as the club itself by winning the title for the first time since 1940 (almost incidentally, the Canucks have never won it at all). NY coach Mike Keenan has previously lost in the final with Philadelphia & Chicago. Mark Messier, who scores the deciding goal, won the Cup five times with Edmonton.

NHL (Stanley Cup) 1994-95

A pay dispute (millionaires v billionaires) leads to an owners' lock-out which lasts 103 days, leading to a reduction in the number of matches played.

British National League 1993-94

Premier division	P	W	D	L	F	A	Pts
Cardiff Devils	44	39	0	5	422	220	78
Fife Flyers	44	27	2	15	304	192	56
Sheffield Steelers	44	28	4	12	313	198	55
Nottingham Panthers	44	26	4	12	288	224	54
Murrayfield Racers	44	27	2	15	385	286	51
Durham Wasps	44	24	2	18	316	284	50
Whitley Warriors	44	23	4	17	282	298	50
Humberside Hawks	44	18	4	22	301	308	40
Basingstoke Beavers	44	11	6	27	255	344	28
Bracknell Bees	44	11	3	20	220	320	25
Peterborough Pirates	44	9	3	32	239	398	21
Teesside Bombers	44	5	0	39	238	491	10

Sheffield & Murrayfield each have five points deducted for an illegal wage structure.

British Championship

Final
24 April 1994 Wembley

Cardiff	12	Sheffield	1
Chinn 4, McEwen 2,		Neil	
Ruggles 2, Brebant 2,			
Townsend, I Cooper			

The steel bubble bursts in no uncertain terms. In their first season in the Premier Division, Sheffield surprise everyone by going almost all the way, but lose by the biggest margin in any final. Brothers Ian & Stephen Cooper have been on the winning side in seven of the last eight finals.

B&H Cup 1993

Final
4 Dec 1993 Sheffield Arena

Murrayfield	6	Cardiff	2
Palmer 2, Hand 2		Chinn, Brebant	
Pentland, Lovell			

Murrayfield goalminder Moray Hanson saves 37 shots.

B&H Cup 1994

Final
4 Dec 1994 Sheffield

Nottingham	7	Cardiff	2
Blaisdell 3, Brebant 2		McEwen, Cooper	
Hunt, Adey			

Rick Brebant, who scored for Cardiff in the 1993 match, scores against them here. Coach Mike Blaisdell, in his last match as a player, leads the way to Nottingham's first major trophy since 1989.

Judo

World Championships

30 Sep - 3 Oct 1993 Hamilton, Ontario

Men

UNDER 60 kg
1	Ryuki Sonoda	JAP
2	Nazim Guseinov	AZER
3eq	Georgi Vazagachvili	GEO
3eq	Richard Trautmann	GER

UNDER 65 kg
1	Yukimasa Nakamura	JAP
2	Eric Born	SWI
3eq	Udo Quellmalz	GER
3eq	Sergei Kosminin	RUS

UNDER 71 kg
1	Chung Hoon	S KOR
2	Bertalan Hajtos	HUN
3eq	Rogerio Cardoso	BRZ
3eq	Daisuke Hideshima	JAP
7eq	*Danny Kingston*	*UK*

UNDER 78kg
1	Chun Ki-young	S KOR
2	Hidehiko Yoshida	JAP
3eq	Darcel Yandzi	FRA
3eq	Jason Morris	USA

UNDER 86 kg
1	Yoshio Nakamura	JAP
2	Nick Gill	CAN
3eq	Leon Villar	SPA
3eq	Adrian Croitoru	ROM
7eq	*David Southby*	*UK*

UNDER 95 kg
1	Antal Kovacs	HUN
2	Aurelio Miguel	BRZ
3eq	Stéphane Traineau	FRA
3eq	Marc Meiling	GER

OVER 95 kg
1	David Douillet	FRA
2	Dav Khakhaleichvili	GEO
3eq	Frank Möller	GER
3eq	Sergei Kosorotov	RUS

OPEN
1	Rafal Kubacki	POL
2	Henry Stöhr	GER
3eq	Naoyo Ogawa	JAP
3eq	Dav Khakhaleichvili	GEO

Women

UNDER 48 kg
1	Ryoko Tamura	JAP
2	Li Ai-yue	CHN
3eq	Giovanna Tortora	ITA
3eq	Joyce Heron	UK

UNDER 52 kg
1	Verdecia Rodriguez	CUBA
2	Almudena Muñoz	SPA
3eq	Wakaba Suzuki	JAP
3eq	Cécile Nowak	FRA
5eq	*Sharon Rendle*	*UK*

UNDER 56 kg
1	Nicola Fairbrother	UK
2	Chiyori Tateno	JAP
3eq	Jessica Gal	HOL
3eq	Morales Gonzalez	CUBA

UNDER 61 kg
1	Gella Van de Cavaye	BEL
2	Yael Arad	ISR
3eq	Diane Bell	UK
3eq	Zulueta Betran	CUBA

UNDER 66 kg
1	Cho Min-sun	S KOR
2	Liiko Ogasawa	USA
3eq	Zhang Di	CHN
3eq	Odalys Reve Jimenez	CUBA

UNDER 72 kg
1	Leng Chun-hui	CHN
2	Kate Howey	UK
3eq	Kim Mi-jung	S KOR
3eq	Victoria Kazunina	RUS

Howey comes within seven seconds of winning the gold.

OVER 72 kg
1	Johanna Hagn	GER
2	Noriko Anno	JAP
3eq	Monique van der Lee	HOL
3eq	Svetlana Gundarenko	RUS

OPEN

1	Beata Maksymowa	POL
2	Angelique Seriese	HOL
3eq	Zhang Ying	CHN
3eq	Moon Ji-yoon	S KOR

European Championships

INDIVIDUAL 19-22 May 1994 Gdansk

Men

UNDER 60 kg

1	Giovinazzo Girola	ITA
2	Nazim Guseinov	AZER
3eq	Franck Chambily	FRA
3eq	Geor Revazichvili	GEO

UNDER 65 kg

1	Vladimir Drachko	RUS
2	Jaroslaw Lewak	POL
3eq	Salim Abanoz	TURK
3eq	Benoit Campargue	FRA

UNDER 71 kg

1	Sergei Kosminin	RUS
2	Patrick Rosso	FRA
3eq	Beratalan Hajtos	HUN
3eq	René Sporleder	GER

UNDER 78 kg

1	Ryan Birch	UK
2	Johan Laats	BEL
3eq	Mark Huixinga	HOL
3eq	Patrick Reiter	AUT

UNDER 86 kg

1	Oleg Maltsev	RUS
2	Vincent Carabetta	FRA
3eq	Iverl Djikurauki	GEO
3eq	Afrian Croitoru	ROM

UNDER 95 kg

1	Pawel Nastula	POL
2	Ray Stevens	UK
3eq	Dmitry Serfuyev	RUS
3eq	Nike Hax	GER

OVER 95 kg

1	David Douillet	FRA
2	Rafal Kubacki	POL
3eq	Igor Möller	GER
3eq	Selim Tataroglu	TURK

OPEN

1	Laurent Crost	FRA
2	Harry Van Berneveld	BEL
3eq	Yevgeny Pechurov	RUS
3eq	David Khakaleichvili	GEO

Women

UNDER 48 kg

1	Jolanda Soler	SPA
2	Sylvie Meloux	FRA
3eq	Tatyana Kuvchinova	RUS
3eq	Justina Pinheiro	PORT

UNDER 52 kg

1	Ewa Krause	POL
2	Alessandra Giunghi	ITA
3eq	A von Schwichow	GER
3eq	Debbie Allan	UK

UNDER 56 kg

1	Jessica Gal	HOL
2	Nicola Fairbrother	UK
3eq	Magalle Baton	FRA
3eq	Ursula Myren	SWE

UNDER 61 kg

1	Gella Van de Cavaye	BEL
2	Diane Bell	UK
3eq	Miriam Blasco	SPA
3eq	Miroslawa Janosikova	SLVK

UNDER 66 kg

1	Rowena Sweatman	UK
2	A Anglberger	AUT
3eq	Claudia Zwiers	HOL
3eq	Radka Studakova	CZE

UNDER 72 kg

1	Ulla Werbrouck	BEL
2	Estha Essombe	FRA
3eq	Kate Howey	UK
3eq	Cristina Curto	SPA

OVER 72 kg

1	Angelique Seriese	HOL
2	Beata Maksymowa	POL
3eq	Svetlana Gundarenko	RUS
3	Raquel Barrientos	SPA

OPEN

1	Monique van der Lee	HOL
2	Christine Cicot	FRA
3eq	Irina Rodina	RUS
3eq	Beata Maksymowa	POL

TEAM Oct 1994 The Hague

QUARTER-FINALS

Germany	7	Slovenia	0
Belgium	4	Turkey	3
UK	3	Holland	3
UK 30-27 pts			
Belarus	4	Austria	3

SEMI-FINALS

Belarus	3	UK	3
Belarus 25-15 pts			

Germany	4	Belgium	2
FINAL			
Germany	6	Belarus	1

British Open
9 April 1994 NEC, Birmingham

Men

UNDER 60 kg
1. Manuel Orgaz — POL
2. Thierry Dibert — FRA
3eq. Ewan Berton — CAN
3eq. James Johnson — UK

UNDER 65 kg
1. Julian Davies — UK
2. Tsuyoshi Uchida — JAP
3eq. Paul Leishman — UK
3eq. Jürgen Grasmuch — GER

UNDER 71 kg
1. E Zymna — GER
2. Billy Cusack — UK
3eq. T Bucholz — GER
3eq. Patrick Loon — HOL

UNDER 78 kg
1. Ryan Birch — UK
2. Edelmar Zandl — BRZ
3eq. Philip Waydelich — FRA
3eq. Knut Kowak — GER

UNDER 86 kg
1. Tamaz Saakachvili — FRA
2. Stéphane Norris — FRA
3eq. Nick Gill — CAN
3eq. Alex Borderieux — FRA

UNDER 95 kg
1. Ray Stevens — UK
2. M Hax — GER
3eq. M Wirth — GER
3eq. D Knorret — GER

OVER 95 kg
1. Georges Mathonnet — FRA
2. Laurent Crost — FRA
3eq. Kasim Dahu — FRA
3eq. Rolf Koser — GER

Women

UNDER 48 kg
1. Ana Fernandez — SPA
2. Yuko Eto — JAP
3eq. Brite Siemens — GER
3eq. Yolanda Soler — SPA

UNDER 52 kg
1. Fatira Merah — FRA
2. Lizzie Floodgate — UK
3eq. A Takeda — JAP
3eq. Elise Summers — UK

UNDER 56 kg
1. Karina Nedellec — FRA
2. Narelle Hill — AUT
3eq. Barbara Dohmen — GER
3eq. Cheryle Peel — UK

UNDER 61 kg
1. Carol Kelly — UK
2. Miriam Blasco — SPA
3eq. Kirsti Weir — UK
3eq. Yuko Emoto — JAP

UNDER 66 kg
1. Karen Roberts — UK
2. Yoko Nakatachi — JAP
3eq. Sophie Roberge — CAN
3eq. Nicole Bruns — GER

UNDER 72 kg
1. Kate Howey — UK
2. Heli Syrja — FIN
3eq. Laurence Sionneau — FRA
3eq. Katarina Hakansen — SWE

OVER 72 kg
1. Monique van der Lee — HOL
2. Claudia Weber — GER
3eq. Karin Kutz — GER
3eq. Heba Rashid — EGY

British National Championships
Dec 1993 Crystal Palace

Men

Under 60 kg	Jamie Johnson
Under 65	Simon Moss
Under 71	Danny KIngston
Under 78	William Tusack
Under 86	Fitzroy Davis
Under 95	Lloyd Alexander
Over 95	William Etherington

Women

Under 48	Joyce Heron
Under 52	Debbie Allan
Under 56	Cheryle Peel
Under 61	Kirsti Weir
Under 66	Chloe Cowen
Under 72	Kate Howey
Over 72	Michelle Rogers

Lacrosse

World Cup (men)
20-30 July 1994

Premier division
Gigg Lane, Bury

Australia	26	Iroquois Nationals	11
Canada	19	England	11
Australia	28	England	7
USA	33	Japan	2
USA	16	Canada	10
Iroquois Nationals	16	Japan	2
USA	26	Iroquois Nationals	6
England	20	Japan	1
Canada	33	Japan	7
England	19	Iroquois Nationals	6
USA	15	England	4
Canada	19	Australia	11
Canada	20	Iroquois Nationals	16
USA	14	Australia	12
Australia	26	Japan	6

Semi-finals

USA	25	England	3
Australia	18	Canada	17

England lead 1-0 and are level at 1-1 before goalkeeper Alex Rastelli's own goal put the States ahead. The half-time score's 11-1.

5th-place final

Iroquois Nationals	19	Japan	13

3rd-place final

Canada	25	England	10

Final

USA	21	Australia	7

Millon 4, Morrill 4,   *Purdie 2, Buchanan 2,*
Dixon 4, Pietramala 2   *Gibson, Brewer, Toomey*
Marino 2, Shek 2, Cook,
Lockwood, Detommaso

Mark Millon finishes with 26 goals in the tournament, Dave Pietramala plays his last international before retiring. The USA have won six of the seven World Cup tournaments (including the first in 1967), losing only one of their 29 games (to Canada, who won the title, in 1978).

1st division
Manchester University

3rd-place final

Czech Rep	17	Sweden	8

Final

Scotland	12	Wales	7

Germany, appearing in the event for the first time (with a goalkeeper who took up the game a month ago), concede 100 goals (and score 7) in four games.

Modern Pentathlon

World Championships
11-16 Aug 1994 Sheffield

Men

Dmitry Svatovski	RUS	5543
Christophe Ruer	FRA	5518
Janos Martinek	HUN	5505
12 Greg Whyte	*UK*	*5366*

Svatovski wins the title for the first time. Whyte was third with only the cross-country run to come. Defending champion Richard Phelps (UK) finishes 22nd.

Team

France	16 194
UK	15 793
Belarus	15 396

Team Relay

Hungary	5279
Poland	5112
Russia	5070
12 UK	*4081*

Women

Final 13 Aug

Eva Fjellerup	DEN	5590	WR
Zhanna Shubyonik	BYL	5392	
Emese Koblo	HUN	5355	

Defending champion Fjellerup scores over 1000 pts in each discipline to win the title for a record fourth time (in five years).

TEAM

Italy	15 352
Poland	15 352
Hungary	14 683

TEAM RELAY 15 Aug

Poland	5114
Hungary	4969
Denmark	4949

British Open
3 July 1994 Milton Keynes

Men

Dominic Mahony	5433
Richard Phelps	5366
Shawn Morgan	5217

Mahony stops Phelps, the reigning world champion, from equalling Jim Fox's record of ten British titles.

Team: Army

Women

Rachel Wilmot	5487
Kate Houston	5371
Julia Allen	5244

Team: SEA-Lions

Winning is the drug

In 1994, an Italian team official admitted doping the horses of sixteen competitors (including world champion Janusz Piciak-Peciak POL) at the 1982 World Championships, leaving Daniele Masala (ITA) the easy winner. (At the time, none other than the Duke of Edinburgh denounced allegations of doping as 'lurid and satirical'.)

Motor Cycling

500cc World Championship 1994

A reminder of what always threatens: Wayne Rainey (USA), world champion three seasons in a row and winner of 24 Grands Prix, attends this year's events in a wheelchair after being partially paralysed by a fall in Italy last September.

Australian GP
27 March Eastern Creek, nr Sydney
John Kocinski   USA   Cagiva
The first GP since 1976 not won by a Japanese machine. Reigning champion Kevin Schwantz finishes fourth after breaking an arm during fitness training(!).

Malaysian GP
10 April Shah Alam, Kuala Lumpur
Mick Doohan   AUS   Honda

Japanese GP
24 April Suzuka
Kevin Schwantz   USA   Susuki
Doohan (second here) takes the lead in the championship.

Spanish GP
8 May Jerez
Mick Doohan   AUS   Honda
Doohan extends his lead in the championship by beating Schwantz by less than half a second.

Austrian GP
22 May Salzburgring, Salzburg
Mick Doohan   AUS   Honda
Doohan breaks the course record.

German GP 12 June Hockenheim
Mick Doohan   AUS   Honda

Dutch GP
25 June Assen
Mick Doohan   AUS   Honda
Doohan wins on a course he calls unfit for GP racing.

Italian GP
3 July Mugello
Mick Doohan   AUS   Honda

French GP
17 July Le Mans
Mick Doohan   AUS   Honda
Doohan's sixth successive win (which breaks Giacomo

Agostini's 1972 record) and unstoppable progress to the title (he leads by 76 pts) owe something to Schwantz's collision with Alex Criville (SPA) on the last lap. Schwantz, who spent the first half of the season with his wrist in a cast, finishes it on crutches.

British GP
24 July Donington Park
Kevin Schwantz   USA   Suzuki
Schwantz recovers from a bad crash in practice to win a 500 GP for the 25th time in his career. Doohan, who finishes second, leads the championship by 71 pts.

Czech GP
21 Aug Brno
Mick Doohan   AUS   Honda
With three races still to go, Doohan assures himself of winning the overall title for the first time. At the end of the season, he'll award himself the luxury of an operation on his right foot (involving the removal of the knuckle from each toe and other grisly manoeuvres), in which he's had virtually no movement since crashing during the 1992 Dutch TT. He moves to Honda for next season.

U.S. GP
11 Sep Laguna Seca
Luca Cadalora   ITA   Yamaha
Doohan finishes third.

Argentinian GP
25 Sep Buenos Aires
Mick Doohan   AUS   Yamaha

European GP
9 Oct Catalunya, Barcelona
Luca Cadalora   ITA   Yamaha

Final standings

317	Mick Doohan	AUS	Yamaha
174	Luca Cadalora	ITA	Yamaha
172	John Kocinski	USA	Cagiva
169	Kevin Schwantz	USA	Susuki
152	Alberto Puig	SPA	Honda
144	Alex Criville	SPA	Honda
69	*Niall McKenzie*	*UK*	*Yamaha (10th)*

250cc World Championship 1994

Australian GP
27 March Eastern Creek, nr Sydney
Max Biaggi   ITA   Aprilia
Reigning champion Tetsuya Harada (JAP) breaks four bones in his right hand in a crash during the first qualifying session. Biaggi's full christian name is Massimiliano.

Malaysian GP
10 April Shah Alam, Kuala Lumpur
Max Biaggi   ITA   Aprilia

Japanese GP
24 April Suzuka
Tadayuki Okada   JAP   Honda
Okada wins a Grand Prix for the first time.

Spanish GP
8 May Jerez
Jean-Philippe Ruggia FRA   Aprilia

Austrian GP
22 May Salzburg
Loris Capirossi   ITA   Honda

German GP
12 June Hockenheim
Loris Capirossi   ITA   Honda

Dutch GP
25 June Assen
Max Biaggi   ITA   Aprilia

Italian GP
3 July Mugello
Ralf Waldmann   GER   Honda
Biaggi crashes while leading to let Waldmann in for his first 250 GP win.

French GP
17 July Le Mans
Loris Capirossi   ITA   Honda
Biaggi, who finishes third, leads Capirossi by a single point overall.

British GP
24 July Donington Park
Loris Capirossi   ITA   Honda
Capirossi takes the overall lead from Biaggi, who crashes.

Czech GP
21 Aug Brno
Max Biaggi   ITA   Aprilia
Biaggi regains the lead, by a single point, from Capirossi. Kenny Roberts (USA), whose father Kenny snr won the 500cc world title in 1978-79-80, competes in his first GP of the season.

U.S. GP
11 Sep Laguna Seca
Doriano Romboni   ITA   Honda

Argentinian GP
25 Sep Buenos Aires
Tadayuki Okada   JAP   Honda
Okada, the only rider to score points in every race so far this season, trails Biaggi, who finishes second, by eight points with one round left.

European GP
9 Oct Catalunya, Barcelona
Max Biaggi   ITA   Aprilia
Okada finishes fourth, three seconds behind.

Final standings

234	Max Biaggi	ITA	Aprilia
214	Tadayuki Okada	JAP	Honda
199	Loris Capirossi	ITA	Honda
170	Doriano Romboni	ITA	Honda
156	Ralf Waldmann	GER	Honda
149	Jean-Philippe Ruggia	FRA	Aprilia

Biaggi & Aprilia win the title for the first time, a European machine for the first time since Mario Lega on a Morbidelli in 1977.

125cc World Championship 1994

Australian GP
27 March Eastern Creek, nr Sydney
Kazuto Sakata   JAP   Aprilia

Malaysian GP
10 April Shah Alam, Kuala Lumpur
Noboru Ueda   JAP

Japanese GP
24 April Suzuka
Takeshi Tsujimura JAP   Honda

Spanish GP
8 May Jerez
Kazuko Sakata   JAP   Aprilia

Austrian GP
22 May Salzburg
Dirk Raudies   GER   Honda

German GP
12 June Hockenheim
Dirk Raudies   GER   Honda

Dutch GP
25 June Assen
Takeshi Tsujimura JAP   Honda

Italian GP
3 July Mugello
Noboru Ueda   JAP   Honda

French GP
17 July Le Mans
Noboru Ueda   JAP   Honda

British GP
24 July Donington Park
Takeshi Tsujimura JAP   Honda

Czech GP
21 Aug Brno
Kazuko Sakata   JAP   Aprilia
Sakata's easy win brings him to the brink of the overall title: he leads Ueda 208-157 with only three rounds left.

U.S. GP
11 Sep Laguna Seca
Takeshi Tsujimura JAP   Honda
Sakata doesn't finish but still leads the table by 40 pts.

Argentinian GP
25 Sep Buenos Aires
Jorge Martínez   SPA   Yamaha
Sakata, who finishes ninth, does enough to become the first Japanese to win a world title on a European machine. Martínez, a former world champion, wins a GP for the 37th time, Yamaha's first in the 125 class since 1974.

European GP
9 Oct Catalunya, Barcelona
Dirk Raudies   GER   Honda
Raudies takes some late consolation for the loss of the overall title.

Final standings
224	Kazuko Sakata	JAP	Aprilia
194	Noboru Ueda	JAP	Honda
190	Takeshi Tsujimura	JAP	Honda
162	Dirk Raudies	GER	Honda
160	Peter Oettl	GER	Aprilia
135	Jorge Martínez	SPA	Yamaha

Last year, Sakata finished second to Raudies in nine races.

Sidecars World Championship 1994

British GP 1
2 May Donington Park
Derek Brindley & Paul Hutchinson   UK   LCR

German GP
12 June Hockenheim
Rolf Biland & Kurt Waltisperg   SWI   Swissauto

Dutch GP
25 June Assen
Rolf Biland & Kurt Waltisperg   SWI   Swissauto

Austrian GP
17 July Zeltweg
Darren Dixon & Andy Hetherington   UK   Padgett-LCR-ADM

British GP 2
23 July Donington Park
Rolf Biland & Kurt Waltisperg   SWI   Swissauto

Czech GP
21 Aug Brno
Rolf Biland & Kurt Waltisperg   SWI   Swissauto

Dutch GP
11 Sep Assen
Rolf Biland & Kurt Waltisperg   SWI   Swissauto
Biland & Waltisperg retain the overall title, Biland setting a new record by winning it for the 7th time (his first was in 1978). This is his 75th GP win; no-one else has won more than 27.

European GP
9 Oct Catalunya, Barcelona
Darren Dixon & Andy Hetherington   UK   Padgett-LCR-ADM

Final Standings
141	Rolf Biland & Kurt Waltisperg	SWI	Swissauto
104	Steve Webster & Adolf Hanni	UK/SWI	LCR
96	David Brindley & Paul Hutchinson	UK	LCR

Superbikes World Championship 1994

British
1 May Donington Park
Race 1	Carl Fogarty	UK	Ducati
Race 2	Scott Russell	USA	Kawasaki

Illegal fuel costs Aaron Slight (NZ, Honda) half the 34 points he wins for two second places (they're restored later in the season, then lost again at an appeal tribunal).

German
8 May Hockenheim
Race 1	Scott Russell	USA	Kawasaki
Race 2	Scott Russell	USA	Kawasaki

In the absence of Fogarty, who breaks an arm in qualifying, Russell seems to have put himself firmly on course towards retaining the title.

Italian
29 May Misano
Race 1	Scott Russell	USA	Kawasaki
Race 2	Giancarlo Falappa	ITA	Ducati

Falappa would have challenged even more strongly for the overall title (he takes his total to 72 points here) but for a near-fatal crash (which cost him over 30 lbs in weight) during testing for the next round, in Spain.

Spanish
19 June Albacete

| Race 1 | Carl Fogarty | UK | Ducati |
| Race 2 | Carl Fogarty | UK | Ducati |

Austrian
17 July Zeltweg

| Race 1 | Carl Fogarty | UK | Ducati |
| Race 2 | Carl Fogarty | UK | Ducati |

Indonesian
21 Aug Sentul

| Race 1 | James Whitham | UK | Ducati |
| Race 2 | Carl Fogarty | UK | Ducati |

Whitham wins a World Superbike race for the first time. Fogarty doesn't finish the first race and trails Slight overall, despite his six wins to the N Zealander's none.

Japanese
28 Aug Sugo

| Race 1 | Scott Russell | USA | Kawasaki |
| Race 2 | Scott Russell | USA | Kawasaki |

Russell closes to within six points of Slight.

Dutch
11 Sep Assen

| Race 1 | Carl Fogarty | UK | Ducati |
| Race 2 | Carl Fogarty | UK | Ducati |

San Marino
25 Sep Mugello

| Race 1 | Scott Russell | USA | Kawasaki |
| Race 2 | Carl Fogarty | UK | Ducati |

Fogarty, who finishes second in the first race, increases his lead over Slight to 18 points.

Spanish
2 Oct Jerez

| Race 1 | Scott Russell | USA | Kawasaki |
| Race 2 | Scott Russell | USA | Kawasaki |

Russell moves to within five points of Fogarty, who chooses the wrong tyres and finishes only 14th & fifth but leads Slight (eighth & tenth) by 17 overall. Ducati compound the error by not instructing other riders to let Fogarty through, which costs him at least another two points.

Australian
30 Oct Phillip Island, Victoria

| Race 1 | Carl Fogarty | UK | Ducati |
| Race 2 | Anthony Gobert | AUS | Kawasaki |

The two title challengers exchange the lead in the first race before Fogarty breaks the lap record to win it. Russell, eight points behind going into the second, punctures and loses his title. Gobert, who recently became the youngest ever winner of his national title (19), wins only the second world championship race he starts.

Final standings

305	Carl Fogarty	UK	Ducati
280	Scott Russell	USA	Kawasaki
277	Aaron Slight	NZ	Honda
158	Doug Polen	USA	Honda
153	Simon Crafar	NZ	Honda
148	Andy Meklau	FRA	Ducati

Fogarty becomes the first British rider to win a solo world road racing title since Barry Sheene in the 1977 500cc.

Superbikes British Championship 1994

Ian Simpson	Norton	319 pts
Jim Moodie	Yamaha	287
Phil Borley	Norton	284

Isle of Man TT Races 1994

They could only take place on an island with no speed restrictions outside its towns and villages. Since the current course was first used, in 1911, an average of two riders per year have died during the TT races. Mark Farmer & Rob Mitchell keep the grisly trend going in practice this time (Nos.162 & 163 on the toll roll). Barry Sheene, whose heart certainly wasn't faint, raced there once and only once: 'It's impossible to make the course even reasonably safe.'

Formula 1 4 June
Steve Hislop　　　　　Honda　　1h53:37.2
Joey Dunlop's brother Robert undergoes six hours of surgery, then a second operation, after breaking an arm and a leg in a collision with a wall.

Sidecar A 4 June
Rob Fisher & Michael Wynn　Yamaha　1h04:14.6

125 cc 6 June
Joey Dunlop　　　　　Honda　　1h25:38.0

Single Cylinder 6 June
Jim Moodie　　　　　Yamaha　　1h21:21.6
Moodie's first win on the island.

Supersport 600 6 June
Iain Duffus　　　　　Yamaha　　1h18:32.0

Junior 8 June
Joey Dunlop　　　　　Honda　　1h18:57.8
The 42-y-o Dunlop's 17th TT win adds to his own record.

Supersport 400 8 June
Jim Moodie　　　　　Yamaha　　1h23:41.2

Sidecar B 8 June
Rob Fisher & Michael Wynn　Yamaha　1h05:41.0

Senior 10 June

Steve Hislop	Honda	1h53:53.8

Hislop's 11th TT win and third in this event. Dunlop, trying to become the first rider ever to win three TT races in one week, finishes third.

Endurance

World Championship 1994

Le Mans
17 April (24 hrs)
Terry Rymer (UK), Adrien Morillas (FRA),
Jean-Louis Battistini (FRA)   Kawasaki

Belgian
10 July, Spa (24 hrs)
Adrien Morillas (FRA), Jean-Louis
Battistini (FRA), Denis Bonoris (FRA)   Kawasaki

Suzuka
31 July (8 hrs)
Doug Polen (USA), Aaron Slight (NZ)   Honda

Bol D'Or
18 Sep, Paul Ricard
Christian Sarron (FRA), Dominique
Sarron (FRA), Yasutomo Nagai (JAP)   Yamaha

After starting from pole (and leading the race) five times, C Sarron at last wins the event for the first time, partnered by his younger brother and the first Japanese to win the race. Morillas' sixth place is enough for the overall title.

Final Standings

Adrien Morillas	FRA	100
Eric Gomez	FRA	90
Philippe Monneret	FRA	90

Moto Cross

Open World Championship 1994

Swiss GP
10 April Payerne

Gert-Jan van Doorn	HOL	Honda

Van Doorn's only other Grand Prix win was in the 1988 Swedish 250cc.

Austrian GP
24 April Sittendorf

Joel Smets	BEL	Vertamati

Ulster GP
8 May Ballykelly

Marcus Hansson	SWE	Honda

British GP
15 May Hawkstone Park

Jacky Martens	BEL	Husqvarna

Italian GP
29 May Arco di Trento

Billy Liles	USA	Honda

Smets & Martens crash out.

Slovakian GP
5 June Svereepec, Bratislava

Mervyn Anstie	UK	Honda

Smets, championship leader Marcus Hansson (SWE) and reigning world champion Martens boycott the second race when heavy rain turns the course to mud.

Dutch GP
19 June Mill, Nijmegen

Jacky Martens	BEL	Husqvarna

Portuguese GP
3 July Agueda

Jacky Martens	BEL	Husqvarna

Belgian GP
7 Aug Namu

Marcus Hansson	SWE	Honda

German GP
21 Aug Holzerlingen, Stuttgart

Joel Smets	BEL	Vertemati

Drama to the very end. In the first race of the day, Hansson finishes only 13th then comes to blows with Van Doorn, whom he accuses of obstruction. In the second, the last of the championship, Martens (now joint overall leader) crashes and finishes 10th, leaving Hansson to hold on for fourth and become the first Swede to win the title since Hakan Carlqvist in 1983 and the first non-factory rider since Gary Hocking of Rhodesia in 1961.

Final Standings

328	Marcus Hansson	SWE	Honda
321	Jacky Martens	BEL	Husqvarna
299	Joel Smets	BEL	Vertemati

British Open Championship 1994

Kurt Nicoll	Honda	420
Mark Eastwood	Honda	320
Rob Herring	Kawasaki	267

Nicoll, who retains the title, wins it for the sixth time, breaking the record he shared with Graham Noyce & Dave Thorpe.

250cc World Championship 1994

Spanish GP
20 March Talavera

Donny Schmit	USA	Yamaha

Dutch GP
27 March Valkenswaard

Stefan Everts	BEL	Kawasaki

Italian GP
24 April Montevarchi

Stefan Everts	BEL	Kawasaki

Austrian GP
1 May Schwanenstadt

Stefan Everts	BEL	Kawasaki

French GP
8 May Ernée

Greg Albertijn	SAF	Suzuki

Polish GP
15 May Gdynia

Greg Albertijn	SAF	Suzuki

Belgian GP
12 June Lommel

Stefan Everts	BEL	Kawasaki

Albertijn loses his overall lead in the championship when his machine runs out of fuel in both races.

British GP
19 June Foxhill, Wiltshire

Yves Demaria	FRA	Honda

Demaria wins a GP for the first time. Albertijn, who wins the first of the day's two races, regains the championship lead.

Czech GP
26 June Holice

Yves Demaria	FRA	Honda

Swedish GP
10 July Uddevalla

Stefan Everts	BEL	Kawasaki

Everts regains the overall lead from Albertijn.

Finnish GP
17 July Heinola

Yves Demaria	FRA	Honda

Albertijn's path to the title is cleared by the crash that breaks Everts' collarbone in practice.

U.S. GP
31 July Budds Creek

Yves Demaria	FRA	Honda

Venezuelan GP
7 Aug Maracay

Yves Demaria	FRA	Honda

Japanese GP
21 Aug

Yves Demaria	FRA	Honda

Albertijn, who finishes fifth, leads the championship by 17 pts with one round to go.

German GP
4 Sep Gaildorf, Stuttgart

Kurt Nicoll	UK	Honda

Nicoll, winner of ten GPs, four times runner-up in the 500cc world championship, wins a 250 GP for the first time.

Final Standings

Greg Albertijn	SAF	Suzuki	403
Stefan Everts	BEL	Kawasaki	392
Yves Demaria	FRA	Honda	367
5 Kurt Nicoll	*UK*	*Honda*	*299*

No British rider's won the title since Neil Hudson in 1982.

125cc World Championship 1994

Italian GP
27 March Bra

Bob Moore	USA	Yamaha

French GP
10 April Chaulieu

Mickael Pichon	FRA	Honda

Spanish GP
15 May Bellpuig

Alessio Chiodi	ITA	Honda

Swedish GP
5 June Hagabanen

Bob Moore	USA	Yamaha

Hungarian GP
19 June Kaposvar

Alessio Chiodi	ITA	Honda

Dutch GP
3 July Oss

Dave Strijbos	HOL	Suzuki

San Marino GP
17 July Borgo Maggiore

Alessio Chiodi	ITA	Honda

German GP
31 July Goldbach

Bob Moore	USA	Yamaha

British GP
7 Aug Foxhill, Swindon

Bob Moore	USA	Yamaha

Belgian GP
28 Aug Borgloon
Bob Moore	USA	Yamaha

Final Standings
Bob Moore	USA	Yamaha	364
Alessio Chiodi	ITA	Honda	316
Pedro Tragter	HOL	Suzuki	264

British 125cc Championship 1994

Neil Prince	Kawasaki	302
John Barfoot	Yamaha	283
Rikki Priest	Kawasaki	271

Prince wins the title for the first time.

Sidecar World Championship 1994

24 April Wohlen, Switzerland
Karl Fussenegger & Jo Meusberger	AUT	Zabel

1 May Betecom, Belgium
Andreas Führer & Adi Kaeser	GER	Kawasaki

8 May Oss, Holland
Jacky Janssen & Wiljam Janssen	HOL	KTMEML

15 May Hawkstone Park, England
Chris Etheridge & Gary Withers	UK	Zabel VMC

12 June Castelnau de Levis, France
Klaus Weinmann & Thomas Weinmann
	GER	KTMEML

10 July Bielstein, Germany
Wolfgang Kühn & Jochen Zimmermann
	GER	Kawasaki

14 Aug Rudersberg, Germany
Andreas Führer & Adi Kaeser	GER	KTMEML

21 Aug Lierop, Holland
Günther Goovaerts & Sven Verbrugge	BEL	KTMEML

18 Sep Oubenice, Czech Rep
Dietmar Schmid & Lothar Jehle	GER	Zabel EML

25 Sep Niederwil, Switzerland
Klaus Weinmann & Thomas Weinmann
	GER	KTMEML

Etheridge (broken shoulder) and Withers (twisted knee) are hospitalised by a bad crash.

Final Standings
232 Andreas Führer & Adi Kaeser	GER	KTMEML
204 Karl Fussenegger & Jo Meusberger	AUT	Zabel
199 Klaus Weinmann & Thomas Weinmann		
	GER	KTMEML
108 Chris Etheridge & Gary Withers	*UK*	*Zabel*

Führer & Kaeser retain the title. Etheridge and Withers finish 10th.

British Championship

Chris Etheridge & Gary Withers	338 pts
Colin Philpott & Jason Peters	334
Simon Brown & David Keene	266

Etheridge & Withers take the title for the fourth consecutive year.

Moto Cross des Nations
11 Sep 1994 Roggenburg, SWI

Heat 1	Yves Demaria	FRA	Honda
Heat 2	Marnicq Bervoerts	BEL	Suzuki
Heat 3	Mike LaRocco	USA	Kawasaki

Overall
G Britain	9
USA	11
France	13
Belgium	18
Germany	28
Holland	29

The USA had won the event for the last 13 years, Britain not since 1967. British team: Kurt Nicoll (500 Honda), Rob Herring (250 Kawasaki), Paul Malin (125 Yamaha).

Motor Racing

Formula 1 World Championship 1993

JAPANESE GP
24 Oct Suzuka

Ayrton Senna	BRZ	McLaren	1h 40: 27.912
Alain Prost	FRA	Williams	11.435s behind
Mika Hakkinen	FIN	McLaren	26.129
Damon Hill	UK	Williams	1m 23.538
Rubens Barrichello	BRZ	Jordan	1m 35.101
Eddie Irvine	UK	Jordan	1m 46.421

POLE: Prost

OVERALL: Prost 93, Hill 65, Senna 63, Schumacher 52

In December, Senna receives a suspended two-race suspension for hitting Irvine with a left hook after the race.

AUSTRALIAN GP
7 Nov Adelaide

Ayrton Senna	BRZ	McLaren	1h43:27.476
Alain Prost	FRA	Williams	9.259s
Damon Hill	UK	Williams	33.902
Jean Alesi	FRA	Ferrari	1 lap
Gerhard Berger	AUT	Ferrari	1 lap
Martin Brundle	UK	Ligier	1 lap

POLE: Senna

Final Standings 1993

DRIVERS

99	Alain Prost	FRA	Williams
73	Ayrton Senna	BRZ	McLaren
69	Damon Hill	UK	Williams
52	Michael Schumacher	GER	Benetton
20	Riccardo Patrese	ITA	Benetton
16	Jean Alesi	FRA	Ferrari
11	Johnny Herbert	UK	Lotus
10	Mark Blundell	UK	Ligier

CONSTRUCTORS

168	Williams
84	McLaren
72	Benetton
28	Ferrari
23	Ligier
12	Lotus, Sauber

Where to begin? The 1994 Formula 1 season had everything. Sadly, that included several accidents. Roland Ratzenberger's death shouldn't have been mourned any less than Ayrton Senna's but inevitably was, partly because it proved that the sport can kill even its very best. Talk of an end to motor racing was bandied about as usual, and as usual not for long – before attention switched to a vibrant, overheated two-horse race for the title: Michael Schumacher versus Damon Hill.

It took the ingredients of famous championships from the past. The points deducted from Benetton (James Hunt 1976), the decisive last race (Hunt v Lauda, Hawthorn v Moss 1958, Surtees v Hill's father Graham 1964) ending with the championship leader ramming his closest challenger out of contention (Prost to Senna 1989, Senna to Prost 1990). Great stuff.

Hill, outclassed by Schumacher for most of the season, suddenly drove like a champion elect in Japan but ultimately finished another dignified British second (voted BBC Sports Personality of the Year in a classic nearly-man award) and would have been an unsatisfactory champion after all the points taken from the German, who won the title (probably just the first of several for him) deservedly as well as controversially. Next season, with David Coulthard confirmed alongside Hill at Williams and Nigel Mansell installed at McLaren, should be a scorcher, even a classic .

Formula 1 World Championship 1994

BRAZILIAN GP
27 March Interlagos

Michael Schumacher	GER	Benetton	1h35:38.759
Damon Hill	UK	Williams	1 lap
Jean Alesi	FRA	Ferrari	1 lap
Rubens Barrichello	BRZ	Jordan	1 lap
Ukyo Katayama	JAP	Tyrell	2 laps
Karl Wendlinger	AUT	Sauber	2 laps

POLE: Senna
OVERALL: Schumacher 10, Hill 6, Alesi 3

Ayrton Senna spins out after 55 laps when lying second.

PACIFIC GP
17 April Aida, Japan

Michael Schumacher	GER	Benetton	1h46:01.693
Gerhard Berger	AUT	Ferrari	1:15.30
Rubens Barrichello	BRZ	Jordan	1 lap
Christian Fittipaldi	BRZ	Footwork	1 lap
Heinz-Harald Frentzen	GER	Sauber	1 lap
Erik Comas	FRA	Larrousse	3 laps

POLE: Senna
OVERALL: Schumacher 20, Barrichello 7, Hill, Berger 6

Senna crashes out at the very first corner.

SAN MARINO GP
1 May Imola

Michael Schumacher	GER	Benetton	1h28:28.642
Nicola Larini	ITA	Ferrari	54.942
Mika Hakkinen	FIN	McLaren	1:10.679
Karl Wendlinger	AUT	Sauber	1:13.658
Ukyo Katayama	JAP	Tyrell	1 lap
Damon Hill	UK	Williams	1 lap

POLE: Senna
OVERALL: Schumacher 30, Barrichello, Hill 7, Larini, Berger 6

Benetton win again, but their controversial season begins here: it's bruited that they use a kind of illegal 'launch computer' to set Schumacher on his way. All of which is of course overshadowed by the deaths of Ratzenberger & Senna.

Most pole positions
Formula 1 world championship races

65	Ayrton Senna	BRZ	1985-94
34	Nigel Mansell	UK	1984-94
33	Jim Clark	UK	1962-68
33	Alain Prost	FRA	1981-93
29	Juan Manuel Fangio	ARG	1950-58

MONACO GP
15 May Monte Carlo

Michael Schumacher	GER	Benetton	1h49:55.372
Martin Brundle	UK	McLaren	37.546
Gerhard Berger	AUT	Ferrari	1:16.824
Andrea de Cesaris	ITA	Jordan	1 lap
Jean Alesi	FRA	Ferrari	1 lap
Michele Alboreto	ITA	Minardi	1 lap

POLE: Schumacher *(in Senna's absence, his first)*
OVERALL: Schumacher 40, Berger 10, Barrichello, Hill 7

Like the San Marino, the race is run in the shadow of a bad crash, which leaves Wendlinger in a coma after the first day of practice. It takes him three weeks to recover consciousness.

SPANISH GP
29 May Barcelona

Damon Hill	UK	Williams	1h36:14.474
Michael Schumacher	GER	Benetton	24.166
Mark Blundell	UK	Tyrell	1m26.969
Jean Alesi	FRA	Ferrari	1 lap
Pier-Luigi Martini	ITA	Minardi	1 lap
Eddie Irvine	UK	Jordan	1 lap

POLE: Schumacher
OVERALL: Schumacher 46, Hill 17, Berger 10

The crashes pile up. Portuguese driver Pedro Lamy (Mugen) breaks both kneecaps at Silverstone while practising for the race in Spain, then – after the newly-formed Grand Prix Drivers' Association calls off its threatened boycott of the GP – Andrea Montermini (Simtek) is hospitalised by a crash in qualifying. A faulty gearbox leaves Schumacher in fifth gear virtually throughout and Mansell's 1992 record of starting the season with five consecutive wins survives. Hill dedicates his win to Senna.

CANADIAN GP
12 June Montreal

Michael Schumacher	GER	Benetton	1h44:31.887
Damon Hill	UK	Williams	39.660
Jean Alesi	FRA	Ferrari	1m13.388
Gerhard Berger	AUT	Ferrari	1m15.609
David Coulthard	UK	Williams	1 lap
JJ Lehto	FIN	Benetton	1 lap

POLE: Schumacher
OVERALL: Schumacher 56, Hill 23, Berger, Alesi 13

Christian Fittipaldi (BRZ, Footwork) is disqualified after finishing sixth. In only his second Grand Prix, Coulthard scores his first points.

FRENCH GP
3 July Magny-Cours

Michael Schumacher	GER	Benetton	1h38:35.704
Damon Hill	UK	Williams	12.642
Gerhard Berger	AUT	Ferrari	52.765
Heinz-Harald Frentzen	GER	Sauber	1 lap

| Pierluigi Martini | ITA | Minardi | 2 laps |
| Andrea de Cesaris | ITA | Sauber | 2 laps |

POLE: Hill *(Mansell second, the first time since 1977 that two British drivers start on the front row)*
OVERALL: Schumacher 66, Hill 29, Berger 17

Schumacher restores order after all the British excitement. Mansell finishes fourteenth.

BRITISH GP
10 July Silverstone

Damon Hill	UK	Williams	1h30:03.640
Michael Schumacher	GER	Benetton	18.778
Jean Alesi	FRA	Ferrari	1:08.128
Mika Hakkinen	FIN	McLaren	1:40.659
Rubens Barrichello	BRZ	Jordan	1:41.751
David Coulthard	UK	Williams	1 lap

POLE: Hill
OVERALL: Schumacher 72, Hill 39, Alesi & Berger 17

Hill succeeds in a GP never won by his father. A five-second penalty is imposed on Schumacher for overtaking during the formation lap prior to the race (he also ignores the black flag calling him in, which costs him a two-race ban and the six pts he wins here). Berger's fined $10 000 for exceeding 80kph in the pit lane during practice.

GERMAN GP
31 July Hockenheim

Gerhard Berger	AUT	Ferrari	1h22:37.272
Olivier Panis	FRA	Ligier	54.779
Eric Bernard	FRA	Ligier	1:05.042
Christian Fittipaldi	BRZ	Footwork	1:21.609
Gianni Morbidelli	ITA	Footwork	1:30.544
Erik Comas	FRA	Larrousse	1:45.445

POLE: Berger
OVERALL: Schumacher 66 (6 deducted), Hill 39, Berger 27

Schumacher, originally banned from this race after what happened at Silverstone, decides to race first and appeal later; his engine problems and a mistake by Hill lead to Ferrari's first GP win since 1990, a drought of 58 races. Behind Berger, the supporting cast take a few bows (Olivier Beretta is seventh in the other Larrousse), though one of them gets the wrong kind of exposure: Jos Verstappen (HOL) and the Benetton crew suffer facial burns after a sudden fire in the pit lane. After the allegations at Imola and the black flag incident at Silverstone, the team's troubles have certainly arrived in threes.

HUNGARIAN GP
14 Aug Budapest

Michael Schumacher	GER	Benetton	1h48:00.185
Damon Hill	UK	Williams	20.827
Jos Verstappen	HOL	Benetton	1:10.329
Martin Brundle	UK	McLaren	1 lap

This sport in life
Milan's superintendent for cultural heritage Lucia Gremmo originally cancelled the Italian GP because 123 trees would have had to be cut down to widen some of the run-off areas. Lombardy's regional council managed to persuade the government to overrule.

| Mark Blundell | UK | Tyrrell | 1 lap |
| Olivier Panis | FRA | Ligier | 1 lap |

POLE: Schumacher
OVERALL: Schumacher 76, Hill 45, Berger 27

In retrospect, Williams feel they make a mistake in coming in for only two pit stops instead of Schumacher's three.

BELGIAN GP
28 Aug Spa

Damon Hill	UK	Williams	1h28:47.170
Mika Hakkinen	FIN	McLaren	51.381
Jos Verstappen	HOL	Benetton	1:10.453
David Coulthard	UK	Williams	1:45.787
Mark Blundell	UK	Tyrrell	1 lap
Gianni Morbidelli	ITA	Footwork	1 lap

POLE: Barrichello *(a first for him, and for Jordan, who've never had a driver on even provisional pole before)*
OVERALL: Schumacher 76, Hill 55, Berger 27

Somebody up there really doesn't care for Benetton. Schumacher, who finishes first for the eighth time in the season so far, loses the ten points when his car is found to have an undersized skidblock. Instead of an untouchable 35, Schumacher's lead in the OVERALL is down to 21 points. Coulthard leads for a lap.

ITALIAN GP
11 Sep Monza

Damon Hill	UK	Williams	1h18:02.754
Gerhard Berger	AUT	Ferrari	04.9
Mika Hakkinen	FIN	McLaren	25.6
Rubens Barrichello	BRZ	Jordan	50.6
Martin Brundle	UK	McLaren	1:25.5
David Coulthard	UK	Williams	1 lap

POLE: Alesi *(perhaps surprisingly, his first ever; he's yet to win a GP)*
OVERALL: Schumacher 76, Hill 65, Berger 33

Hill takes advantage of Schumacher's ban to win the race for the second year in a row.

PORTUGUESE GP
25 Sep Estoril

Damon Hill	UK	Williams	1h41:10.165
David Coulthard	UK	Williams	0.603
Mika Hakkinen	FIN	McLaren	20.193

Rubens Barrichello	BRZ	Jordan	28.003
Jos Verstappen	HOL	Benetton	29.385
Martin Brundle	UK	McLaren	52.702

POLE: Berger
OVERALL: Schumacher 76, Hill 75, Berger 33

With Schumacher still banned, Hill leads a Williams 1-2 as Coulthard finishes in the top three for the first time. Berger's car stops on Lap 8.

EUROPEAN GP
16 Oct Jerez (replaces the cancelled Argentinian GP scheduled for Buenos Aires)

Michael Schumacher	GER	Benetton	1h40:26.289
Damon Hill	UK	Williams	24.689
Mika Hakkinen	FIN	McLaren	1:09.648
Eddie Irvine	UK	Jordan	1:18.446
Gerhard Berger	AUT	Ferrari	1 lap
Heinz-Harald Frentzen	GER	Sauber	1 lap

POLE: Schumacher
OVERALL: Schumacher 86, Hill 85, Berger 35

Hill's only been keeping the podium warm. Three exceptional pit stops (one of which takes less than seven seconds) help Schumacher put his talent where his mouth is (he apparently described Hill as 'not a No.1 driver' before the race). Hill's handicapped by a faulty gauge which makes him carry too much fuel. Mansell, making another F1 return, spins out on Lap 48, not far from a placard that reads 'Nige! We love ya, but give Coulthard the keys.' Williams evntually do just that for 1995, giving Coulthard the second driver's place in preference to Mansell.

JAPANESE GP
6 Nov Suzuka

Damon Hill	UK	Williams	1h55:53.532
Michael Schumacher	GER	Benetton	3.365
Jean Alesi	FRA	Ferrari	52.045
Nigel Mansell	UK	Williams	56.074
Eddie Irvine	UK	Jordan	1:42.107
Heinz-Harald Frentzen	GER	Sauber	1:59.863

POLE: Schumacher
OVERALL: Schumacher 92, Hill 91, Berger 35

Hill drives the race of his career to overtake and close the gap on Schumacher - though the race, stopped then restarted in heavy rain, should arguably never have taken place: Martin Brundle, one of the best wet-weather drivers, can't avoid hitting a marshal, who's lucky to escape with a broken leg. After the race, Hill complains about wages and Williams' lack of belief in his abilities. He seems to have a point: his own technical director Patrick Head mentions that if he were a betting man 'and I had $100 000, I would put it on Schumacher. But that is not meant to undermine Damon.'

Grand Prix wins

51	Alain Prost	FRA	1981-93
41	Ayrton Senna	BRZ	1985-93
31	Nigel Mansell	UK	1985-94
27	Jackie Stewart	UK	1965-73
25	Jim Clark	UK	1962-68
25	Niki Lauda	AUT	1974-85
24	Juan Manuel Fangio	ARG	1950-57
23	Nelson Piquet	BRZ	1980-91

Fangio's total includes two drives shared with another driver.

AUSTRALIAN GP
13 Nov Adelaide

Nigel Mansell	UK	Williams	1h47:51.480
Gerhard Berger	AUT	Ferrari	2.511
Martin Brundle	UK	McLaren	52.487
Rubens Barrichello	BRZ	Jordan	1:10.530
Olivier Panis	FRA	Ligier	1 lap
Jean Alesi	FRA	Ferrari	1 lap

POLE: Mansell

At the very end, luck and controversy fuel Schumacher's overall win: with Hill in his mirrors, he locks his brakes into a turn, crosses the run-off area, bounces back off a wall onto the track, then moves across when Hill tries to overtake. The consequent collision smashes Schumacher off the track but also breaks Hill's wishbone (appropriately enough), putting them both out of the race. Schumacher's not confirmed as champion until after an inquiry. At the eighth attempt, Mansell wins the Australian for the first time.

Final Standings 1994

Drivers

92	Michael Schumacher	GER	Benetton
91	Damon Hill	UK	Williams
41	Gerhard Berger	AUT	Ferrari
26	Mika Hakkinen	FIN	McLaren
24	Jean Alesi	FRA	Ferrari
19	Rubens Barrichello	BRZ	Jordan
16	Martin Brundle	UK	McLaren
14	David Coulthard	UK	Williams
13	Nigel Mansell	UK	Williams
8	Mark Blundell	UK	Tyrrell
6	Eddie Irvine	UK	Jordan

Youngest world champions

yrs days

25 273	Emerson Fittipaldi	BRZ	1972
25 314	Michael Schumacher	GER	1994
26 176	Nikki Lauda	AUT	1975
27 188	Jim Clark	UK	1963
28 237	Ayrton Senna	BRZ	1988

(Age on the day the title was officially confirmed)

Constructors

118	Williams
103	Benetton
71	Ferrari
42	McLaren
28	Jordan
13	Ligier, Tyrrell

The mighty have fallen...Lotus, who score no points at all, lay off their entire workforce and pull out of the 1995 Championship.

Indycars: PPG World Series 1994

20 March Surfers' Paradise, Australia
Michael Andretti   USA   Reynard
Mansell (Newman-Haas) 9th, from pole

The thick-skinned bodywork of Andretti's car allows him to bounce off assorted walls and corners and survive to enjoy his return from a poor season in Formula 1. His father Mario finishes third after being accused of cutting across Mansell. 'Let's settle this right now,' says narked Nige. 'Let's put the boxing gloves on.'

10 April Phoenix (Slick 50)
Emerson Fittipaldi   BRZ   Penske
Mansell 3rd

With no run-offs on the banking of oval tracks, a pile-up involving Paul Tracy (CAN), Hiro Matsushita (JAP) & Jacques Villeneuve (CAN) comes within inches of being fatal.

17 April Long Beach (Toyota GP)
Al Unser jnr   USA   Penske
Mansell 2nd

The twentieth win of Unser's IndyCar career is his fifth in this event, a record.

29 May Indianapolis 500

Al Unser jnr	USA	Penske	200 laps
Jacques Villeneuve	CAN	Reynard	200
			(8.6s behind)
Bobby Rahal	USA	Penske	199

Mansell crashes after 92 laps.

Emerson Fittipaldi had it won. Formula 1 world champion back in 1972 & 1974, now 47 but winner of the Indy only last year as well as in 1989, he takes the lead when Unser stalls, holds it for all but sixteen of the remaining laps, then makes a mistake coming out of a turn. Unser, the 1992 winner, starts from pole for the first time. His father Al senior, winner of the race four times, announces his retirement ten days earlier. Mario Andretti, in his 29th & last Indy, finishes sixth. Mansell survives being set on fire when his car leaks methanol after a collision.

6 June Milwaukee Mile
Al Unser jnr   USA   Penske
Mansell 5th (on the track where, last year, he won an IndyCar race for the first time).

Not for the last time, Penske finish 1-2-3.

12 June Detroit GP
Paul Tracy   CAN   Penske
Mansell doesn't finish (despite starting from pole after breaking the lap record)

Unser leads until Tracy hits him from behind near the finish. Penske win five in a row for the first time.

26 June Portland, Oregon
Al Unser jnr   USA   Penske
Mansell 5th

10 July Cleveland, Ohio
Al Unser jnr   USA   Penske
Mansell 2nd, moving up to third in the championship.

17 July Toronto, Ontario
Michael Andretti   USA   Reynard
Mansell retires on the 68th lap, Unser on the first.

31 July Michigan 500
Scott Goodyear   CAN   Lola
Mansell 26th (from pole, having set the fastest lap in any IndyCar race: 235.639 mph).

Goodyear comes through from twelfth place on the grid (after Mansell, among others, has mechanical trouble while leading) to win the race for the second time (his only two wins in a seven-year IndyCar career).

14 Aug Lexington (Mid-Ohio)
Al Unser jnr   USA   Penske
Mansell 4th

The three Penskes sum up the season by lapping the entire field.

21 Aug Loudon (New Hampshire 200)
Al Unser jnr   USA   Penske

Another Penske 1-2-3. Mansell, who won the race last year, survives a practice crash this year, but not the collision with Mario Andretti during the race itself.
'I was hit by my team mate,' says Nigel. 'He drove right into me,' says Andretti snr.

4 Sep Vancouver, British Columbia
Al Unser jnr   USA   Penske
Mansell crashes and finishes 10th.

11 Sep Elkhart Lake
Jacques Villeneuve   CAN
Mansell punctures and finishes 13th.

Unser finishes second to win the overall title. Villeneuve, in his first season, wins an IndyCar event for the first time. His father Gilles was a Formula 1 driver.

18 Sep Nazareth, Pennsylvania
Paul Tracy   CAN   Penske
Mansell fails to finish.

Tracy wins an IndyCar race for the first time, on the circuit where Mansell clinched the title last year. Penske fill the first three places for the fifth time this season.

9 Oct 1994 Laguna Seca, Bank of America 300
Paul Tracy   CAN   Penske
Mansell 8th (no Americans ahead of him)

Mansell finishes a forgettable season in the shadow of Mario Andretti, who retires at the age of 54 after a record 407 IndyCar races. Penske win a record twelve races in the season.

Final Standings

Al Unser jnr	USA	Penske	225
Emerson Fittipaldi	BRZ	Penske	178
Paul Tracy	CAN	Penske	152
8 Nigel Mansell	*UK*	*Newman-Haas*	*88*

Unser, who won only one race last season, takes the title in his first season with Penske.

Other Races

Le Mans 24 hours
18-19 June 1994

Porsche	344 laps	(Hurley Haywood USA, Yannick Dalmas FRA, Mauro Baldi ITA)
Toyota	343	(Eddie Irvine UK, Pierluigi Martini ITA, Jeff Krosnoff USA)
Porsche	343	(Thierry Boutsen BEL, Hans Stuck GER, Danny Sullivan USA)

Porsche win for the first time since 1987 and the twelfth in all, adding to their record, thanks to a broken gear linkage which cripples the Toyota when it was leading with less than an hour to go.

Touring Cars (saloons)
BRITISH CHAMPIONSHIP 1994

FINAL STANDINGS

Gabriele Tarquini	ITA	Alfa Romeo	298
Alain Menu	SWI	Renault	222
Paul Radisich	NZ	Ford	204

Tarquini seals the title (at Silverstone) with a round to spare.

WORLD CUP
16 Oct 1994 Donington Park

DRIVERS

Paul Radisich	NZ	Ford	41:56.73
Steve Soper	UK	BMW	1.91
Joachim Winkelhock	GER	BMW	7.11

Radisich retains the inaugural title comfortably enough from pole, but is lucky that the race has to be restarted after a crash on the first lap, during which he's overtaken by John Cleland (UK)'s Vauxhall. The drive of the day comes from Gabriele Tarquini (ITA) who finishes fourth despite spinning off. Johnny Cecotto (VEN), who finishes sixth, was the youngest ever motorcycling world champion (1975).

MANUFACTURERS
BMW 54, Ford 48, Alfa Romeo 20

NATIONS CUP
Germany 53, UK 44, Italy 31

British Formula 3 Championship 1994

FINAL OVERALL STANDINGS

Jan Magnussen	DEN	308 pts
Vincent Radermecker	BEL	183
Gareth Rees	UK	171

Magnussen wins a record fourteen races in the season, breaking the record (twelve) set by Ayrton Senna.

Formula 3000 Championship 1994

FINAL OVERALL STANDINGS

Jules Bouillon	FRA	36
Franck Lagorce	FRA	34
Gil De Ferran	BRZ	28

Bouillon overtakes Lagorce, who led from the start of the season, by winning the last round, at Magny-Cours on 2 Oct.

Rallying

World Championship 1993

RAC Nov
Juha Kankkunen   FIN   Toyota

Kankkunen's twentieth win in World Championship races, a record.

FINAL STANDINGS
123	Juha Kankkunen	FIN	Toyota
102	François Delecour	FRA	Ford Escort
86	Didier Auriol	FRA	Toyota

Manufacturers: Toyota

World Championship 1994

MONTE CARLO 24-27 Feb
François Delecour	FRA	Ford
Juha Kankkunen	FIN	Toyota
Carlos Sainz	SPA	Subaru
10 Colin McRae	*UK*	*Subaru*

PORTUGUESE 1-4 March
Juha Kankkunen   FIN   Toyota

SAFARI 31 March - 3 April
Ian Duncan   KEN   Toyota

Duncan, winning a World Championship event for the first time, becomes the first Kenyan to win the race since 1982.

CORSICA 5-7 May
Didier Auriol   FRA   Toyota

Auriol's fifth win in the event, which takes place entirely on tarmac.

ACROPOLIS 28 May - 1 June, Greece
Carlos Sainz   SPA   Subaru

ARGENTINA July
Didier Auriol   FRA   Toyota

Carlos Sainz (SPA), who finishes only six seconds behind, takes the lead in the drivers' championship.

NEW ZEALAND 29-31 July
Colin McRae   UK   Subaru

McRae wins the event for the second year in a row.

1000 LAKES 25-28 Aug, Finland
Tommi Makinen   FIN   Ford Escort

Makinen wins a world championship event for the first time.

SAN REMO 10-12 Oct
Didier Auriol   FRA   Toyota

Auriol overhauls early leader Sainz over the closing two stages to win the event for the third time and increase his world championship lead from six to eleven points with only one round left, while Kankkunen loses his last chance of retaining the title.

RAC 20-23 Nov
Colin McRae	UK	Subaru
Juha Kankkunen	FIN	Toyota
Bruno Thiry	BEL	Ford Escort

For the fourth year in a row, McRae takes the lead during the race, and this time holds to it to become the first British driver to win the event since Roger Clark in 1976. Auriol, whose world title chance seems to have disappeared when he rolls his car during the first stage of the second day, losing ten minutes, receives it on a plate when Sainz retires after going off the road on the last day, soon after negotiating two logs which seem to have been deliberately put in his path.

FINAL STANDINGS
116	Didier Auriol	FRA	Toyota
99	Carlos Sainz	SPA	Subaru
93	Juha Kankkunen	FIN	Toyota
49	*Colin McRae (4th)*	*UK*	*Subaru*

Manufacturers: Toyota (151 points, exactly the same as the previous year).

British Championship 1994

Overall winner: Malcolm Wilson (Ford Escort).
Overall winner 2-wheel drive F2: David Llewellyn (Vauxhall Astra)

Hong Kong to Beijing Oct 1994

Possum Bourne   NZ   Subaru

Richard Burns (UK) finishes second in another Subaru, only 30 seconds behind, in the world's longest race (2356 miles).

Netball

ENGLAND v TRINIDAD & TOBAGO

England	40	Trinidad	35	*27 Oct 1993 Birmingham*
England	40	Trinidad	36	*30 Oct 1993 Sheffield*
England	50	Trinidad	37	*3 Nov 1993 Gateshead*
England	48	Trinidad	36	*6 Nov 1993 Wembley*

T&T arrive at Heathrow only twelve hours before the first game, in which England captain Kendra Slawinski wins her 100th cap.

ENGLAND v S AFRICA

England	44	S Africa	57	*3 Nov 1994 Manchester*
England	36	S Africa	55	*5 Nov 1994 Wembley*

Slawinski gives her all but can do nothing about the player she has to mark, the 6'4 Irene Viljoen, who scores an astonishing 53 points.

England	46	S Africa	58	*9 Nov 1994 Gateshead*
England	45	S Africa	46	*12 Nov 1994 Ponds Forge, Sheffield*

The final whistle goes with Tracy Miller poised to shoot the equaliser - but England's improved showing owes much to Viljoen being left out until the last quarter.

England	47	S Africa	52	*17 Nov 1994 Birmingham*

English National League 1993-94

	P	W	D	L	F	A	Pts
New Cambell	7	6	1	0	348	274	33
Linden	7	5	1	1	355	322	29
Aquila	7	5	0	2	314	304	27
Harborne	7	3	1	3	345	350	21
Tongham	7	3	0	4	304	343	19
Hertford Hornets	7	2	1	4	302	330	17
Toucans	7	1	2	4	267	281	15
BICC	7	0	0	7	265	296	7

Toucans & BICC relegated.

English Knockout Cup 1993-94

ROUND 2
Selected results: Oakwood bt Christchurch 77-33 away,
Kelly bt Aztec 69-38, The Downs bt Pinehurst 63-39

ROUND 3
Selected results: Leeds Athletic bt Pennine 61-25, GEC
bt Sheffield Open 91-10 away

ROUND 4

Falcons	44	Chester	46
Leeds Athletic	42	Kent County	33
All Stars	48	Kelly	53
Auto Electric	38	Watford Premier	42
Bramhall	30	Dudley Leisure	51
The Downs	65	Hillcrest	49
Ipswich	40	GEC	46
Oakwood	65	Grasshoppers	43

QUARTER-FINALS

Chester	27	Leeds Athletic	38
Kelly	36	Watford Premier	41
Dudley Leisure	38	The Downs	44
GEC	49	Oakwood	57

Semi-finals & Final 23 April 1994
Bentham CC, Gloucester

SEMI-FINALS

Leeds	44	Watford	33
Oakwood	59	The Downs	48

FINAL

Oakwood	44	Leeds Athletic	37

Counties League 1993-94

DIVISION 1	P	W	L	F	A	Pts
Essex Met	7	7	0	384	252	35
Surrey	7	6	1	365	292	31
Middlesex	7	4	3	308	261	23
Birmingham	7	3	4	322	346	19
East Essex	7	3	4	268	349	19
Bedfordshire	7	3	4	264	244	18
Hampshire North	7	1	6	295	331	11
Mid Hampshire	7	1	6	249	380	10

DIVISION 2 winners: Derbyshire
DIVISION 3 winners: Gloucestershire

Inter-counties tournament

FINAL April 1994 Anerley, South London

Essex Met	16	Surrey	10

Orienteering

World Championships
10-14 Oct 1993 West Point, USA

Men

SHORT RACE 4.75 km

Petter Thoresen	NOR	22:34
Timo Karppinen	FIN	23:00
Martin Johansson	SWE	23:26
4eq Steve Hale	*UK*	*23:27*

CLASSIC RACE 13.475 km

Allan Mogensen	DEN	1h27:36
Jorgen Martensson	SWE	1h28:07
Petter Thoresen	NOR	1h29:28
16 Steve Palmer	*UK*	*1h34:37*

RELAY 4x10 km
Switzerland
UK
Finland

Women

SHORT RACE 3.66 km

Anna Bogron	SWE	20:39
Marita Skogum	SWE	21:10
Eija Kostivaara	FIN	21:11
9 Yvette Hague	*UK*	*22:32*

CLASSIC RACE 8.62 km

Marita Skogum	SWE	1h)2:27
Annika Viilo	FIN	1h04:42
Yvette Hague	UK	1h06:09

In Aug 1994, Hague recovers from 26th place in the fourth World Cup race to take the overall lead.

RELAY 4x6.8 km
Sweden
Finland
Czech Rep
8 UK

British Championships
19-20 March 1994 Charlton Forest, Sussex

MEN 16 km

Neil Conway	1h29:31
Jonathan Musgrave	1h32:25
Robert Lee	1h33:28

WOMEN 10 km

Yvette Hague	1h09:40
Heather Monro	1h11:12
Jenny James	1h:14:15

Monro was the defending champion.

MEN'S RELAY 3 x 7.8 km

South Yorkshire	1h13:54
Guildford Orienteers	1h15:10
Warrior O	1h16:48

WOMEN'S RELAY 3 x 5.3 km

South Yorkshire	2h13:23
Merseyside	2h16:58
Warrior O	2h22:39

British Night Championships
26 Feb 1994 Delamere Forest, Cheshire

MEN 10.2 km

Steve Nicholson	1h03:06
Dickie Jones	1h06:36
Simon Bourne	1h15:24

WOMEN 7 km

Heather Monro	57:09
Kay Tonkin	1:11.56
Una Creagh	1h14:13

Polo

Rackets

Queen's Cup

5 June 1994

Black Bears	12	Ellerston White	11

Cowdray Trophy

18 June 1994

Young England	8	Young North America	2.5

British Open Championships (Davidoff Gold Cup)

Final *17 July 1994 Cowdray Park*

Ellerston Black	13	Pegasus	11

Ellerston come back from 5-1 down to win the Cup for the first time. Carlos Gracida is on the winning team in a final for the eighth time.

Coronation Cup

24 July 1994

England	11	S Africa	1

European Championship

7-11 Sep Beaufort PC

1 England
2 Italy
3 France
4 Spain

England (Will Hine (capt), Tim Stakemire, Adrian Wade & Jack Kidd) seal the title by beating France 9-4.5. Italy take second place by beating Spain 7-4.

World Doubles Challenge

FIRST LEG *6 Nov 1993 New York*

Neil Smith & Shannon Hazell	4-3
James Male & John Prenn	

15-5 15-10 12-15 10-15 15-7 14-17 15-7

SECOND LEG *13 Nov 1993 Queen's Club, London*

Male & Prenn	Smith & Hazell	4-3

7-15 9-15 15-3 8-15 15-11 15-7 15-4

Smith & Hazell retain the title 166-160. Male later has trials as a hitter with the Atlanta Braves, who believe he has more baseball potential than Michael Jordan, which sounds like damning with faint praise.

British Open

2-13 Feb 1994 Queen's Club, London

SEMI-FINALS

Neil Smith	Tim Cockcroft

17-18 15-10 15-8 15-9 15-12

Rupert Owen-Browne	Willie Boone

17-16 15-10 15-7 15-3

FINAL

Smith	Owen-Browne

15-7 15-12 15-9 11-15 6-15 8-15 15-6

In the absence of world champion Male, Smith retains the title against an opponent playing in his first final in the event. Owen-Browne beat the No.3 seed in the quarter-finals and the No.2 in the semis.

DOUBLES FINAL *24 April 1994 Queen's Club, London*

Boone & Cockcroft	Owen-Browne & Prenn

18-13 15-12 15-7 7-15 15-4

British Professional Championship

28-30 Jan 1994 Malvern College, Worcs

SEMI-FINALS

Peter Brake	Robert Wakeley

7-15 11-15 15-3 15-3 15-1

Norwood Cripps	David Makey

15-5 14-15 15-12 12-15 15-8

FINAL
Brake   Cripps
15-12 15-6 15-9

Brake (28) beats a man 20 years his senior to win the title for the first time.

DOUBLES FINAL
Tolchard & John Eaton Roger & Martin Crosby
9-15 15-4 15-7

The Crosbys are father and son.

British Amateur Championship 1993
Queen's Club, London

SEMI-FINALS
Willie Boone   Tim Cockcroft
15-13 17-16 15-7
John Prenn   Mark Hue Williams
10-15 15-18 15-7 15-18 15-13

FINAL *4 Dec*
Boone   Prenn
18-13 9-15 15-2 15-9

DOUBLES FINAL
16 March 1994 Queen's Club, London
Boone & Cockcroft Prenn & Owen-Browne
7-15 17-18 15-8 15-7 15-7 15-7

British Amateur Championship 1994
Queen's Club, London

SEMI-FINALS
James Male   Tim Cockcroft
15-6 13-15 15-6 15-8
Willie Boone   Rupert Owen-Browne
17-16 15-2 15-10

FINAL *12 Dec*
Male   Boone
13-16 15-2 15-8 15-4

Male, back after a year playing baseball in Atlanta, wins the title for the fifth time by beating a 44-y-o playing in the final for the twentieth time in a row.

English National League
Finals Day 27 March 1994 Marlborough

FINAL
Manchester 4 Old Etonians 2

Real Tennis

World Championship

1st leg, 1st day *1 March 1994 Hobart*
Robert Fahey (AUS) Wayne Davies (USA) 6-0 6-5 6-2 6-3

In the first world title leg ever played in Australia, Fahey starts as he means to go on, winning the first set with a Winning Gallery, a drive to the base of the Tambour and two fiercely cut shots under the Grille. Davies does better in the second with lobs, demi-piqués and sidewalls, but the match is probably settled at 5-5, when Fahey produces two big forces into the Dedans followed by two short chases.

1st leg, 2nd day *3 March Hobart*
Fahey   Davies 6-5 5-6 6-4 6-4

More of the same from Fahey, taking the first game with a Winning Gallery, Tambour winner, ace railroad and fine cut into the galleries, then overcoming Davies' famous Grille defences and harsh main wall forces.

2nd leg, 1st day *14 March New York Racquet Club*
Davies   Fahey 6-4 6-5 6-5 0-6

Davies fights back in his New York lair, where he's lost only twelve sets in thirteen years, six of them in one match, none in the seven US Opens he's won.

2nd leg, 2nd day *16 March New York Racquet Club*
Davies   Fahey 6-1 2-6

Needing only two sets in the NY leg, Fahey makes rather heavy weather of it before serving a railroad at 5-2 40-30, then volleying a winner to win by nine sets to five and become the youngest undisputed winner (25) of the oldest championship in any sport, and the first to win it at his first attempt. The last six world champions were all 31 when they first won the title, including Davies, champion since 1987.

British Open Singles 1993

SEMI-FINALS
Julian Snow James Male 6-2 6-1 6-4
Robert Fahey (AUS) Chris Bray 6-2 6-1 6-2

FINAL *29 Nov Queen's Club, London*
Snow   Fahey 4-6 2-1 ret

Snow retains the title when a pulled groin muscle stops Fahey becoming the first player since 1984 to win the Grand Slam of Open titles.

British Open Singles 1994

SEMI-FINALS

| Julian Snow | Wayne Davies (AUS) | 3-6 0-6 6-5 6-4 6-4 |
| Lachie Deuchar (AUS) | Robert Fahey (AUS) | 6-4 6-4 2-6 6-2 |

The holder recovers from two sets and 4-1 down.

FINAL *27 Nov Queen's Club, London*

| Snow | Deuchar | 6-3 6-5 1-6 6-3 |

Snow wins the title for the third successive year.

British Open Doubles 1994

FINAL *10 Jan 1994 Queen's Club, London*

Chris Bray & Mike Gooding bt Wayne Davies (AUS) & Lachie Deuchar (AUS)   6-5 6-4 6-2

British Professional Singles

SEMI-FINALS

| Lachie Deuchar (AUS) | Chris Bray | 6-2 6-5 6-2 |
| Mark Devine | Robert Fahey (AUS) | 6-4 6-2 6-2 |

FINAL *2 May 1994 Holyport*

| Deuchar | Devine | 6-5 6-3 6-2 |

British Professional Doubles

FINAL *10 Jan 1994 Queen's Club, London*

Robert Fahey & Lachie Deuchar
Chris Bray & Mike Gooding   5-6 6-3 6-0 6-3

The Australians win the title for the first time.

British Amateur Singles

SEMI-FINALS

| Julian Snow | Mark Howard | 6-0 6-1 6-2 |
| Nigel Pendrigh | Ivan Snell | 6-2 6-0 6-3 |

FINAL *20 March 1994 Queen's Club, London*

| Snow | Pendrigh | 6-3 6-3 6-3 |

British Amateur Doubles

FINAL *3 May 1994 Hatfield House*

Nigel Pendrigh & James Acheson Gray
Julian Snow & Mike McMurrugh   1-6 6-5 5-6 6-1 6-3

Pendrigh & Acheson Gray beat the holders to win the title for the first time.

British Women's Open Singles

27 April - 1 May 1994 Seacourt, Hayling Island

SEMI-FINALS

| Alex Garside | Charlotte Cornwallis | 6-4 6-2 |
| Sally Jones | Katrina Allen | 6-4 5-6 6-5 |

Allen won the title in 1983-84-85.

FINAL

| Garside | Jones | 6-3 6-1 |

Garside, playing on her home court, beats her doubles partner, the world champion & No.1 seed, to win the title for the first time. She adds the French Open title in October when four months pregnant.

British Women's Open Doubles

14-16 Jan 1994 Canford

FINAL

Fiona Deuchar & Mandy Happell
Alex Garside & Sally Jones   w.o.

The Australians win when the holders are defaulted because Jones arrives too late.

U S Open

SEMI-FINALS

| Wayne Davies (USA) | Mark Devine (UK) | 6-4 6-0 6-2 |
| Robert Fahey (AUS) | Chris Bray (UK) | 5-6 6-5 4-6 6-4 6-5 |

FINAL

| Davies | Fahey | 6-4 3-6 6-2 6-0 |

Rowing

World Championships

12-18 Sep 1994
Eagle Creek Reservoir, Indianapolis

Men

Single sculls

André Wilms	GER	6:46.33
Xeno Müller	SWI	6:48.02
Iztok Cop	SLVN	6:49.33

Lightweight single sculls

Peter Haining	UK	6:53.48
Niall O'Toole	EIRE	6:56.33
Karsten Nielsen	DEN	6:56.

Haining dominates the second half of the race to overtake 1991 champion O'Toole and retain the title.

Double sculls

R Thorsen & L Bjoness	NOR	6:08.33
P Uhrig & C Händle	GER	6:08.88
Y Lamarque & S Barathay	FRA	6:10.03

Lightweight double sculls

Francesco Esposito & M Crispi	ITA	6:18.01
R Hamill & M Rodger	NZ	6:20.14
Markus Gier & Michael Gier	SWI	6:20.85

The remarkable 37-y-o Esposito wins his 10th world title. Andy Sinton & Stuart Whitelaw (UK), expected to do well, finish sixth.

Quadruple sculls

Italy	5:37.68 WR	
Ukraine	5:39.11	
Germany	5:39.71	

Lightweight quadruple sculls

W Sigi, G Faderbauer, C Schmölzer, W Rantansa	AUT	5:46.75
E Gandola, I Zasio, M Gugliemi, P Pittino	ITA	5:48.83
J Leitão, L Fonseca, L Teixeira, H Baixinno	PORT	5:49.64

Eights

USA	5:24.50 WR	
Holland	5:25.10	
Romania	5:27.08	

Lightweight eights

UK	5:31.00	
Denmark	5:31.36	
Italy	5:34.63	

UK: Chris Bates, Somin Cox, David Lemon, Carl Smith, Stephen Ellis, Jim McNiven, Tom Kay, Toby Hessian, cox John Deakin

Denmark finish second for the second successive year. Defending champions Canada didn't take part.

Coxed pairs

Croatia	6:42.16 WR	
Italy	6:42.98	
Romania	6:46.99	

The favourites, the Searle brothers, take part in the coxless fours. Steve Redgrave, fresh (?) from his win in the coxless pairs, adds to his legend by replacing Jon Singfield and helping Martin Cross (at 37 competing in his 18th successive world championships) to win the B final.

Coxless pairs

Matthew Pinsent & Steve Redgrave	UK	6:18.65
Peter Höltzenbein & Thorsten Streppelhoff	GER	6:19.75
R Walker & R Wearne	AUS	6:20.25

Pinsent & Redgrave (who miss their own world record by 00.01) win the title for the fourth consecutive time, Redgrave for the fifth in all. The two Germans helped Cambridge win this year's university boat race.

Lightweight coxless pairs

L Pettinari & C Gaddi	ITA	6:34.70
V Mityuchev & A Ustinov	RUS	6:39.92
N Maxwell & A O'Connor	EIRE	6:39.96

Coxless fours

Italy	5:48.44 WR	
France	5:49.82	
UK	5:50.37	

Jonny Searle, Greg Searle, Rupert Oberholzer, Tim Foster.

Italy (only seventh last year) beat defending champions France. The Searle brothers took up the event because the coxed pairs (in which they're reigning world & Olympic champions) has been dropped from the next Olympics.

Lightweight coxless fours

Denmark	5:53.77
Australia	5:56.24
Germany	5:57.07

Britain (Andy Butt, Ian Watson, Nick Strange, Ben Helm), who set a world record earlier in the year, fail to reach the final.

Coxed fours

Romania	6:06.68
USA	6:07.07
Holland	6:07.73

Women

Single sculls

Trine Hansen	DEN	7:23.96
Kathrin Boron	GER	7:24.90
Annelise Braedel	BEL	7:25.56

Hansen finished third last year. The 1991 champion, Silke Laumann (CAN), back after a series of injuries, falls foul of inadequate starting arrangements and is eliminated after two false starts.

Lightweight single sculls

Constanta Pipota	ROM	7:34.17
Laurien Vermulst	HOL	7:35.81
Pia Vogel	SWI	7:38.63

Double sculls

P Baker & B Lawson	NZ	6:45.30
M McBean & K Heddle	CAN	6:46.17
J Thieme & A Schuster	GER	6:47.16

Lightweight double sculls

Coleen Miller & Wendy Weebe	CAN	6:54.85
Zhong Ai-fang & Ou Shao-yan	CHN	6:56.83
L Burns & T Zarceczny	USA	6:57.76

Quadruple sculls

Germany	6:11.73 WR
China	6:15.74
Ukraine	6:18.05

Eights

Germany	6:07.42
USA	6:08.24
Romania	6:08.55

Coxless pairs

C Gosse & H Mortin	FRA	7:01.77
I Bobeica & E Lipa	ROM	7:05.45
A Ozolins & C Klomp	AUS	7:07.60

Britain (Miriam Batten & Jo Turvey), favoured for a medal, finish fifth.

Coxless fours

Holland	6:30.76
USA	6:31.92
Australia	6:32.85

Lightweight coxless fours

USA	6:36.40
UK	6:37.28
China	6:38.27

UK: Alison Brownless, Jane Hall, Annemarie Stapleton, Tonia Williams

Britain, the defending champions hampered by Stapleton's injury earlier in the year, leave their finishing burst too late.

Commonwealth Championships

29-31 Aug 1994 Fanshawe Lake, London, Ontario
(Not part of the Commonwealth Games)

Men

Single sculls

Derek Porter	CAN
Jason Day	AUS
Wade Hall-Craggs	ENG
No times taken.	

Lightweight single sculls

T Prince	CAN	7:52.96
S Hawkins	AUS	8:02.84
J Armstrong	N IRE	8:05.32

Double sculls

	NZ	6:52.65
	AUS	6:55.02
A Warnock & M Holmes	SCOT	7:05.22

Lightweight double sculls

M Rodger & R Hamill	NZ	6:41.05
	CAN	6:45.50
	AUS	6:47.09

Quadruple sculls

C Pearson, S Purves,		
A Edwards, S Burgess	AUS	6:00.71
J McGarva, R Burdett,		
N Kittoe, R Redpath	ENG	6:05.56
	CAN	6:07.27

Coxless pairs

P Graham & D Barber	CAN	6:35.12
	AUS	6:42.28
	NZ	6:44.60

Lightweight coxless pairs

	AUS	7:17.54
M Harris & G Gillespie	SCOT	7:22.33
	CAN	7:25.49

Coxed fours

S McLaughlin, D Weightman, N Porzig,		
J Fernandez, cox B Hayman	AUS	6:15.91
R Brown, T McAdams, C Unwin, S Larkin,		
cox R Thomas	ENG	6:16.50
	NZ	6:18.32

Coxless fours

A Parfitt, S Walsh, M Forgerson,		
B Crombie	CAN	6:06.01
	AUS	6:09.01
B Poulton, E Wild, A Green,		
M Kettle	ENG	6:10.01

Lightweight coxless fours

Australia	6:32.30
N Zealand	6:35.60
Canada	6:40.50

Eights

England	5:45.69
Canada	5:46.97
Australia	5:49.80

England: M Partridge, R Evans, M Johnson,
M Harris, R Brown, C McAdams, C Unwin, S Larkin,
cox R Thomas

Lightweight eights

England
Australia
Canada
No times taken.

England: M Williams, J Warnock, J Cooney,
J Williamson, W Baker, S Pearson, R Everington,
J Keys, cox T Richmond

Women

Single sculls

Marnie McBean	CAN	7:36.01
G Toogood	AUS	7:42.04
Fiona Freckleton	SCOT	8:06.90

Lightweight single sculls

Michelle Darville	CAN	8:21.44
Sue Appelboom	ENG	8:27.62
Claire McDougall-Smith	SCOT	8:29.39

Darville's the world champion.

Double sculls

	NZ	7:32.87
	CAN	7:37.65
H Bruce & R Rudkin	ENG	8:11.08

Lightweight double sculls

C Miller & W Wiebe	CAN	7:10.47
	AUS	7:19.07
L Hart & M Stevens	ENG	7:31.19

Quadruple sculls

	AUS	6:54.51
	CAN	7:00.05
	NZ	7:13.34

Coxless pairs

Anna Ozolins & Carmen Klomp	AUS	7:26.02
Kate Grose & Patricia (Tish) Reid	ENG	7:31.03
	CAN	7:34.04

Coxless fours

M Maunder, J Browett,		
E Robinson, Kelly Mahon	CAN	6:45.07
	AUS	6:47.02
K Marwick, N Robinson,		
A Bruce, G Lindsay	SCOT	6:53.03

Lightweight coxless fours

Canada	7:26.29
Australia	7:31.11
England	7:35.99

England: Alison Brownless, Jane Hall,
Annemarie Stapleton, Tonia Williams

Eights

Canada	6:25.04
Australia	6:26.31
England	6:39.86

England: A Mowbray, J Eastwood, S Walker,
R Carroll, H Raine, C Bishop, C Glackin, E Henshilwood,
cox S Ellis

Oxford v Cambridge

Women

20 March 1994 Henley

CAMBRIDGE bt OXFORD 1 length (6min 11sec)

Cambridge: R Gordon, JF Mara, KJ Gill, LC Page, AR
Rowland, AM Moore, Alison Mowbray, MA Hunter;
cox: K Baker.
Oxford: Alison Palmer, LEM Jowitt, EL Haynes, I
Grimberg, L Callaghan, PR Eyres, L Bannon, Elizabeth
Ayling; cox: Richard Craig.

Cambridge win the race for the 3rd year in a row.

Men

26 March Putney to Mortlake

CAMBRIDGE bt OXFORD 6.5 lengths (18min 09sec)

Cambridge: Roger Taylor, Will Mason, Sinclair Gore,
Richard Phelps, Jon Bernstein, Matt Parish, Peter
Höltzenbein, Thorsten Streppelhoff; cox Martin Haycock
Oxford: Harry MacMillan, Chris Mahne, Joe Michels,

Andy Gordon-Brown, Rob Clegg, Sverke Lorgen, Snorre Lorken, Kingsley Poole; cox Liz Chick

Oxford replace coach Richard Tinkler with Fred Smallbone late on, to not much avail against one of the strongest teams Cambridge have ever put out: Bernstein an American international, Streppelhoff & Höltzenbein world championship medallists, Parish & Phelps members of the British eight at the last world championships. Both clubs immediately build for the future, Oxford re-appointing Dan Topolski, who set up their 10 successive wins 1976-85, as coach alongside former national coaching director Penny Chuter.

Cambridge offer cash bursaries to attract international rowers from abroad.

Wingfield Sculls
11 May 1994 Putney to Mortlake

Peter Haining	19:58
Guy Pooley	20:07
Wade Hall-Craggs	20:33

Haining, who won the Scullers Head in 19:54, becomes the first to row the course in less than 20 mins in each direction. Pooley, who also breaks the old record, won the Wingfield in 1991 & 1992.

Doggett's Coat & Badge
19 July 1994 London Bridge to Chelsea (4.75 miles)

Christian George Bullas	c.28m20
Robert Franklin	
Robert Coleman	
David McCarthy	

Although Bullas is the British Under-23 sculling champion, the overall standard isn't particularly high - Coleman's overtaken by the spectators' launches and McCarthy entered only to make up the numbers and so stop the event being thrown open to all comers - but it's arguably the oldest sporting event still taking place in Britain (first run in 1715) and therefore worth its place here.

Henley Regatta
Finals 3 July 1994

Britannia Cup	Belfast University
Diamond Sculls	Xeno Müller (SWI)
Women's Single Sculls	Marnie McBean (CAN)
Double Sculls	G Mitring &
	Zoltán Dani (HUN)
Fawley Cup	Windsorian
Grand Challenge Cup	Charles River &
	San Diego (USA)
Q Elizabeth Cup	St Paul's School
P Philip Cup	Notts County
Q Mother Cup	Treviris & Bollberg
Silver Goblets & Nickalls Cup	Steve Redgrave &
	Matthew Pinsent
Stewards' Cup	Boulogne & Lyon (FRA)
Temple Cup	Imperial College A
Thames Cup	Brown University (USA)
Visitors' Cup	Imperial College
Wyfold Cup	Notts County
Ladies' Plate	College BC (USA)

Lucerne International Regatta
Finals 17 July 1994

Men

Lightweight Single Sculls	UK	Peter Haining
Lightweight Double Sculls	ITA	Francesco Esposito & M Crispi
Lightweight Quadruple Sculls	AUT	
Lightweight Pairs	EIRE	A O'Connor & N Maxwell
Lightweight Fours	DEN	
Lightweight Eights	UK	
World Cup Single Sculls	SWI	Xeno Müller
Double Sculls	NOR	Thorsen & Bjonness
Quadruple Sculls	AUS	
Coxless Pairs	UK	Steve Redgrave & Matthew Pinsent
Coxed Pairs	CRO	T Frankovic & I Boroska
Coxless Fours	FRA	
Eights	GER	

Redgrave & Pinsent set a world record of 6:18.34

Women

Lightweight Double Sculls	CAN	Coleen Miller & Wendy Wiebe
Lightweight Fours	USA	
Pairs	FRA	H Mortin & C Gosse
Fours	HOL	
Single Sculls	ROM	Constanta Pipota
World Cup Single Sculls	CAN	Silke Laumann
Double Sculls	GER	Thieme & Schuster
Quadruple Sculls	GER	

Laumann sets a world record of 7:17.09

Rugby League

A couple of bricks fell out of the wall at the end of the 1992-93 season. Andy Platt & Dean Bell joined Auckland Warriors, suggesting that Wigan's endless domination might just be coming to an…no, only kidding. They won the League for the fifth time in a row, the Challenge Cup for the seventh, filled the gaps with slabs from rugby union: Va'iga Tuigamala (a brick outhouse if ever there was one) and Scott Quinnell, and began the 1994-95 season by equalling the First Division record of 13 successive wins. At the end of it they'll lose two more cornerstones – Dennis Betts to the Warriors, Phil Clarke to Eastern Suburbs – but don't expect the edifice to come tumbling down just yet. Whatever they use for mortar (probably money from sponsors and success) seems to work. Still, it has to come to an end sometime. Doesn't it?

The British game as a whole probably hopes so. By the usual mighty yardstick, it still lags behind Australia, who came, averaged 38 points and seven tries per match (both records) and seemed as far in front as ever, despite the efforts (and genuine successes, such as the one at Wembley) of the last decade. Australian coach Bobby Fulton thinks today's British teams would beat their 1980s equivalents by 30 points, which shows just how far ahead Australia still are. But at least they're still the measuring rod; the British game isn't sliding back into being happy with wins over New Zealand.

International Matches 1993-94

3 Oct 1993 Vetch Field, Swansea
6073, referee John Connolly (ENG)

WALES 19   T: Cordle 2, G: Davies 5; DG: Griffiths
N ZEALAND 24 T:Hoppe, Mackie, Ropati; G: Halligan 6

Wales: Phil Ford, Gerald Cardle, Allan Bateman, John Devereux, Anthony Sullivan, Jonathan Davies (c), Kevin Ellis, Mark Jones, Barry Williams (Adrian Hadley 67), David Young, Ian Marlow (Robert Ackerman 41), Rowland Phillips, Jonathan Griffiths

NZ: Morvin Edwards (Jason Williams 69), Daryl Halligan, Iva Ropati, Whetu Taewa, Sean Hoppe, Gene Ngamu, Gary Freeman (c), John Lomax (Robert Piva 62), Duane Mann, Brent Stuart, Stephen Kearney, Quentin Pongia, Jason Mackie (Logan Edwards 75)

Devereux's late touchdown behind the posts is disallowed for offside against another Welsh player. Cordle scores two tries in only his second match since breaking his jaw against England a year earlier on the same ground.

16 Oct 1993 Wembley
36 131, Greg McCallum (AUS)

G BRITAIN 17 T: Robinson 2, Devereux; G: Davies 2; DG: Davies
N ZEALAND 0

GB: Jonathan Davies, Jason Robinson, Paul Newlove (Daryl Powell 68), Gary Connolly, John Devereux (Alan Tait 77), Garry Schofield (c), Shaun Edwards, Karl Harrison, Martin Dermott, Karl Fairbank (Sonny Nickle 54), Denis Betts, Chris Joynt (Richie Eyres 63), Phil Clarke

NZ: M Edwards (Williams 62), Halligan (Taewa 76), Kevin Iro, Dave Watson, Hoppe, Ngamu, Freeman (c), John Lomax (Jason Lowrie 58), Mann, Stuart, Kearney, Pongia, Tawera Nikau (Mackie 69)

N Zealand lose an opening Test in Britain for the first time since 1965, and fail to score in a Test here for the first time ever. Robinson scores two tries on his Test debut.

30 Oct 1993 Central Park, Wigan
16 502, Greg McCallum (AUS)

G BRITAIN 29   T: Devereux 2, Schofield, Offiah,
Newlove; G: Davies 4; DG: Schofield
N ZEALAND 12   T: Watson, Ropati; G: Botica 2

GB: Davies, Devereux, Connolly (Tait 73), Newlove,
Martin Offiah, Schofield (c), Edwards, Harrison (Powell
67), Lee Jackson, Fairbank (Michael Jackson 29), Nickle
(Eyres 59), Joynt, Clarke

NZ: Watson, Frano Botica, Iro, Ropati, Hoppe (Williams
50), Tony Kemp, Freeman (c), Se'e Solomona (J Lomax
59), Mann (Taewa 73), Stuart, Kearney, Pongia, Mackie
(Gary Mercer 46)

Man of the Match: Devereux

Devereux scores his 100th try in rugby league.

6 Nov 1993 Headingley, Leeds
15 139, Greg McCallum (AUS)

G BRITAIN 29   T: Fairbank, Clarke, Davies, Offiah,
Farrell; G: Davies 4; DG: Davies
N ZEALAND 10   T: Williams; G: Botica 3

GB: Davies, Devereux, Connolly, Newlove (M Jackson
70), Offiah, Schofield (c) (Powell 11, Tait h/t)),
Edwards, Kelvin Skerrett, L Jackson, Fairbank (Nickle
48), Andrew Farrell, Joynt, Clarke

NZ: Watson (Richard Blackmore 48), Botica, Iro, Ropati
(Taewa 70), Williams, Kemp, Aaron Whittaker,
Solomona (J Lomax 48), Denvour Johnston, Stuart,
Kearney (c), Pongia, Mackie (David Lomax 70)

Man of the Match: Clarke

*Farrell's the youngest forward (18 yrs 160 days) to play
for Britain, who whitewash the Kiwis in a series for the
first time since 1951. The British back row of Farrell,
Clarke & Joynt, which gives a storming collective
performance, has an average age of barely 20. A series
of controversial selections (players with British clubs
being preferred to members of the tour party and vice
versa) costs coach Howie Tamati his job.*

21 Nov 1993 Carcassone
3500, John Holdsworth (ENG)

FRANCE 11   T:Sirvent, Llong; G: Chamorin;
DG: Chamorin
N ZEALAND 36   T: Halligan, Iro 2, Taewa, Freeman,
Mackie; G: Halligan 6

France: Frantz Martial, Claude Sirvent, Pierre Chamorin,
David Fraisse, Pascal Bomati, Jean-Marc Garcia, Patrick
Entat (c), Bernard Llong, Mathieu Khedimi, Lilian
Herbert, Ezzedine Attia, Mark Bourneville, Daniel Divet.
Subs used: Pascal Jampy, Thierry Valero, Jean Frison

NZ: M Edwards, Halligan, Iro, Taewa, Williams, Kemp,

Freeman (c), J Lomax, Johnston, Stuart, Lowrie,
Pongia, Mackie. Subs used: D Lomax, L Edwards,
P Edwards, Ropati

20 March 1994 Carcassone
7000, John Connolly (ENG)

FRANCE 4   T: Martial
G BRITAIN 12   T: Newlove, Edwards; G: Crooks,
Farrell

France: Frison, Garcia, Martial (Alexander Couttet 73),
Fraisse, Sirvent (Bomati h/t), Pascal Fages, Entat (c),
Frédéric Teixido, Patrick Torreilles, Llong (Théo Anast 58),
Divet, Didier Cabestany, Georges Grandjean (Attia 37)

GB: Graham Steadman, John Bentley (St John Ellis 73),
Connolly, Newlove (Powell 58), Offiah, Schofield (c),
Edwards, Crooks (Paul Moriarty 67), L Jackson, Steve
Molloy, Farrell, Fairbank (Barrie-Jon Mather 51), Joynt

*Almost a shock for an experimental GB team, who trail
4-2 until the last minute of the first half.*

4 March 1994 Ninian Park, Cardiff
6287, David Campbell (ENG)

WALES 13   T: Webster; G: Davies 4; DG: Davies
FRANCE 12   T: Entat, Garcia; G: Torreilles 2

Wales: Phil Ford (Daio Powell 68), Gerald Cordle, Allan
Bateman, Jonathan Davies (c), Anthony Sullivan,
Jonathan Griffiths, Kevin Ellis, Mark Jones (Ian Marlow
74), Barry Williams, David Young (Richard Webster 74),
Paul Moriarty, Rowland Phillips, Mark Perrett

France: Jean Frison, Jean-Marc Garcia, David Despin
(Christophe Martinez 24), David Fraisse, Claude Sirvent,
Pascal Fages, Patrick Entat (c), Frédéric Teixido
(Ezzedine Attia h/t), Patrick Torreilles, Bernard Llong
(Pascal Jampy 72), Daniel Divet, Didier Cabestany,
Thierry Valero

*Webster, who won 13 rugby union caps for Wales
1987-93, scores the winning try with his second touch
of the ball in his first rugby league international.*

International Matches 1994-95

22 Oct 1994 Wembley
57 034, Graham Annesley (AUS)

G BRITAIN 8   T: Davies; G: Davies, Goulding
AUSTRALIA 4   T: Renouf

GB: J Davies (Bateman 58), Robinson, Connolly, Allan
Hunte, Offiah, Powell (Barrie McDermott 23), Edwards
(c), Harrison (Mick Cassidy 61), L Jackson, Joynt,
Betts, Farrell (Bobby Goulding 31), Clarke

Winning is the drug

Dean Pay of Australia fails a drug test (for pseudoephedrine) on his international debut, but the tour management doesn't consider the offence serious enough to warrant a ban.

Australia: Brett Mullins, Andrew Ettingshausen, Mal Meninga (c), Steve Renouf, Wendell Sailor, Laurie Daley (Ricky Stuart 56), Allan Langer, Ian Roberts, Steve Walters, Paul Harragon, Paul Sironen (Dean Pay 52), Bradley Clyde (David Furner 40), Brad Fittler

A record crowd for an Ashes Test bites its nails through some heroic stuff. After Edwards becomes the first GB captain ever to be sent off in an international (for a 25th-minute high tackle that hospitalises Clyde) the twelve good men go 6-0 up by half-time and hold out to beat Australia at home for only the second time since 1978: an unexpected start for brand new coach Ellery Hanley, whose team were 3-1 underdogs. The two countries have now played each other 109 times, Britain leading 53-52 with four drawn.

Meninga, who sets records by touring here for the fourth time & the second as captain, fails to score v GB for the first time (in eleven previous matches, he scored 108 pts).

Sailor's the only new cap (and black player) in the Australian starting line-up. Pay & Furner also win their first. The latter's father Don toured Britain with the 1956 team, Clarke's father Colin scored a try for GB v Australia at Wembley in 1973.

Between scoring the winning try in the last World Cup final and playing in this series, Renouf contracts diabetes, requiring four daily insulin injections.

30 Oct 1994 Cardiff
John Connolly (ENG)

WALES 4   T: Powell
AUSTRALIA 46   T: Furner, Renouf 2, Mullins, Wishart, Meninga, Florimo, Fittler; G: Wishart 7

Wales: Ford, Sullivan, Scott Gibbs, Devereux (Cordle 10, Jason Lee 76), Hadley (Daio Powell 41), Iestyn Harris, Kevin Ellis, Young (c) (Webster 65), Griffiths, Marlow, Moriarty, Phillips, Perrett

Australia: Mullins, Rod Wishart, Meninga (c), Renouf, Sailor, Kevin Walters, Langer, Glenn Lazarus, S Walters (Greg Florimo 41), Roberts (Sironen 61), Sironen (David Fairleigh 41), Furner (Harragon 41), Fittler
[Yes, Sironen substituted then a substitute]

Wales, without Jonathan Davies (injured in the GB Test), are overwhelmed in every department in this record defeat: Devereux suffers a broken jaw, Young a

cut that needs twelve stitches; (Sironen, Ellis & Ford are sin binned); the vaunted rugby union recruit Gibbs misses two tackles that lead to tries; even their lone try has the suspicion of a forward pass about it. Australia don't regard this as an official international. A bit beneath them, probably.

5 Nov 1994 Old Trafford
43 930, Graham Annesley (AUS)

G BRITAIN 8   T: Newlove; G: Goulding 2
AUSTRALIA 38   T: Ettingshausen, Clyde, Mullins 2, Daley, Renouf; G: Wishart 7

GB: Steadman, Robinson, Connolly, Hunte (Newlove h/t), Offiah, Darryl Powell (Schofield h/t), Goulding, Harrison (McDermott 50), Jackson, Joynt (Cassidy 58), Betts (McDermott 62), Farrell, Clarke (c)

Australia: Mullins, Ettingshausen, Meninga (c), Renouf, Wishart, Daley (Sironen 69), Stuart, Lazarus, S Walters, Roberts (Florimo 20, Langer 53), Pay, Clyde, Fittler

Britain, without the injured Davies and the suspended Edwards, lead 4-2 till Meninga intercepts Goulding's pass in the 26th minute to set up Ettingshausen – then the fireworks start. Britain lose at Old Trafford for the fourth time in a row. Schofield plays in a record sixth Ashes series. McDermott (within two minutes of coming on) & Walters are sin-binned at the same time.

20 Nov 1994 Elland Road, Leeds
39 468, Bill Harrigan (AUS)

G BRITAIN 4   G: Farrell 2
AUSTRALIA 23   T: Daley, Wishart, Walters, Pay; G: Wishart 3; DG: Stuart

GB: Connolly, Robinson, Hunte (Darryl Powell 12), Newlove, Offiah, Clarke (Schofield 22), Edwards (c), Harrison, Jackson, McDermott (Nickle 32), Betts, Joynt (Goulding 71), Farrell

Australia: Mullins, Ettingshausen (Tim Brasher 51), Meninga (c), Renouf, Wishart, Daley, Stuart, Lazarus (Fairleigh 76), S Walters (Langer 76), Roberts (Florimo 13), Pay, Clyde, Fittler

The experiment which could only happen in League (Clarke, normally a flank forward, playing at fly-half) is wrecked by injury, a few of the early refereeing decisions

G Britain caps

46	Mick Sullivan	1954-63
46	Garry Schofield	1984-94
36	Ellery Hanley	1984-93
36	Shaun Edwards	1985-94

Sullivan also played twice v France before they were given Test status. His record of 36 consecutive caps still stands.

don't help (Pay stays on the field after a retributional late tackle on Edwards), and Daley's opening try, against the run of play with Britain leading 2-0, is the result of a lucky deflection – but there are no good excuses: Australia are simply a class above; Daley & Stuart brilliant, Walters deservedly man of the match. For the second tour in a row, Britain win at Wembley before losing the series up north. They haven't won the Ashes since 1970, or a home series against Australia since 1959 (this is the eighth here since then). Before the third Test, Australia complete their programme against English club sides. They've now won exactly 50 since their last defeat, by a single point, by Widnes in 1978.

4 Dec 1994 Béziers
11 000

FRANCE 0
AUSTRALIA 74 T: Ettingshausen 3, Mullins 2, Daley, Wishart, Renouf 2, Harragon, Stuart, Fairleigh, Meninga; G: Wishart 11

In the most fitting of finales, Meninga scores the last try three minutes from the end of his international career.

Stones Bitter (English) Championship 1993-94

	P	W	D	L	F	A	Pts
Wigan	30	23	0	7	780	403	46
Bradford N	30	23	0	7	784	555	46
Warrington	30	23	0	7	628	430	46
Castleford	30	19	1	10	787	466	39
Halifax	30	17	2	11	682	581	36
Sheffield E	30	16	2	12	704	671	34
Leeds	30	15	2	13	673	680	32
St Helens	30	15	1	14	704	537	31
Hull	30	14	2	14	536	530	30
Widnes	30	14	0	16	523	530	38
Featherstone R	30	13	1	16	651	681	27
Salford	30	11	0	19	554	650	22
Oldham	30	10	1	19	552	651	21
Wakefield T	30	9	1	20	458	708	19
Hull KR	30	9	0	21	493	782	18
Leigh	30	2	1	27	370	912	5

Wigan add to their own record by winning the title for the fifth successive season (no other club has won it more than twice in a row), Hull KR & Leigh are relegated, Leigh for the third time in ten years.

For the first time ever, three clubs finish level on points at the top. There's some fuss from Bradford Northern about the last matches of the season not being played at exactly the same time, but it's hard to believe Wigan would have dropped a point at Oldham (they win 52-10), and their winning margin on points difference

(148) doesn't really brook much argument. Warrington pay for not taking a single point off Wigan or Northern.

Division 2

	P	W	D	L	F	A	Pts
Workington	30	22	2	6	760	331	46
Doncaster	30	22	1	7	729	486	45
London C	30	21	2	7	842	522	44
Batley	30	21	1	8	707	426	43
Huddersfield	30	20	0	10	661	518	40
Keighley C	30	19	1	10	856	472	39
Dewsbury	30	18	1	11	766	448	37
Rochdale H	30	18	0	12	704	532	36
Ryedale-York	30	17	1	12	662	516	35
Whitehaven	30	14	4	12	571	437	32
Barrow	30	13	1	16	581	743	27
Swinton	30	11	0	19	528	681	22
Carlisle	30	9	0	21	540	878	18
Hunslet	30	3	1	26	45	814	7
Bramley	30	3	0	27	376	957	6
Highfield	30	1	1	28	267	1234	3

Workington & Doncaster are promoted, Doncaster (founded 1951) for the first time ever. Highfield suffer a league record 96-0 defeat at Doncaster in March.

Winning is the drug
In November 1994 Doncaster's South African full-back Jamie Bloem becomes the first League player ever to be banned for taking steroids.

Premiership 1993-94

1st ROUND
Bradford N	42	Leeds	16
Castleford	28	Halifax	23
Warrington	16	Sheffield E	32
Wigan	34	St Helens	16

SEMI-FINALS
Bradford N	16	Castleford	24
Wigan	52	Sheffield E	18

Martin Offiah (Wigan) & Simon Middleton (Castleford) score three tries each.

FINAL
22 May 1994 Old Trafford
35 644, referee Stuart Cummings

WIGAN   (16)24   CASTLEFORD   (8)20
T: Farrell, Panapa   T: Sampson, Sykes,
Botica, Betts   Steadman
G: Botica 4   G: Crooks 2, Steadman 2

Wigan: Paul Atcheson, Jason Robinson, Sam Panapa (Joe Lydon 72), Gary Connolly, Martin Offiah, Frano Botica, Shaun Edwards (c), Kelvin Skerrett, Martin Hall, Neil Cowie (Mick Cassidy 54), Denis Betts, Andrew Farrell, Phil Clarke

Castleford: St John Ellis, Chris Smith, Richard Blackmore, Tony Smith, Simon Middleton, Graham Steadman, Mike Ford, Lee Crooks (c) (Nathan Sykes 72), Richard Russell, Dean Sampson, Martin Ketteridge (Ian Smales 49), Andy Hay, Tawera Nikau

A slightly under-strength Wigan recover from Skerrett's fractured cheekbone to lead 24-6 after 70 minutes, avenge their Regal Trophy defeat, repeat their 1992 treble, and win the Premiership for the third time. In their only previous appearance in the final (1984), Castleford lost to Hull KR. Sykes scores his try after the ball rebounds from his head.

2nd Division

1st ROUND

Batley	28	Huddersfield	17
Doncaster	48	Dewsbury	18
London Crusaders	66	Keighley C	12
Workington Town	50	Rochdale H	6

SEMI-FINALS

Doncaster	6	London C	16
Workington T	19	Batley	4

FINAL
22 May 1994 Old Trafford
referee John Connolly

WORKINGTON	(24)30	LONDON	(6)22
T: Cocker 2, Byrne, Kay		T: Johnson 3, Campbell	
Drummond, Mulligan		G: Gallagher 3	
G: Marwood 3			

Workington: Mark Mulligan, Des Drummond, Tony Kay, Paul Burns, Stuart Cocker, Wayne Kitchin, Dean Marwood, James Pickering (Peter Riley 46), Phil McKenzie, Colin Armstrong (c), Brad Hepi, Martin Oglanby, Ged Byrne (Paul Penrice 50)

Crusaders: André Stoop, John Gallagher, Scott Roskell, Logan Campbell, Mark Johnson, Dixon McIvor, Mark Riley (Geoff Luxon 13), Chris Whiteley, Scott Carter (Kris Smith 6), Dave Rotheram, Steve Rosolen, Sam Stewart (c), Neville Ramsey

Man of the Match: Marwood

Workington, beaten finalists the previous year, complete the 2nd Division Double against a club playing in any final for the first time in their 14-season existence. Johnson's three tries equal the record set by Darryl Powell (Sheffield Eagles) in the finals of 1989 & 1992.

Challenge Cup 1993-94

4th ROUND

Barrow	30	Bradford N	58
Batley	8	Keighley C	29
Bramley	11	Widnes	20
Carlisle	12	Workington T	13
Castleford	36	Salford	4
Doncaster	18	Dewsbury	6
Halifax	18	Warrington	22
Highfield	4	Whitehaven	15
Huddersfield	16	St Helens	23
Hull KR	16	Ryedale-York	6
Hunslet	20	Oldham	30
London C	14	Featherstone R	28
Rochdale H	18	Leeds	40
Sheffield E	42	Leigh	10
Swinton	12	Hull	18
Wigan	24	Wakefield T	16

5th ROUND

Doncaster	20	Oldham	0
Hull	21	Wigan	22
Hull KR	8	Featherstone R	30
Keighley C	14	Castleford	52
Leeds	38	Warrington	4
Whitehaven	4	St Helens	46
Widnes	22	Sheffield E	6
Workington T	0	Bradford N	32

6th ROUND

Castleford	30	Widnes	6
Leeds	33	Bradford N	10
St Helens	40	Doncaster	9
Wigan	32	Featherstone R	14

SEMI-FINALS

Wigan	20	Castleford	6	*at Leeds*
Leeds	20	St Helens	8	*at Wigan*

FINAL
30 April 1994 Wembley
78 348, referee David Campbell

WIGAN	(12)26	LEEDS	(0)16
T: Offiah 2, Farrell, Panapa		T: Fallon, Schofield,	
G: Botica 5		Cummins	
		G: Holroyd 2	

Wigan: Gary Connolly, Va'aiga Tuigamala, Dean Bell (c), Barrie-Jon Mather, Martin Offiah, Frano Botica, Shaun Edwards, Kelvin Skerrett, Martin Dermott, Andy Platt (Sam Panapa 59), Denis Betts, Andrew Farrell (Mick Cassidy 52), Phil Clarke

Leeds: Alan Tait, Jim Fallon, Kevin Iro, Craig Innes, Francis Cummins, Graham Holroyd, Garry Schofield, Neil Harmon (Mike O'Neill 62), James Lowes, Harvey

Howard, Gary Mercer, Richard Eyres, Ellery Hanley (c) (Marcus Vassilakopoulos 69)

Lance Todd Trophy (Man of the Match): Offiah

The records keep mounting up. Wigan win the Cup for the 14th time and the seventh in succession (no-one else has ever won it more than twice in a row) to complete their fifth consecutive Double. Mather is one of the two tallest players (6'7) ever to take part in a Wembley final (matching John Harrison of St Helens in 1991), Cummins (17 yrs 200 days) is the youngest ever player, Vassilakopoulos (also 17) the youngest ever forward. O'Neill becomes the first player to take part in finals 15 years apart: his first (this is his fifth) was in 1979, when he was with Widnes. Fallon is the only player to appear in a rugby union and rugby league English cup final.

Regal Trophy 1993-94

3rd ROUND

Batley	8	Salford	12
Bradford N	16	Halifax	8
Carlisle	34	Bramley	4
Castleford	54	Leigh	14
Hull	10	Widnes	6
Oldham	8	Wigan	16
Ryedale-York	10	London C	42
St Helens	8	Wartrington	16

4th ROUND

Castleford	44	Carlisle	4
London C	10	Bradford N	22
Salford	26	Hull	6
Warrington	10	Wigan	27

SEMI-FINALS

Bradford N	10	Castleford	23
Salford	12	Wigan	18

FINAL

22 Jan 1994 Headingley, Leeds
15 626, referee David Campbell

CASTLEFORD (20)33 WIGAN (2)2
T: Ketteridge 2, Nikau G: Botica
T: Anderson, Crooks
G: Crooks 6 DG: Kemp

Castleford: Graham Steadman, St John Ellis, Richard Blackmore, Grant Anderson (Andy Hay 63), Simon Middleton, Tony Kemp, Mike Ford, Lee Crooks (c), Richard Russell, Martin Ketteridge (Dean Sampson 74), Tony Morrison, Ian Smales, Tawera Nikau

Wigan: Joe Lydon, Jason Robinson, Barrie-Jon Mather, Gary Connolly, Martin Offiah, Frano Botica, Shaun

Tries in Challenge Cup finals

6	Kevin Iro	1988-89-90
4	Stan Moorhouse	1913-15
4	Allan Edwards	1942-43-48
4	Eric Batten	1944-45-49-52
4	Johnny Lawrenson	1941-52
4	Martin Offiah	1992-94

Iro scored two in each of three matches.

Goals in Challenge Cup finals

16	Frano Botica	1991-92-93-94
15	Neil Fox	1960-62-63
12	Joe Lydon	1988-89-90-92
11	Mick Burke	1981-82
10	Ray Dutton	1975-76-77

Points in Challenge Cup finals

39	Neil Fox	1960-62-63
36	Frano Botica	1991-92-93-94
34	Joe Lydon	1984-88-89-90-92

In today's values, Fox scored 42.

Winning the Lance Todd Trophy more than once

Gerry Helme	Warrington	1950	1954
Andy Gregory	Wigan	1988	1990
Martin Offiah	Wigan	1992	1994

Helme won his second award in a replay.

Edwards (Sam Panapa 51), Kelvin Skerrett, Martin Dermott, Andy Platt (c), Neil Cowie (Mick Cassidy 30), Andrew Farrell, Phil Clarke

Man of the Match: Ketteridge

Castleford set three records for a final in beating the holders (and preventing Wigan's Grand Slam): most points by one side (previously their own 25 v Blackpool Borough in 1977, their only other appearance in the final), record winning margin (previously 24-0 by Widnes v Leeds in 1992), most points by one player (16, previously 15 by Derek Whitehead of Warrington in 1974, worth 16 today). Crooks' six goals also equal Whitehead's record.

Regal Trophy 1994-95

In the first round, Huddersfield beat Blackpool G 142-4 to break the record, also set by Huddersfield: 119-2 v Swinton Park in 1914, worth 145-2 today. They and Barrow, who beat Nottingham 138-0 the following day, each score 26 tries.

3rd ROUND

Keighley	26	Sheffield	10
Widnes	20	Oldham	6
Batley	22	St Helens	22
St Helens	50	Batley	22
Whitehaven	14	Bradford	34
Hull	14	Wigan	38
Salford	24	Warrington	31
Dewsbury	2	Castleford	30
Workington	14	Leeds	18

QUARTER-FINALS

Leeds	14	Castleford	34
Keighley	18	Warrington	20
Widnes	23	Bradford	10
Wigan	24	St Helens	22

SEMI-FINALS
(14-15 Jan): Widnes v Warrington, Wigan v Castleford

Leading Scorers 1993-94

TRIES

43	Mark Johnson	London C
40	St John Ellis	Castleford
37	Paul Newlove	Bradford N
37	Martin Offiah	Wigan

GOALS

188	Frano Botica	Wigan
159	John Gallagher	London C
148	Deryck Fox	Bradford N

POINTS

422	Frano Botica	Wigan
384	John Gallagher	London C
338	Jonathan Davies	Warrington

TRIES IN A MATCH

5	Stuart Cocker	Workington T	v Barrow
5	James Grant	Hull	v Leigh
5	Carl Hall	Doncaster	v Mysons
5	Tommy Oldroyd	Batley	v Highfield

GOALS IN A MATCH

12	Steve Turner	Rochdale H	v Blackpool G
12	Robert Turner	Doncaster	v Highfield

POINTS IN A MATCH

36	John Wasyliw	Keighley C	v Nottingham
32	Steve Turner	Rochdale H	v Blackpool G

Awards 1993-94

Man of Steel	Jonathan Davies	Warrington
Div 1 Player	Jonathan Davies	Warrington
Div 2 Player	Martin Oglanby	Workington T
Young Player	Andrew Farrell	Wigan
Coach	John Joyner	Castleford

Wigan's dissatisfaction with John Dorahy (he leaves after less than a year despite winning three major trophies) is reflected in Joyner's nomination, which seems to belong to the Anyone Can Coach Wigan With All The Players They've Got school of thought.

Winfield Cup 1993
Australian club championship

	P	W	D	L	F	A	Pts
Canterbury-Bankstown	22	17	0	5	464	254	34
St George	22	17	0	5	418	258	34
Canberra Raiders	22	16	1	5	587	272	33
Manly-Waringah	22	16	0	6	442	232	32
Brisbane Broncos	22	16	0	6	517	330	32
North Sydney	22	14	1	7	448	325	29
Illawarra	22	12	0	10	373	253	24
Eastern Suburbs	22	11	1	10	343	356	23
Newcastle	22	10	0	12	337	381	20
Cronulla-Sutherland	22	9	0	13	272	399	18
Parramatta	22	9	0	13	237	439	18
Penrith	22	7	0	15	314	428	14
Western Suburbs	22	7	0	15	319	475	14
South Sydney	22	6	0	16	319	560	12
Balmain	22	6	1	15	327	412	11
Gold Coast	22	1	0	21	229	572	2

Balmain have two pts deducted for breaking the player replacement rule v Penrith.

LEADING SCORERS

Tries	Noa Nadruku	Canberra
Goals	Darryl Halligan	N Sydney
Points	Darryl Halligan	N Sydney

Play-offs

Brisbane	36	Manly	10
St George	31	Canberra	10
Brisbane	30	Canberra	12
St George	27	Canterbury	12
Brisbane	23	Canterbury	16

Grand Final

26 Sep 1993 Sydney Football Stadium
42 239, referee Greg McCallum

BRISBANE BRONCOS(10)14 St GEORGE (6)6
T: Johns, Matterson, Carne   G: Herron 3
G: O'Neill

Brisbane: Julian O'Neill, Michael Hancock, Steve Renouf, Chris Johns, Willie Carne, Kevin Walters, Allan Langer (c), Glenn Lazarus, Kerrod Walters, Mark Hohn (Andrew Gee, Peter Ryan), Trevor Gillmeister, Alan Cann, Terry Matterson (John Plath)

St George: Michael Potter (c), Ricky Walford, Graeme Bradley, Mark Coyne, Ian Herron, Tony Smith (Phil Blake), Noel Goldthorpe, Tony Priddle, Wayne Collins (Nathan Brown), Jason Stevens (Jeff Hardy), David Barnhill (Gorden Tallis), Scott Gourley, Brad Mackay

Man of the Match (Clive Churchill Medal): Mackay

The Broncos, who retain the Cup (beating the same team as in the previous year's final), are the first club to win it after finishing as low as fifth in the league.

Winfield Cup 1994

GRAND FINAL 25 Sep, Sydney Football Stadium
Canberra Raiders   36   Canterbury-Bankstown 12

Canberra, who lead 18-6 at half-time, score 7 tries. Full report in 1996 Yearbook.

World Club Challenge
1 June 1994 ANZ, Brisbane
54 220, referee Greg McCallum (AUS)

BRISBANE BRONCOS(4)14	WIGAN	(12)20
T: Sailor, Hancock, O'Neill	T: Betts, Mather, Robinson	
G: O'Neill	G: Botica 4	

Broncos: Sailor, Hancock, Renouf (Ryan 23), Johns, Carne, Kevin Walters (Plath 6, McKenna 74), Langer, Lazarus, Kerrod Walters, Gee (Galea 65), Hohn, Cann, O'Neill

Wigan: Connolly, Robinson, Panapa, Mather (Atcheson 50), Offiah, Botica, Edwards, Cowie, Dermott (Hall 23), McGinty (Cassidy 26), Betts, Farrell, Clarke

Man of the Match: Edwards

Wigan, under caretaker coach Graeme West, missing both their first-choice props, avenge their defeat of the previous year to win the Challenge for the third time (after 1987 & 1991), the first away from home.

World Sevens 1994

FINAL Sydney
Manly   44   St George   12

Rugby Union

Like Wigan, Bath dominated the English domestic scene, winning the League for the fourth consecutive season and the Cup for the eighth time. At the end of the season, they lost coach Jack Rowell and three linchpins (Stuart Barnes, Gareth Chilcott, Richard Hill) but the opposition's eyes didn't light up for long: Bath picked up internationals Simon Geoghegan & Andy Nicol, moved Mike Catt to fly-half, and carried on as before: a record number of successive League wins and (at the time of writing) clear water at the top of Division 1.

Unlike Wigan, the effects on the national team weren't so demonstrably negative. True, Ireland won at Twickenham, Scotland came close and South Africa won 27-9 – but there were wins against New Zealand and South Africa (32-15 in a faultless performance), and Wales were beaten more easily than the scoreline suggests. The huge wins over Romania & Canada haven't proved anything yet, but England still look the best of the Five Nations.

That they didn't actually win the title shows the kind of a season it was: win some, lose some. Wales, without ever really looking the part, at least climbed some of the way back up from the nadir against Canada – but defeats by Western Samoa & South Africa were probably more realistic signposts on the way to the World Cup. France lost to Wales, England & Canada – then twice beat the All Blacks away from home. Ireland beat England but no-one else to speak of. Scotland didn't beat anyone at all.

Even the All Blacks caught the bug, losing to England, France & Australia, who won every match in 1994 and are probably favourites to retain the world title. But anything can happen at the end of the long season that looms ahead. Very long, in domestic as well as international rugby. If the top players are getting paid (and one way or another they surely are) they appear to deserve every penny.

Five Nations Championship 1994

15 Jan National Stadium, Cardiff

WALES 29	T: Rayer 2, I Evans; C: N Jenkins; PG: N Jenkins 4
SCOTLAND 6	PG: G Hastings 2

Wales: Tony Clement, Ieuan Evans (c), Mike Hall, Nigel Davies, Nigel Walker (Mark Rayer 11), Neil Jenkins, Rupert Moon, Ricky Evans, Garin Jenkins, John Davies, Phil Davies, Gareth Llewellyn, Emyr Lewis, Scott Quinnell

Scotland: Gavin Hastings (c), Tony Stanger, Gregor Townsend, Iain Jardine, Kenny Logan, Craig Chalmers (Doug Wyllie 55), Andy Nicol, Peter Wright, Keny Milne, Paul Burnell, Neil Edwards, Shade Munro, Derek Turnbull, Rob Wainwright, Iain Morrison (George [Doddie] Weir 18)

Hastings' 47th cap equals Andy Irvine's record for a Scotland full-back.

15 Jan Parc des Princes

FRANCE 35	T: Benetton, Saint-André, Lacroix, Merle; C: Lacroix 3; PG: Lacroix 3
IRELAND 15	PG: Elwood 5

France: Jean-Luc Sadourny, Philippe Bernat-Salles, Philippe Sella, Thierry Lacroix, Philippe Saint-André, Alain Penaud, Fabien Galthié, Louis Armary, Jean-Michel Gonzalez*, Philippe Gallart, Olivier Merle, Olivier Roumat (c), Philippe Benetton, Marc Cecillon, Abdelatif Benazzi

* One source calls him Jean-Marie.

Ireland: Conor O'Shea, Richard Wallace, Vinny Cunningham, Philip Danahar, Simon Geoghegan, Eric Elwood, Michael Bradley (c) (Rob Saunders temp), Nick Popplewell, Terry Kingston, Peter Clohessy (Garrett Halpin 56), Paddy Johns, Neil Francis, Mick Galwey, Brian Robinson, Ken O'Connell

France have won their last nine matches v Ireland, who've won only once in Paris (1972) since 1952 and haven't scored a try there since 1980. Jim Fleming referees an international match for the 18th time, breaking Alan Hosie's Scottish record.

5 Feb Murrayfield

SCOTLAND 14   T: Wainwright; PG: G Hastings 2; DG: Townsend
ENGLAND 15   PG: Callard 5

Scotland: G Hastings (c), Stanger, Scott Hastings (Ian Jardine 71), Wyllie, Logan, Townsend, Gary Armstrong (Bryan Redpath 48-50), Alan Sharp, Milne, Burnell, Munro, Andy Reed, Peter Walton, Weir, Wainwright (Ian Smith 67)

England: Jonathan Callard, Tony Underwood, Will Carling (c), Phil de Glanville, Rory Underwood, Rob Andrew, Kyran Bracken, Jason Leonard, Brian Moore, Victor Ubogu, Martin Bayfield, Martin Johnson, Jon Hall, Ben Clarke, Neil Back

Callard kicks an injury-time penalty, dubiously awarded against Jardine, just after Townsend's last-minute dropped goal seems to have made up for G Hastings' five missed kicks. Hastings' total of 59 pts breaks Andy Irvine's record in Scotland-England matches.

5 Feb Lansdowne Road

IRELAND 15   PG: Elwood 5
WALES 17   T: N Jenkins; PG: N Jenkins 4

Ireland: O'Shea, Wallace, Mark McCall, Danahar, Geoghegan, Elwood, Bradley (c), Popplewell, Kingston, Clohessy, Galwey, Francis, Robinson, Johns, Denis McBride

Wales: Clement (Rayer 52), I Evans (c), Hall, N Davies (Robert Jones 75), Wayne Proctor (Simon Hill 43), N Jenkins, Moon, R Evans, G Jenkins, J Davies, P Davies, Llewellyn, Lewis, Quinnell, Mark Perego

Elwood hits the post with a penalty from twenty yards with seven minutes to go.

19 Feb Twickenham

ENGLAND 12   PG: Callard 4
IRELAND 13   T: Geoghegan; C: Elwood; PG: Elwood 2

England: Callard, T Underwood, Carling (c), de Glanville, R Underwood, Andrew, Bracken, Leonard, Moore,

Ubogu, Johnson, Bayfield, Tim Rodber, Steve Ojomoh, Back

Ireland: O'Shea, Wallace, Maurice Field, Danaher, Geoghegan, Elwood, Bradley (c), Popplewell, Kingston, Clohessy, Galwey, Francis, Robinson (KD O'Connell temp), Johns, McBride

England's first home defeat in the Championship since 1988 owes something to Elwood's controversial late penalty, awarded after Geoghegan's tackle on Andrew.

19 Feb National Stadium, Cardiff

WALES 24   T: Quinnell, Walker; C: N Jenkins; PG: N Jenkins 4
FRANCE 15   T: Roumat, Sella; C: Lacroix; PG: Lacroix

Wales: Rayer, Hill, Hall, Clement, Walker, N Jenkins, Moon, R Evans, G Jenkins, J Davies, P Davies, Llewellyn (c), Lewis, Quinnell, Perego

France: Sadourny, Émile N'Tamack, Sella, Lacroix, Saint-André, Penaud, Galthié, Armary, Gonzalez, Gallart, Merle, Roumat (c), Benetton, Cecillon, Benazzi

After twelve consecutive defeats v France (Sella played in each one) Wales beat them for the first time since 1982 and win successive Championship matches for the first time since 1988.

5 March Parc des Princes

FRANCE 14   T: Benazzi; PG: Lacroix 3
ENGLAND 18   PG: Andrew 5; DG: Andrew

France: Sadourny, William Téchoueyres, Sella, Lacroix, Saint-André, Penaud, Galthié, Laurent Benezech, Gonzalez, Gallart, Merle, Roumat (c), Benazzi, Benetton, Laurent Cabannes

England: David Pears, Ian Hunter, Carling (c), de Glanville, R Underwood, Andrew, Dewi Morris, Leonard, Moore, Ubogu, Johnson, Nigel Redman, Rodber, Ojomoh, Clarke

For the fifth match in a row, England fail to score a try - but are quite happy to let Andrew kick five penalties out of five to bring about their seventh successive win over France, four of them in Paris.

5 March Lansdowne Road

IRELAND 6   PG: Elwood 2
SCOTLAND 6   PG: G Hastings 2

Ireland: O'Shea, Wallace, Field, Danaher, Geoghegan, Elwood, Bradley (c), Popplewell, Kingston, Clohessy, Galwey, Francis, Robinson, Johns, D McBride

Scotland: G Hastings (c) (Michael Dods temp), Stanger, S Hastings, Wyllie, Logan, Townsend, Armstrong, Sharp, Milne, Burnell, Munro, Reed, Walton, Weir, Smith

19 March Murrayfield

SCOTLAND 12 PG: G Hastings 4
FRANCE 20 T: Sadourny, Saint-André; C:
Lacroix, Montlaur; PG: Lacroix 2

Scotland: G Hastings (c), Stanger, Hastings, Wyllie, Logan, Townsend, Redpath, Sharp, Milne, Burnell, Munro, Reed, Walton, Weir, Smith

France: Sadourny, Téchoueyres, Sella, Yann Delaigue, Saint-André (c), Lacroix (Pierre Montlaur 52), Alain Macabiau, Benezech, Gonzalez, Laurent Seigne, Olivier Brouzet, Benetton, Benazzi, Cabannes

The Hastings brothers are both capped for the 50th time but can't stop France winning in Edinburgh for the first time since 1978, in their first match there since the old stadium was revamped.

19 March Twickenham

ENGLAND 15 T: R Underwood, Rodber;
C: Andrew; PG: Andrew
WALES 8 T:Walker; PG: N Jenkins

England: Hunter, T Underwood, Carling (c), de Glanville, R Underwood, Andrew (Mike Catt 77), Morris, Leonard, Moore, Ubogu, Johnson, Redman, Rodber, Dean Richards, Clarke

Wales: Rayer, I Evans (c), Hall, N Davies, Walker, N Jenkins, Moon, R Evans, G Jenkins, J Davies, P Davies, Llewellyn, Lewis (Tony Copsey 49), Quinnell, Perego

Needing to win the 100th match between the two countries by 16 points to take the title, England bring back the incomparable Richards (who teaches the rampaging young Quinnell more in one match than he's learned throughout the Championship so far). It isn't quite enough: England lead 15-3 with 26 minutes left before the collective foot mysteriously lifts off the gas pedal. Moore wins his 50th cap. R Underwood celebrates becoming the first Englishman to play twelve times v Wales by scoring England's first international try for 438 mins, twelve short of their all-time record.

Final standings

	P	W	D	L	F	A	Pts
Wales	4	3	0	1	78	51	6
England	4	3	0	1	60	49	6
France	4	2	0	2	84	69	4
Ireland	4	1	1	2	49	70	3
Scotland	4	0	1	3	38	70	1

Wales win the title outright for the first time since 1979 and the 22nd time in all. If England had won it, both countries would be on 21 apiece.

England

27 Nov 1993 Twickenham

ENGLAND 15 PG: Callard 4; DG: Andrew
N ZEALAND 9 PG: Wilson 3

England: Jonathan Callard, T Underwood, Carling (c), de Glanville, Underwood, Andrew, Kyran Bracken, Leonard, Moore, Ubogu, Redman, Johnson, Rodber, Clarke, Richards

N Zealand: John Timu, Jeff Wilson, Frank Bunce, Eroni Clarke, Va'iga Tuigamala, Mark Ellis, Stu Forster, C Dowd, Sean Fitzpatrick (c), Olo Brown, Ian Jones, S Gordon, Zinzan Brooke, Jamie Joseph, Aron Pene

The Daily Telegraph talked of a Black outlook for England against opposition who wouldn't lose a wink of sleep over the match; the occasional bad dream probably follows. Carling leads a team to victory against every other senior International Board country - but England are lucky that a) Grant Fox didn't make the tour, and b) Cooper, in prolific form as his replacement, suffered a groin injury v Scotland. Wilson, coming down from his Murrayfield heights, misses five kicks at goal. Meanwhile England's two new caps do well, Callard kicking the goals, Bracken bossing things despite having his ankle trampled on by Joseph.

4 June 1994 Loftus Versfeld, Pretoria

S AFRICA 15 PG: Joubert 5
ENGLAND 32 T: Clarke, Andrew; C: Andrew 2;
PG: Andrew 5; DG: Andrew

S Africa: André Joubert, James Small, Pieter Müller, Brendon Venter, Chester Williams, Hennie Le Roux, Joost van der Westhuizen, Ollie Le Roux, John Allan, Balie Swart, H Strydom, Steve Atherton, François Pienaar (c), Fritz van Heerden, Christiaan (Tiaan) Strauss

England: Paul Hull, T Underwood, Carling (c), de Glanville, Underwood, Andrew, Morris, Leonard, Moore, Ubogu, Bayfield, Redman, Rodber, Clarke, Richards (Ojomoh 55)

Andrew's 27 points set a new England individual points-scoring record for a single match (although his dropped goal, from a free kick, should have been disallowed because no opponent had touched the ball

Most dropped goals in internationals

25	Hugo Porta	Argentina	1971-90
19	Rob Andrew	England	1985-94
18	Naas Botha	S Africa	1980-92

Andrew also scored two for the British Lions 1989-93.

Elandré van den Bergh (Eastern Province) is cleared of malpractice after raking Jonathan Callard so badly that he needs 25 stitches in his face. In the same full-blooded tour match, Tim Rodber becomes only the second man to be sent off while playing for England (the first: Mike Burton v Australia 1975). The great god No Further Action swiftly comes into play: Rodber plays in the second Test and goes unpunished. Arguably just about fair enough (he was sorely provoked), though so was the sending-off: he hit his opponent ten times! To the consternation of Callard, among others, Van den Bergh's picked for the subsequent tour to Britain.

Meanwhile, Stuart Barnes is reprimanded for comments in his newspaper column after a reception in Bloemfontein, at which he alleges the visitors are 'vilified in Afrikaans by their malignant hosts' who don't realise that England player Mike Catt, a South African, understands the lingo! Jack Rowell calls the article 'naughty'.

first). Rory Underwood's 66th cap adds to his England record. South Africa concede a record number of points in a home match. Williams' brother Avril, one of the first black players to play for the Springboks, had won two caps in 1984, both v England. Allan won nine caps for Scotland 1990-91.

11 June 1994 Newlands, Cape Town

S AFRICA 27	T: H Le Roux, Joubert; C: Joubert; PG: H Le Roux 3, Joubert 2
ENGLAND 9	PG: Andrew 3

S Africa: Joubert, Small, Müller, Venter, Williams (van der Westhuizen 32), Le Roux, Johan Roux, Swart, Allan, L Le Roux, Mark Andrews, Atherton, Pienaar (c), Ian MacDonald (F van Heerden 68), Adriaan Richter

Englan: unchanged except for Ojomoh in place of Richards

S Africa's first home win since their return to international rugby.

12 Nov 1994 Twickenham

ENGLAND 54	T: T Underwood 2, Carling, penalty try, Rodber, R Underwood; C: Andrew 6; PG: Andrew 4
ROMANIA 3	PG: Ivanciuc

England: Hull, T Underwood, Carling (c), Jeremy Guscott, Underwood, Andrew, Morris, Leonard, Moore, Ubogu, Johnson, Bayfield, Rodber, Clarke, Ojomoh

Romania: V Brici, G Solomie, Mihai Vioreanu, S Tofan, R Cioca, Ilie Ivanciuc, Daniel Neaga, Leodor Costea (Florin Marioara 52), Ion Negreci (Cristian Gheorghe 65), J Vlad, Constantin Cojocariu, C Branescu (A Guranescu 78), Traian Oroian (Catalin Draguceanu 51), Alexandru Gealapu, Tiberiu Brinza (c)

Romania take the lead with a third-minute kick from near half-way, then the floodgates open - though England don't quite pour through. Errors of handling and judgment get in the way, Guscott has two tries disallowed, and England run several kickable penalties in the second half, preventing Andrew (who misses only one of eleven kicks at goal) from breaking his own national record of 27 points in an international (he scored 18 points v Romania at Twickenham on his international debut in 1985). Carling celebrates his 50th cap with a try.

10 Dec 1994 Twickenham

ENGLAND 60	T: T Underwood, R Underwood 2, Bracken, Catt 2: C: Andrew 6; PG: Andrew 6
CANADA 19	T: Lougheed 2, Evans; C: Rees 2

England: Hull (Catt 26), T Underwood (de Glanville 63), Carling, Guscott, R Underwood, Andrew, Bracken, Leonard,. Moore, Ubogu, Johnson, Bayfield, Rodber, Clarke, Richards

Canada: Scott Stewart, Ron Toews, Christian Stewart (Steve Gray 40-43 temp), Ian Stuart (c) (Steve Gray 65), Dave Lougheed, Gareth Rees, John Graf, Eddie Evans, Mark Cardinal, D Jackart, Mike James, Norm Hadley, Ian Gordon, Gord MacKinnon, Colin McKenzie

The scoreline doesn't say it all: Canada play well and certainly tackle ferociously (Stuart's cautioned by the referee), Lougheed looks good on the wing, and it takes England 48 minutes to score the first try, an interception at that - but by then Andrew's boot has set up the kill: his penalty goals put England 18-0 ahead. His last conversion, the final kick of the match, equals the world record for most points in an international between major countries. Twelve successful place kicks out of twelve (he missed only a drop at goal) definitely constitute a record, achieved in the teeth of a typically difficult Twickenham wind. His only problem's the loss of a contact lens.

Most points in an international

33	Didier Camberabero	FRA	1987	(30)
30	Rob Andrew	ENG	1994	(30)

Between major countries. All scores recalculated using today's points values. Actual scores in brackets

England most points in a match

82-0	1881	v Wales	(-)
70-8	1987	v Japan	(60-7)
68-27	1989	v Fiji	(58-23)
67-3	1989	v Romania	(58-3)
60-19	1994	v Canada	(60-19)

All totals recalculated using today's points values. Actual totals in brackets (no points awarded in 1881).

England caps

69	Rory Underwood	1984-94
61	Rob Andrew	1985-94
58	Peter Winterbottom	1982-93
55	Wade Dooley	1985-93
54	Brian Moore	1987-94
51	Will Carling	1988-94

England points

301	Jonathan Webb	1987-93	(297)
242	WH 'Dusty' Hare	1978-84	(240)
265	Rob Andrew	1985-94	(264)
204	Simon Hodgkinson	1989-91	(203)
200	Rory Underwood	1984-94	(165)

All totals recalculated using today's points values. If Andrew had been first choice kicker in the reigns of Webb, Hodgkinson & Marcus Rose...

England tries

40	Rory Underwood	1984-94
18	Cyril Lowe	1914-23
16	Jeremy Guscott	1989-93
10	John GG Birkett	1907-12
10	David Duckham	1969-76

Most times captain in internationals

44	Will Carling	ENG
43	Hugo Porta	ARG*
36	Nick Farr-Jones	AUS
34	Jean-Pierre Rives	FRA
30	Wilson Whineray	NZ

* and South America

Scotland

20 Nov 1993 Murrayfield

SCOTLAND 15 PG: G Hastings 4 ,Chalmers
N ZEALAND 51 T: Ellis 2, Wilson 3, Brooke, Bunce;
C: Cooper 4,Wilson; PG: Cooper 2

Scotland: G Hastings (c) (Logan 35-40 temp), Stanger, Jardine, Graham Shiel, S Hastings, Chalmers (Wyllie 59), Nicol (Redpath 7-10 temp), Watt, Milne, Burnell, Damian Cronin (Carl Hogg 62), Macdonald, McIvor, Wainwright, G Weir

N Zealand: Timu, Wilson, Bunce, Matthew Cooper, Tuigamala, Ellis, Forster, Dowd, Fitzpatrick (c), Brown, Jones, Gordon, Joseph, Brooke, Pene

G Hastings passes 500 points in intenationals, but the day belongs to Wilson, the youngest player (20yrs 27 days) to score three tries on his international debut. New Zealand's highest score in any international in Europe, and their biggest winning margin v Scotland, is no surprise: ten days earlier they scored twelve tries in beating South of Scotland 84-5 (a century there for the taking but they eased off near the end). The All Blacks' previous record score in Britain was 63-0 by the first touring team, in 1905 v the Combined Hartlepool Clubs. Under 1905 points values, South of Scotland would have lost only 60-0.

4 June 1994 Buenos Aires

ARGENTINA 16 T: Teran; C: Meson; PG: Meson 3
SCOTLAND 15 PG: Dods 5

Argentina: Santiago Meson, Martin Teran, D Cuesta Silva, Marcelo Loffreda (c), Gustavo Jorge, Guillermo del Castillo, NF Miranda, Matias Corral, JJ Angelillo, Ernesto Noriega, Pedro Sporleder, German Llanes, C Viel, Pablo Camerlinckx, Christian Viel-Temperley

Scotland: Michael Dods, C Joiner, I Jardine, G Shiel, K Logan, G Townsend, B Redpath, A Sharp, Kevin McKenzie, P Burnell, S Munro, A Reed (c), P Walton, C Hogg, I Smith

11 June 1994 Buenos Aires

ARGENTINA 19 T: Martin; C: Meson; PG: Meson 3;
DG: Del Castillo
SCOTLAND 17 T: Logan; PG: Shiel 2;
DG: Townsend 2

Argentina: Meson, Teran, Cuesta Silva, Loffreda (c), Jorge, del Castillo, Miranda, Grau, JJ Angelillo, Noriega, Llanes, Sporleder, Martin, Viel-Temperley, José Santamaría

Scotland unchanged

Dods, who missed five penalty kicks in the first international, misses one in the last minute here.

19 Nov 1994 Murrayfield

SCOTLAND 10 T: Stanger; C: G Hastings;
PG: G Hastings

S AFRICA 34 T: Van der Westhuizen 2, Williams, Straeuli, Mulder; C: Joubert 3; PG: Joubert

Scotland: G Hastings (c), Stanger, S Hastings, Shiel, Logan, Chalmers, Derrick Patterson, Redpath, Sharp,

Scotland: most points conceded

62-0	1951	S Africa	(44-0)
51-15	1993	N Zealand	(51-15)
48-14	1911	Wales	(32-10)
47-17	1981	N Zealand	(40-16)
45-14	1972	Wales	(35-12)
43-10	1943*	England	(29-6)
42-15	1992	Australia	(37-13)
42-12	1953	England	(26-8)

*All scores amended to current points values. Actual score in brackets. The top three were in home matches. * Wartime match (unofficial).*

Scotland tries

24	Ian Smith	1924-33
16	Tony Stanger	1989-94
15	Iwan Tukalo	1987-91

Milne, Burnell, McIvor, Jeremy Richardson, Reed, Morrison, Weir

S Africa: Joubert, Henriks, Muller, Japie Mulder, Williams, H le Roux, J van der Westhuizen, Pieter du Randt, Schmidt, Tommy Laubscher, Andrews, Philip Schutte, Ruben Kruger, Staeuli, Pienaar (c)

Scotland pick their team early, leaving out Rob Wainwright, Ian Jardine & Damian Cronin who all contribute to the A team's win over South Africa - but it hardly matters: the tourists, only 8-0 ahead after the first half, run riot early in the second. Their 14st scrum-half scores the first try by a South African in an international at Murrayfield since Janie Engelbrecht (the current tour manager) in 1965. Scotland haven't won any of their last nine internationals spread over nearly two years. Jim Aitken, who captained them to the 1984 Grand Slam, believes 'defeat at the hands of the Ivory Coast in next year's World Cup is a real possibility.'

Ireland

13 Nov 1993 Lansdowne Road, Dublin

IRELAND 25	T:Geoghegan; C: Elwood; PG: Elwood 6
ROMANIA 3	PG: Rosu

Ireland: O'Shea, Wallace, Cunningham, Danaher, Geoghegan, Elwood, Bradley (c), Popplewell, Kingston, Halpin, Johns, Francis, Galwey, McBride, Robinson

Romania: Brici, S Catalin, Solomie, Fulina, Kolceriu, Rosu, Neaga, Leonte, Gheorghe, Vlad, T Oroian, A Girbu (Cojocariu 43, N Marin 67 temp), Dumitras (c), Guranescu, Brinza

5 June 1994 Brisbane

AUSTRALIA 33	T: Tabua, Lynagh, Campese, Burke, Smith; C: Lynagh; PG: Lynagh 2
IRELAND 13	T: Johns, C: Elwood, PG: Elwood, O'Shea

Australia: Matt Pini, Damian Smith, Matt Burke, Matthew O'Connor, David Campese, Michael Lynagh (c), Peter Slattery, Tony Daly, Phil Kearns, Ewen McKenzie, John Eales, Garrick Morgan, Ilie Tabua, David Wilson, Tim Gavin

Ireland: O'Shea, Geoghegan, Jonathan Bell, Danahar, Niall Woods, Elwood, Bradley (c), John Fitzgerald, Keith Wood, Clohessy, Galwey (McBride 28), Francis, Robinson, David Corkery, Johns

Campese's 58th international try adds to his world record.

11 June 1994 Sydney

AUSTRALIA 32	T: Herbert, Wilson, Tabua; C: Lynagh,; PG: Lynagh 5
IRELAND 18	T: Clohessy, Francis; C: O'Shea; PG: O'Shea; DG: O'Shea

Australia: Burke, Campese, Richard Tombs, Dan Herbert, Smith, Lynagh (c), Slattery, Daly, Kearns, McKenzie, Eales, Morgan, Tabua, Wilson, Gavin

Ireland: O'Shea, Geoghegan, Bell, Danahar, Woods, Elwood, Bradley (c), Fitzgerald, Wood, Clohessy, Gabriel Fulcher, Francis, Robinson, Corkery, Johns

Lynagh, already the only player to score 650 international points, becomes the first to pass 800.

5 Nov 1994 Lansdowne Road, Dublin

IRELAND 26	T: Geoghegan, Bradley; C: McGowan 2; PG: McGowan 3, O'Shea
USA 15	T: Anitoni, Bachelet; C: Williams; PG: Williams

Ireland: O'Shea, Geoghegan, Brendan Mullin (Malone 39), Danaher, Bell, Alan McGowan, Bradley (c) (A Rolland 73), Popplewell, Wood, Clohessy, Johns (Galwey 79), Francis, G Fulcher, Corkery, Brendan Cronin.

USA: M Sika, C Schlereth, T Takau, Ray Green, V Anitoni, M Williams, A Bachelet (c), C Lippert, T Billups, D James, Dan Lyle, W Leversee, R Randall, Richard Tardits, R Lumkong

McGowan does well on his international debut, made as a late replacement for Elwood.

Wales

16 Oct 1993 National Stadium, Cardiff

WALES 55   T: I Evans 2, Gibbs 2, Jenkins, Moon, Lewis, Rayer, Clement; C: Jenkins 5

JAPAN 5   T: Williams

Wales: Clement, Evans (c)(Roger Bidgood 73), Scott Gibbs, N Jenkins, Walker (Rayer 27), Adrian Davies, Moon, Mike Griffiths, Andrew Lamerton, J Davies, Tony Copsey, Llewellyn, Stuart Davies, Lewis, Lyn Jones

Japan: T Matsuda, Ian Williams, Mitsuo Fujikake, F Kutsuki, Yoshihito Yoshida, S Aoki, Yoji Nagatomo, O Ota, M Kunda (c), K Takahashi, Y Sakuraba, Bruce Ferguson, S Kaleta, S Latu, Hirofumi Ouchi

Japan's reinforcements (Williams won 17 caps for Australia 1987-90, Ferguson peviously played for Fiji Schools) do them little good: Evans touches down after only 45 seconds, apparently a record for Wales, who rack up their highest score and widest margin of victory in any full international so far (they beat Japan 82-6 away in an unofficial match in 1975). The aptly named Ouchi, apparently about to become a Buddhist monk, was sent off v Dunvant.

10 Nov 1993 Arms Park, Cardiff

WALES 24   PG: N Jenkins 8

CANADA 26   T: Stuart, Charron; C: Rees 2; PG: Rees 4

Wales: Clement, Evans (c), Gibbs, N Jenkins, Proctor, A Davies, Moon, M Griffiths, G Jenkins, J Davies, Copsey, Llewellyn, Quinnell, R Jones, Lewis

Canada: Mark Williams, Toews, Gray, Stuart (c), D Stewart, Rees, Chris Tynan, P Szabo, I Kennedy, Jackart, N Knauer, Charron, Gordon, J Hutchinson, McKenzie

It takes a try 40 seconds from the end (and a conversion from a player whose father had emigrated from Llantrisant) to beat the Welsh, who lead three times, but Canada match them throughout. What odds, after this, on Wales winning the Five Nations..? Rees, a world class thinker and goalkicker, is also one of the stockiest international fly-halves: even as an 18-y-o he was wearing 38-inch shorts.

17 May 1994 Lisbon

PORTUGAL 11   T: Murinello; PG: Vilar-Gomes 2

WALES 102   T:Quinnell, Llewellyn, Walker 4, Hall 3, Jones 2, I Evans 3, Taylor, penalty try; C: Jenkins 11

Portugal: M Vilar-Gomes, P Murinello, R Pereira, N Mourão, T Morais, J Quimado (c), P Netto Fernandes, S Pereira, M Batista, P Domingos, A Pecas, A Andrade, P Arsenio, P Eusebio, J Pires

Wales: Clement, I Evans (c), Hall, N Davies, Walker, N Jenkins, Robert Jones, R Evans, G Jenkins, J Davies, Copsey, Llewellyn, Hemi Taylor, Lewis, Quinnell

For what it's worth (not much) it's the highest score by a British country, and Nigel Walker's four tries equal the Welsh record for a single international. Taylor becomes the first New Zealander (he had a trial with the national Colts team) to be capped by Wales, who are captained by Ieuan Evans for the 19th time, a new record.

21 May 1994 Madrid

SPAIN 0

WALES 54   T: Quinnell, I Evans 3, penalty try, Walker, G Jenkins; C: N Jenkins 5; PG: N Jenkins 3

SPAIN: J Azkargorta, P Martin, A Mino, A Enciso, J Torres Morote, F Puertas, J Hernandez-Gil, J Alvarez (S Espina 40), J Aguiar, J Diez (I de Lazaro 45, O Solano 49), A Malo, J Villa, J Exteberria (F Calle 68), J Gutierrez (c), J Lopez

Wales: Clement, I Evans (c), Hall, N Davies, Walker, N Jenkins, Moon, R Evans, G Jenkins, J Davies, Llewellyn, Paul Arnold, Lewis (Copsey 40), Perego, Quinnell

If not quite the nonsense against Portugal, at least half a nonsense. When Ieuan Evans breaks the Welsh record for international tries, he'll have had it a mite easier than Gareth Edwards & Gerald Davies.

11 June 1994 Markham

CANADA 15   PG: Rees 5

WALES 33   T: Hall 2, I Evans; C: Jenkins 3; PG: Jenkins 4

Most successful penalty goals in an international match

8	Mark Wyatt	Canada v Scotland	1991
8	Neil Jenkins	Wales v Canada	1993
8	Diego Dominguez	Italy v Romania	1994
7	Simon Hodgkinson	England v Wales	1991
7	Grant Fox	N Zealand v W Samoa	1993
7	Neil Jenkins	Wales v Italy	1994

100 points in an international

164-13	Hong Kong	1994	v Singapore
111-0	Zimbabwe	1987	v Nigeria
104-8	Italy	1994	v Czech Rep
102-11	Wales	1994	v Portugal

HK, stuffed with expatriates, score a preposterous world record 26 tries in winning a World Cup qualifier against a team which lost its two previous matches 90-3 to S Korea and 69-5 to Thailand. Full-back Ashley Billington's 50 points are also a record, made up of 10 tries that double the previous world record shared by Rory Underwood. Jamie McKee kicks a world best 17 conversions, but nine others are missed, surely yet another record.

In 1979, in an international for which French caps weren't awarded, France beat Tahiti 92-12 (worth 112-13 now) despite missing 14 out of 20 conversions.

Canada: S Stewart, Toews, Gray, Stuart (c), Lougheed, Rees, Graf, Evans, Svoboda, Jackart, James, Charron, Gordon, McKenzie (G Ennis 54), MacKinnon

Wales: Rayer, I Evans (c) (Clement 57), Hall, N Davies, Proctor, N Jenkins, Moon, R Evans, G Jenkins, J Davies, P Davies, Llewellyn, Taylor, Quinnell, Richie Collins

Ieuan Evans's 20th international try equals the Welsh record. Dr Lynne Manson of Hamilton General Hospital claims Wales put Collins' life at risk by picking him. She says he was concussed in the match v Canada A, the Welsh management agree he was dazed but deny concussion.

18 June 1994 Suva

FIJI 8   T: Veitayaki; PG: Bogisa

WALES 23   T: Rayer, Collins; C: A Davies 2;
              PG: A Davies 3

Fiji: R Bogisa, J Vidiri, J Toloi, E Nauga, P Tuidraki, F Rayasi, J McLennan, R Williams, E Batimala, J Veitayaki, I Tawake (c), I Savai, S Matalulu, J Campbell (M Korovou 58), A Mocelutu

Wales: Rayer, I Evans (c), Neil Boobyer, N Davies, Proctor, A Davies, Moon, R Evans, R McBryde, Hugh Williams-Jones, Copsey, Arnold, Taylor, Collins, Lewis (P Davies 73)

Phil Davies' 41st cap equals Graham Price's record for a Welsh forward.

22 June 1994

TONGA 9   PG:S Tu'ipulotu 3

WALES 18   PG: N Jenkins 6

Tonga: S Tu'ipulotu, T Va'enuku, F Manukia, P Latu, S Taupeaafu, E Vunipola, M Vunipola, T Lutua, F Vunipola (c), U Fa, F Mali, V Taumoepeaw, T Loto'ahea, T Vikilani, K Tu'ipulotu

Wales: Clement, I Evans (c), Hall (N Davies 63), Boobyer, Gwilym Wilkins, Jenkins, Paul John, Ian Buckett, G Jenkins, Williams-Jones, Copsey, Llewellyn, Taylor, Steve Williams, Collins

Jenkins succeeds with six kicks out of six.

26 June 1994 Apia

W SAMOA 34   T: Lima 2, Lam; C: Kellett 2;
                PG: Kellett 5

WALES 9   PG: N Jenkins 3

W Samoa: Anetelea Aiolupo, Brian Lima, T Vaega, F Tuilagi, T Samania, Darren Kellett, V Vitale, Peter Fatialofa (c), T Leiasamaivao, G Latu, M Birtwhistle, Matt Keenan (S Kaleta 30-32 & 58 temp), Sila Vaifale, M Iupeli, Pat Lam (D Mika 76 temp)

Wales: Rayer, I Evans (c), Clement, N Davies, Proctor, N Jenkins, Moon, R Evans (Williams-Jones 76 temp), G Jenkins, J Davies (Copsey 45 temp) , P Davies, Llewellyn, Lewis, Collins, Quinnell (Taylor 79 temp)

No easy pickings this time for Ieuan Evans - or revenge for Wales, knocked out of the last World Cup by the same country. Jenkins has now scored with 16 consecutive kicks in internationals. Davies breaks Price's record.

17 Sep1994 Bucharest

ROMANIA 9   PG: Nichitean 3

WALES 16   T: I Evans; C: N Jenkins;
              PG: N Jenkins 3

Romania: Vasile Brici, L Colceriu, Nicolae Racean, Nicolae Fulina, Gheorghe Solomie, Necula Nichitean, Daniel Neaga, G Leonte (C Stan 70), Gheorghe Ion, G Vlad, Traian Oroian, Sandu Ciorescu, C Cojocariu, A Guranescu, T Brinza (c) (C Draguceanu 61)

Wales: Rayer, I Evans (c), N Davies, Hall, Proctor, N Jenkins, R Moon, R Evans, G Jenkins, J Davies, Taylor, P Davies, Llewellyn, Collins, Lewis

Ieuan Evans' 21st try for Wales breaks the national record. One of Jenkins' successful penalties is awarded on the halfway line for a foul by Racean on Evans after he scores the try.

12 Oct 1994 National Stadium, Cardiff

WALES 29   T: N Davies; PG: Jenkins 7; DG: Jenkins

ITALY 19   T: Francescato; C: Dominguez; PG: Dominguez 4

Wales: Rayer, Proctor, Hall, N Davies, Clement, N Jenkins, Moon, R Evans, G Jenkins, J Davies, P Davies, Llewellyn (c), Taylor, Collins, Lewis

Italy: P Vaccari, Mario Gerosa, S Bordon, Massimo Bonomi, Ivan Francescato, Diego Dominguez, Alessandro Troncon, Massimo Cuttitta (c), C Orlandi, G Grespan, R Favaro, D Scaglia, O Arancio, A Sgorlon, C Checchinato

In the first match between the two countries, Jenkins equals the Welsh record for most points in one international and reaches 308 pts in total to overhaul Paul Thorburn's national record of 304. Clement emulates Phil Bennett by playing for Wales in four different positions. Cuttitta captains Italy for the first time. Francescato is usually Italy's scrum-half, Vaccari often a winger. Wales qualify for a slightly easier World Cup group.

26 Nov 1994 National Stadium, Cardiff

WALES 12   PG: N Jenkins 4

S AFRICA 20   T: Staeuli, Joubert, Williams; C: Le Roux; PG: Le Roux

Wales: Clement, Proctor, Hall, Mark Taylor, Hill, N Jenkins, Moon, R Evans, G Jenkins (McBryde 32-37 temp), J Davies, Taylor, Derwyn Jones, Llewellyn (c), Collins, Lewis

S Africa: unchanged (for the first time in the last 17 matches) from the game v Scotland (Pienaar again captain)

The two new caps don't let anyone down: 6'10 Derwyn Jones wins his share of lineout ball, Mark Taylor becomes the first Pontypool threequarter capped since Fenton Coles in 1960. Jenkins' penalties (he's now kicked a record 73 for Wales) produce a 12-10 lead with twenty minutes to go, but after eight matches against S Africa Wales are still the only British country not to have beaten them. Admittedly the other seven were close: this is South Africa's biggest win in Cardiff.

England Women 1994-95

18 Dec 1994 Repton Avenue (Wasps RUFC), London

ENGLAND 30
HOLLAND 5

England's first international since winning the World Cup.

Other Internationals

2 Oct 1993 Riverside, California

USA 22   T: Schurfield; C: O'Brien; PG: O'Brien 5

AUSTRALIA 26   T: Tabua, Lea, Wilson, Howard; C: Lynagh 3

USA: M Sika, Gary Hein, E Schram (S Hiatt 65), M Scharrenberg, R Schurfield, C O'Brien, A Bachelet, C Lippert, T Billups, D James, K Swords (c), R Randell, Chris Campbell, R Tardits, J Wilkerson

Australia: Burke, BPJ Lea, Jason Little, PW Howard, D Smith, Lynagh (c), Slattery, Daly, David Nucifora, McKenzie, McCall, W Waugh, Tabua, F Finau, Wilson

Australia award caps v Canada but not the USA, so Michael Lynagh's six points don't count towards his world record total.

9 Oct 1993 Kingsland, Calgary

CANADA 16   T: Kennedy, Jackart; PG: Graf 2

AUSTRALIA 43   T: Campese 3, Smith, Horan, Daly; C: Lynagh 2; PG: Lynagh 3

Canada: S Stewart, J Loveday, M Williams (c), Stuart, Gray, Graf, I MacKay, Paul Szabo, I Kennedy (Cardinal 58), Jackart, C Whittaker, Al Charron J Hutchinson, McKenzie, Gordon

Australia: Marty Roebuck, Campese, Tim Horan, Little, Smith, Lynagh (c), Slattery, Daly (Dan Crowley 62), Kearns (Nucifora 68), McKenzie, Morgan, McCall, Wilson, Tabua, Gavin

17 Oct 1993 Brive

FRANCE 51   T: Bernat-Salles 3, Sella, Merle, Loppy; C: Lacroix 6; PG: Lacroix 3

ROMANIA 0

France: Sadourny, Bernat-Salles, Sella (Olivier Campan 56), Lacroix, David Berty, Penaud, Aubin Hueber, Armary (Seigne 56), Gonzalez, Stéphane Graou, Merle, Roumat, Benetton, Cecillon, Léon Loppy

Romania: Solomie, A Mitocaru, M Nedelcu, Fulina, M Dumitru, F Ion, M Foca, Leonte, G Ion, G Vlad, H Dumitras (c), Cojocariu, I Seceleanu (Girbu 48), Brinza, G Dinu (N Marin 60)

30 Oct 1993 Parc Lescure, Bordeaux

FRANCE 16   T: Hueber; C: Lacroix; PG: Lacroix; DG: Penaud, Sadourny

AUSTRALIA 13   T: Gavin; C: Lynagh; PG: Lynagh 2

France: Sadourny, Bernat-Salles, Sella, Lacroix,

Saint-André, Penaud, Hueber, Armary, Gonzales, Seigne, Merle, Roumat (c), Benetton, Benazzi, Cecillon

Australia: Burke, A Murdoch, Little, Horan, Campese, Lynagh (c), Slattery, Daly, Kearns, McKenzie, McCall, Morgan, Tabua, Wilson, TGavin

Australia have never won a series in France.

6 Nov 1993 Parc des Princes, Paris

FRANCE 3   PG: Lacroix

AUSTRALIA 24   T: Roebuck, Gavin; C: Roebuck;
                  PG: Roebuck 4

France: unchanged (Roumat captain again). Graou sub'd Seigne 79)

Australia: Roebuck, Campese, Little, Horan, D Smith, Lynagh, Slattery, Daly, Kearns, McKenzie, McCall, Morgan, MC Brial, Wilson, Gavin

Australia's widest ever winning margin over France, who suffer their heaviest home defeat since the Parc was refurbished in the early '70s. Sella's 94th cap breaks Serge Blanco's world record.

6 Nov 1993 Ferrocaril Oeste, Buenos Aires

ARGENTINA 26   T:Cuesta Silva, Meson; C: Meson 2;
                  PG: Meson 4

S AFRICA 29   T:Small 2, Van der Westhuizen,
                  Joubert; C: Stransky 3; PG: Stransky

Argentina: Meson, Teran, Sebastien Salvat, D Cuesta Silva, Jorge, L Arbizu (c), G Camardon, Corral, R le Fort (S Peretti 65), Noriega, Sporleder, Llanes, RN Perez, Guillermo Ugartemendia, P Fernandez-Bravo

S Africa: Joubert, Small, Heinrich Fuls, Müller, Jacques Olivier, Stransky, van der Westhuizen, Swart (K Andrews 46), Allan, Guy Kebble, J Strydom, Atherton, Pienaar (c), Strauss, Kruger

13 Nov 1993 Ferrocaril Oeste, Buenos Aires

ARGENTINA 23   T: Camardon, Jorge; C: Meson 2;
                  PG: Meson 2; DG: Arbizu

S AFRICA 52   T: Strauss 2, Small 2, Van der
                  Westhuizen, Williams, Johnson;
                  C: Johnson 4; PG: Johnson 3

Argentina: unchanged (Arbizu captain again) except for M Bertranou in place of Perez. Rafael Bullrich sub'd Camardon 50, L Criscuolo sub'd Salvat 60.

S Africa: Gavin Johnson, Small, Müller, Fuls, Williams, Henry Honiball, van der Westhuizen, Kebble, N Drotske, Andrews, Strydom, Atherton, Pienaar (c) (Allan h/t), Strauss, Kruger

Johnson, a tour replacement making his international debut, scores 22 points to equal the national record for

a single match set by Gerald Bosch in 1975, when Johnson's score would have been worth 21. Williams, the only black player in the team, scores a try on his international debut.

5 June 1994 Twin Elms Park, Nepean, Ontario

CANADA 18   PG: Rees 6

FRANCE 16   T: N'Tamack; C: Lacroix;
                  PG: Lacroix 3

Canada: S Stewart, Toews, Gray, Stuart (c), Lougheed, Rees, Graf, Evans, Cardinal, Jackart, Sharron, James, Gordon, MacKinnon, McKenzie (Karl Svoboda 30)

France: Sadourny, N'Tamack, Sella, Lacroix, Saint-André (c), Sébastien Viars, Christophe Deylaud, Macabiau, Benezech, Gonzales, Seigne, Merle, Roumat, Benetton, Cabannes, Benazzi

Philippe Sella adds to his world record by winning his 99th cap before being sent off in the second half. Cardinal is sent off in the first.

18 June 1994 Ballymoe, Brisbane

AUSTRALIA 23   T: Herbert, Burke; C: Lynagh,
                  Wallace; PG: Lynagh 2, Wallace

ITALY 20   T: Bonomi; PG: Troiani 5

Australia: Burke, D Smith, Herbert, Tombs, Campese, Lynagh (c) (T Wallace 60), George Gregan, Daly, Kearns, McKenzie, Morgan, Eales, Tabua, Gavin, Wilson

Italy: Vaccari, Gerosa, EG Filizzola (Bordon ht), Bonomi, Marcello Cuttitta, L Troiani, Troncon, Massimo Cuttitta, Orlandi, F Properzi Curti , Favaro, M Giacheri, Arancio, Checchinato, M Giovanelli (c)

An injury puts a (temporary?) halt to Lynagh's record-breaking points scoring.

Most points in internationals

821	Michael Lynagh	Australia	1984-94
645	Grant Fox	N Zealand	1985-93
471	Gavin Hastings	Scotland	1986-94
354	Didier Camberabero	France	1982-93
320	Neil Jenkins	Wales	1991-94
312	Naas Botha	S Africa	1980-92

Hastings also scored a record 66 for the British Lions (1989-93). Hugo Porta scored 568 points for Argentina & South America, Stefano Bettarello 483 for Italy.

Most conversions	138	Lynagh
Most penalty goals	164	Lynagh

26 June 1994 Melbourne

AUSTRALIA 20   T: Campese; PG: Wallace 5

ITALY 7   T: Orlandi; C: Troiani

Australia: Pini, Smith, Herbert, Burke, Campese, Wallace, Gregan, Daly, Kearns, McKenzie, McCall, Eales, Tabua, Gavin, Wilson

Italy: unchanged except for Bordon in place of Filizzola

David Campese's try is his 59th in internationals, again adding to his world record.

26 June 1994 Lancaster Park, Christchurch

N ZEALAND 8   T: Bunce; PG: Cooper

FRANCE 22   T:Benetton; C: Lacroix; PG: Lacroix 2; DG: Sadourny, Deylaud 2

N Zealand: Timu, John Kirwan, Bunce, Jonah Lomu, Cooper, S Mannix, Forster, Brown, Fitzpatrick (c), Richard Loe, Blair Larsen, Mark Cooksley, Jones, Mike Brewer, Pene

France: Sadourny, N'Tamack, Sella, Saint-André, Lacroix, Deylaud, G Accoceberry, Benezech, Gonzalez, Califano, Benazzi, Merle, Roumat, Cabannes (Armary 68), Benetton

Sella becomes the first player from any county to win 100 caps. Lomu is one of the youngest players (18) ever to play for N Zealand.

3 July 1994 Eden Park, Auckland

N ZEALAND 20   T: Fitzpatrick; PG: Cooper 5

FRANCE 23   T: N'Tamack, Sadourny; C: Lacroix 2; PG: Lacroix 3

N Zealand: Timu, Kirwan, Bunce, Cooper, Lomu, Steve Bachop, Forster, Brown, Fitzpatrick (c), Loe, M Cooksley, Jones, Brewer, Brooke (Pene 76), Larsen

France: Sadourny, N'Tamack, Sella, Saint-André, Lacroix (Delaigue), Deylaud, Accoceberry, Benetton (Xavier Blond 73 temp, Brouzet 80), Cabannes, Roumat, Merle, Benazzi, C Califano, Gonzalez, Benezech

For the first time ever, France win a series in N Zealand, who lose one at home for the first time since 1986 and consecutive Tests at home for the first time since 1949, when Australia beat a B team in all but name.

9 July 1994 Carisbrook, Dunedin

N ZEALAND 22   T: Kirwan; C: Howarth; PG: Howarth 5

S AFRICA 14   T: Straeuli; PG: Joubert 3

NZ: Shane Howarth, Kirwan, Bunce, A Ieremia, Timu, Bachop, Graham Bachop, Loe, Fitzpatrick (c), Brown, Larsen, Jones (Pene 9, C Dowd 75), Cooksley, Brewer, Brooke

SAF: Joubert, Small, Müller, Venter, Williams, H le Roux, Swart (Kebble 23), Allan, Johan Le Roux, Strauss (c), Andrews, Atherton, Straeuli, Richter

Serious injuries all round (Jones fractured cheekbone, Swart concussion, Müller torn neck ligaments) as the All Blacks avoid losing three successive home matches for the first time. South Africa have still never won at Carisbrook.

23 July 1994 Athletic Park, Wellington

N ZEALAND 13   T: Timu, Z Brooke; PG: Howarth

S AFRICA 9   PG: Van Rensburg 3

NZ: Howarth, Kirwan, Bunce (Walter Little 73), A Ieremia, Timu, S Bachop, G Bachop, Loe, Fitzpatrick (c), Brown, Brooke, Cooksley, BLarsen, Brewer, Brooke

SAF: Theo van Rensburg (Joubert 76), Small, Mulder, Venter, Williams, H Le Roux, Roux, Kebble, Allan, J Le Roux, Andrews, Atherton, Pienaar (c), Richter

J Le Roux is sent home (and banned from Test rugby until after the next World Cup) for biting Sean Fitzpatrick's ear. He seems to have a taste for this kind of thing: Will Carling claims Le Roux bit Paul Hull in the Transvaal–England match earlier in the season.

6 Aug 1994 Eden Park, Auckland

N ZEALAND 18   PG: Howarth 6

S AFRICA 18   T: Johnson, Venter; C: Johnson; PG: Johnson 2

NZ: Howarth, Kirwan, Bunce, Ieremia, Timu, S Bachop, G Bachop, Loe, Fitzpatrick (c), Brown, Jones, Brooke, Larsen (Jones 70), Brewer, Brooke

SAF: Joubert, Johnson (Small 30-35 temp), Mulder, Venter, Williams, H Le Roux, Roux, B Stewart, Allan, K Andrews, S Andrews, Atherton, Pienaar (c), F Van Heerden, Richter

NZ just miss becoming the first All Black team to whitewash South Africa in a series. Fitzpatrick, uneaten this time, is the recipient of a punch from Venter which costs South Africa three points.

6 Aug 1994 Sydney Football Stadium

AUSTRALIA 73   T: Little 2, Smith 2, Ofahengaue, Howard, Campese, Gavin, Pini, Junee, Gregan; C: Knox 6; PG: Knox 2

W SAMOA 3   PG: Kellett

Australia: Pini (D Junee), D Smith, Little, P Howard, Campese, D Knox, Gregan, McKenzie, Kearns (c), Daly, Morgan, Eales, Viliame (Willy) Ofahengaue, Wilson, Gavin

International Tries

up to & including 31 Dec 1994

				matches
60	David Campese	Australia	1982-94	86
40	Rory Underwood	England	1984-94	69
38	Serge Blanco	France	1981-91	93
35	John Kirwan	N Zealand	1985-94	63
30	Philippe Sella	France	1982-94	102
24	Ian Smith	Scotland	1924-33	32
23	Christian Darrouy	France	1957-66	40
21	Ieuan Evans	Wales	1987-94	48
20	Gareth Edwards	Wales	1968-78	53
20	Gerald Davies	Wales	1967-78	46
20	Patrice Lagisquet	France	1987-91	46

Dates of first & last (or latest) tries, not beginning & end of international career. Test tries for the British Lions (not included above): Davies two, Underwood & Evans one each. Kirwan, still only 29, retired from international rugby in Oct 1994.

W Samoa: Aiolupo, Lima Vaega, Tuilagi, Samania, Kellett, Vitale, Fatialofa (c), S To'omalatai, Latu, Keenan, Birtwistle, Vaifale, Mika, Lam

Despite fielding two second-choice half-backs, Australia record their biggest win in any international, (previously 67-9 v the USA in 1990) against virtually the same line-up that beat Wales 34-9 five weeks earlier. Campese adds another to his record try total.

17 Aug 1994 Sydney Football Stadium

AUSTRALIA 20   T: Little, Kearns; C: Knox 2; PG: Knox 2

N ZEALAND 16   T: Howarth; C: Howarth; PG: Howarth 3

Australia: Pini, Campese, Little, Howard, Smith, Knox, Gregan, Daly, Kearns (c), McKenzie, Morgan, Eales Ofahengaue, Wilson, Gavin

NZ: Howarth, Wilson, Bunce, Little, Timu, S Bachop, G Bachop, Loe, Fitzpatrick (c), Brown, Cooksley, I Jones, Brewer, Michael Jones, Brooke

Australia regain the Bledisloe Cup thanks to a last-ditch tackle by Gregan on Wilson with only a few minutes to go. For the first time in any season, the All Blacks lose more matches than they win. Timu later moves to rugby league, the third winger (after Tuigamala & Kirwan) lost to the All Blacks within a year.

1 Oct 1994 Catania

ITALY 24   PG: Dominguez 8

ROMANIA 6   PG: Nichitean 2

Italy: Dotto, Vaccari, Bordon, Francescato, Gerosa, Dominguez (c), Troncon, M del Sie, Orlandi, G Grespan, Favaro, Diego Scaglia, Arancio, Checcchinato, Andrea Sgorlon (C de Rossi 58)

Romania: Brici, Colceriu, Fulina, Solomie, R Cioca, Nichitean, Neaga, Vlad, G Ion (c), Leonte, Branescu, Cojocariu, Oroian, Draguceanu, Gealapu

The Argentinian-born Dominguez, captaining Italy for the first time, equals a world record (see Wales v Canada) to send Romania into the toughest World Cup group. Nichitean, having an even worse day than against Wales, misses six out of eight kicks at goal.

8 Oct 1994 Boet Erasmus, Port Elizabeth

S AFRICA 42   T: Roux 2, Stransky, Strauss, Williams; C: Stransky 4; PG: Stransky 3

ARGENTINA 22   T: Loffreda, Pfister, Teran; C: Del Castillo 2; PG: Del Castillo

SAF: Johnson, Small, Christiaan Scholtz, Venter, Williams, JStransky, Roux, Os du Randt, Schmidt, Laubscher, M Andrews, Drikus Hattingh, Staeuli, Pienaar (c), Strauss

Argentina: Salvat, Martin Pfister, Loffreda (c), Cuesta Silva (F del Castillo 60), Teran, del Castillo, Bullrich, Corral, Federico Mendez, Noriega, Sporleder, Llanes, Viel-Temperley, Rolando Martin, Ugartemendia

After Argentina twice take a first-half lead (once through their 36-y-o captain), South Africa win the first official match between the countries (more than once, Argentina provided the entire team when South America played in South Africa). Stransky's 22 points equal the national record for a single international but would have been worth 21 at the time the record was set. Mendez, the hooker, is best known in Britain as the young prop sent off for punching Paul Ackford at Twickenham. Schmidt's father Louis won two caps 1958-62.

Consecutive caps

60	Sean Fitzpatrick	NZ	1987-94
53	Gareth Edwards	WAL	1967-78
52	Willie John McBride	IRE	1964-75
49	Sandy Carmichael	SCOT	1967-78
49	Phil Orr	IRE	1976-86

Fitzpatrick's run is still unbroken. Edwards didn't miss a game throughout his international career.

15 Oct 1994 Ellis Park, Johannesburg

S AFRICA 46   T: Badenhorst 2, Stransky, Andrews,
Staeuli, Williams, Van der
Westhuizen; C: Stransky 4;
PG: Stransky

ARGENTINA 26   T: Llanes, Cilley; C:Cilley 2; PG: 4

SAF: Joubert, Chris Badenhorst, H le Roux, Venter, Williams, Stransky, van der Westhuizen, du Randt, Schmidt, Laubscher (Swart 63), M Andrews, Hattingh, Strauss (Elandré van der Bergh 42), Straeuli, Pienaar (c)

Argentina: Salvat, Teran, Francisco Garcia, Loffreda (c), Pfister, José Cilley, Bullrich, Corral, Mendez, Noriega, Sporleder, Llanes, Viel-Temperley, Martin, Ugartemedia.

Success for two new caps: the 30-y-o Badenhorst - and Cilley, who arrives as a replacement just three hours before the match. Straeuli scores his try after just eleven seconds of the second half.

17 Dec 1994 Stade Léo Lagrange, Besançon

FRANCE 28   T: Benetton, Sadourny, Sella;
C: Lacroix 2; PG: Lacroix 2;
DG: Delaigue

CANADA 9   PG: Rees 3

France: Sadourny, N'Tamack, Sella, Lacroix, Saint-André (c), Delaigue, Accoceberry, Benezech, Gonzales, Califano, Merle, Roumat, Benazzi, Benetton, Costes

Canada: S Stewart, Winston Stanley, C Stewart, Gray, Lougheed, Rees (c), Graf, Evans, Svoboda (Cardinal 75), Jackart, James, Hadley, Gordon, MacKinnon, McKenzie

International caps

102	Philippe Sella	FRA	1982-94
93	Serge Blanco	FRA	1980-91
86	David Campese	AUS	1982-94
69	Mike Gibson	IRE	1964-79
69	Rory Underwood	ENG	1984-94
65	Roland Bertranne	FRA	1971-81
66	Michael Lynagh	AUS	1984-94
63	Michel Crauste	FRA	1957-66
63	Willie John McBride	IRE	1962-75
63	Benoit Dauga	FRA	1964-72
63	Nick Farr-Jones	AUS	1984-93
63	John Kirwan	NZ	1984-94
62	Sean Fitzpatrick	NZ	1986-94
61	Jean Condom	FRA	1982-90
61	Fergus Slattery	IRE	1970-84
61	Rob Andrew	ENG	1985-94

*British Lions Tests (not included above):
Gibson 12, Underwood 6, McBride 17,
Slattery 4, Andrew 5.*

FIRA Championship

A1 (Division 1)

17 Oct 1993 Brive	France	51	Romania	0
6 Nov 1993 Moscow	Russia	19	Italy	30
11 Nov 1993 Treviso	Italy	16	France	9
20 Mar 1994 Sarlat	France	49	Spain	3
10 Apr 1994 Madrid	Spain	9	Russia	16
24 Apr 1994 Zaragoza	Spain	3	Romania	11
7 May 1994 Bucharest	Romania	30	Russia	0
7 May 1994 Parma	Italy	62	Spain	15
14 May 1994 Bucharest	Romania	26	Italy	12
28 May 1994 Moscow	Russia	9	France	11

*After 45 matches since 1936 (43 defeats, two draws)
Italy win for the first time v France, who take the
championship by a single score in Moscow.*

	P	W	D	L	F	A	Pts
France	4	3	0	1	120	28	10
Italy	4	3	0	1	120	69	10
Romania	4	3	0	1	67	66	10
Russia	4	1	0	3	44	80	6
Spain	4	0	0	4	30	138	4

Women's World Championship

11-24 April 1994 Scotland

QUARTER-FINALS

England	24	Canada	10
Wales	8	Scotland	0
USA	76	Ireland	0
France	99	Japan	0

SEMI-FINALS

England	18	France	6
USA	56	Wales	15

Full-back Jen Crawford scores five tries.

FINAL 24 April 1994 Edinburgh Academicals RUFC

ENGLAND 38   T: Mitchell, Burns, Edwards,
2 penalty tries; C: Almond 5;
PG: Almond

USA 23   T:Crawford 2, Jervey, Huffer;
PG: Bergman

England: J Mitchell, V Blackett, J Edwards, G Pragnelle, A Cole, K Almond (c), E Mitchell J Mangham,N Ponsford, S Ewing, S Wen, H Stirrup, J Ross, G Burns, J Shore

USA: J Crawford, K McFarren, C Orsini, E Huffer, P Jervey, J Bergman, P Connell, A Flavin, J Gray, M Sorrensen, J Rutkowski, T Flanagan, S Hunt, B Bond, L Spicer-Bourdon

Almond sets a record for most points in a final (13). The USA scored 364 pts in their first four games, beating Sweden 111-0 then Japan 121-0 in group matches. Japan concede 220 pts in two matches, which is probably an international record before Singapore's men get involved (see above).

English Club League 1993-94

DIVISION 1	P	W	D	L	F	A	Pts
Bath	18	17	0	1	431	181	34
Leicester	18	14	0	4	425	210	28
Wasps	18	10	1	7	362	340	21
Bristol	18	10	0	8	331	276	20
Northampton	18	9	0	9	305	342	18
Harlequins	18	8	0	10	333	287	16
Orrell	18	8	0	10	327	302	16
Gloucester	18	6	2	10	247	356	14
London Irish	18	4	0	14	217	391	8
Newcastle Gosforth	18	2	1	15	190	483	5

Bath champions (for the fourth successive season and fifth in six years), London Irish & Newcastle Gosforth relegated.

Leading points scorer: Jez Harris (Leicester) 202 (a Div I record).

DIVISION 2
Promoted: Sale, West Hartlepool. Relegated: Rugby, Otley

DIVISION 3
Promoted: Coventry, Fylde. Relegated: Havant, Redruth

DIVISION 4
Promoted: Clifton, Harrogate. Relegated: Sheffield, Sudbury

DIVISION 5 NORTH
Promoted: Rotherham
Relegated: Durham City, Bradford & Bingley

DIVISION 5 SOUTH
Promoted: Reading
Relegated: Southend, Maidstone

Divisional Championship 1993-94

North	21	London	22
South & S West	31	Midland	3
South & S West	29	North	16
Midland	14	London	23
Midland	9	North	31
London	17	South & S West	25

	P	W	D	L	F	A	Pts
South & S West	3	3	0	0	85	36	6
London	3	2	0	1	62	60	4
North	3	1	0	2	68	60	2
Midland	3	0	0	3	26	85	0

English Clubs Cup 1993-94

5th ROUND
Bath	14	Bristol	9
Gloucester	11	Northampton	6
Harlequins	23	West Hartlepool	15
Leicester	43	London Irish	10
Moseley	15	Fylde	6
Newcastle Gosforth	7	Orrell	12
Otley	7	Sale	58
Rosslyn Park	12	Saracens	29

QUARTER-FINALS
Gloucester	3	Orrell	10
Harlequins	26	Sale	13
Leicester	12	Moseley	6
Saracens	6	Bath	23

SEMI-FINALS
Harlequins	25	Bath	26
Orrell	18	Leicester	31

Tony Swift's 50th try for the club, converted by Jonathan Callard with three minutes left, wins the game for Bath, who lead 19-0 before falling behind 25-19.

FINAL
7 May 1994 Twickenham
68 000, referee Ed Morrison

BATH	21	LEICESTER	9
T: Swift, Catt		PG: Harris 3	
C: Callard; PG: Callard 3			

Bath: Jonathan Callard, Tony Swift, Phil de Glanville, Mike Catt, Adedayo Adebayo, Stuart Barnes, Richard Hill, D Hilton, Graham Dawe, Victor Ubogu, Nigel Redman, Andy Reed, Andy Robinson (Steve Ojomoh 49), Ben Clarke, Jon Hall (c)

Leicester: WA Kilford, Tony Underwood, Stuart Potter, LS Boyle, Rory Underwood, Jez Harris, Aadel Kardooni, GC Rowntree, R Cockerill, Darren Garforth, Martin Johnson, Matt Poole, JM Wells, Dean Richards (c), Neil Back

A world record crowd for a club match watches Bath win the Cup for the eighth time (adding to their own record), all since 1984. Hill, who plays his last game for the club, has appeared in every one of those winning teams.

English County Championship 1993-94

North

Durham	38	Northumberland	11
Lancashire	3	Yorkshire	26
Durham	16	Lancashire	22
Yorkshire	27	Northumberland	3
Northumberland	30	Lancashire	15
Yorkshire	30	Durham	8

	P	W	D	L	F	A	Pts
Yorkshire	3	3	0	0	83	14	6
Durham	3	1	0	2	62	63	2
Northumberland	3	1	0	2	44	80	2
Lancashire	3	1	0	2	40	72	2

South

Cornwall	19	Gloucestershire	17
Hampshire	21	Middlesex	7
Cornwall	14	Hampshire	6
Middlesex	17	Gloucestershire	26
Gloucestershire	35	Hampshire	3
Middlesex	14	Cornwall	15

	P	W	D	L	F	A	Pts
Cornwall	3	3	0	0	48	37	6
Gloucestershire	3	2	0	1	78	39	4
Hampshire	3	1	0	2	30	56	2
Middlesex	3	0	0	3	38	62	0

SEMI-FINALS

| Yorkshire | 13 | Gloucestershire | 13 |
| Cornwall | 9 | Durham | 14 |

FINAL

16 April 1994 Twickenham
15 000, referee Tony Spreadbury

YORKSHIRE	26	DURHAM	3
T: Barley, Harrison		PG: Parker	
C: Plant 2; PG: Plant 4			

Yorks: D Breakwell, M Harrison, B Barley (c), S Burnhill, C Thornton, K Plant, G Easterby, R Szabo, R Whyley, S McMain, I Carroll, C Raducanu, C West, C Vyvyan, N Hargreaves

Durham: GD Spearman (JMA Brown 75), O Evans (KR McCallum 35), I Bell, PJT Nickalls, CA Mattison, A Parker, S Kirkup, RG Naisbitt (c), IR Parnaby, M Douthwaite, GR Wanless, C Aldus, S Musgrove, B Dixon, D McKinnon

Mike Harrison, who captained Yorkshire to their last win in the Championship (1987), is called in as a late replacement to provide a fairytale ending. He and another former England threequarter, Bryan Barley, are playing their last match for Yorks. Harrison is 38, Kevin Plant 37, Christian Raducanu a Romanian international.

Varsity Match 1993-94

7 Dec 1993 Twickenham

OXFORD	20	CAMBRIDGE	8
T: Du Toit		T: Boyd	
PG: Rees 3		DG: Kennedy	
DG: Boyle, Rees			

Oxford: Mike Joy, RV Wintle, Lawrence Boyle, EJ Rayner, TCS Watson, Gareth Rees, Fanie du Toit, Ben Fennell, Dave Henderson, CJ Clark, John Daniell, DR Evans, Chad Lion-Cachet (c), Andy Aitken, Neil Martin

Cambridge: Tony Dalwood, Andy Arentsen, JP Flood (CW Thompson 59), Adam Palfrey, Adrian Boyd, AJS Kennedy, Chris Tynan, TJ Hughes, AJG Read, PG Callow (c)(JF Duckworth temp), Richard Bramley, Stuart Roy, PCM Irons, Ally Meadows, Nigel Richardson

Rees & Tynan were Canada's half-backs v Wales a month earlier.

Varsity Match 1994-95

6 Dec 1994 Twickenham

CAMBRIDGE	26	OXFORD	21
T: Reynolds 2, Harrison		T: Rees, Martin	
C: McCarthy		C: Rees	
PG: McCarthy		PG: Rees 2	
DG: McCarthy 2		DG: Rees	

Cambridge: Tony Dalwood, Nick Walne, Glenn Harrison (Adrian Spencer 54), Adam Palfrey (Richard Dix 82), James Reynolds, Matt McCarthy, Justin Davies, Liam Mooney, Ivan Mackenzie, MQ Cox, Alistair Metcalfe, Ally Meadows, Richard Bramley, Nigel Richardson (c), Eban Rollitt

Oxford: Mike Joy, Innes Gray, Spencer Bromley (Nick Marval 66), Mike Nolan, Tyrone Howe, Gareth Rees, Mike Kirsten, Andy Bryce, Dave Henderson (c), Simon Thompson, Neil Martin, Pat Coveney, John Daniell, Gareth Allison, Richard Yeabsley

Oxford almost come back from 20-6 & 23-13 down, but Cambridge, taking on the holders at their running game, deserve to win a fine match. Reynolds scores two tries on his 22nd birthday. Rees' 16 points and McCarthy's two dropped goals are records for their respective universities in the history of the match. Spencer has played rugby league as well as union for Cambridge. A neck injury to Tynan (see 1993) allows Justin Davies, in his sixth year at the university, to win a blue at last. Rollitt's father Dave won eleven England caps 1967-75.

UAU Final 1993-94

23 March 1993 Twickenham

Northumbria	13	West London Institute	9
T: Miller		PG: Lee 3	
C: Eley; PG: Eley 2			

Hong Kong Sevens 1994

QUARTER-FINALS

W Samoa	21	President's VII	12
Australia	43	Argentina	0
N Zealand	21	France	12
Fiji	14	S Africa	12

SEMI-FINALS

Australia	20	W Samoa	17 aet
N Zealand	28	Fiji	14

FINAL

N Zealand	32	Australia	20
T: Rush 2, Lomu		T: Williams 2, Wilson	
T: Erenavula		T: Gregan	
T: Osborne			
C: Osborne 2			
PG: Osborne			

NZ: Luke Erenavula, Glen Osborne, Joe Tauiwi, P Woods, D Seymour, Eric Rush (c), Jonah Lomu

AUS: Jason Little, Tim Horan, David Campese (c), George Gregan, Ilie Tabua (J Fenwicke), David Wilson, Jim Williams

New Zealand win the event for the first time since 1989 and the fourth in all. Australia last won it in 1988.

Middlesex Sevens 1994

7th ROUND

Rosslyn Park	21	Harlequins	10
Orrell	10	Fiji Spartans	7
Bath	24	Loughboro' Univ	0
Saracens	26	London Irish	5

SEMI-FINALS

Orrell	10	Rosslyn Park	7
Bath	19	Saracens	0

FINAL

Bath	19	Orrell	12
T: Rayner, Lumsden		T: Naylor, Johnson	
T: Callard		C: Johnson	
C: Callard 2			

Bath: Audley Lumsden, E Rayner, Jonathan Callard (c), I Sanders, E Peters, G Adams, M Haag

Orrell: Jim Naylor, I Wynn, Paul Johnson (c), Austin Healey, M Farr, J Clayton, H Parr

Bath win the title for the first time to complete a League-Cup-Sevens treble. Orrell, who level the final at 12-12, have never won it.

Scottish Club League 1993-94

DIVISION 1	P	W	D	L	F	A	Pts
Melrose	13	12	0	1	410	192	24
Gala	12	9	0	3	274	214	18
Edinburgh Academicals	13	8	1	4	265	183	17
Heriot's Former Pupils	12	7	0	5	230	224	14
Watsonians	13	7	0	6	276	337	14
Stirling County	12	6	1	5	227	163	13
Hawick	12	6	1	5	218	178	13
Jedforest	13	6	0	7	231	199	12
Currie	12	6	0	6	230	285	12
Stewart's-Melville	13	5	1	7	157	190	11
Boroughmuir	12	5	0	7	214	228	10
West of Scotland	13	4	1	8	235	279	9
Kelso	13	4	0	9	175	296	8
Selkirk	13	0	1	12	138	312	1

Melrose win the title for the third season in a row and the fourth in all, losing only their opening match, at home to Gala. Kelso (champions in 1987-88 & 1988-89) & Selkirk are relegated.

DIVISION 2
Promoted: Glasgow High/Kelvinside, Dundee High School Former Pupils
Relegated: Clarkston, Ayr

DIVISION 3
Promoted: Gordonians, Corstorphine
Relegated: Howe of Fife, Perthshire

District Championship 1993-94

South	2	2	0	0	65	27	4
Glasgow	2	1	0	1	35	34	2
Edinburgh	2	1	0	1	34	46	2
North & Midlands	2	0	0	2	38	65	0

The South, who win the title for the third successive year, lose 84-5 to New Zealand.

District Championship 1994-95

	P	W	D	L	F	A	Pts
Exiles	4	4	0	0	119	51	8
Edinburgh	4	1	2	1	62	62	4
North & Midlands	4	1	1	2	69	84	3
South	4	1	1	2	61	81	3
Glasgow	4	1	0	3	62	05	2

Welsh Club League 1993-94

DIVISION 1	P	W	D	L	F	A	Pts
Swansea	22	20	0	2	549	264	40
Neath	22	17	2	3	581	286	36
Pontypridd	22	17	1	4	571	299	35
Cardiff	22	15	2	5	668	240	32
Llanelli	22	13	1	8	461	366	27
Bridgend	22	10	1	11	466	434	21
Newport	22	8	2	12	362	472	18
Newbridge	22	7	1	14	367	440	15
Pontypool	22	7	0	15	312	626	14
Dunvant	22	6	1	15	288	464	13
Aberavon	22	6	1	15	242	464	13
Cross Keys	22	0	0	22	239	751	0

Swansea, unbeaten at home, become the first club to regain the title, Aberavon & Cross Keys are relegated.

DIVISION 2
Promoted: Teorchy & Abertillery. Relegated: Mountain Ash & Glamorgan Wanderers.

DIVISION 3
Promoted: Abercynon, Bonymaen
Relegated: St Peter's, Tumble

DIVISION 4
Promoted: Builth Wells, Caerphilly
Relegated: Rumney, Cardiff Quins, Wrexham, Garndiffaith

Welsh Club Cup 1993-94

6th ROUND
Cardiff	15	Bridgend	6
Dunvant	8	Newbridge	16
Llanelli	57	Llandovery	5
Maesteg	11	Bonymaen	9
Maesteg Celtic	14	S Wales Police	37
Pontypridd	13	Swansea	3
Tenby Utd	25	Narberth	14
Ystradgynlais	3	Neath	26

7th ROUND
Cardiff	20	S Wales Police	13
Maesteg	35	Tenby Utd	17

Neath	3	Llanelli	7
Pontypridd	32	Newbridge	10

SEMI-FINALS
Llanelli	23	Maesteg	7 at Neath
Cardiff	9	Pontypridd	6 at Newport

FINAL
7 May 1994 National Stadium, Cardiff
referee R Yeman

Cardiff	15	Llanelli	8
T: Hall, Rayer		T: I Evans	
C: Davies; PG: Davies		PG: Stephens	

Cardiff: Mike Rayer, S Ford, Mike Hall (c), Colin Laity, Nigel Walker, Adrian Davies, Andy Moore, Mike Griffiths, J Humphreys, L Mustoe, AP Rees, Derwyn Jones, M Bennett, O Williams, M Budd (V Davies temp)

Llanelli: Neil Boobyer, Ieuan Evans, Simon Davies (IW Jones 53), NG Davies, Wayne Proctor, Colin Stephens, Rupert Moon (c), Ricky Evans, Andrew Lamerton, Hugh Williams-Jones, Phil Davies (PM Jones 58), Tony Copsey, Emyr Lewis, Scott Quinnell, Mark Perego

Man of the Match (Lloyd Lewis Memorial): Moore

By winning the Cup for the sixth time, the first since 1987, Cardiff stop Llanelli taking it for the fourth year in a row and and the tenth in all (nine is already the record). I Evans adds to his own records by scoring his 45th Cup try and seventh in a final.

All-Ireland Club League 1993-94

DIVISION 1	P	W	D	L	F	A	Pts
Garryowen	10	8	0	2	172	108	16
Cork Constitution	10	7	0	3	201	123	14
Blackrock College	10	7	0	3	137	99	14
Dungannon	10	5	0	5	181	130	10
Lansdowne	10	5	0	5	162	167	10
St Mary's College	10	5	0	5	157	163	10
Young Munster	10	5	0	5	102	149	10
Shannon	10	4	0	6	107	104	8
Old Wesley	10	4	0	6	114	138	8
Greystones	10	4	0	6	97	156	8
Wanderers	10	1	0	9	141	234	2

Garryowen regain the title (the only club to win it twice in its four-season existence), Greystones & Wanderers are relegated.

DIVISION 2
Promoted: Instonians, Sunday's Well
Relegated: Galwegians, Ballina

Inter-Provincial Tournament

	P	W	D	L	F	A	Pts
Leinster	4	3	0	1	72	40	6
Ulster	4	3	0	1	84	59	6
Munster	4	3	0	1	91	71	6
Exiles	4	1	0	3	72	80	2
Connacht	4	0	0	4	42	111	0

New Zealand Provincial Championship 1993

DIVISION 1	P	W	D	L	F	A	Pts
Waikato	8	6	0	2	219	106	26
Auckland	8	6	0	2	356	131	25
North Harbour	8	6	0	2	257	161	24
Otago	8	5	1	2	221	141	23
Wellington	8	4	1	3	174	166	20
Canterbury	8	4	0	4	188	235	16
King Country	8	2	0	6	90	317	9
Taranaki	8	2	0	6	175	338	8
Hawke's Bay	8	0	0	8	157	242	0

Hawke's Bay relegated

SEMI-FINALS

Auckland	43	North Harbour	20
Otago	36	Waikato	22

FINAL

Auckland	27	Otago	18

DIVISION 2	P	W	D	L	F	A	Pts
North Auckland	8	7	0	1	322	162	29
South Canterbury	8	6	0	2	238	138	25
Counties	8	6	0	2	401	135	24
Bay of Plenty	8	6	0	2	318	189	24
Manawatu	8	4	1	3	224	242	18
Southland	8	3	0	5	199	230	14
Nelson Bays	8	2	0	6	182	275	9
Wirarapa-Bush	8	0	2	6	105	300	4
Poverty Bay	8	0	1	7	80	393	3

Poverty Bay relegated

SEMI-FINALS

Bay of Plenty	41	N Auckland	26
Counties	33	S Canterbury	18

FINAL

Counties	33	Bay of Plenty	10

Counties promoted

DIVISION 3

Promoted: Horowhenua
Bottom: West Coast (P8 L8)

Ranfurly Shield

Auckland	80	Horowhenua	17
Auckland	48	Buller	3
Auckland	69	Hawke's Bay	31
Auckland	139	North Otago	5
Auckland	51	Wellington	14
Waikato	17	Auckland	6
Waikato	28	Otago	11

Waikato bring to an end one of the longest unbeaten sequences in any sport: Auckland had held the Shield since 1985, a run of 61 successful defences.

New Zealand Provincial Championship 1994

FINAL

Auckland	22	North Harbour	16

Eric Rush (N Harbour) & Robin Brooke (Auckland) are sent off, Mark Carter (Auckland) is taken off with blood pouring from a head wound after being kicked by Graham Dowd, who's allowed to stay on. League tables in 1996 Yearbook.

South Africa

Currie Cup Final 1993

TRANSVAAL 21   T: Johnson, Schmidt; C: Johnson; PG: Johnson 3

NATAL 15   PG: Stransky 5

Natal: André Joubert, C van der Westhuizen, R Muir, Pieter Müller, James Small, Joel Stransky, K Putt, Guy Kebble, John Allan, L Müller, Steve Atherton, Mark Andrews, Wahl Bartmann (c), A Blakeway, G Teichmann

Transvaal: Gavin Johnson, Pieter Hendriks, B Fourie, Japie Mulder, C Dirks, Hennie le Roux, Johan Roux, Balie Swart, Uli Schmidt, H Rodgers, K Wiese, H Strydom, Ian Macdonald, Rudolf Strauli, François Pienaar (c)(D Lotter 46)

Currie Cup Final 1994

TRANSVAAL 56   T: Roussouw, Le Roux, Roux, Grobler, penalty try, Hendriks, Schmidt; C: Johnson 6; PG: Johnson 3

ORANGE FREE STATE 33   T: Venter 2, Badenhorst; C: Herbert 3; PG: Herbert 4

Transvaal: G Grobler, Gavin Johnson, Japie Mulder
(C Scholz 48), B Fourie, P Hendriks, Hennie le Roux,
Johan Roux, Balie Swart, Uli Schmidt, Drikus Hattingh,
K Wiese, P Schutte, François Pienaar (c), C Roussouw,
G Combrinck

OFS: A Pawson (F Smith 55), H Truter, H Müller (c),
Brendon Venter, Chris Badenhorst, Derek Herbert,
T Kirkham, P du Randt, Ollie Le Roux, D Heymans
(N Drotske 43), R Opperman, B Els, A Venter, J Coetzee

*Johnson kicks nine goals, Herbert doesn't miss one in
the match.*

French Club Championship Final
28 June 1994 Parc des Princes

Toulouse 22 T: Cazalbou; C: Deylaud;
  PG: Deylaud 3

Montferrand 16 T: Juillet; C: Pradier; PG: Pradier 3

Toulouse: J Dupuy, Émile N'Tamack, P Carbonneau (D
Lacroix), O Carbonneau, David Berty, Christophe
Deylaud, J Cazalbou, C Califano, P Soula (C Guiter), C
Portolan, H Miorin, F Belot, JL Cester, A Cigagna (c), R
Sonnes

Montferrand: G Darlet, Philippe Saint-André,
F Ribeyrolles, R Saint-André, F Bertrank, E Nicol,
M Pradier, E Menieu, Philippe Marocco, C Duchène,
E Lecomte, JP Versailles, A Costes, C Juillet,
JM Lhermet (c)

*Toulouse come from 9-0 down to take the title for the
11th time. Montferrand have never won it.*

Super 10 Series

POOL A	P	W	D	L	F	A	Pts
Queensland	4	3	0	1	85	61	13
North Harbour	4	3	0	1	95	56	13
Otago	4	2	0	2	119	109	9
Transavaal	4	2	0	2	95	74	8
Eastern Province	4	0	0	4	70	164	0

*Queensland qualify for the final by virtue of having
beaten North Harbour.*

POOL B							
Natal	3	3	0	0	92	62	16
New South Wales	3	3	0	1	90	58	12
Western Samoa	4	2	0	2	96	102	9
Auckland	4	1	0	3	71	62	7
Waikato	4	0	0	4	66	132	1

*Natal awarded four pts when NSW refuse to travel to
Durban.*

FINAL
14 May 1994 Kings Park, Durban

Natal 10 T: Van der Westhuizen; C: Joubert;
  PG: Joubert

Queensland 21 T: Lea, Scott-Young; C: Lynagh;
  PG: Lynagh 2; DG: Lynagh

Natal: André Joubert, C van der Westhuizen, J
Thomson, Pieter Müller (A Marinos), James Small,
Henry Honiball, R du Preez, Guy Kebble, John Allan, A
Garvey, J Slade, Steve Atherton, Wahl Bartmann (c), G
Teichmann

Queensland: Matt Pini, Damian Smith, Tim Horan
(A Herbert), Jason Little (Paul Carozza), B Lea, Michael
Lynagh, Peter Slattery (c), Cameron Lillicrap, M Foley,
A Skeggs, Rod McCall, Garrick Morgan, David Wilson,
Sam Scott-Young, Ilie Tabua (John Eales)

Sydney Premiership

GRAND FINAL
19 Sep 1994 Concord Oval
Randwick 36 Warringah 16

*Warringah lose in the final for the second
successive year.*

Shinty

Camanchd Cup

FINAL
4 June 1994 Bught Park, Inverness
KYLES ATHLETIC (2) 3 FORT WILLIAM (0) 1
Mobeck 2 *MacLeod*
Nicholson pen

Kyles: Macdonald, Irvine, MacDonald, MacPhail,
Taylor (c), White, D MacRae, Allen, MacVicar,
Nicholson, Mobeck, I MacRae

F William: MacMillan, MacNeil, A Robertson, J Clark,
Gibson, N Robertson, A Clark, W MacDonald (c),
Smith, Wood, Cameron, Ferguson; sub MacLeod

*Kyles, from Tighnabruaich, win the Cup for the first
time since 1983. Fort William, the 1992 champions,
are in the final for the third time in four years.*

Shooting

World Champions 1994

Men

300m RIFLE

3x40m Free	Glenn Dubis	USA
60 x Prone Free	Bernd Rücker	GER
3x20m Standard	Jukka Salonen	FIN

50m RIFLE

3x40m	Petr Kurka	CZE
60 x Prone Free	Li Wen-je	CHN

AIR RIFLE	Boris Polyak	BYL
AIR PISTOL	Franck Dumoulin	FRA
FREE PISTOL	Wang Yi-fu	CHN
RAPID FIRE PISTOL	Krzystof Kucharcznyk	POL
CENTRE FIRE PISTOL	Pal Hembre	NOR
STANDARD PISTOL	Hak Lee-Sang	S KOR

50m RUNNING TARGET

30+30	Shu Qing-kwan	CHN
Mixed	Lubos Racansky	CZE

10m RUNNING TARGET

30+30	Manfred Kurzer	GER
Mixed	Roy Hill	USA

TRAP	Dmitry Monakov	UKR
DOUBLE TRAP	Mark Russell	AUS
SKEET	Bruno Rosetti	ITA

Women

50m RIFLE

3x20m	Anna Malukhina	RUS
60xProne	Petra Horneber	GER

AIR RIFLE	Sonja Pfeilschifter	GER
SPORT PISTOL	Hee Boo-Soon	S KOR
AIR PISTOL	Jasna Sekaric	YUG
RUNNING TARGET	Sun Kim-moon	S KOR
TRAP	Paola Tattini	ITA
DOUBLE TRAP	Satu Pusila	FIN
SKEET	Erdanik Avetisian	ARM

National Rifle Association Imperial

June-July 1994 Bisley

QUEEN'S PRIZE 23 June

Martin Millar	291.34
John Jackman	291.29
Anthony Ringer	289.35

Millar ties with Jackman on 291 but wins on the V-bull count. Ringer won the title in 1992.

Grand Aggregate	Andrew Luckman	595.80
Allcomers' Aggregate	Andrew Luckman	321.45
Prince of Wales Prize	Nick Brasier	75.13
St George's Vase	Stuart Collings	150.21
The Albert	Stuart Collings	214.24
The Hopton Challenge Cup	Stuart Collings	986.118
National Trophy	England	2050.259
Kolapore Cup	G Britain	1183.169
Chancellor's Trophy	Cambridge Univ	1156.131
Musketeers Cup	Birmingham Univ	591.79
Vizianagram Trophy	House of Lord's	677.27
County Long-range	Suffolk	443.56
Mackinnon Challenge Cup	Scotland	1146.115
The Elcho	England	1720.171
The Ashburton	Epsom	525.44

Epsom win it for the fifth time in a row.

British Open Air Rifle Championship

13 Feb 1994 Wolverhampton

MEN

David Rattray	681.5
Nigel Wallace	680.3
A Morris	672.7

Wallace is runner-up for the second successive year.

WOMEN

T Lunn	473.4
H Jones	472
D Lawrence	470.9

Lunn & Jones finish in the same order as 1993.

JUNIOR MEN	C Miles	681.7
JUNIOR WOMEN	L Minett	497

British Air Pistol Championship

20 Feb 1994 Aldersley

MEN

Mick Gault	685.3	UKR
N Freeland	672.1	
S Haynes	670.1	

Gault sets two UK records in regaining the title: the 685.9 for 70 shots, and 586 for 60.

WOMEN

Carol Page	475.9

Laura Elsworth 467.9
C Lind 466.9

Page wins the title for the fourth consecutive year.

Junior men: Simon Preston.
Junior women: Helen Preston

The Prestons are brother and sister.

British Championship for Disabled
20 Feb 1994

T Budgen 613.2
R Osborn 604.9
S Duguid 582.6

English Air Gun Championships
March 1994

Men's rifle N Wallace
Men's pistol Steve Haynes
Women's rifle K Morton
Women's pistol Carol Paige

Page retains the title by beating Wendy Haynes, Steve's wife, into second place.

British Pistol Championships
Aug 1994 Bisley

50 yards M Kemp
Free Pistol I Robinson
Short Range B Smith
Sport Pistol (women) Barbara Barber
Standard Pistol B Smith
Rapid Fire M Estaque (FRA)
NSRA 900 Aggregate B Smith
Standard Handgun J Harrison
Centre Fire A Lamont
Clubs London & Middlesex Club

British Pistol Club Championships
Sep 1994

MEN
Overall Paul Leatherdale
Standard R Duckworth
Rapid Fire N Freeland
Free Pistol Paul Leatherdale
Air Pistol Paul Leatherdale
Sport Pistol Paul Leatherdale
Centre-Fire B Smith *(fractionally ahead of Leatherdale)*

Centre-Fire Aggregate Paul Leatherdale

WOMEN
Overall Barbara Barber

Sport Pistol Bryony Young
Air Pistol Carol Page
Centre-Fire Aggregate Barbara Barber
Barber also finishes second to Page and third behind Young

British Small-bore Championships
13-21 Aug 1994 Bisley

Men Harry Hancox
Women I Andrew
Hancox, who finishes two shots ahead of Bill Brown (781-779) reaches the final for the first time in 28 years of competition.

Small-bore Home Championships

MEN
England 3760
Wales 3714
Scotland 3697
Ireland 3686

WOMEN
England 1849
Scotland 1835
Wales 1790

JUNIORS
England 1144
Wales 1087

No other entries in the Juniors. England retain all three team titles.

English Clay Pigeon Championships
May 1994 Chatcombe

M Rouse 189
R Borsley 180
J Grice 177

British Clay Pigeon Championships (Double Rise)
March 1994 Sutton Coldfield

Men P Cockle
Women K Dinenage

British Clay Pigeon Open
14 Aug 1994 Hodnet, Shropshire

Men George Digweed
Women V Ellis

Digweed wins a shoot-off with Carl Bloxham after they both shoot 97 out of 100.

Skiing

Alpine Skiing

World Cup 1993-94

Men

Solden (AUT) 30 Oct

G Slalom	Franck Piccard	FRA

The first Frenchman to win a World Cup Giant Slalom since Henri Duvillard at Megeve in 1973.

Park City (USA) 27-28 Nov

Slalom	Thomas Stangassinger	AUT
G Slalom	Günther Mader	AUT

Stoneham (CAN) 4-5 Dec

Slalom	Alberto Tomba	ITA

Val d'Isère (FRA) 12-14 Dec

Slalom	Alberto Tomba	ITA
G Slalom	Christian Mayer	AUT
Super G	Günther Mader	AUT

Mayer's first World Cup win.

Val Gardena (ITA) 17-18 Dec

Downhill 1	Markus Foser	LIECH
Downhill 2	Patrick Ortlieb	AUT

Alta Badia (ITA) 19 Dec

G Slalom	Steve Locher	SWI

Madonna di Campiglio (ITA) 20 Dec

Slalom	Jure Kosir	SLVN

Slovenia's first World Cup title since independence.

Lech am Arlberg (AUT) 22 Dec

Super G	Hannes Trinkl	AUT

Bormio ITA) 29 Dec

Downhill	Hannes Trinkl	AUT

Saalbach (AUT) 6 Jan

Downhill	Ed Podivinsky	CAN

Cary Mullen's being announced as the winner while his team mate makes a late charge.

Kranjska Gora (SLVN) 8-9 Jan

Slalom	Finn Christian Jägge	NOR
G Slalom	Fredrik Nyberg	SWE

Hinterstoder (AUT) 11 Jan

G Slalom	Kjetil-André Aamodt	NOR

Kitzbühel (AUT) 15-16 Jan

Downhill	Patrick Ortlieb	AUT
Slalom	Thomas Stangassinger	AUT
Combined	Lasse Kjus	NOR

Graham Bell's 12th place in the Downhill is the best ever by a British racer on the Hahnenkamm, beating the 14th of his brother Martin in 1986.

Crans-Montana (SWI) 18 Jan

G Slalom	Jan Einar Thorsen	NOR

Wengen (SWI) 22-23 Jan

Downhill	William Besse	SWI
Super G	Marc Girardelli	LUX

Chamonix (FRA) 29-30 Jan

Downhill	Kjetil André Aamodt	NOR
Slalom	Alberto Tomba	ITA
Combined	Kjetil André Aamodt	NOR

Aamodt's first win in a World Cup Downhill.

Garmisch-Partenkirchen (GER) 6 Feb

Slalom	Alberto Tomba	ITA

The Downhill due to be run on 5 Feb, on the same Kandahar piste where Ulrike Maier died, is moved to Aspen.

Aspen (USA) 4-6 Feb

Downhill 1	Hannes Trinkl	AUT
Downhill 2	Cary Mullen	CAN
G Slalom	Fredrik Nyberg	SWE

After twice finishing second this season, Mullen wins a World Cup Downhill for the first time.

Whistler Mountain (CAN) 12-13 March

Downhill	Atle Skaardal	NOR
Super G	Tommy Moe	USA

Skaardal wins the event for the second successive year.

Vail (USA) 17-20 March

G Slalom	Kjetil André Aamodt	NOR
Super G	Jan Einar Thorsen	NOR

FINAL STANDINGS

Overall	Kjetil André Aamodt	NOR
Downhill	Marc Girardelli	LUX
Slalom	Alberto Tomba	ITA
G Slalom	Christian Mayer	AUT
Super G	Jan Einar Thorsen	NOR

Aamodt, still only 22, wins the overall title for the first time, Tomba the Slalom title for the third.

Women

Solden (AUT) 31 Oct

G Slalom	Anita Wachter	AUT

Santa Caterina (ITA) 26-28 Nov

Slalom	Vreni Schneider	SWI
G Slalom 1	Anita Wachter	AUT
G Slalom 2	Ulrike Maier	GER

Tignes (FRA) 4-5 Dec

Downhill	Kate Pace	CAN
G Slalom	Deborah Compagnoni	ITA

Veysonnaz (SWI) 11-12 Dec

Slalom	Pernilla Wiberg	SWE
G Slalom	Deborah Compagnoni	ITA

St Anton (AUT) 18-19 Dec

Downhill	Anja Haas	AUT
Slalom	Vreni Schneider	SWI

Flachau (AUT) 21 Dec

Super G	Katja Koren	SLVN

Morzine (FRA) 5-6 Jan

Slalom	Pernilla Wiberg	SWE
G Slalom	Deborah Compagnoni	ITA

Altenmarkt (AUT) 8-9 Jan

Slalom	Vreni Schneider	SWI
Super G	abandoned	

Bad luck for Heidi Zurbriggen, sister of the famous Pirmin, who's been trying to win a World Cup race since 1985 and is leading when the event's called off for safety reasons. She's originally awarded the race, but it's eventually declared void because only 33 of the field of 85 started.

Cortina d'Ampezzo (ITA) 14-17 Jan

Downhill	Katja Seizinger	GER
G Slalom	Anita Wachter	AUT
Super G 1	Katja Seizinger	GER
Super G 2	1 eq Pernilla Wiberg	SWE
	1 eq Alenka Dozvan	SLVN

Dozvan is only 16.

Maribor (SLVN) 22-23 Jan

Slalom 1	Urska Hrovat	SLVN
Slalom 2	Vreni Schneider	SWI
G Slalom	Ulrike Maier	AUT

Hrovat, a former world junior champion, wins a senior World Cup race for the first time.

Garmisch Partenkirchen (GER) 29 Jan

Downhill	Isolde Kostner	ITA

In her first World Cup season, the 18-y-o Kostner wins an event interrupted by the death of Ulrike Maier, the first woman to die in a World Cup race. The Kandahar piste doesn't stage any World Cup events in 1994-95 At the beginning of the new season the governing body asks skiers to sign a disclaimer waiving all rights to legal action against piste organisers on safety grounds.

Sierra Nevada (SPA) 2-6 Feb

Downhill	Hilary Lindh	USA
Slalom	Vreni Schneider	SWI
Super G	Hilde Gerg	GER
Combined	Pernilla Wiberg	SWE

Whistler Mountain (CAN) 5-6 March

Downhill 1	Katja Seizinger	GER

Mammoth Mountain (USA) 9-10 March

Slalom	Vreni Schneider	SWI
Super G	Katja Seizinger	GER

Vail (USA) 17-20 March

Downhill	Katja Seizinger	GER
Slalom	Vreni Schneider	SWI
G Slalom	Martina Ertl	GER
Super G	Diann Roffe Steinrotter	USA

Roffe, recent surprise Olympic gold medallist, retires after winning a World Cup event for only the second time in ten years. She was Giant Slalom world champion in 1985.

FINAL STANDINGS

Overall	Vreni Schneider	SWI
Downhill	Katja Seizinger	GER
Slalom	Vreni Schneider	SWI
G Slalom	Anita Wachter	AUT
Super G	Katja Seizinger	GER

Schneider regains the overall title she won in 1989. Seizinger is Downhill champion for the third season in a row.

World Cup 1994-95

Men

Saas Fee (SWI) 6 Nov
Parallel Slalom   cancelled (high winds)

Sestriere (ITA) 26-27 Nov

Slalom	cancelled (melting snow)
G Slalom	ditto

Tignes (FRA) 3-4 Dec (moved from Val d'Isère)

Slalom	Alberto Tomba	ITA
Super G	Achim Vogt	LIECH

Vogt wins a World Cup event for the first time.

Tignes (FRA) 11 Dec (moved from Val Gardena)

Super G	Patrick Ortlieb	AUT

Sestriere (ITA) 12 Dec (from Madonna di Campiglio)

Slalom	Alberto Tomba	ITA

The local favourite makes light of a rib injury to finish 0.06 seconds ahead of Thomas Fogdoe (SWE) and win the first World Cup event ever staged under floodlights.

Val d'Isère (FRA)16-18 Dec

Downhill 1	Josef Ströbl	AUT
Downhill 2	Armin Assinger	AUT
G Slalom	Michael Grünigen	SWI

Ströbl not only becomes the first skier ever to win the first World Cup race he contests, he sets the fastest time in practice the day before. He then finishes third behind Assinger (Austrians fill the first four places).

Lech am Arlberg (AUT) 20-21 Dec

Slalom	Alberto Tomba	ITA
G Slalom	Alberto Tomba	ITA

In the days immediately after his birthday, the Bomba's ribs can't stop him maintaining his 100% record in slalom this season, or winning a World Cup Giant Slalom for the first time since 1991. His current overall total of 550 points is 248 ahead of Grünigen in second place.

Women

Saas Fee (SWI) 5 Nov

Slalom	cancelled (high winds)

Park City, Utah (USA) 26-27 Nov

Slalom	Heidi Zeller-Bähler	SWI
G Slalom	Vreni Scheider	SWI
Super G	Sylvia Eder	AUT

After ten years on the circuit, Zeller-Bähler wins a World Cup event for the first time (and doesn't have long to wait for the second).

Vail, Colorado (USA) 3-5 Dec

Downhill	Hilary Lindh	USA
G Slalom	Heidi Zeller-Bähler	SWI
Super G	Sylvia Eder	AUT

Lake Louise (CAN) 10-11 Dec

Downhill 1	Picabo Street	USA
Downhill 2	Hilary Lindh	USA

Super G	Katja Seizinger	GER

Lindh finishes second in the first Downhill.

Sestriere (ITA) 18 Dec

Slalom	Vreni Scheider	SWI

Schneider's 53rd World Cup win takes her ever closer to Annemarie Moser-Pröll's record 62.

Alta Badia (ITA) 21 Dec

G Slalom	Sabina Panzanini	ITA

Panzanini wins a World Cup race for the first time.

Méribel (FRA) 30 Dec

Slalom	Urska Hrovat	SLVN

Hrovat beats Vreni Schneider by 0.09 seconds.

Ski Jumping

Four Hills Tournament
Dec 1993 – Jan 1994

FINAL STANDINGS

Espen Bredesen	NOR	931.3
Jens Weissflog	GER	923.3
Andreas Goldberger	AUT	891.8

World Cup 1993-94

FINAL POSITIONS

Espen Bredesen	NOR	1203
Jens Weissflog	GER	1110
Andreas Goldberger	AUT	927

Cross Country

World Cup 1993-94

FINAL POSITIONS

Men	Vladimir Smirnov	KAZ
Women	Manuela Di Centa	ITA

Snooker

It was possible to see cracks in Stephen Hendry's game during 1994, but they were hairline to say the least, and anyway the most significant one was caused in his elbow by a slip on a hotel bathroom, which ultimately frightened the opposition more than it affected him: he immediately beat Dave Harold 13-2 and went on to retain the world title. Simply bionic.

Even so, even though he appeared to lose only when winning everything became a chore, all that supremacy depended on a single shot, the easy black missed by Jimmy White while compiling the winning break in the last frame of the world final, leaving him as runner-up for the fifth successive year. The Buffalo Bills story has nothing on this.

As for the younger generation (the really young; Hendry's only 25), it arrived mob-handed but perhaps not as menacingly as expected. Alan McManus began winning tournaments at last (beating Hendry in both) but lost in too many semis and finals; Ronnie O'Sullivan beat Hendry in another final but lost to him in the very next, went out early in the world championship and by the end of the year was muttering about retirement – at 18! The threat to the champion may not be quite as intense as some would hope.

Still, if the youth of today have an uncertain future, the youth of yesterday had problems of his own. Worrying about that elusive world title seems to have gone to Jimmy White's head: in Dec 1994 he withdrew from an exhibition match in the Midlands after undergoing an operation to cover up his bald spot. No hairline cracks required.

World Professional Championship
16 April - 2 May 1994 Crucible Theatre, Sheffield

47-y-o Ashot Potikyan, the first Russian to enter the event, loses 5-3 to Damon Zeid (ENG) in the first qualifying round in Blackpool.

ROUND 8

Surinder Gill	Matthew Couch	10-8
Dave Harold	Wayne Jones	10-8
Cliff Thorburn	Rod Lawler	10-6
Mark Davis	Jim Wych	10-4
Stefan Mazrocis	Nick Terry	10-8
Brian Morgan	Jason Weston	10-3
Les Dodd	Nigel Gilbert	10-3
Stephen Lee	Anthony S Hamilton	10-6
Billy Snaddon	Steve Newbury	10-4
Anthony Davies	Noppadon Noppachorn	10-8
Alex Higgins	Andrew Cairns	10-5
Fergal O'Brien	Mark O'Sullivan	10-9
Gary Ponting	Adrian Rose	10-6
Mark A King	Sean Lanigan	10-8
Ronnie O'Sullivan	Andy Hicks	10-8
Drew Henry	Sean Storey	10-5

ROUND 9

Surinder Gill	Mark Bennett	10-7
Dave Harold	Alain Robidoux	10-8
Cliff Thorburn	Tony Drago	10-5
Mark Davis	Jason Ferguson	10-9
Peter Ebdon	Stefan Mazrocis	10-4
Brian Morgan	Dean Reynolds	10-8
Les Dodd	Doug Mountjoy	10-9
Dene O'Kane	Stephen Lee	10-6
Billy Snaddon	Joe Swail	10-4
Anthony Davies	Joe Johnson	10-9
Alex Higgins	Tony Knowles	10-9
Fergal O'Brien	Mick Price	10-4
Gary Ponting	Mark Johnston-Allen	10-9
Mark A King	Gary Wilkinson	10-9
Ronnie O'Sullivan	Tony Jones	10-8
Drew Henry	Mike Hallett	10-5

ROUND 10

(televised stage) 17 April – 2 May 1994
Crucible Theatre, Sheffield

Stephen Hendry	Surinder Gill	10-1
Dave Harold	David Roe	10-8
Nigel Bond	Cliff Thorburn	10-9

Thorburn, competing in the championship for the 21st time, loses the last eight frames. He lost the last nine v Dene O'Kane in 1987.

Terry Griffiths	Mark Davis	10-7
James Wattana	Peter Ebdon	10-6
Brian Morgan	Martin Clark	10-9
Steve James	Les Dodd	10-9
Steve Davis	Dene O'Kane	10-3
Jimmy White	Billy Snaddon	10-6
Neal Foulds	Anthony Davies	10-7
Ken Doherty	Alex Higgins	10-6

The Hurricane has frank and meaningful discussions with referee John Williams, who he claims is standing in his eye-line. Higgins, after Williams stands his ground: 'Some of the referees don't know to walk backwards. I can with six Guinnesses down me.'

Alan McManus	Fergal O'Brien	10-7
Willie Thorne	Gary Ponting	10-2
Darren Morgan	Mark A King	10-5
Ronnie O'Sullivan	Dennis Taylor	10-6

Taylor drops out of the world's top 16 for the first time since rankings were inroduced (1976).

John Parrott	Drew Henry	10-9

Henry leads 9-8 and 66-6, but a kick on a red ends his break of 66.

ROUND 11

Stephen Hendry	Dave Harold	13-2

Harold finds it hard to cope with Hendry's fractured left arm.

Nigel Bond	Terry Griffiths	13-8
James Wattana	Brian Morgan	13-9
Steve Davis	Steve James	13-3
Jimmy White	Neal Foulds	13-10
Ken Doherty	Alan McManus	13-11

The first Republic of Ireland player to reach the quarter-finals since Patsy Fagan in 1978.

Darren Morgan	Willie Thorne	13-12
John Parrott	Ronnie O'Sullivan	13-3

Parrott wins the last eight frames against the young sensation

QUARTER-FINALS

Stephen Hendry	Nigel Bond	13-8
Steve Davis	James Wattana	13-9
Jimmy White	Ken Doherty	13-10
Darren Morgan	John Parrott	13-11

SEMI-FINALS

Stephen Hendry	Steve Davis	16-9
Jimmy White	Darren Morgan	16-8

FINAL

Stephen Hendry	Jimmy White	18-17

Hendry wins the title for the third time in a row and fourth in all (beating White in the final every time). White, who's never won the title, loses in the final for the fifth consecutive year and sixth in all. Exactly like last year, Hendry leads 5-2, but this time White goes ahead 9-7 & 11-9. Putting together the championship-winning break in the last frame, he misses an easy black to let Hendry in for the deciding break of 58.

Consecutive world championship finals

Since restructuring in 1969

7	Steve Davis	1983-89
5	Jimmy White	1990-94
4	Ray Reardon	1973-76
3	Stephen Hendry	1992-94

Professional Ranking Tournaments 1993-94

Dubai Classic

SEMI-FINALS
Stephen Hendry	Ronnie O'Sullivan	6-2
Steve Davis	Alan McManus	6-3

FINAL 8 Oct 1993 Al Nasr Sports Hall, Dubai
Hendry	Davis	9-3

One MBE beats another as Hendry wins the title for the third time.

Skoda Grand Prix

SEMI-FINALS
Peter Ebdon	John Parrott	9-5
Ken Doherty	Steve Davis	9-4

FINAL 31 Oct 1993 Hexagon, Reading
Ebdon	Doherty	9-6

Ebdon wins a ranking title for the 1st time.

UK Championship

SEMI-FINALS
Ronnie O'Sullivan	Darren Morgan	9-5
Stephen Hendry	John Parrott	9-3

Hendry scores 443 consecutive points without reply, a world record he breaks in the same tournament the following year. O'Sullivan becomes the youngest finalist (17yrs 358 days) in any ranking tournament.

FINAL 28 Nov 1993 Guild Hall, Preston
O'Sullivan   Hendry   10-6

European Open

SEMI-FINALS
Stephen Hendry	John Parrott	6-1
Ronnie O'Sullivan	Jimmy White	6-3

FINAL 19 Dec 1993 Arenahal, Antwerp
Hendry   O'Sullivan   9-5

Welsh Open

SEMI-FINALS
Steve Davis	James Wattana	6-1
Alan McManus	Peter Ebdon	6-2

FINAL 5 Feb 1994 Newport
Davis   McManus   9-6

McManus finishes runner-up in the event for the second successive year. Davis appears in his 90th major final.

International Open

SEMI-FINALS
John Parrott	Jimmy White	6-4
James Wattana	Alan McManus	6-3

FINAL 19 Feb 1994 Bournemouth
Parrott   Wattana   9-5

Parrott's first tournament win in Britain since the 1991 UK Championship.

Thailand Open

SEMI-FINALS
James Wattana	Jimmy White	5-1
Steve Davis	Alan McManus	5-4

FINAL 12 March Bangkok
Wattana   Davis   9-7

By winning his major home event for the first time, Wattana (real name Wattana Pu-Ob-Orm) prevents Davis from adding to his record 27 ranking titles. Hendry, trying to win the three overseas events in the same season, loses 5-2 in the first round to world amateur champion Chuchart Triratanaprandit, playing under the name Tai Pichit.

British Open

David McDonnell, ranked No.92, shoots a maximum 147 during his 5-3 win over Nic Barrow in the 4th qualifying round.

SEMI-FINALS
Ronnie O'Sullivan	Stephen Hendry	6-2

James Wattana	Steve Davis	6-4

FINAL 7 April 1994 Plymouth Pavilions
O'Sullivan   Wattana   9-4

Wattana loses in the final for the third year in a row.

World Professional Championship
see separate entry

Other Leading Tournaments 1993-94

B&H
10 Nov 1993 Edinburgh
Ronnie O'Sullivan   John Lardner   9-6
O'Sullivan (17) scores two centuries to equal Stephen Hendry's world record of ten in a professional tournament. Lardner (21) is ranked No.273.

MASTERS
13 Feb 1994 Wembley Conference Centre
Alan McManus   Stephen Hendry   9-8
In his sixth major final, McManus wins one for the first time to inflict Hendry's first ever defeat in the event after 23 matches and five titles going back to his debut in 1989.

IRISH MASTERS
27 March 1994 Goffs, Co.Kildare
Steve Davis   Alan McManus   9-8
Davis wins the title for the eighth time.

EUROPEAN LEAGUE
29 May 1994 Bingen, Germany
Stephen Hendry   John Parrott   10-7
Hendry wins the last five frames.

AUSTRALIAN OPEN
Bentleigh Club, Melbourne
John Higgins   Willie Thorne   9-5
During the tournament, Higgins breaks the Australian all-comers' record for the highest break three times (140, 141, 144) on the way to winning a professional event for the first time.

Professional Ranking Tournaments 1994-95

Dubai Classic

SEMI-FINALS
Peter Ebdon	Ronnie O'Sullivan	6-4
Alan McManus	Stephen Hendry	6-4

Ebdon wins four frames in a row to beat the 18-y-o O'Sullivan for the first time as a professional. McManus profits from a missed yellow that would have put Hendry 4-0 up.

FINAL 7 Oct 1994 Al Nasr Sports Hall, Dubai

McManus	Ebdon	9-6

McManus, appearing in his fourth ranking tournament final, wins one for the first time by taking the first three and last three frames.

Skoda Grand Prix

SEMI-FINALS

John Higgins	Joe Swail	9-5
Dave Harold	Andy Hicks	9-8

Higgins reaches the final of a ranking tournament for the first time. Harold wins the last three frames.

FINAL 23 Oct 1994 Assembly Rooms, Derby

Higgins	Harold	9-6

Higgins becomes the youngest player apart from Hendry and O'Sullivan to win a ranking tournament.

UK Championship

SEMI-FINALS

Stephen Hendry	Peter Ebdon	9-8
Ken Doherty	James Wattana	9-6

A six-frame streak takes Doherty to 7-2 in his attempt to become the first Republic of Ireland player to win the title since Patsy Fagan won in the inaugural year (1978). Hendry wins after leading 8-5, winning the decider 53-36.

FINAL 27 Nov 1994 Guild Hall, Preston

Hendry	Doherty	10-5

Hendry regains the title in a welter of centuries: three in a row, a record seven in all, twelve in the tournament, breaking his own record of ten; against Willie Thorne in the third round, he breaks another of his records by scoring 454 points in a row - all this after having to win the last five frames to beat Dean Reynolds 9-8 in the second, the same round in which Steve Davis, trying to win the title for the seventh time, playing with a cue borrowed from his father after breaking the one he's used for the past fifteen years, loses 9-6 to Dave Harold who hadn't taken a frame off him in two previous matches.

Winning is the drug

World No.111 Chris Scanlon is fined £195 and docked 400 ranking points after failing a dope test.

European Open

SEMI-FINALS

John Parrott	Nigel Bond	6-4
Stephen Hendry	Ronnie O'Sullivan	6-5

FINAL 17 Dec 1994 Arenahal, Antwerp

Hendry	Parrott	9-3

A mere three centuries this time by Hendry, who retains the title and wins a major title for the 50th time.

Other Leading Tournaments 1994-95

TOP RANK CLASSIC
Sep 1994 Bangkok

Stephen Hendry	James Wattana	6-5

Hendry wins the five-man round-robin competition by beating Wattana on the re-spotted black of the last frame. Wattana would have won the tournament himself if he hadn't missed an easy pink in front of his home supporters.

REGAL MASTERS
25 Sep 1994 Civic Centre, Motherwell

Ken Doherty	Stephen Hendry	9-7

Doherty retains the title by beating the 1989 & 1990 champion and 5-2-on favourite.

B&H
6 Nov 1994 Edinburgh

Mark Williams	Rod Lawler	9-5

GRAND PRIX
4 Dec 1994 Malta

John Parrott	Tony Drago	7-6

The local boy tries too hard after leading 5-1. Allison Fisher loses 4-1 to Joe Swail in the quarter-finals.

World Amateur Championship 1993

QUARTER-FINALS

Chuchat Triratanapradit	Paul Reeve	5-0
Patrick Wallace	Kieran Irwin	5-2
Graeme Dott	Adrian Tan	5-2
Prapruet Chaitanasakun	Raymond Fabrie	5-3

SEMI-FINALS

Triratanapradit	Wallace	8-7
Chaitanasakun	Dott	8-4

FINAL
16-17 Dec 1993 Karachi

Chuchart Triratanapradit	THAI	
Prapruet Chaitanasakun	THAI	11-6

The first World Amateur final involving players from the same country, and the third Thai to win the event, following James Wattana (1989) and Noppadon Noppachorn (1991). In the first frame, Triratanapradit, a 31-y-o former monk, equals the championship record break of 141.

World Amateur 1994

FINAL
26 Nov 1994 Johannesburg

Mohamed Yusuf	PAK	
Johannes Johannesson	ICE	11-9

The Icelandic teenager doesn't quite go all the way. The last British survivor, Ron Jones of Wales, loses 5-1 in the quarter-finals to Somporn Kunthawung (THAI).

World Under-21 1994
Helsinki

QUARTER-FINALS

David Gray	ENG	Flan Hayes	EIRE	5-1
Johannes Johannesson	ICE	Reind Duut	HOL	5-3
Jonathan Nelson	N IRE	Chris Shade	SCOT	5-2
Quinten Hann	AUS	Anan Terananon	THAI	5-0

Johannesson reaches the semis for the second successive year.

SEMI-FINALS

Gray	Johannesson	8-3
Hann	Nelson	8-4

FINAL

Hann	Gray	11-10

After losing six consecutive frames, Hann (17) overtakes the 15-y-o favourite (who'd beaten him 4-0 at the round-robin stage) to become the first Australian to win a world amateur title.

Women's Snooker

World Championship

1st ROUND

Valerie Dalgleish	Valerie Van Beiilinghen	4-0
Dawn Wells	Margaret Browne	4-1
Pam Beevers	Nicola Barker	4-2
Anita Kuczma	Tracy Warren	4-0
Jane Moss	Martina Lemsden	4-2
Christel Leclerq	Sue Parrish	4-2
Mary Talbot	Mary Winn	4-2
Helen Lazell	Sarah Ellerby	4-3
Louise King	Lyn Cast	4-3
Ann McMahon	Miranda Wauters	4-2
Nicla Golley	Clare Heseldine	4-0
Liliane Van Riel	Doreen Buckton	4-0
Martine Vanderaerden	Sheila Pook	4-1
Paula Darby	Saskia Smits	w.o.
Laura Stoddard	Maureen Twomey	4-1
Julie Billings	Rachel Ozier	4-3

2nd ROUND

Valerie Dalgleish	Mary Hawkes	4-0
Kathy Parashis (AUS)	Dawn Wells	4-0
Carla Jolly	Pam Beevers	4-1
Anita Kuczma	Teresa Carlisle	4-3
Julie Kelly	Jane Moss	4-1
Jenny Poulter	Christel Leclerq	4-2
Maria Tart	Mary Talbot	4-0
Kirsten Miners	Helen Lazell	4-1
Gaye Jones	Louise King	4-3
Helen Audus	Ann McMahon	4-1
Lisa Gordon	Nicla Golley	4-3
Margaret Campion	Liliane Van Riel	4-1
Emma Bonney	Martine Vanderaerden	4-2
Maureen Seto	Paula Darby	4-2
Maryann McConnell (CAN)	Laura Stoddard	4-3
Julie Billings	Jane 'Neill	4-1

3rd ROUND

Allison Fisher	Valerie Dalgleish	4-0
Julie Gillespie	Kathy Parashis	4-0
Sarah Smith	Carla Jolly	4-2
Mandy Fisher	Anita Kuczma	4-2
Ann-Marie Farren	Julie Kelly	4-1
Kelly Fisher	Jenny Poulter	4-0
Caroline Walch	Maria Tart	4-0
Tessa Davidson	Kirsten Miners	4-1
Stacey Hillyard	Gaye Jones	4-0
Helen Audus	Georgina Aplin	4-3
Lisa Gordon	Lisa Quick	4-3
Kim Shaw	Margaret Campion	4-2
Lynette Horsburgh	Emma Bonney	4-2
Sharon Dickson	Maureen Seto	4-1
June Banks	Maryann McConnell	4-2
Karen Corr	Julie Billings	4-0

4th ROUND

Allison Fisher	Julie Gillespie	4-0
Sarah Smith	Mandy Fisher	4-1
Kelly Fisher	Ann-Marie Farren	4-2
Tessa Davidson	Caroline Walch	4-2
Stacey Hillyard	Helen Audus	4-1
Kim Shaw	Lisa Gordon	4-2

| Sharon Dickson | Lynette Horsburgh | 4-1 |
| Karen Corr | June Banks | 4-1 |

Final stages 19-21 May 1994
Le Meridien Hotel, New Delhi

QUARTER-FINALS

Allison Fisher	Sarah Smith	5-0
Tessa Davidson	Kelly Fisher	5-4
Stacey Hillyard	Kim Shaw	5-0
Karen Corr	Sharon Dickson	5-3

Davidson comes from 3-1 down to beat the 15-y-o Fisher. Hillyard plays in her ninth World Championship quarter-final...

SEMI-FINALS

| Allison Fisher | Tessa Davidson | 6-3 |
| Stacey Hillyard | Karen Corr | 6-3 |

...eighth semi-final...

FINAL

| Allison Fisher | Stacey Hillyard | 7-3 |

...and sixth final. Fisher, who beat Hillyard in last year's decider, wins the last five frames to take the title for the third time in a row and the seventh in all. She's never lost in the final. Hillyard's won the championship once, in 1984 when it was an amateur event and she was just 15 (she beat the 16-y-o Fisher in the semi-final)

Highest Break: 108 Hillyard (v Jones)

Major Tournaments

Connie Gough Memorial

SEMI-FINALS

| Kelly Fisher | Kim Shaw | 3-1 |
| Tessa Davidson | Stacey Hillyard | 3-0 |

FINAL 22 Aug 1993

| K Fisher | Davidson | 3-1 |

Fisher, still only 14, wins a world ranking tournament for the first time.

Regal Masters

SEMI-FINALS

| Stacey Hillyard | Lynette Horsburgh | 4-3 |
| Ann-Marie Farren | Karen Corr | 4-1 |

FINAL 13-14 Nov Stirling

| Hillyard | Farren | 4-3 |

British Open

SEMI-FINALS

| Allison Fisher | Tessa Davidson | 3-1 |
| Karen Corr | Kim Shaw | 3-1 |

FINAL 4-5 Dec 1993 Prestatyn

| A Fisher | Corr | 3-1 |

National Championship

SEMI-FINALS

| Karen Corr | Stacey Hillyard | 4-2 |
| Allison Fisher | Ann-Marie Farren | 4-0 |

FINAL 6 March 1994 Mayfair SC, Tooting Bec, London

| Corr | A Fisher | 4-0 |

Fisher's good form deserts her: she totals only 105 points in the final.

UK Championship

Three Fishers (all unrelated) reach the quarter-finals: Allison, Kelly and Mandy.

SEMI-FINALS

| Karen Corr | Lynette Horsburgh | 4-1 |
| Stacey Hillyard | Tessa Davidson | 4-3 |

FINAL 19-20 March 1994 Pakefield, Lowestoft

| Corr | Hillyard | 4-3 |

A black ball win in the fifth frame helps Corr take the title for the first time (she comes from behind to win the decider).

Green Baize Classic

SEMI-FINALS

| Allison Fisher | Tessa Davidson | 3-1 |
| Karen Corr | Stacey Hillyard | 3-1 |

FINAL 17 April 1994 Cirencester

| A Fisher | Corr | 3-2 |

Fisher wins the inaugural event on the very last black.

Spring Bowl

SEMI-FINALS

| Karen Corr | Kim Shaw | 3-1 |
| Lisa Quick | Kelly Fisher | 3-2 |

FINAL 7-14 May Prestatyn

| Corr | Quick | 4-1 |

The tournament's in its last year as a ranking event. Kelly Fisher is now 15.

Llanelli Classic

SEMI-FINALS

| Allison Fisher | Kelly Fisher | 4-1 |
| Stacey Hillyard | Tessa Davidson | 4-0 |

FINAL 27-28 Aug 1994 Llanelli

| A Fisher | Hillyard | 4-2 |

Despite a highest break of only 33 in the final, Fisher regains the World No.1 ranking from Corr.

Speed Skating

World Championships

Men *12-13 March 1994 Gothenburg*

OVERALL

Johann Olav Koss	NOR	167.233
Ids Postma	HOL	168.457
Rintje Rintsma	HOL	168.567

Koss regains the title he won in 1990 & 1991.

500

Ids Postma	HOL	38.39
Hiroyuki Noake	JAP	38.50
Naoki Kotake	JAP	38.90

1500

Johann Olav Koss	NOR	1:59.68
Andrei Anufriyenko	RUS	2:00.76
Hiroyuki Noakle	JAP	2:00.95

5000

Kjell Storelid	NOR	7:11.63
Johann Olav Koss	NOR	7:14.21
Jaromir Radke	POL	7:16.05

10 000

Johann Olav Koss	NOR	14:49.58
Kjell Storelid	NOR	14:51.68
Ids Postma	HOL	14:54.93

Women *5-6 Feb 1994 Butte, Montana*

OVERALL

Emese Hunyady	AUT	177.480
Ulrike Adeberg	GER	178.733
Mihaela Dascalu	ROM	178.859

The first Austrian to win the title adds to the unbroken succession of German-speaking winners since 1982.

500

Ulrike Adeberg	GER	41.36
Emese Hunyady	AUT	41.80
Emese Antal	AUT	41.84

1500

Emese Hunyady	AUT	2:07.13
Mihaela Dascalu	ROM	2:07.22
Anni Friesinger	GER	2:07.93

3000

Emese Hunyady	AUT	4:30.59
Ulrike Adeberg	GER	4:30.71
Mihaela Dascalu	ROM	4:32.41

5000

Emese Hunyady	AUT	8:02.06
Anni Friesinger	GER	8:04.77
Lyudmila Prokashyev	KAZ	8:04.97

World Sprint Championships
29-30 Jan 1994 Calgary

Men

OVERALL

Dan Jansen	USA	144.815	WR
Sergei Klevchenya	RUS	145.315	
Junichi Inoue	JAP	145.670	

Race winners: both 500s Jansen, 1000 Klevchenya, 1000 Scott. Jansen's 35.76 breaks his own 500 WR (35.92) set in 1993.

Women

OVERALL

Bonnie Blair	USA	157.405	WR
Angela Hauck	GER	159.020	
Xue Rui-hong	CHN	159.080	

Race winners: all four (two 500s, two 1000s) Blair

European Championships
7-9 Jan 1994 Hamar, Norway

Men

OVERALL

Rintje Risma	HOL	156.201
Johann Olav Koss	NOR	157.257
Falko Zandstra	HOL	157.686

Race winners: 500, 1500, 5000 Ritsma, 10 000 Koss

Women

OVERALL

Gunda Niemann	GER	167.282	WR
Svetlana Bazhanova	RUS	170.263	
Emese Hunyady	AUT	170.473	

Race winners: 500, 1500 Hunyady, 3000, 5000 Niemann

World Short track Championships

Men *31 Mar - 2 Apr 1994*
Guildford Spectrum, Surrey

OVERALL

Marc Gagnon	CAN	10 pts
Frederic Blackburn	CAN	9
Chae Ji-hoon	S KOR	9

Race winners: 500 Blackburn, 1000 Gagnon, 1500 Chae, 3000 Orazio Fagone (ITA), 5000 relay JAP (Yuichi Akasaka, Hideto Imai, Tatsuyoshi Ishihara, Satoru Terao)

Gagnon, still only 18, retains the overall title. In the 1500 final, Nicky Gooch (UK), skating on his home rink, is elbowed in the face by Fagone and brought down by Blackburn, finishes fifth, then falls in the 500 semi-final.

Women

OVERALL

Nathalie Lambert	CAN	16
Kim So-hee	S KOR	8
Kim Ryang-hee	S KOR	7

Race winners: 500 Marinella Caclini (ITA), 1000, 3000 Lambert, 1500 Kim So-hee, 3000 relay CAN (Lambert, Sylvie Daigle, Isabelle Charest, Angela Cutrone)

Lambert, who retains the overall title, retires, as does five-time world champion Daigle, who first won the overall title in 1979. Kim So-hee won the world junior overall title in Jan 1994.

European Short track Championships

Men Overall	Nicky Gooch	UK
Women Overall	Marina Pilayeva	RUS

Gooch wins the 1500 & 3000, Pilayeva the 500 & 1000.

Speedway

World Championship

British Final *1 May 1994 Coventry*

Andy Smith	12
Joe Screen	11
Gary Havelock	11
Dean Barker	10
Mark Loram	9
Jeremy Doncaster	9
Martin Dugard	9
Simon Cross	9
Chris Louis	7

Smith wins his last three rides to retain the title. The top nine qualify for the Commonwealth Final.

Commonwealth Final *22 May 1994 King's Lynn*

Mark Loram	ENG	14
Martin Dugard	ENG	13
Joe Screen	ENG	12
Leigh Adams	AUS	11
Chris Louis	ENG	10
Jeremy Doncaster	ENG	9
Craig Boyce	AUS	8
Jason Lyons	AUS	8
Gary Havelock	ENG	7
Jason Crump	AUS	7

A British rider wins the Commonwealth title for the first time. The top ten qualify for the Overseas Final.

Overseas Final *12 June 1994 Coventry*

Sam Ermolenko	USA	14
Greg Hancock	USA	12
Craig Boyce	AUS	12
Leigh Adams	AUS	11
Jason Crump	AUS	9
Josh Larsen	USA	9
Billy Hamill	USA	8
Mark Loram	ENG	8
Chris Louis	ENG	8

England's worst ever world championship performance: only two qualifiers for the semi-finals. Among those eliminated, two world champions: Gary Havelock (who broke his collarbone less than two weeks earlier), and Joe Screen (Under-21).

Nordic Final *12 June 1994 Eskilstuna, Sweden*

Hans Nielsen	DEN	13
Tommy Knudsen	DEN	12
Tony Rickardsson	SWE	12
Henrik Gustafsson	SWE	10

Per Jonsson	SWE	10
Lars Gunnestad	NOR	10
Stefan Dannö	SWE	8
Gert Handberg	DEN	8
Jan Staechmann	DEN	8

Nielsen wins the event for the ninth time.

World Semi-final *10 July 1994 Bradford*

Mark Loram	ENG	14
Hans Nielsen	DEN	13
Henrik Gustafsson	SWE	12
Marvyn Cox	ENG	11
Josh Larsen	USA	11
Chris Louis	ENG	9
Piotr Swist	POL	8
Craig Boyce	AUS	8

Eight qualify for the World Final. Cox competes under a German licence.

World Semi-final *10 July 1994 Prague*

Tomasz Gollob	POL	14
Tony Rickardsson	SWE	12
Jan Staechmann	DEN	11
Sam Ermolenko	USA	11
Stefan Dannö	SWE	11
Tommy Knudsen	DEN	11
Jason Crump	AUS	9
Greg Hancock	USA	8

Eight qualify for the World Final.

World Final *20 Aug 1994 Vojens, Denmark*

Tony Rickardsson	SWE	12
Hans Nielsen	DEN	12
Craig Boyce	AUS	12
Greg Hancock	USA	11
Tommy Knudsen	DEN	10
Marvyn Cox	ENG	9
Mark Loram	ENG	8
Henrik Gustafsson	SWE	9
Josh Larsen	USA	9
Jan Staechmann	DEN	7
Chris Louis	ENG	6
Jason Crump	AUS	6
Sam Ermolenko	USA	6
Stefan Dannö	SWE	2
Piotr Swist	POL	1
Tomasz Gollob	POL	0
Roman Jankowski	POL	0

In the last world final to be decided on a single night (replaced next season by a series of races), Rickardsson's late run in the three-man ride-off brings him the title for the first time (he was runner-up in 1991), deprives Nielsen (riding in a cast after breaking three bones in his right foot) of a fourth win in the event, and prevents Boyce from becoming the first Australian world champion since Jack Young in 1952. Ermolenko was the defending champion. The 1992 champion Per Jonsson (SWE) is in a wheelchair after suffering spinal injuries in a crash in June.

World Team Final

18 Sep 1994 Brokstedt, Germany

Tony Rickardsson 12, Henrik Gustafsson 11, Mikael Karlsson DNR	SWE	23
Tomasz Gollob 16, Jacek Gollob 4, Dariusz Sledz 0	POL	20
Tommy Knudsen 12, Hans Nielsen 5, Jan Staechmann 0	DEN	17
Craig Boyce 9, Leigh Adams 8, Jason Crump DNR	AUS	17
Sam Ermolenko 12, Greg Hancock 5, Bily Hamill DNR	USA	17
Mark Loram 9, Chris Louis 4, Gary Havelock 3	ENG	16
Gerd Riss 12, André Pöhlen 3, Robert Barth 1	GER	16

Knudsen wins the third-place race-off ahead of Boyce & Ermolenko. English team manager John Louis rather controversially picks his son ahead of Martin Dugard & Joe Screen. It doesn't work: England finish last for the second year in a row. Sweden retain the title, all seven teams criticise the hard track, which allows only three overtaking moves in 21 races.

World Long Track Final

25 Sep 1994 Marianske Lazne, Czech Rep

Simon Wigg	ENG	25
André Pollehn	GER	20
Gerd Riss	GER	17
Egon Müller	GER	17
A Dryml	CZE	16
B Diener	GER	15
M Gerhard	SWI	11

At Adolf Hitler's favourite spa town, Wigg wins the title for the fifth time, breaking the record he shared with Müller & Karl Maier (WG). Riss wins a ride-off for third place against the 46-y-o Müller.

World Under-21 Final

14 Aug 1994 Elgane, Oslo

Mikael Karlsson	SWE	14
Rune Holta	NOR	14
Jason Crump	AUS	12
Tomas Topinka	CZE	12
Tomasz Bajerski	POL	11
Ronni Pedersen	DEN	10
Jiri Stancl	CZE	10

Karlsson & Crump win run-offs.

Division 1 Riders' Championship

9 Oct 1994 Swindon

Sam Ermolenko	Wolverhampton	15
Hans Nielsen	Coventry	13
Martin Dugard	Eastbourne	11

Ermolenko's maximum, which gives him the title for the second time in four years, stops Nielsen winning one last major event before retiring from British speedway.

Division 2 Riders' Championship

17 Sep 1994 Coventry

Paul Bentley	Middlesbrough	13
Tony Olsson	Swindon	12
Tony Langdon	Swindon	11

England v USA 1993

24 Sep Arena Essex	England	43	USA	65
11 Oct Wolverhampton	England	50	USA	58
14 Oct Sheffield	England	53	USA	55

Australia v British Lions 1993-94

31 Dec Sydney	Australia	68	Lions	40
2 Jan Brisbane	Australia	56	Lions	52
5 Jan Newcastle	Australia	69	Lions	39
8 Jan Avalon	*rained off*			
12 Jan Adelaide	Australia	61	Lions	46

England v Sweden 1994

17 July Exeter	England	70	Sweden	38
21 July Ipswich	England	65	Sweden	43
22 July Oxford	England	75	Sweden	32

England v USA 1994

4 Sep Eastbourne	England	67	USA	41
23 Sep Arena Essex	England	54	USA	54
18 Oct Poole	England	68	USA	40

British Knockout Cup 1994

1st round

Cradley Heath	70	Ipswich	25
Ipswich	61	Cradley Heath	33
Poole	56	King's Lynn	40
King's Lynn	58	Poole	38
Belle Vue	47	Eastbourne	49
Eastbourne	59	Belle Vue	37

2nd round

Bradford	49	King's Lynn	47
King's Lynn	61	Bradford	35
Arena Essex	52	Cradley Heath	44
Cradley Heath	59	Arena Essex	24
Reading	52	Coventry	43
Coventry	59	Reading	34
Wolverhampton	50	Eastbourne	46
Eastbourne	51	Wolverhampton	45

Semi-finals

Cradley Heath	55	Coventry	41
Coventry	48	Cradley Heath	47
King's Lynn	55	Eastbourne	41
Eastbourne	55	King's Lynn	41

Replay

Eastbourne	62	King's Lynn	33
King's Lynn	45	Eastbourne	51

FINAL

23 Oct

Eastbourne	59	Cradley Heath	37

M Dugard 14, Barker 12, Dannö 12, P Dugard 8, Norris 7, Andersson 5, Swain 1

Hancock 13, Nahlin 9, Hamill 7, Cross 6, Forsgren 2, Smith 0, Sealey 0

1 Nov

Cradley Heath	49	Eastbourne	47

Cross 14, Hamill 14, Nahlin 9, Hancock 7, Forsgren 4 Smith 1 Sealey 0

M Dugard 10, Barker 10, Dannö 9, Norris 8, Andersson 4, P Dugard 4 Swain 2

Eastbourne win their first title as a Division 1 club. In the 29 years of the competition, only seven clubs have won it after losing the first leg, or in this case the second, which was staged first when the first was postponed (!).

Division 2 Final

14 Oct 1994

Edinburgh	50	Glasgow	46

16 Oct 1994

Glasgow	55	Edinburgh	41

Glasgow become only the second club (after Eastbourne in 1987) to do the divisional double in successive years.

British League 1993

Division 1	M	W	D	L	F	A	Bonus	Pts
Belle Vue	40	24	1	15	2287	2017	14	63
Wolverhampton	40	23	0	17	2284	2029	17	63
Eastbourne	40	23	1	16	2189	2087	14	61
Arena Essex	40	21	1	18	2203	2113	10	53
Coventry	40	18	3	19	2172	2142	13	52
Reading	40	20	1	19	2181	2129	10	51
Bradford	40	19	3	18	2109	2174	7	48
Ipswich	40	17	0	23	2081.5	2202.5	8	42
King's Lynn	40	15	4	21	2002.5	2215.5	6	40
Poole	40	17	0	23	2033	2281	6	40
Cradley Heath	40	16	0	24	2080	2232	5	37

Belle Vue effectively win the title by a single race point, late in the season, beating long-time leaders Wolverhampton 54-53. Amazingly, the champions finish bottom the following season and are threatened with dissolution after the Greyhound Racing Association raise the rent at Kirkmanshulme Stadium.

Division 2	M	W	D	L	F	A	Bonus	Pts
Glasgow	40	27	1	12	2416	1900	19	74
Long Eaton	40	25	0	15	2302	1970	13	63
Peterborough	40	24	0	16	2260	2012	13	61
Swindon	40	23	1	16	2217.5	2088.5	13	60
Edinburgh	40	20	1	19	2272	2041	15	56
Newcastle	40	21	2	17	2138.5	2133.5	8	52
Middlesbrough	40	21	0	19	2125	2189	8	50
Rye House	40	20	0	20	2133	2177	9	49
Sheffield	40	15	0	25	1959	2320	5	35
Exeter	40	12	0	28	1881	2429	3	27
Oxford	40	9	1	30	1934	2378	4	23

British League 1994

Division 1	M	W	D	L	F	A	Bonus	Pts
Poole	40	30	1	9	2081	1670	16	77
Eastbourne	40	23	2	15	1978	1767	14	62
Wolverhampton	40	20	2	18	1925.5	1902.5	12	54
Coventry	40	19	3	18	1925	1853	11	52
King's Lynn	40	20	1	19	1799	1985	10	51
Ipswich	40	19	2	19	1944	1890	10	50
Bradford	40	18	1	21	1891	1901	11	48
Arena Essex	40	19	0	21	1868	1948	7	46
Cradley Heath	40	16	3	21	1871	1895	7	42
Reading	40	14	2	24	1815.5	2018.5	6	36
Belle Vue	40	13	1	26	1781	2049	5	32

Poole rise from tenth last year to win the championship for the first time since 1969,

Division 2	M	W	D	L	F	A	Bonus	Pts
Glasgow	36	26	1	9	1955	1494	14	67
Long Eaton	36	24	2	10	1835	1614	15	65
Edinburgh	36	20	1	15	1760	1690	10	51
Swindon	36	18	1	17	1752	1698	12	49
Peterborough	36	18	2	16	1752	1681	10	48
Middlesbrough	36	19	1	16	1744.5	1706.5	9	48
Newcastle	36	15	1	20	1729.5	1714.5	9	40
Oxford	36	15	1	20	1691	1743	7	38
Sheffield	36	10	1	25	1537	1914	3	24
Exeter	36	9	1	26	1474	1975	1	20

Glasgow retain the title, Newcastle are forced to fold. Berwick win the first ever Division 3 championship.

Squash

In some ways, the same old story. Britain settled mob-handed around the top of the world rankings, but couldn't oust the leading Pakistani man or Australian woman, neither of whom looks about to step down in '95. This plus another traditional power (Egypt) rising again from the junior ranks. So the No.1 spot will have to be earned - but the British are still paying their way, still arguably the strongest all-round country, and the likes of Marshall, Nicol & Jackman may be ready to make the final step. Although that's been said for the last few years, it's still worth watching this space.

World Open 1993

Men

Nov 1993 Karachi

QUARTER-FINALS

Jansher Khan	PAK	Rodney Eyles	AUS 15-7 15-7 15-7
Chris Walker	ENG	Brett Martin	AUS 13-15 17-14 15-10 15-11
Peter Marshall	ENG	Tony Hands	ENG 15-8 15-12 15-14
Jahangir Khan	PAK	Rodney Martin	AUS 17-16 17-15 15-11

The only other English player to reach the semis was Gawain Briars in 1985.

SEMI-FINALS

Jansher	Marshall	15-5 15-6 15-8
Jahangir	Walker	15-7 15-5 9-15 15-4

FINAL

Jansher	Jahangir	14-15 15-9 15-5 15-5

No.1 seed Jansher wins the title for the fifth time. The unseeded Jahangir, world champion six times, British Open champion ten years in a row, retires from international squash after the team event.

Men's team

Nov 1993 Karachi

SEMI-FINALS

PAKISTAN	ENGLAND	2-1
Jansher Khan	Peter Marshall	9-4 9-10 9-2 9-1
Jahangir Khan	Phil Whitlock	9-5 9-5 9-3
Zarak Jahan Zhan	Chris Walker	5-9 1-9 9-7 9-5 5-9

AUSTRALIA	FINLAND	2-1
Rodney Martin	Sami Elopuro	10-8 10-9 4-9 4-9 0-9
Brett Martin	P Pekkanen	9-0 9-8 9-6
Rodney Eyles	J Raumolin	9-4 9-4 9-3

3RD-PLACE FINAL

England	Finland	3-0

FINAL

PAKISTAN	AUSTRALIA	3-0
Jansher Khan	Rodney Martin	9-2 9-0 9-0
Jahangir Khan	Brett Martin	5-9 9-19-5 9-3
Zarak Jahan Khan	Rodney Eales	9-4 9-2 6-9 2-9 10-9

World Open 1994

Men

14-18 Sep 1994 Barcelona

QUARTER-FINALS

Jansher Khan	PAK	Chris Walker	ENG 15-11 15-6 15-10
Rodney Eyles	AUS	Anthony Hill	AUS 15-6 15-10 15-8
Peter Marshall	ENG	Rodney Martin	AUS 15-13 13-15 15-10 15-11
Peter Nicol	ENG	Brett Martin	AUS 15-10 15-11 6-15 15-10

The Peters beat the Martin brothers to set up a semi-final that ensures Britain a player in the final for the first time.

SEMI-FINALS

Jansher	Eyles	15-7 15-12 15-13
Marshall	Nicol	15-7 13-15 15-5 15-3

Including this one, there have been 18 World finals, not one without a Pakistani player.

FINAL

Jansher	Marshall	10-15 15-11 15-8 15-5

Even with an ankle injury, Jansher (as Marshall admits) is 'too good again.'

Most world titles (men)

6	Jahangir Khan	PAK	1981-82-83-84-85-88
6	Jansher Khan	PAK	1987-89-90-92-93-94
4	Geoff Hunt	AUS	1976-77-79-80

Most world finals

9	Jahangir Khan	PAK	as above,
			plus 1986-91-93
7	Jansher Khan	PAK	as above, plus 1988
5	Geoff Hunt	PAK	as above plus 1981
5	Chris Dittmar	AUS	1983-87-89-90-92

Women

4-9 Oct 1994 Beau Sejour Centre,
St Peter Port, Guernsey

In the 1st Round, Horner wins a match in the fastest time ever recorded at the World Open, beating Adriana Moura (BRZ) who retires with a knee injury after losing the first set 9-0 in two (no misprint) minutes. Jackman beats Miyuki Adachi (JAP) 9-0 9-0 9-0 in twelve minutes. 1989 world champion Martine Le Moignan, playing on home territory, retires from the game after losing to Linda Charman (ENG) in the 2nd Round. In the 3rd, Jackman beats 39-y-o 15th seed Vicki Cardwell (AUS), champion in 1983. The top eight seeds reach the quarter-finals.

QUARTER-FINALS

Michelle Martin	AUS	Sue Wright	ENG	9-2 9-7 9-1
Suzanne Horner	ENG	Sarah		
		Fitz-Gerald	AUS	9-4 10-8 9-2
Fiona Geaves	ENG	Liz Irving	AUS	9-7 2-9 9-3 0-9
				9-7
Cassie Jackman	ENG	Carol Owens	AUS	9-6 3-9 9-5 9-1

Geaves loses thirteen pts in a row, falls 4-0 & 7-4 down in the last game, then recovers to reach the semis for the first time by producing what looks like the upset of the tournament, beating the No.2 seed - but Irving plays with a bad back

SEMI-FINALS

| Martin | Horner | 9-4 9-4 9-6 |
| Jackman | Geaves | 9-4 9-1 9-2 |

Martin reaches the final for the third year in a row. Jackman has never lost to Geaves.

FINAL

| Martin | Jackman | 9-1 9-0 9-6 |

Martin retains the title, again winning the final in straight games. Jackman was the last British player to beat her (1992), not that you'd know it from this match: 8-3 down in the third game, she saves four match balls but loses in 33 mins, by the widest margin since the very first final, in 1976.

Women's team

10-15 Oct 1994 Beau Sejour Centre,
St Peter Port, Guernsey

SEMI-FINALS

AUSTRALIA	N ZEALAND	3-0
Michelle Martin	P Beams	9-4 9-3 9-0
Sarah Fitz-Gerald	L Marsh	9-1 9-0 9-2
Liz Irving	J Wilson	9-1 9-4 9-4
ENGLAND	S AFRICA	3-0
Suzanne Horner	Claire Nitch	6-9 9-3 9-2 9-3
Cassie Jackman	C Clifton-Parks	9-0 9-0 9-1
Sue Wright	N Grainger	9-3 9-2 9-1

FINAL

AUSTRALIA	ENGLAND	3-0
Michelle Martin	Suzanne Horner	9-6 9-2 9-6
Liz Irving	Sue Wright	9-1 9-5 9-6
Sarah Fitz-Gerald	Cassie Jackman	9-3 9-0 9-4

Australia retain the title with the easiest win in any final. Fitzgerald, for instance, beats Jackman in 27 mins.

British Open 1994

Men

QUARTER-FINALS

Jansher Khan	PAK	Rodney Eyles	AUS	9-2 9-4 9-5
Peter Marshall	ENG	Anthony Hill	AUS	9-1 9-1 9-1
Chris Walker	ENG	Mark Cairns	ENG	9-7 4-9 9-3 9-2
Brett Martin	AUS	Zarak		
		Jahan Khan	PAK	9-3 9-5 9-0

SEMI-FINALS

| Jansher | Marshall | 9-2 7-9 9-4 9-3 |
| Martin | Walker | 9-7 7-9 9-7 9-4 |

FINAL

| Jansher | Martin | 9-1 9-0 9-10 9-1 |

Jansher wins the event for the third consecutive year. Martin, who reaches the final for the first time, is the brother of Rodney Martin, who lost 3 in a row 1988-89-90. The last Australian to win the title was Geoff Hunt in 1981. The event moves to Cardiff in 1995, the first time it will have been held outside England.

Women

QUARTER-FINALS

Michelle Martin	AUS	Martine		
		LeMoignan	ENG	9-2 9-3 9-2
Sarah				
Fitz-Gerald	AUS	Claire Nitch	SAF	9-3 3-9 9-2
				10-8

Suzanne				
Horner	ENG	Fiona Geaves	ENG	9-2 9-2 9-3
Liz Irving	AUS	Carol Owens	AUS	9-4 9-1 8-10
				9-4

SEMI-FINALS

Martin	Fitz-Gerald	9-6 9-6 9-5
Irving	Horner	7-9 9-7 9-2 9-1

FINAL

Martin	Irving	9-1 9-5 9-3

The Martin brothers' sister retains the title. Irving also lost in the 1988 final.

Pakistan Open

SEMI-FINALS

Jansher Khan	PAK	Rodney Eales	AUS	15-10 15-11
				13-15 15-7
Peter Marshall	ENG	Del Harris	ENG	15-3 12-15
				15-6 15-8

The first British player, and only the third from outside Pakistan, to reach the final.

FINAL

Jansher	Marshall	14-15 15-14 15-10
		9-15 15-6

UK National Championships

13-18 Jan 1994 Herts Country Club, Welwyn Garden City

Men

QUARTER-FINALS

Peter Nicol	Phil Whitlock	10-8 9-5 10-8
Jason Nicolle	Chris Walker	5-9 2-9 9-4 9-3 9-1
Tony Hands	Simon Parke	10-8 9-0 9-4
Peter Marshall	Stephen Meads	9-2 10-8 9-6

SEMI-FINALS

Nicol	Nicolle	9-5 10-9 9-0
Marshall	Hands	9-4 9-2 9-5

FINAL

Marshall	Nicol	9-6 9-7 9-4

Women

QUARTER-FINALS

Jane Martin	Cassie Jackman	9-6 9-10 10-9 6-9
		9-5
Suzanne Horner	Linda Charman	9-2 7-9 9-3 9-0

Lisa Opie	Rebecca		
	O'Callaghan	9-3 9-6 9-0	
Sue Wright	Fiona Geaves	1-9 10-8 9-4 9-0	

SEMI-FINALS

Horner	Martin	9-6 9-2 9-6
Wright	Opie	9-6 9-5 8-10 9-4

FINAL

Horner	Wright	9-4 9-1 9-1

Horner (30), who lost in three consecutive finals 1989-90-91, wins the title for the first time at the thirteenth attempt.

British National League

DIVISION 1	P	W	D	L	F	A	Pts
Leekes Wizards	10	6	3	1	28	12	44
Village Manchester	10	6	1	3	24	16	38
Manchester Northern	10	3	6	1	21	19	37
Rackets Club	10	5	1	4	21	19	32
Herts Country Club	10	1	3	6	15	25	21
Lingfield	10	1	2	7	11	29	16

Leekes win the title for the third time in five seasons after top London teams Cannons and Lambs withdraw before the start. Cannons, who come back the following season, are unbeaten in the league at the time of writing. 21-y-o Cassie Jackman (playing for Barnham Broom) beats Mike Herridge (Duffield) to become the first woman to win a National League match against a man: 8-10 9-2 3-9 9-4 9-3

British Club Championships 1994

Manor Club, Ilkeston, Derbyshire

Men

SEMI-FINALS

Durham	4	Edgbaston Priory	1
Devon & Exeter	3	Cumberland LTC	2

FINAL

Durham	4	Devon & Exeter	1

Durham retain the title.

Women

SEMI-FINALS

Pontefract	5	Edgbaston Priory	0
Lee-on-Solent	4	Redwood Lodge	1

FINAL

Pontefract	3	Lee-on-Solent	2

European Championships

28 April - 1 May 1994 Zoetermeer, Holland

Men

SEMI-FINALS

England	4	France	0
Germany	2	Scotland	2

Germany 8-6 on games countback

3rd-PLACE FINAL

Scotland	2	France	2

Scotland 100-99 on pts countback

FINAL

ENGLAND	4	GERMANY	0	
Tony Hands		Hansi Wiens	1-9 9-3 9-3 9-1	
Phil Whitlock		Simon Frenz	9-1 9-4 9-5	
Jason Nicolle		Oliver Rucks	9-4 9-1 6-9 9-2	
Stephen Meads		Florian Possl	9-2 9-1 9-4	

England retain the title despite the absence of their two leading players Peter Marshall & Chris Walker.

Women

SEMI-FINALS

England	3	Holland	0
Germany	3	Ireland	0

3rd-PLACE FINAL

Holland	2	Ireland	1

FINAL

ENGLAND		GERMANY	3-0	
Suzanne Horner		Sabine Schöne	9-1 9-0 9-6	
Cassie Jackman		Sabine Baum	9-2 9-5 9-3	
Fiona Geaves		Silke Bartel	9-3 9-5 9-0	

England have never failed to win the title.

European Champion of Champions

Finals 29 Oct 1994 Lisbon

Men

Peter Nicol (SCOT) bt Derek Ryan (EIRE)
3-9 9-7 9-6 9-4

Women

Suzanne Horner (ENG) bt Sabine Schöne (GER)
9-2 9-0 6-9 9-1

World Junior Championships (Men)

July-Aug 1994 Christchurch, N Zealand

Individual

QUARTER-FINALS

Ahmed Barada	EGY	bt	
Chris Tomlinson	ENG		10-8 9-7 9-4
Thierry Lincou	FRA	bt	
Michael Fiteni	AUS		4-9 8-10 9-7 9-4 9-5
Iaian Higgins	ENG	bt	
Ahmed Fayzi	EHY		9-6 4-9 10-8 9-5
Omar El Borolossy	EGY	bt	
Jackie Lee	HK		9-0 9-0 9-5

Despite benefitting from a contentious penalty stroke awarded against Tomlinson when he leads 8-5 in the first game, Barada has little need to feel shamefaced: the warm favourite, No.58 in the senior rankings, he looks the class of the field throughout.

SEMI-FINALS

Barada	Lincou	9-2 9-0 9-2
El Borolossy	Higgins	9-7 9-2 9-5

3rd-PLACE FINAL

Lincou	Higgins	7-9 9-7 9-6 9-6

FINAL

Barada	El Borolossy	9-0 7-9 3-9 9-3 9-2

For the third time, following Australia in 1980 and England 1990, the same country provides both finalists.

Team

QUARTER-FINALS

Egypt	3	Pakistan	0
Finland	2	Germany	1
Australia	2	France	1
England	3	Canada	0

SEMI-FINALS

Egypt	3	Finland	0
England	2	Australia	1

England beat the holders and No.1 seeds.

3rd-PLACE FINAL

Finland	2	Australia	1

FINAL

EGYPT	3	ENGLAND	0

Ahmed Barada bt Chris Tomlinson 9-2 9-3 4-9 9-7
Omar El Borolossy bt Iain Higgins 9-5 9-0 3-9 9-3
Ahmed Fayzi bt Marcus Cowie 2-9 7-9 9-6 9-6 9-2

Tomlinson loses to the new individual champion for the second time, having beaten him in a 'dead' group match, as Egypt win the title for the first time.

Swimming

World Championships
1-11 Sep 1994 Stadio del Nuoto, Rome
(postponed for a day after the first rain for two months)

Men

Freestyle

50 metres

Aleksandr Popov	RUS	22.17
Gary Hall	USA	22.44
Raimundas Mazuolis	LITH	22.52

Hall's father Gary senior set ten individual world records 1968-72, at backstroke, butterfly & medley.

100 metres

Aleksandr Popov	RUS	49.12
Gary Hall	USA	49.41
Gustavo Borges	BRZ	49.52

Popov has it all now at 100m: World, Olympic & European gold, world record.

200 metres

Antti Kasvio	FIN	1:47.32
Anders Holmertz	SWE	1:48.24
Danyon (Dan) Loader	NZ	1:48.49

The first Finn to win a world swimming title.

400 metres

Kieren Perkins	AUS	3:43.80	WR
Antti Kasvio	FIN	3:48.55	
Dan Loader	*NZ*	*3:4.62*	

Perkins regains the world record.

1500 metres

Kieren Perkins	AUS	14:50.52
Dan Kowalski	AUS	14:53.42
Steffen Zesner	GER	15:09.20

Perkins improves on his second place of 1991, when Zesner was second in the 200 free. Jörg Hoffmann (GER), who won the 400-1500 double in 1991, finishes fourth here, but his championship record survives (Perkins swims a leisurely race) by 0.16 secs.

Marathon (25km)

Greg Streppel	CAN	5h35:26
David Bates	AUS	5h36:31
Alexei Akatiyev	RUS	5h37:26

Defending champion Chad Hundeby (USA) finishes seventh in 5h43:07.

Backstroke

100 metres

Martin Lopez Zubero	SPA	55.17	ChR
Jeff Rouse	USA	55.51	
Támas Deutsch	HUN	55.69	

Rouse, the Olympic gold medallist & world record holder, was the defending champion, beating Lopez Zubero into third place in 1991.

200 metres

Vladimir Selkov	RUS	1:57.42	ChR
Martin Lopez Zubero	SPA	1:58.75	
Roy Sharp	USA	1:58.86	

Lopez Zubero was the defending champion. 19-y-o Adam Ruckwood, who broke the British record in winning the Commonwealth title, does it again, this time twice in ten hours: 2:00.61 in qualifying, 2:00.15 while finishing sixth in the final.

Breaststroke

100 metres

Norbert Rózsa	HUN	1:01.24	ChR
Károly Güttler	HUN	1:01.44	
Frédéric Deburghgraeve	BEL	1:01.79	

Rózsa retains the title he won by beating Adrian Moorhouse in 1991. Güttler, the 1988 Olympic silver medallist (behind Moorhouse), took the world record from Rózsa in 1993.

200 metres

Norbert Rózsa	HUN	2:12.81
Eric Wunderlich	USA	2:12.87
Károly Guttler	HUN	2:14.12

Rózsa, second in 1991, completes the double this time, the first since David Wilkie (UK) in 1975. Nick Gillingham, third in 1991, finishes fourth (2:14.25), Britain's best placing at the championships, the first one in which they don't win a single medal.

Butterfly

100 metres

Rafal Szukala	POL	53.51
Lars Frolander	SWE	53.65
Denis Pankratov	RUS	53.68

For the first time, Europeans take all three medals in the event.

200 metres

Denis Pankratov	RUS	1:56.54
Dan Loader	NZ	1:57.99
Chris-Carol Bremer	GER	1:58.11

Medley

200 metres

Jani Sievinen	FIN	1:58.16	WR
Greg Burgess	USA	2:00.86	
Attila Czene	HUN	2:01.84	

Sievinen breaks the world record set by the great Támas Darnyi (HUN) at the last world championships.

400 metres

Tom Dolan	USA	4:12.30	WR
Jani Sievinen	FIN	4:13.29	
Eric Namesnik	USA	4:15.69	

Namesnik was second at the 1991 championships behind Darnyi, who's now seen both his world records broken within two months of his retirement.

4x100m Free

Jon Olsen, Josh Davis, Ugur Taner, Gary Hall	USA	3:16.90	ChR
Roman Tchegolev, Vladimir Predkin, Vladimir Pishnyenko, Aleksandr Popov	RUS	3:18.12	
Fernando Scherer, Teofilo Ferreira, André Teixeira, Gustavo Borges	BRZ	3:19.35	

4x200m Free

Christer Wallin, Tommy Werner, Lars Frolander, Anders Holmertz	SWE	7:17.74
Yuri Mukhin, Vladimir Pishnyenko, Denis Pankratov, Roman Tchegolev	RUS	7:18.13
Andreas Szigat, Christian Keller, Oliver Lampe, Steffen Zesner	GER	7:19.10

4x100m Medley

Jeff Rouse, Eric Wunderlich, Mark Henderson, Gary Hall	USA	3:37.74	ChR
Vladimir Selkov, Vasily Ivanov, Denis Pankratov, Aleksandr Popov	RUS	3:38.28	
Támas Deutsch, Norbert Rózsa, Peter Horvath, Attila Czene	HUN	3:39.47	

Diving

1m Springboard

Evan Stewart	ZIM	382.14
Lan Wei	CHN	375.18
Brian Earley	USA	361.59

The 19-y-o Stewart, who won only silver & bronze at the Commonwealth Games, beats the usual Chinese favourite to become the first African ever to win a medal in any event at the championships.

3m Springboard

Yu Zhuo-cheng	CHN	655.44
Dmitry Sautin	RUS	646.59
Wang Tian-ling	CHN	638.22

10m Highboard

Dmitry Sautin	RUS	634.71
Sun Shu Wei	CHN	630.03
Vladimir Timoshinin	RUS	607.32

Sautin's brilliant last dive, a backward 1.5 somersault with 3.5 twists, brings him a 9.5 and three 9.0s to leave defending champion Sun needing 83.00 from his last to win; he scores 78.54. Robert Morgan (UK) leads in the early stages but falls back to finish sixth on 552.06.

Women

Freestyle

50 metres

Le Jing-yi	CHN	24.51	WR
Natalya Mersheryakova	RUS	25.18	ER
Amy Van Dyken	USA	25.18	

100 metres

Le Jing-yi	CHN	54.01	WR
Lu Bin	CHN	54.15	
Franziska Van Almsick	GER	54.77	
7 eq Karen Pickering	*UK*	*55.79*	*UKR*

Lu Bin also beat the previous world's best. Later in the year she fails a drug test.

200 metres

Franziska Van Almsick	GER	1:56.78	WR
Lu Bin	CHN	1:56.89	
Claudia Poll	C RICA	1:57.61	

After Van Almsick reaches the final only because her team mate Dagmar Hase is withdrawn by the German management, the question's raised: if swimmers can be exchanged with impunity by officials, why bother with heats? Van Almsick breaks a world record set by Heike Friedrich in 1986.

400 metres

Yang Ai-hua	CHN	4:09.64
Christina Teuscher	USA	4:10.21
Claudia Poll	C RICA	4:10.61

The slowest winning time in the event since 1975. The defending champion, the once unbeatable Janet Evans (USA), finishes fifth. Ironically, Hase (see above) finishes ninth fastest in the heats - but finds team mate Jana Henke unwilling to trade places. The 16-y-o Yang is later, like Lu Bin, banned for use of steroids.

800 metres

Janet Evans	USA	8:29.85
Hayley Lewis	AUS	8:29.94
Brooke Bennett	USA	8:31.30

Evans retains the title in the slowest winning time since 1975. The leading Chinese, Luo Ping, finishes fifth.

Marathon (25km)

Melissa Cunningham	AUS	5h48:25
Rita Kovacs	HUN	5h50:13
Shelley Taylor-Smith	AUS	5h53:12

Taylor-Smith was the defending champion. Like

Hundeby in the men's event, her 1991 championship record (5h21:05.53) was set in the river at Perth, Australia.

Backstroke

100 metres

He Ci-hong	CHN	1:00.57	ChR
Nina Zhivanevskaya	RUS	1:00.83	
Barbara Bedford	USA	1:01.32	

Defending champion & world record holder Egerszegi, unbeaten in any major competition for five years, finishes fifth.

200 metres

He Ci-hong	CHN	2:07.40
Krisztina Egerszegi	HUN	2:09.19
Lorenza Vigarani	ITA	2:10.92

Breaststroke

100 metres

Sam Riley	AUS	1:07.69	WR
Dai Guo-hong	CHN	1:09.26	
Yuan Yuan	CHN	1:10.19	

The first Australian to set a world best in the event since Clare Dennis in 1933, Riley breaks the record set by one of the inevitable East Germans (Silke Hörner) in 1987.

200 metres

Sam Riley	AUS	2:26.87	ChR
Yuan Yuan	CHN	2:27.38	
Brigitte Becue	BEL	2:28.85	

As in the men's breaststroke, the first 100/200 double at these championships since 1975 (Hannelore Anke of E Germany).

Butterfly

100 metres

Liu Li-min	CHN	58.98	ChR
Qu Yin	CHN	59.69	
Sue O'Neill	AUS	1:00.11	

200 metres

Liu Li-min	CHN	2:07.25
Qu Yin	CHN	2:07.42
Sue O'Neill	AUS	2:09.54

The first woman to do the butterfly double at the world championships. Both world records have been held by Mary T Meagher (USA) since 1981: 57.93 & 2:05.96.

Medley

200 metres

Lu Bin	CHN	2:12.34	ChR
Allison Wagner	USA	2:14.40	
Elli Overton	AUS	2:15.26	

400 metres

Dai Guo-hong	CHN	4:39.14
Allison Wagner	USA	4:39.98
Kristine Quance	USA	4:42.21

Dai's only 16.

4x100m

Le Jing-yi, Shan Ying,			
Le Ying, Lu Bin	CHN	3:37.91	WR
Angel Martino, Amy Van Dyken, Nicole Haislett,			
Jenny Thompson	USA	3:41.50	
Franziska Van Almsick, Katrin Meissner, Kerstin			
Kielgass, Daniela Hunger	GER	3:42.94	

Haislett & Thompson were in the team that won the title in 1991.

4x200m Free

Shan Ying, Yang Ai-hua,			
Zhou Guan-bin, Le Ying	CHN	7:57.96	ChR
Kerstin Kielgass, Franziska Van Almsick,			
Julia Jung, Dagmar Hase	GER	8:01.37	
Cristina Teuscher, Jenny Thompson,			
Janet Evans, Nicole Haislett	USA	8:03.16	

4x100m Medley

He Ci-hong, Dai Gu -hong,			
Liu Li-min, Le Jing-yi	CHN	4:01.67	WR
Lea Loveless, Christine Quance, Amy Van Dyken,			
Jenny Thompson	USA	4:06.53	
Nina Zhivanevskaya, Olga Prokhorova,			
Svetlana Pozdeyeva,			
Natalya Mesheryakova	RUS	4:06.70	

Egerszegi's eclipse is completed by the 19-y-o He, who sets a world record of 1:00.16 on the first (backstroke) leg. Anchorwoman Le (also 19) takes her fourth gold medal of the championships, all won in world record times.

Diving

1m Springboard

Chen Li-xia	CHN	279.30
Tan Shu-ping	CHN	276.00
Annie Pelletier	CAN	273.84

3m Springboard

Tan Shu-ping	CHN	548.49
Vyera Ilyina	RUS	498.60
Claudia Böckner	GER	480.15

10m Highboard

Fu Ming-xia	CHN	434.04
Chi Bin	CHN	420.24
María José Alcala	MEX	396.48

Fu, awarded 75.48 for her last dive, retains the title she won as a 12-y-o in 1991 (the age limit was subsequently raised to 14).

Men and Women combined

Marathon Team 25 km

AUS	17h17:35.41
GER	17h37:19.47
HUN	17h37:34.58

This sport in life

The most successful diver in Olympic history, Greg Louganis, announces he's gay, welcoming people to the Gay Games held in New York at the same time as the football World Cup.
Bruce Hayes, US swimming gold medallist from 1984, also came out.

Water polo

Men

3rd-Place final

Russia	14	Croatia	13

Final

Italy	10	Spain	5

Italy win the title for the first time since 1978, Spain lose in the final for the second successive time. N Zealand lose all six of their matches: 28-4, 35-1, 26-2 15-2, 8-2, 13-3.

Italy: Marco D'Altrui, Alessandro Bovo, Giuseppe Porzio, Alessandro Campagna, Roberto Calcaterra, Mario Fiorillo, Franco Porzio, Amedeo Pomilio, Ferdinando Gandolfi, Massimiliano Ferretti, Carlo Silippo

Spain: Sergio Pedrerol, Josep Pico, Gustavo Marcos, Manuel Estiarte, Daniel Ballart, Jordi Paia, Jordi Sans, Salvador Gómez, Miguel Angel Oca, Gabriel Hernandez, Pedro Garcia

Russia: Aleksandr Ogorodnikov, Sergei Yevstigneyev, Nikolai Kozlov, Sergei Garbuzov, Aleksandr Yerishov, Maksim Apanasenko, Dmitry Apanasenko, Dmitry Gorshkov, Dmitry Markotsch, Yuri Smolovy, Sergei Ivlyev

Women

3rd-Place final

Italy	14	USA	9

Final

Hungary	7	Holland	5

Hungary beat the defending champions.

Hungary: Gabriella Tóth, Katalin Kisne Dancsa, Andrea Eke, Mercedes Stieber, Katalin Redei, Ildikó Kuna, Iren Rafael, Krisztina Szremko, Zsuzsa Dunkel, Edit Sipos, Noemi Tóth

Holland: Jany Spijker, Edmee Hiemstra, Stella Kriekaard, Ingrid Leijen Dekker, Alice Lindhout, Karin Kuipers, Ellen Bast, Gillian van den Berg, Rianne Shram, Sandra Scherrenburg, Hedda Verdam

Italy: Martina Micelli, Carmela Allucci, Stefania Lariucci, Milena Virzi, Monica Vaillant, Antonella Di Giacinto, Cristina Consoli, Giusi Malato, Oriana Di Siena, Nicoletta Abbate, Melania Greco

Synchro

Solo

Becky Dyroen Lancer	USA	191.040
Fumiko Okuno	JAP	187.306
Lisa Alexander	CAN	186.826

Duet

Jill Sudduth & Becky Dyroen-Lancer	USA	187.009
Lisa Alexander & Erin Woodley	CAN	186.259
Fimuiko Okuno & Miya Tachibana	JAP	186.259

The Canadians & Japanese share second place.
Alexander was third in 1991 with a different partner.

Team

USA	185.883
Canada	183.263
Japan	183.215

USA: Margot Thien, Heather Simmons, Jill Savery, Tammy Cleland, Jill Sudduth, Nathalie Schneyder, Becky Dyroen Lancer, Suzannah Bianco

Canada: Carrie Deguerre, Janice Bremner, Karen Fonteyne, Erin Woodley, Cari Read, Kasia Kulesza, Karen Clark, Lisa Alexander

Japan: Miho Takeda, Kaori Takahashi, Rei Jinbo, Miya Tachibana, Masayo Yajima, Raika Fujii, Akiko Kawase, Fumiko Okuno

World Short Course Championships

2-5 Dec 1993 Palma, Majorca
(inaugural championships)

Men

Freestyle

50	Mark Foster	UK	21.84	
100	Fernando Scherer	BRZ	48.38	
200	Antti Kasvio	FIN	1:45.21	
400	Dan Kowalski	AUS	3:42.95	
	3 Paul Palmer	UK	3:45.07	
1500	Dan Kowalski	AUS	14:42.04	
	4 Graeme Smith	UK	14:54.45	UKR

Backstroke

100	Tripp Schwenk	USA	52.98	
	2 Martin Harris	UK	53.93	

| 200 | Tripp Schwenk | USA | 1:54.19 | |

Breaststroke

| 100 | Phil Rogers | AUS | 59.56 | |
| 200 | Nick Gillingham | UK | 2:07.91 | ER |

Butterfly

| 100 | Milos Milosevic | CRO | 52.79 | |
| 200 | Franck Esposito | FRA | 1:55.42 | |

Individual Medley

200	Christian Keller	GER	1:56.80	
	2 Fraser Walker	UK	1:58.35	UKR
400	Curtis Myden	CAN	4:10.41	

Relays

4x100 Free		BRZ	3:12.11	WR
4x200 Free		SWE	7:05.92	
4x100 Medley		USA	3:32.57	WR

3 UK (Martin Harris, Nick Gillingham, Mike Fibbens, Mark Foster) 3:37.27 (UKR)

Women

Freestyle

50	Le Jing-yi	CHN	24.23	WR
100	Le Jing-yi	CHN	53.01	WR
	3 Karen Pickering	UK	54.39	UKR
200	Karen Pickering	UK	1:56.25	ComR

Pickering wins the first world championship gold medal by a British woman, and (in the 100) the first medal since Natalie Steward's 100m bronze at the 1960 Olympics.

| 400 | Janet Evans | USA | 4:05.64 | |
| 800 | Janet Evans | USA | 8:22.43 | |

Backstroke

100	Angel Martino	USA	58.50	WR
200	He Ci-hong	CHN	2:06.09	
	6 Joanne Deakins	UK	2:09.99	UKR

Breaststroke

| 100 | Dai Guo-hong | CHN | 1:06.58 | |
| 200 | Dai Guo-hong | CHN | 2:21.99 | WR |

Butterfly

| 100 | Sue O'Neill | AUS | 59.19 | |
| 200 | Liu Li-min | CHN | | |

Individual medley

| 200 | Allison Wagner | USA | 2:07.79 | WR |
| 400 | Dai Guo-hong | CHN | 4:29.00 | WR |

Relays

4x100 Free		CHN	3:35.97	
4x200 Free		CHN	7:52.45	WR
4x100 Medley		CHN	3:57.73	WR

Winning is the drug

Zhong Wei-yue, who broke two butterfly world records at the 1994 World Cup short course meeting in Peking, and Ren Zin, triple gold medallist at the Goodwill Games, were banned for two years after failing drug tests.

Dave Haller, long-serving UK head coach, was just one of many who believed other Chinese record-breaking women were taking the tablets: 'I cannot see any other way to come from oblivion to total domination of the world in such a short period...It has all the hallmarks of East Germany.' (Kornelia Ender, the multiple Olympic medallist, now admits to having taken steroids).

Still, this was all just suspicions and educated guesswork (FINA announced that all 169 drug tests at the World Championships were negative) until at the Asian Games, eleven Chinese competitors failed drug tests, among them seven swimmers including two big fish: Yang Ai-hua, world 400m freestyle champion, and Lu Bin, who won four golds at the worlds. Both were caught taking testosterone and banned for two years (swimming's maximum penalty, only half that of athletics) but allowed to keep their titles. The other aquatic miscreants were Zhou Guan-bin and four men: Xiong Guo-ming, Hu Bin, Zhang Bin, Fu Young.

Chinese officials still maintained that only a few individuals were involved but others weren't convinced: the German swimming federation boycotted the World Cup short course meeting in Jan 1995 in protest against 'an event that is a doping nest' and Australian swimming coaches asked FINA to ban China for four years.

Meanwhile, at the other end of things, British diving champion Antonio Ali's banned for six months, missing the World Championships, for missing a drugs test because he has to get back to sign on the dole.

European Sprint Championships 1993

13-14 Nov Gateshead

Men

50 Free	Joakim Holmquist	SWE	22.26
50 Back	Patrick Hermanspann	GER	25.76
50 Breast	Vasily Ivanov	RUS	27.82
50 Butterfly	Carlos Sánchez	SPA	24.04
100 IM	Ron Dekker	HOL	55.77
4x50 Free	SWE		1:36.53
	3 UK		*1:33.30*
4x50 Back	GER		1:44.97
	2 UK		*1:48.28*
4x50 Breast	GER		1:55.53
	2 UK		*1:58.24*
4x50 Butterfly	SWE		1:36.53
	3 UK		*1:40.27*
4x50 Medley	SWE		1:39.54

Women

50 Free	Sandra Volker	GER	25.55	
50 Back	Sandra Volker	GER	28.26	WR
50 Breast	Sylvia Gerasch	GER	31.57	
	3 Karen Rake	*UK*	*31.89*	
50 Butterfly	Louise Karlsson	SWE	27.49	
100 IM	Louise Karlsson	SWE	1:01.45	
4x50 Free	SWE		1:41.27	
4x50 Back	GER		2:01.15	
	2 UK		*2:02.45*	
4x50 Breast	UK		2:11.28	
4x50 Butterfly	GER		1:53.06	
	2 UK		*1:55.62*	
4x50 Medley	GER		1:53.26	
	3 UK		*1:57.13*	

Gerasch is banned from European competition for two years after testing positive for drugs (as does her team mate Steffen Smollich). She first broke the 100m world record back in 1984.

European Sprint Championships 1994

3-4 Dec Stavanger, Norway

Men

50 Free	K Cwalina	POL	22.01
50 Back	J Letzin	GER	25.47
50 Breast	M Warnecke	GER	27.58
50 Butterfly	A Akesson	SWE	24.25

100 IM	D Kalchev	BUL	55.51	
4x50 Free	SWE		1:27.62	WR
4x50 Medley	GER		1:38.01	WR

Women

50 Free	Sandra Volker	GER	25.29	
	3 Susan Rolph	*UK*	*25.55*	*UKR*
50 Back	Sandra Volker	GER	27.96	
50 Breast	E Ingelström	SWE	32.13	
50 Butterfly	A Postma	HOL	27.48	
100 IM	Louise Karlsson	SWE	1:01.89	
	2 Susan Rolph	*UK*	*1:02.21*	*UKR*
4x50 Free	GER		1:41.20	
4x50 Medley	GER		1:53.58	

These are the fourth Euro Sprint Championships; Volker (in the backstroke) & Karlsson have won their events every time. The 16-y-o Rolph sets three British records in all.

British National Championships

28-31 July 1994 Crystal Palace

Men

Freestyle

50	Mike Fibbens		23.33
100	Nick Shackell		51.49
200	James Salter		1:52.61
400	Steven Mellor		3:57.72
1500	Ian Wilson		15:19.70

Wilson beats defending champion Graeme Smith to win the title for the fourth time.

Backstroke

50	Martin Harris		26.18
100	Martin Harris		55.73 UKR
200	Adam Ruckwood		2:02.49

Harris finishes second.

Breaststroke

50	Gavin Brettell		29.60
100	James Parrack		1:03.48
200	Alex Clapper		2:17.74

Butterfly

50	Mike Fibbens		25.15
100	Janko Gojkovic		55.80
200	James Hickman		2:02.24

Individual medley

200	David Warren		2:06.42
400	David Warren		4:27.86

Grant Robins finishes second in both events.

Relays

4x100 Free	City of Sheffield	3:28.35
4x200 Free	City of Leeds	7:47.83
4x100 Medley	City of Leeds	3:49.22

Women

Freestyle

50	Susan Rolph	
100	Susan Rolph	56.74

Karen Pickering finishes second in each event.

200	Karen Pickering	2:02.59
400	Sarah Hardcastle	4:13.37
800	Susan Colling	8:56.13

Backstroke

50	Kathy Osher	30.48
100	Emma Tattum	1:03.82

Osher, trying to win the title for the tenth time, finishes second. She won all three dorsal events last year.

200	Kathy Osher	2:16.38

Osher's ninth national title at the distance.

Breaststroke

50	Lorraine Coombes	33.59
100	Marie Hardiman	1:11.87
200	Marie Hardiman	2:30.63 UKR

Nicole Thornley finishes second behind Hardiman in both events.

Butterfly

50	Susan Rolph	28.84
100	Samantha Greenep	1:03.27
200	Helen Slatter	2:15.75

Individual medley

200	Susan Rolph	2:18.02
400	Helen Slatter	4:52.15

Rolph wins four individual titles at the age of 15.

Relays

4x50 Free	Nova Centurion	1:53.30
4x100 Free	Portsmouth Northsea	3:59.07
4x200 Free	Portsmouth Northsea	8:36.86
4x100 Medley	Portsmouth Northsea	4:21.79

British Club Team Championships

5-6 March 1994 Stockport

Overall	City of Leeds
Men	City of Leeds
Women	Nova Centurion

Synchronised Swimming

Europa Cup

May 1994

Individual	Kerry Shacklock	UK
Team	Italy	
	3 UK	

In December 1993, after an appeal by the International Swimming Federation, the IOC award Sylvie Frechette (CAN) the 1992 Olympic individual gold, accepting that a mistake had been made on the computer marking system. Bizarrely, Kristen Babb-Sprague (USA) is allowed to keep her gold medal, and no silver's awarded.

UK National Diving Championships

July 1994 Sheffield

Men

1m Springboard	Antonio (Tony) Ali
3m Springboard	Robert Morgan
Platform	Robert Morgan

Women

1m Springboard	V Stenning
3m Springboard	O Clark
Platform	H Allen

Water Polo

World championships: see Swimming

Goodwill Games

26-30 July St Petersburg (men only)

Semi-finals

Russia	9	Italy	7
Germany	11	Spain	8

3rd-Place final

Italy	9	Spain	8

Final

Russia	11	Germany	9

British Championship

In 1994, Polytechnic win the title for the fourth successive year by beating Nova 9-0 to overhaul Lancaster, winning on goals scored after both clubs finish the season (18 games) with 29 points and an identical goal difference.

Table Tennis

World Cup
Taipei

QUARTER-FINALS
Jean-Michel Saive	BEL	Chang Peng-lung	TAIW	21-16 20-22 19-21 21-16 21-14
Zoran Primorac	CRO	Johnny Huang	CAN	21-15 21-19 18-21 21-12
Jean-Pierre Gatien	FRA	W Tao	CHN	15-21 21-19 21-18 22-20
Jan-Ove Waldner	SWE	K Ling-hui	CHN	13-21 21-18 8-21 21-13 21-17

SEMI-FINALS
Saive	Primorac	18-21 21-19 21-12 21-18
Gatien	Waldner	21-19 17-21 13-21 21-10 21-12

FINAL 18 Dec 1994
Gatien	Saive	17-21 15-21 21-18 26-24 21-19

Same players, result and number of sets as the 1993 World Championship final, but even more excruciatingly close for the Belgian.

European Championships
25 March - 4 April 1994 Birmingham

Men's Singles

QUARTER-FINALS
Jean-Michel Saive	BEL	Chen Xin Hua	UK	21-11 21-12 15-21 21-19
Patrick Chila	FRA	Philippe Saive	BEL	19-21 20-22 21-19 21-6 21-19
Zoran Primorac	CRO	Daniel Cioca	GRE	15-21 21-18 23-21 21-23 21-13
Jan-Ove Waldner	SWE	Jörg Rosskopf	GER	21-11 22-20 21-17

SEMI-FINALS
JM Saive	Chila	21-12 21-15 21-8
Waldner	Primorac	21-18 16-21 17-21 21-19 21-16

FINAL
JM Saive	Waldner	23-25 21-10 21-17 21-16

Women's Singles

QUARTER-FINALS
Gerdie Keen	HOL	Csilla Batorfi	HUN	21-16 11-21 21-17 21-14
Nicole Struse	GER	Wang-Drechou Xiao Ming	FRA	21-16 21-14 21-8
Jie Scöpp	GER	Otilia Badescu	ROM	21-12 21-14 21-18
Marie Svensson	SWE	Krisztina Tóth	HUN	21-12 21-16 21-15

SEMI-FINALS
Keen	Struse	22-20 21-16 19-21 16-21 22-20
Svensson	Scöpp	16-21 21-18 21-14 21-17

FINAL
Svensson	Keen	16-21 21-18 21-14 21-17

Keen, ranked only 31 in Europe, reaches the final unseeded.

Men's Doubles

FINAL

Calin Cranga (GRE) & Zoran Kalinic (YUG) bt
Jean-Michel Saive (BEL) & Zoran Primorac CRO)   21-17 23-21

Women's Doubles

FINAL

Csilla Batorfi (HUN) & Krysztina Tóth (HUN) bt
Yelena Timina (RUS) & Irina Palina (RUS)   21-17 21-9

Mixed Doubles

FINAL

Zoran Primorac (CRO) & Csilla Batorfi (HUN) bt
Calin Creanga (GRE) & Otilia Badescu (ROM)   21-16 21-13

Men's Team

SEMI-FINALS

SWEDEN	ENGLAND	4-1
Thomas Von Scheele	Chen Xin-hua	14-21 21-18 21-18
Jan-Ove Waldner	Carl Prean	21-17 17-21 21-13
Peter Karlsson	Matthew Syed	21-7 20-22 18-21
Waldner & Erik Lindh	Alan Cooke & Prean	21-18 21-19
Waldner	Chen	12-21 21-16 21-3

FRANCE	GERMANY	4-3
Jean-Philippe Gatien	Steffen Fetzner	21-19 21-13
Patrick Chila	Jörg Rosskopf	18-21 21-17 10-21
Christophe Legout	Peter Franz	20-22 17-21
Gatien & Damien Eloi	Fetzner & Rosskopf	21-11 14-21 21-18
Chila	Franz	21-13 21-14
Legout	Fetzner	21-16 20-22 21-18

3rd-PLACE FINAL

GERMANY	ENGLAND	4-2
Christian Dreher	Cooke	12-21 13-21
Rosskopf	Andrew Eden	21-23 21-23
Richard Prause	Syed	13-21 21-12 22-20
Fetzner & Rosskopf	Cooke & Prean	21-15 21-15
Rosskopf	Cooke	15-21 21-13 21-15
Prause	Eden	21-14 21-19

FINAL

FRANCE	SWEDEN	4-3
Legout	Waldner	23-25 12-21
Gatien	Karlsson	15-21 16-21
Chila	Lindh	21-19 21-14
Gatien & Eloi	Waldner & Lindh	21-16 21-16
Gatien	Waldner	21-18 19-21 14-21
Chila	Karlsson	14-21 21-19 21-19
Legout	Lindh	18-21 21-10 21-17

Sweden were the holders.

Women's Team

SEMI-FINALS

RUSSIA	ENGLAND	4-1
Galina Melnik	Lisa Lomas	21-14 21-15
Yelena Timina	Andrea Holt	21-19 23-25 17-21
Irina Palina	Alison Gordon	21-8 21-14
Timina & Palina	Holt & Lomas	21-15 21-12
Timina	Lomas	21-14 22-20 21-17

GERMANY	HUNGARY	4-0
Nicole Struse	Krisztina Tóth	21-11 17-21 21-6
Olga Nemes	Csilla Batorfi	18-21 21-16 21-19
Jie Schöpp	Vivien Éllö	17-21 21-15 21-15
Struse & Christina Fischer	Batorfi & Tóth	21-14 21-18

3rd-PLACE FINAL

HUNGARY	ENGLAND	4-0
Vivien Éllö	Lisa Lomas	21-15 21-23 21-18
Csilla Batorfi	Andrea Holt	23-21 22-20
Krisztina Tóth	Alison Gordon	21-19 22-20
Batorfi & Tóth	Holt & Lomas	21-17 21-12

FINAL

RUSSIA	GERMANY	4-1
Timina	Schöpp	21-16 12-21 13-21
Melnik	Struse	21-16 21-14
Palina	Nemes	18-21 21-13 21-12
Palina & Timina	Fischer & Struse	21-13 16-21 21-19
Timina	Struse	21-12 19-21 21-16

European Nations Cup (Men)

FINAL 16 Jan 1994 Bayreuth, Germany

SWEDEN	3	FRANCE	2	
Jan-Ove Waldner	lost to	Patrick Chila		21-19 22-24 21-23
Peter Karlsson	beat	Jean-Philippe Gatien		21-17 21-19
Waldner, T Von Scheele	lost to	Gatien, Damien Eloi		21-18 13-21 13-21
Waldner	beat	Gatien		21-15 21-19
Karlsson	beat	Chila		21-14 21-23 21-16

European Super League 1993 (Men)

SEMI-FINALS

Belgium	4	England	2
England	4	Belgium	3
Germany	1	Sweden	4
Sweden	4	Germany	0

FINAL

Belgium	4	Sweden	0
Sweden	2	Belgium	4

European League (Women)

FINAL Feb 1994 Crewe & Stuttgart

England	1	Germany	4
Germany	4	England	0

European Youth Championships

Finals July 1994 Paris

JUNIOR BOYS SINGLES

K Lengerov	AUT	T Schröder	GER	21-14 21-15

JUNIOR GIRLS SINGLES

S Ganina	RUS	T Logaskaya	BYL	22-20 21-12

JUNIOR BOYS DOUBLES

A Smirnov (RUS) & D Gavrilov (RUS)	K Lengerov (AUT) & V Dolezel (CZE)	18-21 21-16

JUNIOR GIRLS DOUBLES

A Manac (ROM) & M Stef (ROM)	S Ganina (RUS) & V Pavlovich (BYL)	9-21 21-17 22-20

Commonwealth Championships

25 Jan - 1 Feb 1994 Hyderabad

MEN'S TEAM FINAL

ENGLAND	CANADA	5-3
Matthew Syed	Joe Ng	21-8 16-21 21-15
Alan Cooke	Francis Trudel	21-17 21-15
Andrew Eden	Johnny Huang	18-21 13-21
Cooke	Ng	21-15 21-15
Syed	Huang	19-21 21-23
Eden	Trudel	21-10 21-15
Cooke	Huang	21-18 12-21 19-21
Eden	Ng	21-13 21-18

Ng (born in Vietnam) has been playing for Canada for 15 years.

WOMEN'S TEAM FINAL

HONG KONG	ENGLAND	3-1
Chai Po Wa	Lisa Lomas	21-14 21-10
Chan Tan Lui	Alison Gordon	21-23 27-25 21-18
Chai & Chan	Lomas & Andrea Holt	21-14 18-21 15-21
Chai	Gordon	21-16 21-18

MEN'S SINGLES

QUARTER-FINALS

Johnny Huang	CAN	C Baboor	INDIA	17-21 21-15 21-18 21-15
Matthew Syed	ENG	A Basak	INDIA	21-10 21-13 21-9
Joe Ng	CAN	Chris Oldfield	ENG	22-20 13-21 22-24 21-12 21-19
Alan Cooke	ENG	K Mehta	INDIA	22-20 21-17 21-16

SEMI-FINALS

Huang	Syed	21-11 22-20 21-10
Cooke	Ng	29-27 16-21 22-24 21-19 24-22

FINAL

| Huang | Cooke | 21-15 21-17 21-17 |

Huang, real name Huang Weng-guan, was the tournament favourite.

WOMEN'S SINGLES

QUARTER-FINALS

Chai Po Wa	HK	Gaop Dong Ping	SING	21-9 21-17 21-16
Cheng To	HK	Sim Phua Been	MAL	21-10 21-11 21-13
Chan Tan Lui	HK	Barbara Chiu	CAN	21-14 21-19 21-10
Jing Jun Hong	SING	K Tepper	AUS	21-14 21-13 15-21 21-16

SEMI-FINALS

| Chi Po Wa | Cheng To | 21-10 21-19 21-13 |
| Jing Jun Hong | Chan Tan Lui | 21-18 22-20 17-21 21-14 |

FINAL

| Chai Po Wa | Jing Jun Hong | 21-23 21-14 21-7 21-15 |

MEN'S DOUBLES
Winners: Johnny Huang & Joe Ng (CAN)

WOMEN'S DOUBLES
Winners: Chai Po Wa & Chan Tan Lui (HK)

MIXED DOUBLES
Winners: Johnny Huang & Barbara Chiu (CAN)

Huang wins all three titles.

English National Championships
5-6 March King's Lynn

MEN'S SINGLES

QUARTER-FINALS

Chen Xin-hua	Andrew Eden	21-12 21-6 21-11
Matthew Syed	G Solder	21-6 21-17 21-7
Nicky Mason	Carl Prean	21-16 15-21 21-16 21-17
Alan Cooke	Skylet Andrew	21-15 21-14 21-10

SEMI-FINALS

| Chen | Syed | 15-21 21-14 14-21 21-14 1-15 |
| Cooke | Mason | 21-15 1-18 21-15 |

FINAL

| Chen | Cooke | 21-12 21-13 18-21 21-8 |

Chen wins the title for the second time.

WOMEN'S SINGLES

QUARTER-FINALS

Lisa Lomas	L Radford	21-11 21-16 21-4
Sally Marling	K Goodall	22-20 21-15 18-21 19-21 21-19
Alison Gordon	Fiona Mommessin	21-10 21-18 13-21 18-21 21-19
Andrea Holt	N Deaton	21-14 20-22 21-13 21-13

SEMI-FINALS

| Lomas | Marling | 21-7 21-10 21-12 |
| Holt | Gordon | 22-20 14-21 21-14 21-14 |

FINAL

Lomas	Holt	21-17 21-17 22-24 21-19

Lomas beats the holder to win the title for the third time, the first for five years.

MEN'S DOUBLES Final

Skylet Andrew & Nicky Mason	Alan Cooke & John Holland	21-16 1-13

WOMEN'S DOUBLES Final

Lisa Lomas & Fiona Mommessin	Andrea Holt & K Goodall	19-21 22-20 21-10

MIXED DOUBLES Final

Skylet Andrew & Fiona Mommessin	A Perry & Sally Marling	21-19 21-9

British League 1993-94

Men

PREMIER DIVISION

BFL Grove	14	14	0	0	28
Team Peniel	14	11	1	2	23
Sedgefield	14	7	3	4	17
DML Launceston	14	6	0	8	12
Horsham Angels	14	5	1	8	11
St Neots	14	5	1	8	11
Vymura Int.	14	2	1	11	5
Bathwick Tyres	11	2	1	11	5

Bathwick, one point ahead of Vymura before the last day, are relegated.

Div 1 North	BFL Grove II
Div 1 South	BFL Grove III
Div 2 North	Uxbridge Burton
Div 2 S East	Linda Farrow
Div 2 S West	Horsham Angels II
Div 3 East	Peterborough
Div 3 Midlands	Bribar Colley II
Div 3 North	Drumchapel Glasgow
Div 3 South	Barclays
Boys	BFL Grove

Women

PREMIER DIVISION

BFL Grove	10	10	0	0	20
Hull Sandhill	10	8	0	2	16
S Kesteven Sov.	10	6	0	4	12
Hull Sandhill II	10	3	1	6	7
Graham Spicer	10	1	1	8	3
Welsh Ladies	10	0	2	8	2

Grove win the title for the fifth consecutive year.

Div 1	BFL Grove II
Div 2	Olivetti Bribar

Div 3a	Westminster
Div 3b	Gonerby
Girls	BFL Grove

English County Championship 1993-94

PREMIER DIVISION

Essex	7	6	1	0	13
Derbyshire	7	4	1	2	9
Middlesex	7	4	0	3	8
Lancashire	7	2	3	2	7
Staffordshire	7	3	1	3	7
Devon	7	1	3	3	5
Sussex	7	1	2	4	4
Surrey	7	1	1	5	3

Div 1a	Leicestershire
Div 1b	Middlesex II
Div 2a	Lancashire II
Div 2b	Worcestershire
Div 2c	Buckinghamshire
Div 2d	Kent

National Disabled Championships

Aug 1994 Reading

MEN'S SINGLES FINAL

David Russell	Arthur Wade	21-5 21-18

WOMEN'S SINGLES FINAL

Lynne Ridings	Kathy Mitton	21-17 16-21 21-9
Martine Hubert		BEL
Evelien Hengstman		HOL

Tennis

The reign of Spain? Nearly but probably not quite. True, Bruguera & Berasategui dominated the French and Sánchez Vicário made it a Spanish double there as well as winning the US Open – but her success owed a great deal to one of Steffi Graf's years of self-doubt and especially the continued absence of Monica Seles – and the men's game, when it wasn't being played on clay, was dominated by Pistol Pete and the other big guns, so much so that calls were made, yet again, for a change in ball pressure or the abolition of the second serve – something, anything, to bring back the good old, gentler days.

Ho hum, 'twas ever thus. The same cries were heard when Smith was beating Nastase, Connors crushing little old Rosewall, Curran beating McEnroe. They went quiet and they'll do so again, especially when people can point to Agassi's US Open win as a sign that a great returner can still beat the heavy servers. Expect no drastic developments in the near future.

Dark mutterings apart, the big story was Navratilova's run to the Wimbledon final (in the absence of Graf, whom she hasn't beaten there since 1987) and subsequent retirement, after an eternity on the tour, to some typically restrained fanfares in New York (meanwhile another Czech who made it big in America also bowed out: Ivan Lendl, more quietly, not missed so much). The best of all time? They all seemed to think so, and her record would appear to say it all: a record 167 singles titles, 165 doubles, 51 Grand Slams including 18 singles, and the world No.1 ranking for a record 381 weeks (7 yrs 17 weeks). But most of this was built on the muscularity and big left-handed serve that works well on fast surfaces (she won the French only twice), and even her Wimbledon record doesn't quite stand comparison with those of Helen Wills Moody (who won her last 50 matches there and would have taken the title at least ten times if she'd bothered to cross the Atlantic every year), or Suzanne Lenglen (who lost only one match in her entire career).

Still and all, her importance to the women's game will never be in doubt. Some of her biggest battles have been off the court – in 1994 she was refused fertility treatment by one doctor because she was a lesbian – and not always in fair fights.

Not so the poor Brits, who had arguably their worst year ever. By the end of November '94, the highest ranked players were the 32-y-o Bates (who had another good Wimbledon and even won a tournament) at No.74 and Clare Wood at 136. Successive defeats brought relegation to the bowels of the Davis Cup, and the women followed suit in the European team championship they'd actually won in 1992.

Still, this was only to be expected as the public courts continue to go unused (especially by the working class) and the private clubs still play mainly social mixed doubles. As ever, Britain's a tennis-playing country for just two weeks of the year, all of which makes Wimbledon's record profits of £27.9 million (a staggering 70% up on 1993) look more bizarre than encouraging.

Wimbledon
Seeds in capitals, seeding numbers in brackets

Men's Singles

1st ROUND

PETE SAMPRAS (USA,1)	Jared Palmer	7-6 7-5 6-3
Richey Reneberg (USA)	Jonathan Canter (USA)	7-6 6-3 7-6
Andrew Foster (UK)	Guillaume Raoux (FRA)	3-6 6-2 6-2 6-1
Chuck Adams (USA)	José Francisco Altur (SPA)	6-1 7-5 6-4
Mark Woodforde (AUS)	Shuzo Matsuoka (JAP)	6-2 7-5 6-4
Daniel Vacek (CZE)	Gérard Solves (FRA)	6-4 6-2 4-6 2-6 6-2
Karsten Braasch (GER)	Jonathan Stark (USA)	6-2 6-4 3-6 4-6 6-3
YEVGENY KAFELNIKOV (RUS, 15)	Laurence Tieleman (ITA)	7-5 6-7 7-5 6-7 11-9
MICHAEL CHANG (USA, 10)	Alberto Costa (SPA)	7-6 6-4 6-2
Michael Tebbutt (AUS)	Robbie Weiss (USA)	6-3 6-0 6-3
Jaime Yzaga (PERU)	Nick Gould (UK)	6-3 7-6 6-7 4-6 7-5
Grant Connell (CAN)	Stefano Pescosolido (ITA)	6-4 6-4 6-4
Christian Saceanu (GER)	Stéphane Simian (FRA)	6-4 6-4 6-3
Jean-Philippe Fleurian (FRA)	Simon Youl (AUS)	6-3 6-4 6-7 6-7 6-1
Patrick Rafter (AUS)	Jamie Morgan (AUS)	6-4 5-7 6-4 7-6
SERGI BRUGUERA (SPA, 8)	Barry Cowan (UK)	6-2 4-6 6-4 6-3
STEFAN EDBERG (SWE, 3)	Ellis Ferreira (SAF)	6-2 7-6 6-4
Kenneth Carlsen (DEN)	Marc Göllner (GER)	6-4 6-3 7-6
Marcos Ondruska (SAF)	Karel Novacek (CZE)	7-6 6-2 7-5
Jonas Björkman (SWE)	Mark Petchey (UK)	6-2 6-1 2-6 2-6 6-1
Carlos Costa (SPA)	Alex O'Brien (USA)	2-6 3-6 7-6 6-4 6-1
Chris Wilkinson (UK)	Omar Camporese (ITA)	6-3 3-6 6-3 3-6 7-5
Wayne Ferreira (SAF)	Mauricio Hadad (COL)	6-4 3-6 7-5 6-3
MARC ROSSET (SWI, 14)	David Witt (USA)	6-2 6-4 7-6
ANDRÉ AGASSI (USA, 12)	Andrea Gaudenzi (ITA)	6-2 6-7 6-3 6-2
Nicolas Pereira (VEN)	Renzo Furlan (ITA)	2-6 6-4 6-3 6-4
Aaron Krickstein (USA)	David Rikl (CZE)	6-3 6-2 6-0
Olivier Delaitre (FRA)	Rodolphe Gilbert (FRA)	6-2 7-5 7-5
Martin Damm (CZE)	Patrick McEnroe (USA)	6-7 6-3 6-4 6-2
Mark Knowles (BAH)	Andrei Cherkasov (RUS)	6-4 7-5 7-6
Patrick Kuhnen (GER)	Maurice Ruah (VEN)	6-3 7-5 0-6 5-7 6-4
TODD MARTIN (USA, 6)	Grant Stafford (SAF)	6-4 6-2 6-7 6-7 6-1
Jim Courier (USA, 5)	Byron Black (ZIM)	6-1 6-7 6-3 6-4
Guy Forget (FRA)	Doug Flach (USA)	6-1 6-2 6-2
Wally Masur (AUS)	Alex Antonitsch (AUT)	6-1 6-2 3-6 6-3
Jakob Hlasek (SWI)	Steve Bryan (USA)	5-7 6-1 7-5 6-3
Jörn Renzenbrink (GER)	Malivai Washington (USA)	7-6 6-4 7-6
Jeremy Bates (UK)	Gianluca Pozzi (ITA)	7-5 6-4 6-1
Markus Zöcke (GER)	Miles McLagan (UK)	6-4 6-2 6-4
PETR KORDA (CZE, 11)	John Fitzgerald (AUS)	6-2 6-1 6-4
Brett Steven (NZ)	CÉDRIC PIOLINE (FRA, 13)	6-2 4-6 6-3 6-1
Aleksandr Volkov (RUS)	Jeff Tarango (USA)	6-4 6-2 6-2
Jacco Eltingh (HOL)	Sebastien Lareau (CAN)	6-3 6-2 6-0
David Prinosil (GER)	Tim Henman (UK)	4-6 6-3 6-2 6-2
Amos Mansdorf (ISR)	Tomás Carbonell (SPA)	7-5 2-6 4-6 6-1 6-4
Kenny Thorne (USA)	Jim Grabb (USA)	3-2 ret
Alexander Mronz(GER)	Thomas Muster(AUT)	5-7 7-6 6-7 6-4 8-6
GORAN IVANISEVIC (CRO, 4)	Fernando Meligeni (BRZ)	6-1 6-3 6-4
BORIS BECKER (GER, 7)	David Wheaton (USA)	6-2 6-4 6-3

Arne Thoms (GER)	Bernd Karbacher (GER)	3-6 6-3 2-6 6-4 11-9
Javier Frana (ARG)	Chris Bailey (UK)	3-6 7-6 7-5 6-3
Brad Gilbert (USA)	Karol Kucera (SLVK)	6-3 7-6 4-6 6-2
Alex Corretja (SPA)	Henri Leconte (FRA)	2-6 4-6 7-5 7-6 3-2 ret
Richard Fromberg (AUS)	Hendrik Dreekman (GER)	6-4 6-7 7-5 2-6 6-3
Ctislav (Slava) Dosedel (SLVK)	Younes El Aynaoui (MOR)	6-1 6-4 6-4
ANDREI MEDVEDEV (UKR, 9)	Ronald Agenor (HAITI)	6-4 5-7 6-3 6-2
Andrei Olhovskiy (RUS)	ARNAUD BOETSCH (FRA, 16)	6-2 6-3 7-5
Jordi Burillo (SPA)	Lars Jonsson (SWE)	6-2 6-2 4-6 5-7 6-4
Christian Bergström (SWE)	Diego Nargiso (ITA)	6-1 7-5 6-2
Greg Rusedski (CAN)	Nicklas Kulti (SWE)	6-3 6-4 6-2
Darren Cahill (AUS)	Richard Krajicek (HOL)	6-3 6-2 5-7 7-6
Jason Stoltenberg (AUS)	Paul Haarhuis (HOL)	7-6 6-1 6-4
Karim Alami (MOR)	Magnus Larsson (SWE)	7-6 7-6 7-5
Bryan Shelton (USA)	MICHAEL STICH (GER, 2)	6-3 6-3 6-4

First seed (of either sex) to go out: Pioline, who incurs two $500 fines in the process.

2nd ROUND

SAMPRAS	Reneberg	6-3 6-4 6-2
Adams	Foster	6-2 6-4 7-6
Vacek	Woodforde	6-3 7-6 6-4
KAFELNIKOV	Braasch	6-1 6-1 6-3
CHANG	Tebbutt	3-6 6-3 7-6 6-7 6-4
Connell	Yzaga	6-3 1-6 6-1 7-6
Fleurian	Saceanu	7-5 6-3 6-4
BRUGUERA	Rafter	7-63-6 4-6 7-5 13-11
Carlsen	EDBERG	6-7 6-7 6-2 6-4 6-4
Björkman	Ondruska	6-3 4-6 6-3 3-6 6-3
Wilkinson	C Costa	6-1 6-4 6-1
W Ferreira	ROSSET	6-7 6-3 6-4 6-4
AGASSI	Pereira	6-7 6-3 6-4 6-7 6-4
Krickstein	Delaître	6-7 7-5 1-6 7-6 6-2
Damm	Knowles	6-3 6-4 2-6 6-1
MARTIN	Kuhnen	6-2 6-2 6-4
Forget	COURIER	3-6 6-3 3-6 6-3 6-4
Hlasek	Masur	6-1 6-4 7-6
Bates	Renzenbrink	6-2 7-6 6-4
Zöcke	KORDA	4-6 -7 6-3 6-2 6-4
Volkov	Steven	4-6 6-4 3-6 7-5 6-3
Prinosil	Eltingh	3-6 6-2 6-3 6-4
Mansdorf	Thorne	7-6 6-3 6-7 6-1
IVANISEVIC	Mronz	6-2 7-6 6-1
BECKER	Thoms	7-6 6-2 6-4
Frana	Gilbert	6-3 4-6 6-1 6-2
Fromberg	Corretja	6-2 7-6 7-5
MEDVEDEV	Dosedel	3-6 7-5 6-1 6-4
Burillo	Olhovskiy	6-0 6-1 6-3
Bergström	Rusedski	6-4 6-4 5-7 7-6
Stoltenberg	Cahill	6-3 ret
Shelton	Alami	6-3 7-5 1-6 6-7 6-2

British tennis has to take what crumbs of success it can get. Wilkinson becomes the first home player to reach the men's 3rd Round in successive years since John Lloyd 1984-85. Forget, after a year's absence with damaged knee ligaments, is ranked 1,130 in the world. Surely a Centre Court rarity: Becker, Thoms, and German umpire.

3rd ROUND

SAMPRAS	Adams	6-1 6-2 6-4
Vacek	KAFELNIKOV	4-6 7-5 6-4 3-6 6-4
CHANG	Connell	7-6 6-4 6-2

BRUGUERA	Fleurian	7-6 6-4 2-6 7-5
Björkman	Carlsen	6-4 6-4 1-0 ret
W Ferreira	Wilkinson	6-2 6-2 6-3
AGASSI	Krickstein	6-4 6-3 7-6
MARTIN	Damm	6-2 6-7 4-6 6-3 11-9
Forget	Hlasek	6-4 6-4 7-6
Bates	Zöcke	6-4 6-4 3-6 6-3
Volkov	Prinosil	7-6 6-3 6-2
IVANISEVIC	Mansdorf	6-3 7-5 6-4
BECKER	Frana	7-6 6-4 1-6 6-3
MEDVEDEV	Fromberg	7-6 6-3 5-7 6-4
Bergström	Burillo	6-3 6-3 6-4
Shelton	Stoltenberg	7-6 5-7 5-7 7-5 6-4

4th ROUND

SAMPRAS	Vacek	6-4 6-1 7-6
CHANG	BRUGUERA	6-4 7-6 6-0
W Ferreira	Björkman	6-3 6-7 6-4 6-3
MARTIN	AGASSI	6-3 7-5 6-7 4-6 6-1
Forget	Bates	2-6 6-1 6-3 6-1
IVANISEVIC	Volkov	7-6 7-6 4-6 6-2
BECKER	MEDVEDEV	6-7 7-5 7-6 6-7 7-5
Bergström	Shelton	3-6 6-3 3-6 6-3 10-8

QUARTER-FINALS

SAMPRAS	CHANG	6-4 6-1 6-3
MARTIN	W Ferreira	6-3 6-2 3-6 5-7 7-5
IVANISEVIC	Forget	7-6 7-6 6-4
BECKER	Bergström	7-6 6-4 6-3

SEMI-FINALS

| SAMPRAS | MARTIN | 6-4 6-4 3-6 6-3 |
| IVANISEVIC | BECKER | 6-2 7-6 6-4 |

FINAL 3 July 1994

| SAMPRAS | IVANISEVIC | 7-6 7-6 6-0 |

In the first final since 1936 to end in a love set, Sampras beats the 1992 runner-up to retain the title .

Women's Singles

1st ROUND

Lori McNeil (USA)	STEFFI GRAF (GER, 1)	7-5 7-6
Yone Kamio (JAP)	Petra Bergerow (GER)	6-0 6-2
Kristie Boogert (HOL)	Liz Smylie (AUS)	6-4 4-6 6-2
Alexia Dechaume-Balleret (FRA)	Kyoko Nagatsuka (JAP)	6-3 7-5
Rachel McQuillan (AUS)	Patty Fendick (USA)	6-3 2-6 6-3
Pam Shriver (USA)	Amy Frazier (USA)	6-7 6-2 8-6
Petra Langrova (CZE)	Helen Kelesi (CAN)	7-6 6-2
Florencia Labat (ARG)	SABINE HACK (GER, 15)	6-3 3-6 6-4
AMANDA COETZER (SAF, 14)	Yelena Likhovtseva (KAZ)	6-3 3-6 6-4
Louise Field (AUS)	Chanda Rubin (USA)	6-2 6-7 8-6
Claire Wegink (HOL)	Amanda Wainwright (UK)	6-2 6-3
Ginger Helgeson (USA)	Veronika Martinek (GER)	6-3 6-2
Larissa Savchenko Neiland (LAT)	Katrina Adams (USA)	6-4 6-3
Anna Smashnova (ISR)	Yevgenia Maniokova (RUS)	6-4 -6 7-5
Shirli-Ann Siddall (UK)	Christina Singer (GER)	6-4 5-7 7-5
KIMIKO DATE (JAP, 6)	Ai Sugiyama (JAP)	6-3 7-6
CONCHITA MARTÎNEZ (SPA, 3)	René Simpson-Alter (CAN)	6-1 6-3

Nana Miyagi (JAP)	Lisa Raymond (USA)	4-6 7-5 8-6
Nathalie Tauziat (FRA)	Asa Carlsson (SWE)	6-2 6-1
Elna Reinach (SAF)	Joannette Kruger (SAF)	7-6 6-3
Kristine Radford (AUS)	Angelica Gavaldon (MEX)	6-0 6-0
Irina Spirlea (ROM)	Monique Javer (UK)	6-1 6-2
Ines Gorrochategui (ARG)	Debbie Graham (USA)	6-3 6-1
ANKE HUBER (GER, 12)	Jo Durie (UK)	7-5 6-2
GABRIELA SABATINI (ARG, 10)	Judith Wiesner (AUT)	2-6 6-4 6-1
Jenny Byrne (AUS)	Janette Husarova (SLVK)	6-3 6-0
Caroline Kuhlman (USA)	Karine Quentrec (FRA)	3-6 7-5 6-4
Meredith McGrath (USA)	Julie Pullin (UK)	6-2 6-4
Ruxandra Dragomir (ROM)	Clare Wood (UK)	6-3 6-1
Barbara Rittner (GER)	Sabine Appelmans (BEL)	6-0 6-4
Tessa Price (SAF)	Andrea Strnadova (CZE)	6-3 7-5
LINDSAY DAVENPORT (USA, 9)	Julie Halard (FRA)	6-1 6-4
JANA NOVOTNA (CZE, 5)	Miriam Oremans (HOL)	6-4 4-6 6-4
Wiltrud Probst (GER)	Sandrine Testud (FRA)	6-2 6-1
Yelena Brioukhovets (UKR)	Aléxandra Fusai (FRA)	7-5 7-5
Dominique Monami (BEL)	Jo Ward (UK)	6-0 6-2
Naoko Sawamatsu (JAP)	Caroline Vis (HOL)	7-6 6-3
Radka Bobkova (CZE)	Ludmila Richterova (CZE)	6-3 6-1
Brenda Schultz (HOL)	Leila Meshki (GEO)	2-6 6-3 6-4
MARY JOE FERNANDEZ (USA, 11)	Karina Habdusova (SLVK)	6-4 6-2
HELENA SUKOVA (CZE, 17)	Tami Whitlinger Jones (USA)	6-7 6-0 6-3
Patricia Tarabini (ARG)	Petra Ritter (AUT)	6-3 3-6 8-6
Silke Frankl (GER)	Barbara Schett (AUT)	6-1 7-6
Sandra Cacic (USA)	Iva Majoli (CRO)	4-6 6-3 6-4
Linda Harvey-Wild (USA)	Manon Bollegraf (HOL)	6-1 4-6 6-3
Meike Babel (GER)	Paola Suarez (ARG)	4-6 6-2 6-1
Anna Maria 'Sandra' Cecchini (ITA)	Patricia Hy (CAN)	6-2 6-4
MARTINA NAVRATILOVA (USA, 4)	Claire Taylor (UK)	6-2 6-3
Mana Endo (JAP)	NATALYA ZVEREVA (BYL, 8)	4-6 6-4 6-1
Jolene Watanabe (USA)	Karen Cross (UK)	6-0 6-1
Kimberly Po (USA)	Marketa Kochta (GER)	6-2 6-4
Gigi Fernandez (PR)	Marzia Grossi (ITA)	6-2 6-1
Ann Grossman (USA)	Silvia Farina (ITA)	6-2 6-4
Nicole Arendt (USA)	Nicole Muns-Jagerman (HOL)	6-3 6-2
Yayuk Basuki (INDO)	Natalya Medvedeva (UKR)	6-3 6-2
MAGDALENA MALEEVA (BUL, 16)	Shaun Stafford (USA)	6-7 6-2 6-4
ZINA GARRISON JACKSON (USA,13)	Katarina Studenikova (SLVK)	6-3 7-6
Mercedes Paz (ARG)	Sandra Dopfer (AUT)	6-1 7-6
Fang Li (CHN)	Emanuela Zardo (SWI)	6-4 6-3
Laura Golarsa (ITA)	Isabelle Demongeot (FRA)	6-3 7-6
Marianne Werdel (USA)	Bettina Fulco-Villella (ARG)	6-2 5-7 6-2
Nancy Feber (BEL)	Laurence Courtois (BEL)	6-0 6-1
María José Gaidano (ARG)	Beate Reinstadler (AUT)	7-6 7-5
ARANTXA SÁNCHEZ VICÁRIO (2)	Katerina Maleeva (BUL)	6-1 6-2

First seed to go out: Hack.

Graf, the hottest favourite of all time, becomes the first defending champion to lose in the First Round of the women's singles.

Navratilova's seeded for the 20th time, a record.

Sukova's number is no misprint: she was seeded when Mary Pierce (7) dropped out.

Siddall aside, the eight other British women win only 33 games in 16 sets, the most dismal showing ever. And the overall situation's even worse. Another seven players who were allowed in as wild cards went out in the first round of the pre-tournament qualifying competition.

2nd ROUND

McNeil	Kamio	6-3 6-7 6-3
Boogert	Dechaume-Balleret	6-3 7-5
Shriver	McQuillen	5-7 6-2 8-6
Labat	Langrova	6-2 6-2
COETZER	Field	6-4 6-0
Helgeson	Wegink	6-2 6-2
Savchenko Neiland	Smashnova	6-3 6-4
DATE	Siddall	6-2 6-0
MARTÍNEZ	Miyagi	6-1 7-6
Tauziat	Reinach	6-3 6-7 6-2
Radford	Spirlea	7-5 3-6 6-4
Gorrochategui	HUBER	6-3 6-4
SABATINI	Byrne	6-2 6-3
McGrath	Kuhlman	6-1 6-3
Rittner	Dragomir	6-2 6-1
DAVENPORT	Price	6-4 6-2
NOVOTNA	Probst	6-2 6-1
Monami	Brioukhovets	6-1 4-6 6-2
Sawamatsu	Bobkova	6-1 6-3
MJ FERNANDEZ	Schultz	6-4 6-4
SUKOVA	Tarabini	6-4 6-2
Frankl	Cacic	2-6 6-1 6-3
Harvey-Wild	Babel	6-2 2-6 6-2
NAVRATILOVA	Cecchini	6-2 6-0
Endo	Watanabe	6-3 6-4
G Fernandez	Po	6-2 1-6 9-7
Grossman	Arendt	6-4 3-6 6-4
Basuki	M MALEEVA	5-7 7-6 6-4
GARRISON JACKSON	Paz	7-5 6-0
Golarsa	Fang Li	6-3 6-0
Feber	Werdel	6-4 6-4
SÁNCHEZ VICÁRIO	Gaidano	6-2 6-1

3rd ROUND

McNeil	Boogert	6-2 6-4
Labat	Shriver	6-4 4-6 6-2
Coetzer	Helgeson	6-0 6-3
Savchenko Neiland	DATE	6-3 6-2
MARTÍNEZ	Tauziat	6-1 6-3
Radford	Gorrochategui	w.o.
SABATINI	McGrath	6-4 6-1
DAVENPORT	Rittner	6-4 3-6 6-1
NOVOTNA	Monami	6-0 4-6 6-0
Sawamatsu	MJ FERNANDEZ	6-0 7-5
SUKOVA	Frankl	6-3 6-2
NAVRATILOVA	Harvey-Wild	6-3 6-2
G Fernandez	Endo	4-6 6-3 6-3
Basuki	Grosman	6-0 6-2
GARRISON JACKSON	Golarsa	6-2 4-1 ret
SÁNCHEZ VICÁRIO	Feber	6-2 6-1

4th ROUND

McNeil	Labat	7-6 7-6
Savchenko Neiland	COETZER	-6 6-3 6-4
MARTÍNEZ	Radford	3-6 6-3 6-4
DAVENPORT	SABATINI	6-1 6-3
NOVOTNA	Sawamatsu	6-3 6-3

NAVRATILOVA	SUKOVA	6-1 6-2
G Fernandez	Basuki	6-4 6-1
GARRISON JACKSON	SÁNCHEZ VICÁRIO	7-5 4-6 6-3

For the first time since 1981, a Grand Slam singles title will be won by someone other than the top two seeds. For the first time ever at Wimbledon, neither of the top two reaches the women's quarter-finals. Navratilova does, for the 20th consecutive year.

QUARTER-FINALS

McNeil	Savchenko Neiland	6-3 6-4
MARTÍNEZ	DAVENPORT	6-2 6-7 6-3
NAVRATILOVA	NOVOTNA	5-7 6-0 6-1
G Fernandez	GARRISON JACKSON	6-4 6-4

Navratilova's 17th semi-final, equalling Chris Evert Lloyd's record.

SEMI-FINALS

| MARTÍNEZ | McNeil | 3-6 6-2 10-8 |
| NAVRATILOVA | G Fernandez | 6-4 7-6 |

FINAL

| MARTÍNEZ | NAVRATILOVA | 6-4 3-6 6-3 |

Martínez, the only Spaniard to reach the final since Lili de Alvárez in 1926-27-28, becomes the first to win it.

Wimbledon: greatest age differences between singles finalists

yrs	days		
20	264	1919	Dolly Douglass Chambers (40) Suzanne Lenglen (20)
18	33	1919	Norman Brookes (41) Gerald Patterson (23)
17	304	1974	Ken Rosewall (39) Jimmy Connors (21)
15	302	1910	Arthur W Gore (42) Tony Wilding (26)
15	180	1994	Martina Navratilova (37) Conchita Martínez (22)
13	243	1930	Elizabeth Ryan (38)

Wimbledon: most singles titles

9	Martina Navratilova	1978-90
8	Helen Wills Moody	1927-38
7	Willie Renshaw	1881-89
7	Dolly Douglass Chambers	1903-14

Wimbledon: most singles finals

13	Blanche Bingley Hillyard	1885-1901
12	Martina Navratilova	1978-94
11	Chattie Cooper Sterry	1895-1912
11	Dolly Douglass Chambers	1903-20
10	Chris Evert Lloyd	1973-85

Navratilova never failed to win a set.

Men's singles:

| 8 | Willie Renshaw | 1881-90 |

Men's Doubles

QUARTER-FINALS

TODD WOODBRIDGE	AUS	JACCO ELTINGH	HOL	4-6 7-6 6-2 6-7 9-7
MARK WOODFORDE	AUS	PAUL HAARHUIS	HOL	
WAYNE FERREIRA	SAF	Marius Barnard	SAF	6-3 7-5 6-2
MICHAEL STICH	GER	Brent Haygarth	SAF	
MARC GOELLNER	GER	Tom Nijssen	HOL	6-4 6-7 6-4 3-6 6-4
YEVGENY KAFELNIKOV	RUS	Cyril Suk	CZE	

GRANT CONNELL	CAN	Lan Bale	SAF	7-6 7-6 6-2
PATRICK GALBRAITH	USA	Brett Steven	NZ	

SEMI-FINALS

WOODBRIDGE & WOODFORDE	FERREIRA & STICH			6-2 7-6 6-2
CONNELL & GALBRAITH	GOELLNER & KAFELNIKOV			4-6 6-3 6-4 6-2

FINAL

WOODBRIDGE & WOODFORDE	CONNELL & GALBRAITH	7-6 6-3 6-1

The Woods become the first pair since 1905 to beat the same opponents in successive finals.

Women's Doubles

QUARTER-FINALS

GIGI FERNANDEZ	PR	Linda Harvey-Wild	USA	6-1 4-6 6-0
NATALYA ZVEREVA	BYL	Chanda Rubin	USA	
Nicole Arendt	USA	Natalya Medvedeva	UKR	2-6 6-3 6-1
Kristine Radford	AUS	Larissa Savchenko Neiland	LAT	
MANON BOLLEGRAF	HOL	Ingelise Driehuis	HOL	6-4 6-2
MARTINA NAVRATILOVA	USA	Maja Muric	CRO	
JANA NOVOTNA	CZE	PAM SHRIVER	USA	6-2 6-4
ARANTXA SÁNCHEZ VICÁRIO	SPA	LIZ SMYLIE	AUS	

SEMI-FINALS

FERNANDEZ & ZVEREVA	BOLLEGRAF & NAVRATILOVA	6-4 6-4
NOVOTNA & SANCHEZ VICARIO	Arendt & Radford	4-6 7-5 6-3

FINAL

FERNANDEZ & ZVEREVA	NOVOTNA & SÁNCHEZ VICÁRIO	6-4 6-1

Fernandez & Zvereva win the title for the third time in succession. Novotna, in the final for the sixth consecutive year, becomes the first to lose four in a row

Mixed Doubles

QUARTER-FINALS

TODD WOODBRIDGE	AUS	ANDREI OLHOVSKIY	RUS	6-2 6-4
HELENA SUKOVA	CZE	LARISSA S NEILAND	LAT	
GRANT CONNELL	CAN	JOHN FITZGERALD	AUS	6-3 7-6
LINDSAY DAVENPORT	USA	LIZ SMYLIE	AUS	
TJ (Todd) Middleton	USA	Maurice Ruah	VEN	6-3 6-2
Lori McNeil	USA	Florencia Labat	ARG	
BYRON BLACK	ZIM	MARK WOODFORDE	AUS	7-6 3-6 7-5
PAM SHRIVER	USA	MERDITH McGRATH	USA	

SEMI-FINALS

Middleton & McNeil	BLACK & SHRIVER	6-3 7-6
WOODBRIDGE & SUKOVA	CONNELL & DAVENPORT	6-3 6-4

FINAL

WOODBRIDGE & SUKOVA	Middleton & McNeil	3-6 7-5 6-3

Junior Men's Singles

FINAL
Scott Humphries   USA   Mark Phillippousis   AUS   7-6 3-6 6-4

Junior Women's Singles

FINAL
Martina Hingis   SWI   Jeon Ma-Ri   S KOR   7-5 6-4

Hingis beat an almost equally well-known and precocious 13-y-o, Anna Kournikova (RUS) in the quarter-finals. In the US Open, she beats her 6-0 6-0. A few days after her 14th birthday, Hingis (born in Czechoslovakia, apparently named after Navratilova) wins her first senior match, beating Patty Fendick 6-4 6-3 in Zürich. In her second pro tournament, she beats Helena Sukova 6-2 6-1 in 45 mins. Another heavily hyped 14-y-o, Venus Williams (USA) also wins her first match as a professional, beating Shaun Stafford in October before taking a set off Arantxa Sánchez in the next round.

The only British winner at Wimbledon 94: Lizzie Jelfs, who partners Nannie De Villiers (SAF) to beat No.2 seeds Corina Morariu (ROM) & Lyudmila Varmuzova (RUS) in the girls doubles final, and Virginia Wade, who partners Wendy Turnbull (AUS) to beat Betsy Nagelsen & Joanne Russell (both USA) in the Over-35 women's doubles.

Australian Open

Seeds in capitals, seeding numbers in brackets

Men's Singles

1st ROUND

PETE SAMPRAS (USA, 1)	Joshua Eagle (AUS)	6-4 6-0 7-6
Yevgeny Kafelnikov (RUS)	Steve Bryan (USA)	4-5 ret
Stéphane Simian (FRA)	Christo van Rensburg (SAF)	1-6 6-3 4-6 6-4 6-1
Jared Palmer (USA)	David Prinosil (GER)	6-7 4-6 6-1 6-1 8-6
Paul Haarhuis (HOL)	David Nainkin (SAF)	6-2 6-2 6-4
Jonathan Stark (USA)	Tommy Ho (USA)	7-5 6-7 7-6 6-3
Richey Reneberg (USA)	Brian MacPhie (USA)	7-5 6-4 6-0
IVAN LENDL (USA, 15)	Greg Rusedski (CAN)	6-4 7-6 7-5
MAGNUS GUSTAFSSON (SWE, 10)	Roger Smith (BAH)	3-6 7-5 6-2 2-6 6-2
Brett Steven (NZ)	Bernd Karbacher (GER)	6-2 5-2 ret
Filip Dewulf (BEL)	Jeff Tarango (USA)	7-5 6-4 6-1
Jörn Renzenbrink (GER)	Cristiano Caratti (ITA)	6-1 6-4 6-4
Amos Mansdorf (ISR)	Mikael Pernfors (SWE)	6-3 6-4 6-2
Brent Larkham (AUS)	Ryuso Tsujino (JAP)	6-0 7-5 6-4
Henri Leconte (FRA)	Kent Kinnear (USA)	6-4 6-0 6-1
Martin Damm (CZE)	CÉDRIC PIOLINE (FRA, 7)	7-5 3-6 7-6 6-3
JIM COURIER (USA, 3)	Brian Shelton (USA)	4-6 6-1 6-7 6-2 6-4
Marcus Ondruska (SAF)	Gianluca Pozzi (ITA)	6-3 6-1 6-3
Nicklas Kulti (SWE)	Jean-Philippe Fleurian (FRA)	6-4 6-2 7-5
Sandon Stolle (AUS)	Sebastien Lareau (CAN)	6-3 3-6 7-5 3-6 6-2
Daniel Vacek (CZE)	Christian Bergström (SWE)	6-3 1-1 ret
Andrea Gaudenzi (ITA)	Karsten Braasch (GER)	6-4 6-2 6-0
David Rikl (CZE)	Magnus Larsson (SWE)	1-6 7-6 6-3 6-0
WAYNE FERREIRA (SAF)	Fernando Meligeni (BRZ)	6-4 6-3 7-6
MARC ROSSET (SWI, 11)	Chris Wilkinson (UK)	6-2 7-6 6-3
Jakob Hlasek (SWI)	Mark Knowles (BAH)	7-5 4-6 6-3 6-4
Emilio Sánchez (SPA)	Tomás Carbonell (SPA)	2-6 6-1 6-4 6-3

Grant Stafford (SAF)	Mark Philippousis (AUS)	6-2 6-2 6-0
Tomas Nydahl (SWE)	Andrew Kratzmann (AUS)	6-4 3-6 6-1 7-5
Aaron Krickstein (USA)	Renzo Furlan (ITA)	6-3 2-6 7-6 6-3
Jason Stoltenberg (AUS)	Maurice Ruah (VEN)	6-3 6-3 6-3
GORAN IVANISEVIC (CRO, 5)	Alex O'Brien (USA)	6-4 6-0 6-2
THOMAS MUSTER (AUT, 6)	Robbie Weiss (USA)	6-3 6-3 6-3
Kenneth Carlsen (DEN)	Darren Cahill (AUS)	6-4 3-6 6-3 3-6 8-6
Guillaume Raoux (FRA)	Markus Naewie (GER)	4-6 6-2 6-3 6-0
Patrick Kuhnen (GER)	Andrei Olhovskiy (RUS)	6-7 7-6 6-2 6-4
Todd Woodbridge (AUS)	John Sullivan	5-7 4-6 7-6 6-4 6-3
Henrik Holm (SWE)	Hendrik Dreekman (GER)	7-5 6-4 6-4
Richard Fromberg (AUS)	Patrick McEnroe (USA)	1-6 7-6 6-3 6-4
ALEKSANDR VOLKOV (RUS, 12)	Wally Masur (AUS)	6-4 6-4 6-2
KAREL NOVACEK (CZE, 14)	Daniel Orsanic (ARG)	6-3 4-6 6-1 6-4
Lars Wahlgren (SWE)	Anders Jarryd (SWE)	0-6 6-4 6-0 1-0 ret
Lars Jonsson (SWE)	Byron Black (ZIM)	6-3 7-5 6-4
Younes El Aynaoui (MOR)	Neil Borwick (AUS)	6-1 6-2 ret
Rodolphe Gilbert (FRA)	Jordi Burillo (SPA)	5-7 7-5 6-3 6-1
Fabrice Santoro (FRA)	Dmitry Poliakov (UKR)	6-2 6-3 6-2
Jan Siemerink (HOL)	Markus Zöcke (GER)	6-3 7-6 4-6 6-3
STEFAN EDBERG (SWE, 4)	Javier Sánchez (SPA)	6-3 6-0 6-3
Thomas Enqvist (SWE)	PETR KORDA (CZE, 8)	6-3 6-4 7-6
Xavier Daufresne (BEL)	Thomas Johansson (SWE)	6-7 6-2 7-5 6-3
Patrick Rafter (AUS)	Paul Wekesa (KEN)	6-1 3-6 6-1 6-2
Jacco Eltingh (HOL)	Chris Garner (USA)	6-4 6-4 6-4
Stefano Pescosolido (ITA)	Doug Flach (USA)	6-4 6-3 6-4
Jonas Svensson (SWE)	Michael Tebbutt (AUS)	5-7 7-6 6-0 6-3
Jonas Björkman (SWE)	Kenny Thorne (USA)	3-6 6-4 6-7 7-5 6-2
TODD MARTIN (USA, 9)	Jaime Yzaga (PERU)	6-3 7-6 6-2
ARNAUD BOETSCH (FRA, 16)	Ryan Blake (USA)	6-2 6-4 6-0
Alexander Mronz (GER)	Paul Kilderry (AUS)	6-1 6-2 6-4
Olivier Delaitre (FRA)	Diego Nargiso (ITA)	6-4 6-2 4-6 6-2
Mats Wilander (SWE)	Milen Velev (BUL)	6-1 4-6 6-0 6-0
Alex Antonitsch (AUT)	Shuzo Matsuoka (JAP)	4-6 7-6 7-6 6-4
Jamie Morgan (AUS)	Andrei Chesnokov (RUS)	6-3 6-7 7-6 4-6 6-4
Andrei Cherkasov (RUS)	Mark Woodforde (AUS)	6-1 2-6 6-1 7-5
Malivai Washington (USA)	MICHAEL STICH (GER, 2)	7-6 6-3 3-6 6-2

Causes of the rash of retirements: Bergström & Borwick stomach upsets, Karbacher tonsilitis, Bryan eye injury, Leconte (2nd Round) heat exhaustion.

2nd ROUND

SAMPRAS	Kafelnikov	6-3 2-6 6-3 1-6 9-7
Simian	Palmer	3-6 7-6 4-6 6-4 8-6
Haarhuis	Stark	6-2 6-4 6-4
LENDL	Reneberg	5-7 6-2 6-2 6-2
GUSTAFSSON	Steven	7-6 6-2 4-6 6-2
Renzenbrink	Dewulf	6-1 6-4 6-3
Larkham	Mansdorf	7-5 7-6 6-4
Damm	Leconte	1-6 7-6 6-4 4-2
COURIER	Ondruska	6-1 6-4 6-4
Kulti	Stolle	6-4 6-2 6-1
Vacek	Gaudenzi	6-3 6-2 6-2
W FERREIRA	Rikl	6-3 6-4 6-2
ROSSET	Hlasek	6-4 7-6 3-6 6-2
Stafford	E Sánchez	6-1 6-2 6-2
Krickstein	Nydahl	7-6 6-1 6-7 6-2
IVANISEVIC	Stoltenberg	3-6 6-3 6-4 6-3
MUSTER	Carlsen	6-4 6-4 6-2

Raoux	Kuhnen	6-2 7-5 6-4
Holm	Woodbridge	6-4 7-6 5-7 4-6 7-5
VOLKOV	Fromberg	7-6 6-3 6-3
NOVACEK	Wahlgren	6-4 7-6 7-6
Jonsson	El Aynaoui	7-6 6-7 6-1 6-3
Santoro	R Gilbert	7-5 5-7 2-6 7-5 6-0
EDBERG	Siemerink	4-6 6-2 6-1 6-1
Daufresne	Enqvist	6-3 6-2 7-6
Rafter	Eltingh	6-4 6-4 6-4
Svensson	Pescosolido	6-2 7-5 7-5
MARTIN	Bjorkmän	6-3 6-4 6-0
Mronz	BOETSCH	w.o.
Wilander	Delaître	6-1 2-6 7-5 6-4
Antonitsch	Morgan	7-5 1-0 ret
Washington	Cherkasov	6-4 2-6 6-2 3-6 6-2

3rd ROUND

SAMPRAS	Simian	7-5 6-1 1-6 6-4
LENDL	Haarhuis	4-6 6-2 6-2 6-4
GUSTAFSSON	Renzenbrink	6-2 6-2 6-2
Damm	Larkham	6-4 6-4 3-6 2-6 6-2
COURIER	Kulti	6-3 6-3 7-6
W FERREIRA	Vacek	4-6 6-2 7-6 6-4
Stafford	ROSSET	3-6 6-2 6-2 6-1
IVANISEVIC	Krickstein	3-6 7-5 6-3 6-4
MUSTER	Raoux	6-3 6-3 6-2
VOLKOV	Holm	7-5 2-6 4-6 6-3 6-4
Jonsson	NOVACEK	6-1 7-5 7-5
EDBERG	Santoro	6-2 6-1 6-1
Daufresne	Rafter	5-7 6-2 6-1 6-4
MARTIN	Svensson	6-1 5-7 6-2 6-2
Wilander	Mronz	4-6 5-7 6-3 6-4 6-3
Washington	Antonitsch	4-6 7-6 6-3 6-3

4th ROUND

SAMPRAS	LENDL	7-6 6-2 7-6
GUSTAFSSON	Damm	2-6 6-3 6-1 6-1
COURIER	Ferreira	6-3 6-4 6-2
IVANISEVIC	Stafford	6-3 6-2 7-6
MUSTER	VOLKOV	6-3 6-3 6-2
EDBERG	Jonsson	6-4 6-4 6-4
MARTIN	Daufresne	6-7 7-6 6-3 6-3
Washington	Wilander	6-7 6-2 6-7 6-4 6-1

QUARTER-FINALS

SAMPRAS	GUSTAFSSON	7-6 2-6 6-3 7-6
COURIER	IVANISEVIC	7-6 6-4 6-2
EDBERG	MUSTER	6-2 6-3 6-4
MARTIN	Washington	6-2 7-6 7-6

SEMI-FINALS

SAMPRAS	COURIER	6-3 6-4 6-4
MARTIN	EDBERG	3-6 7-6 7-6 7-6

FINAL 30 Jan 1994

SAMPRAS	MARTIN	7-6 6-4 6-4

The first man since Rod Laver in 1969 to win three successive Grand Slam singles titles.

Women's Singles

1st ROUND

STEFFI GRAF (GER, 1)	Kimberly Po (USA)	6-1 2-0 ret
Nicole Provis (AUS)	Clare Wood (UK)	7-5 6-4
Pam Shriver (USA)	Laurence Courtois (BEL)	2-6 6-1 6-4
Barbara Rittner (GER)	Federica Bonsignori(ITA)	6-0 6-0
Sandrine Testud (FRA)	Marzia Grossi (ITA)	6-1 6-3
Lisa Raymond (USA)	Miriam Oremans (HOL)	6-2 2-6 6-4
Mana Endo (JAP)	Dominique Monami (BEL)	6-4 6-3
HELENA SUKOVA (CZE, 13)	Jenny Byrne (AUS)	6-7 7-6 6-2
LINDSAY DAVENPORT (USA, 16)	Patricia Hy (CAN)	3-6 6-2 7-5
Wiltrud Probst (GER)	Petra Langrova (CZE)	7-6 5-7 6-4
Yelena Makarova (RUS)	Sandra Wasserman (BEL)	6-4 6-3
René Simpson-Alter (CAN)	Nicole Pratt (AUS)	6-3 6-0
Nadin Ercegovic (CRO)	Robin White (USA)	4-6 6-3 7-5
Caroline Kuhlman (USA)	Karin Kschwendt (GER)	6-4 6-1
Inés Gorrochategui (ARG)	Kristin Godridge (AUS)	6-4 6-3
MARY JOE FERNANDEZ (USA, 6)	Elly Hakami (USA)	6-4 6-3
CONCHITA MARTINEZ (SPA, 3)	Natalya Zvereva (BYL)	5-7 6-4 6-3
Patty Fendick (USA)	Tina Krizan (SLVN)	6-4 6-4
Amy Frazier (USA)	Liz Smylie (AUS)	6-1 2-6 6-2
Radka Bobkova (CZE)	Christina Papadaki (GRE)	6-1 6-3
Kristine Radford (AUS)	Janette Husarova (SLVK)	3-6 7-6 7-5
Marketa Kochta (GER)	Joanette Kruger (SAF)	6-2 4-6 7-5
Chanda Rubin (USA)	Katerina Maleeva (BUL	6-4 6-0
AMANDA COETZER (SAF, 12)	Petra Begerow (GER)	6-1 6-3
KIMIKO DATE (JAP, 10)	Kathy Rinaldi Stunkel (USA)	6-1 6-1
Meredith McGrath (USA)	Larissa Savchenko Neiland (LAT)	3-6 6-4 6-4
Debbie Graham (USA)	Rennae Stubbs (AUS)	3-6 7-5 6-0
Rachel McQuillan (AUS)	Petra Ritter (AUT)	6-1 6-3
Kristie Boogert (HOL)	Manon Bollegraf (HOL)	6-3 6-3
Ginger Helgeson (USA)	Veronika Martinek (GER)	6-3 6-2
Julie Halard (FRA)	Kerry-Anne Guse (AUS)	6-0 6-2
ANKE HUBER (GER, 7)	Leila Meshki (GEO)	6-1 6-3
JANA NOVOTNA (CZE, 5)	Fang Li (CHN)	6-1 6-3
Helen Kelesi (CAN)	Silvia Farina (ITA)	6-1 6-1
Christina Singer (GER)	Irina Spirlea (ROM)	6-2 6-4
Jane Taylor (AUS)	Caroline Vis (HOL)	6-2 6-7 6-4
Gigi Fernandez (PR)	Naoko Kijimuta (JAP)	6-1 6-4
Yone Kamio (JAP)	Lisa McShea (AUS)	6-1 6-3
Emanuela Zardo (SWI)	Katarina Studenikova (SLVK)	6-4 7-5
Yayuk Basuki (INDO)	NATHALIE TAUZIAT (FRA, 15)	6-4 7-6
MARY PIERCE (FRA, 9)	Nathalie Baudone (ITA)	6-2 6-1
Linda Harvey-Wild (USA)	Sandra Dopfer (AUT)	6-3 6-2
Florencia Labat (ARG)	Virginia Ruano Pascual (SPA)	6-3 6-1
Sabine Appelmans (BEL)	Noelle Van Lottum (FRA)	5-7 6-2 3-0 ret
Tami Whitlinger (USA)	Maria José Gaidano (ARG)	6-3 6-2
Linda Ferrando (ITA)	Jolene Watanabe (USA)	6-4 6-3
Natalya Medvedeva (UKR)	Nicole Muns-Jagerman (HOL)	7-5 6-2
GABRIELA SABATINI (ARG, 4)	Stephanie Rottier (HOL)	7-6 6-3
MANUELA M-FRAGNIÈRE (SWI)	Laura Golarsa (ITA)	6-0 6-3
Catalina Cristea (ROM)	Joanne Limmer (AUS)	7-6 6-3
Patricia Tarabini (ARG)	Angelica Gavaldon (MEX)	6-4 7-6
Romana Tedjakusuma (INDO)	Karine Quentrec (FRA)	6-0 6-4
Nanne Dahlman (FIN)	Radka Zrubakova (CZE)	6-2 6-7 7-5
Beate Reinstadler (AUT)	Shaun Stafford (USA)	6-2 6-4

Tracy Austin (USA)	Elna Reinach (SAF)	6-1 7-5
Sabine Hack (GER)	ZINA GARRISON JACKSON (USA, 11)	7-5 6-3
Magdalena Maleeva (BUL)	Sandra Cacic (USA)	6-3 6-1
Naoko Sawamatsu (JAP)	Michelle Jaggard-Lai (AUS)	6-4 6-1
Anna Smashnova (ISR)	Ruxandra Dragomir (ROM)	6-2 6-2
Yelena Likhovtseva (KAZ)	Rosana de los Rios (PAR)	6-2 6-2
Tatiana Ignatieva (BYL)	Magdalena Mroz (POL)	6-1 6-2
Ann Grossman (USA)	Nicole Arendt (USA)	6-7 6-3 6-0
Wang Shi-ting (TAIW)	Audra Keller (USA)	6-4 6-0
ARANTXA SÁNCHEZ V. (SPA, 2)	Karina Habsudova (SLVK)	6-1 6-3

2nd ROUND

GRAF	Provis	6-1 6-4
Rittner	Shriver	6-4 3-6 6-2
Testud	Raymond	7-5 3-6 6-3
SUKOVA	Endo	6-4 5-7 7-5
DAVENPORT	Probst	6-1 7-5
Makarova	Simpson-Alter	6-3 7-6
Kuhlman	Ercegovic	7-5 4-6 6-1
MJ FERNANDEZ	Gorrochategui	6-3 2-6 9-7
MARTÍNEZ	Fendick	6-7 6-1 6-4
Frazier	Bobkova	6-2 6-1
Radford	Kochta	7-5 6-2
Rubin	COETZER	6-1 2-6 6-3
DATE	McGrath	6-4 6-2
McQuillan	Graham	6-2 3-6 6-4
Helgeson	Boogert	6-2 6-0
HUBER	Halard	7-6 3-6 6-3
NOVOTNA	Kelesi	6-3 6-1
Taylor	Singer	7-5 4-6 7-5
G Fernandez	Kamio	6-3 6-2
Zardo	Basuki	6-2 7-6
PIERCE	Harvey-Wild	6-7 7-5 6-3
Appelmans	Labat	6-2 6-3
Ferrando	Whitlinger	6-4 6-1
SABATINI	Medvedeva	6-1 3-6 7-5
MALEEVA-FRAGNIÈRE	Cristea	5-7 6-4 6-4
Tedjakusuma	Tarabini	6-2 7-6
Reinstadler	Dahlman	6-3 4-6 7-5
Hack	Austin	6-1 5-7 6-2
Magd. MALEEVA	Sawamatsu	6-2 6-4
Likhovtseva	Smashnova	2-6 6-2 6-1
Grossman	Ignatieva	6-1 6-0
SÁNCHEZ VICÁRIO	Wang	6-2 6-4

3rd ROUND

GRAF	Rittner	6-2 6-4
Testud	SUKOVA	6-4 6-3
DAVENPORT	Makarova	6-1 6-2
MJ FERNANDEZ	Kuhlman	6-4 6-1
MARTÍNEZ	Frazier	6-3 6-0
Rubin	Radford	6-3 7-6
DATE	McQuillan	6-3 7-5
Helgeson	HUBER	3-6 7-6 6-4
NOVOTNA	Taylor	6-4 6-2
Zardo	G Fernandez	7-6 6-4
PIERCE	Appelmans	6-3 6-2
SABATINI	Ferrando	6-2 6-1
MALEEVA-FRAGNIÈRE	Tedjakusuma	6-0 6-1

Hack	Reinstadler	6-3 3-6 7-5
Magd. MALEEVA	Likhovtseva	6-4 6-2
SÁNCHEZ VICÁRIO	Grossman	6-2 6-3

4th ROUND

GRAF	Testud	6-1 6-2
DAVENPORT	MJ FERNANDEZ	6-2 6-7 6-2
MARTÍNEZ	Rubin	7-6 6-3
DATE	Helgeson	7-5 6-1
NOVOTNA	Zardo	6-2 7-5
SABATINI	PIERCE	6-3 6-3
MALEEVA-FRAGNIÈRE	Hack	7-6 6-7 7-5
SÁNCHEZ VICÁRIO	Magd, Maleeva	4-6 6-1 6-3

QUARTER-FINALS

GRAF	DAVENPORT	6-3 6-2
DATE	MARTÍNEZ	6-2 4-6 6-3
SABATINI	NOVOTNA	6-3 6-4
SÁNCHEZ VICÁRIO	MALEEVA-FRAGNÈRE	7-6 6-4

Date becomes the first Japanese woman to reach a Grand Slam semi-final since Kazuko Sawamatsu at the same championships in 1973. Sánchez Vicário beats two of the Maleeva sisters in consecutive matches.

SEMI-FINALS

| GRAF | DATE | 6-3 6-3 |
| SÁNCHEZ VICÁRIO | SABATINI | 6-1 6-2 |

FINAL 29 Jan 1994

| GRAF | SÁNCHEZ VICÁRIO | 6-0 6-2 |

By winning the briefest Australian final since Margaret Court beat Jan Lehane in 1962, Graf becomes the only player to twice hold all four Grand Slam titles simultaneously.

Men's Doubles

SEMI-FINALS

Jacco Eltingh	HOL	Martin Damm	CZE	6-1 6-4 6-2
Paul Haarhuis	HOL	Karel Novacek		
Byron Black	ZIM	Jan Apell	SWE	6-1 6-4 6-4
Jonathan Stark	USA	Jonas Björkman	SWE	

FINAL

| Eltingh & Haarhuis | Black & Stark | 6-7 6-3 6-4 6-3 |

Women's Doubles

SEMI-FINALS

Gigi Fernandez	PR	Pam Shriver	USA	6-3 6-3
Natalya Zvereva	LAT	Liz Smylie	AUS	
Patty Fendick	USA	Jana Novotna	CZE	6-3 7-5
Meredith McGrath	USA	Arantxa Sánchez Vicário	SPA	

FINAL

| Fernandez & Zvereva | Fendick & McGrath | 6-3 4-6 6-4 |

Mixed Doubles

SEMI-FINALS

Todd Woodbridge	AUS	Emilio Sánchez	SPA	6-3 6-4	
Helena Sukova	CZE	Arantxa Sánchez Vicário	SPA		
Andrei Olhovskiy	RUS	Paul Haarhuis	HOL	6-1 1-0 ret	
Larissa Savchenko Neiland	LAT	Natalya Medvedeva	UKR		

FINAL

Olhovskiy & Savchenko Neiland	Woodbridge & Sukova	7-5 6-7 6-2	

Junior Men

FINAL

Ben Ellwood	AUS	Andrew Ilie	AUS	5-7 6-3 6-3

Junior Women

FINAL

Trudi Musgrave	AUS	Barbara Schett	AUT	4-6 6-4 6-2

French Open

Seeds in capitals

Men's Singles

1st ROUND

PETE SAMPRAS (USA)	Alberto Costa (SPA)	6-3 6-4 6-4
Marcelo Rios (CHILE)	Joshua Eagle (AUS)	6-2 6-3 6-2
Lars Jonsson (SWE)	Mikail Pernfors (SWE)	7-5 6-2 1-0 ret
Paul Haarhuis (HOL)	Henri Leconte (FRA)	6-4 6-4 6-2
Mikael Tillström (SWE)	Markus Zöcke (GER)	6-4 3-6 6-3 6-4
Andrei Olhovskiy (RUS)	Steve Bryan (USA)	6-3 6-3 6-3
Thierry Champion (FRA)	Jamie Morgan (AUS)	4-6 7-5 3-6 7-6 9-7
Richard Krajicek (HOL)	Karel Novacek (CZE)	6-1 7-5 7-5
Jonathan Stark (USA)	Brent Larkham (AUS)	6-2 6-3 6-7 6-3
Fabrice Santoro (FRA)	Kenneth Carlsen (DEN)	7-6 6-3 6-4
Agustin Garizzio (ARG)	Gérard Solves (FRA)	3-6 6-1 6-2 6-4
Olivier Delaitre (FRA)	Luis Mattar (BRZ)	7-6 7-6 ret
Ctislav (Slava) Dosedel (SLVK)	Alex Antonitsch (AUT)	6-3 6-4 6-4
Jonas Björkman (SWE)	Patricio Arnold (ARG)	6-7 7-6 6-1 3-6 9-7
Stefano Pescosolido (ITA)	Karsten Braasch (GER)	4-6 7-6 7-5 6-3
JIM COURIER (USA)	Jean-Philippe Fleurian (FRA)	6-1 6-4 6-4
ANDREI MEDVEDEV (UKR)	Wally Masur (AUS)	6-2 6-4 6-2
Nicklas Kulti (SWE)	Frédéric Fontang (FRA)	6-3 6-4 6-7 3-6 6-1
Greg Rusedski (CAN)	Markus Göllner (GER)	7-6 6-3 7-6
Aleksandr Volkov (RUS)	Marcus Ondruska (SAF)	6-7 6-3 6-2 6-3
Jacco Eltingh (HOL)	Carl-Uwe Steeb (GER)	7-6 6-2 6-3
David Wheaton (USA)	Thomas Enqvist (SWE)	7-6 6-2 6-3
Daniel Vacek (CZE)	Javier Sánchez (SPA)	7-6 0-6 6-2 6-4
MAGNUS GUSTAFSSON (SWE)	Jordi Burillo (SPA)	7-5 3-6 7-5 6-2
THOMAS MUSTER (AUT)	Andrei Cherkasov (RUS)	6-0 7-5 6-1
André Agassi (USA)	Mats Wilander (SWE)	6-2 7-5 6-1
Patrick Rafter (AUS)	Franco Davin (ARG)	6-7 6-4 2-6 6-4

Lionel Roux (FRA)	Gabriel Markus (ARG)	7-5 6-1 7-6
David Prinosil (GER)	Emilio Sánchez (SPA)	2-6 7-6 6-3 7-6
Ronald Agenor (HAITI)	Lionel Barthez (FRA)	2-6 1-6 6-2 6-4 6-2
Christian Ruud (NOR)	Gilbert Schaller (AUT)	6-4 6-4 6-2
SERGI BRUGUERA (SPA)	Martin Damm (CZE)	6-1 6-1 7-6
GORAN IVANISEVIC (CRO)	Jörn Renzenbrink (GER)	7-6 7-6 6-2
Brian Shelton (USA)	Martin Blackman (USA)	4-6 6-3 7-6 6-3
Alex O'Brien (USA)	Marc Rosset (SWI)	6-2 6-7 6-7 6-3 8-6
Alex Corretja (SPA)	Fernando Meligeni (BRZ)	6-3 6-1 1-6 5-7 6-3
Karol Kucera (SLVK)	Maurice Ruah (VEN)	6-2 6-3 6-1
Arnaud Boetsch (FRA)	Ivan Lendl (USA)	6-4 6-3 6-4
Brad Gilbert (USA)	Cristiano Caratti (ITA)	6-2 6-2 6-3
Andrea Gaudenzi (ITA)	PETR KORDA (CZE)	6-2 5-7 6-7 6-2 6-2
CÉDRIC PIOLINE (FRA)	Jakob Hlasek (SWI)	6-4 3-6 6-4 6-3
Alberto Berasategui (SPA)	Wayne Ferreira (SAF)	6-3 ret
Bernd Karbacher (GER)	Tomás Carbonell (SPA)	7-5 6-2 3-6 4-6 6-0
Yevgeny Kafelnikov (RUS)	Thierry Guardiola (FRA)	4-6 7-5 6-4 4-6 6-4
Richard Fromberg (AUS)	Byron Black (ZIM)	7-6 5-7 7-6 6-1
Mark Woodforde (AUS)	Lars Wahlgren (SWE)	4-6 6-2 6-1 7-6
Javier Frana (ARG)	Malivai Washington (USA)	7-5 6-1 6-3
Henrik Holm (SWE)	STEFAN EDBERG (SWE)	7-5 7-6 6-7 6-7 6-4
MICHAEL CHANG (USA)	Jim Grabb (USA)	6-3 7-6 6-1
Jordi Arrese (SPA)	Rodolphe Gilbert (FRA)	4-6 6-3 6-1 6-3
Jaime Yzaga (PERU)	Patrick McEnroe (USA)	6-2 6-3 6-2
Jared Palmer (USA)	Amos Mansdorf (ISR)	6-4 6-0 6-2
Jeff Tarango (USA)	Chuck Adams (USA)	6-4 3-6 6-2 6-1
Magnus Larsson (SWE)	Brett Steven (NZ)	6-2 6-2 6-2
Francisco Clavet (SPA)	Darren Cahill (AUS)	4-6 4-6 6-4 6-4 6-1
TODD MARTIN (USA)	Stéphane Simian (FRA)	6-2 7-6 3-6 6-1
CARLOS COSTA (SPA)	Guillaume Raoux (FRA)	6-1 7-6 6-1
Hendrik Dreekmann (GER)	Adrian Voinea (ROM)	6-2 4-6 7-5 6-4
David Rikl (CZE)	Andrei Chesnokov (RUS)	6-1 2-1 ret
Richey Reneberg (USA)	Jason Stoltenberg (AUS)	1-6 6-3 6-3 6-3 7-5
Dmitry Poliakov (UKR)	Grant Stafford (SAF)	6-2 7-6 6-4
Radomir Vasek (CZE)	Younes El Aynaoui (MOR)	6-3 6-4 7-6
Aaron Krickstein (USA)	Horacio de la Peña (ARG)	6-3 6-4 6-1
MICHAEL STICH (GER)	Renzo Furlan (ITA)	6-1 7-5 6-4

2nd ROUND

SAMPRAS	Rios	7-6 7-6 6-4
Haarhuis	Jonsson	6-3 2-6 1-6 7-5 6-3
Tillström	Olhovskiy	6-3 7-6 6-4
KRAJICEK	Champion	6-3 6-3 4-6 6-2
Santoro	Stark	6-2 6-2 6-2
Delaître	Garizzio	6-4 6-0 7-6
Björkman	Dosedel	6-0 7-5 6-3
COURIER	Pescosolido	7-5 6-0 6-7 6-4
MEDVEDEV	Kulti	6-4 7-6 4-6 7-5
Rusedski	Volkov	7-5 6-3 2-6 6-3
Eltingh	Wheaton	6-3 4-6 7-6 6-7 6-4
Vacek	GUSTAFSSON	0-6 6-4 7-6 6-4
MUSTER	Agassi	6-3 6-7 7-5 2-6 7-5
Rafter	Roux	6-2 6-4 6-4
Agenor	Prinosil	6-7 6-7 6-3 6-4 6-1
BRUGUERA	Ruud	6-2 6-2 7-6
IVANISEVIC	Shelton	1-6 6-1 6-2 6-4
Corretja	O'Brien	6-2 4-6 6-2 6-4
Boetsch	Kucera	6-2 6-2 6-3

Gaudenzi	B Gilbert	7-5 6-3 6-3
Berasategui	PIOLINE	6-4 7-5 6-3
Kafelnikov	Karbacher	6-2 1-6 6-2 6-2
Woodforde	Fromberg	6-2 7-5 7-6
Frana	Holm	6-4 6-4 6-4
CHANG	Arrese	4-6 6-0 6-4 6-2
Yzaga	Palmer	7-6 6-4 4-6 6-1
Larsson	Tarango	6-2 6-4 6-3
MARTIN	Clavet	6-0 6-0 6-2
Dreekmann	C COSTA	7-6 6-4 6-4
Reneberg	Rikl	7-6 6-1 5-7 6-3
Vasek	Poliakov	4-6 2-6 7-5 6-3 6-1
Krickstein	STICH	6-3 6-3 6-4

3rd ROUND

SAMPRAS	Haarhuis	6-1 6-4 6-1
Tillström	KRAJICEK	7-6 6-2 6-3
Delaître	Santoro	1-6 3-6 7-6 6-4 6-2
COURIER	Björkman	6-3 6-1 6-1
MEDVEDEV	Rusedski	2-6 6-3 6-4 3-6 6-2
Eltingh	Vacek	7-6 7-6 2-6 6-3
Rafter	MUSTER	6-4 5-7 6-3 6-3
BRUGUERA	Agenor	6-3 6-3 6-3
IVANISEVIC	Corretja	6-7 3-6 6-1 6-2 6-3
Gaudenzi	Boetsch	6-1 2-1 ret
Berasategui	Kafelnikov	6-3 6-2 6-2
Frana	Woodforde	6-4 3-6 6-0 4-6 10-8
Yzaga	CHANG	6-2 6-3 5-7 1-6 7-5
Larsson	MARTIN	6-7 6-3 6-0 1-6 6-3
Dreekmann	Reneberg	4-6 3-6 6-4 6-4 6-4
Krickstein	Vasek	6-3 1-6 6-3 6-3

4th ROUND

SAMPRAS	Tillström	6-4 6-4 1-6 6-4
COURIER	Delaître	6-1 6-7 6-1 7-6
MEDVEDEV	Eltingh	6-4 3-6 6-4 6-1
BRUGUERA	Rafter	6-4 6-3 6-1
IVANISEVIC	Gaudenzi	6-2 5-7 6-4 6-3
Berasategui	Frana	6-2 6-0 ret
Larsson	Yzaga	6-3 6-2 6-2
Dreekmann	Krickstein	6-4 6-4 6-4

Dreekmann (19) is only the third player to reach the quarter-finals in his first Grand Slam tournament.

QUARTER-FINALS

COURIER	SAMPRAS	6-4 5-7 6-4 6-4
BRUGUERA	MEDVEDEV	6-3 6-2 7-5
Berasategui	IVANISEVIC	6-4 6-3 6-3
Larsson	Dreekmann	3-6 6-7 7-6 6-0 6-1

Two Spaniards in the last four for the first time since 1972. Larsson saves six match points.

SEMI-FINALS

BRUGUERA	COURIER	6-3 5-7 6-3 6-3
Berasategui	Larsson	6-3 6-4 6-1

FINAL 5 June 1994

BRUGUERA	Berasategui	6-3 7-5 2-6 6-1

Bruguera beats the unseeded Berasategui (the only ranked player to use the ancient Western Grip, holding the racquet the same way for forehand & backhand) to retain the title in the first Grand Slam final between two Spanish players and complete another unique feat: both French singles titles won by Spaniards.

Women's Singles

1st ROUND

STEFFI GRAF (GER)	Katarina Studenikova (SLVK)	6-2 6-2
Stephanie Rottier (HOL)	Natalya Medvedeva (UKR)	6-2 3-6 6-3
Radka Zrubakova (SLVK)	Nathalie Herreman (FRA)	6-0 61
Joanette Kruger (SAF)	Eugenia Maniokova (RUS)	4-6 6-0 6-3
Karine Quentrec (FRA)	Eva Martincova (CZE)	6-2 3-6 6-4
Irina Spirlea (ROM)	Katerina Kroupova (CZE)	6-3 6-1
Angelica Gavaldon (MEX)	Christine Singer (GER)	7-5 6-0
MARY JOE FERNANDEZ (USA)	Karina Habsudova (SLVK)	6-4 3-6 6-1
HELENA SUKOVA (CZE)	Laurence Courtois (BEL)	6-3 7-5
Clare Wood (UK)	Gigi Fernandez (PR)	6-3 2-6 6-2
Naoko Sawamatsu (JAP)	Laura Garrone (ITA)	4-6 6-4 6-0
Inés Gorochategui (ARG)	Michelle Jaggard-Lai (AUS)	6-3 6-2
Karin Kschwendt (GER)	Angelique Olivier (FRA)	5-7 6-4 9-7
Kimblerly Po (USA)	Catherine Mothes (FRA)	6-1 6-1
Iva Majoli (CRO)	Dominique Monami (BEL)	6-1 7-5
Silvia Farina (ITA)	GABRIELA SABATINI (ARG)	2-6 6-2 6-4
Miriam Oremans (HOL)	MARTINA NAVRATILOVA (USA)	6-4 6-4
Sabine Appelmans (BEL)	Amelie Castera (FRA)	6-4 6-1
Nathalie Tauziat (FRA)	Beate Reinstadler (AUT)	7-5 6-2
Petra Ritter (AUT)	Lisa Raymond (USA)	3-6 6-2 11-9
Ludmila Richterova (CZE)	Barbara Schett (AUT)	6-1 7-6
Tami Whitlinger Jones (USA)	Kyoko Nagatsuka (JAP)	6-4 2-6 6-3
Anna-Maria (Sandra) Cecchini (ITA)	Amy Frazier (USA)	3-6 6-1 7-5
Ruxandra Dragomir (ROM)	MAGDALENA MALEEVA (BUL)	6-3 7-5
MARY PIERCE (FRA)	Nicole Provis (AUS)	6-1 6-0
Maria-Francesca Bentivoglio (ITA)	Patricia Hy (CAN)	4-6 4-2 ret
Kristie Boogert (HOL)	Isabelle Demongeot (FRA)	6-2 6-2
Lori McNeil (USA)	Caroline Vis (HOL)	6-0 6-2
Marketa Kochta (GER)	Tracy Austin (USA)	6-0 6-1
Katerina Maleeva (BUL)	Linda Harvey-Wild (USA)	6-1 6-4
Radka Bobkova (CZE)	Rachel McQuillan (AUS)	6-3 5-7 7-5
Amanda Coetzer (SAF)	KIMIKO DATE (JAP)	6-2 6-1
Anna Smashnova (ISR)	JANA NOVOTNA (CZE	6-4 6-2
Shaun Stafford (USA)	Yelena Makarova (RUS)	6-2 6-1
Ann Grossman (USA)	Maria Angeles Montolio (SPA)	6-2 6-1
Petra Langrova (CZE)	Bettina Fulco-Villella (ARG)	7-5 2-6 6-3
Fang Li (CHN)	Helen Kelesi (CAN)	6-7 6-1 6-3
Aléxandra Fusai (FRA)	Nicole Muns-Jagerman (HOL)	6-3 7-5
Yelena Brioukhovets (UKR)	Manon Bollegraf (HOL)	6-4 6-3
SABINE HACK (GER)	Maria José Gaidano (ARG)	6-2 6-1
Silke Frankl (GER)	ZINA GARRISON JACKSON (USA)	6-3 4-6 6-2
Marzia Grossi (ITA)	Caroline Kuhlman (USA)	6-4 6-4
Alexia Dechaume-Balleret (FRA)	Emanuela Zardo (SWI)	6-3 6-1
Wiltrud Probst (GER)	Carole Lucarelli (FRA)	6-4 6-1
Marianne Werdel (USA)	Pam Shriver (USA)	6-3 6-2
Brenda Schultz (HOL)	Paola Suarez (ARG)	6-1 6-1
Ginger Helgeson (USA)	Elna Reinach (SAF)	4-6 6-4 6-3
CONCHITA MARTÍNEZ (SPA)	Larissa Savchenko Neiland (LAT)	6-2 6-3
NATALYA ZVEREVA (BYL)	Romana Tedjakusuma (INDO)	6-0 6-1
Judith Wiesner (AUT)	Petra Kamstra (HOL)	7-5 6-1
Silke Meier (GER)	Yone Kamio (JAP)	6-1 6-3
Wang Shi-ting (TAI)	Asa Carlsson (SWE)	7-5 7-6
Petra Begerow (GER)	Meredith McGrath (USA)	6-2 4-6 9-7
Julie Halard (FRA)	Patricia Tarabini (ARG)	6-3 6-2

Katarzyna Nowak POL	Lea Ghirardi (FRA)	6-4 6-2
LINDSAY DAVENPORT (USA)	Chanda Rubin (USA)	6-7 6-4 6-3
ANKE HUBER (GER)	Sandrine Testud (FRA)	7-6 6-3
Meike Babel (GER)	Patty Fendick (USA)	6-3 6-4
Leila Meshki (GEO)	Catalina Cristea (ROM)	6-2 4-6 6-4
Sandra Cacic (USA)	Mana Endo (JAP)	6-3 6-4
Barbara Rittner (GER)	Kristine Radford (AUS)	6-1 6-2
Sandra Dopfer (AUS)	Laura Golarsa (ITA)	6-3 3-6 6-1
Noelle Van Lottum (FRA)	Linda Ferrando (ITA)	6-2 6-2
ARANTXA SÁNCHEZ VICÁRIO (SPA)	Florencia Labat (ARG)	6-4 6-1

Navratilova goes out in the first round for only the fourth time in 64 Grand Slam tournaments (the first since 1976). Sabatini loses to an opponent she'd beaten 6-0 6-0 in both their previous matches.

2nd ROUND

GRAF	Rottier	7-5 6-3
Kruger	Zrubakova	4-6 7-5 6-3
Spirlea	Quentrec	7-5 6-0
MJ FERNANDEZ	Gavaldon	6-0 6-1
SUKOVA	Wood	2-6 6-3 6-2
Gorrochategui	Sawamatsu	7-5 6-4
Kschwendt	Po	2-6 6-1 7-5
Majoli	Farina	6-4 6-1
Oremans	Appelmans	6-3 1-6 6-4
Ritter	Tauziat	6-3 6-1
Richterova	Whitlinger	6-4 6-2
Dragomir	Cecchini	6-2 4-6 6-1
PIERCE	Bentivoglio	6-0 6-1
McNeil	Boogert	4-6 6-1 6-2
Kochta	K Maleeva	0-6 6-3 6-2
Coetzer	Bobkova	6-4 6-4
Stafford	Smashnova	6-4 6-1
Grossman	Langrova	3-6 6-4 6-3
Fusai	Fang Li	6-0 6-2
HACK	Brioukhovets	6-2 3-6 6-1
Grossi	Frankl	6-3 6-1
Dechaume-Balleret	Probst	7-6 6-2
Schultz	Werdel	6-4 7-6
MARTÍNEZ	Helgson	6-2 6-3
ZVEREVA	Wiesner	7-5 7-5
Wang	Meier	6-4 6-2
Halard	Begerow	7-5 4-6 6-4
DAVENPORT	Nowak	6-4 6-2
HUBER	Babel	7-6 6-2
Meshki	Cacic	7-6 4-6 7-5
Rittner	Dopfer	6-2 6-3
SÁNCHEZ VICÁRIO	Van Lottum	6-1 6-0

3rd ROUND

GRAF	Kruger	6-0 4-6 6-2
Spirlea	MJ FERNANDEZ	6-4 6-1
Gorrochategui	SUKOVA	7-6 7-6
Majoli	Kschwendt	3-6 6-3 6-2
Ritter	Oremans	4-6 6-2 6-1
Dragomir	Richterova	6-3 6-4
PIERCE	McNeil	6-0 6-0
Coetzer	Kochta	6-0 6-3
Stafford	Grossman	6-7 6-3 6-3
HACK	Fusai	6-0 6-7 6-1

Dechaume-Balleret	Grossi	6-3 6-2
MARTÍNEZ	Schultz	7-5 6-3
ZVEREVA	Wang Shi Ting	6-2 6-1
Halard	DAVENPORT	6-4 6-2
HUBER	Meshki	6-1 6-4
SÁNCHEZ VICÁRIO	Rittner	6-4 6-2

4th ROUND

GRAF	Spirlea	6-0 6-1
Gorrochategui	Majoli	7-5 6-4
Ritter	Dragomir	7-6 4-6 6-0
PIERCE	Coetzer	6-1 6-1
HACK	Stafford	6-4 6-2
MARTÍNEZ	Dechaume-Balleret	6-1 6-2
Halard	ZVEREVA	7-6 7-5
SÁNCHEZ VICÁRIO	HUBER	6-3 6-2

QUARTER-FINALS

GRAF	Gorochategui	6-4 6-1
PIERCE	Ritter	6-0 6-2
MARTÍNEZ	HACK	2-6 6-0 6-2
SÁNCHEZ VICÁRIO	Halard	6-1 7-6

Pierce, of the infamous American father, reaches the semis after dropping only six games in five matches, a record for a Grand Slam event since tennis went Open. Only her compatriot (so to speak) Suzanne Lenglen ever matched this kind of domination, conceding only five games in five matches at Wimbledon in 1925 and six games in the 1926 French.

SEMI-FINALS

PIERCE	GRAF	6-2 6-2
SÁNCHEZ VICÁRIO	MARTÍNEZ	6-3 6-1

For the first time since 1990, someone other than Graf or Monica Seles will win a Grand Slam singles tournament. Pierce becomes the first 'French' woman to reach the final since Françoise Durr won it in 1967.

FINAL 5 June 1994

SÁNCHEZ VICÁRIO	PIERCE	6-4 6-4

Rain postpones the final for a day with Pierce leading 3-1 in the first set.

Men's Doubles

SEMI-FINALS

Jan APELL	SWE	GRANT CONNELL	CAN	7-6 6-3
JONAS BJÖRKMAN	SWE	PATRICK GALBRAITH	USA	
BYRON BLACK	ZIM	DAVID ADAMS	AUS	6-3 6-3
JONATHAN STARK	USA	ANDREI OLHOVSKIY	RUS	

FINAL

BLACK & STARK	APELL & BJÖRKMAN	6-4 7-6

Women's Doubles

SEMI-FINALS

LINDSAY DAVENPORT	USA	AMANDA COETZER	SAF	7-6 6-7 6-4
LISA RAYMOND	USA	INÉS GORROCHATEGUI	ARG	
GIGI FERNANDEZ	PR	JULIE HALARD	FRA	4-6 6-2 6-4
NATALYA ZVEREVA	BYL	NATHALIE TAUZIAT	FRA	

FINAL

FERNANDEZ & ZVEREVA	DAVENPORT & RAYMOND	6-2 6-2

Mixed Doubles

SEMI-FINALS

LARISSA NEILAND	LAT	HELENA SUKOVA	CZE	7-6 6-2
ANDREI OLHOVSKIY	RUS	ANDREI OLHOVSKIY	RUS	
Kristie Boogert	HOL	MEREDITH McGRATH	USA	0-6 6-2 6-3
Menno Oosting	HOL	S MELVILLE	USA	

FINAL

| Boogert & Oosting | NEILAND & OLHOVSKIY | 7-5 3-6 7-5 |

Junior Men's Singles

FINAL

| Jacobo Diaz (SPA) | Giorgio Galimbert (ITA) | 6-3 7-6 |

Junior Women's Singles

FINAL

| Martina Hingis (SWI) | Sonya Jeyaseelan (CAN) | 6-3 6-1 |

The astonishingly precocious Hingis retains the title at the age of 13.

US Open

Seeds in capitals, seeding numbers in brackets

Men's Singles

1st ROUND

PETE SAMPRAS (USA, 1)	Kevin Ullyett (USA)	6-2 6-2 6-2
Daniel Vacek (CZE)	Younes El Aynaoui (MOR)	6-7 7-5 6-1 6-1
Henrik Holm (SWE)	Greg Rusedski (CAN)	6-3 6-2 3-6 7-5
Roger Smith (BAH)	Diego Nargiso (ITA)	7-6 6-4 6-0
David Witt (USA)	Wally Masur (AUS)	6-2 3-6 7-5 6-1
Jaime Yzaga (PERU)	Gabriel Markus (ARG)	7-6 6-2 6-2
Rodolphe Gilbert (FRA)	Mauricio Hadad (COL)	6-4 6-2 6-7 2-6 7-6
Cédric Pioline (FRA)	Oliver Gross (GER)	6-2 7-5 4-6 6-4
Marius Ondruska (SAF)	ALBERTO BERASATEGUI (SPA, 10)	6-1 2-6 6-3 6-3
Christian Bergström (SWE)	Tommy Ho (USA)	6-3 6-3 7-6
Vincent Spadea (USA)	Tamir El Sawy (EGY)	7-6 4-6 6-4 6-2
Javier Frana (ARG)	Mark Merklein (USA)	6-4 1-6 4-6 7-6 6-0
Mark Petchey (UK)	Karol Kucera (SLVK)	6-4 7-6 6-3
Todd Woodbridge (AUS)	Paul Kilderry (AUS)	6-2 7-5 6-2
Karel Novacek (CZE)	Aleksandr Volkov (RUS)	6-2 3-6 6-1 7-5
ANDREI MEDVEDEV (UKR, 8)	Gilbert Schaller (AUT)	6-3 6-4 6-0
MICHAEL STICH (GER, 4)	Olivier Delaitre (FRA)	7-6 6-3 6-3
Steve Bryan (USA)	Franco Davin (ARG)	6-0 6-1 6-1
Francisco Clavet (SPA)	Jean-Philippe Fleurian (FRA)	6-3 4-6 6-3 7-6
Byron Black (ZIM)	Patrick McEnroe (USA)	7-6 6-2 6-4
Richard Krajicek (HOL)	Jan Siemerink (HOL)	7-6 6-4 6-7 6-7 6-4
Carlos Costa (SPA)	Nicolas Pereira (VEN)	4-6 7-5 6-4 5-7 6-4
Martin Damm (CZE)	Fernando Meligeni (BRZ)	6-2 6-3 4-6 6-4
YEVGENY KAFELNIKOV (RUS, 14)	Jacco Eltingh (HOL)	7-6 7-5 6-3
JIM COURIER (USA, 11)	Aaron Krickstein (USA)	6-3 6-4 6-4

Andrea Gaudenzi (ITA)	Albert Chang (CAN)	7-6 6-1 7-6
Karim Alami (MOR)	Alberto Costa (SPA)	6-1 7-5 6-2
Jörn Renzenbrink (GER)	Grant Stafford (SAF)	6-1 6-4 6-4
Alex O'Brien (USA)	Paul Haarhuis (HOL)	6-3 7-6 6-3
Jonas Björkman (SWE)	Jonathan Stark (USA	6-2 6-2 7-5
Jeff Tarango (USA)	Lars Wahlgren (SWE)	4-6 7-5 6-4 3-6 6-3
STEFAN EDBERG (SWE, 5)	Lars Jonsson (SWE)	7-5 6-1 6-1
MICHAEL CHANG (USA, 6)	Andrei Cherkasov (RUS)	6-4 6-2 6-2
Malivai Washington (USA)	Karsten Braasch (GER)	6-7 6-3 3-6 6-3 6-3
Jim Grabb (USA)	Magnus Larsson (SWE)	6-7 5-7 6-3 6-3 6-3
Ellis Ferreira (SAF)	Arnaud Boetsch (FRA)	7-6 6-4 6-4
André Agassi (USA)	Robert Eriksson (SWE)	6-3 6-2 6-0
Guy Forget (FRA)	Mats Wilander (SWE)	7-5 6-1 6-4
Marcelo Rios (CHILE)	Jared Palmer (USA)	6-2 7-6 6-2
WAYNE FERREIRA (SAF, 12)	Wade McGuire (USA)	7-5 6-2 6-2
THOMAS MUSTER (AUT, 13)	Daniel Musa (ITA)	6-3 6-2 6-0
Maurice Ruah (VEN)	Jeremy Bates (UK)	6-7 7-6 6-4 2-6 6-4
Thomas Enqvist (SWE)	Alex Corretja (SPA)	4-6 6-3 6-4 6-7 6-1
Hendrik Dreekman (GER)	Jonas Svensson (SWE)	6-4 6-4 6-2
Marc Göllner (GER)	Brett Steven (NZ)	7-6 6-4 3-6 6-1
Tomás Carbonell (SPA)	Alex Antonitsch (AUT)	1-6 6-7 7-6 6-2 6-3
Andrei Olhovskiy (UKR)	Jason Stoltenberg (AUS)	1-6 4-6 6-4 6-3 6-4
SERGI BRUGUERA (SPA, 3)	Brian Shelton (USA)	6-0 6-2 7-5
Richey Reneberg (USA)	BORIS BECKER (GER, 7)	6-1 6-4 4-6 1-6 7-6
Jordi Burillo (SPA)	Kenneth Carlsen (DEN)	6-3 7-6 6-7 6-4
Richard Fromberg (AUS)	David Wheaton (USA)	4-6 6-4 6-2 3-6 6-3
Ronald Agenor (HAITI)	Paul Goldstein (USA)	6-4 6-3 6-4
Patrick Rafter (AUS)	David Rikl (CZE)	6-4 6-1 6-4
Jan Apell (SWE)	Stefano Pescosolido (ITA)	3-6 6-3 6-4 6-4
Andrei Chesnokov (RUS)	Javier Sánchez (SPA)	6-3 2-6 7-6 6-2
TODD MARTIN (USA, 9)	Guillaume Raoux (FRA)	6-7 4-6 6-3 6-4 7-6
MARC ROSSET (SWI, 15)	Mark Woodforde (AUS)	4-6 1-6 6-3 7-6 6-3
Nicklas Kulti (SWE)	Chuck Adams (USA)	7-6 2-6 3-6 6-4 6-4
Bernd Karbacher (GER)	Leander Paes (INDIA)	6-4 6-4 6-2
Ivan Lendl (USA)	Neil Borwick (AUS)	7-5 6-2 6-3
Gianluca Pozzi (ITA)	Renzo Furlan (ITA)	6-2 6-2 6-4
Amos Mansdorf (ISR)	Emilio Sánchez (SPA)	6-4 6-4 3-6 6-3
Robbie Weiss (USA)	Grant Doyle (AUS)	4-6 6-2 6-3 6-3
Markus Zöcke (GER)	GORAN IVANISEVIC (CRO, 2)	6-2 7-5 3-6 7-5

2nd ROUND

SAMPRAS	Vacek	6-3 6-4 6-4
Smith	Holm	4-6 7-6 6-3 1-6 7-6
Yzaga	Witt	6-1 6-7 6-4 6-4
Pioline	Gilbert	2-6 6-3 7-6 6-3
Ondruska	Bergström	7-6 6-3 6-0
Frana	Spadea	6-4 6-1 0-6 7-5
Woodbridge	Petchey	6-3 6-2 6-4
Novacek	MEDVEDEV	6-3 6-2 6-2
STICH	Bryan	6-1 6-4 6-2
Black	Clavet	7-5 1-6 3-6 6-1 6-4
Costa	Krajicek	4-6 7-6 6-3 1-6 7-6
KAFELNIKOV	Damm	6-3 7-6 7-6
Gaudenzi	COURIER	7-5 6-2 3-6 6-3
Renzenbrink	Alami	6-3 6-4 6-7 6-3
Björkman	O'Brien	6-2 6-3 6-4
EDBERG	Tarango	6-2 6-3 6-2
CHANG	Washington	4-6 6-2 6-3 7-6

Grabb	E Ferreira	4-6 6-4 6-2 6-3
Agassi	Forget	6-3 7-5 6-7 6-2
W FERREIRA	Rios	6-4 6-2 6-4
MUSTER	Ruah	6-4 4-6 6-4 6-2
Enqvist	Dreekman	7-6 7-6 6-7 7-5
Göllner	Carbonell	7-6 3-2 ret
BRUGUERA	Olhovskiy	7-5 6-2 7-6
Reneberg	Burillo	6-3 7-5 6-3
Fromberg	Agenor	6-3 6-3 6-4
Rafter	Apell	7-5 4-6 7-6 6-3
MARTIN	Chesnokov	6-3 6-2 7-5
ROSSET	Kulti	6-4 6-2 6-7 6-2
Karbacher	Lendl	6-4 7-6 1-0 ret
Pozzi	Mansdorf	4-6 7-5 3-6 7-5 6-3
Zöcke	Weiss	6-1 7-5 6-2

3rd ROUND

SAMPRAS	Smith	4-6 6-2 6-4 6-3
Yzaga	Pioline	1-6 5-7 7-5 6-1 6-4
Frana	Ondruska	6-3 6-1 6-7 3-6 6-4
Novacek	Woodbridge	1-6 5-7 7-6 6-2 7-6
STICH	Black	7-6 6-2 6-1
KAFELNIKOV	Costa	6-3 6-4 6-2
Renzenbrink	Gaudenzi	6-4 6-1 6-3
Björkman	EDBERG	6-4 6-4 6-0
CHANG	Grabb	6-1 4-1 ret
Agassi	W FERREIRA	7-5 6-1 7-5
MUSTER	Enqvist	6-0 6-4 6-1
BRUGUERA	Göllner	1-6 6-4 6-2 6-7 6-1
Reneberg	Fromberg	2-6 6-1 7-6 6-2
MARTIN	Rafter	7-5 6-3 6-7 6-2
Karbacher	ROSSET	4-6 6-4 4-6 6-1 6-2
Pozzi	Zöcke	2-6 6-4 6-2 6-2

4th ROUND

Yzaga	SAMPRAS	3-6 6-3 4-6 7-6 7-5
Novacek	Frana	6-3 6-3 6-7 6-3
STICH	KAFELNIKOV	7-6 6-3 6-2
Björkman	Renzenbrink	3-6 6-3 6-2 6-7 6-3
Agassi	CHANG	6-1 6-7 6-3 3-6 6-1
MUSTER	BRUGUERA	6-4 7-6 6-4
MARTIN	Reneberg	3-6 3-0 ret
Karbacher	Pozzi	6-2 4-6 6-3 6-4

For the first time since seeding was introduced (1927) only one of the top four seeds (Stich) reaches the quarter-finals.

QUARTER-FINALS

Novacek	Yzaga	6-2 6-7 6-1 5-7 6-3
STICH	Björkman	6-4 6-4 6-7 6-4
Agassi	MUSTER	7-6 6-3 6-0
MARTIN	Karbacher	6-4 7-6 4-6 6-4

SEMI-FINALS

STICH	Novacek	7-5 6-3 7-6
Agassi	MARTIN	6-3 4-6 6-2 6-3

FINAL 11 Sep 1994

Agassi	STICH	6-1 7-6 7-5

Stich, who lost in the opening round the previous year and won only one match in the three other Grand Slam tournaments this year, reaches a GS singles final for the first time since winning Wimbledon in 1991, but has no answer to a restored Agassi, the first unseeded player to reach the final since Jan Kodes (CZE) in 1971 and the first to win it since Fred Stolle (AUS) in 1966. The grandfather of his girlfriend Brooke Shields, Frank Shields, reached the US final in 1930 and scratched from the Wimbledon final a year later.

Women's Singles

1st ROUND

STEFFI GRAF (GER, 1)	Anne Mall (USA)	6-2 6-1
Sandra Cacic (USA)	Maria Angeles Montolio (SPA)	7-5 6-3
Nicole Provis Bradtke (AUS)	Jolene Watanabe (USA)	6-3 6-4
Radka Bobkova (CZE)	Kimberly Po (USA)	3-6 7-5 7-6
María José Gaidano (ARG)	Angela Lettiere (USA)	6-1 7-6
Alexia Dechaume-Balleret (FRA)	Miriam Oremans (HOL)	6-4 6-3
Paola Suarez (ARG)	Julie Steven (USA)	7-6 6-2
ZINA GARRISON JACKSON (USA, 10)	Kristine Radford (AUS)	6-3 6-4
AMANDA COETZER (SAF, 11)	Petra Ritter (AUT)	6-1 7-6
Eugenia Maniokova (RUS)	Helen Kelesi (CAN)	4-6 6-2 6-0
Marianne Werdel (USA)	Ludmila Richterova (CZE)	6-3 2-6 6-4
Mariaan De Swardt (SAF)	Yayuk Basuki (INDON)	6-3 6-4
Julie Halard (FRA)	Petra Langova (CZE)	6-1 3-6 6-2
Mana Endo (JAP)	Tami Whitlinger Jones (USA)	6-4 7-6
Pam Shriver (USA)	Beate Reinstadler (AUT)	7-6 6-4
LYNDSAY DAVENPORT (USA, 6)	Marzia Grossi (ITA)	6-1 6-1
MARY PIERCE (FRA, 4)	Andrea Temesvari (HUN)	6-3 6-2
Katarina Studenikova (SLVK)	Debbie Graham (USA)	6-3 3-6 6-4
Caroline Kuhlman (USA)	Silke Frankl (GER)	6-3 6-1
Judith Wiesner (AUT)	Romana Tedjakusuma (INDO)	6-2 6-0
Iva Majoli (CRO)	Noelle Van Lottum (FRA)	6-1 2-0 ret
Elna Reinach (SAF)	Dinky Van Rensburg (SAF)	6-3 2-6 6-4
Nicole Muns Jagerman (HOL)	Janette Husarova (SLVK)	7-5 6-1
Anna Smashnova (ISR)	LORI McNEIL (USA, 13)	6-2 6-4
MAGDALENA MALEEVA (BUL, 15)	Chanda Rubin (USA)	6-3 6-3
Ruxandra Dragomir (ROM)	Kristie Boogert (HOL)	7-5 6-2
Linda Harvey-Wild (USA)	Adriana Serra-Zanetti (ITA)	6-0 6-4
Shaun Stafford (USA)	Naoko Sawamatsu (JAP)	2-6 7-6 6-4
Angelica Gavaldon (MEX)	Bettina Fulco-Villella (ARG)	7-5 7-6
Patricia Hy (CAN)	Florencia Labat (ARG)	6-1 7-6
Karina Habsudova (SLVK)	Dominique Monami (BEL)	6-3 6-2
JANA NOVOTNA (CZE, 7)	Yelena Makarova (RUS)	7-5 7-5
GABRIELA SABATINI (ARG, 8)	Larissa Savchenko Neiland (LAT)	6-0 6-1
Meredith McGrath (USA)	Tessa Price (SAF)	6-1 6-2
Radka Zrubakova (SLVK)	Patricia Tarabini (ARG)	6-2 6-2
Isabelle Demongeot (FRA)	Lea Ghirardi (FRA)	6-2 6-3
Silvia Farina (ITA)	Meilen Tu (USA)	7-5 6-7 6-1
Yelena Likhovtseva (KAZ)	Joanette Kruger (SAF)	6-2 6-4
Natalya Medvedeva (UKR)	Barbara Schett (AUT)	4-6 6-2 7-6
AMY FRAZIER (USA, 16)	Rachel McQuillan (AUS)	6-0 6-3
Gigi Fernandez (PR)	SABINE HACK (GER, 12)	6-2 2-6 7-6
Sandrine Testud (FRA)	Yelena Brioukhovets (RUS)	7-5 7-5
Wang Shi-ting (TAIW)	Fang Li (CHN)	7-5 6-4
Kyoko Nagatsuka (JAP)	Sandra Dopfer (AUT)	6-1 6-3
Ginger Helgeson (USA)	Karin Kschwendt (GER)	6-2 6-1
Asa Carlsson (SWE)	Nancy Feber (BEL)	4-6 6-16-2
Nicole Arendt (USA)	Clare Wood (UK)	6-2 7-6
CONCHITA MARTÍNEZ (SPA, 3)	Veronika Martinek (GER)	6-1 6-0

KIMIKO DATE (JAP, 5)	Rika Hiraki (JAP)	6-0 6-2
Yone Kamio (JAP)	Laura Golarsa (ITA)	6-4 6-4
Aléxandra Fusai (FRA)	Brenda Schultz (HOL)	6-4 6-3
Lisa Raymond (USA)	Carrie Cunningham (USA)	7-6 6-4
Barbara Rittner (GER)	Manon Bollegraf (HOL)	6-2 6-1
Emanuela Zardo (SWI)	Eva Martincova (CZE)	6-3 6-0
Leila Meshki (GEO)	Ai Sugiyama (JAP)	6-1 6-4
ANKE HUBER (GER, 14)	Irina Spirlea (ROM)	6-4 6-2
MARY JOE FERNANDEZ (USA, 9)	Sabine Appelmans (BEL)	6-4 6-3
Patty Fendick (USA)	Katrina Adams (USA)	6-7 6-4 6-3
Ann Grossman (USA)	Christina Singer (GER)	6-3 6-4
Katerina Maleeva (BUL)	Marketa Kochta (GER)	6-1 6-2
Anna Maria 'Sandra' Cecchini (ITA)	Silke Meier (GER)	6-3 6-1
Audra Keller (USA)	Laurence Courtois (BEL)	6-1 6-3
Nathalie Tauziat (FRA)	Stephanie Rottier (HOL)	7-5 2-6 7-5
ARANTXA SÁNCHEZ V. (SPA, 2)	Linda Ferrando (ITA)	7-5 6-1

Hack reprises her Wimbledon rôle of first seed to fall.

2nd ROUND

GRAF	Cacic	6-0 6-2
Bobkova	Provis Bradtke	6-7 6-4 6-2
Dechaume-Balleret	Gaidano	7-5 6-3
GARRISON JACKSON	Suarez	6-4 6-3
COETZER	Maniokova	6-2 6-0
De Swardt	Werdel	6-4 2-6 7-6
Endo	Halard	6-1 7-5
DAVENPORT	Shriver	6-1 6-2
PIERCE	Studenikova	6-3 2-6 6-4
Wiesner	Kuhlman	6-2 6-2
Majoli	Reinach	6-2 6-2
Smashnova	Muns-Jagerman	6-2 3-6 6-3
M MALEEVA	Dragomir	7-5 6-3
Stafford	Harvey-Wild	6-0 6-7 6-2
Hy	Gavaldon	6-3 6-2
NOVOTNA	Habsudova	6-2 6-3
SABATINI	McGrath	6-4 6-7 6-1
Demongeot	Zrubakova	3-6 6-1 6-2
Likhovtseva	Farina	7-5 2-6 6-3
Medvedeva	FRAZIER	6-2 6-7 6-4
G Fernandez	Testud	7-5 6-3
Wang	Nagatsuka	4-6 6-0 6-2
Helgeson	Carlsson	6-1 6-1
MARTÍNEZ	Arendt	6-3 6-3
DATE	Kamio	6-0 6-2
Raymond	Fusai	6-2 3-6 6-1
Rittner	Zardo	6-0 6-3
Meshki	HUBER	6-2 6-2
MJ FERNANDEZ	Fendick	6-2 2-6 7-6
Grossman	K Maleeva	6-4 1-6 6-1
Cecchini	Keller	6-3 3-6 6-4
SÁNCHEZ VICÁRIO	Tauziat	6-2 7-6

3rd ROUND

GRAF	Bobkova	6-2 6-2
GARRISON JACKSON	Dechaume-Balleret	2-6 6-4 7-6
COETZER	De Swardt	6-1 6-3
Endo	DAVENPORT	6-3 7-6
PIERCE	Wiesner	6-2 6-4

Majoli	Smashnova	6-2 6-3
M MALEEVA	Stafford	6-3 7-6
NOVOTNA	Hy	6-1 6-2
SABATINI	Demongeot	6-0 6-2
Likhovtseva	Medvedeva	7-6 7-6
G Fernandez	Wang	6-3 6-2
Helgeson	MARTÍNEZ	3-6 6-4 6-1
DATE	Raymond	6-4 6-2
Meshki	Rittner	4-6 6-3 6-2
Grossman	MJ FERNANDEZ	6-4 6-4
SÁNCHEZ VICÁRIO	Cecchini	6-2 6-1

4th ROUND

GRAF	GARRISON JACKSON	6-1 6-2
COETZER	Endo	6-3 6-0
PIERCE	Majoli	6-1 6-2
NOVOTNA	M MALEEVA	6-0 6-4
SABATINI	Likhovtseva	6-2 6-1
G Fernandez	Helgeson	6-3 6-4
DATE	Meshki	6-2 6-7 7-5
SÁNCHEZ VICÁRIO	Grossman	6-2 6-0

QUARTER-FINALS

GRAF	COETZER	6-0 6-2
NOVOTNA	PIERCE	6-4 6-0
SABATINI	G Fernandez	6-2 7-5
SÁNCHEZ VICÁRIO	DATE	6-3 6-0

SEMI-FINALS

GRAF	NOVOTNA	6-3 7-5
SÁNCHEZ VICÁRIO	SABATINI	6-1 7-6

Graf reaches the final for the sixth time with her tenth consecutive win over Novotna, who collapses in much the same way as she did in the 1993 Wimbledon final between the two: leading 5-2 in the second, she misses two set points and loses the last five games, serving three double faults at the very end. Sabatini also misses a set point.

FINAL 10 Sep 1994

SÁNCHEZ VICÁRIO	GRAF	1-6 7-6 6-4

Like Martínez at Wimbledon, Sánchez becomes the first Spaniard to win the event, thanks to Graf's well-documented fallibility: she makes 46 unforced errors (a bad back doesn't help; she has treatment on court). For the third time this year, Sánchez beats her after losing the first set (on each of the two previous occasions, after saving a match point).

Men's Doubles

SEMI-FINALS

TODD WOODBRIDGE	AUS	Nicklas Kulti	SWE	6-3 7-6
MARK WOODFORDE	AUS	Magnus Larsson	SWE	
JACCO ELTINGH	HOL	WAYNE FERREIRA	SAF	6-3 7-5
PAUL HAARHUIS	HOL	MARK KNOWLES	BAH	

FINAL

ELTINGH & HAARHUIS	WOODBRIDGE & WOODFORDE	6-3 7-6

Having won the first Grand Slam event of the season, the Australian Open, Eltingh & Haarhuis win the last.

Women's Doubles

SEMI-FINALS

JANA NOVOTNA	CZE	LARISSA NEILAND	LAT	7-6 6-2
ARANTXA SÁNCHEZ V	SPA	GABRIELA SABATINI	ARG	

| Katerina Maleeva | BUL | GIGI FERNANDEZ | PR | 7-6 1-6 6-3 |
| Robin White | USA | NATALYA ZVEREVA | BYL | |

For the second successive year, Fernandez & Zvereva win the first three Grand Slam titles before losing the last.

FINAL

| NOVOTNA & SÁNCHEZ VICÁRIO | | K Maleeva & White | | 6-3 6-3 |

Mixed Doubles

SEMI-FINALS

JANA NOVOTNA	CZE	GIGI FERNANDEZ	PR	
TODD WOODBRIDGE	AUS	CYRIL SUK	CZE	7-5 6-4
ELNA REINACH	SAF	Jill Hetherington	CAN	7-6 6-7 6-1
PATRICK GALBRAITH	USA	John-Laffnie de Jager	SAF	

FINAL

| REINACH & GALBRAITH | | NOVOTNA & WOODBRIDGE | | 6-2 6-4 |

Galbraith loses $5000 to his coach David Cox who bet him he'd win the title.

Junior Boys

FINAL

| Sjeng Schalken | HOL | Mehdi Tahiri | MOR | 6-2 7-6 |

Junior Girls

FINAL

| Meilen Tu | USA | Martina Hingis | SWI | 6-2 6-4 |

The 16-y-o Tu beats the 13-y-o favourite. Lizzie Jelfs (UK) & Nannie De Villiers (SAF) lose 4-6 6-4 6-2 in the doubles final to Surina De Beer (SAF) & Chantal Reuter (HOL).

Italian Open

Men's Singles

SEMI-FINALS

| Pete Sampras | USA | Ctislav (Slava) Dosedel | CZE | 6-1 6-2 |
| Boris Becker | GER | Goran Ivanisevic | CRO | 6-2 7-6 |

FINAL 15 May 1994 Foro Italico, Rome

| Sampras | | Becker | 6-1 6-2 6-2 |

Becker, the first German to reach the final, in his twelfth year on the circuit, shows why he still hasn't won a title on clay.

Doubles winners: Yevgeny Kafelnikov (RUS) & David Rikl (CZE)

Women's Singles

SEMI-FINALS

| Conchita Martínez | SPA | Karina Habsudova | SLVK | 6-1 6-2 |
| Martina Navratilova | USA | Irina Spirlea | ROM | 6-2 6-3 |

FINAL 8 May 1994 Foro Italico, Rome

| Martínez | | Navratilova | 7-6 6-4 |

Doubles winners: Gigi Fernandez (PR) & Natalya Zvereva (BYL)

German Open

Men's Singles

SEMI-FINALS

| Andrei Medvedev | UKR | Javier Sánchez | SPA | 6-4 6-1 |
| Yevgeny Kafelnikov | RUS | Michael Stich | GER | 6-3 6-4 |

FINAL 8 May 1994 Hamburg

| Medvedev | Kafelnikov | 6-4 6-4 3-6 6-3 |

Doubles winners: Scott Melville (USA) & Piet Norval (SAF)

Women's Singles

SEMI-FINALS

| Steffi Graf | GER | Jana Novotna | CZE | 6-2 6-3 |
| Brenda Schultz | HOL | Anke Huber | GER | 7-6 6-3 |

FINAL 15 May 1994 Berlin

| Graf | Schultz | 7-6 6-4 |

Graf, who retains the title, wins it for the seventh time. The big-serving Schultz hadn't dropped a set throughout the tournament. Doubles winners: Gigi Fernandez (PR) & Natalya Zvereva (BYL)

Davis Cup 1993

FINAL 3-5 Dec Düsseldorf

GERMANY	4	AUSTRALIA	1
Michael Stich	W	Jason Stoltenberg	6-7 6-3 6-1 4-6 6-3
Marc Goellner	L	Richard Fromberg	6-3 7-5 6-7 2-6 7-9
Stich & Patrick Kuhnen	W	Todd Woodbridge	
		& Mark Woodforde	7-6 4-6 6-3 7-6
Stich	W	Fromberg	6-4 6-2 6-2
Goellner	W	Stoltenberg	6-1 6-7 7-6

Germany win the Cup for the third time, the first without Becker.

Davis Cup 1994

World Group

ROUND 1 25-27 March					QUARTER-FINALS 15-17 July			
India	0	USA	5					
Holland	5	Belgium	0		Germany	3	Spain	1
Sweden	5	Denmark	0					
France	4	Hungary	1		Russia	3	Czech Rep	2
Israel	1	Czech Rep	4					
Russia	4	Australia	1		France	2	Sweden	3
Spain	4	Italy	1					
Austria	2	Germany	3		Holland	2	USA	3

SEMI-FINALS 23-25 Sep

Germany	1	Russia	4
Sweden	3	USA	2

After surviving a match point in the decisive doubles, Russia reach the final for the first time by knocking out the holders, who lose at home for the first time since 1985 after death threats against Michael Stich. Thanks to Sampras' knee injury (he retires after losing the first set 6-3 to Stefan Edberg), Sweden become the first team to recover from 2-0 down in a semi-final.

FINAL 2-4 Dec St Petersburg

RUSSIA	1	SWEDEN	4
Aleksandr Volkov	L	Stefan Edberg	4-6 2-6 7-6 6-0 6-8
Yevgeny Kafelnikov	L	Magnus Larsson	0-6 2-6 6-3 6-2 3-6
Kafelnikov & Andrei Olhovskiy	L	Jan Apell & Jonas Björkman	6-7 6-2 6-3 1-6 8-6
Kafelnikov	W	Edberg	4-6 6-4 6-0
Volkov	L	Larsson	6-7 4-6

Sweden, who reached the final seven years in a row during the '80s, win it for the first time in the next decade. Russia lose within two days, but become the first finalists ever to lose each of the first three matches in five sets, and the whole thing may have been decided by Volkov's match point at 5-4 on his own serve, saved by a backhand down the line from Edberg, who becomes the first European to play on Davis Cup winning teams ten years apart (the record, fourteen, is held by Rod Laver 1959-73 & John McEnroe 1978-92).

Euro-African Zone: Group 1, Round 1

25-27 March Oporto

PORTUGAL	4	G BRITAIN	1
Nuno Marques	W	Mark Petchey	6-1 7-6 6-1
Emanuel Couto	W	Jeremy Bates	6-3 5-7 4-6 6-1 6-0
Marques & João Cunha Silva	L	Bates & Petchey	5-7 6-4 7-6 3-6 6-8
Marques	W	Bates	4-6 6-1 6-4 6-0
Couto	W	Petchey	6-1 6-2

Britain, eliminated by a country they beat 5-0 in 1949 & 1985, lose four consecutive Davis Cup ties for the first time. Bates does his bit towards this achievement by losing to Couto, a 20-y-o ranked 348 in the world, making his Davis Cup debut and struggling with cramp. Portugal had won only twelve of their previous 51 ties, since 1925. GB now have to beat Romania in July to avoid relegation to a virtual 3rd Division. In December, Portugal also beat Britain in the European Team Championship, relegating them to the 2nd Division.

Euro-African Zone: Relegation Match

15-17 July 1994 Didsbury, Manchester

G BRITAIN	2	ROMANIA	3
Jeremy Bates	L	Razvan Sabau	6-0 6-3 6-7 2-6 2-6
Mark Petchey	L	Andrei Pavel	6-3 3-6 4-6 2-6
Bates & Petchey	W	Dinu Pescariu & Gheorghe Cosac	6-2 6-7 5-7 6-2 6-1
Bates	W	Pavel	6-3 7-6 6-2
Petchey	L	Sabau	7-5 4-6 7-6 3-6 2-6

You people are in the pits. Next season you'll enter the draw with the likes of Estonia, Kenya, Monaco & Senegal (no disrespect intended). It could have been worse, if not much: the doubles match is won only after Piscariu injures an ankle and has to hobble through the last set. In a match of two halves, Bates leads 6-0 6-3 5-1 before losing to a 17-y-o ranked more than 700 places below him, which sounds terrible (it wasn't great) but it's worth mentioning that Sabau's not a complete novice on grass: he was Wimbledon junior champion in 1993. Pavel too is better than his ranking suggests: French Open junior champion in 1992. The match against Pavel was Bates' 50th and last Davis Cup singles. Ilie Nastase, banned from taking part, becomes (surprise, surprise) the first to achieve this as both player and captain.

Federation Cup

18-24 July Frankfurt

1st ROUND

Argentina	3	Cuba	0
Germany	3	Colombia	0
France	3	S Korea	0
Japan	2	China	1
S Africa	3	Paraguay	0
Slovakia	2	Finland	1
Sweden	2	Belgium	1
Holland	2	Belarus	1
Spain	3	Chile	0
USA	3	Czech Rep	0
Bulgaria	2	Croatia	1
Indonesia	2	Chinese Taipei	1
Italy	2	Denmark	1
Austria	2	Poland	1
Canada	3	Switzerland	0
Australia	2	Latvia	1

2nd ROUND

Germany	2	Slovakia	1
France	3	Italy	0
Japan	3	Sweden	0
S Africa	2	Holland	1
USA	3	Canada	0
Bulgaria	3	Indonesia	0
Austria	2	Australia	1
Spain	3	Argentina	0

QUARTER-FINALS

Germany	3	S Africa	0
Spain	3	Japan	0
USA	3	Austria	0
France	2	Bulgaria	1

SEMI-FINALS

Spain	2	Germany	1
USA	3	France	0

FINAL

SPAIN	3	USA	0
Conchita Martínez		Mary Joe Fernandez	
6-2 6-2			
Arantxa Sánchez Vicário		Lindsay Davenport	
6-2 6-1			
Martínez & Sánchez V		MJ & Gigi Fernandez	
6-3 6-4			

Spain, in their fourth consecutive final, retain the title they also won in 1991.

ATP Tour 1994 (Men)

Outdoor unless specified otherwise. Surface in brackets after venue.

QATAR OPEN 3-9 Jan Doha (hard)
Stefan Edberg (SWE) bt Paul Haarhuis (HOL) 6-3 6-2
Doubles winners: Olivier Delaitre (FRA) & Stéphane Simian (FRA)

HAWAII OPEN 3-9 Jan Oahu (hard)
Wayne Ferreira (SAF) bt Richey Reneberg (USA) 6-4 6-7 6-1
Tom Nijssen (HOL) & Cyril Suk (CZE)

AUSTRALIAN HARDCOURT CHAMPIONSHIP 3-9 Jan Adelaide (hard)
Yevgeny Kafelnikov (RUS) bt Aleksandr Volkov (RUS) 6-4 6-3
Andrew Kratzmann (AUS) & Mark Kratzmann (AUS)

NEW SOUTH WALES OPEN 10-15 Jan Sydney (hard)
Pete Sampras (USA) bt Ivan Lendl (USA) 7-6 6-4
Darren Cahill (AUS) & Sandon Stolle (AUS)

INDONESIAN OPEN 10-15 Jan Jakarta (hard)
Michael Chang (USA) bt David Rikl (CZE) 6-3 6-3
Jonas Björkman (SWE) & Neil Borwick (AUS)

B&H OPEN 10-15 Jan Auckland (hard)
Magnus Gustafsson (SWE) bt Patrick McEnroe (USA) 6-4 6-0
Patrick McEnroe (USA) & Jared Palmer (USA)

AUSTRALIAN OPEN 17-30 Jan see separate entry

DUBAI OPEN 31 Jan - 6 Feb (hard)
Magnus Gustafsson (SWE) bt Sergi Bruguera (SPA) 6-4 6-2
Todd Woodbridge (AUS) & Mark Woodforde (AUS)

OPEN 13 31 Jan - 6 Feb Marseille (hard)
Marc Rosset (SWI) bt Arnaud Boetsch (FRA) 7-6 7-6
Jan Siemerink (HOL) & Daniel Vacek (CZE)

SAN JOSÉ OPEN 31 Jan - 6 Feb (hard)
Renzo Furlan (ITA) bt Michael Chang (USA) 3-6 6-2 7-5
Rick Leach (USA) & Jared Palmer (USA)

MURATTI TIME INDOOR 7-13 Feb Milan (indoor; Supreme)
Boris Becker (GER) bt Petr Korda (CZE) 6-2 3-6 6-3
Tom Nijssen (HOL) & Cyril Suk (CZE)

KROGER ST JUDE INTERNATIONAL 7-13 Feb Memphis (hard)
Todd Martin (USA) bt Brad Gilbert (USA) 6-4 7-5
Byron Black (ZIM) & Jonathan Stark (USA)

EUROCARD OPEN 14-20 Feb Stuttgart (indoor; Supreme)
Stefan Edberg (SWE) bt Goran Ivanisevic (CRO) 4-6 6-4 6-2 6-2
David Adams (AUS) & Andrei Olhovskiy (RUS)

US INDOOR 14-20 Feb Philadelphia (hard)
Michael Chang (USA) bt Paul Haarhuis (HOL) 6-3 6-2
Jacco Eltingh (HOL) & Paul Haarhuis (HOL)

ARIZONA CHAMPIONSHIP 21-27 Feb Scottsdale (hard)
André Agassi (USA) bt Luiz Mattar (BRZ) 6-4 6-3
Jan Apell (SWE) & Doug Flach (USA)

ABN/AMRO WEREID 21-27 Feb Rotterdam (Supreme)
Michael Stich (GER) bt Wayne Ferreira (SAF) 4-6 6-3 6-0
Jeremy Bates (UK) & Jonas Björkman (SWE)

ABIERTO MEXICANO (Mexican Open) 21-27 Feb Mexico City (clay)
Thomas Muster (AUT) bt Roberto Jabali (BRZ) 6-3 6-1
Jeremy Bates (UK) & Jonas Björkman (SWE)

NEWSWEEK CHAMPIONS CUP 28 Feb - 6 March Indian Wells (hard)
Pete Sampras (USA) bt Petr Korda (CZE) 4-6 6-3 3-6 6-3 6-2
Grant Connell (CAN) & Patrick Galbraith (USA)

COPENHAGEN OPEN 28 Feb - 6 March (indoor)
Yevgeny Kafelnikov (RUS) bt Daniel Vacek (CZE) 6-3 7-5
Martin Damm (CZE) & Brett Steven (NZ)

LIPTON CHAMPIONSHIP 7-20 March Key Biscayne, Florida (hard)
Pete Sampras (USA) bt André Agassi (USA) 5-7 6-3 6-3
Jacco Eltingh (HOL) & Paul Haarhuis (HOL)

ZARAGOZA OPEN 7-13 March (Supreme)
Magnus Larsson (SWE) bt Lars Rehmann (GER) 6-4 6-4
Henrik Holm (SWE) & Anders Jarryd (SWE)

HASSAN II GRAND PRIX 14-21 March Casablanca (clay)
Renzo Furlan (ITA) bt Karim Alami (MOR) 6-2 6-2
David Adams (AUS) & Menno Oosting (HOL)

SALEM OPEN 28 March - 3 April Osaka (hard)
Pete Sampras (USA) bt Guillaume Raoux (FRA) 6-2 6-2
Martin Damm (CZE) & Sandon Stolle (AUS)

ESTORIL OPEN 28 March - 3 April Estoril (clay)
Carlos Costa (SPA) bt Andrei Medvedev (UKR) 4-6 7-5 6-4
Cristian Brandi (ITA) & Federico Mordegan (ITA)

SOUTH AFRICAN OPEN 28 March - 3 April Sun City (hard)
Markus Zöcke (GER) bt Henrik Dreekman (GER) 6-4 6-1
Marius Barnard (SAF) & Brent Haygarth (SAF)

JAPAN OPEN 4-10 April Tokyo
Pete Sampras (USA) bt Michael Chang (USA) 6-4 6-2
Henrik Holm (SWE) & Anders Jarryd (SWE)

TROFEO CONDE de GODO 4-10 April Barcelona (clay)
Richard Krajicek (HOL) bt Carlos Costa (SPA) 6-4 6-7 6-2
Yevgeny Kafelnikov (RUS) & David Rikl (CZE)

SALEM OPEN 11-17 April Hong Kong (hard)
Michael Chang (USA) bt Patrick Rafter (AUS) 6-1 6-3
Jim Grabb (USA) & Brett Steven (NZ)

PHILIPS OPEN 11-17 April Nice (clay)
Alberto Berasategui (SPA) bt Jim Courier (USA) 6-4 6-2
Javier Sánchez (SPA) & Mark Woodforde (AUS)

US CLAY COURT CHAMPIONSHIP 11-17 April Birmingham, Alabama (clay)
Jason Stoltenberg (AUS) bt Gabriel Markus (ARG) 6-3 6-4
Richey Reneberg (USA) & Christo Van Rensburg (SAF)

MONTE CARLO OPEN 18-24 April (clay)
Andrei Medvedev (UKR) bt Sergi Bruguera (SPA) 7-5 6-1 6-3
Nicklas Kulti (SWE) & Magnus Larsson (SWE)

KOREA OPEN 18-24 April Seoul (hard)
Jeremy Bates (UK) bt Jörn Renzenbrink (GER) 6-4 6-7 6-3
Stéphane Simian (FRA) & Kenny Thorne (USA)

The first British player to reach the final of a Tour event since Nick Brown at Bristol in 1989 and the first to win one since Mark Cox at Helsinki in 1977. Normal service is resumed (and broken) in his next match: he loses 6-2 6-4 to Daniel Nestor (CAN) in the first round of the Taipei Challenger.

TROFEO GRUPO ZETA 25 April - 1 May Madrid (clay)
Thomas Muster (AUT) bt Sergi Bruguera (SPA) 6-2 3-6 6-4 7-5
Ricard Bergh (SWE) & Menno Oosting (HOL)

BMW OPEN 25 April - 1 May Munich (clay)
Michael Stich (GER) bt Petr Korda (CZE) 6-2 2-6 6-3
Yevgeny Kafelnikov (RUS) & David Rikl (CZE)

AT & T CHALLENGE 25 April - 1 May Atlanta (clay)
Michael Chang (USA) bt Todd Martin (USA) 6-7 7-6 6-0
Jared Palmer (USA) & Richey Reneberg (USA)

GERMAN OPEN 2-8 May see separate entry

US CLAY COURT CLASSIC 2-8 May Pinehurst (clay)
Jared Palmer (USA) bt Todd Martin (USA) 6-4 7-6
Todd Woodbridge (AUS) & Mark Woodforde (AUS)

ITALIAN OPEN 9-15 May see separate entry

RED CLAY CHAMPIONSHIP 9-15 May Coral Springs
(clay)
Luiz Mattar (BRZ) bt Jamie Morgan (AUS) 6-4 3-6 6-3
Lan Bale (SAF) & Brett Steven (NZ)

INTERNAZIONALE del RS PARMIO 16-22 May Bologna
(clay)
Javier Sánchez (SPA) bt Alberto Berasategui (SPA) 7-6
4-6 6-3
John Fitzgerald (AUS) & Patrick Rafter (AUS)

WORLD TEAM CUP May 1994 Düsseldorf (clay)
Final: Germany bt Spain.

FRENCH OPEN 23-30 May see separate entry

STELLA ARTOIS 6-12 June Queen's Club, London
(grass)
Todd Martin (USA) bt Pete Sampras (USA) 7-6 7-6
Jan Apell (SWE) & Jonas Björkman (SWE)

FLORENCE INTERNATIONAL 6-12 June (clay)
Marcelo Filippini (URU) bt Richard Fromberg (AUS) 3-6
6-3 6-3
Jon Ireland (USA) & Kenny Thorne (USA)

CONTINENTAL CHAMPIONSHIP 6-12 June Rosmalen,
Holland (grass)
Richard Krajicek (HOL) bt Karsten Braasch (GER) 6-3
6-4
Stephen Noteboom (HOL) & Fernon Wibier (HOL)

GERRY WEBER OPEN 13-19 June Halle (grass)
Michael Stich (GER) bt Magnus Larsson (SWE) 6-4 4-6
6-3
Olivier Delaitre (FRA) & Guy Forget (FRA)

RAIFFEISEN GRAND PRIX 13-19 June St Polten,
Austria (clay)
Thomas Muster (AUT) bt Tomas Carbonell (SPA) 4-6
6-2 6-4
Vojtech Flegl (CZE) & Andrew Florent (AUS)

MANCHESTER OPEN 13-19 June (grass)
Patrick Rafter (AUS) bt Wayne Ferreira (SAF) 7-6 7-6
Rick Leach (USA) & Danie Visser (SAF)

WIMBLEDON 20 June - 3 July see separate entry

SWISS OPEN 4-10 July Gstaad (clay)
Sergi Bruguera (SPA) bt Guy Forget (FRA) 3-6 7-5 6-2
6-1
Sergio Casal (SPA) & Emilio Sánchez (SPA)

SWEDISH OPEN 4-10 July Bastad (clay)
Bernd Karbacher (GER) bt Horst Skoff (AUT) 6-4 6-3
Jan Apell (SWE) & Jonas Björkman (SWE)

HALL OF FAME 4-10 July Newport, Rhode Island
(grass)
David Wheaton (USA) bt Todd Woodbridge (AUS) 6-4
3-6 7-6
Alex Antonitsch (AUT) & Greg Rusedski (CAN)

MERCEDES CUP 18-24 July Stuttgart (clay)
Alberto Berasategui (SPA) bt Andrea Gaudenzi (ITA) 7-5
3-6 7-6
Scott Melville (USA) & Piet Norval (SAF)

NEWSWEEK CLASSIC 18-24 July Washington DC
(hard)
Stefan Edberg (SWE) bt Jason Stoltenberg (AUS) 6-4
6-2
Grant Connell (CAN) & Patrick Galbraith (USA)

CANADIAN OPEN 25-31 July Toronto (hard)
André Agassi (USA) bt Jason Stoltenberg (AUS) 6-4 6-4
Byron Black (ZIM) & Jonathan Stark (USA)

DUTCH INTERNATIONAL 25-31 July Hilversum (clay)
Karel Novacek (CZE) bt Richard Fromberg (AUS) 7-5
6-4 7-6
Daniel Orsanic (ARG) & Jan Siemerink (HOL)

EA GENERALI OPEN 1-7 Aug Kitzbühel (clay)
Goran Ivanisevic (CRO) & Fabrice Santoro (FRA) 6-2
4-6 4-6 6-3 6-2
David Adams (AUS) & Andrei Olhovskiy (RUS)

CZECH OPEN 1-7 Aug Prague (clay)
Sergi Bruguera (SPA) bt Andrei Medvedev (UKR) 6-3
6-4
Karel Novacek (CZE) & Mats Wilander (SWE)

LOS ANGELES OPEN 1-7 Aug (hard)
Boris Becker (GER) bt Mark Woodforde (AUS) 6-2 6-2
John Fitzgerald (AUS) & Mark Woodforde (AUS)

ATP CHAMPIONSHIP 8-14 Aug Cincinnati (hard)
Michael Chang (USA) bt Stefan Edberg (SWE) 6-2 7-5
Alex O'Brien (USA) & Sandon Stolle (AUS)

SAN MARINO INTERNATIONAL 9-14 Aug (clay)
Carlos Costa (SPA) bt Oliver Gross (GER) 6-1 6-3
Neil Broad (UK) & Greg van Emburgh (USA)

RCA CHAMPIONSHIP 15-21 Aug Indianapolis (hard)
Wayne Ferreira (SAF) bt Olivier Delaitre (FRA) 6-2 6-1
Todd Woodbridge (AUS) & Mark Woodforde (AUS)

VOLVO INTERNATIONAL 15-21 Aug New Haven (hard)
Boris Becker (GER) bt Marc Rosset (SWI) 6-3 7-5
Grant Connell (CAN) & Patrick Galbraith (USA)

CROATIAN INTERNATIONAL 22-28 Aug Umag (clay)
Alberto Berasategui (SPA) bt Karol Kucera (SLVK) 6-2
6-4
Diego Perez (URUG) & Francisco Roig (SPA)

HAMLET CUP 22-28 Aug Long Island (hard)
Yevgeny Kafelnikov (RUS) bt Cédric Pioline (FRA) 5-7 6-1 6-2
Olivier Delaitre (FRA) & Guy Forget (FRA)

OTB INTERNATIONAL 22-28 Aug Schenectady (hard)
Jacco Eltingh (HOL) bt Chuck Adams (USA) 6-3 6-4
Jan Apell (SWE) & Jonas Björkman (SWE)

US OPEN 29 Aug - 4 Sep see separate entry

ROMANIAN OPEN 12-18 Sep Bucharest (clay)
Franco Davin (ARG) bt Goran Ivanisevic (CRO) 6-2 6-4
Wayne Arthurs (AUS) & Simon Youl (AUS)

PASSING SHOT GRAND PRIX 12-18 Sep Bordeaux (clay)
Wayne Ferreira (SAF) bt Jeff Tarango (USA) 6-0 7-5
Olivier Delaitre (FRA) & Guy Forget (FRA)

COLOMBIAN OPEN 12-18 Sep Bogotá (clay)
Nicolas Pereira (VEN) bt Mauricio Hadad (COL) 6-3 3-6 6-4
Mark Knowles (BAH) & Daniel Nestor (CAN)

SWISS INDOOR 26 Sep - 2 Oct Basle (hard)
Wayne Ferreira (SAF) bt Patrick McEnroe (USA) 4-6 6-2 7-6 6-3
Patrick McEnroe (USA) & Jared Palmer (USA)

SICILIAN INTERNATIONAL 26 Sep - 2 Oct Palermo (clay)
Alberto Berasategui (SPA) bt Alex Corretja (SPA) 2-6 7-6 6-4
Tom Kempers (HOL) & Jack Waite (USA)

SALEM OPEN 26 Sep - 2 Oct Kuala Lumpur (indoor)
Jacco Eltingh (HOL) bt Andrei Olhovskiy (RUS) 7-6 2-6 6-4
Jacco Eltingh (HOL) & Paul Haarhuis (HOL)

AUSTRALIAN INDOOR 3-9 Oct Sydney (hard)
Richard Krajicek (HOL) bt Boris Becker (GER) 7-6 7-6 2-6 6-3
Jacco Eltingh (HOL) & Paul Haarhuis (HOL)

TOULOUSE GRAND PRIX 3-9 Oct (hard)
Magnus Larsson (SWE) bt Jared Palmer (AUS) 6-1 6-3
Menno Oosting (HOL) & Daniel Vacek (CZE)

ATHENS CUP 3-9 Oct (clay)
Alberto Berasategui (SPA) bt O Martínez 4-6 7-6 6-3
Luis Lobo (ARG) & Javier Sánchez (SPA)

SEIKO SUPER TENNIS 10-16 Oct Tokyo (indoor)
Goran Ivanisevic (CRO) bt Michael Chang (USA) 6-4 6-4
Grant Connell (CAN) & Patrick Galbraith (USA)

CZECH INDOOR 10-16 Oct Ostrava (Supreme)
Malivai Washington (USA) bt Arnaud Boetsch (FRA) 4-6 6-3 6-3
Martin Damm (CZE) & Karel Novacek (CZE)

ISRAEL OPEN 10-16 Oct Tel Aviv (hard)
Wayne Ferreira (SAF) bt Amos Mansdorf (ISR) 7-6 6-3
Lan Bale (SAF) & John-Laffnie de Jager (SAF)

Mansdorf retires at the end of the season.

LYONS GRAND PRIX 17-23 Oct (indoor)
Marc Rosset (SWI) bt Jim Courier (USA) 6-4 7-6
Jakob Hlasek (SWI) & Yevgeny Kafelnikov (RUS)

CA TROPHY 17-23 Oct Vienna (indoor)
André Agassi (USA) bt Michael Stich (GER) 7-6 4-6 6-2 6-3
Mike Bauer (USA) & David Rikl (CZE)

SALEM OPEN 17-23 Oct Beijing (indoor)
Michael Chang (USA) bt Anders Jarryd (SWE) 7-5 7-5
Tommy Ho (USA) & Kent Kinnear (USA)

STOCKHOLM OPEN 24-30 Oct (Supreme)
Boris Becker (GER) bt Goran Ivanisevic (CRO) 4-6 6-4 6-3 7-6
Todd Woodbridge (AUS) & Mark Woodforde (AUS)

HELLMANN'S CUP 24-30 Oct Santiago (clay)
Alberto Berasategui (SPA) bt Francisco Clavet (SPA) 6-3 6-4
Karel Novacek (CZE) & Mats Wilander (SWE)

PARIS OPEN 31 Oct - 6 Nov (indoor)
André Agassi (USA) bt Marc Rosset (SWI) 6-3 6-3 4-6 7-5
Jacco Eltingh (HOL) & Paul Haarhuis (HOL)

TOPPER OPEN 31 Oct - 6 Nov Montevideo (clay)
Alberto Berasategui (SPA) bt Francisco Clavet (SPA) 6-4 6-0
Marcelo Filippini (URUG) & Luiz Mattar (BRZ)

SOUTH AMERICAN OPEN 7-13 Nov Buenos Aires (clay)
Alex Corretja (SPA) bt Javier Frana (ARG) 6-3 5-7 7-6
Sergio Casal (SPA) & Emilio Sánchez (SPA)

KREMLIN CUP 7-13 Nov Moscow (indoor)
Aleksandr Volkov (RUS) bt Chuck Adams (USA) 6-2 6-4
Jacco Eltingh (HOL) & Paul Haarhuis (HOL)

EUROPEAN COMMUNITY CHAMPIONSHIP 7-13 Nov Antwerp (Supreme)
Pete Sampras (USA) bt Magnus Larsson (SWE) 7-6 6-4
Jan Apell (SWE) & Jonas Björkman (SWE)

ATP WORLD CHAMPIONSHIP 15-20 Nov Frankfurt
Pete Sampras (USA) bt Boris Becker (GER) 4-6 6-3 7-5 6-4

Becker, twice the champion, is runner-up for the fourth time.

GRAND SLAM CUP FINAL 11 Dec 1994 Munich
Magnus Larsson (SWE) bt Pete Sampras (USA) 7-6 4-6 7-6 6-4
Larsson picks up the usual inflated cheque for this event: $1.5 million.

WTA Tour 1994 (Women)

AUSTRALIAN HARDCOURT 3-9 Jan Brisbane (hard)
Lindsay Davenport (USA) bt Florencia Labat (ARG) 6-1
2-6 6-3
*Doubles winners: Laura Golarsa (ITA) & Natalya
Medvedeva (UKR)*

NEW SOUTH WALES OPEN 10-16 Jan Sydney (hard)
Kimiko Date (JAP) bt Mary Joe Fernandez (USA) 6-4
6-2
Patty Fendick (USA) & Meredith McGrath (USA)

TASMANIAN INTERNATIONAL OPEN 10-15 Jan Hobart
(hard)
Mana Endo (JAP) bt Rachel McQuillan (AUS) 6-1 6-7
6-4
Linda Harvey-Wild (USA) & Chanda Rubin (USA)

AUSTRALIAN OPEN 17-30 Jan see separate entry

PAN PACIFIC OPEN 1-6 Feb Tokyo (hard)
Steffi Graf (GER) bt Martina Navratilova (USA) 6-2 6-4
Pam Shriver (USA) & Liz Smylie (AUS)

AMWAY CLASSIC 31 Jan - 6 Feb Auckland (hard)
Ginger Helgeson (USA) bt Inés Gorrochategui (ARG)
7-6 6-3
Patricia Hy (CAN) & Mercedes Paz (ARG)

VIRGINIA SLIMS OF CHICAGO 5-13 Feb Chicago
(indoor)
Natalya Zvereva (BYL) bt Chanda Rubin (USA) 6-3 7-5
Gigi Fernandez (PR) & Natalya Zvereva (BYL)

ASIAN OPEN 8-13 Feb Osaka (indoor)
Manuela Maleeva-Fragnière (SWI) bt Iva Majoli (CRO)
6-1 4-6 7-5
*Larissa Savchenko Neiland (LAT) & Rennae Stubbs
(USA)*

EA-GENERALI 5-13 Feb Linz, Austria (indoor)
Sabine Appelmans (BEL) bt Meike Babel (GER) 6-1 4-6
7-6
Hana Mandlikova (AUS) & Leila Meshki (GEO)

PARIS OPEN 15-20 Feb Paris (indoor)
Martina Navratilova (USA) bt Julie Halard (FRA) 7-5 6-3
Sabine Appelmans (BEL) & Laurence Courtois (BEL)

IGA CLASSIC 14-20 Feb Oklahoma City (hard)
Meredith McGrath (USA) bt Brenda Schultz (HOL) 7-6
7-6
Patty Fendick (USA) & Meredith McGrath (USA)

CHINA OPEN 14-20 Feb Beijing (hard)
Yayuk Basuki (INDON) bt Kyoko Nagatsuka (JAP) 6-4
6-2
Chen Li (CHN) & Fang Li (CHN)

EVERT CUP 21-27 Feb Indian Wells (hard)
Steffi Graf (GER) bt Amanda Coetzer (SAF) 6-0 6-4
Lindsay Davenport (USA) & Lisa Raymond (USA)

VIRGINIA SLIMS OF FLORIDA 28 Feb - 6 March Delray
Beach (hard)
Steffi Graf (GER) bt Arantxa Sánchez Vicário (SPA) 6-3
7-5
Jana Novotna (CZE) & Arantxa Sánchez Vicário (SPA)

LIPTON CHAMPIONSHIPS 11-20 March Key Biscayne,
Florida (hard)
Steffi Graf (GER) bt Natalya Zvereva (BYL) 4-6 6-1 6-2
Gigi Fernandez (PR) & Natalya Zvereva (BYL)

WESLEY CHAPEL (Doubles only) 24-27 March (clay)
Jana Novotna (CZE) & Arantxa Sánchez Vicário (SPA)

FAMILY CIRCLE CUP 28 March - 3 April Hilton Head
Island (clay)
Conchita Martínez (SPA) bt Natalya Zvereva (BYL) 6-4
6-0
Lori McNeil (USA) & Arantxa Sánchez Vicário (SPA)

BAUSCH & LOMB CHAMPIONSHIPS 4-10 April Amelia
Island (clay)
Arantxa Sánchez Vicário (SPA) bt Gabriela Sabatini
(ARG) 6-1 6-4
*Larissa Savchenko Neiland (LAT) & Arantxa Sánchez
Vicário (SPA)*

JAPAN OPEN 4-10 April Tokyo (hard)
Kimiko Date (JAP) bt Amy Frazier (USA) 7-5 6-0
Mami Nonoshiro (JAP) & Ai Sugiyama (JAP)

VOLVO OPEN 11-17 April Pattaya, Thailand (hard)
Sabine Appelmans (BEL) bt Patty Fendick (USA) 6-7 7-6
6-2
Patty Fendick (USA) & Meredith McGrath (USA)

SINGAPORE OPEN 18-24 April Kailang (hard)
Naoko Sawamatsu (JAP) bt Florencia Labat (ARG) 7-5 7-5
Patty Fendick (USA) & Meredith McGrath (USA)

LA FAMILIA OPEN 19-24 April Barcelona (clay)
Arantxa Sánchez Vicário (SPA) bt Iva Majoli (CRO) 6-0 6-2
*Larissa Savchenko Neiland (LAT) & Arantxa Sánchez
Vicário (SPA)*

CITIZEN CUP 25 April - 1 May Hamburg (clay)
Arantxa Sánchez Vicário (SPA) bt Steffi Graf (GER) 4-6
7-6 7-6
Jana Novotna (CZE) & Arantxa Sánchez Vicário (SPA)

TROFEO ILVA 25 April - 1 May Taranto, Italy (clay)
Julie Halard (FRA) bt Irina Spirlea (ROM) 6-2 6-3
Irina Spirlea (ROM) & Noelle van Lottum (FRA)

INDONESIAN OPEN 25 April - 1 May Jakarta (hard)
Yayuk Basuki (INDON) bt Florencia Labat (ARG) 6-4 3-6
7-6
Nicole Arendt (USA) & Kristine Radford (AUS)

ITALIAN OPEN 2-9 May see separate entry

GERMAN OPEN 9-15 May see separate entry

INTERNATIONAUX DE STRASBOURG 16-22 May
Strasbourg (clay)

Mary Joe Fernandez (USA) bt Gabriela Sabatini (ARG) 2-6 6-4 6-0
Lori McNeil (USA) & Rennae Stubbs (USA)

EUROCARD OPEN 16-21 May Lucerne (clay)
Lindsay Davenport (USA) bt Lisa Raymond (USA) 7-6 6-4
Doubles cancelled (rain)

FRENCH OPEN 23 May - 5 June see separate entry

DFS CLASSIC 6-12 June Birmingham, England (grass)
Lori McNeil (USA) bt Zina Garrison Jackson (USA) 6-2 6-2
Zina Garrison Jackson (USA) & Larissa Savchenko Neiland (LAT)

VOLKSWAGEN CUP 13-18 June Eastbourne (grass)
Meredith McGrath (USA) bt Linda Harvey-Wild (USA) 6-2 6-4
Gigi Fernandez (PR) & Natalya Zvereva (BYL)

WIMBLEDON 20 June - 3 July see separate entry

PALERMO INTERNATIONAL 5-10 July Palermo (clay)
Irina Spirlea (ROM) bt Brenda Schultz (HOL) 6-4 1-6 7-6
Ruxandra Dragomir (ROM) & Laura Garrone (ITA)

FEDERATION CUP 18-24 July see separate entry

US HARDCOURT CHAMPIONSHIPS 25-31 July Stratton Mountain (hard)
Conchita Martínez (SPA) bt Arantxa Sánchez Vicário (SPA) 4-6 6-3 6-4
Pam Shriver (USA) & Liz Smylie (AUS)

STYRIA OPEN 25-31 July Styria, Austria (clay)
Anke Huber (GER) bt Judith Wiesner (AUT) 6-3 6-3
Anna Maria 'Sandra' Cecchini (ITA) & Patricia Tarabini (ARG)

MAZDA CLASSIC 1-7 Aug San Diego (hard)
Steffi Graf (GER) bt Arantxa Sánchez Vicário (SPA) 6-2 6-1
Jana Novotna (CZE) & Arantxa Sánchez Vicário (SPA)

VIRGINIA SLIMS OF LA 8-14 Aug Manhattan Beach (hard)
Amy Frazier (USA) bt Ann Grossman (USA) 6-1 6-3
Julie Halard (FRA) & Nathalie Tauziat (FRA)

CANADIAN OPEN 15-21 Aug Montreal (hard)
Arantxa Sánchez Vicário (SPA) bt Steffi Graf (GER) 7-5 1-6 7-6
Meredith McGrath (USA) & Arantxa Sánchez Vicário (SPA)

US OPEN 29 Aug - 5 Sep see separate entry

MOSCOW 19-24 Sep (Supreme)
Magdalena Maleeva (BUL) bt Anna Maria 'Sandra' Cecchini (ITA) 7-5 6-1
Manon Bollegraf (HOL) & Larissa Savchenko Neiland (LAT)

TOKYO 20-25 Sep (hard)
Arantxa Sánchez Vicário (SPA) bt Amy Frazier (USA) 6-1 6-2
Julie Halard (FRA) & Arantxa Sánchez Vicário (SPA)

VOLKSWAGEN GRAND PRIX 26 Sep - 2 Oct Leipzig (Supreme)
Jana Novotna (CZE) bt Mary Pierce (FRA) 7-5 6-1
Patty Fendick (USA) & Meredith McGrath (USA)

BARILLA 3-9 Oct Zürich (indoor)
Magdalena Maleeva (BUL) bt Helena Sukova (CZE) 7-5 3-6 6-4
Manon Bollegraf (HOL) & Martina Navratilova (USA)

PORSCHE GRAND PRIX 10-16 Oct Filderstadt (hard)
Anke Huber (GER) bt Mary Pierce (FRA) 6-4 6-2
Gigi Fernandez (PR) & Natalya Zvereva (BYL)

AUTOGLASS CLASSIC 18-23 Oct Brighton (Supreme)
Jana Novotna (CZE) bt Helena Sukova (CZE) 6-7 6-3 6-4
Manon Bollegraf (HOL) & Larissa Savchenko Neiland (LAT)

NOKIA GRAND PRIX 24-30 Oct Essen (Supreme)
Jana Novotna (CZE) bt Iva Majoli (CRO) 6-2 6-4
Maria Lindström & Maria Strandlund (SWE)

BANK OF THE WEST CLASSIC 31 Oct - 6 Nov Oakland (Supreme)
Arantxa Sánchez Vicário (SPA) bt Martina Navratilova (USA) 1-6 7-6 7-6
Lindsay Davenport (USA) & Arantxa Sánchez Vicário (SPA)

BELL C6 31 Oct - 6 Nov Quebec City (hard)
Katerina Maleeva (BUL) bt Brenda Schultz (HOL) 6-4 6-7 6-4
Elna Reinach (SAF) & Nathalie Tauziat (FRA)

VIRGINIA SLIMS OF PHILADELPHIA 7-13 Nov Philadelphia (Supreme)
Anke Huber (GER) bt Mary Pierce (FRA) 6-0 6-7 7-5
Gigi Fernandez (PR) & Natalya Zvereva (BYL)

SURABAYA 7-13 Nov Surabaya, Hong Kong (hard)
Elena Wagner (BUL) bt Ai Sugiyama (JAP) 2-6 6-0 ret
Yayuk Basuki (INDON) & Romana Tedjakusuma (INDON)

TAIPEI 4-20 Nov Taipei (hard)
Wang Shi-ting (TAI) bt Kyoko Nagatsuka (JAP) 2-6 7-6 6-3
Michelle Jaggard-Lai (AUS) & Renée Simpson-Alter (CAN)

VIRGINIA SLIMS CHAMPIONSHIP 14-20 Nov New York City (Supreme)
Gabriela Sabatini (ARG) bt Lindsay Davenport (USA) 6-3 6-2 6-4
Gigi Fernandez (PR) & Natalya Zvereva (BYL)

Sabatini wins in three straight sets to take a singles title for the first time in two years.

ATP World Doubles 1993

Nov Johannesburg

SEMI-FINALS

Jacco Eltingh	HOL Grant Connell	CAN 4-6 7-6 7-5
Paul Haarhuis	HOL Patrick Galbraith USA	

Todd Woodbridge	AUS David Adams	AUS 6-2 7-5
Mark Woodforde	AUS Andrei Olhovskiy RUS	

FINAL

Eltingh & Haarhuis	Woodbridge & Woodforde	
7-6 7-6 6-4		

ATP World Doubles 1994

Nov Jakarta

SEMI-FINALS

Jan Apell	SWE David Adams	AUS 6-3 6-2
Jonas Björkman	SWE Andrei Olhovskiy RUS	

Todd Woodbridge	AUS Jacco Eltingh	HOL 6-7 6-4 6-4
Mark Woodforde	AUS Paul Haarhuis	HOL

FINAL

Apell & Björkman	Woodbridge & Woodforde	
6-4 4-6 4-6 7-6 7-6		

A double fault costs the Woods dear when they serve for the match at 5-4 in the fourth set. They lose each tie-break 7-5.

British National Championships 1993

Telford

Men

SEMI-FINALS

Jeremy Bates	Colin Beecher	6-2 6-3
Chris Bailey	Miles McLagan	6-1 6-4

FINAL

Bates	Bailey	6-3 6-3

Women

SEMI-FINALS

Clare Wood	Amanda Wainwright	6-2 6-2

Karen Cross	Jo Durie	2-6 6-2 6-4

FINAL

Wood	Cross	7-5 6-0

Wood regains the title she won in 1989.

British National Championships 1994

Telford

Men

SEMI-FINALS

Jeremy Bates	Danny Sapsford	6-1 6-2
Miles McLagan	Jamie Delgado	7-6 6-4

Sapsford reached the semis unseeded.

FINAL

Bates	McLagan	6-4 6-2

Bates adds to his record by winning the title for the sixth time, the third in a row without conceding a set.

Women

SEMI-FINALS

Jo Ward	Clare Wood	6-3 5-7 6-3
Kaye Hand	Shirli-Ann Siddall	1-6 7-5 8-6

The 19-y-o Ward, world ranked 432, beats the holder and No.1 seed to become the first unseeded player ever to reach the final, and is immediately followed by the second (ranked 567) who beats the No.2 seed.

FINAL

Ward	Hand	6-0 6-2

Wheelchair World Championships

Aug 1994 Nottingham

MEN'S FINAL			
Australia	3	France	0

WOMEN'S FINAL			
USA	3	Austria	0

Tenpin Bowling

World Cup 1993

Nov, Johannesburg

MEN'S CHAMPIONSHIP GAME

Rainer Puisis	GER	
Tomas Leandersson	SWE	258-184

WOMEN'S CHAMPIONSHIP GAME

Pauline Smith	UK	
Rosalind Greiner	HOL	178-177

The biggest event in the sport outside the USA. Smith first won the title in 1981.

World Cup 1994

Nov, Hermosillo, Mexico

MEN'S CHAMPIONSHIP GAME

Tore Torgersen	NOR	
Mohamed Khalifa	UAE	217-212

Torgersen leads all the way (i.e. after 24, 40 & 48 games) before beating the 1988 champion in the final.

WOMEN'S CHAMPIONSHIP GAME

Anne Jacobs	SAF	
Lucy Giovinco	USA	226-204

Giovinco is a previous holder of the title.

World Open

16-17 July 1994 Super Bowl, Swindon

MEN

George Patel	4881
Chris Buck	4490
Lol Ellis	4433

WOMEN

Gema Burden	3007
Carol Callow	3000
Pauline Smith	2999

British Open

15-18 Sep 1994 Nottingham Bowl

MEN'S STEPLADDER

Chris Van Damme (BEL) bt Mats Karlsson (SWE)
248-244

3rd Mike Machnig (GER)

Van Damme wins the title at last after finishing six times in the top ten.

WOMEN'S STEPLADDER

Gina Wardle (UK) bt Jette Bergendorff (SWE)   188-172
3rd Pauline Smith (UK)

UK Championships

15 May 1994 Solar Bowl, Ipswich

MEN

Leslie Miranda	1829
Ron Oldfield	1810
Steve Gomersall	1785

WOMEN

Gem Burden	2021
Pauline Smith	1786
Kimberley Oakley	1738

Burden, who wins gold at the European Championships (see below), beats the defending champion and 1993 World Cup winner into second place. Mother & daughter Shirley & Ruth Molineaux both reach the quarter-finals.

European Championships

Rome

MEN'S FINAL

Philippe Dubois	FRA	Raymond
Jansson	SWE	458-385
5 Kevin Hills	*UK*	

WOMEN'S FINAL

Asa Larsson	SWE	
Leena Pulliainen	FIN	421-415
6 Pauline (Smith) Buck	*UK*	

Trampolining

World Cup Final
13 Nov 1993 Frankfurt

Men

Fabrice Scwertz	FRA	38.10
Martin Kuicka	GER	37.50
Fabrice Hennique	FRA	37.40

Synchro pairs

Kasak & Morozov	BYL	47.60
Buhkhotsyev & Tjabus	UKR	46.80
Fabrice Hennique & Fabrice Schwertz	FRA	46.60

Women

Andrea Holmes	ENG	37.20
Anna Dogonadze	GEO	36.70
Sue Challis	ENG	36.70

Dogonadze & Challis equal second.

Synchro pairs

Anna Dogonadze & Khoperia	GEO	45.80
Ludwig & Röwe	GER	45.00
Karpenkova & Pisheyko	BYL	44.50

European Championship
14-16 Oct 1993 Sursee, Switzerland

Men

Fabrice Schwertz	FRA	38.70
Dmitry Poliarus	BYL	38.30
Anders Christiansen	DEN	38.10

Synchro pairs

Dalsten & Ledstrup	DEN	46.40
Kemmer & Kubicka	GER	45.20
Villafuerte & Villafuerte	HOL	45.10

Team

Belarus	193.70
France	190.60
Germany	189.40

Women

Sue Challis	UK	37.30
Anna Dogonadze	GEO	36.50
Rusudan Khoperia	GEO	36.50

The Georgians share second place.

Synchro pairs

Movchan & Chiguleva	UKR	46.70
Dogonadze & Khoperia	GEO	46.30
Sue Challis & Andrea Holmes	UK	45.20

Team

Germany	189.90
Ukraine	189.40
Belarus	188.10
UK	188.10

Third place shared.

British Championships
8-10 July 1994 Gillingham

Men

Theo Kypri	103.90
Paul Smyth	103.80
D Herring	102.00

Women

Andrea Holmes	101.30
Lorraine Lyon	98.00
C Wright	95.80

Triathlon

World Series

OVERALL (MEN)
Brad Bevan	AUS	440
Miles Stewart	AUS	370
B Braun	USA	368

OVERALL (WOMEN)
Jo-Anne Richie	CAN	465
C Montgomery	CAN	460
M Jones	AUS	400

Ironman Championships 1993
Hawaii

MEN
Mark Allen	USA	8h07:45
P Kiuru	FIN	8h14.27
W Dittrich	GER	8h20:13

The 35-y-o Allen sets a new course record in winning the title for the fifth consecutive year. In 1994 Greg Welch (AUS) becomes the first non-American to win it. Details in 1996 Yearbook.

WOMEN
Paula Newby-Fraser	ZIM	8h58:23
E Baker	NZ	9h08:04
S Latshaw	USA	9h20:40

Newby-Fraser, who wins the title for the sixth time, retains it in 1994.

World Long Distance Championships
27 June 1994 Nice
(4km swim, 120km cycle, 30km run)

MEN
Rob Barel	HOL	5h59:47
Lothar Ledr	GER	6h00:18
Yves Cordier	FRA	6h03:09

A puncture puts paid to the chances of Simon Lessing (UK), one of the favourites.

WOMEN
Isabelle Mouthon	FRA	6h41:50
Karen Smyers	USA	6h57:21
Lydie Reuze	FRA	7h01:17

European Olympic Distance Championships
2 July 1994 Eichstatt, Germany
(1500m swim, 40km cycle, 10km run)

MEN
Simon Lessing	UK	1h50:38
Ralf Eggert	GER	1h52:34
Rainer Müller	GER	1h53:37

The winner, born in S Africa, is a nephew of the novelist Doris Lessing.

WOMEN
Sonja Krolik	GER	2h02:51
Sabine Westhoff	GER	2h05:23
Isabelle Mouthon	FRA	2h05:58
18 Ali Hollington	*UK*	*2h13:16*

European Middle Distance Championships
6 Aug 1994 Novomesto, Slovenia

MEN
Rob Barel	HOL	3h48:19
Christopher Mauch	SWI	3h50:37
Peter Kropko	HUN	3h51:13

WOMEN
Isabele Mouthon	FRA	4h17:45
Natascha Badmann	SWI	4h20:27
Simone Mortier	GER	4h22:16

Goodwill Games (Olympic distance)
28 July 1994 Kavgolovo

MEN
Simon Lessing	UK	1h55:32.8
Dmitry Gaag	RUS	1h56:46.3
Aleksandr Merzlov	RUS	1h57:18.4

Lessing's eighth consecutive Triathlon win.

WOMEN
Isabelle Mouthon	FRA	
Rena Bradshaw	CAN	
Katie Webb	USA	

World Duathlon Championships

20 Nov 1994 Tasmania

MEN

Norman Stadler	GER	1h48:29
Urs Dellsperger	SWI	1h50:07
A Noble	AUS	1h50:32

WOMEN

Irma Heeren	HOL	2h03:00
Natascha Badmann	SWI	2h04:37
J Gallagher	AUS	2h07:15

World Olympic Distance Championships

27 Nov 1994 Wellington NZ

MEN

Spencer Smith	UK	1h51:04
Brad Bevan	AUS	1h51:49
Ralf Eggert	GER	1h52:40

Smith retains the title. Richard Allen (UK) finishes second in the junior event to Ben Bright (AUS).

WOMEN

Emma Carney	AUS	2h03:18
Anette Pedersen	DEN	2h05:31
Sarah Harrow	NZ	2h06:52

The champion for the last two years, Michelle Jones, another Australian, is kept out by injury. Carney's sister Clare takes the junior title won last year by Harrow.

British Duathlon Championship

24 April 1994 Chertsey, Surrey

MEN

Richard Allen	1h16:38
Craig Ball	1h17:26
Steve Burton	1h17:52

WOMEN

Helen Cawthorne	1h27:47
Melissa Watson	1h28:28
Kate Burge	1h31:46

British Sprint Championship

8 May 1994 Market Bosworth, Leics

MEN

Robin Brew	55:42
Steve Burton	56.57
Craig Ball	57:14

WOMEN

Helen Cawthorne	1h04:31
Loretta Sollars	1h04:56
Ali Hollington	1h05:34

British Olympic Distance Championship

21 Aug 1994 Wakefield

MEN

Steve Burton	2h01:15
Tim Stewart	2h02:14
Richard Hobson	2h02:40

Burton breaks the course record by 5 mins.

WOMEN

Ali Hollington	2h18:02
Helen Cawthorne	2h21:00
Annie Emmeron	2h23:12

Cawthorne, the defending champion, misses out on a treble, having won this year's national sprint & duathlon titles.

British Middle Distance Championship

4 Sep 1994 Guernsey

MEN

Tim Stewart	3h52:54
Mark Edmonds	3h54:55
Julian Jenkinson	3h55:37

WOMEN

Ali Hollington	4h25:34
Shirley Yarde	4h41:36
Helen Cawthorne	4h52:32

Home International Championship

4 Sep 1994 Port Rush, N Ireland

MEN

Craig Ball	ENG	2h00:57
Steven Barkess	ENG	2h01:11
Eugene Galbraith	IRE	2h02:42

WOMEN

Loretta Sollars	ENG	2h14:58
Fiona Lothian	SCOT	2h21:01
Ann Paul	IRE	2h21:39

Volleyball

World Championships

Men

Sep-Oct 1994 Athens

Quarter-finals

Italy	Russia	3-1	15-4 16-17 15-3 15-5
Cuba	Brazil	3-2	15-12 1-15 15-12 8-15 15-12
USA	S Korea	3-0	15-2 15-4 16-14
Holland	Greece	3-0	15-12 15-5 15-5

Semi-finals

Italy	Cuba	3-1	15-12 8-15 15-9 15-2
Holland	USA	3-2	5-15 16-14 10-15 15-8 15-11

3rd-place final

USA	Cuba	3-1	15-6 14-16 15-8 15-9

Final

Italy	Holland	3-1	15-10 11-15 15-11 15-1

Italy retain the title they also won in 1990. The Dutch, who beat them on the way to the 1992 Olympic silver, have never won it.

Women

Oct 1994 Belo Horizonte & São Paulo, Brazil

Quarter-finals

Cuba	Germany	3-0	15-9 15-5 15-5
Brazil	Japan	3-0	15-10 17-15 15-7
Russia	USA	3-1	15-9 9-15 15-9 16-14
S Korea	China	3-1	15-5 4-15 15-5 15-11

Semi-finals

Brazil	Russia	3-2	15-7 14-16 12-15 15-8 15-10
Cuba	S Korea	3-0	15-4 15-9 15-5

Brazil knock out the holders (USSR 1990).

3rd-place final

Russia	S Korea	14-16 15-11 15-6 15-8

Final

Cuba	Brazil	3-0	15-2 15-10 15-5

The reigning Olympic champions win the title for the second time, the first since 1978.

UK National League 1993-94 (Men)

Division 1	P	W	F	A	Pts
Malory Lewisham	14	14	42	5	28
Polonia Ealing	14	9	31	21	18
Newcastle Staffs	14	9	30	24	18
Liverpool City	14	8	30	28	16
Tooting Aquila	14	7	29	26	14
Wessex	14	5	23	33	10
Whitefield	14	3	14	36	6
Leeds	14	1	14	40	2

Divisional Winners

I	Malory	II	Lewisham
III North	Chester	III South	Solent
IV North	Ashton	IV Central	Varsovia
IV South	Mayfield Portsmouth		

UK National Cup 1993-94 (Men)

Semi-finals

Malory Lewisham	Liverpool City	15-5 15-8 15-8
Tooting Aquila	Polonia Ealing	15-10 15-8 4-15 15-8

Final *19 March Sheffield*

Malory Lewisham	Tooting Aquila	15-4 15-11 15-8

In winning the Cup for the seventh time in eight seasons, Malory stake a strong claim to being the most successful domestic team in any sport. They've already won the league title for the seventh sucessive year, have lost only two out of 79 league and cup matches in four seasons, and are unbeaten in 38 since Feb 1992.

UK National League 1993-94 (W)

Division 1	P	W	F	A	Pts
Woolwich Brixton	13	11	35	14	22
Sale	13	9	34	16	18
Britannia Music City	13	8	32	20	16
Dynamo London	13	5	18	29	10

Divisional winners

II	Birmingham Ladies
III North	Loughborough Students
III Central	Orpington Ladies
III South	Speedwell Ladies

UK National Cup 1993-94 (Women)

Semi-finals

Sale	Dynamo London	15-6 15-7 16-14
Britannia Music City	Woolwich Brixton	15-8 9-15 15-9 11-15 15-8

Final *19 March 1994 Sheffield*

Britannia Music City	Sale	15-9 15-10 7-15 15-13

Sale, the holders, appear in the final for the seventh time in eight years.

Water Sports

Water Skiing

British Championships
*July 1994 National Training Site,
Holme Pierrepont, Notts*

Men

Overall

Jodi Fisher	2678.8 pts
Jason Seels	2666.9
Matt Southam	2428.7

Slalom

Jodi Fisher	3 buoys at 11.25m
John Battleday	2@11.25
Jeremy Newby-Ricci	2@11.25

Fisher stops Battleday winning the title for the 10th time in a row.

Tricks

Jason Seels	7230
Nick Heaney	6640
Mike Hay	6320

Seels wins the title for the first time. Heaney, the defending champion, scored 7630 in the semi-final.

Jump

Danny Budd	53.1m
Jason Seels	52.0
Jodi Fisher	51.5

Budd wins the event for the second time.

Women

Overall

Philippa Roberts	3000.0
Nicola Huntridge	2458.2
Sarah Blake	2239.0

Roberts' perfect score beats defending champion Huntridge (15 years her junior) to win her the title for a record 11th time.

Slalom

Philippa Roberts	2@12
Nicola Huntridge	1@12

Sarah Gatty Saunt	2.5@13

Tricks

Philippa Roberts	6040
Rachel Crosland	4830
Lisa Ringrose	4600

Roberts sets a personal best to win the event for the 12th time, a total which already looks within the scope of either of the other medallists: Ringrose (who also sets a PB) is 15, Crosland only 13.

Jump

Philippa Roberts	41.7
Nicola Huntridge	40.6
Heidi Birr	33.0

Roberts sets another personal best, Birr improves hers in every round.

Carlsberg Masters
29 May 1994 Reading

Men

Overall

Claude Perez	FRA	2202
Jason Seels	UK	1934
Matt Southam	UK	1792

Tricks

O Nadin	BYL	7810
Julian Heaney	UK	6060
A Minenok	BYL	5990

Slalom

John Battleday	UK	2@11
Jodi Fisher	UK	1.5@11
Shawn Bronson	UK	3.5@12

Battleday wins the event for the fifth time.

Jump

Steffen Wild	GER	54.70m
Franz Oberleitner	AUT	53.70
Claude Perez	FRA	52.60

Women

Overall

Philippa Roberts	UK	2436

Olga Gubarenko	RUS	2382
Natalya Rumiantseva	RUS	2357

Rumiantseva's the reigning overall world champion.

Tricks

M Mosti	ITA	6120
A Andriopoulou	GRE	5740
Natalya Rumiantseva	RUS	5580

Slalom

G Jamin	FRA	3@12
Olga Gubarenko	RUS	2.5@12
C Gusenbauer	AUT	2@12

Jump

Nicola Huntridge	UK	36.70
Philippa Roberts	UK	35.90
Olga Gubarenko	RUS	35.80

World Junior Championships

9 Aug 1994 Guadalajara, Mexico

Boys

J Javier	ARG
G Hatzis	GRE
Tom Asher	UK

Asher, only 13, wins the Tricks, Paul Price (UK), who finishes fourth overall, wins the Jump.

Girls

B Hunte	USA
Marie Toms	UK
M Nightingale	USA

Team

USA
UK
France

Windsurfing

World Championships

Sep 1994 Ronbhjerg, Denmark
International funnelboards, slalom & course racing

Men

		pen
A Albeau	FRA	1.4
M Jensen	DEN	6.0
G Pelleau	FRA	13
13 J Anderson	*UK*	*29.0*

Women

G Hibaudo	FRA	1.4
E Duby	FRA	7.0
N Drurzer	GER	7.0
18 C Patterson	*UK*	*34.0*

A tie for second place.

Surfing

1994 world champion
Kelly Slater (USA)
Slater wins the title for the second time.

Powerboats

Class I Offshore

World Champion 1993
Khalfan Harib (UAE) Throttleman: 45-y-o Ed Colyer (USA)

C6 I Offshore

World Champion 1994
Saeed Al Tayer (UAE) Throttleman: Félix Serralles (PR)

Class II O6

World Champions 1994

2 litre	Phil Duggan	UK
8 litre	Phil Duggan	UK

Formula 1

World Champion 1994
Guido Cappellini (ITA)
Cappellini sets a record 18 pole positions in retaining the title. Second overall: 1986-89-91 (a record three wins) champion Jonathan Jones (UK).

British GP
24 July 1994 Cardiff

Michael Werner	GER
Danny Bertels	BEL
Guido Cappellini	ITA

Cappellini awarded third place despite being forced out by a collision with Steve Kerton (UK).

European Championships
21 Aug 1994 Bournemouth

Class 1	M Capoferri	ITA
Class 2	M Mansbridge	UK
4 Litre	C Stoneman	UK
2 Litre	M Mumford	UK

Weightlifting

World Championships 1993

Nov, Melbourne

Men

54 kg

Ivan Ivanov	BUL	277.5 kg	WR
Halil Mutlu	TURK	275.0	
Ko Kwang-Ku	S KOR	270.0	

Snatch gold: Yan Bin (CHN) 122.5, Jerk gold: Ivanov 157.5

Ivanov, the 1990 &1991 champion, wins the overall title with his last attempt.

59 kg

Nikolai Peshalov	BUL	305.0	WR
Hafiz Suleymanoglu	TURK	295.0	
Tang Ning-sheng	CHN	292.5	

Snatch: Peshalov 137.5, Jerk: Peshalov 167.5 WR

Suleymanoglu's no relation to to the famous Naim (64 kg).

64 kg

Naim Suleimanoglu	TURK	322.5
Ri Hi-Bong	N KOR	317.5
Yurik Sarkisian	ARM	315.0

Snatch: Suleymanoglu 145.0, Jerk: Suleymanoglu 177.5

Suleymanoglu, the 1991 champion and pound for pound arguably the greatest lifter of all time, is run quite close but nevertheless wins by taking only two lifts in all. Ming Feng (CHN), who finishes seventh overall, breaks six world junior records.

70 kg

Yoto Yotov	BUL	342.5
Ergun Batmaz	TURK	332.5
Andreas Behm	GER	330.0

Snatch: Yotov 155.0, Jerk: Yotov 187.5

Yotov, who won the 1991 title on bodyweight, this time dominates the competition.

76 kg

| Altim Orazdurdiev | TKM | 370.0 | WR |
| Ruslan Savchenko | UKR | 370.0 | WR |

| Kim Myong-Nam | N KOR | 362.5 |

Snatch: Savchenko 170.0, Jerk: Orazdurdiev 202.5 WR

Orazdurdiev won the 82.5 kg overall title in 1990.

83 kg

Pyros Dimas	GRE	377.5
Marc Huster	GER	375.0
Kiril Kounev	AUS	372.5

Snatch: Dimas 175.0, Jerk: Huster 210.0 WR

Andrew Callard (UK) finishes effectively last with 132.5 in the snatch and no lift in the jerk.

91 kg

Ivan Tchakarov	BUL	407.5	WR
Khaki Khakiashvili	GEO	402.5	
Anatoly Khrapatyi	KAZ	395.0	

Snatch: Tchakarov 185.0 WR, Jerk: Khakiashvili 222.5

99 kg

Viktor Tregubov	RUS	407.5
Sergei Sirtsov	RUS	407.5
Boris Burov	ECU	395.0

Snatch: Sirtsov 190.0, Jerk: Tregubov 222.5

Sirtsov won the 90 kg title in 1991. His gold medal attempt at 222.5 looks perfectly good but is controversially called a no-lift. The favourite Nicu Vlad, who won the 1984 Olympic 90 kg gold medal for Romania, represents Australia for the first time, surprisingly misses at 192.5, loses the snatch gold medal because he weighs 0.08 kg more than Sirtsov, fails at 222.5 in the jerk, and finishes last.

108 kg

Timur Taimazov	UKR	420.0
Stefan Botev	AUS	417.5
Igor Razorenov	UKR	415.0

Snatch: Taimazov 195.0, Jerk: Botev

Razorenov, who would have won the jerk if he'd lifted 232.5, attempts 237.5 for the overall gold. Botev won the 1989 & 1990 110 kg overall title for Bulgaria and totalled 445.0 to win the 1990 European title.

Over 108 kg

Ronnie Weller	GER	442.5
Manfred Nerlinger	GER	440.0
Andrei Chemerkin	RUS	435.0

Snatch: Weller 200.0 WR, Jerk: Nerlinger 247.5

Nerlinger also finished second overall in 1991.

Women

46 kg
Chu Nan-Mei	TAIW	152.5
Yu Shiu-Fen	TAIW	147.5
Satomi Saito	JAP	147.5

Snatch: Chu 67.5, Jerk Chu 85.0

50 kg
Liu Xiu-hua	CHN	187.5
Guan Hong	CHN	177.5
Kuo Chiu-Chun	TAIW	170.0

Snatch: Guan 77.5, Jerk: Liu 110.0

Liu, the hot favourite, takes only one lift after 77.5 to let Guan have the snatch gold. Choi Myung-Shik (N KOR) finishes without a medal despite lifting exactly the same weights as Kuo.

54 kg
Chen Xiao-min	CHN	200.0
Robin Byrd	USA	177.5
Karnam Malleswari	INDIA	177.5

Snatch: Chen 90.0, Jerk: Chen 110.0

Byrd, Malleswari & Janeta Georgieva (BUL) lift exactly the same totals in both diciplines.

59 kg
Sun Cai-yan	CHN	217.5
Gergana Kirilova	BUL	202.5
Maria Christoforidou	GRE	197.5

Snatch: Sun 97.5, Jerk Sun 120.0

64 kg
Li Hong-yun	CHN	220.0	WR
Won Soon-Li	S KOR	202.5	
Julie Malenfant	CAN	195.0	

Snatch: Li 102.5 WR, Jerk: Li 117.5

In every sense a frightening thought: Li, who breaks the snatch world record three times and would have won two golds in the next weight class up, is only 17.

70 kg
Milena Trendafilova	BUL	220.0	WR
Kumi Haseba	JAP	207.5	
Kim Dong-hee	S KOR	205.0	

Snatch: Trendafilova 100.0, Jerk: Trendafilova 120.0

Despite the world record, Trendafilova's rather lucky to win. Only six competitors take part, none of them Chinese.

76 kg
Hua Ju	CHN	230.0	WR

Li Chang-ping	CHN	220.0
Maria Takacs	HUN	207.5

Snatch: Hua 105.0 WR, Jerk: Li 127.5 WR

Double trouble for the future: Hua & Li are both juniors.

83 kg
Panagiota

Snatch: Xing Shu-wen (CHN) 107.5, Jerk: Chen 127.5

Over 83 kg
Li Ya-juan	CHN	260.0
Carla Garret	USA	232.5
Lyubov Grigurko	UKR	215.0

Snatch: Li 105.0, Jerk: Li 155.0

Garret weighs 126 kg, Li 125, Grigurko only 86. Myrtle Augee (UK), the 1990 gold medallist and 1994 silver medallist in the Commonwealth Games shot putt, finishes sixth (192.5 kg) of the nine competitors but does better at the European Championships.

World Championships 1994
18-27 Nov Istanbul

Men

54 kg
Halil Mutlu	TURK	290.0	WR
Ivan Ivanov	BUL	275.0	
Sevdalin Michev	BUL	270.0	

Snatch: Mutlu 130.0 WR, Jerk: Mutlu 160.0 WR

Mutlu turns last year's tables on Ivanov by setting seven world records.

59 kg
Nikolai Peshalov	BUL	302.5
Hafiz Suleymanoglu	TURK	297.5
Radostin Panayotov	BUL	287.5

Snatch: Peshalov 135.0, Jerk: Peshalov 167.5

Peshalov, taking an extra lift, breaks the world record in the jerk: 168.

64 kg
Naim Suleymanoglu	TURK	330.0	WR
Valerios Leonidis	GRE	325.0	
Attila Czanka	HUN	312.5	

Snatch: Suleymanoglu 147.5 WR, Jerk: Suleymanoglu 182.5 WR

The mighty mite rises to the Greek challenge: Leonidis sets world records in both disciplines (146.5 & 180.5) but Naim breaks five in all.

70 kg

Fedail Guler	TURK	350.0	WR
Yoto Yotov	BUL	345.0	
Anghel Guentchev	BUL	340.0	

Snatch: Guler 160.0 WR, Jerk: Attila Feri (HUN) 190.0

76 kg

Pablo Lara	CUBA	365.0
Ingo Steinhöfel	GER	362.5
Ruslan Savchenko	UKR	360.0

Snatch: Steinhöfel 165.0, Jerk: Lara 202.5

83 kg

Marc Huster	GER	382.5	WR
Sergo Tchakoian	ARM	380.0	
Sunay Bulut	TURK	375.0	

Snatch: Tchakoian 175.0 WR, Jerk: Huster 210.0

Bulut takes an extra lift to break the jerk WR (210.5)

91 kg

Alexei Petrov	RUS	412.5
Khaki Khakiashvili	GEO	397.5
V Belyatski	BYL	380.0

Snatch: Tschakarov 185.0, Jerk: Petrov 227.5

Still only a junior, Petrov sets two world senior records (with extra lifts) and puts on so much pressure that defending champion Ivan Tchakarov fails all three lifts in the jerk.

99 kg

Sergei Sirtsov	RUS	417.5	WR
Viktor Tregubov	RUS	405.0	
S Rybalchenko	UKR	395.0	

Snatch: Sirtsov 192.5 WR, Jerk: Sirtsov 225.0 WR

The Russians' battle continues from the previous year, with the older man this time a clear winner, setting three world records during the actual competition (no extra lifts).

108 kg

Timur Taimazov	UKR	435.0	WR
Nicu Vlad	AUS	422.5	
Artur Akoyev	RUS	420.0	

Snatch: Taimazov 200.0 WR, Jerk: Taimazov 235.0

This time Taimazov wins all three golds, setting four world records in the process.

Over 108 kg

Aleksandr Kurlovich	BYL	457.5	WR
Andrei Chemerkin	RUS	452.5	
Stefan Botev	AUS	435.0	

Snatch: Kurlovich 205.0 WR, Jerk: Kurlovich 252.5 WR

Kurlovich, the favourite, who didn't take part last year,

sets six world records - and needs them to hold off Chemerkin (he matches Kurlovich's WR in the jerk). Botev & Vlad switch weights, to no great avail. Chemerkin outweighs Botev by five stone. The weights in this category range from 17st 7 (Mamoru Sato of Japan) to 28st 10 (Ernesto Aguero of Cuba, who finishes next to last)

Women

46 kg

Yun Yan-hong	CHN	180.0
Nameir Kunjarani	INDIA	167.5
Tsai Huey-Woan	TAIW	155.0

Snatch: Yun 80.0 WR, Jerk: Yun 100.0

50 kg

Robin Byrd	USA	175.0
I Rifatova	BUL	165.0
Chen Li-chuan	TAIW	165.0

Snatch: Byrd 80.0, Jerk:Rifatova 95.0

54 kg

Wang Sheng	CHN	197.5
Karnam Maleswari	INDIA	197.5
Li Feng-ying	CHN	195.0

Snatch: Li 87.5, Jerk: Wang 110.0

Maleswari misses out on all three golds solely on bodyweight.

59 kg

Zou Feie	CHN	220.0
Gergana Kirilova	BUL	202.5
K Suta	THAI	197.5

Snatch: Zou 97.5, Jerk: Zou 122.5

Zou, another Chinese taking golds away from Kirilova, takes extra lifts to set world records in both snatch & jerk.

64 kg

Li Hong-yun	CHN	235.0	WR
Kuo Su-fen	TAIW	205.0	
Erzsebet Markus	HUN	197.5	

Snatch: Li 105.0 WR, Jerk: Li 130.0 WR

Li dominates, setting five world records.

70 kg

Zhou Mei-hong	CHN	222.5
Qu Li-hua	CHN	220.0
W Puncharkarn	THAI	210.0

Snatch: Qu 97.5, Jerk: Zhou 127.5

Zhou takes an extra lift to set a WR in the jerk: 128.5

76 kg

Maria Takacs	HUN	217.5
Albina Khomich	RUS	212.5

Snatch: Khomich 97.5, Jerk: 127.5

83 kg

Maria Urrutia	COL	237.5
Chen Shu-chih	TAIW	235.0
Derya Acikgoz	TURK	220.0

Snatch: Urrutia 105.0, Jerk: Urrutia 132.5

For once, the absence of the Chinese doesn't affect the standard at the top: Chen sets a short-lived WR of 130.0 in the jerk.

Over 83 kg

Li Dan	CHN	242.5
Karolina Lundahl	FIN	230.0
Chen Hsiao-Lien	TAIW	217.5

Snatch: Li 107.5 WR, Jerk: Li 135.0

Li sets two WRs in the snatch. Augee finishes fourth overall, with the same total as Chen.

European Championships

Men 1994

May, Sokolov, Czech Republic

54 kg

Halil Mutlu	TURK	277.5
Sevdalin Minchev	BUL	275.0
Iakovos Polanidis	GRE	260.0

Snatch: Minchev 125.0, Jerk: Mutlu 155.0

Minchev sets a world junior record in the snatch.

59 kg

Nikolai Peshalov	BUL	297.5
Radostin Panayotov	BUL	290.0
Giorgios Tzelilis	GRE	

Snatch: Peshalov 135.0, Jerk: 162.5

64 kg

Naim Suleymanoglu	TURK	325.0	WR
Valerios Leonidis	GRE	317.5	
Ilian Tzankov	BUL	312.5	

Snatch: Suleymanoglu 245.0 WR, Jerk: 180.0 WR

Suleymanoglu, dominant as ever, takes only one lift in the snatch, enough to break his own world record. Ben Devonshire (UK) finishes 15th & last.

70 kg

Yoto Yotov	BUL	345.0	WR
Fedail Guler	TURK	342.5	
Ergun Batmaz	TURK	332.5	

Snatch: Israel Militosian (ARM) 157.5 WR, Jerk: Yotov 192.5 WR

Militosian lifts 5kg more than Yotov in the snatch but fails at his opening jerk of 180 and finishes last.

76 kg

Ruslan Savchenko	UKR	355.0
Khat Kiapanaktsian	ARM	355.0
Roman Sevosteyev	UKR	355.0

Snatch: Kiapanaktsian 165.0, Jerk: Savchenko 195.0

A rare event: all three overall medals decided on bodyweight.

83 kg

Vadim Bazhan	UKR	377.5
Alexandr Blychtchik	UKR	372.5
Vadim Vakartchiouk	MOLD	370.0

Snatch: Bazhan 172.5, Jerk: Vakartchiouk 205.0

91 kg

Alexei Petrov	RUS	412.5
Kakhi Kakhiashvili	GEO	400.0
Ivan Tchakarov	BUL	395.0

Snatch: Igor Alexeyev (RUS) 185.0, Jerk: Petrov 227.5

Petrov sets six world junior records.

99 kg

Sergei Sirtsov	RUS	415.0	WR
Oleg Tchiritso	BYL	387.5	
Moukhran Gogia	GEO	387.5	

Snatch: Sirtsov 190.0 WReq, Jerk: Sirtsov 225.0 WR

Sirtsov sets four world records in all.

108 kg

Timur Taimazov	UKR	430.0	WR
Vadim Stasenko	RUS	405.0	
Igor Razorenov	UKR	402.5	

Snatch: Taimazov 195.0, Jerk: Taimazov 235.0 WR

Over 108 kg

Andrei Chemerkin	RUS	450.0	WR
Sergei Naguirnyi	UKR	412.5	
Artur Skripkin	RUS	410.0	

Snatch: Chemerkin 200.0 WReq, Jerk: Chemerkin 250.0 WR

The emergent Chemerkin, perhaps the lifter of the championships, almost equals Suleymanoglu's feat of setting new world records in all three categories. Petr Sobotka (CZE), who finishes ninth overall, sets world junior records for the snatch and total.

Women 1993

46 kg

Csilla Földi	HUN	150.0
Blanca Fernandez	SPA	137.5
Danila Manca	ITA	132.5

Snatch: Földi 67.5, Jerk: Földi 82.5

Földi retains the overall title.

50 kg

Anna Stroboli	GRE	160.0
Neli lankova	BUL	155.0
María Dolores Sotoca	SPA	147.5

Snatch: Stroboli 72.5, Jerk: Stroboli 87.5

54 kg

Janeta Georgieva	BUL	177.5
Konstantina Misirli	GRE	165.0
Aurore Ernault	FRA	140.0

Snatch: Georgieva 82.5, Jerk: Georgieva 95.0

Georgieva retains the overall title.

59 kg

Gergana Kirilova	BUL	200.0
Timea Ray	HUN	167.5
Diane Greenidge	UK	165.0

Snatch: Kirilova 90.0, Jerk: Kirilova 110.0

Kirilova retains the overall title.

64 kg

Maria Christoforidou	GRE	192.5
Erzsebet Markus	HUN	192.5
Stephanie Utsch	GER	187.5

Snatch: Markus 90.0, Jerk: Christoforidou 107.5

Cristoforidou, the heavy favourite, wins because she's lighter.

70 kg

Milena Trendafilova	BUL	210.0
Maria Tákacs	HUN	207.5
Daniela Kerkelova	BUL	205.0

Snatch: Trendafilova 95.0, Jerk: Trendafilova 115.0

76 kg

Senka Asenova	BUL	220.0
Panagiota Antonopoulou	GRE	210.0
Valkana Tosheva	BUL	195.0

Snatch: Asenova 100.0, Jerk: Asenova 120.0

Antonopoulou wins all three silvers.

83 kg

Theodoula Spanou	GRE	202.5
Karolina Lundahl	FIN	195.0
Line Mary	FRA	182.5

Snatch: Spanou 90.0, Jerk: Spanou 112.5

Sandra Smith-Vokroj finishes fourth (with a British record 175.0) of the five competitors. Line Mary is correct, not 'Mary Line.'

Over 83 kg

Myrtle Augee	UK	200.0
N Chiriavela	RUS	192.5
Bernadette Nagy	HUN	192.5

Snatch: Erika Tákacs (HUN) 87.5, Jerk: Augee 115.0

Augee, the shot putter (see World Championships), clears 85.0 in the snatch, missing a medal on bodyweight, but wins two golds when Tákacs fails to lift a weight in the jerk. Her feat's put into perspective by the winning total, which is lower than in any of the three divisions below.

Women 1994

Rome

46 kg

Donka Mincheva	BUL	147.5
Lyubov Averyanova	RUS	137.5
Csilla Foldi	HUN	135.0

Snatch: Mincheva 67.0, Jerk: Averyanova 80.0

50 kg

Izabela Rifatova	BUL	160.0
Anna Stroubou	GRE	150.0
Siika Stoyeva	BUL	150.0

Snatch: Rifatova 70.0, Jerk: Rifatova 90.0

54 kg

Neli Yankova	BUL	177.5
Janeda Georgieva	BUL	177.5
Konstantina Misirli	GRE	160.0

Snatch: Georgieva 82.5, Jerk: Yankova 102.5

59 kg

Gergana Kirilova	BUL	192.5
Bénédicte Comblez	FRA	172.5
Diana Greenidge	UK	167.5

Snatch: Kirilova 87.5, Jerk Kirilova 105.0

Kirilova easily retains all three titles. Greenidge finishes fourth in both snatch & jerk.

64 kg

Daniela Kerkelova	BUL	192.5
Erzsebet Markus	HUN	190.0
Alexia Papageorgiou	GRE	182.5

Snatch: Markus 90.0, Jerk: Kerkelova 107.5

70 kg

Milena Trendafilova	BUL	207.5
Theodoula Spanou	GRE	200.0
Ilona Danko	HUN	192.5

Snatch: Trendafilova 95.0, Jerk: Trendafilova 112.5

Trendafilova retains all three titles.

76 kg

MariaTákacs	HUN	215.0
Derya Acikgoz	TURK	210.0
Irina Kasimova	RUS	207.5

Snatch: Acikgoz 95.0, Jerk: Kasimova 122.5

No Bulgarians enter this or the 83kg division. The British Weightlifter magazine spell Acikgoz's first name Diarrhoea.

83 kg

Karolina Lundahl	FIN	222.5
Panagiota Antonopoulou	GRE	212.5
Venera Mananova	RUS	210.0

Snatch: Lundahl 97.5, Jerk: Lundahl 125.0

Lundahl herself feels that Antonopoulou's mistake hands her the jerk & total golds.

Over 83 kg

Lyubov Grigurko	UKR	217.5
Myrtle Augee	UK	212.5
Erika Tákacs	HUN	207.5

Snatch: Grigurko 100.0, Jerk: Grigurko 117.5

Augee takes three silvers, losing the jerk gold on bodyweight. Tákacs is Maria's sister. Fourth in all three categories: the splendidly named Grit Hammer (GER).

British Championships 1993

54 kg

Alan Ogilvie	207.5
Charles Revolta	160.0

As in 1994, only two lifters take part.

59 kg

Ben Devonshire	232.5
John Lubin	217.5
Lucas Witts	190.0

64 kg

Stewart Cruikshank	255.0
Paul Richard	232.5
William Eveson	227.5

70 kg

Tony Morgan	292.5
Marius Hardiman	262.5
Leon Griffin	250.0

76 kg

Ed Halsted	270.0
Andy Littler	260.0
Gary Carthew	255.0

Winning is the drug

Powerlifter John Povey, suspended for four years by the British Weightlifting Association for taking steroids, is the first disabled British athlete to be banned. Two Iranians competing in the World Cup are caught taking nandronolone: Rabek Kazem & Jahangir Chosbari.

83 kg

Andy Callard	327.5
Kamran Majid	270.0
Mike Mahoney	265.0

91 kg

Peter May	325.0
Jimmy Singh	320.0
Gary Williams	282.5

99 kg

Andrew Saxton	305.0
Brian Clifton	292.5
Dave Swayer	280.0

Only three take part. Just a year earlier, Saxton was caught taking drugs at the Olympics.

108 kg

Giles Greenwood	315.0
Ray Kopka	302.5
Mark Thomas	-

Again, only three take part.

Over 108 kg

Fraser Thomas	297.0
Nat Cooper	280.0

Only two in this one.

British Championships 1994

4 June 1994 Meadowbank, Edinburgh

54 kg

A Jones	172.5 kg
James Power	-

The most foregone of conclusions after the snatch: Power misses all three lifts, and only two competitors take part.

59 kg

Ben Devonshire	235.0
Sam Hayer	220.0
S Green	182.5

Devonshire sets British records in the snatch (105.0) and total, but (here we go again) only two others take part.

64 kg

C Byrne		230.0
Steve Warman		225.0
D Leverage		217.5

The favourite, John Lubin, leads after the snatch but misses all three jerks.

70 kg

Stuart Cruikshank		290.0
Brendon Cook		232.5
S See		227.5

Cruikshank sets a British record (160.0) in the jerk.

76 kg

David Morgan	310.0	ChR
Anthony Arthur	292.5	
Leon Griffin	285.0	

Morgan breaks four British records, at least one in each category: 140.0, 170.0, and the total set just before him in the competition by Arthur.

83 kg

Steve Ward		317.5
J McEwan		280.0
Ray Vaughan		272.5

91 kg

Peter May	350.0	ChR
Andy Callard	325.0	
Keith Boxell	312.5	

Five lifts are enough for May to break six records. Boxell totalled 350 to win the 90 kg Commonwealth Games title in 1986.

99 kg

Karl Grant		315.0
Brian Clifton		310.0
Dave Sawyer		287.0

108 kg

Giles Greenwood		332.5

Over 108 kg

Nat Cooper		290.0
Fraser Thomas		260.0

As in 1993, only two (the same two) take part - but Greenwood (108 kg) takes the biscuit: no-one else competed for it.

World Junior Championships 1993

Cheb, Czech Rep

54 kg

Halillvan Mutlu	TURK	275.0
Sevdalin Minchev	BUL	275.0
Ham Jung-hoon	S KOR	252.5

Treble, in fact quintuple, frustration for Minchev: after losing two golds at the senior European Championships to team mate Ivan Ivanov, he goes one better by losing all three here, again only on bodyweight.

59 kg

Olec Iugai	KAZAK	280.0
Petr Petrov	BUL	270.0
Cho Joon-ho	S KOR	267.5

64 kg

Ilian Tzankov	BUL	300.0
Muchait Yakci	TURK	295.0
Ashot Kazarian	ARM	285.0

70 kg

Zhan Xu-gang	CHN	325.0
Zlatan Vanev	BUL	320.0
Sergei Filimonov	KAZAK	315.0

Zhang wins all three golds.

76 kg

Nikolai Kocheilov	RUS	332.5
Karen Igitian	ARM	330.0
Krasimir Ivanov	BUL	325.0

83 kg

Vyacheslav Osipov	RUS	347.5
Vyacheslav Kanutkin	RUS	345.0
Iurie Conjuhari	MOLD	342.5

91 kg

Alexei Petrov	RUS	400.0
Marin Kehayov	BUL	357.5
Denys Gotfrid	UKR	357.5

Petrov, whose performances would have won all six gold medals in the higher classes, completely dominates both disciplines to produce the year's highest total at this weight by a junior or senior.

99 kg

Ara Vardanian	ARM	380.0
E Chichliannikov	RUS	375.0
Dmitry Smirnov	RUS	365.0

Vardanian & Chichliannikov, who have the same bodyweight, share first place in the jerk, the Armenian winning the other two golds.

108 kg

Ruslan Doroschuk	BYL	382.5
Sergei Lukyanchikov	UKR	372.5
Pavel Najdek	POL	370.0

Over 108 kg

Aleksandr Manushev	UZB	372.5
V Chtcherbatykh	LAT	370.0
Achot Danielian	ARM	367.5

Chtcherbatykh misses the snatch gold because he weighs 0.05 kg more than Popov. As often happens in the juniors, the three lower classes all produce higher winning totals.

Wrestling

World Champions

Freestyle

FINALS 24-28 Aug 1994 Istanbul

48 kg	Alexis Vila	CUBA
52 kg	Valentin Yordanov	BUL
57 kg	Alejandro Puerto	CUBA
62 kg	Magomed Azizov	RUS
68 kg	Alexander Leopold	GER
74 kg	Turan Ceylan	TURK
82 kg	Lukman Shabraylov	MOLD
90 kg	Rasul Khadem Azghadi	IRAN
100 kg	Aravet Sabeyev	GER
130 kg	Mahmut Demir	TURK

Graeco-Roman

MEN 8-11 Sep 1994 Tampere, Finland

48 kg	Wilber Sánchez	CUBA
52 kg	Alfred Ter-Mkrytschan	GER
57 kg	Yuri Melnitchyenko	KAZ
62 kg	Sergei Martinov	RUS
68 kg	Islam Dugutyev	RUS
74 kg	Mnatasakan Eskandarian	RUS
82 kg	Thomas Zander	GER
90 kg	Gogi Koguashvili	RUS
100 kg	Andrzej Wronski	POL
130 kg	Aleksandr Karelin	RUS

WOMEN 6-7 Aug Sofia

44 kg	Shoko Yoshimura	JAP
47 kg	Misho Kamibayashi	JAP
50 kg	Miyo Yamamoto	JAP
53 kg	Akemi Kawasaki	JAP
57 kg	Line Johansen	NOR
61 kg	Nikola Hartmann	AUT
65 kg	Yaoi Urano	JAP
70 kg	Chrissie Nordhagen	CAN
75 kg	Mitsuko Funakoshi	JAP

British Champions

Finals 7 May 1994 Lancing

MEN

52 kg	Andrew Hutchinson
57 kg	Darren Rigby
62 kg	John Melling
68 kg	Brian Aspen
74 kg	Calum McNeil
82 kg	Gurchetan Kooner
90 kg	Graeme English
100 kg	Noel Loban
130 kg	Amerjit Singh

WOMEN

53 kg	Amanda Broadbent
57 kg	Tara Williams

The only two weight classes staged.

Yachting

World Champions 1994

CENTREBOARD DINGHY

420	John Merricks & Ian Lavering	UK
470 (men)	Ben & Jan Kouwenhoven	HOL
470 (women)	Ines Bohn & Sabine Rotazsch	GER
505	Chris & Darren Nicolson	AUS
	2 Ian Barker & Tim Hancock	*UK*
Cadet	Juan de la Fuente	ARG
Contender	Scott Graham	UK
Enterprise	Ian Fisher & Richard Sadler	UK
Europe	Kristine Roug	DEN
Finn	Fredrik Loof	SWE
Fireball	Ian Pinnell & Daniel Cripps	UK
Flying Junior	Jan Boultman	HOL
Flying Dutchman	Jorgen Boysen Moller	DEN
Int. 14 foot	Ian Walker & Chris Fox	UK
Laser	Nik Burfoot	NZ
Laser II	Roger Ward & Suzi Mistlin	UK
Lightning	Manfred Kaufmann	BRZ
Mirror	T King	AUS
Moth	Toby Collyer	UK
OK Dinghy	Leith Armit	NZ
Optimist	Martin Jenkins	ARG
Snipe	Santiago Lange & Mariano Parada ARG	
Sunfish	Eduardo Cordero	VEN
Vaurien	K Diem & M Kalkowski	AUT

KEEL BOAT

Dragon	Jesper Bank	DEN
Etchells	Dennis Conner, Steve Jarvin, Brad Rodi	USA
8 metre	Ronald B Palms	USA
5.5 metre	Dominiq Lauener	SWI
Flying Fifteen	Roger Craddock	NZ
H Boat	Christian Rasmussen	GER
J22	Chris Larson	USA
J24	Ken Read	USA
6 metre	A Bassain	ITA
Soling	Manuel Doreste	SPA
Star	Ross MacDonald & Eric Jespersen	CAN
Tempest	Vincent Hösch	GER
2.4 metre	Patrik Farsgren	SWE
Yngling	Soren Edrup	DEN

MODEL YACHT

Class A	Derek Priestley	UK
Marblehead	Graham Bantock	UK
Ten Rater	Paul Lucas	FRA

MULTIHULL

Class A	Mitch Booth	AUS
Class C	S McKeon	AUS
Dart 18	Kim Furniss	UK
Hobie 14	Allan Lawrence	SAF
Hobie 16	Enrique Figueroa & Carla Malatrasi	PR
Hobie 17	Bob Seaman	USA
Hobie 18	Donna Kennedy	AUS
Tornado	Fernando Leon & John Ballester	SPA

MATCH RACING Oct 1994 La Rochelle

Semi-finals

Bertrand Pace	FRA	Rod Davis	USA	3-0
Paul Cayard	USA	Peter Gilmour	AUS	3-0

3rd-place final

Davis	Gilmour	2-1

Final

Pace	Cayard	2-1

The first Frenchman to win the event, in a final reduced to best of three from best of five. Chris Law (UK) is expelled from the event for using abusive language to an official.

AMERICA'S CUP CLASS Oct-Nov 1994 San Diego

oneAustralia (John Bertrand)	3
America3 (Dawn Riley)	13
Nippon '94 (J Cutler)	17

The first two names are apparently written as above. America3 has an all-woman crew.

World Sailing Championships

26 June - 7 Aug La Rochelle
(inaugural IYRU championships)

MEN

Finn

Francesco Bruni	ITA
Robert Scheidt	BRZ
Alfonso Domingos	PORT

470

John Merricks & Ian Walker	UK
Kan Yamada & Seiji Saito	JAP

Paolo Cian & Marco Scotto	ITA

Keelboat

Magnus Gravare	SWE
P Ahlby	SWE
C King	UK

WOMEN

Europe

Kristine Roug	DEN
Tine Moberg-Parker	CAN
Margriet Matthysee	HOL

470

Teresa Zabell & Begonis via Dufresne	SPA
Ruslana Taran & Natalya Hapanovich	UKR
Peggy Hardwiger & Christina Pinnow	GER

Keelboat

Christine Briand	FRA
B Kristiansen	NOR
A McGaw	SWE

Multihull

Kerry Ireland & Vicki Tanner	AUS
Margot Brache & Belinda Klaase	SAF
Judy Herald & Lisa Holman	SAF

OPEN

Multihull

Enrique Figueroa & Carla Malatrasi	PR
Blaine Dodds & Steve Arnold	SAF
Shaun Ferry & Lewis Alison	SAF

When the organisers can't find a recording of the Puerto Rican national anthem, Figueroa sings it unaccompanied.

OVERALL (IYRU Cup)

Italy	73 pens
Sweden	74
France	75

World Youth Sailing Championships
Marathon, Greece

BOYS

Boards	Amir Lebinson	ISR
Single-handed	Daniel Slater	NZ
Double-handed	David Ames & PJ Buhler	USA

GIRLS

Boards	Amelie Lux	GER
Single-handed	Shelley Hesson	NZ
Double-handed	Storm Nuttal & Sally Cutherbert	UK

Round the World Race (Crews)
Sep 1993 - June 1994

1st Leg Southampton to Punta del Este (URU)
5950 miles, finish 11 Oct 1993
New Zealand Endeavour
Grant Dalton (NZ)   24 days 07h 19m

2nd leg Punta del Este to Fremantle (AUS)
7558 miles, finish 9 Dec 1993
Intrum Justitia
Lawrie Smith (UK)   25 days 14h 39m

3rd leg Fremantle to Auckland
3272 miles, finish 22 Jan 1994
New Zealand Endeavour
Grant Dalton (NZ)   13 days 08h 15m

4th leg Auckland to Punta del Este
4914 miles, finish 13 March 1994
New Zealand Endeavour
Grant Dalton (NZ)   21 days 02h 26m

5th leg Punta del Este to Fort Lauderdale (USA)
5600 miles, finish 25 April 1994
Yamaha Ross Field (NZ)   22 days 05h 13m

6th leg Fort Lauderdale to Southampton
3818 miles, finish 3 June 1994
Tokio   Chris Dickson (NZ)   12 days 19h 36m

OVERALL
New Zealand Endeavour
Grant Dalton (NZ)   120 days 5h 9m

60-FOOTERS
Yamaha Ross Field (NZ)   120 days 14h 55m

Steinlager II's record for the race is broken by more than eight days.

Allegations of cheating are made against Field, who seems to have received weather information during the first leg from Adrienne Cahalan, navigator of Heineken, in contravention of Rule 75 which forbids no outside assistance. The allegations are brought by Nance Frank, who plans to sue the owners of Yamaha & Heineken, alleging collusion to have her removed from the race. It doesn't affect the result of the 60-foot class, which Field wins thanks to Tokio's broken mast on the fifth leg.

Dawn Riley's all-woman crew, beset by problems to the end (the last straw a broken tiller), finish the race on 8 June.

Round the World Race (Solo)

1st Leg Charleston, S Carolina to Cape Town
6865 miles, finish 21 Oct 1994
Ecureuil Poitou-Charentes 2
Isabelle Autissier (FRA) 35 days 08h 52m 18s

The only woman in the event becomes the first ever to win a leg in the race, breaking the record (set over a shorter distance) by 2 days 2h 20m 21s in the process of finishing 1200 miles ahead of the first man, Steve Petengill, whose time (nearly six days slower than Autissier) is the fastest ever by an American in the race! Autissier's compatriot Christophe Auguin, winner of the race the last time it was held (1990) trails her by 1700 miles. She takes half as long as Harry Mitchell, who uses a day for every year of his age (70), finishing the leg just as most of the rest of the fleet start the second.

2nd Leg Cape Town to Sydney
6698 miles, finish 21 Dec 1994
Sceta Calberson
Christophr Auguin (FRA) 24 days 23h 40m 16s

Auguin sets a record for the leg, as well as covering 350.9 miles in 24 hours, apparently another world best – but is very lucky that Autissier loses her mast early on; it may well cost her the entire race, which she was dominating till then.

Records

On 7 May 1994, trying to break the record for sailing non-stop, solo, and 'the wrong way' round the world, Mike Golding's 67-foot steel yacht Group 4 makes the usual topical joke of its name by being marooned on Shingles Bank in the Solent for a frustrating eight hours, but there was a little time in hand: he cut Chay Blyth's 1971 record time almost in half. By 125 days in fact, taking only 167 of them, plus 7 hours & 42 mins.

Laurent Bourgnon (FRA) sets a new record for the voyage from New York to the Lizard in Cornwall: 7 days 2h 34m, beating the previous fastest by more than 25 hours. En route, he sets a record of 538.7 miles in 24 hours.

In Oct 1994, Steve Fossett (USA) destroys Robin Knox-Johnston's 1976 record (11 days 8 hrs) when he circumnavigates Britain & Ireland in 4 days 21 hrs 5 mins.

Sydney – Hobart 1993
26-29 Dec, 630 nautical miles

Ninety Seven
Andrew Strachan (AUS) 4days 00h 54:11
Micropay Cuckoo's Nest
Nigel Holman (AUS) 4days 02h 54:59
Wild Thing
G Wharington (AUS) 4days 07h 44.30

Strachan, returning to ocean racing after an absence of ten years, skippers the smallest boat (47 feet) to win the event in the past forty years. Bad weather forces 67 of the 105 entries to drop out, and generally slows things down somewhat: the record stands at 2 days 14h 36:56.

Sydney – Hobart 1994
26-29 Dec

Tasmania Bob Clifford
Brindabella George Snow

Clifford finishes two minutes (about a mile) ahead of Snow to win the 50th edition of the race.

Goodwill Games
2-5 Aug 1994 St Petersburg

MEN
Finn Craig Monk NZ
Mistral Murray McCraig CAN

WOMEN
Europe Ausling Bowman EIRE
Mistral Lisa Neuberger VIRG

Boardsailing

World Champions 1994

MEN
Funboard	Antoine Albeau	FRA
Mistral	Aaron McIntosh	NZ
Raceboard	Nick Keeling	UK
Windsurfer	Bean Moulson	AUS

WOMEN
Mistral	Maud Herbert	FRA
Raceboard	Fabienne Allandrieu	FRA
Windsurfer	Lanee Butler	USA

Winter Olympics

In Britain they'll be remembered for Torvill & Dean's comeback, which wasn't quite given its golden finale in the end, but to the rest of the sporting world, Lillehammer 94 rose above the tawdry Harding-Kerrigan sideshow to provide probably the most satisfying Winter Olympics of all time, just reward for its small-town approach. From 58-y-o Olav Bekken rubbing two sticks together to light the flame, through Tore Haugen making plans to sell earrings made of moose droppings (for the German market), to the £25 000 a day donated to Bosnia in roadside collections, the Games were a success with a smile on its face.

Watched by a record ten billion television viewers, they provided the hosts with ten gold medals, including Bredersen's heroic comeback, and some great memories – Dan Jansen, Tomba's fantastic second run, and the Mongolian who broke his national 500m speed skating record after an eight-day train journey.

MEDALS	G	S	B
Russia	11	8	4
Norway	10	11	5
Germany	9	7	8
Italy	7	5	8
USA	6	5	2
S Korea	4	1	1
Canada	3	6	4
Switzerland	3	4	2
Austria	2	3	4
Sweden	2	1	0
Japan	1	2	2
Kazakhstan	1	2	0
Ukraine	1	0	1
Uzbekistan	1	0	0
UK	*0*	*0*	*2*

Alpine Skiing

Men

DOWNHILL 13 Feb

Tommy Moe	USA	1:45.75
Kjetil-André Aamodt	NOR	1:45.79
Ed Podivinsky	CAN	1:45.87
26 Graham Bell	*UK*	*1:47.39*
28 Martin Bell	*UK*	*1:47.49*

SLALOM 27 Feb

Thomas Stangassinger	AUT	2:02.02
Alberto Tomba	ITA	2:02.17
Jure Kosir	SLVN	2:02.53
DNF: Bill Gaylord	*UK*	

A typically uninhibited finish just fails to win Tomba his fourth Olympic gold. Stangassinger, the last man down, wins his first after leading Tomba by 1.84s on the first run.

GIANT SLALOM 23 Feb

Markus Wasmeier	GER	2:52.46
Urs Kaelin	SWI	2:52.48
Christian Mayer	AUT	2:52.58

The closest finish ever to a men's Olympic Alpine race.

SUPER GIANT SLALOM 17 Feb

Markus Wasmeier	GER	1:32.53
Tommy Moe	USA	1:32.61
Kjetil-André Aamodt	NOR	1:32.93
DNF Graham Bell	*UK*	
DNF Spencer Pession	*UK*	

Wasmeier, the 1985 giant slalom world champion, wins the first Olympic gold by a German male skier since Franz Pfnür in 1936.

COMBINED 14-21 Feb

Lasse Kjus	NOR	3:17.53
Kjetil-André Aamodt	NOR	3:18.55
Harald Christian Nilsen	NOR	3:19.14

Only the third time, following the 1956 men's Giant Slalom and 1964 women's downhill, that one country has taken all three medals in an Olympic Alpine event.

Women

DOWNHILL 19 Feb

Katya Seizinger	GER	1:35.93
Picabo Street	USA	1:36.59
Isolde Kostner	ITA	1:36.85

Street's first name is pronounced Peek-a-boo.

SLALOM 26 Feb

Vreni Schneider	SWI	1:56.01
Alfriede Eder	AUT	1:56.35
Katja Koren	SLVN	1:56.61

Schneider wins her third Olympic gold by regaining the title she won in 1988.

GIANT SLALOM 24 Feb

Deborah Compagnoni	ITA	2:30.97
Martina Ertl	GER	2:32.19
Vreni Schneider	SWI	2:32.97

DNF: Emma Carrick-Anderson (UK)
DNS: Claire de Portales (UK)

Compagnoni won the 1992 Olympic Super GS.

SUPER GIANT SLALOM 15 Feb

Diann Roffe Steinrotter	USA	1:22.15
Svetlana Gladisheva	RUS	1:22.44
Isolde Kostner	ITA	1:22.45

The first Olympic Alpine skiing medal by a woman from any USSR republic.

COMBINED 20-21 Feb

Pernilla Wiberg	SWE	3:05.16
Vreni Schneider	SWI	3:05.29
Alenka Dozvan	SLVN	3:06.64

Biathlon

Men

10 KM 23 Feb

Sergei Chepikov	RUS	28:07.0
Ricco Gross	GER	28:13.0
Sergei Tarasov	RUS	28:27.4
49 Ian Woods	*UK*	*31:58.3*

20 KM 20 Feb

Sergei Tarasov	RUS	57:25.3
Frank Luck	GER	57:28.7
Sven Fischer	GER	57:41.9
54 eq Ian Woods	*UK*	*1h03:44*
54eq Mike Dixon	*UK*	*1h03:44*

Luck & Fischer are brothers-in-law.

4x7.5 RELAY 26 Feb

Ricco Gross, Frank Luck,
Mark Kirchner, Sven Fischer   GER 1h30:22.1

Valery Kirienko, Vladimir Drachev,
Sergei Tarasov, Sergei Chepikov   RUS 1h31:23.6
Thierry Dusserre, Patrice Bailly-Salins,
Lionel Laurent, Hervé Flandin   FRA 1h32:31.3

Women

7.5 KM 23 Feb

Myriam Bedard	CAN	26:08.8
Svetlana Paramygina	BYL	26:09.9
Valentina Tserbe	UKR	26:10.0

15 KM 18 Feb

Myriam Bedard	CAN	52:06.6
Anne Briand	FRA	52:53.3
Ursula Disl	GER	53:15.3

4x7.5 RELAY 25 Feb

Nadyeshda Talanova, Natalya Snytina,
Louiza Noskova, Anfisa Restzova   RUS 1h47m19.5
Ursula Disl, Antje Harvey, Simone Greiner-
Petter-Memm, Petra Schaaf   GER 1h51:16.5
Corinne Niogret, Véronique Claudel,
Delphyne Heymann, Anne Briand   FRA 1h52:28.3

Bobsleigh

Men only

TWO MAN 19-20 Feb

Gustav Weder & Donat Acklin	SWI I	3:30.81
Reto Goetschi & Guido Acklin	SWI II	3:30.86
Gunther Huber & Stefano TIcci	ITA I	3:31.01
6 Mark Tout & Lenny Paul	*UK I*	*3:32.15*
10 eq Sean Olsson & Paul Field	*UK II*	*3:32.83*

The Jamaican team (Dudley Stokes & Wayne Thomas) are disqualified for being 8lb overweight.

FOUR MAN 26-27 Feb

Harald Czudaj, Karsten Brannasch,
Olaf Hampel, Alexander Szelig   GER II 3:27.78
Gustav Weder, Donat Acklin,
Kurt Meier, Domenico Semeraro   SWI I 3:27.84
Wolfgang Hoppe, Ulf Hielscher, René
Hannemann, Carsten Embach   GER I 3:28.01
5 Mark Tout, George Farrell,
Jason Wing, Lenny Paul   *UK I   3:28.87*
8 Sean Olsson, John Herbert,
Dean Ward, Paul Field   *UK II 3:29.41*

Winning is the drug

Two-man bobsleigher Gerhard Rainer (AUT) is expelled from the Austrian team after failing a test for steroids two weeks earlier.

Cross-Country Skiing

Men

10 km CLASSICAL 17 Feb

Bjorn Daehlie	NOR	24:20.1
Vladimir Smirnov	KAZ	24:38.3
Marco Albarello	ITA	24:42.3

50 km CLASSICAL 27 Feb

Vladimir Smirnov	KAZ	2h07:20.3
Mika Myllylae	FIN	2h08:41.9
Sture Sivertsen	NOR	2h08:49.0
DNS: David Belam	*UK*	

15 km FREESTYLE 19 Feb

Bjorn Daehlie	NOR	35:48.8
Vladimir Smirnov	KAZ	36:00.0
Silvio Fauner	ITA	36:40.6
63 David Belam	*UK*	*41:17.8*

30 km FREESTYLE 14 Feb

Thomas Alsgaard	NOR	1h12:26.4
Bjorn Daehlie	NOR	1h13:13.6
Mika Myllylae	FIN	1h14:14.0
60 David Belam	*UK*	

4x10 km RELAY 22 Feb

Maurillio De Zolt, Marco Albarello,		
G Vanzetta, Silvio Fauner	ITA	1h41:15.0
Sture Sivertsen, Vegard Ulvang,		
Thomas Alsgaard, Bjorn Dahlie	NOR	1h41:15.4
Mika Myllylae, Harri Kirviesniemi,		
Jari Raesaenen, Jari Isometsae	FIN	1h42:15.6

Italy, second to Norway in the world championships and last Olympics, win the race of the Games against the hosts' superteam. Fair and square, too: although Ulvang mutters about Albarello breaking Kirviesniemi's pole, Albarello counter-claims that Kirviesniemi & Ulvang blocked his path. There's no official protest.

Women

5 km CLASSICAL 15 Feb

Lyubov Yegorova	RUS	14:08.8
Manuela Di Centa	ITA	14:28.3
Marja-Liisa Kirvesniemi	FIN	14:36.0

10 km FREESTYLE 17 Feb

Decided on an unusual basis: results of a 10km race and the 5km classical put together. Final standings:

Lyubov Yegorova	RUS	41:38.1
Manuela Di Centa	ITA	41:46.4
Stefania Belmondo	ITA	42:21.1

15 km FREESTYLE 13 Feb

Manuela Di Centa	ITA	39:44.5
Lyubov Yegorova	RUS	41:03.0
Nina Gavriluk	RUS	41:10.4

30 km CLASSICAL 24 Feb

Manuela Di Centa	ITA	1h25:41.6
Marit Wold	NOR	1h25:57.8
Marja-Liisa Kirvesniemi	FIN	1h26:13.6

4x5 km RELAY 21 Feb

Yelena Vaelbe, Larisa Lazutina,		
Nina Gavriluk, Lyubov Yegorova	RUS	57:12.5
Trude Dybendahl, Inger Helene		
Nybrten, Elin Nilsen, Anita Moen	NOR	57:42.6
Bice Vanzetta, Manuela Di Centa, Gabriella Paruzzi,		
Stefania Belmondo	ITA	58:42.6

Figure Skating

MEN 17-19 Feb

Alexei Urmanov	RUS	1.5
Elvis Stojko	CAN	3.0
Philippe Candeloro	FRA	6.5
9 Steven Cousins	*UK*	*12.5*

In the course of his best international placing yet, Cousins becomes the first British skater to land a triple axel.

WOMEN 23-25 Feb

Oksana Baiul	UKR	2.0
Nancy Kerrigan	USA	2.5
Chen Lu	CHN	5.0
15 Charlene Von Saher	*UK*	*22.5*

By the narrowest of margins, the Kerrigan gravy train is jolted by the 16-y-o Baiul (the youngest winner of the event since Sonia Henie in 1928) who cut her leg during practice in a collision with Tanja Szewczenko (GER). In June the US Association strips Tonya Harding of her national title after she finally admits involvement in the attack that injured Kerrigan's knee on 6 Jan.

PAIRS 13-15 Feb

Yekaterina Gordeyeva,		
Sergei Grinkov	RUS	1.5
Natalya Mishkutenok,		
Artur Dmitriyev	RUS	3.0
Isabelle Brasseur, Lloyd Eisler	CAN	4.5
15 Jacqueline Soames,		
John Jenkins	*UK*	*23.0*

The winners, champions in 1988, had competed in 1980 when he was 14 and she 10. No pair from outside the Soviet bloc has won the event since 1960.

DANCE 18-21 Feb

Yevgeny Platov, Oksana Gritschuk	RUS	3.4
Maia Usova, Aleksandr Zhulin	RUS	3.8
Jayne Torvill, Christopher Dean	UK	4.8

After seeing the writing on the wall at the Europeans, T&D change their free dance - to no avail, though the British judge Mary Parry gives them a 6.0 at the death.

Freestyle Skiing

Men

MOGULS 15-16 Feb

Jean-Luc Brassard	CAN	27.24 pts
Sergei Shoupletsov	RUS	26.90
Edgar Grospiron	FRA	26.64

AERIALS 21-24 Feb

Andreas Schönbächler	SWI	234.67 pts
Philippe Laroche	CAN	228.63
Lloyd Langlois	CAN	222.44
10 Richard Cobbing	*UK*	*196.58*

Cobbing has a place in the Guinness Book of Records as the only man to turn 51 somersaults on a trampoline while wearing skis. Why? Why not?

Women

MOGULS 15-16 Feb

Stine Lise Hattestad	NOR	25.97
Liz McIntyre	USA	25.89
Yelizaveta Kojevnikova	RUS	25.81

AERIALS 21-24 Feb

Lina Tcherjazova	UZB	166.84
Marie Lindgen	SWE	165.88
Hilde Synnove Lid	NOR	164.13
21 Jilly Curry	*UK*	*74.21*

Ice Hockey

Men only 12-27 Feb

POOL A

Finland	5	5	0	0	25	4	10
Germany	5	3	0	2	11	14	6
Czech Rep	5	3	0	2	16	11	6
Russia	5	3	0	2	20	14	6
Austria	5	1	0	4	13	28	2
Norway	5		0	0	5	19	0

POOL B

Slovakia	5	3	2	0	26	14	8
Canada	5	3	1	1	17	11	7
Sweden	5	3	1	1	23	13	7
USA	5	1	3	1	21	17	5
Italy	5	1	0	4	15	31	2
France	5	0	1	4	11	27	1

QUARTER-FINALS

Sweden	3	Germany	0
Russia	3	Slovakia	2
Finland	6	USA	1
Canada	3	Czech Rep	2

SEMI-FINALS

Sweden	4	Russia	3
Canada	5	Finland	3

3rd PLACE FINAL

Finland	4	Russia	0

FINAL

Sweden	2	Canada	2

Sweden win 3-2 on penalties, the first shoot-out to decide an Olympic final, when Peter Forsberg scores and Paul Kariya misses.

Luge

Men

SINGLE 13-14 Feb

Georg Hackl	GER	3:21.571
Manfred Prock	AUT	3:21.584
Armin Zoggeler	ITA	3:21.833
26 Paul Hix	*UK*	*3:29.115*

Hackl retains the title.

DOUBLE 18 Feb

Kurt Brugger, Wilfried Huber	ITA	1:36.720
Hansjörg Raffl, Norbert Huber	ITA	1:36.769
Stefan Krausse, Jan Behrendt	GER	1:36.945

The Hubers are brothers appearing in different pairs.

Women

SINGLE 15-16 Feb

Gerda Weissensteiner	ITA	3:15.517
Susi Erdmann	GER	3:16.276
Andrea Tagwerker	AUT	3:16.652

No women's double seater.

Nordic Combined

Men only

INDIVIDUAL 18-19 Feb

		Jump	*15 km*
Fred Borre Lundberg	NOR	247.0 pts	39:07.9
Takanori Kono	JAP	239.5	39:35.4
Bjarte Engen Vik	NOR	240.5	39:43.2

TEAM 23-24 Feb

Takanori Kono, Masashi Abe,			
Kenji Ogiwara	JAP	733.5	27:55.2
Knut Tore Apeland, Bjarte Engen Vik,			
Fred Borre Lundberg	NOR	672.0	1h22:33.9
Hippolyte Kempf, Jean-Yves Cündet,			
Andreas Schaad	SWI	643.5	1h23:09.9

Ski Jumping

Men only

90m HILL 25 Feb

Espen Bredesen	NOR	282.0 pts
Lasse Ottesen	NOR	268.0
Dieter Thoma	GER	260.5

Bredesen, christened Espen the Eagle (in honour of the immortal Eddie) after finishing last in the event in 1992, recovers from relative failure on the big hill to become the first Norwegian since 1964 to win Olympic gold in a sport they used to dominate.

120m HILL 20 Feb

Jens Weissflog	GER	274.5
Espen Bredesen	NOR	266.5
Andreas Goldberger	AUT	255.0

Weissflog, the Flying Flea, had won the short hill gold medal in 1984.

120m HILL TEAM 22 Feb

Hansjörg Jäkle, Christof Duffner, Dieter Thoma, Jens Weissflog	GER	970.1
Jinya Nishikata, Takanobu Okabe, Noriaki Kasai, Masahiko Harada	JAP	956.9
Heinz Kuttin, Christian Moser, Stefan Horngacher, Andreas Goldberger	AUT	918.9

Weissflog comes in for heavy criticism (and some heartfelt crowd reaction before the 90m competition) for deliberately trying to distract the Japanese. Not so much trying as succeeding rather well. A bad third jump costs Japan the gold.

Speed Skating

Men

500m 14 Feb

Alekandr Golubyev	RUS	36.33	OR
Sergei Klevchenya	RUS	36.39	
Manabu Horii	JAP	36.53	

World record holder Dan Jansen (USA), competing in his fourth Games, slips, finishes eighth, and has yet to win an Olympic medal.

1000m 18 Feb

Dan Jansen	USA	1:12.43	WR
Igor Zhelozovsky	BYL	1:12.72	
Sergei Klevchenya	RUS	1:12.85	

Not for long.

1500m 16 Feb

Johann-Olav Koss	NOR	1:51.29	WR
Rintje Ritsma	HOL	1:51.99	
Falko Zandstra	HOL	1:52.38	

Koss breaks Ritsma's world record.

5000m 13 Feb

Johann-Olav Koss	NOR	6:34.96	WR
Kjell Storelid	NOR	6:42.68	
Rintje Risma	HOL	6:43.94	

10 000m 20 Feb

Johann-Olav Koss	NOR	13:30.55	WR
Kjell Storelid	NOR	13:49.25	
Bart Veldkamp	HOL	13:56.73	

'Koss the Boss' breaks his own world record by nearly thirteen seconds to set his third of the Games.

Women

500m 19 Feb

Bonnie Blair	USA	39.25
Susan Auch	CAN	39.61
Franziska Schenk	GER	39.70

Blair wins the event for the third successive time.

1000m 23 Feb

Bonnie Blair	USA	1:18.74
Anke Baier	GER	1:20.22
Ye Qiao Bo	CHN	1:20.22

By successfully defending her title, Blair wins her fifth Olympic gold, a new record for an American woman in any sport.

1500m 21 Feb

Emese Hunyady	AUT	2:02.19
Svetlana Fedotkina	RUS	2:02.69
Gunda Niemann	GER	2:03.41

3000m 17 Feb

Svetlana Bazhanova	RUS	4:17.43
Emese Hunyady	AUT	4:18.14
Claudia Pechstein	GER	4:18.34

5000m 25 Feb

Claudia Pechstein	GER	7:14.37
Gunda Niemann	GER	7:14.88
Hiromi Yamamoto	JAP	7:19.68

Short Track Speed Skating

Men

500m 24-26 Feb

Chae Ji-hoon	S KOR	43.45
Mirko Vuillermin	ITA	43.47
Nicky Gooch	UK	43.68

Vuillermin throws away victory off the last bend.
Wilf O'Reilly (UK), not allowed to change a damaged
skate, finishes last in his first round heat.

1000m 22 Feb

Kim Ki-hoon	S KOR	1:34.57
Chae Ji-hoon	S KOR	1:34.92
Marc Gagnon	CAN	1:33.03
		(B final)

Disq: Nicky Gooch (UK) 2nd

There are falls galore (including O'Reilly in the
qualifiers), Gooch suffers just one of several
contentious disqualifications, Gagnon's given the
bronze for winning a race between the four beaten
semi-finalists. This branch of the sport has a way to go.

5000m RELAY 24-26 Feb

M Carnino, H Herrnhos, Orazio Fagone,			
Mirko Vuillermin	ITA	7:11.74	OR
R Bartz, John Coyle, Eric Flaim,			
Andy Gabel	USA	7:13.37	
Steve Bradbury, Kieran Hansen,			
A Murtha, Richard Nizielski	AUS	7:13.68	

Flaim was overall world long track champion in 1988.

Women

500m 24 Feb

Cathy Turner	USA	45.98	OR
Zhang Yan-mei	CHN	46.44	
Amy Peterson	USA	46.76	

1000m 26 Feb

Chun Lee-kyung	SK	1:36.87	OR
Nathalie Lambert	CAN	1:36.97	
Kim So-hee	SK	1:37.09	

3000m RELAY 22 Feb

S Korea	4:26.64	OR
Canada	4:32.04	
USA	4:39.34	

Paralympics (British placings)

10-20 March 1994 Lillehammer

ICE SLEDGE HOCKEY
3rd-place final

Canada	2	UK	0

Britain finish fourth despite scoring only two goals in
five matches, both v Estonia (scorers John Lambert &
David Hall) in the opener.

Final

Sweden	1	Norway	0

CROSS-COUNTRY
5 km Classic (Class B1)

Terje Lovaas	NOR	15:40.6
Magne Lunde	NOR	16:22.9
Peter Young	UK	16:23.2

20 km Classic (Class B2)

Terje Lovass	NOR	1h01:37.1
V Kupchinski	RUS	1h02:19.3
Magne Lunde	NOR	1h02:25.9
4 Peter Young	*UK*	*1h03:45.7*

ALPINE SKI-ING
Men's Downhill (Class LW X1)

Wendi Eberle	SWI	1:32.74
Bill Bowness	USA	1:34.59
Jim Barker	UK	1:39.12

Men's Slalom (Class LW2)

Alexander Spitz	GER	1:15.78
Michael Milton	AUS	1:18.05
Monte Meier	USA	1:20.29
10 Johnathan Morris	*UK*	*1:52.02*

Morris finishes last, but at least he finishes. 22 others
don't.

Men's Slalom (Class B3)

Brian Santos	USA	1:41.11
Bruno Oberhammer	ITA	
Manfred Persler	ITA	

Men's Giant Slalom (Class B3)

Brian Santos	USA	2:36.74
Bruno Oberhammer	ITA	2:39.58
Richard Burt	UK	2:46.79

Men's Super GS (Class B3)

Brian Santos	USA	1:27.74
Bruno Oberhammer	ITA	1:29.48
Richard Burt	UK	1:35.19

Santos & Oberhammer also finish first and second in
the B3 Slalom.

Men's Giant Slalom (Class LW1 & LW3)

Bernard Bauden	FRA	2:35.60
Jozef Mistina	SLVK	2:42.70
Alexei Mochkin	RUS	2:45.25
5 Ed Suckling	*UK*	*4:38.24*

Because of the low turn-out, LW1 & LW3 are
combined, which leaves the likes of Suckling (LW1,
more disabled than LW3) at a disadvantage. All three
medallists are LW3.

Commonwealth Games

19-28 Aug 1994 Victoria, British Columbia

Once again the 'Friendly Games' were just that, more or less, but they always have to be: in a crowded international calendar, it's the best argument for their continued existence. Australia, England and Canada picked up a pile of easy gold medals (158 between them, out of 217). Linford was still ageless, Kieren Perkins spearheaded Australia's clean-up in the pool, Canada dominated the wrestling.

For the first time, events specifically for the disabled were included (although Neroli Fairhall had struck archery gold from a wheelchair in 1982). Of the 3500 competitors 55 were handicapped.

MEDALS	G	S	B
Australia	87	52	43
Canada	40	42	46
England	31	45	49
Nigeria	11	13	13
Kenya	7	4	8
India	6	11	7
Scotland	6	3	11
New Zealand	5	16	41
Wales	5	8	6
N Ireland	5	2	3
Nauru	3	0	0
South Africa	2	4	5
Jamaica	2	4	2
Malaysia	2	3	2
Cyprus	2	1	2
Sri Lanka	1	2	0
Zambia	1	1	2
Namibia	1	0	1
Zimbabwe	0	3	3
Papua NG, W Samoa	0	1	0
Hong Kong	0	0	4
Pakistan	0	0	3
Trinidad & T, Uganda	0	0	2
Bermuda, Botswana, Ghana, Guernsey, Norfolk Is, Seychelles, Tanzania, Tonga	0	0	1

Athletics
Centennial Stadium

Men

100	Linford Christie	ENG	9.91	ChR
	Michael Green	JAM	10.05	
	Frankie Fredericks	NAM	10.06	

Christie, who retains the title, also finished second behind Ben Johnson's powerful chemistry in 1986. Horace Dove-Edwin, who runs 10.02, seems to have won Sierra Leone's first ever Games medal in any sport, and uses his performance to highlight the plight of his country. Back home, he says, 'people do not have enough to eat, but we produce gold, diamonds...' Then he spoils it all by failing a drugs test, which costs him his place in an American college.

200	Frankie Fredericks	NAM	19.97	ChR
	John Regis	ENG	20.25	
	Daniel Effiong	NIG	20.40	

Regis wins his second successive silver in the event, behind the first Namibian to win a Commonwealth gold.

400	Charles Gitonga	KEN	45.00
	Du'aine Ladejo	ENG	45.11
	Sunday Bada	NIG	45.45

Now he knows how Roger Black felt. Two championships in quick succession (and four races in two days here) catch up with Ladejo, who can't do the same to the Kenyan setting a personal best in his first major championship.

800	Patrick Konchellah	KEN	1:45.18
	Hezekiel Sepeng	SAF	1:45.76
	Savieri Ngidhi	ZIM	1:46.06

The first black South African to win a Commonwealth Games medal. Konchellah's brother Billy won the world title at this distance in 1987 & 1991. Tom McKean, the only runner to finish last in two World Championship 800m finals, brings up the rear here.

Wheelchair 800			
	Jeff Adams	CAN	1:44.94
	David Holding	ENG	1:45.13
	Paul Wiggins	AUS	1:45.40

The wheels get there faster than the legs.

1500 Reuben Chesang	KEN	3:36.70
Kevin Sullivan	CAN	3:36.78
John Mayock	ENG	3:37.22

Perhaps surprisingly, only the second Kenyan to win the event (after Kip Keino in 1966 & 1970). A sign of how far back British miling has slipped: this is the first time since 1974 that the event's won by someone other than an English runner - and David Strang (SCOT), who finished last in the European Championship final, repeats the feat here.

5000 Rob Denmark	ENG	13:23.00
Philemon Hanneck	ZIM	13:23.20
John Nuttall	ENG	13:23.54

10 000		
Lameck Aguta	KEN	28:38.22
Tendai Chimusasa	ZIM	28:47.72
Fackson Nkandu	ZAM	28:51.72

Marathon		
Steve Moneghetti	AUS	2h11:50
Sean Quilty	AUS	2h14:58
Mark Hudspith	ENG	2h15:11

The winner's worked his way up from third in 1986 and second in 1990. Hudspith, coached by the 1966 winner and 1970 silver medallist Jim Alder, runs a Marathon for only the second time.

Wheelchair Marathon		
Paul Wiggins	AUS	1h37:33
Ivan Newman	ENG	1h41:55
Ben Lucas	NZ	1h42:19

Wiggins holds the lead from the 5km mark to become the first athlete ever to win Commonwealth Games medals in both the 800 & Marathon.

3000 St		
Johnson Kipkoech	KEN	8:14.72 ChR
Gideon Chirchir	KEN	8:15.25
Graeme Fell	CAN	8:23.28

Kenya have won the event at every Commonwealth Games they've entered since 1970. Fell completes his set of medals: silver in 1982 (running for England), gold in 1986.

110 H		
Colin Jackson	WAL	13.08 ChR eq
Tony Jarrett	ENG	13.22
Paul Gray	WAL	13.54

Robert Foster (JAM), who finished sixth, tests positive for ephedrine. Jackson (who equals his own Games record) and Jarrett finish in the same positions as in 1990.

400 H		
Samuel Matete	ZAM	48.67 ChR
Sammy Biwoit	KEN	49.43
Barnabas Kinyor	KEN	49.50

Matete breaks the Games record set by Alan Pascoe (ENG) in 1974.

30 km W		
Nick A'Hern	AUS	2h07:53
Tim Berrett	CAN	2h08:22
Scott Nelson	NZ	2h09:10

A'Hern sets a personal best.

4x100		
Donovan Bailey, Glenroy Gilbert, Carlton Chambers, Bruny Surin	CAN	38.39 ChR
Shane Naylor, Paul Henderson, Tim Jackson, Damien Marsh	AUS	38.88
Jason John, Tobias (Toby) Box, Phil Goedluck, Terry Williams	ENG	39.39

Williams' fierce anchor leg wins the bronze for the England B team (no Christie, Regis or Jarrett). Gilbert is a former Olympic bobsleigh brakeman.

4x400		
Dave McKenzie, Peter Crampton, Adrian Patrick, Du'aine Ladejo	ENG	3:02.14 ChR
Orville Taylor, Dennis Blake, Lindell Laird, Garth Robinson	JAM	3:02.32
Patrick Delice, Neil De Silva, Hayden Stephen, Ian Morris	TRIN	3:02.78

Another reserve team (no Black, Regis or Grindley), another strong anchor. Ladejo's 44.2 is just enough to run down Robinson who doesn't help the cause by going out too quickly (he led by ten metres round the last bend) - or by running in the 4x100 a little earlier!

High Jump		
Tim Forsyth	AUS	2.32
Steve Smith	ENG	2.32
Geoff Parsons	SCOT	2.31

Forsyth & Smith tie at 2.31, miss at 2.34, clear 2.32, miss at 2.34, then try again at 2.32. Parsons, the former British record holder who now sets a personal best outdoors, won silver in 1986 and bronze in 1990.

Long Jump		
Obinna Eregbu	NIG	8.05
David Culbert	AUS	8.00
Ian James	CAN	7.93

Culbert wins his second successive silver in the event.

Triple Jump		
Julian Golley	ENG	17.03 ChR
Jonathan Edwards	ENG	17.00
Brian Wellman	BERM	17.00

Golley's personal best is a Games record (wind-assisted marks aside). Edwards, who beats Wellman into third by virtue of a longer second-best jump, wins his second successive silver in the event. If he'd jumped a total of two inches further he'd have won two golds (see Heptathlon).

Pole V

Neil Winter	WAL	5.40	ChR
Curtis Heywood	CAN	5.30	
Jim Miller	AUS	5.30	

Thanks to hot favourite Ockert Brits (SAF), who deigns to enter the competition at 5.50 and fails three times, the 20-y-o Winter becomes the first Welsh athlete to win a Commonwealth Games field event since Lynn Davies in the 1970 long jump.

Shot	Matt Simson	ENG	19.49
	Courtney Ireland	NZ	19.38
	Chima Ugwu	NIG	19.26

Discus

Werner Reiterer	AUS	62.78	
Adewale Olukoju	NIG	62.46	
Bob Weir	ENG	60.86	

Reiterer takes the Moneghetti route to gold: he was third in 1986 and second in 1990. Olukoju was the defending champion, Weir won the 1982 hammer gold.

Hammer

Sean Carlin	AUS	73.48	
Paul Head	ENG	70.18	
Peter Vivian	ENG	69.80	

Carlin retains the title.

Javelin

Steve Backley	ENG	82.74	
Mick Hill	ENG	81.884	
Gavin Lovegrove	NZ	80.42	

The same medallists, in the same order, as 1990. In fact, the same first four (Nigel Bevan of Wales threw 80.38). Hill & Lovegrove also won the same medals in 1986. The only other example of the same three competitors winning identical medals in a major championship was in the European shot putt of 1966 & 1969: Nadyeschda Chizhova, Margitta Gummel, Marita Lange (they finished Chizhova-Lange-Gummel in 1971).

Decathlon

Mike Smith	CAN	8326	
Peter Winter	AUS	8074	
Simon Shirley	ENG	7980	

Smith retains the title. Winter breaks the Australian record set by...Shirley, who changed allegiances. Dean Smith (AUS), who leads after four rounds, holds the world record among deaf athletes.

Women

100	Mary Onyali	NIG	11.06
	Christy Opara-Thompson	NIG	11.22
	Paula Thomas	ENG	11.23

Thomas, as Paula Dunn, finished second in 1982 and eighth in 1990.

200	Cathy Freeman	AUS	22.25	ChR
	Mary Onyali	NIG	22.35	
	Melinda Gainsford	AUS	22.68	

After winning the 400, Freeman emulates Valerie Brisco-Hooks (USA 1984) in doing the 200/400 double at a major championship. Her winning time is only 0.06 outside Merlene Ottey's wind-assisted Games record.

400	Cathy Freeman	AUS	50.38	ChR
	Fatima Yousuf	NIG	50.53	
	Sandie Richards	JAM	50.69	

Freeman, who won a gold in the sprint relay four years earlier, beats defending champion Yousuf to become the first Aborigine woman to win a major championship event. All three medallists break the oldest Games track and field record in the book, the 51.02 of Marilyn Neufville (JAM) in 1970, a world record at the time, set when Neufville was 17.

800	Inez Turner	JAM	2:01.74
	Charmaine Crooks	CAN	2:02.35
	Gladys Wamuyu	KEN	2:03.12

Crooks won a 4x400 relay gold in the 1982 Games and was in the quartet who won Olympic silver in 1984, setting a Commonwealth record that was later deleted after accusations of drug taking.

1500	Kelly Holmes	ENG	4:08.06
	Paula Schnurr	CAN	4:09.65
	Gwen Griffiths	SAF	4:10.16

3000	Angela Chalmers	CAN	8:32.17	ChR
	Robin Meagher	CAN	8:45.59	
	Alison Wyeth	ENG	8:47.98	

Chalmers breaks her own Games record (and sets a personal best) in retaining the title. She and Meagher are competing in their home town.

10 000			
Yvonne Murray	SCOT	31:56.97	
Elana Meyer	SAF	32:06.02	
Jane Omoro	KEN	32:13.01	

Meyer wins South Africa's first Commonwealth track and field medal since 1958. When it's announced that the medals are to be presented by Roger Bannister, Murray & Meyer's excitement is plain to see on the podium. Just one thing. It isn't the Roger Bannister of sub-four-minute fame but Roger Bannister of the Games Federation. Not that Murray's immediately aware of the difference: 'What a privilege,' she says as she bows her head to receive her medal.

Marathon			
Carole Rouillard	CAN	2h30:41	
Lizanne Bussières	CAN	2h31:07	
Yvonne Danson	ENG	2h32:24	

The 35-y-o Danson is 4'11.

Commonwealth Games: athletics gold medals

7	Marjorie Jackson Nelson	AUS	1950-54	(3)
7	Raelene Boyle	AUS	1970-82	(2)
6	Pam Kilborn	AUS	1962-70	(2)
6	Don Quarrie	JAM	1970-78	(1)
5	Decima Norman	AUS	1938	(2)
5	Val Sloper Young	NZ	1958-66	(0)
5	Sally Gunnell	ENG	1986-94	(2)

Figures in brackets: relay golds.

100 H
Michelle Freeman	JAM	13.12
Jacqui Agyepong	ENG	13.14
Samantha Farquharson	ENG	13.38

400 H
Sally Gunnell	ENG	54.51	ChR
Deon Hemmings	JAM	55.11	
Debbie-Ann Parris	JAM	55.25	

Gunnell retains the title and wins her fourth Commonwealth Games gold medal in all.

10 km W
Kerry Junna-Saxby	AUS	44:25	ChR
Anne Manning	AUS	44:37	
Janice McCaffrey	CAN	44:54	

The event's been held twice in the Games, Saxby winning each time.

4x100
Faith Idehen, Mary Tombiri, Christy Opara-Thompson, Mary Onyali	NIG	42.99	ChR
M Miers, Cathy Freeman, Melinda Gainsford, Kathy Sambell	AUS	43.43	
Stephanie Douglas, Geraldine McLeod, Simmone Jacobs, Paula Thomas	ENG	43.46	

An African team (in fact, a country apart from Canada, Australia & England) wins the event for the first time. The previous Games record was set by England (Wendy Hoyte, Kathy Smallwood, Bev Callender, Sonia Lannaman) in 1982. Freeman & Sambell were in the gold medal winning quartet in 1990, Jacobs in the Olympic bronze medal team of 1984.

4x400
Phylis Smith, Tracy Goddard, Linda Keough, Sally Gunnell	ENG	3:27.06	ChR
R Campbell, Deon Hemmings, Inez Turner, Sandie Richards	JAM	3:27.63	
A Yakiwchuk, S Bowen, Donalda Duprey, Charmaine Crooks	CAN	3:32.52	

Australia finish first in a Games record 3:26.84 but are disqualified (rather harshly) for Cathy Freeman's baulking of Fatima Yousuf (NIG) on the last bend. For some reason, Nigeria are also disqualified, as (even more preposterously) are England, who are then reinstated. A shambles.

High Jump
Alison Inverarity	AUS	1.94	ChR
Charmaine Weavers	SAF	1.94	ChR
Debbie Marti	ENG	1.91	

Inverarity will be sick of hearing this, but...her father John played cricket for Australia (6 Tests 1968-72).

Long Jump
Nicole Boegman	AUS	6.82w
Yinka Idowu	ENG	6.73
Christy Opara-Thompson	NIG	6.72

Boegman married Gary Staines (ENG), the former European 5000m silver medallist, in 1990. Unusually, all her six jumps in the final are wind-assisted. Opara-Thompson becomes the first woman to win Commonwealth medals in 100m & long jump since Decima Norman (AUS) took gold in both in 1938.

Shot
Judy Oakes	ENG	18.16
Myrtle Augee	ENG	17.64
Lisa-Marie Vizaniari	AUS	16.61

The 36-y-o Oakes, who retired (again) in 1993, beats defending champion Augee (Vizaniari won the discus in 1990) to become the only athlete to win medals five times in the same event at the same championships over a full 16-year period (Igor Ter-Ovanesian won five in the European Championship long jump 1958-71): she finished third in 1978, first in 1982, second in 1986 & 1990, and is still campaigning to have the 1986 silver turned into gold: Gael Mulhall Martin (AUS), who won the title after serving a doping suspension, has admitted (on oath) taking drugs throughout her career.

Discus
Daniela Costian	AUS	63.72	ChR
Beatrice Faumuina	NZ	57.12	
Lizette Etzebeth	SAF	55.74	

Javelin
Louise McPaul	AUS	63.76
Kirsten Hellier	NZ	60.40
Sharon Gibson	ENG	58.20

Heptathlon
Denise Lewis	ENG	6325
Jane Flemming	AUS	6317
Catherine Bond-Mills	CAN	6193

Without a javelin throw of 53.68 (easily a personal best and 13m further than any other in the competition), Lewis wouldn't have beaten Flemming, the defending champion who's in tears after the last event. She also finished second in 1986. If she'd gained just twelve more points in all, she'd have won the title three times in a row.

Badminton

Men's singles

SEMI-FINALS

Rashid Sidek	MALAY	Anders Nielsen	ENG
15-3 15-11

Ong Ewe Hock	MALAY	N Hall	NZ
15-4 15-5

FINAL

Sidek	Oong	15-6 15-4

Sidek retains the title.

Men's Doubles

FINAL

Cheah Soon Kit & Soo Beng Kiang (MALAY)
bt Simon Archer & Chris Hunt (ENG)   15-10 15-9

Women's Singles

SEMI-FINALS

Deng Si-an	CAN	S Yang	AUS
8-11 11-9 11-5

Lisa Campbell	AUS	Rhona Robertson	NZ
11-1 12-10

FINAL

Campbell	Deng	11-2 11-5

The first unseeded player ever to win either of the singles titles.

Women's Doubles

FINAL

Jo Muggeridge & Joanne Wright (ENG)
bt Gill Clark & Julie Bradbury (ENG)   15-9 15-11

Mixed Doubles

FINAL

Chris Hunt & Gill Clark (ENG)
bt Simon Archer & Julie Bradbury (ENG)   15-11 15-4

Gill Clark finishes with twelve Games medals, a badminton record, including six golds. The Games record for a woman in any sport is seven (see Athletics).

Team

SEMI-FINALS

England	4	Australia	1
Malaysia	3	Hong Kong	2

FINAL

ENGLAND	3	MALAYSIA	2

Peter Knowles lost to Rashid Sidek	8-15 5-15
Jo Muggeridge beat Lee Wai Leng	11-2 11-8
Chris Hunt & S Archer lost to Cheah Soo Kit & Soo Beng Kiang	12-15 4-15

Gillian Clark & Julie Bradbury beat
Lee & Tan Lee Wai   15-3 15-3
Nick Ponting & Joanne Wright beat
Tan Kim Her & Zamalia Sidek   15-4 16-18 18-16

A desperately tight finish (the mixed doubles is the decider).

Bowls

Men

SINGLES
Richard Corsie (SCOT) bt Tony Allcock (ENG) 25-20
3eq Rob Parrella (AUS) & K Wallis (HK)

Parrella was the defending champion.

SINGLES (PARTIALLY SIGHTED)
Lawson Brand (SCOT) bt John Hubbard (AUS) 21-18
3eq Carlos Martinez (HK) & Craig Nolan (NZ)

The 62-y-o Brand wins Scotland's first gold of the Games, in any sport. Some reports refer to him as Robert Brand, but he's known by his second christian name.

PAIRS
Cameron Curtis & Rex Johnston (AUS) bt John Pice & Robert Weale (WAL) 18-14
3eq Gary Smith & Andy Thomson (ENG) & N IRE

FOURS
S Africa bt Australia 21-18
3eq N Zealand & N Ireland

Women

SINGLES
Margaret Johnston (N IRE) bt Rita Jones (WAL) 25-17
3eq Norma Shaw (ENG) & C Anderson (Norfolk Is.)

The 51-y-o Johnston, at various times world outdoor and indoor champion, won the Commonwealth pairs in 1986.

SINGLES (PARTIALLY SIGHTED)
Katie Pintas (NZ) bt Gloria Hopkins (WAL) 21-6
3eq Margaret Lyne (ENG) & Kit Lan (HK)

Hopkins, who's completely blind, is guided by her husband (and sighted coach) Ken.

PAIRS
Scotland (Sarah Gourlay & Frances Whyte) bt SAF 32-18
3eq: Brenda Atherton & Mary Price (ENG), Noree Watson & Millie Khan (NZ)

FOURS
S Africa bt Papua N Guinea 24-17
3eq N Zealand & Scotland

Boxing

Light-fly

SEMI-FINALS

Victor Kasote pts 20-15	ZAM	Domenic Filane	CAN
Haman Ramadhani pts 24-8	KEN	Birju Sah	INDIA

FINAL
Ramadhani   Kasote   pts 15-4

Fly

SEMI-FINALS

Dancan Karanja pts 26-8	KEN	Boniface Mukuka	ZAM
Paul Shepherd pts 16-10	SCOT	Danny Costello	ENG

FINAL
Shepherd   Karanja   pts 20-9

Shepherd & Wilson (see Light-Heavy) took up boxing at the same school, where their mothers were catering assistants.

Bantam

SEMI-FINALS

Spencer Oliver pts 23-12	ENG	Godson Sowah	GHA
Robert Peden pts 17-11	AUS	Fred Muteweta	UGA

FINAL
Peden   Oliver   pts 20-18

Sowah is caught taking furosemide, a banned diuretic.

Feather

SEMI-FINALS

Casey Patton pts 21-8	CAN	James Swan	AUS
Jason Cook pts 19-8	WAL	Matumia Hassan	TANZ

FINAL
Patton   Cook   pts 22-7

The 19-y-o Cook was trying to become the first Welsh boxer since Howard Winstone in 1958 to win a Commonwealth gold. medal.

Light

SEMI-FINALS

Mike Strange pts 12-2	CAN	Kalolo Fiaui	NZ
Martin Renaghan pts 20-11	N IRE	Hussain Arshad	PAK

FINAL
Strange   Renaghan   pts 18-11

Light-welter

SEMI-FINALS

Mark Winters pts 11-7	N IRE	Trevor Shaller	NZ
Peter Richardson pts 11-7	ENG	Tijani Moro	GHA

FINAL
Richardson   Winters   pts 20-17

Richardson survives having to take a standing count in the last round.

Welter

SEMI-FINALS

Neil Sinclair rsf	N IRE	Richard Vowles	AUS
Albert Eromosele pts 25-6	NIG	Wald Fleming	CAN

FINAL
Sinclair   Eromosele   pts 25-16

Light-middle

SEMI-FINALS

Jim Webb w.o.	N IRE	Rival Cadeau	SEY
Bob Gasio pts 12-0	W SAM	Joe Townsley	SCOT

FINAL
Webb   Gasio   pts 10-4

Middle

SEMI-FINALS

Rowan Donaldson pts 18-13	CAN	Mervyn Penniston-John	TRIN
Rasmus Ojemaye pts 15-3	NIG	Peter Wanyoike	KEN

FINAL
Donaldson   Ojemaye   pts 26-13

Light-heavy

SEMI-FINALS

Dale Brown pts 12-7	CAN	Odhiambo Opiyo	KEN
John Wilson pts 13-8	SCOT	France Mabiletsa	BOTS

FINAL
Brown   Wilson   rsf 1

Brown improves on the silver medal he won in 1990. Wilson was added to the Scottish team only when Liz McColgan dropped out!

Heavy

SEMI-FINALS

Omaar Ahmed rsf	KEN	Charles Kizza	UGA
Stephen Gallinger w.o.	CAN	Ezwell Ndlovu	ZIM

FINAL
Ahmed   Gallinger   pts 23-3

Super-heavy

SEMI-FINALS

Miriambo Anyim pts 9-5	KEN	Paea Wolfgramm	TONGA
Duncan Dokiwari pts 24-13	NIG	Danny Williams	ENG

FINAL
Dokiwari   Anyim   pts 13-9

Cycling

Men

SPRINT

Gary Neiwand	AUS
Curt Harnett	CAN
Darryn Hill	AUS

Neiwand, persuaded by a knee injury to defend the Commonwealth rather than the world title, becomes the first rider to win this event three times in a row.

1000m TIME TRIAL

Shane Kelly	AUS	1:05.386	ChR
Darryn Hill	AUS	1:05.632	
Tim O'Shannessey	AUS	1:06.789	

POINTS RACE (40 km)

Brett Aitken	AUS	38 pts
Stuart O'Grady	AUS	37
Dean Woods	AUS	23

4000m PURSUIT

Brad McGee	AUS	4:31.371ComR
Shaun Wallace	ENG	4:34.662
Stuart O'Grady	AUS	4:35.203

McGee, 18-y-o world junior champion at two events, is fourteen years younger than Wallace, who also won the silver in this event in 1982.

4000m TEAM PURSUIT

Brett Aitken, Brad McGee, Stuart O'Grady, Tim O'Shannessey	AUS	4:10.485
Tony Doyle, Rob Hayles, Chris Newton, Bryan Steel	ENG	
	NZ	

Australia catch Britain before carrying on to break the Games record by over ten secs.

10 MILE SCRATCH RACE

Stuart O'Grady	AUS 18:50.520
Glenn McCleay	NZ
Brian Walton	CAN

O'Grady, who tangles with three NZ riders at the end, wins the title after an outbreak of protests.

100km TEAM TIME TRIAL

Phil Anderson, Brett Dennis, Henk Vogels, Damian McDonald	AUS	1h53.19 ChR
Matt Illingworth, Paul Jennings, Simon Lillistone, Peter Longbottom	ENG	1h56.40
Brian Fowler, Paul Leitch, Tim Pawson, Mark Rendell	NZ	1h56.52

In winning the title for the first time, Australia take thirteen minutes off the championship record set by N Zealand in 1990. Anderson, riding with a bandaged left knee and hairline fracture of the elbow sustained in the recent Tour of Britain, was a Games gold medallist back in 1978.

ROAD RACE 113 miles/81.96 km

Mark Rendell	NZ	4h46:07
Brian Fowler	NZ	4h48:09
Willie Engelbrecht	SAF	4h48:10

Chris Lillywhite (ENG), who finishes third, was relegated to fourth (but not disqualified...) for pulling Grant Rice (AUS)'s jersey, leaving Engelbrecht to become S Africa's first Games medallist since 1958.

Women

SPRINT

Tanya Dubnicoff	CAN
Michelle Ferris	AUS
Donna Wynd	NZ

Dubnicoff beats the 17-y-o Ferris to pick up some consolation for losing her world title in Sicily.

3000m PURSUIT

Kathy Watt	AUS	3:48.522
Sarah Ulmer	NZ	3:50.953
Jacqui Nelson	NZ	3:55.241

Watt's third gold of the Games.

POINTS RACE (25 km)

Yvonne McGregor	ENG	5 pts
Jacqui Nelson	NZ	32 (1 lap)
Sally Hodge	WAL	28 (1 lap)

The 33-y-o McGregor, previously a world championship competitor at fell running and triathlon, causes a sensation in her first ever points race by lapping every other competitor. Hodge wins Wales' only cycling medal of the Games.

50km TEAM TIME TRIAL

Jill Nolan, Cathy Reardon, Rachel Victor,		
Kathy Watt	AUS	1h04:03
Clara Hughes, Anne Samplonius, Alison Sydor,		
Leslie Tomlinson	CAN	1h04:18

No bronze medal is awarded because only four teams take part in this inaugural event (the decision is changed more than once). England (Maxine Johnson, Maria Lawrence, Yvonne McGregor, Julie Freeman) finish third in 1h05:32 after Freeman & McGregor crash into each other pushing off from the start!

ROAD RACE 36.5 miles/58.5 km

Kathy Watt	AUS	2h48:04
Linda Jackson	CAN	2h48:34
Alison Sydor	CAN	2h50:17

Watt, the Olympic champion, retains the title.

Gymnastics

Men

TEAM

Alan Nolet, Kristan Burley,		
Richard Ikeda, Travis Romagnoli	CAN	164.700
Peter Hogan, Brennon Dowrick,		
Bret Hudson, Nathan Kingston	AUS	164.500
Neil Thomas, Lee McDermott,		
Bob Barber, Paul Bowler	ENG	162.375

Canada retain the title after England have to finish the competition with only three men when Bowler pulls out injured during his floor routine while the team's in the overall lead.

OVERALL

Neil Thomas	ENG	55.950
Brennon Dowrick	AUS	55.525
Peter Hogan	AUS	54.950

Thomas carried the England flag in the opening ceremony.

FLOOR

Neil Thomas	ENG	9.662
Kristan Burley	CAN	9.437
Alan Nolet	CAN	9.150

RINGS

Lee McDermott	ENG	9.475
Peter Hogan	AUS	9.275
Brennon Dowrick	AUS	9.150
Richard Ikeda	CAN	9.150

POMMEL HORSE

Brennon Dowrick	AUS	9.425
Nathan Kingston	AUS	9.400
Richard Ikeda	CAN	9.225

VAULT

Bret Hudson	AUS	9.375
Kristan Burley	CAN	9.350
Neil Thomas	ENG	9.306

PARALLEL BARS

Peter Hogan	AUS	9.400
Kristan Burley	CAN	9.350
Brennon Dowrick	AUS	9.250

HORIZONTAL BAR

Alan Nolet	CAN	9.512
Richard Ikeda	CAN	9.500
Nathan Kingston	AUS	9.325

Women

TEAM

Jackie Brady, Zita Lusack,		
Annika Reeder, Karin Szymko	ENG	114.225
Stella Umeh, Stacey Galloway,		
Jaime Hill, Lisa Simes	CAN	113.650
Ruth Stoyel, Salli Wills,		
Ruth Moniz, Joanna Hughes	AUS	113.625

England owe their first win in the event to Galloway's injury: she dislocates a kneecap and receives her silver medal on crutches. Brady (18) is the oldest in the team. Lusack is 16, and Reeder (who stands 4'6 and weighs 5st) 14 yrs 326 days (apparently the youngest ever Commonwealth Games gold medallist).

OVERALL

Stella Umeh	CAN	38.400
Ruth Stoyel	AUS	38.037
Zita Lusack	ENG	37.725

Umeh retires (again) after the Games.

ASYMMETRICAL BARS

Ruth Stoyel	AUS	9.525
Stella Umeh	CAN	9.450
Sarah Thompson	NZ	9.337

VAULT

Stella Umeh	CAN	9.556
Sonia Lawrence	WAL	9.543
Lisa Simes	CAN	9.506

The 14-y-o Lawrence becomes the first Welsh competitor to win a Commonwealth Games gymnastics medal.

BEAM

Salli Wills	AUS	9.075
Zita Lusack	ENG	8.987
Ruth Moniz	AUS	8.900

FLOOR

Annika Reeder	ENG	9.750
Jacky Brady	ENG	9.662
Lisa Simes	CAN	9.550

The 14-y-o Reeder wins the only individual event she contests.

RHYTHMIC GYMNASTICS

TEAM

Lindsay Richards, Camille Martens, Gretchen McLennan	CAN	106.900
Katie Mitchell, Leigh Marning, Kasumi Takahashi	AUS	105.300
Aicha McKenzie, Debbie Southwick, Linda Southwick	ENG	103.300

HOOP

Kasumi Takahashi	AUS	9.300
Lindsay Richards	CAN	9.050
Aicha McKenzie	ENG	8.900
J Walker	SCOT	8.900

BALL

Kasumi Takahashi	AUS	9.200
Camille Martens	CAN	9.000
Gretchen McLennan	CAN	8.800
Aicha McKenzie	ENG	8.800

CLUBS

Kasumi Takahashi	AUS	9.400
Camille Martens	CAN	9.150
Leigh Marning	AUS	9.000

RIBBON

Kasumi Takahashi	AUS	9.200
Camille Martens	CAN	9.050
Gretchen McLennan	CAN	9.000

Takahashi, a Japanese American, came to Australia a year ago.

Shooting

Men

RUNNING TARGET

Bryan Wilson	AUS	657.9
Mark Bedlington	CAN	656.0
Paul Carmine	NZ	650.7

RUNNING TARGET PAIRS

Mark Bedlington & Matthew Bedlington	CAN	1088
Bryan Wilson & P Zutenis	AUS	1088
A Clarke & Paul Carmine	NZ	1079

Tough on the Australians. They come as close as it's possible to come, but the Bedlingtons win the gold - and no other medals are awarded.

AIR PISTOL

Jean-Pierre Huot	CAN	672.4
Jaspal Rana	INDIA	670.7
Greg Yelavich	NZ	668.5

The 43-y-o Huot holds off a late surge by the Indian teenager.

AIR PISTOL PAIRS

M Giustiniano & Bengt Sandstrom	AUS	1137
Jean-Pierre Huot & J Rochon	CAN	1135
Jaspal Rana & V Singh	INDIA	1133

Sandstrom retains the title with a new partner.

AIR RIFLE

Chris Hector	ENG	685.9	ChR
Jean-François Senecal	CAN	683	
Nigel Wallace	ENG	680	

Hector wins despite the borrowed rifle (see below) and an attack of 'flu. Senecal won the title in 1982.

AIR RIFLE PAIRS

Jean-François Senecal & Wayne Sorensen	CAN	1166	ChR
Chris Hector & Nigel Wallace	ENG	1161	
David Rattray & Robert Law	SCOT	1145	

Senecal, a smallbore gold medallist in 1990, shot a perfect 100 in the last round. Hector who'd also finished second in this event four years earlier, had to use Wallace's spare rifle after finding water in his own.

SMALLBORE RIFLE PRONE

Stephen Petterson	NZ	694.4
Jim Cornish	ENG	696.9
Michel Dion	CAN	694.6

SMALLBORE RIFLE PRONE PAIRS

Stephen Petterson & L Arthur	NZ	1181
S Chandrasiri & L Rajasinghe	SRI	1177
D Clifton & D Turley	AUS	1176

Petterson retains the title with a new partner.

SMALLBORE RIFLE 3 POSITIONS

Michel Dion	CAN	234.2
Wayne Sorensen	CAN	228.7
Alister Allan	SCOT	224.8

SMALLBORE RIFLE 3 POSITIONS PAIRS

Michel Dion & W Sorensen	CAN	2300
Alister Allan & W Murray	SCOT	2271
Chris Hector & T Langridge	ENG	2259

CENTRE-FIRE PISTOL

Jaspal Rana	INDIA	581
Mick Gault	ENG	581
Greg Yelavich	NZ	575

Rana beats Gault in a shoot-off.

FREE PISTOL

Mick Gault	ENG	654.1	ChR
Phillip Adams	AUS	647.0	
Bengt Sandstrom	AUS	642.5	

The 40-y-o Gault beats defending champion Adams, who finishes with sixteen medals (seven golds) since 1982, a Games record.

FREE PISTOL PAIRS

Phillip Adams & Bengt Sandstrom	AUS	1104
J Lawton & G Yelavich	NZ	1094
Mick Gault & Paul Leatherdale	ENG	1082

Adams & Sandstrom retain the title.

RAPID FIRE PISTOL

Michael Jay	WAL	670.2	ChR
Robert Dowling	AUS	668.4	
Patrick Murray	AUS	668.1	

RAPID FIRE PISTOL PAIRS

Patrick Murray & Rpbert Dowling	AUS	1148
Richard Craven & Michael Jay	WAL	1142
A Breton & G Le Maître	GUER	1131

Women

SPORT PISTOL

Christine Trefry	AUS	679.4
Margaret Thomas	ENG	675.0
Annette Woodward	AUS	674.0

Trefry wins her third gold of the Games.

SPORT PISTOL PAIRS

Christine Trefry & Annette Woodward	AUS	1134
Sharon Corrazin & Helen Smith	CAN	1132
Carol Page & Margaret Thomas	ENG	1129

Page competed for Jersey in the 1978 Games.

AIR PISTOL

Helen Smith	CAN	474.2
Annette Woodward	AUS	466.1
Sharon Cozzarin	CAN	465.8

AIR PISTOL PAIRS

Christine Trefry & Annette Woodward	AUS	747
G Barkman & J Lees	NZ	745
Carol Page & Margaret Thomas	ENG	744

AIR RIFLE PAIRS

P Ramanayake & K Wickremasinghe	SRI	771
Kate Morton & Louise Minett	ENG	771
C Ashcroft & Sharon Bowes	CAN	766

AIR RIFLE

Fani Theofanous	CYP	488.7
K Wickremasinghe	SRI	488.5
Sharon Bowes	CAN	488.4

AIR RIFLE PRONE PAIRS

Kim Frazier & Sylvia Purdie	AUS	
Pat Littlechild & Shirley McIntosh	ENG	

SMALLBORE RIFLE PRONE

Shirley McIntosh	SCOT	586
Sylvia Purdie	AUS	585
P Littlechild	SCOT	585

SMALLBORE RIFLE PRONE PAIRS

K Frazer & Sylvia Purdie	AUS	1160
Shirley McIntosh & P Littlechild	SCOT	1158
Christina Ashcroft & L Szulga	CAN	1158

SMALLBORE RIFLE 3 POSITION

Sharon Bowes	CAN	666.4
Roopa Unikrishnan	INDIA	662.5
Christina Ashcroft	CAN	661.6

SMALLBORE RIFLE 3 POSITIONS PAIRS

Christrina Ashcroft & Sharon Bowes	CAN	1143
Karen Morton & Lindsay Volpin	ENG	1132
Roopa Unikrishnan & K Gangulee	INDIA	1110

Open

TRAP

Mansher Signh	INDIA	141
George Leary	CAN	140
Andreas Anglou	CYP	137

Anglou beats Bob Barsley (ENG) in a shoot-off.

TRAP PAIRS

T Hewitt & S Allen	N IRE	188
R Bonotto & G Leary	CAN	187
R Borsley & J Grice	ENG	186

FULLBORE RIFLE

David Calvert	N IRE	398
Geoff Smith	NZ	398
Glynn Barnett	ENG	397

FULLBORE RIFLE PAIRS

A Bowden & G Grenfell	AUS	593
G Barnett & A Ringer	ENG	588
D Calvert & M Millar	N IRE	584

SKEET

Ian Hale	AUS	144
Christos Kourtellas	CYP	143
Andrew Austin	ENG	143

Competing in his fifth Commonwealth Games, Hales (who carried the Australian flag in the opening ceremony) wins a gold medal for the first time. Kourtellas takes the silver, Austin the bronze.

SKEET PAIRS

A Andreou & C Kourtellas	CYP	189
B Thompson & G Jukes	NZ	186
M Thompson & I Marsden	ENG	186

Four pairs scored 186. Thompson & Jukes won the silver, Thompson & Marsden the bronze.

Swimming

Men

FREESTYLE

50	Mark Foster	ENG	23.12	
	Darren Lange	NZ	23.13	
	Peter Williams	SAF	23.16	

Williams set a world record of 22.18 (later nullified) in 1988.

100	Darren Clarke	ST LUC	50.21	
	Chris Fydler	AUS	50.51	
	Andrew Baildon	AUS	50.71	

Baildon, the defending champion, is still the Games record holder.

DISABLED 100

	Andrew Haley	CAN	1:03.07	
	Brendan Burkett	AUS	1:03.75	
	Sean Tretheway	NZ	1:05.30	

The event's entitled 'Free Functional'. Haley, whose right leg was amputated above the knee, enjoys the irony of being watched by Arthur Tunstall, the Australian official reported as saying the presence of the disabled athletes was an 'embarrassment'.

200	Kieren Perkins	AUS	1:49.31	ChR
	Trent Bray	NZ	1:49.53	
	Danyon (Dan) Loader	NZ	1:49.53	

400	Kieren Perkins	AUS	3:45.77	
	Dan Loader	NZ	3:49.65	
	Dan Kowalski	AUS	3:50.41	

1500	Kieren Perkins	AUS	14:41.66	WR
	Dan Kowalski	AUS	14:53.61	
	Glen Housman	AUS	15:02.59	

On the way to beating world short-course champion Kowalski, the 21-y-o Perkins breaks another of his own world records by clocking 7:46.00 for the first 800m.

BACKSTROKE

100	Martin Harris	ENG	55.77	ChR
	Steven Dewick	AUS	56.09	
	Adam Ruckwood	ENG	56.52	

200	Adam Ruckwood	ENG	2:00.79	ChR
				UKR
	Kevin Draxinger	CAN	2:02.19	
	Scott Miller	AUS	2:02.43	

BREASTSTROKE

100	Phil Rogers	AUS	1:02.62	
	Nick Gillingham	ENG	1:02.65	
	Jon Cleveland	CAN	1:03.20	

200	Nick Gillingham	ENG	2:12.54	ChR
	Phil Rogers	AUS	2:13.56	
	Jon Cleveland	CAN	2:14.91	

Gillingham at last wins a major Games gold. Cleveland was the defending champion in both events.

BUTTERFLY

100	Scott Miller	AUS	54.39	
	Steve Clarke	CAN	54.45	
	Adam Pine	AUS	54.76	
200	Dan Loader	NZ	1:59.54	
	Scott Miller	AUS	1:59.70	
	Jamie Hickman	ENG	2:00.87	

INDIVIDUAL MEDLEY

200	Matthew Dunn	AUS	2:02.28	
	Curtis Myden	CAN	2:03.47	
	Fraser Walker	SCOT	2:04.28	

Scotland's first Games swimming medal since 1986.

| 400 | Matthew Dunn | AUS | | |
| | Curtis Myden | CAN | | |

Myden faints after the race.

RELAYS

4x100 FREE

Darren Lange, Andrew Baildon, D Sheehan, Chris Fydler	AUS	3:20.89	
J Steel, N Tongue, Dan Loader, Trent Bray	NZ	3:21.79	
Nick Shackell, Mark Foster, Andrew Clayton, Mike Fibbens	ENG	3:22.61	

4x200 FREE

Dan Housman, Dunn, Roberts, Kieren Perkins	AUS	7:20.80	ChR
	NZ	7:21.67	
Andrew Clayton, Mellor, Nick Shackell, Salter	ENG	&;26.19	

4x100 MEDLEY

S Beqir, S Lewis, Adam Pine, Andrew Baildon	AUS	3:40.41	ChR
C Renaud, Jon Cleveland, E Parenti, S Van der Meulen	CAN	3:43.25	
Martin Harris, Nick Gillingham, Jamie Hickman, Nick Shackell	ENG	4:43.72	

Women

FREESTYLE

50	Karen Van Wirdum	AUS	25.90	
	Andrea Nugent	CAN	26.24	
	Shannon Shakespeare	CAN	26.27	

100	Karen Pickering	ENG	56.20	ChR
	Karen Van Wirdum	AUS	56.42	
	Marion Limpert	CAN	56.54	

Pickering beats defending champion Van Wirdum to win England's first gold of the Games (in any sport).

200	Sue O'Neill	AUS	2:00.86
	Nicole Stevenson	AUS	2:01.34
	Karen Pickering	ENG	2:01.50

400	Hayley Lewis	AUS	4:12.56
	Stacey Gartrell	AUS	4:13.06
	Sarah Hardcastle	ENG	4:13.29

Lewis retains the title. Hardcastle, who won the event in 1986, didn't defend it in 1990.

800	Stacey Gantrell	AUS	8:30.18
	Hayley Lewis	AUS	8:30.72
	Nikki Dryden	CAN	8:37.70

DISABLED 100			
	Melissa Carlton	AUS	1:09.61 ChR
	Clare Bishop	ENG	1:11.00
	Kelly Barnes	AUS	1:11.03

Carlton has one arm.

BACKSTROKE

100	Nicole Stevenson	AUS	1:02.68
	Elli Overton	AUS	1:02.90
	Kathy Osher	ENG	1:03.27 UKR

Stevenson retains the title she won as Nicole Livingstone

200	Nicole Stevenson	AUS	2:12.73
	Anna Simcic	NZ	2:13.94
	Elli Overton	AUS	2:14.96

Simcic was the defending champion.

BREASTSTROKE

100	Sam Riley	AUS	1:08.02
	Rebecca Brown	AUS	1:09.40
	Penny Heyns	SAF	1:09.86

200	Sam Riley	AUS	2:25.53
	Rebecca Brown	AUS	2:30.24
	Lisa Flood	CAN	2:31.85

BUTTERFLY

100	Petra Thomas	AUS	1:00.21
	Sue O'Neill	AUS	1:00.24
	Eli Overton	AUS	1:01.88

200	Sue O'Neill	AUS	2:09.96
	Hayley Lewis	AUS	2:12.21
	Julie Majer	AUS	2:12.43

INDIVIDUAL MEDLEY

200	Elli Overton	AUS	2:15.59
	Marion Limpert	CAN	2:15.97
	Nancy Sweetnam	CAN	2:16.67

Sweetnam was the defending champion.

400	Elli Overton	AUS	4:47.95
	Nancy Sweetnam	CAN	4:46.20
	Hayley Lewis	AUs	4:46.62

Lewis was the defending champion.

RELAYS

4x100 FREE

Susan Rolph, Alex Bennett, Claire Huddart,			
Karen Pickering	ENG	3:46.23	ChR
			UKR

Sue O'Neill, Sarah Ryan, Elli Overton,		
Karen Van Wirdum	AUS	3:46.73

Marion Limpert, Shannon Shakespeare,		
J Amey, G Maughan	CAN	3:47.25

4x200 FREE

A Windsor, Nicole Stevenson,		
Hayley Lewis, Sue O'Neill	AUS	8:08.06 ChR

Sarah Hardcastle, Claire Huddart,		
Alex Bennett, Kate Pickering	ENG	8:09.62

Because only four teams take part, no bronze medals are awarded. Canada (S Richardson, D Wu, Joanne Malar, Marion Limpert) finish third in 8:14.97. Lewis finishes with seven golds in all, equalling the Games record for a woman in any sport (see Athletics).

4x100 MEDLEY

Nicole Stevenson, Sam Riley,		
Petra Thomas, Karen van Wirdum	AUS	4:07.89 ChR

Kathie Osher, Marie Hardman,		
Alex Bennett, Karen Pickering	ENG	4:12.83
	CAN	4:14.04

Diving

Men

1m SPRINGBOARD

Jason Napper	CAN	364.080
Michael Murphy	AUS	363.180
Evan Stewart	ZIM	357.780

3m SPRINGBOARD

Michael Murphy	AUS	671.760
Evan Stewart	ZIM	625.860
Jason Napper	CAN	621.030

10m HIGHBOARD

Michael Murphy	AUS	614.700
Robert Morgan	WAL	585.960
Claude Villeneuve	CAN	581.220

World junior champion Murphy beats title holder Morgan.

Women

1m SPRINGBOARD
Annie Pelletier	CAN	279.660
Jodie Rogers	AUS	252.720
Mary DePiero	CAN	245.340

DePiero was the defending champion.

3m SPRINGBOARD
Annie Pelletier	CAN	529.860
Paige Gordon	CAN	529.080
Jodie Rogers	AUS	474.810

10m HIGHBOARD
Anne Montminy	CAN	428.580
Paige Gordon	CAN	414.360
Myriam Boileau	CAN	411.210

Synchronised

SOLO
Lisa Alexander	AUS	189.4835
Kerry Shacklock	ENG	183.9717
Celeste Ferraris	AUS	172.6626

DUET
Lisa Alexander & Erin Woodley	AUS	188.0890
Kerry Shacklock & Laila Vakil	ENG	182.6803
Celeste Ferraris & M Downes	AUS	167.1646

Weightlifting

Men only

54 kg

TOTAL
B Adisekhar	INDIA	237.5 kg
M Veerasamy	INDIA	232.5
François Lagace	CAN	227.5

SNATCH
M Veerasamy	INDIA	105.0
B Adisekhar	INDIA	105.0
François Lagace	CAN	105.0

Medals decided on lighter bodyweight.

JERK
B Adisekhar	INDIA	132.5
M Guntali	MALAY	130,0
M Veerasamy	INDIA	127.5

59 kg

TOTAL
Marcus Stephen	NAU	262.5
Raghavan Chandersekaran	INDIA	255.0
D Aumais	CAN	237.5

SNATCH
Marcus Stephen	NAU	115.0
Raghavan Chandersekaran	INDIA	110.0
D Aumais	CAN	107.5

JERK
Marcus Stephen	NAU	147.5
Raghavan Chandersekaran	INDIA	145.0
Ben Devonshire	ENG	132.5

Chandersekaran won the overall 52 kg title in 1990.

64 kg

TOTAL
S Marinov	AUS	277.5
N Ogbodu	NIG	275.0
O Toby	NIG	272.5

SNATCH
N Ogbodu	NIG	125.0
S Marinov	AUS	125.0
O Toby	NIG	120.0

JERK
O Toby	NIG	152.5
S Marinov	AUS	152.5
N Ogbodu	NIG	150.0

Despite lifting the same weight as the winner each time, Marinov finishes with two silvers instead of all three golds.

70 kg

TOTAL
M Oluwa	NIG	295.0
S Rai	INDIA	292.5
Stewart Cruikshank	ENG	292.5

Rai takes silver, Cruikshank bronze.

SNATCH
L Riliwan	NIG	132.5
Stewart Cruikshank	ENG	132.5
M Oluwa	NIG	130.0

Riliwan takes gold, Cruikshank silver.

JERK
M Oluwa	NIG	165.0
S Rai	INDIA	165.0
Stewart Cruikshank	ENG	160.0

Oluwa takes gold, Rai silver.

76 kg

TOTAL
David Morgan	WAL	327.5
Damien Brown	AUS	325.0
S Tremblay	CAN	317.5

SNATCH

David Morgan	WAL	147.5ComR
S Tremblay	CAN	145.0
Damien Brown	AUS	142.5

JERK

Damien Brown	AUS	182.5
David Morgan	WAL	180.0
S Tremblay	CAN	172.5

Morgan, in his last competition before retirement, wins his 6th & 7th Games medals (the first as an 18-y-o in 1982) but misses the chance to replicate his 1990 feat of winning all three titles by opting to try 185 kg in the jerk while needing only 182.5 to win. When he tries to lower the weight, the judges (rightly, as he admits) refuse to let him.

83 kg

TOTAL

Kiril Kounev	AUS	352.5
S Ward	ENG	335.0
Dan Corbett	CAN	330.5

SNATCH

Kiril Kounev	AUS	152.5
S Ward	ENG	147.5
Dan Corbett	CAN	147.5

Ward takes silver, Corbett bronze.

JERK

Kiril Kounev	AUS	200.0
S Ward	ENG	187.5
Dan Corbett	CAN	182.5

Kounev, like Vlad & Botev (below), is an eastern European import.

91 kg

TOTAL

Harvey Goodman	AUS	362.5
Peter May	ENG	345.0
C Okoth	KEN	240.0

Okoth lifts 90kg less than the bronze medallist in the weight below.

SNATCH

Harvey Goodman	AUS	162.5
Peter May	ENG	155.0
C Okoth	KEN	120.0

JERK

Harvey Goodman	AUS	200.0
Peter May	ENG	190.0
C Okoth	KEN	120.0

99 kg

TOTAL

Andy Callard	ENG	347.5

Andrew Saxton	ENG	347.5
C Onyezie	NIG	345.0

SNATCH

C Onyezie	NIG	155.0
Andrew Saxton	ENG	155.0
P Christou	AUS	152.5

JERK

Andy Callard	ENG	197.5
Andrew Saxton	ENG	192.5
C Onyezie	NIG	190.0

Saxton, who comes within 5.5kg of winning 3 golds, has to settle for 3 silvers; after being caught taking drugs at the Olympics only two years earlier, better than nothing. Callard competed in the 83 kg class at the world championships.

108 kg

TOTAL

Nicu Vlad	AUS	405.0
I Chika	NIG	360.0
Gareth Hives	WAL	290.0

SNATCH

Nicu Vlad	AUS	185.0 ChR
I Chika	NIG	160.0
Gareth Hives	WAL	130.0

JERK

Nicu Vlad	AUS	220.0
I Chika	NIG	200.0
Gareth Hives	WAL	160.0

Hives, caught taking steroids at the 1990 Games, was stripped of the three silver medals he picked up there. Vlad recovers from his world championship disaster: his performances would have won all three golds in the higher weight class.

Over 108 kg

TOTAL

Stefan Botev	AUS	360.0
Steve Kettner	AUS	360.0
V Edem	NIG	345.0

SNATCH

Steve Kettner	AUS	165.0
Stefan Botev	AUS	160.0
V Edem	NIG	155.0

JERK

Stefan Botev	AUS	200.0
Steve Kettner	AUS	195.0
V Edem	NIG	190.0

The policy of allowing world class Europeans to settle Down Under pays off again (see World Championships). Botev, although hampered by a knee injury, needs only two lifts to win two gold medals.

Wrestling

48 kg

Jacob Isaac	NIG
Paul Ragusa	CAN
R Kumar	INDIA

52 kg

Selwyn Tam	CAN
Andrew Hutchinson	ENG
K Shankar	INDIA

57 kg

Bob Dawson	CAN
Ashok Kumar	INDIA
C O'Brien	AUS

62 kg

Marty Calder	CAN
John Melling	ENG
A Barseguian	CYP

68 kg

Chris Wilson	CAN
Ibo Oziti	NIG
Muhammed Umar	PAK

74 kg

Dave Hohl	CAN
Reinhold Ozoline	AUS
Calum McNeil	SCOT

82 kg

Justin Abdou	CAN
Randhir Singh	INDIA
Bhala Bhola	PAK

90 kg

Scott Bianco	CAN
Kodei Victor	NIG
Graham English	SCOT

100 kg

Greg Edgelow	CAN
Noel Loban	ENG
S Verma	INDIA

130 kg

Andy Borodow	CAN
Bidei Jackson	NIG
Amerjit Singh	ENG

Obituaries

from Oct 1993

Xenophon Balaskas
12 May 1994, b 15 Oct 1910 (Xenophon Constantine Balaskas). A leg-spinner whose 5-49 & 4-54 won the 1935 Lord's Test, he took 22 wickets for South Africa in nine Tests 1930-39.

Ralph Banks
Oct 1993, b 28 June 1920. Left-back who was injured while marking Sir Stan in the Matthews Cup Final of 1953. His brother Tommy, also a left-back, won six England caps in 1958.

Ned Barry
12 Dec 1993, b 1905 (Edward Fitzgerald Barry). Flanker capped once by N Zealand, v Australia in 1934. His son & grandson also went on tour (though neither played in a Test), the only family to provide three generations of All Blacks.

Danny Blanchflower
Dec 1993, b 10 Feb 1926 (Robert Dennis Blanchflower). English Footballer Of The Year in 1958 & 1961, captain of the Spurs team that won the 1961 Double & 1963 Cup-Winners' Cup and the N Ireland side which did so well in the 1958 World Cup, he was a skilful and crafty passer, though he was certainly lucky to have Dave Mackay & John White around him at Tottenham. He made a career as an articulate commentator on the game but was a disappointment as manager of Chelsea and N Ireland. Still, anyone who refuses to appear on This Is Your Life deserves a special mention in any book.

Neil Bonnett
Feb 1994 (47). US racing driver, in a crash at Daytona.

Julius Boros
28 May 1994 (74). American golfer who died where he would have wanted to go: in a golf cart on the course. Slightly unsung, he was nevertheless one of the best over a number of years, winning the US Open in 1952 & 1963 and the USPGA (at the age of 48) in 1968, voted PGA Player Of The Year in 1952 (ahead of Hogan & Snead) and 1963 (Palmer & Nicklaus).

Jean Borotra
17 July 1994, b 13 Aug 1898. French tennis player, one of the 'Four Musketeers' who dominated Wimbledon and the Davis Cup in the 1920s. A great gamesman and crowd pleaser, whose volleying did much to disguise his unconvincing technique (Bill Tilden, whom he never beat outdoors, called him a charlatan), he won the French singles title in 1924 & 1931 and the Australian in 1928, but made his greatest mark at Wimbledon, where he reached the singles final five times, winning in 1924 & 1926, won the doubles in 1925-32-33 and played more matches (224) than any other male player.

Geoff Bradford
30 Dec 1994, b 18 July 1927 (Geoffrey Reginald William Bradford). The only footballer to win a full England cap while with Bristol Rovers (where he played for fifteen years), he scored a goal and made another in his only international, v Denmark in 1955.

Frank Broome
Sep 1994, b 11 June 1915. Famously fast footballer who played for England (seven caps 1938-39) in four forward positions, scoring from three of them, including the goal that put England 3-1 ahead on his debut, in the notorious Nazi Salute match in Berlin.

Sam Burns
May 1994, b 20 May 1919 (Samuel Burns). Manager of the fighting Finnegans, Chris & Kevin, Tony Sibson, Chris Pyatt (briefly), all of whom won European boxing titles; and above all Terry Downes, world middleweight champion in 1961.

Matt Busby
20 Jan 1994, b 26 May 1909. Scottish wing-half who won a single peacetime cap (1933 v Wales) before finding immense fame and affection as manager of Man Utd, whom he rebuilt after the War, assembling three distinct and successful teams: the one which won the league in 1952 and a sparkling 1948 FA Cup final; the Babes who won the championship in 1956 & 1957 before Munich struck; the Law-Best-Charlton-Crerand brigade which won the FA Cup in 1963 and the League in 1965 & 1967 before crowning everything with an emotional 1968 European Cup. Until Alex Ferguson, every other United manager lived under his shadow.

Raich Carter
9 Oct 1994, b 21 Dec 1913 (Horatio Stratton Carter). England's greatest inside-forward, a brilliant playmaker-goalscorer, confident, dominating, tetchy (he resented the adulation Stanley Matthews received), reduced to only 13 caps from 1934 to 1947 by Hitler and assorted selectorial despots. The only player to play in FA Cup winning teams before and after the War, he also led Sunderland to the League title in 1936.

Luigi Chinetti
Aug 1994, b 17 July 1901. Brilliant Italian racing driver who emerged from the great Nuvolari's shadow to win Le Mans three times: 1932-34-49 (the last being the first for Ferrari) and finish second in 1933.

Bertie Clarke
14 Oct 1993, b 7 April 1918 (Carlos Bertram Clarke). A leg spinner who took six wickets for West Indies in three Tests, all on the 1939 tour to England, he was suspended from medical practice in the 1970s after being found guilty of performing illegal operations.

Joe Cockcroft
Feb 1994, b 20 June 1911. The oldest player ever to make his First Division debut (37), he played 217 consecutive matches for West Ham 1932-37 and was Sheff Weds' first captain after World War II.

Jack Cowie
3 June 1994, b 30 March 1912 (John Cowie). Strongly built New Zealand seam bowler who took 45 wickets at only 21.53 in nine Tests 1937-49. Particularly effective on his first England tour, he took 19 wickets at 20.78 despite several dropped catches off his bowling, and 114 in all matches at 19.95.

Peter Cranmer
29 May 1994, b 10 Sep 1914. Classic dashing England centre who won 16 caps (all consecutive, two as captain) 1934-38, scoring a try, a penalty and two dropped goals (one in the famous win over the All Blacks in 1936) and captained Warwickshire at cricket 1938-47.

Bob Crisp
March 1994, b 28 May 1911 (Robert James Crisp). S African swing bowler who took twenty wickets in nine Tests 1935-36 and made his name (it's still in the record books) as the only bowler ever to twice take four wickets in four consecutive balls.

John Curry
April 1994 (of an AIDS-related illness), b 9 Sep 1949. British figure skater, the best ever, who overcame the prejudices of judges (and the rest) to introduce some artistry into men's skating at the highest level, becoming the first since 1936 to win European, Olympic and world titles in the same year (1976).

Fred Davies
Nov 1994 (83). The best-known ball-boy in the world, for 45 years he used his coracle to fish balls out of the Severn when they were kicked out of Shrewsbury Town's ground.

Marie Dollinger
10 Aug 1994 (83). Sprinter made famous by the 1936 Olympics. The Germans, having broken the 4x100m relay world record in the heats, were ten yards clear at the last changeover, when Dollinger's pass to Ilse Dörffeldt was dropped (in front of Hitler, too). She never won an Olympic medal (fourth in that year's 100m) but her daughter Brunhilde Hendrix took silver in the 1960 sprint relay.

Clément Dupont
1 Nov 1993 (95). Scrum-half who won 16 caps 1923-29 and played in France's first wins over England (1927) & Wales (1928).

Alex Escobar
2 July 1994, b 13 March 1967. Slim, talented Colombian central defender, shot dead in Medellín, Colombia's drug capital, apparently because his own goal in the World Cup had cost someone some money in bets. First capped in 1988, in only his fifth international he headed the equaliser in the 1-1 draw at Wembley that same year.

Michela Fanini
26 Oct 1994 (21), in a car crash. Italian cyclist who won the 1994 Giro d'Italia.

Mark Farmer
Motorcycle rider, during 1994 Isle of Man TT week.

Heather Farr
late 1993, of cancer (28). American golfer who played in the 1984 Curtis Cup at Muirfield, where a candlelit memorial service was held in her honour.

Barbara Flowers
Nov 1994 (45). Choreographer of Rosalyn Sumners (world figure skating champion in 1983) & Tonya Harding.

Allen Forward
Jan 1994 (72). Aptly-named Welsh flanker & No.8 who won six caps 1951-52.

Bob Frame
Jan 1994 (52). Rugby union centre, integral part of the Warwickshire side which won the County Championship in 1962-63-64-65.

Doug Freeman
31 May 1994, b 8 Sep 1914. 6'3 Australian-born leg-spinner whose first-class career of only sixteen days included six in Test cricket for N Zealand, the two Tests in 1933 v England, for whom Wally Hammond scored 227 & 336 not out. Freeman, who took 1-169 in all, is still the youngest ever to play for N Zealand: 18yrs 197 days.

Alfie Fyles
March 1994 (66). Harry Vardon aside, the only man to win the British Open six times: caddy to Gary Player in 1968 & Tom Watson 1975-77-80-82-83. Amazingly, three others from the same street in Lancashire caddied for British Open winners, including his brother Albert (Tom Weiskopf 1973).

Vitas Gerulaitis
18 Sep 1994 (of mysterious but apparently not suspicious monoxide poisoning), b 26 July 1954.

Crowd-pleasing, dashing blond volleyer of the late 1970s (lived it to the full off-court, too: the all-night dancing fuelled by a cocaine addiction), winner of 27 singles titles in all, including the 1977 Australian. Runner-up at the 1979 US Open, 1980 French, and two Masters.

Harry Golombek
7 Jan 1995, b 1 March 1911. International Grandmaster, British chess champion 1947-49-55, better known for his writing on the game (more than 30 books) and world championship refereeing (1954-72).

Reinaldo Gorno
10 April 1994 (75). Argentinian Marathon runner, Olympic silver medallist in 1952.

Duncan Hamilton
May 1994, b April 30 1920 (James Duncan Hamilton). British racing driver who won Le Mans in 1953.

Johnny Hancocks
19 Feb 1994, b 30 April 1919. A tiny winger with a thunderous shot, he scored twice on his England debut, winning three caps in all (1948-50). Member of the Wolves side which won the FA Cup in 1949 (the final on his 30th birthday) and league title in 1954.

Michael Hardy
13 Jan 1994, b 13 Nov 1927 (Evan Michael Pearce Hardy). Rugby union fly-half, three caps in 1951, during which England scored a total of only eight points.

Marea Hartman
29 Aug 1994 (74). Secretary of the women's AAA for 43 years, women's team manager and general mother hen at many major championships. A classic administrator of the old school, she seems to have been generally regarded with amused affection by her charges.

Christy Henrich
26 July (22), of complications arising from anorexia and bulimia. US gymnast, fourth in the asymmetrical bars at the 1989 world championships.

Terry Hibbitt
4 Aug 1994 (of cancer), b 1 Dec 1947. All-purpose midfielder with Leeds (with whom he won a Fairs Cup winner's medal in 1967), Birmingham and especially Newcastle, where he made countless openings for Malcolm Macdonald. The result of the 1974 FA Cup final (Liverpool 3-0) might just have been different if he hadn't been injured when the score was still 0-0.

Ralph Hill
17 Oct 1994, b 26 Dec 1908. US track runner who would have won the 1932 Olympic 5000m but for being baulked twice by world record holder Lauri Lehtinen (FIN) in the finishing straight. Amid boos from the Los Angeles crowd, Lehtinen finished only inches ahead. A protest would certainly have won Hill his rightful gold, but he didn't make one or accept Lehtinen's offer of a

place beside him on the top step of the podium.

Lew Hoad
July 1994, b 23 Nov 1934 (Lewis Alan Hoad). Australian tennis player who won his major titles after Kramer & Gonzales had turned professional, but there's little doubt about his place among the all-time greats. Blond, built like a welterweight, looking like Robert Mitchum, he could play a bit too. Badly affected by back problems at the end of his career, he was an imposing all-court athlete when fully fit, his competitiveness as famous as his steel wrists. He won three Grand Slam titles in his great year of 1956 (losing to Rosewall in the US final) and Wimbledon again the following year (massacring Ashley Cooper in the final) before turning pro.

Jim Holton
4 Oct 1993, b 11 April 1951 (James Allan Holton). Big, very limited stopper, something of a folk hero at Old Trafford ('Six foot two, eyes of blue, big Jim Holton's after you'), who won 15 Scottish caps 1973-74.

Idris Hopkins
Oct 1994, b 11 Oct 1907 (Idris Morgan Hopkins). Small tricky Brentford winger, inevitably nicknamed Dai, who scored two goals in 12 matches for Wales 1934-39.

Gordon Hudson
Rugby union flanker who played 312 times for Goucester from 1935. Played twice for England in wartime internationals. His father Arthur won eight official caps 1906-10.

Innes Ireland
24 Oct 1993, b 12 June 1930. Talented, cavalier British racing driver sacked by Colin Chapman after giving Lotus their first ever (and his only) Grand Prix win, the 1961 US.

Bosko Jankovic
Oct 1993, b 22 May 1951 (Bozidar Jankovic). Yugoslav forward who played for Middlesbrough 1979-81 after winning two caps in 1972.

Gerald John
26 Oct 1994 (60). The 1951 ABA flyweight champion who lost in the final in 1952 & 1958.

Peter Jones
May 1994, b 24 March 1932. Rawboned All Black loose forward who won 11 caps 1954-60 and scored a famous try to win the deciding Test of the 1956 series v S Africa, then achieved immortality after the match by announcing, live on radio, that he was 'absolutely buggered.'

Larry Klein
Sep 1994 (42), drowned during a race in San Francisco. US Yachtsman Of The Year 1989, world champion in three different classes.

Atanas Komshev
Nov 1994 (35) after eleven days in a coma following a

car crash. Bulgarian wrestler who won the 1988 Olympic Graeco-roman light-heavyweight gold medal.

'Tim' Kirwan-Taylor

Aug 1994, b 29 June 1905 (William John Kirwan-Taylor, also simply Taylor). Rugby union winger who won five caps, all in 1928, when England won every match, including the Grand Slam. Scored a try in each of his first two internationals.

Ina Lamason

30 April 1994, b 2 May 1911 (Ina Mabel Lamason). After missing the 1935 Test v England, she had to wait eleven years to win her first cap, then went on to captain New Zealand in 1948 & 1949.

Ridley Lamb

25 July 1994 (39) when his car drove into a harbour. Jockey who retired not long after riding The Thinker to win the 1987 Cheltenham Gold Cup.

Richard Langhorn

25 Nov 1994 (29), of a heart attack during a back operation. 6'6 Harlequins No.8 who played on the England tour of Canada in 1993.

Mark Lees

14 June 1994, b 28 May 1956. Much admired British rowing coach, in charge at both Boat Race universities, national performance director 1991-92.

Ross Logan

26 Nov 1993 (84). Scottish rugby union scrum-half who won 20 caps 1930-37.

Jimmy McAlinden

Nov 1993, b 31 Dec 1917. Creative inside-forward, no goalscorer, who won four caps for Ireland 1937-48 and two for the Republic in 1946.

Ulrike Maier

Jan 1994 (26), Austrian skier, one of the very best, world Super GS champion 1989 & 1991, the first woman to be killed in a World Cup race. The next downhill was cancelled in her honour.

Zillwood 'Zac' March

Sep 1994, b 25 Oct 1892. Brighton & Portsmouth footballer 1913-23. Before he died, the oldest surviving former League professional.

Antono Martín

11 Feb 1994 (23). Spanish cyclist, in a road accident during training. Voted most promising rider in the 1993 Tour de France,

Wallis Mathias

1 Sep 1994, b 4 Feb 1935. The first non-Muslim cricketer capped by Pakistan, he was given opportunities enough as a batsman (21 Tests 1955-62) but managed just three fifties (highest score 77) in 36 innings at an average of only 23.72.

Peter May

27 Dec 1994, b 31 Dec 1929. Although others exceeded his Test figures of 4537 runs at 46.77, he's still regarded by many good judges as the best batsman produced by England after World War II. An amateur captain with a steely approach, he led England in a record 41 Tests, playing 66 in all (1951-61) before retiring from international cricket at only 31. MCC president 1980-81, his time as chairman of the England selectors left a verdict of not proven.

Jimmy Meadows

Jan 1994, b 21 July 1931. Full-back who might have won more than his single England cap (1955) but for the injury in the 1956 FA Cup final which ended his career.

Jack Metcalfe

Jan 1994 (81). Australian triple jumper, one of the best of his time, Olympic bronze medallist 1936, Commonwealth champion 1934 (also third in the long jump) & 1938 (also third in the javelin!), above all world record holder (15.78m) in 1935.

Rob Mitchell

Motorcycle rider, during 1994 Isle of Man TT week.

Carlos Monzon

8 Jan 1995, b 7 Aug 1942, in a car crash while returning to prison, where he was serving an 11-year sentence for killing his third girlfriend (his first had shot him). Argentinian middleweight, arguably the greatest of all time, world champion 1970-77 (a record 14 defences), unbeaten in his last 82 pro fights.

Bill Mumm

11 Dec 1993 (70). William John Mumm. N Zealand prop who won a single cap, playing for a virtual B team which took on Australia in 1949 while the main All Black party was touring S Africa.

Ira Murchison

28 March 1994 (61). Fast-starting US sprinter who equalled the 100m world record (10.1) in 1956, the same year that he led off the relay team which won the Olympic title, breaking a world record that had lasted twenty years.

Simon Robert Naali

12 Aug (28), hit by a car during a training run. Tanzanian Marathon runner, Commonwealth bronze medallist in 1990.

Wangila Napunyi

24 July 1994. Kenyan boxer, welterwight gold medallist at the 1988 Olympics under the name Robert Wangila, who died of head injuries after a fight in Las Vegas. A legal wrangle over his final resting place (the body was hijacked by a family faction claiming he asked to be buried as a Muslim) was finally resolved by a 103-page Kenyan High Court judgement in November.

Hans Nordahl
late 1993 (75). Midfielder whose international career (1938-54) was the longest for any Norwegian: 16 years 29 days.

Luis Ocaña
19 May 1994 (48, suicide). Brave and rugged Spanish cyclist who gave the mighty Merckx a tough time in more than one Tour de France and won the event himself in 1973.

Ochiro Ogimura
4 Dec 1994 (62). President of the International Table Tennis Federation, member of the Japanese squad which won the Swaythling Cup (world team championship) five times in a row, and winner of all three individual titles: singles 1954 & 1956 (finalist 1957), doubles 1956 & 1959 (finalist 1957), mixed 1957-59-61.

Derek Oldbury
9 July 1994, b 21 March 1924. Small and wasted, unable to speak or move his limbs without difficulty, confined to a wheelchair all his life, Derek Oldbury was one of the most tenacious and dynamic players of all time, retiring as undefeated British draughts champion after 40 years, world champion in 1978 (freestyle) & 1991 (three move).

Arnie Oliver
late 1993 (86). Member of the USA team which reached the semi-finals of the first football World Cup (1930).

Andy Penman
20 July 1994, b 20 Feb 1943 (Andrew Penman). Part of the famous Dundee forward line (Smith-Penman-Cousin-Gilzean-Robertson) which won the Scottish league title in 1961-62 and reached the European Cup semi-finals the following year. A diabetic throughout his career, he won a single cap, as a member of the last Scotland team to include only players with Scottish clubs; it lost 3-0 at home to Holland in 1966.

Bruno Pezzey
31 Dec 1994, b 3 Feb 1955. Tall mop-haired sweeper, one of the very best of his time, who won 84 caps for Austria 1975-90 and was the only defender ever to score twice in a match against England (1979).

George Pope
29 Oct 1993, b 27 Jan 1911 (George Henry Pope). All-rounder called up by England for Tests v Australia in 1938 & 1948 but played in only one, v S Africa in 1947, scoring 8 not out and taking 1-75.

Arthur Porritt
Jan 1994 (93). New Zealand sprinter who won the bronze medal behind Harold Abrahams in the 1924 Olympic 100m.

Christian Pravda
Nov 1994 (67). Austrian alpine skier, world downhill champion in 1954 after winning silver and bronze in the 1952 Olympics.

Simon Prior
June 1994 (40). British sidecar rider, Yoshi Kumanagaya's passenger, who crashed at the German Grand Prix.

'Pipette' Puig-Aubert
(69). Most famous of French rugby league players, skilful playmaker and expert goalkicker, though his missed kick against England cost France the first World Cup (1954).

CR Rangachari
9 Oct 1993, b 14 April 1916 (Commandur Rajagopalachari Rangachari). Genuinely quick bowler with a flailing action and little guile who took nine expensive wickets for India in four Tests in 1948.

Roland Ratzenberger
30 April 1994 (31) during qualifying for the San Marino Grand Prix. Austrian driver in his first Formula 1 season, death overshadowed by that of Senna the following day.

David Rayner
16 Nov 1994 (murdered in a Bradford nightclub), b 4 March 1967. Cyclist who was British junior road race champion in 1984 and won the Milk Race Under-22 award three years in a row.

Norman Read
22 May 1994 (62). British race walker turned down by the AAA, selected by New Zealand, for whom he won the 1956 Olympic 50 km.

Allie Reynolds
Dec 1994 (79). Pitcher who helped the New York Yankees win the World Series six times. Part Creek Indian, he was known (surprise, surprise) as Chief.

Gus Risman
Oct 1994, b 1911. Augustus John Risman. World-famous centre & full-back, captain of G Britain & Wales, who won 17 caps 1932-46 (the longest international career of any British player). His son Bev won eight England rugby union caps 1959-61, four for the British Lions in 1959, and five for GB at rugby league in 1968.

Arthur Rowe
Nov 1994, b 1 Sep 1906. An attacking centre-half who won a single England cap, keeping out the dangerous Jean Nicolas in the 4-1 win over France in 1933, he was better known, and altogether more influential, as the manager of Tottenham's attractive push-and-run team (Ramsey, Nicholson, Burgess, Baily) which won the 1951 League title in their first season back in the First Division.

Wilma Rudolph
12 Nov 1994, b 23 June 1940. One of the greatest runners of all time, star of the 1960 Olympics, where

she won the sprint treble. Her style, which led to fanciful comparisons with gazelles, completely disguised the fact that polio, scarlet fever and double pneumonia had left her unable to walk unaided till she was eleven. Only four years later, she won a bronze in the Olympic sprint relay.

Miguel Angel Rugilo
late 1993 (75). Acrobatic goalkeeper, a Wembley hero in 1951 when Argentina came within ten minutes of becoming the first overseas country to beat England at home.

Rui Felipe
28 Aug 1994 (car crash), b 8 March 1968. Porto midfielder who won six Portuguese caps 1992-93.

Michel Sansen
5 Jan 1994 (59, surely too old for this kind of thing?) Belgian motorcyclist who crashed during the Paris-Dakar rally

Herbert Schade
March 1994 (71). Bespectacled German runner, third in the febrile Olympic 5000m final of 1952.

Alex Scott
30 Sep 1994 (34, killed by a shotgun at his stables). Trained the winner of the Irish Oaks (Possesive Dancer) & Breeders' Cup Sprint (Sheikh Albadou), both in 1991.

Ayrton Senna
1 May 1994 (after a crash during the San Marino Grand Prix), b 21 March 1960. One of the very greatest Formula 1 drivers of all time, winning the world title in 1988-90-91 as well as 41 Grands Prix, starting from pole a record 65 times. Fast, aggressive, simply an obvious talent of the highest order since his days in karting and Formula Ford, a single-minded perfectionist who rarely suffered fools (or any other driver, especially Prost), he won fewer friends than the likes of Stirling Moss and Graham Hill, but no-one could fail to admire. Moss himself ranked him alongside Fangio, the highest possible praise.

Jack Sharkey
Aug 1994, b 6 Oct 1902 (Joseph Paul Zukauskas). Before he died, he was the oldest surviving world heavyweight boxing champion, a title he won from Max Schmeling in 1932, two years after losing a fight for the vacant championship to the same man on a disputed foul. A skilful boxer with a sharp punch, unlucky to lose a controversial fight to Jack Dempsey in 1927, he lost the world title in 1933 to the gigantic Primo Carnera.

John Sichula
(39) Zambian Commonwealth super-featherweight boxing champion 1984 and 1987-89.

Evgeny Smirgis
Dec 1993 (54). A Russian who began his attempt to row round the world three years earlier, he was found

on the shore near La Rochelle.

Charlie Smirke
Dec 1993, b 23 Sep 1906 (Charles James William Smirke). Jockey who rode the winners of eleven English Classics & nine Irish Classics. Warned off for alleged cheating in 1928, he was given his licence back in 1933, winning the following year's Derby. Resented the general adulation of Gordon Richards, whom he considered an inferior jockey. His win on Mahmoud in the 1936 Derby, ahead of Richards on the favourite Taj Akbar, suggested he (along with other good judges) may have been right. While Richards won only one Derby in 27 attempts, Smirke won it for the fourth time (to match his total of wives) in 1958, aged 51.

Anne Smith
Nov 1993 (52). Winner of four AAA titles and the 1966 Commonwealth Games bronze, all at 880y, she was infinitely better at twice the distance, the last British runner to hold the world record for the women's mile, which she set twice in 1967; during the second (the first official FIFA mark) she also set an unofficial world's best for 1500m.

Helen Stephens
Jan 1994 (75). Tall, overpowering US sprinter who never lost a race in senior competition and won golds in the 1936 Olympic 100m & relay. The suspicion that she was actually a man was disproved by a sex test, while an autopsy on the athlete she beat into second place, defending champion and favourite Stanislawa Walasciewiczowna (Stella Walsh), discovered that 'she' had only male sex organs!

Archie Stinchcombe
Oct 1994. Member of the 1936 British ice hockey squad (composed almost entirely, and very controversially, of Canadians) who won the 1936 Olympic gold medal.

Hugh Tayfield
March 1994, b 30 Jan 1929 (Hugh Joseph Tayfield). Perhaps the best of all S African off-spinners, certainly the only South African bowler of any kind to take nine wickets in a Test innings and the first to take 100, his total of 170 (1949-60) is still easily the national Test record. Nicknamed Toey from his habit of stubbing his foot before bowling.

Ferko Tokar
26 Oct 1993 (68). Czech table tennis player, men's doubles world champion 1949, runner-up 1950.

Frithjof Ulleberg
late 1993 (81). Member of the excellent Norwegian team which beat Germany at the 1936 Olympics and lost only 2-1 after extra-time to eventual gold medallists Italy.

Kjetil Ulvang
Oct 1993, lost (then found dead) in the snow during a training run. Norwegian cross-country skier, brother of the famous Vegard,

Vilmos Varju
17 Feb 1994 (56). Hungarian shot putter, best of his generation outside the USA: European champion 1962 & 1966, Olympic bronze medallist 1964.

Roy Vernon
4 Dec 1993, b 14 April 1937 (Thomas Royston Vernon). Slim dangerous striker , a favourite at Goodison, who scored eight goals in 32 matches for Wales 1957-67.

Ellsworth Vines
17 March 1994, b 28 Sep 1911 (Henry Ellsworth Vines). US tennis player, one of the most dynamic of all time. His uncompromising service (one of the fastest ever) and ground strokes carried margins of error that cost him the 1933 Wimbledon final, but they crushed poor hapless little Bunny Austin in the previous year's final (6-0 in the final set, the last point an ace Austin admits he didn't see) and swept him to the US title in 1931 & 1932.

Tony Waddington
Jan 1994, b 9 Nov 1924. Manager of Stoke City when they won their only major trophy, the 1972 League Cup.

Wout Wagtmans
Dutch cyclist who won a Tour de France stage in each of three successive years 1954-55-56.

Jersey Joe Walcott
26 Feb 1994, b 31 Jan 1914 (Arnold Raymond Cream). The oldest boxer before Foreman to win the world heavyweight title. Officially 37y 168d, he may well have been older when he ko'd Ezzard Charles in 1951, having previously lost title challenges to Joe Louis (twice, once controversially) & Charles. Came within a single punch of retaining the title v Rocky Marciano in 1952 before losing to the same fighter in one round the following year, after which he retired.

Ike Williams
5 Sep 1994 (71). US boxer, NBA world lightweight champion in 1945 and undisputed champion 1947-51.

Robbie Williams
Sep 1993 (40), gassed himself and his son. South African boxer who lost a split decision in the first ever WBA cruiserweight fight (1982).

'Tug' Wilson
1 Dec 1993, b 25 Nov 1938 (Kenneth James Wilson). RAF heavyweight boxing champion who won a single England rugby union cap, as prop v France in 1963, before joining rugby league club Oldham.

Cliff Wilson
May 1994 (60). Bulky bespectacled cheerful Welshman who came to professional snooker late in life after beating Joe Johnson to win the world amateur title in 1978.

Steve Wood
May 1994 (26), after falling from a horse at Lingfield. English jockey.

Billy Wright
3 Sep 1994, b 6 Feb 1924 (William Ambrose Wright). Won 59 caps as a wing-half before moving to centre-half in 1954, staying to become the first footballer from any country to win 100 caps (105 1946-59). The first to play 70 consecutive internationals or captain any country 90 times, he was lucky to survive all of England's disasters of the Fifties but was successful in domestic club football: voted Footballer Of The Year in 1951-52, he captained Wolves to the 1949 FA Cup and the League title in 1954-58-59.

Bert Yancey
25 Aug 1994, (56). US golfer. Diagnosed a manic depressive in 1975, he nevertheless won seven US Tour events. Like Boros, he died on a golf course.

Francisco Zuluaga
late 1993, b 4 Feb 1929. Full-back who played in nine internationals 1957-62. In his last, Colombia's first in any World Cup finals, he opened the scoring from the penalty spot v Uruguay.

1995 Calendar

ALPINE SKIING
30 Jan - 12 Feb	World Championships
16-19 March	World Cup finals

AMERICAN FOOTBALL
29 Jan	Superbowl XXIX
3 Sep	NFL regular season begins

ARCHERY
23-26 March	World indoor championships

ATHLETICS
10-12 March	World Indoor Championships
11 March	National Cross-Country, Wigmore Valley, Luton *(men's & women's events held together for first time)*
25 March	World Cross-Country
3-18 March	Pan-American Games
2 April	London Marathon
9 April	World Marathon Cup
24-25 June	European Cup final
27-30 June	European Junior Championships
15-16 July	AAA Championships
4-13 Aug	World Championships
9 Sep	Grand Prix final
1 Oct	World Half-Marathon Championships

BADMINTON
14-18 March	All England Championships
17-21 May	World Championships

BASEBALL
3 Apr	Major League season begins
3 Oct	Major League play-offs begin

BASKETBALL
14 March	European Champions Cup final
26 April	NBA play-offs begin
29-30 April	British men's National Championship finals
8-17 June	European Championship (women)
21 June - 22 July	European Championship (men)

BILLIARDS
7-19 Feb	World Championships
25-26 March	English Championship finals
3-9 April	UK Championship

BOBSLEIGH
16-20 Jan	British Championships
25 Jan - 1 Feb	World Cup final
6-12 Feb	European Cup final
6-19 Feb	World Championships

BOWLS
13-26 Feb	World Indoor Championships
3-7 Jul	British Championships

BOXING
12 April	ABA finals
4-15 May	World Amateur Championships

CANOEING
25 Aug - 3 Sep	World Slalom Championships

CRICKET
26-30 Jan	Australia v England 4th Test
3-7 Feb	Australia v England 5th Test
27 Apr	County Championship begins
24-26-28 May	England v West Indies 1-days
8-12 June	England v W Indies 1st Test
22-26 June	England v W Indies 2nd Test
3-7 July	England v W Indies 3rd Test
15 July	B&H Cup final
27-31 July	England v W Indies 4th Test
10-14 Aug	England v W Indies 5th Test
24-28 Aug	England v W Indies 6th Test
2 Sep	NatWest Trophy final
16-20 Nov	S Africa v England 1st Test
30 Nov - 4 Dec	S Africa v England 2nd Test
14-18 Dec	S Africa v England 3rd Test
26-40 Jan	S Africa v England 4th Test
2-6 Jan 1996	S Africa v England 5th Test

CYCLING
29 Jan	World Cyclo-Cross Championships
23 May - 3 June	Tour of Britain
1-23 July	Tour de France
11-17 Sep	World Mountain Bike Championships
26-30 Sep	World Track Championships
7 Oct	World Professional Road Championships
8 Oct	World Amateur Road Championships

411

EQUESTRIANISM

13-17 April	World Cup final
4-7 May	Badminton
10-14 May	Windsor
8-11 June	Bramham
17-20 Aug	Hickstead Derby
31 Aug - 3 Sep	Burghley
26 Sep - 1 Oct	Horse of the Year Show
14-18 Dec	Olympia

FIGURE SKATING

30 Jan - 5 Feb	European Championships
7-12 March	World Championships

FOOTBALL

2 April	League Cup final
23 April	Women's League Cup final
30 April	Women's FA Cup final
3 & 17 May	UEFA Cup final
5 May	Scottish Cup final
10 May	European Cup-winners' Cup final
20 May	FA Cup final
24 May	European Cup final
3-11 June	International Challenge Tournament
15-18 June	Women's World Cup

GOLF

19-22 Jan	Dubai Desert Classic
26-29 Jan	Johnnie Walker Classic
2-5 Feb	Madeira Open
9-12 Feb	Canary Open
16-19 Feb	S African PGA
23-26 Feb	Mediterranean Open
2-5 March	Andalucian Open
9-12 March	Moroccan Open
16-19 March	Portuguese Open
23-26 March	to be announced
30 Mar - 2 April	Extremadura Open
6-9 April	US Masters
13-16 April	Catalan Open
20-23 April	Cannes Open
27-30 April	Paris Tournament
4-7 May	Italian Open
11-14 May	B&H International Open
18-21 May	Spanish Open
26-29 May	Volvo PGA
1-4 June	English Open
8-11 June	Tournament Players' Championship
15-18 June	US Open
15-18 June	Jersey Open
22-25 June	French Open
29 June - 2 July	BMW International Open
6-9 July	Irish Open
12-15 July	Scottish Open
20-23 July	British Open
27-30 July	Dutch Open
3-6 Aug	Scandinavian Masters
10-13 Aug	USPGA
10-13 Aug	Austrian Open
17-20 Aug	Czech Open
24-27 Aug	German Open
31 Aug- 3 Sep	European Masters
7-10 Sep	Lancôme Trophy
14-17 Sep	British Masters
22-24 Sep	Ryder Cup
28 Sep - 1 Oct	European Open
5-8 Oct	German Masters
12-15 Oct	World Matchplay
19-22 Oct	Dunhill Cup
26-29 Oct	Volvo Masters
2-5 Nov	to be announced
9-12 Nov	World Cup
14-17 Dec	World Championship

GREYHOUNDS

24 June	Derby (final)

GYMNASTICS

6-9 July	European Championships
19-24 Sep	World Championships
17-19 Nov	British Championships
1-3 Dec	European Championships (team final)

HANDBALL

8-21 May	Men's World Championship

HORSE RACING

14 March	Champion Hurdle
16 March	Cheltenham Gold Cup
8 April	Grand National
6 May	2000 Guineas
7 May	1000 Guineas
9 June	Oaks
10 June	Derby
22 July	K George & Q Elizabeth Stakes
9 Sep	St Leger
1 Oct	Arc de Triomphe
28 Oct	Breeders' Cup races
7 Nov	Melbourne Cup
11 Nov	Mackeson Gold Cup
26 Dec	King George VI Chase

ICE HOCKEY

30 Mar - 9 April	British League Premier Division play-offs
15-16 April	British Championship finals
12-21 April	World Championship Pool B including Britain

JUDO

8 April	British Open
11-14 May	European Championships
28 Sep - 1 Oct	World Championships

MODERN PENTATHLON
25-30 July   World Championships

MOTOCROSS
125 World Championship
2 April   Italian GP
9 April   Spanish GP
30 April   Argentine GP
14 May   Polish
21 May   Dutch GP
28 May   Hungarian GP
11 June   British GP
18 June   Czech GP
9 July   French GP
30 July   Indonesian GP
13 Aug   German GP

250 World Championship
26 March   Spanish GP
9 April   Dutch GP
23 April   Swiss GP
30 April   Italian GP
7 May   Austrian GP
21 May   Finnish GP
28 May   Swedish GP
11 June   British GP
18 June   Irish GP
25 June   Belgian GP
16 July   Venezuelan GP
30 July   Polish GP
6 Aug   German GP
20 Aug   Japanese GP
3 Sep   French GP

Open World Championship
2 April   Portuguese GP
23 April   Austrian GP
7 May   German GP
21 May   Czech GP
28 May   Luxembourger GP
11 June   Italian GP
18 June   French GP
2 July   Ulster GP
9 July   British GP
6 Aug   Belgian GP
20 Aug   Dutch GP
27 Aug   German GP
10 Sep   MotoCross des Nations

MOTOR CYCLING
World Championship
26 March   Australian GP
2 April   Malaysian GP
23 April   Japanese GP
7 May   Spanish GP
21 May   German GP
11 June   Italian GP
24 June   Dutch GP

9 July   French GP
23 July   British GP
6 Aug   US GP
20 Aug   Czech GP
17 Sep   Brazilian GP
24 Sep   Argentinian GP
8 Oct   European GP

Superbike World Championship
7 May   German
21 May   Italian 1
28 May   British 1 (Donington Park)
18 June   Italian 2
25 June   Spanish
9 July   Austrian
16 July   French
6 Aug   British 2 (Brands Hatch)
27 Aug   Japanese
3 Sep   Dutch
15 Oct   Indonesian
29 Oct   Australian
US date & venue to be announced

MOTOR RACING
Formula 1 World Championship
26 March   Brazilian GP
9 April   Argentinian GP
30 April   San Marino GP
14 May   Spanish GP
28 May   Monaco GP
11 June   Canadian GP
2 July   French GP
16 July   British GP
30 July   German GP
13 Aug   Hungarian GP
27 Aug   Belgian GP
10 Sep   Italian GP
24 Sep   Portuguese GP
1 Oct   European GP (Nurburgring)
22 Oct   Pacific GP (Aida, Japan)
29 Oct   Japanese GP
12 Nov   Australian GP

17-18 June   Le Mans 24 hour

NETBALL
23 April   British clubs finals
15-29 July   World Championships

RALLYING
19-22 Nov   RAC Rally

ROWING
1 April   Oxford v Cambridge
28 June - 2 July   Henley
7-9 July   Lucerne
20-27 Aug   World Championships

RUGBY LEAGUE

28 Jan	Regal Trophy final
29 April	Challenge Cup final
21 May	Premiership finals
28 Oct	World Cup final

RUGBY UNION

21 Jan	France v Wales, Ireland v England
4 Feb	Scotland v Ireland, England v France
18 Feb	Wales v England, France v Scotland
4 March	Scotland v Wales, Ireland v France
18 March	England v Scotland, Wales v Ireland
22 April	County Championship final
6 May	English & Welsh Cup finals
13 May	Middlesex Sevens
25 May - 24 June	World Cup (see below)

Pool A

25 May	South Africa v Australia	Cape Town
26 May	Canada v Romania	Port Elizabeth
30 May	South Africa v Romania	Cape Town
31 May	Australia v Canada	Port Elizabeth
3 June	Australia v Romania	Stellenbosch
3 June	South Africa v Canada	Port Elizabeth

Pool B

27 May	England v Argentina	Durban
27 May	Western Samoa v Italy	East London
30 May	W Samoa v Argentina	East London
31 May	England v Italy	Durban
4 June	Argentina v Italy	East London
4 June	England v W Samoa	Durban

Pool C

27 May	New Zealand v Ireland	Johannesburg
27 May	Wales v Japan	Bloemfontein
31 May	Ireland v Japan	Bloemfontein
31 May	New Zealand v Wales	Johannesburg
4 June	Ireland v Wales	Johannesburg
4 June	New Zealand v Japan	Bloemfontein

Pool D

26 May	France v Tonga	Pretoria
26 May	Scotland v Ivory Coast	Rustenburg
30 May	France v Ivory Coast	Rustenburg
30 May	Scotland v Tonga	Pretoria
3 June	Scotland v France	Pretoria
3 June	Tonga v Ivory Coast	Rustenburg

Quarter-finals

10 June	1st Pool D v 2nd Pool C	Durban	(1)
10 June	1st Pool A v 2nd Pool B	Johannesburg	(2)
11 June	1st Pool B v 2nd Pool A	Cape Town	(3)
11 June	1st Pool C v 2nd Pool D	Pretoria	(4)
17 June	Winner (1) v Winner (2)	Durban	
18 June	Winner (3) v Winner (4)	Cape Town	
22 June	3rd-place play-off	Pretoria	
24 June	World Cup Final	Johannesburg	

SNOOKER

18-19 Feb	UK Championship (women)
1-9 April	British Open
14-30 April	World Professional Championship
2-5 May	World Championship (women)

SPEEDWAY

World Individual Championship

20 May	Polish GP
11 June	Continental semi-finals, Scandinavian final
17 June	Overseas final (Coventry)
17 June	Austrian GP
8 July	German GP
30 July	Continental semi-final
12 Aug	Swedish GP
19 Aug	Intercontinental final
9 Sep	Danish GP
30 Sep	British GP (Coventry)
8 Oct	Italian GP challenge
24 Sep	World Team final
5 Aug	World Junior final
16 Sep	World Long Track final

SQUASH

12-17 Jan	British Nationals
1-10 April	British Open
25 June - 2 July	World Open (women)
6-12 Nov	World Open (men)

SWIMMING

17-27 Aug	European Championships
30 Nov - 4 Dec	World Short Course Championships

TABLE TENNIS

5-8 Jan	English Open
14-17 April	European Cup-Winners' Cup
29-30 April	County Championship, National finals
1-14 May	World Championships

TENNIS

16-29 Jan	Australian Open
19 May - 11 June	French Open
26 June - 9 July	Wimbledon
28 Aug - 10 Sep	US Open
25-26 Nov	Federation Cup final
1-3 Dec	Davis Cup final

VOLLEYBALL

1-2 April	British cup finals

WATER SKIING

25-27 Aug	European Championships
11-17 Sep	World Championships

YACHTING

6-13 May	America's Cup

Addresses & phone numbers

(Some of the following are merely starting points. Be prepared to follow the initial call with others)

AMERICAN FOOTBALL
British AFA: 92 Palace Gardens Terrace, London W8 4RS, tel 071 727 7760

ARCHERY
Grand National Archery Society: National Agricultural Centre, 7th Street, Stoneleigh Park, Kenilworth, CV8 2LG, tel 0203 696631

ATHLETICS
BAF: Edgbaston House, 3 Duchess Place, Hagley Road, Birmingham B16 8NM, tel 021 440 5000, fax 021 440 0555

BADMINTON
BAoE: National Badminton Centre, Bradwell Road, Loughton Lodge, Milton Keynes MK8 9LA, tel 0908 568822

BASKETBALL
EBA: 48 Bradford Road, Stanningley, Pudsey, W Yorks, LS28 6DF, tel 0532 361166, fax 0532 361022

BILLARDS & SNOOKER
World Ladies B&SA: 3 Felsted Avenue, Wisbech, PE13 3SL
World Professional B&SA: 27 Oakfield Road, Clifton, Bristol, BS8 2AT

BOBSLEIGH
BBA: Springfield House, Woodstock Road, Coulsdon, Surrey CR5 3HS, tel 0737 555152

BOWLS
EBA: Lyndhurst Road, Worthing, E Sussex BN11 2AZ, tel 0903 820222, fax 0903 820444

BOXING
ABA: Francis House, Francis Street, London SW1P 1DE, tel 071 828 8568
Board of Control: 52a Borough High Street, I London SE1 1XW

CANOEING
BCU: Dudderidge House, Adbolto Lane, West Bridgford, Notts NG2 5AS, tel 0602 821100

CRICKET
TCCB: Lord's CG, London NW8 8QN, tel 071 286 4405
Women's Association: 41 St Michael's Lane, Headingley, Leeds LS6 3BR

CROQUET
Croquet Association: Hurlingham Club, Ranelagh Gardens, London SW6 3PR, tel 071 736 3148

CURLING
Royal Caledonian Club: tel 031 5562272

CYCLING
BCF: 36 Rockingham Road, Kettering NN16 8HG, tel 0536 4122211, fax 0536 412142

DARTS
BDO: 2 Pages Lane, London N10 1PS, tel 081 883 5544, fax 081 883 0109

EQUESTRIANISM
BEF: British Equestrian Centre, Stoneleigh Park, Kenilworth CV8 2LR, tel 0203 696697, fax 0203 696484

FENCING
AFA: 1 Baron's Gate, 33-35 Rothschild Road, London W4 5HT, tel 081 742 3032, fax 081 742 3033

FOOTBALL
FA: 16 Lancaster Gate, London W2 3LW, tel 071 262 4542, fax 071 402 0486
League: 319 Clifton Drive South, Lytham St Annes, FY8 1JG, tel 0253 729421, fax 0253 724786

GLIDING
BGA: 47 Vaughan Way, Leicester LE1 4SE, tel 0533 531051

GOLF
PGA: Apollo House, Th Belfry, Wilshaw, Sutton Coldfield B76 9PT, tel 0675 4670333
Women's PGA: Tytherington Club, Dorchester Way, Tytherington, Cheshire SK10 2JP, tel 0625 611444

GREYHOUND RACING
NGRC: 24-28 Oval Road, London NW1 7DA, tel 071 267 9256, fax 071 482 1023

GYMNASTICS
BAGA: Ford Hall, Lilleshall National Sports Centre, Newport, Salop TF10 9NB, tel 0952 820330, fax 0952 820326

HANDBALL
BHA: 60 Church Street, Radcliffe, Manchester M26 8SQ, tel 0706 229354, fax 061 7249656

HANG GLIDING & PARAGLIDING
BHG&PA: Old School Room, Loughborough Road,
Leicester LE4 5PJ, tel 0533 611322, fax 611323

HOCKEY
HA: 102 Saxon Gate West, Milton Keynes MK9 2EP,
tel 0908 241100, fax 0908 241106
Women's HA: 51 High Street, Shrewsbury SY1 1ST,
tel 0743 233572, fax 0704 233583

HORSE RACING
Horse Racing Board: 42 Portman Square,
London W1H 0EN, tel 071 396 0011, fax 071 935 3626
Jockey Club Press Office: 071 486 4921

ICE HOCKEY
BIHA: 517 Christchurch Road, Boscombe,
Bournemouth BH1 4AG,
tel 0202 303946, fax 0202 398005

ICE SKATING
UK National ISA: 15-27 Gee Street, London EC1V 3RE,
tel 071 253 3824, fax 071 490 2589

JUDO
BJA: 7a Rutland Street, Leicester LE1 1RB,
tel 0533 559669

LACROSSE
ELU: Winton House, Winton Road, Bowdon, Altrincham,
WA14 2PB, tel 061 928 9600
Women's LA: 4 Western Court, Bromley Street,
Digbeth, Birmingham B9 4AN, tel 021 773 4422

MODERN PENTATHLON
MPA: Wessex House, Silchester Road, Tadley,
Basingstoke RG26 6PX, tel 0747 855833

MOTORCYCLING
Auto-Cycle Union: ACU House, Wood Street, Rugby
CV21 2YX, tel 0788 540519, fax 0788 573585

MOTOR RACING
BARC: Thruxton Racing Circuit, Andover SP11 8PN,
tel 0264 772607, fax 0264 773794
RAC: Motor Sports House, Riverside Park, Colnbrook,
Slough SL3 0HG, tel 0753 681 736, fax 0753 682938

NETBALL
AENA: 9 Paynes Park, Hitchin SG5 1EH,
tel 0462 442344, fax 0462 442343

ORIENTEERING
BOF: Riversdale, Dale Road North, Darley Dale, Matlock
DE4 2HX, tel 0629 734042, fax 0629 733769

POLO
Hurlingham PA: Winterlake, Kirtlington,
Oxford OX5 3HG, tel 0869 350044

RACKETS
TRA: Queen's Club, PAlliser Road,
London W14 9EQ, tel 071 386 3448

ROWING
ARA: 6 Lower Mall, London W6 9DJ,
tel 081 741 5314, fax 081 741 4658

RUGBY LEAGUE
RFL: 180 Chapeltown Road, Leeds LS7 4HT,
tel 0532 624637, fax 0532 623386

RUGBY UNION
RFU: Rugby Road, Twickenham TW1 1DZ,
tel 081 892 8161, fax 081 892 9816
Women's RFU: Meadow House, Springfield Farm,
Shipston-on-Stour CV36 4HQ, tel 0635 298906

SHOOTING
NRA: Bisley Camp, Brookwood, Woking GU24 0PB,
tel 0483 797777

SKI-ING
BSF: 258 Main Street, East Calder, Livingston
EH53 0EE, tel 0506 884343, fax 0506 882952

SPEEDWAY
tel: 0788 540096, press office 0733 243988

SQUASH
SRA: 33-34 Warple Way, London W3 0RQ,
tel 081 746 1616

SWIMMING
ASA: Harold Fern House, Derby Square, Loughborough
LE11 0AL, tel 0509 230431, fax 0509 610720

TABLE TENNIS
ETTA: Queensbury House, Havelock Road, Hastings
TN34 1HF, tel 0424 722525, fax 0424 422103

TENNIS
All England Club: Church Road, London SW19 5AE,
tel 081 944 1066, fax 081 947 8752

TRIATHLON
BTA: Dover Leisure Centre, Townhall Street,
Dover CT16 1LN

VOLLEYBALL
BVF: 27 South Road, West Bridgford, Notts NG2 7AG,
tel 0602 816324, fax 0602 455429

WATER SKI-ING
BWSF: 390 City Road, London EC1V 2QA,
tel 071 833 2855, fax 071 837 5879

WEIGHTLIFTING
BAWLA: tel 0865 200339

WRESTLING
BAWA: 41 Great Clowes Street, Salford M7 9RQ,
tel 061 832 9209

YACHTING
RYA: RYA House, Romsey Road, Eastleigh SO5 4YA,
tel 0703 629962, fax 0703 629924